A Little Character Goes a Long Way

Other *Ziggy* Books

Ziggy & Friends
Ziggy Faces Life
Ziggy's Big Little Book
Life Is Just a Bunch of Ziggys
Alphabet Soup Isn't Supposed to Make Sense
Ziggy's Place
Ziggy's Ups and Downs
Ziggy in the Fast Lane
Ziggy's Follies
Ziggy's School of Hard Knocks
Ziggy on the Outside Looking In . . .
Look Out World . . . Here I Come!
Ziggy . . . A Rumor in His Own Time
A Day in the Life of Ziggy . . .
1-800-ZIGGY
My Life as a Cartoon
The Z Files
Ziggy's Divine Comedy
Get Ziggy with It
The Zen of Ziggy
Ziggy Goes Hollywood
Character Matters
Ziggy's Gift

Treasuries
The Ziggy Treasury
Encore! Encore!
Ziggy's Star Performance
The First 25 Years Are the Hardest
Ziggy's Friends for Life

A Little Character Goes a Long Way

A 35 Year Collection of ZIGGY Favorites

by Tom Wilson

**Andrews McMeel
Publishing, LLC**

Kansas City

06 07 08 09 10 BAM 10 9 8 7 6 5 4 3 2 1

ISBN-13: 978-0-7407-5824-9
ISBN-10: 0-7407-5824-1

Library of Congress Control Number: 2005935607

www.uComics.com
www.andrewsmcmeel.com

For my dad, Tom Wilson Sr.

It's a Friday night, almost thirty-five years ago, and I'm sitting on the green cracked-vinyl sofa in our basement, anxiously waiting for a beam of light to shine through the windows and onto the wall above our old TV. My twelve-year-old body is exhausted from five straight days of learning, chasing young love, and hours upon hours of swim-team practice, but I don't dare fall asleep. Tonight is the night that I've waited for all week.

It seems like forever, then, at last! The headlights of Dad's car herald his arrival home.

My mom and my sister have gone to bed, and finally I hear my father's heavy footsteps coming down the basement stairs. We share our tired smiles as he takes up his position on the maroon shag carpeting and our midnight "Creature Feature" begins. It's here in this room, with *Godzilla* on the tube, that the two most influential characters in my life lie spread out before me. The first is my superhero as well as the most brilliant man I will ever know. He's wearing his boxer shorts, a rumpled dress shirt and tie, and with a cigarette in one hand, a pen in the other, he's drawing the second character: a short, little bald guy with a big nose named Ziggy.

It doesn't matter that the movie completely sucks or that my dad and I are so physically beat that we'll never see the end of the show. No, these things don't matter. What does is that this is our time and we both know how much it means to each other without ever having to say so.

I fight the urge to sleep while the great man in his underwear works long into the night, drawing beneath the television's projection of one classic character as he continues to create another. Ultimately, as Godzilla wreaks chaos and tears apart Tokyo, my tired eyes fix upon the steady stream of smoke from Dad's burning Kool menthol, gracefully meandering up, up, and away, taking my consciousness along with it.

As I fall asleep, I don't think about the funny little character he draws by night. I haven't yet experienced the pressures of syndication deadlines and I don't know that *Ziggy* is only in eighteen newspapers and struggling to survive. My family never sees whatever fears or stress my dad may carry. Just as we never see that when he's away, my father is building companies and transforming entire industries by virtue of his creative brilliance and charisma. I only know that I rarely see him and these brief, special times we spend together make everything else that's taking place in our respective worlds stop, so that he might share this part of his life with me.

—Tom Wilson Jr.

Chapter I
1971–1975

My husband, Rod, and I were in Cleveland to see the folks at American Greetings, and we called up Tom Wilson to see if he had time for coffee. Generous as always, Tom put aside a day to show us around and told us he'd pick us up at the hotel in his new car. He described it as being a black Mercedes and he was excited to show it off.

It was a sunny day. He apologized for being late (due to some unforeseen family circumstances), and climbed out of a rusting red Peugeot. The doors jammed badly. We seated ourselves and he grimaced as he closed them from the outside. His daughter had taken the new car and Tom was left with hers. Stones rattled in the hubcaps as we rumbled along the highway toward his house.

"I have some beautiful horses," he told us as we entered a long driveway. There was a white fence along the left side. A small barn in a neat pasture was home to two lovely mares who were happily leaning over the fence in anticipation as the familiar car arrived. "You've gotta see them!" he enthused. "They're so friendly!" Tom let us out of the car and as we approached, the horses both trotted back to the barn and one pulled the door shut with its chin. We could see their hind ends. "They don't like me much. They're my daughter's." Tom shrugged. We continued on to the house. "I have two dogs. Real nice ones. Wait till you see the dogs!" He opened the kitchen door and immediately two brown shapes whizzed past us into the woods. Tom ran after them, but soon gave up. "They'll be back sometime," he assured us. "Come and take a look at my kitchen."

Tom had told us about the skylights. They had been specially made with multiple panes of beveled glass, "so that when the sun shines, there are rainbows everywhere!" It was a neat country kitchen. The sky had just clouded over and there were no rainbows. "You'll have to come back when the sun's out," said Tom, sadly.

Disappointed by the car, the horses, the dogs, and now the rainbows, he was keen to show us at least one treasure that was a sure thing. "You've got to see my bed!" he cried. "It's an antique four-poster—one of the most amazing designs you've ever seen!" We declined. Having only just met him as a colleague, we thought that his bedroom might be too intimate a space to share. "Not at all," he insisted. "This is something you really must see!" He gallantly pushed the door to his bedroom aside and gestured with a "Ta-daaa!" motion of his hand. We entered the room and the bed was indeed a showpiece; however, hanging on one of the posts was a pair of worn undershorts that rather took our interest away from the furniture.

Tom stuffed the undies into a drawer and, blushing, led us back to the kitchen. Needless to say, the restaurant he'd planned to take us to was closed for renovations, but we enjoyed a wonderful evening with him anyway.

People ask cartoonists where ideas come from and are the characters really us? We never had to ask if Ziggy was real or imaginary. We spent a day with him!

How lucky I am to know Tom Wilson. Over the years, he's been an adviser, an ally, and an inspiration. He is as kind, as humble, and as endearing as the character he draws so well. Tom Wilson is one of the gifts I'll take with me, wherever I go.

—Lynn Johnston, creator of *For Better or For Worse*

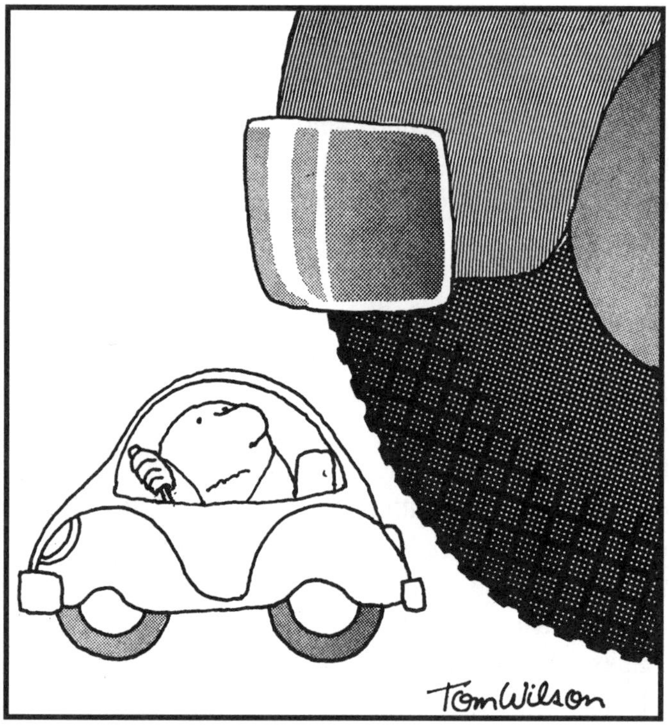
Tom Wilson

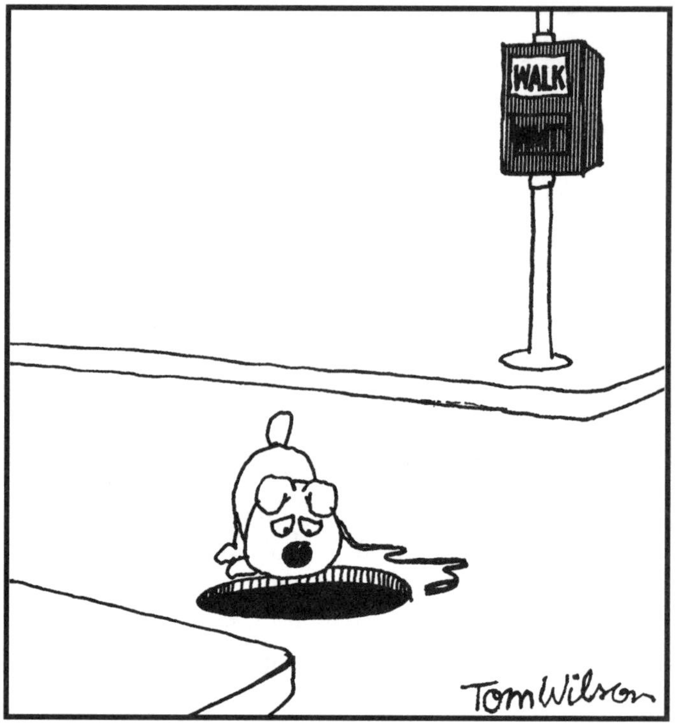
WALK
Tom Wilson

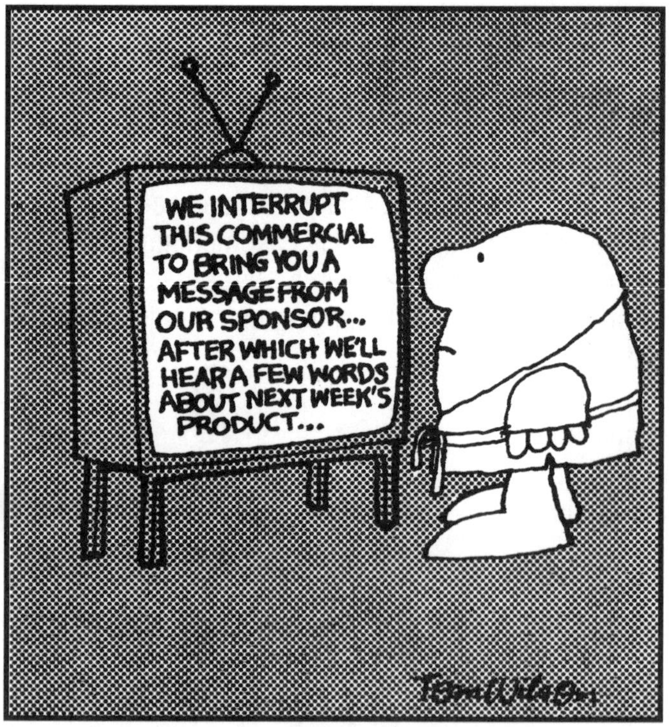
WE INTERRUPT THIS COMMERCIAL TO BRING YOU A MESSAGE FROM OUR SPONSOR... AFTER WHICH WE'LL HEAR A FEW WORDS ABOUT NEXT WEEK'S PRODUCT...
Tom Wilson

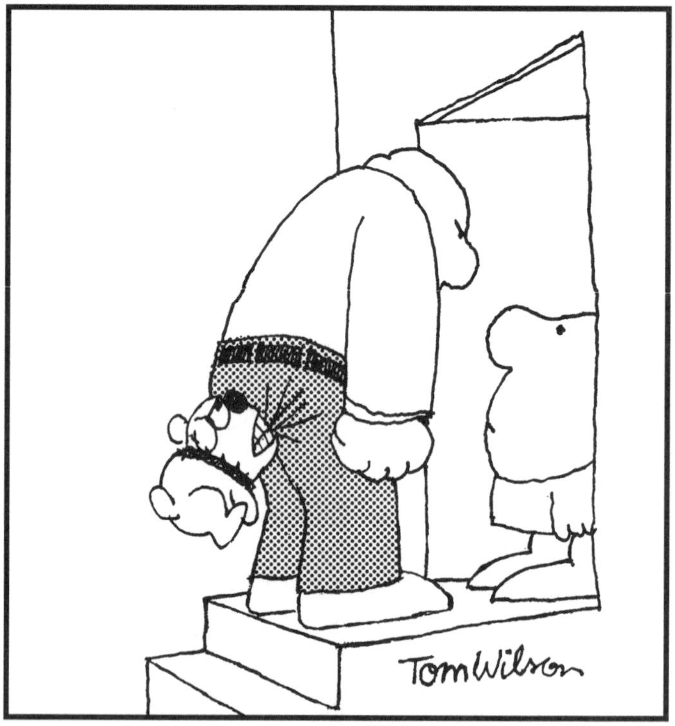
Tom Wilson

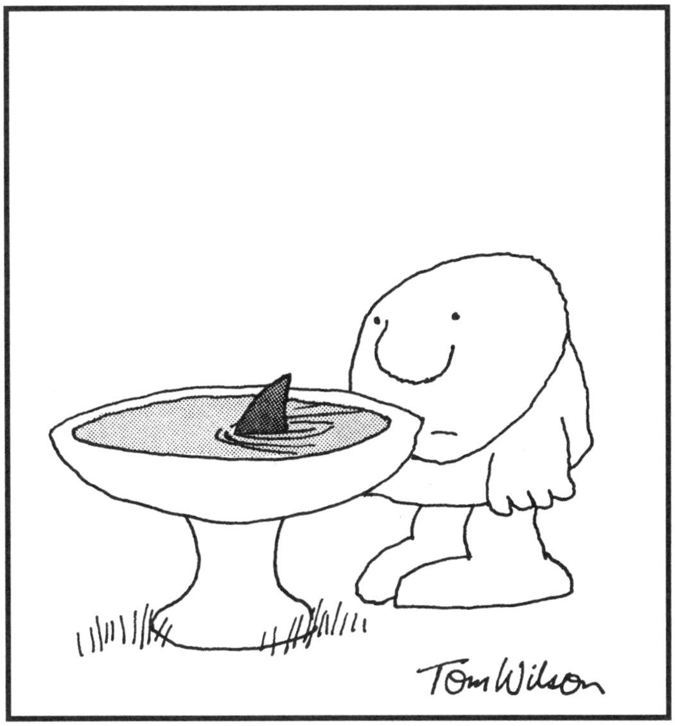
Tom Wilson
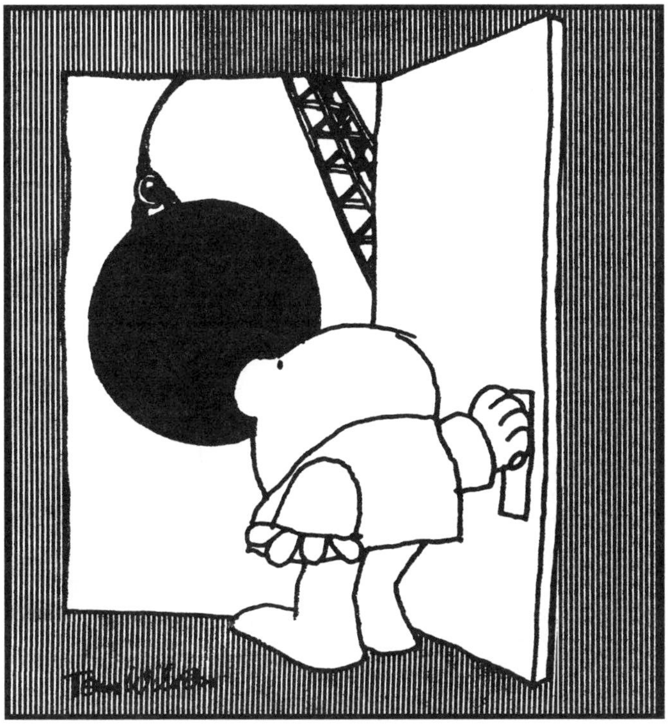
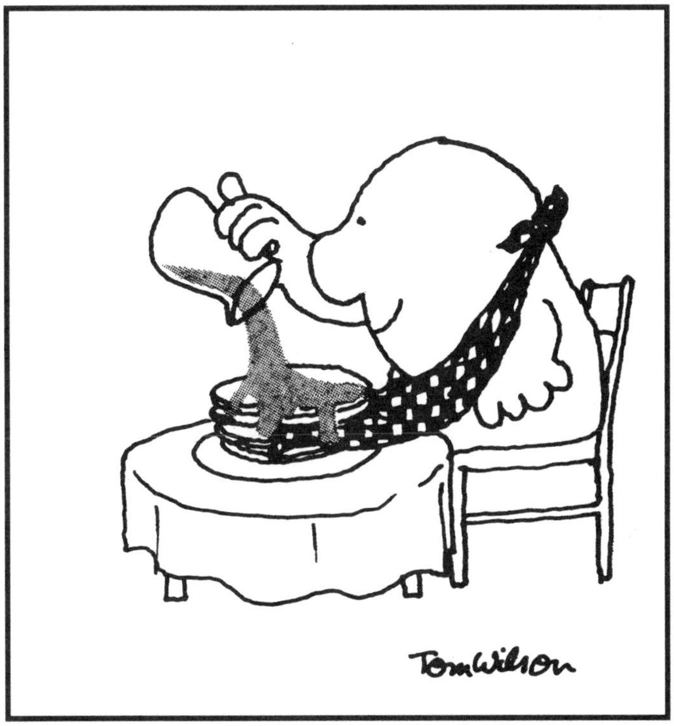
Tom Wilson
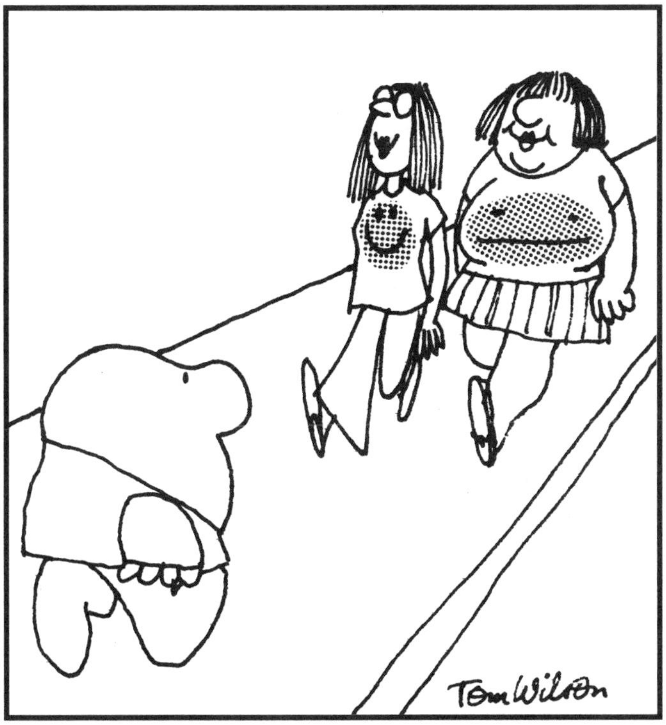
Tom Wilson

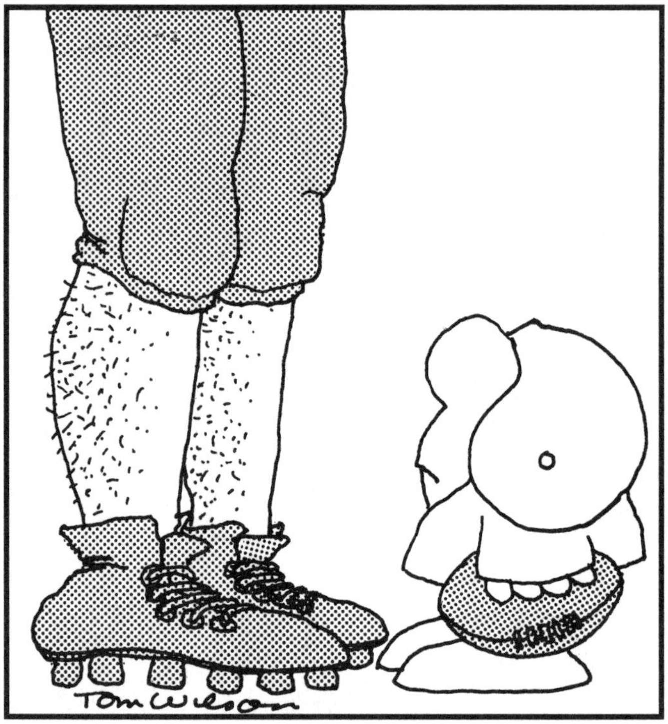
Tom Wilson

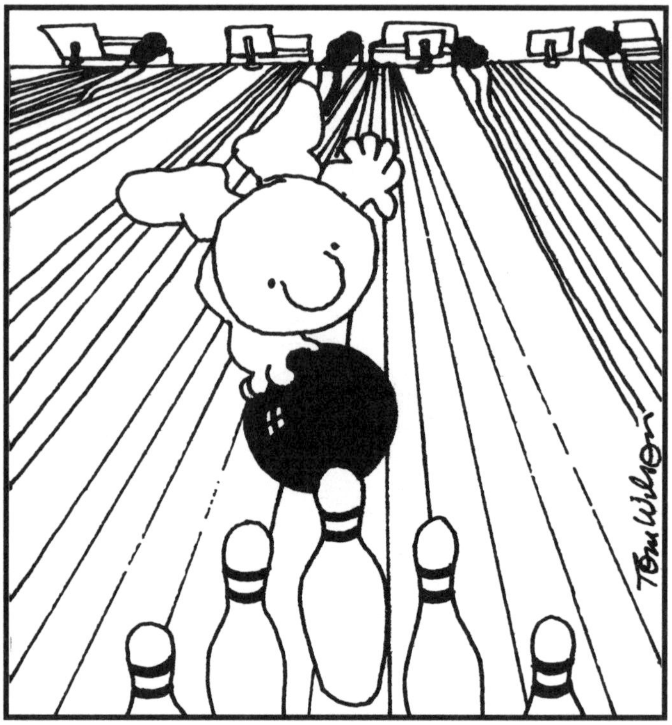
Tom Wilson

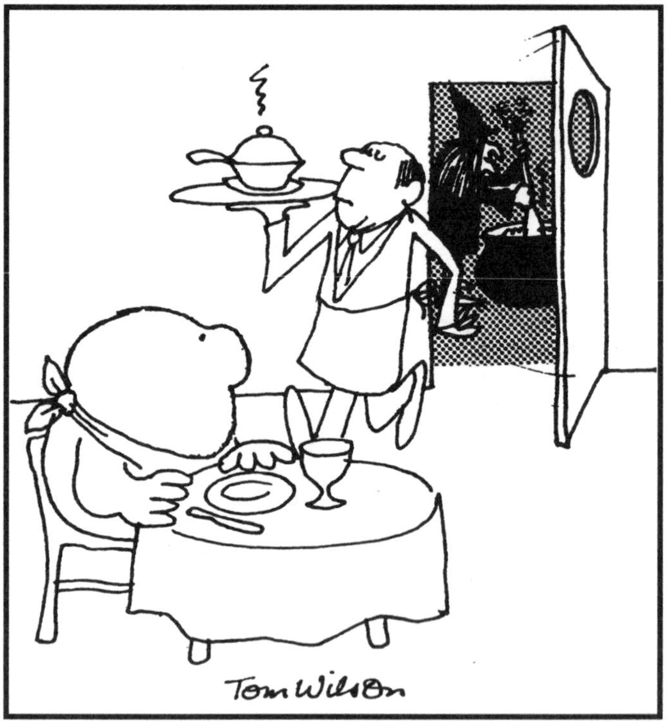
Tom Wilson

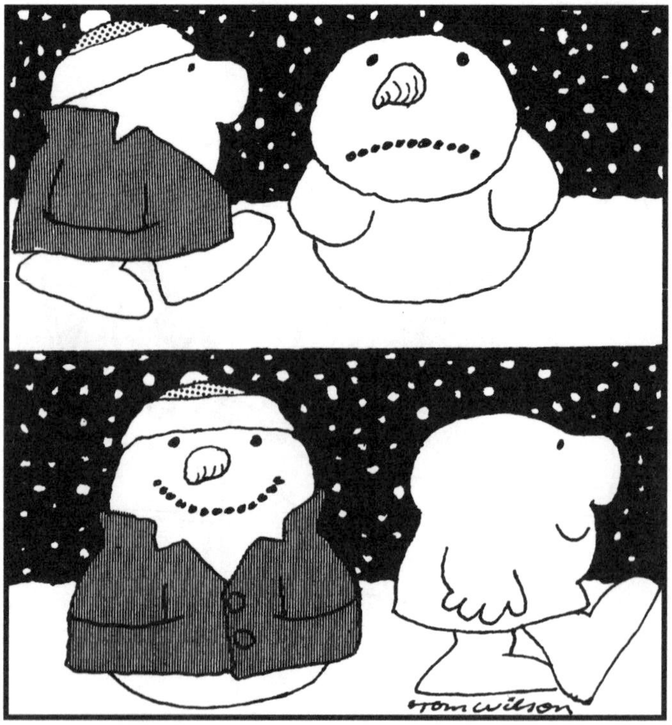
Tom Wilson

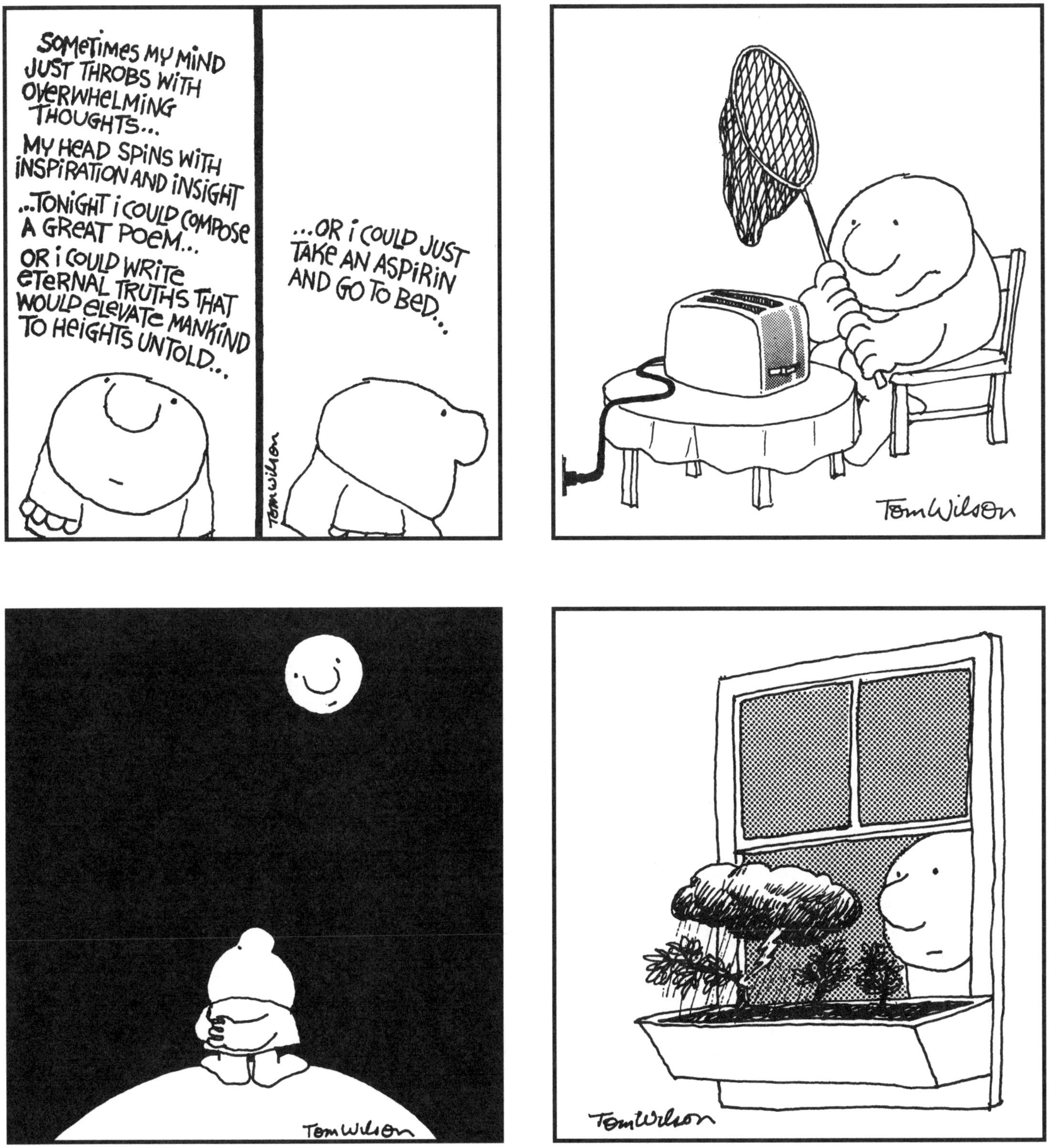
SOMETIMES MY MIND JUST THROBS WITH OVERWHELMING THOUGHTS...
MY HEAD SPINS WITH INSPIRATION AND INSIGHT
...TONIGHT I COULD COMPOSE A GREAT POEM...
OR I COULD WRITE ETERNAL TRUTHS THAT WOULD ELEVATE MANKIND TO HEIGHTS UNTOLD...
...OR I COULD JUST TAKE AN ASPIRIN AND GO TO BED...
Tom Wilson
Tom Wilson
Tom Wilson
Tom Wilson

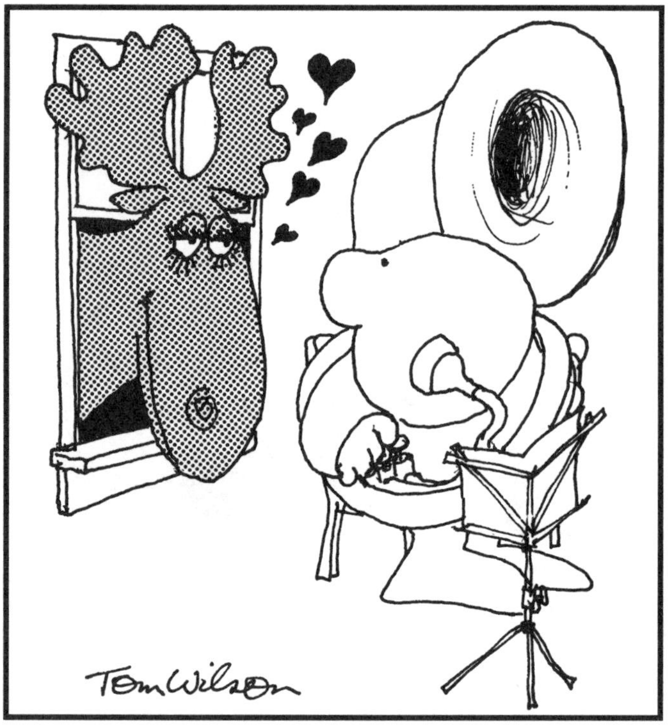
Tom Wilson

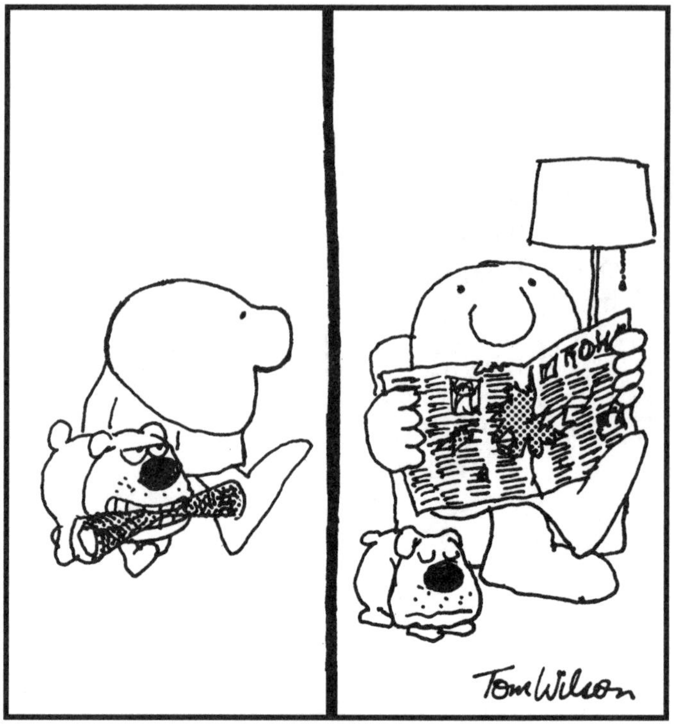
Tom Wilson

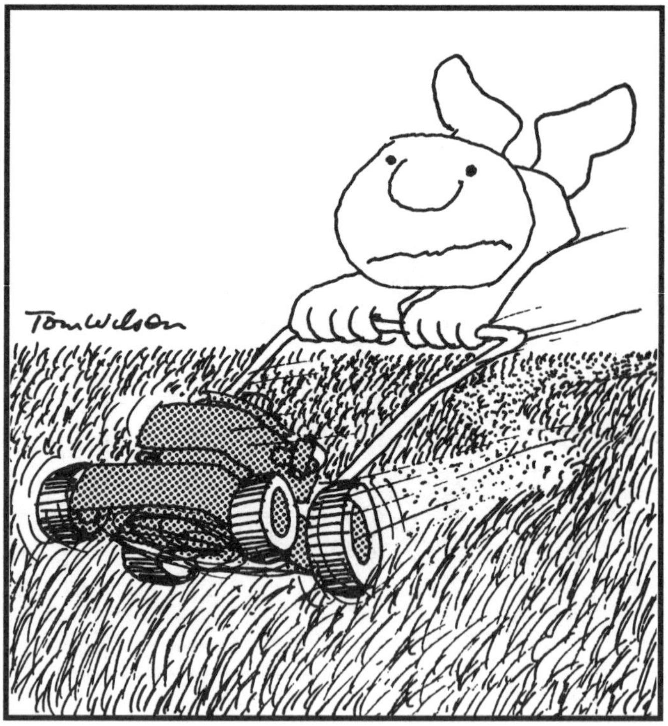
Tom Wilson

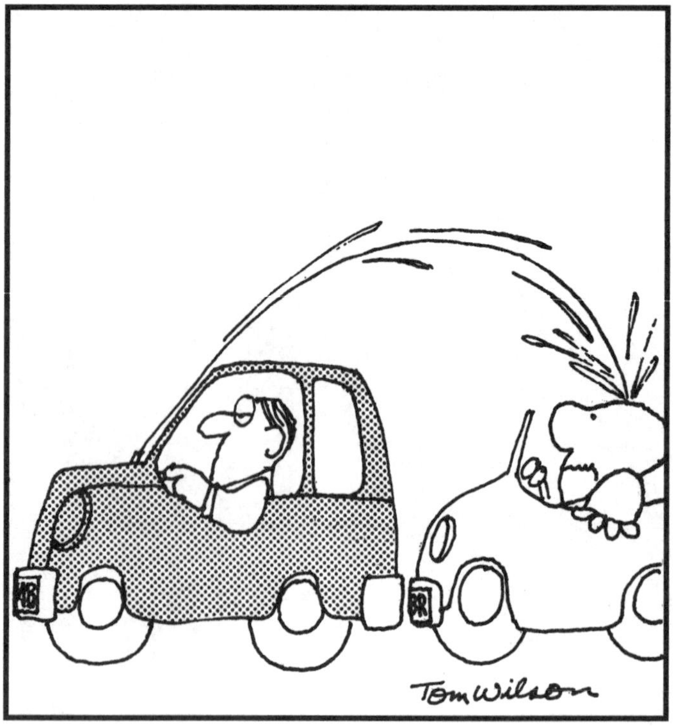
Tom Wilson

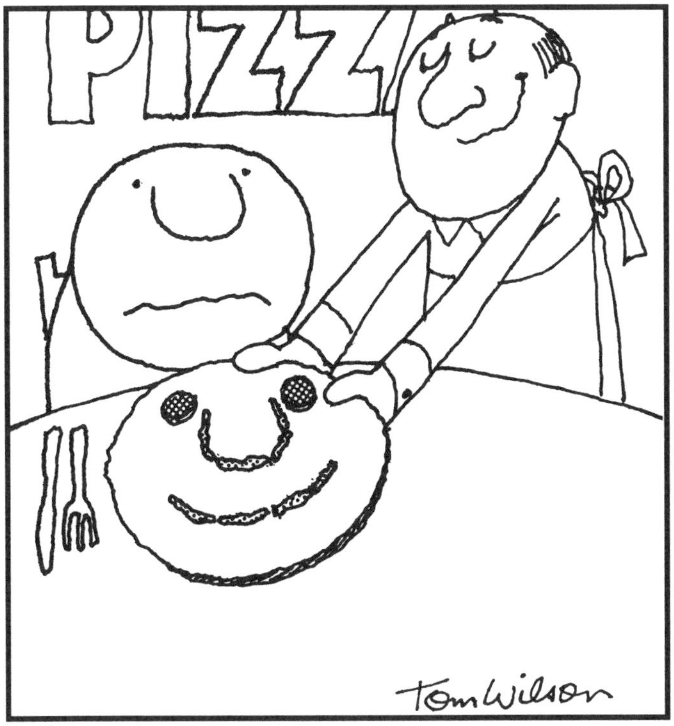
PIZZ
Tom Wilson

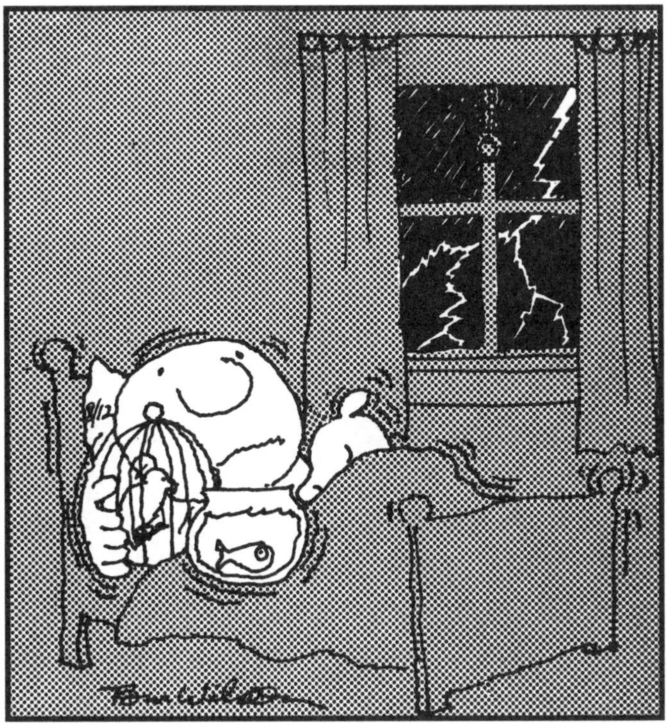

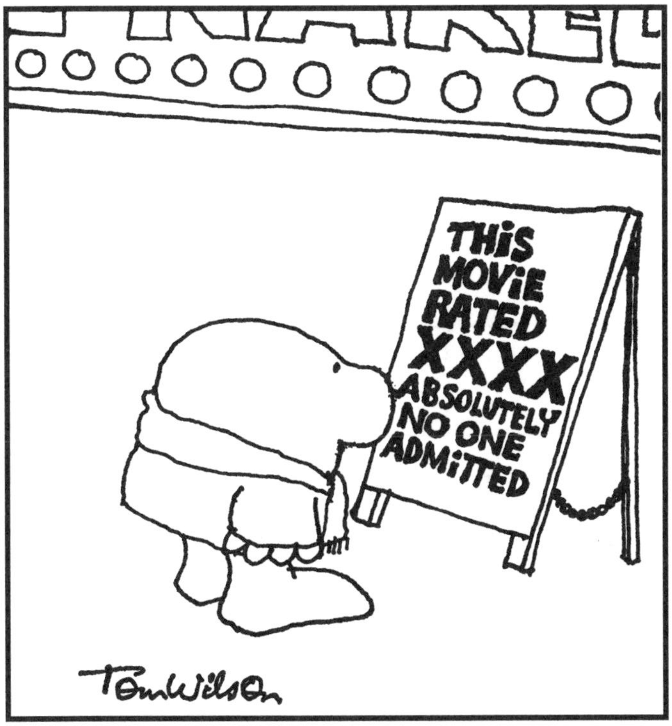
THIS MOVIE RATED XXXX ABSOLUTELY NO ONE ADMITTED
Tom Wilson

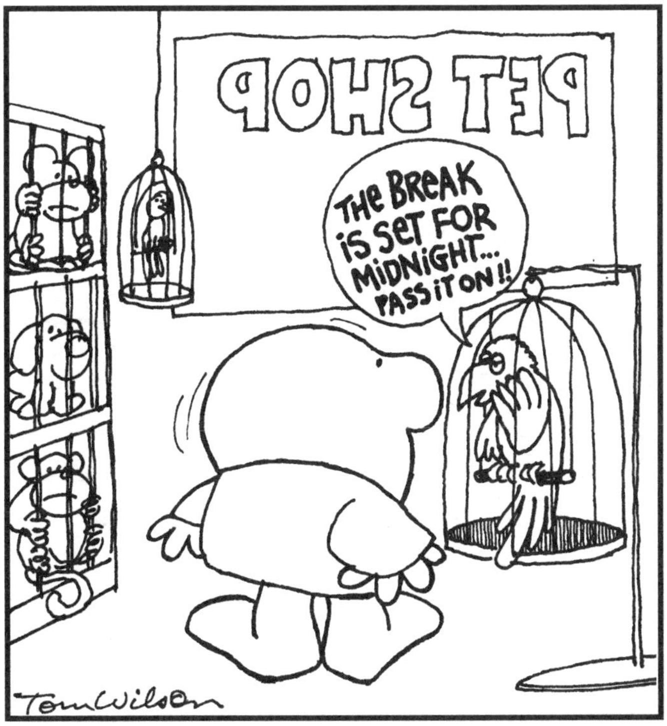
PET SHOP
THE BREAK IS SET FOR MIDNIGHT... PASS IT ON!!
Tom Wilson

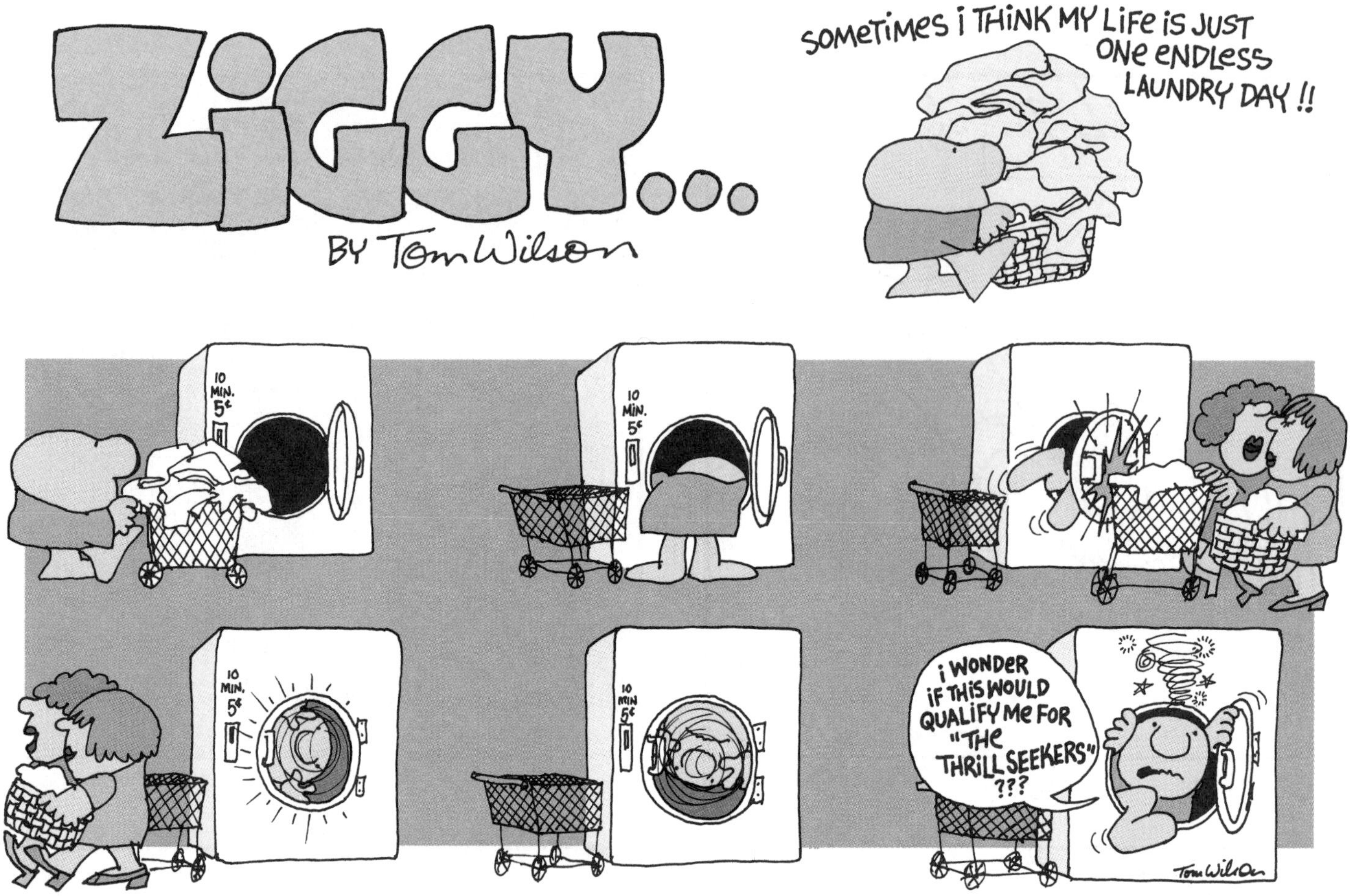
ZIGGY...
BY Tom Wilson
SOMETIMES I THINK MY LIFE IS JUST ONE ENDLESS LAUNDRY DAY !!
10 MIN. 5¢
10 MIN. 5¢
10 MIN. 5¢
10 MIN 5¢
I WONDER IF THIS WOULD QUALIFY ME FOR "THE THRILL SEEKERS" ???
Tom Wilson

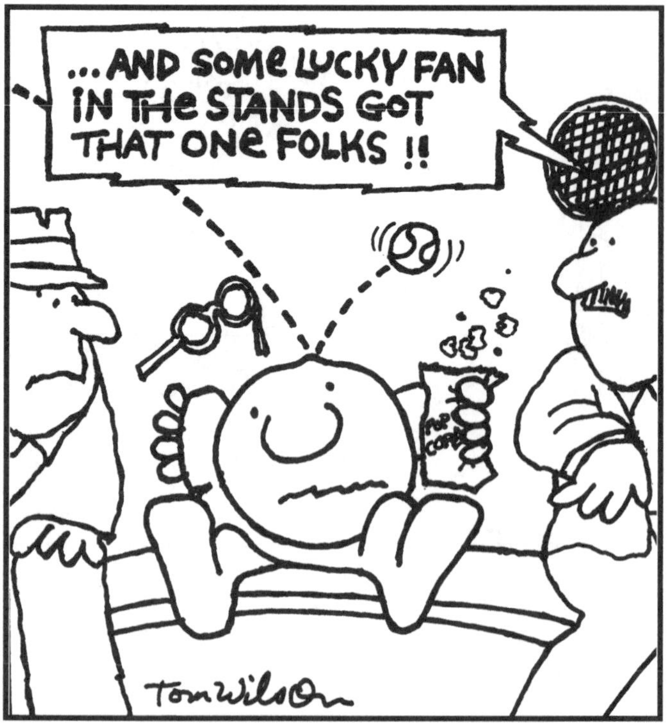
...AND SOME LUCKY FAN IN THE STANDS GOT THAT ONE FOLKS !!
POP CORN
Tom Wilson

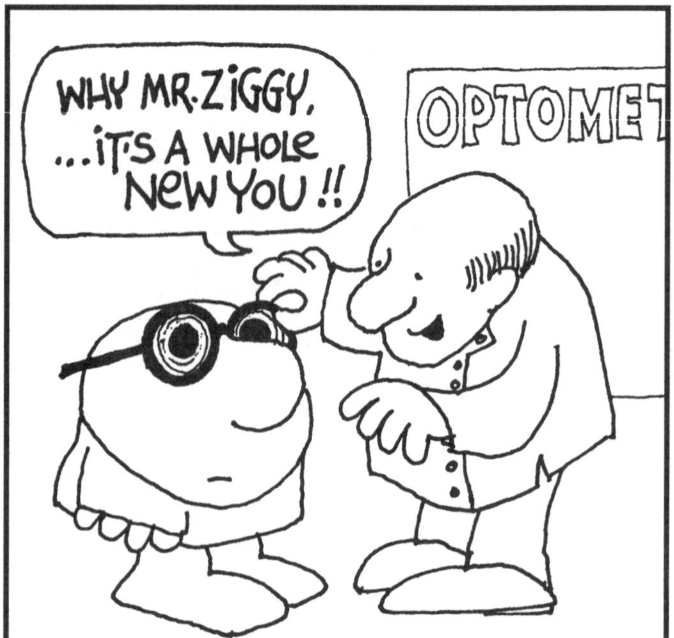
WHY MR. ZIGGY, ...IT'S A WHOLE NEW YOU !!
OPTOMET
Tom Wilson

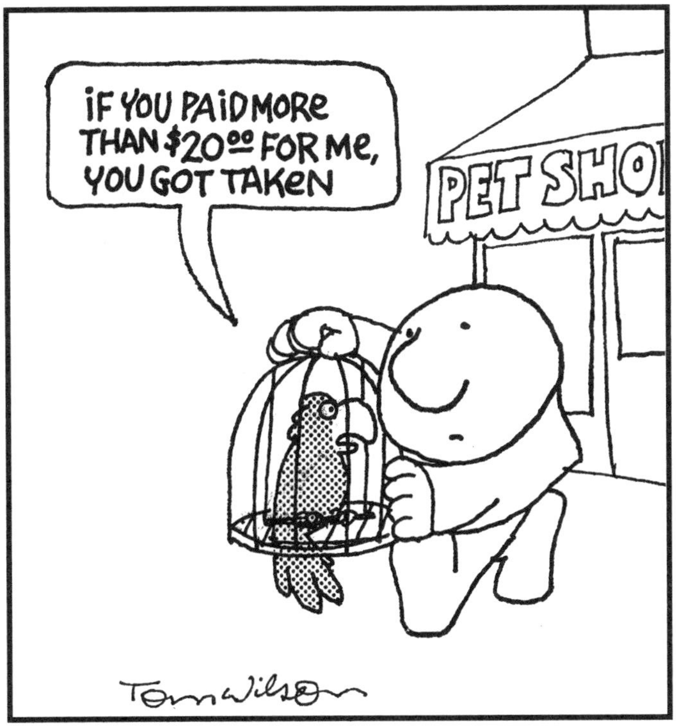
IF YOU PAID MORE THAN $20.00 FOR ME, YOU GOT TAKEN
PET SHO
TOM WILSON

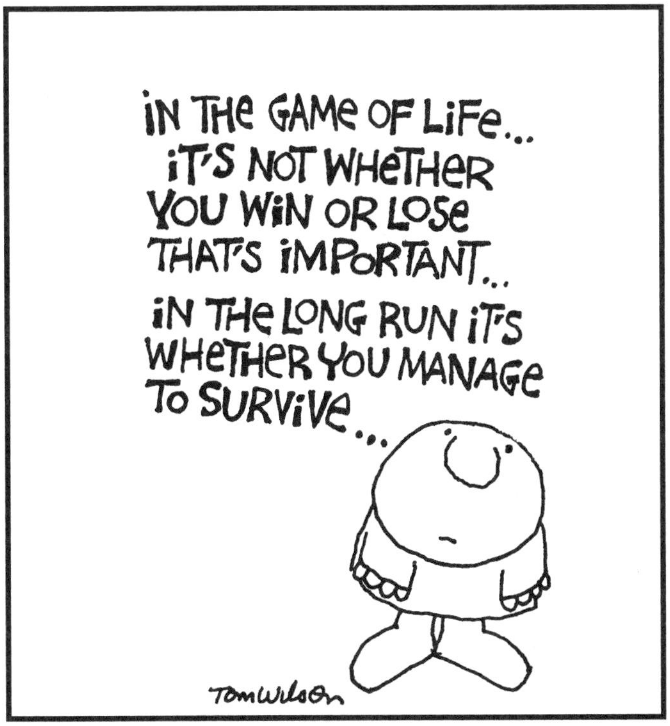
IN THE GAME OF LIFE... IT'S NOT WHETHER YOU WIN OR LOSE THAT'S IMPORTANT... IN THE LONG RUN IT'S WHETHER YOU MANAGE TO SURVIVE...
TOM WILSON

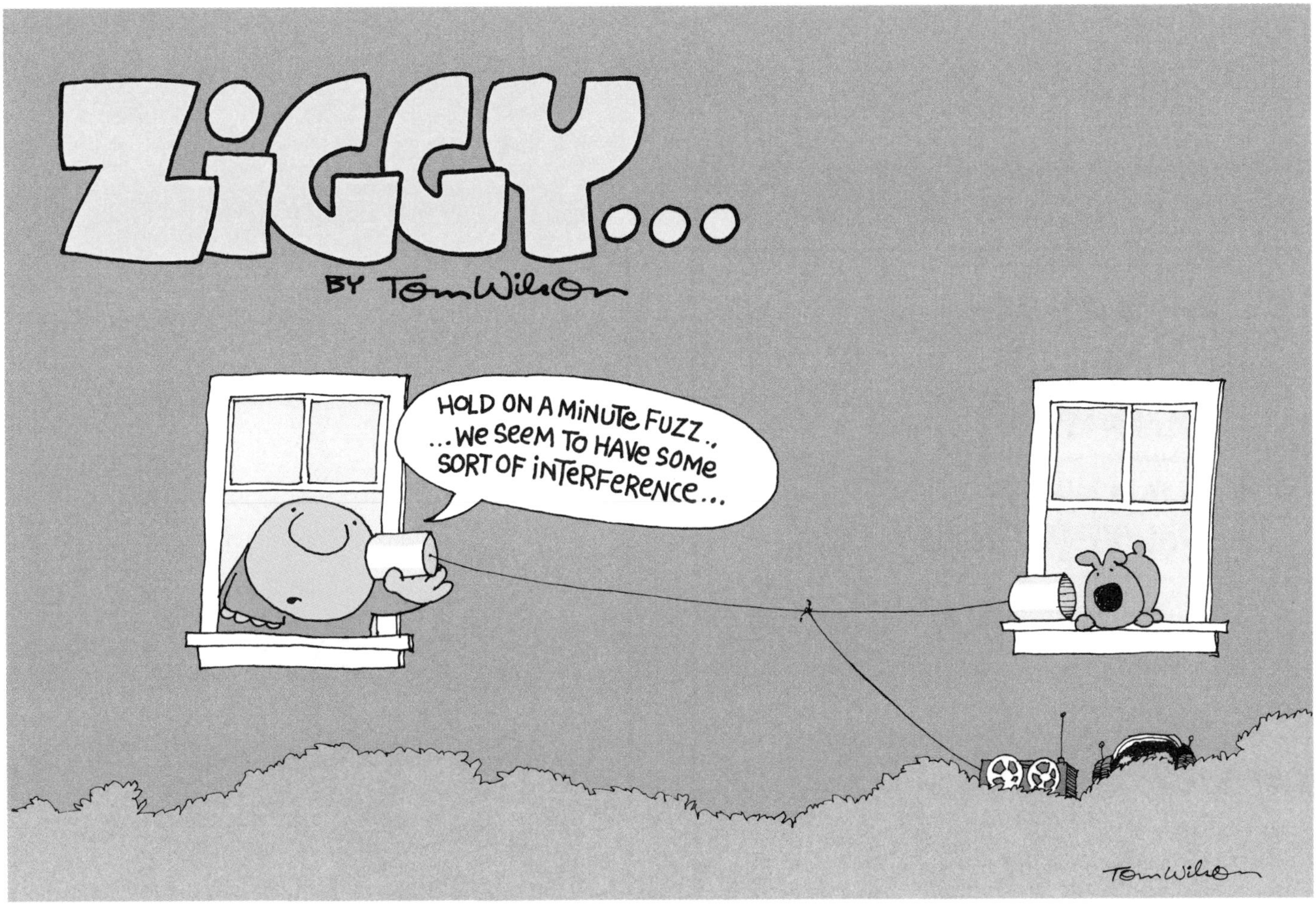
ZIGGY...
BY TOM WILSON
HOLD ON A MINUTE FUZZ.. ...WE SEEM TO HAVE SOME SORT OF INTERFERENCE...
TOM WILSON

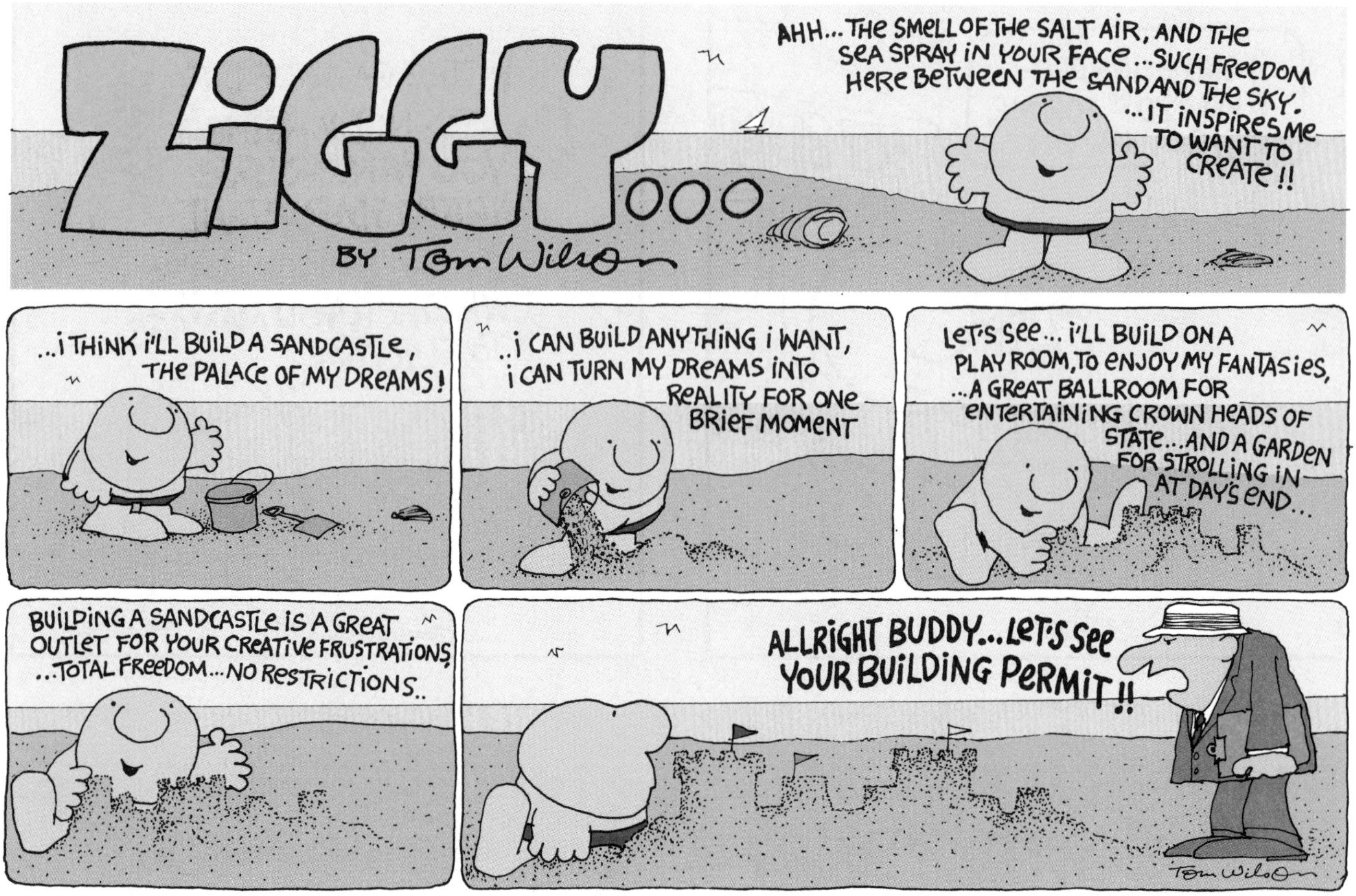
ZIGGY...
BY Tom Wilson
AHH... THE SMELL OF THE SALT AIR, AND THE SEA SPRAY IN YOUR FACE... SUCH FREEDOM HERE BETWEEN THE SAND AND THE SKY. ...IT INSPIRES ME TO WANT TO CREATE!!
...I THINK I'LL BUILD A SANDCASTLE, THE PALACE OF MY DREAMS!
..I CAN BUILD ANYTHING I WANT, I CAN TURN MY DREAMS INTO REALITY FOR ONE BRIEF MOMENT
LET'S SEE... I'LL BUILD ON A PLAY ROOM, TO ENJOY MY FANTASIES, ...A GREAT BALLROOM FOR ENTERTAINING CROWN HEADS OF STATE... AND A GARDEN FOR STROLLING IN AT DAY'S END...
BUILDING A SANDCASTLE IS A GREAT OUTLET FOR YOUR CREATIVE FRUSTRATIONS, ...TOTAL FREEDOM... NO RESTRICTIONS..
ALLRIGHT BUDDY... LET'S SEE YOUR BUILDING PERMIT!!
Tom Wilson

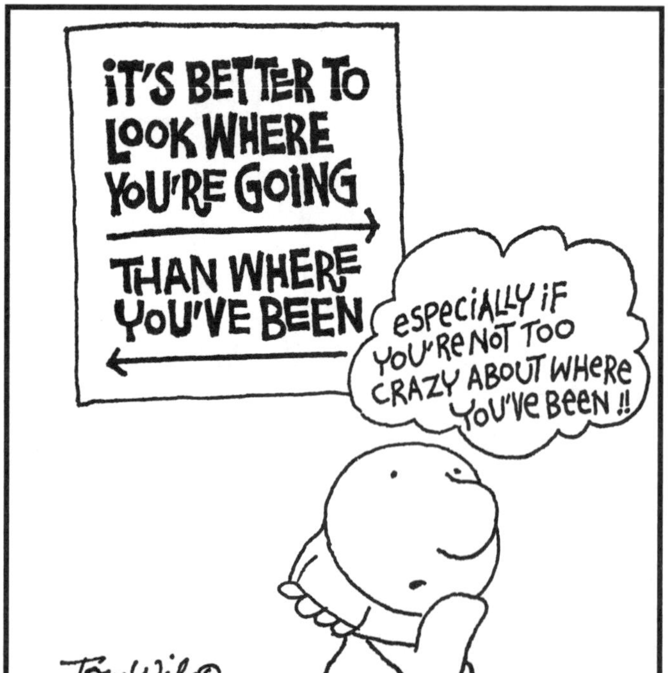
IT'S BETTER TO LOOK WHERE YOU'RE GOING
THAN WHERE YOU'VE BEEN
especially if you're not too crazy about where you've been!!
Tom Wilson

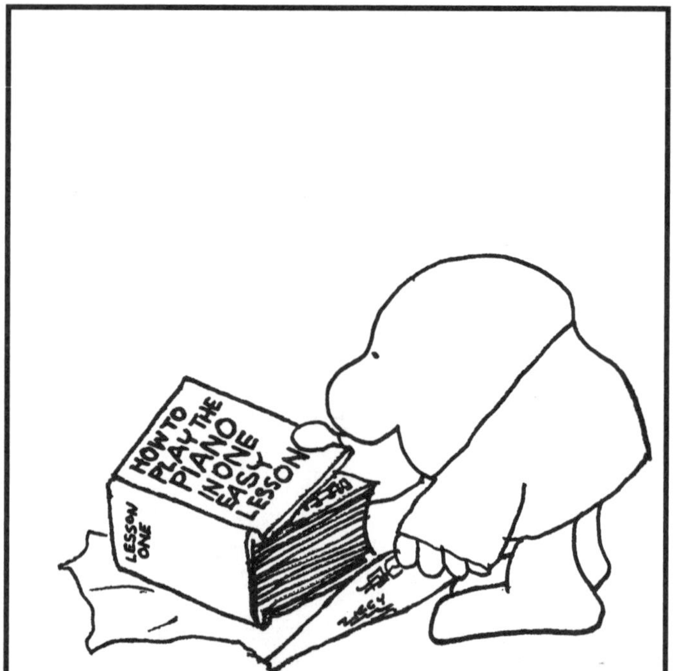
HOW TO PLAY THE PIANO IN ONE EASY LESSON
LESSON ONE
Tom Wilson

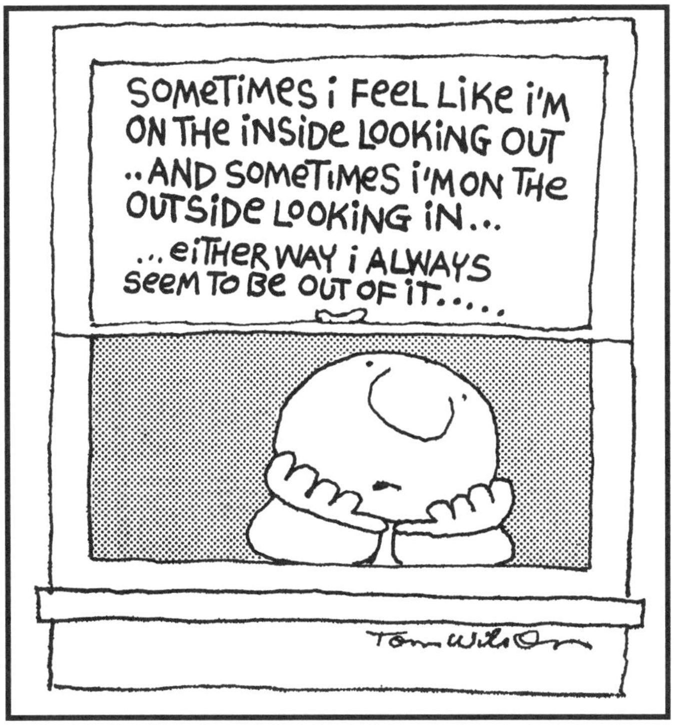
SOMETIMES I FEEL LIKE I'M ON THE INSIDE LOOKING OUT ..AND SOMETIMES I'M ON THE OUTSIDE LOOKING IN... ...EITHER WAY I ALWAYS SEEM TO BE OUT OF IT.....
Tom Wilson

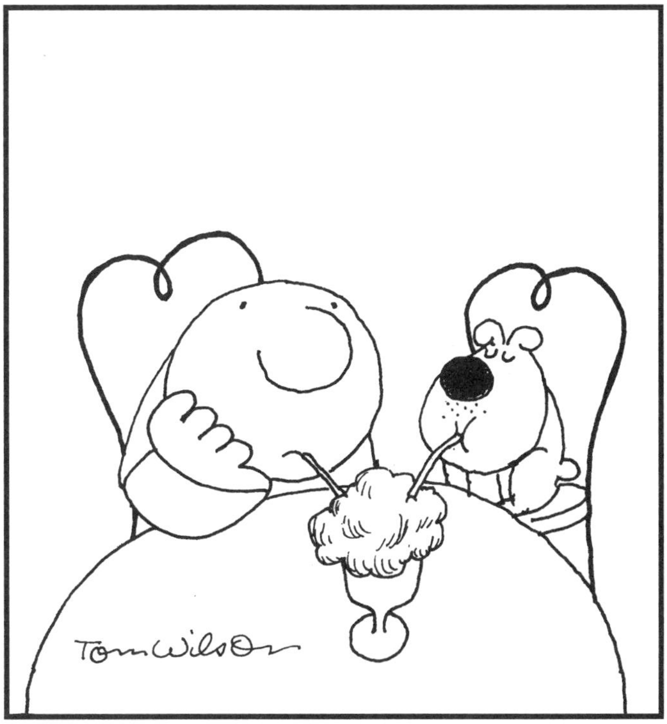
Tom Wilson

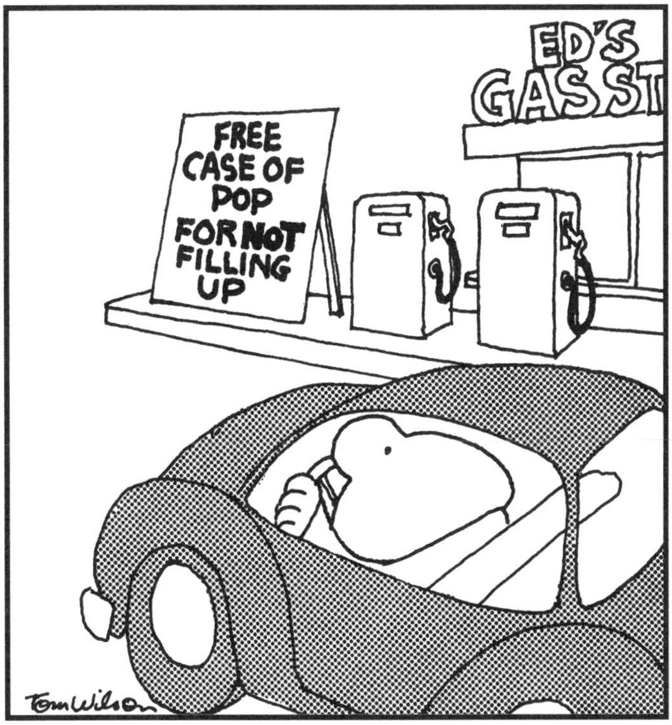
ED'S GAS ST
FREE CASE OF POP FOR NOT FILLING UP
Tom Wilson

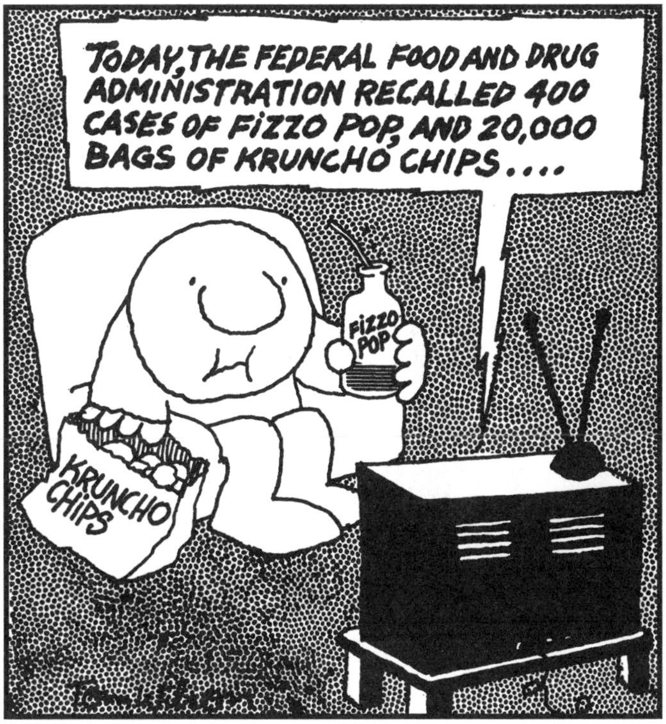
TODAY, THE FEDERAL FOOD AND DRUG ADMINISTRATION RECALLED 400 CASES OF FIZZO POP, AND 20,000 BAGS OF KRUNCHO CHIPS....
FIZZO POP
KRUNCHO CHIPS

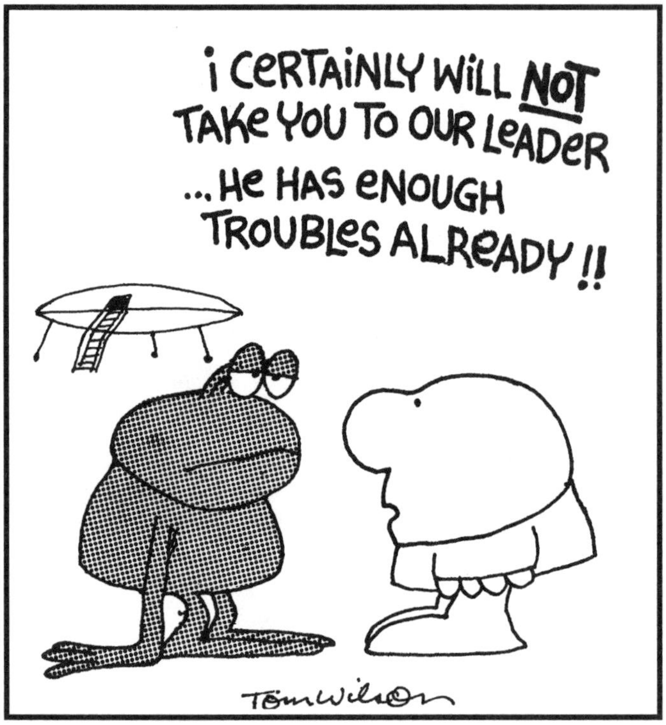
I CERTAINLY WILL NOT TAKE YOU TO OUR LEADER ...HE HAS ENOUGH TROUBLES ALREADY !!

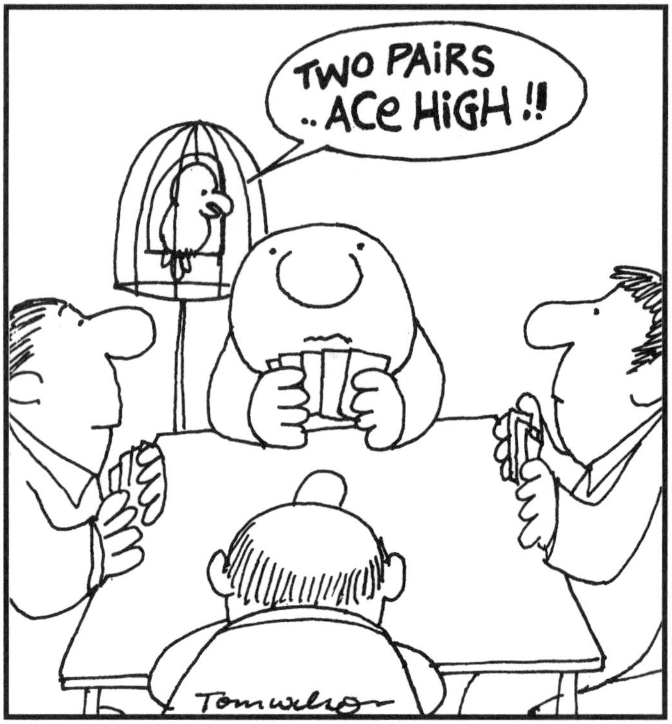
TWO PAIRS ..ACE HIGH !!

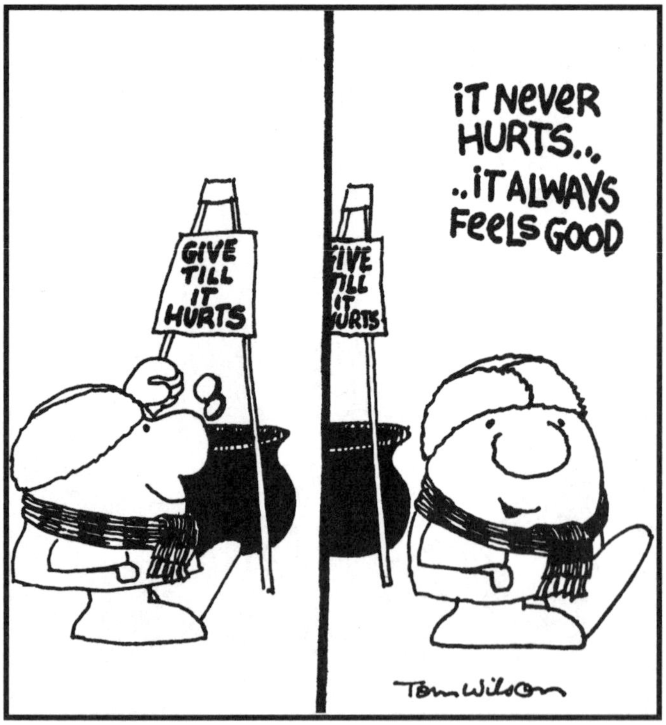
GIVE TILL IT HURTS
IT NEVER HURTS.. ..IT ALWAYS FEELS GOOD

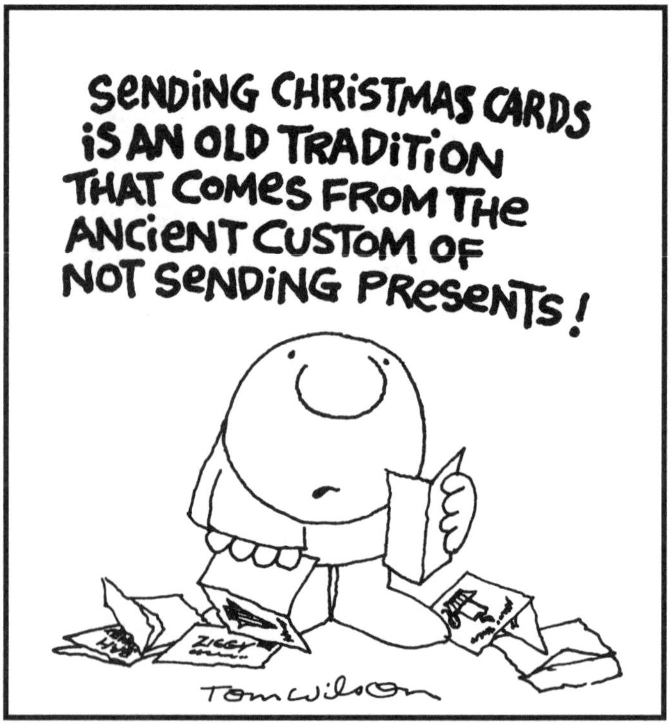
SENDING CHRISTMAS CARDS IS AN OLD TRADITION THAT COMES FROM THE ANCIENT CUSTOM OF NOT SENDING PRESENTS !

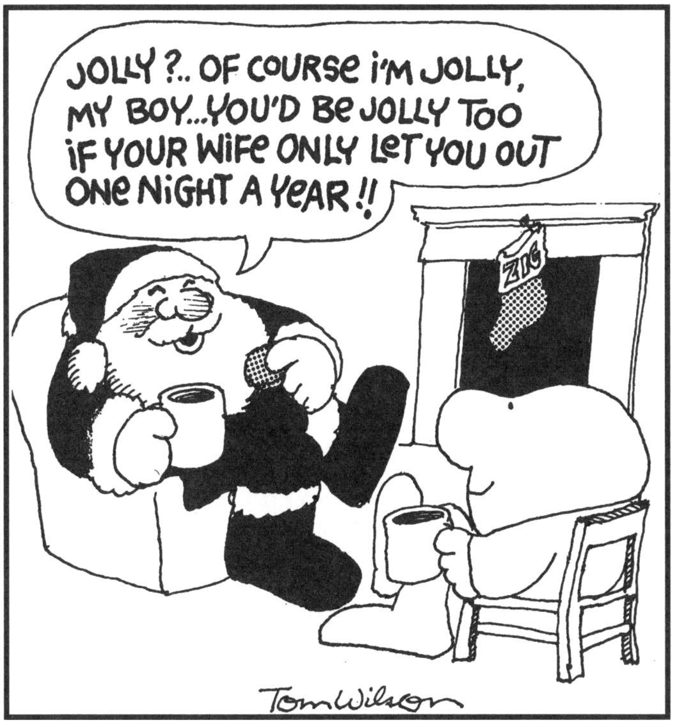
JOLLY ?.. OF COURSE I'M JOLLY, MY BOY...YOU'D BE JOLLY TOO IF YOUR WIFE ONLY LET YOU OUT ONE NIGHT A YEAR !!
ZIG
Tom Wilson

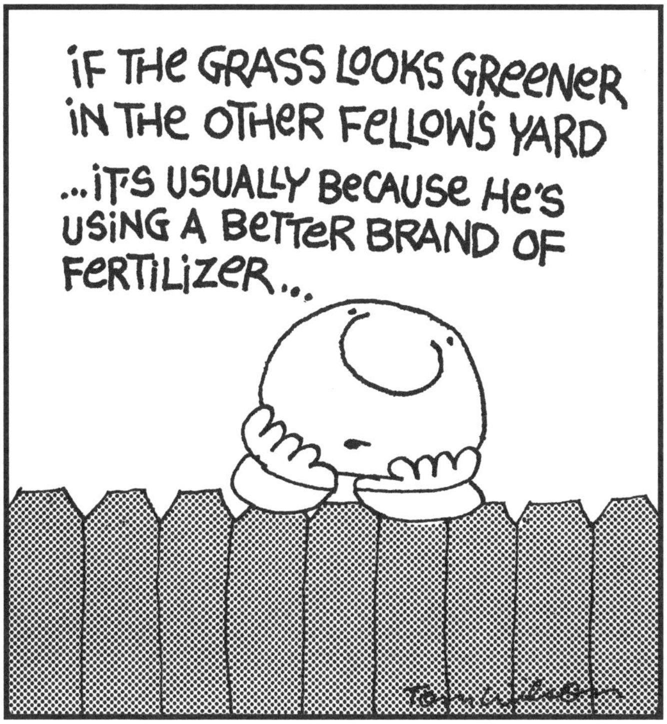
IF THE GRASS LOOKS GREENER IN THE OTHER FELLOW'S YARD
...IT'S USUALLY BECAUSE HE'S USING A BETTER BRAND OF FERTILIZER...
Tom Wilson

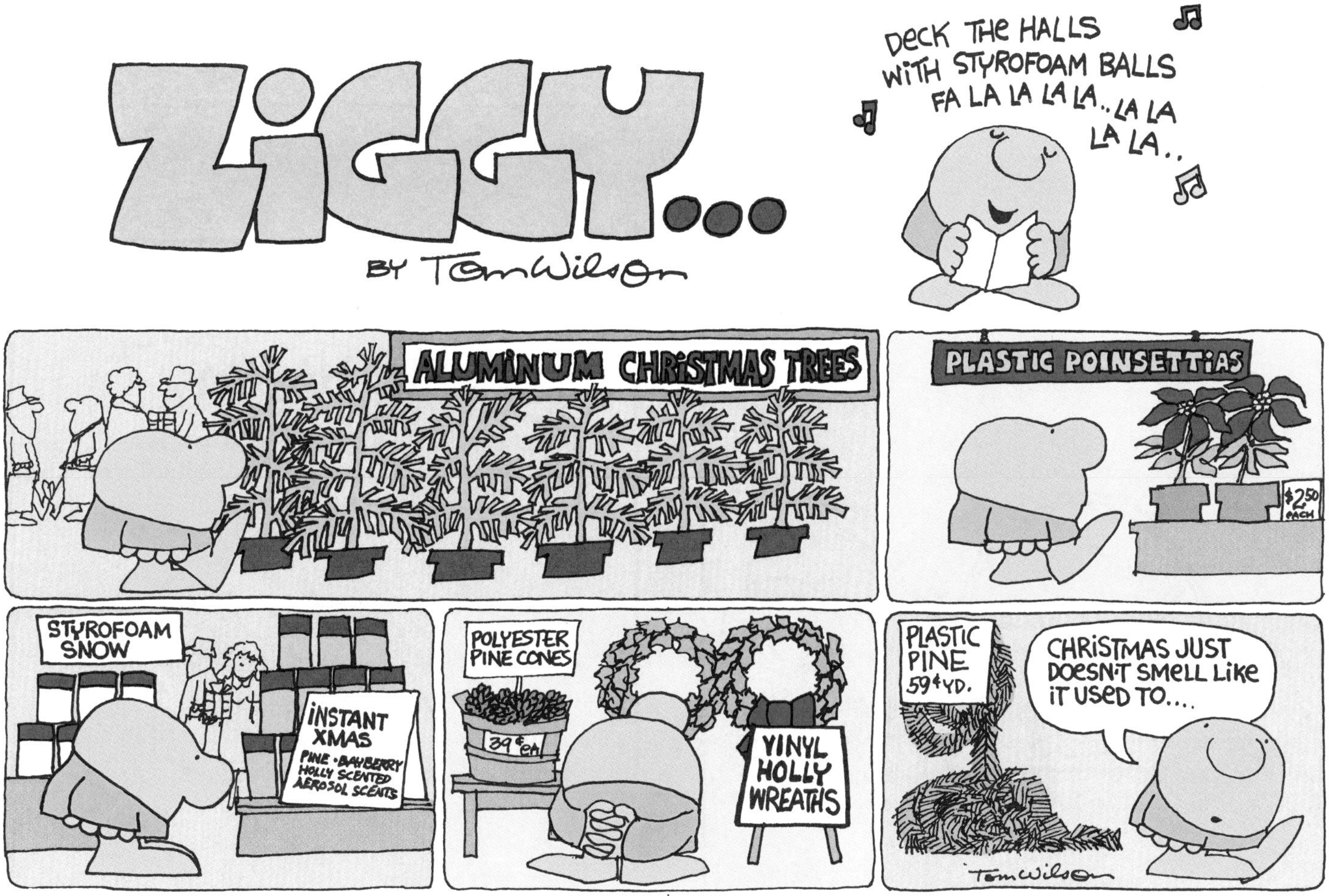
ZIGGY...
BY Tom Wilson
DECK THE HALLS WITH STYROFOAM BALLS FA LA LA LA LA.. LA LA LA LA..
ALUMINUM CHRISTMAS TREES
PLASTIC POINSETTIAS
$2.50 EACH
STYROFOAM SNOW
INSTANT XMAS
PINE • BAYBERRY HOLLY SCENTED AEROSOL SCENTS
POLYESTER PINE CONES
39¢ EA
VINYL HOLLY WREATHS
PLASTIC PINE 59¢ YD.
CHRISTMAS JUST DOESN'T SMELL LIKE IT USED TO....
Tom Wilson

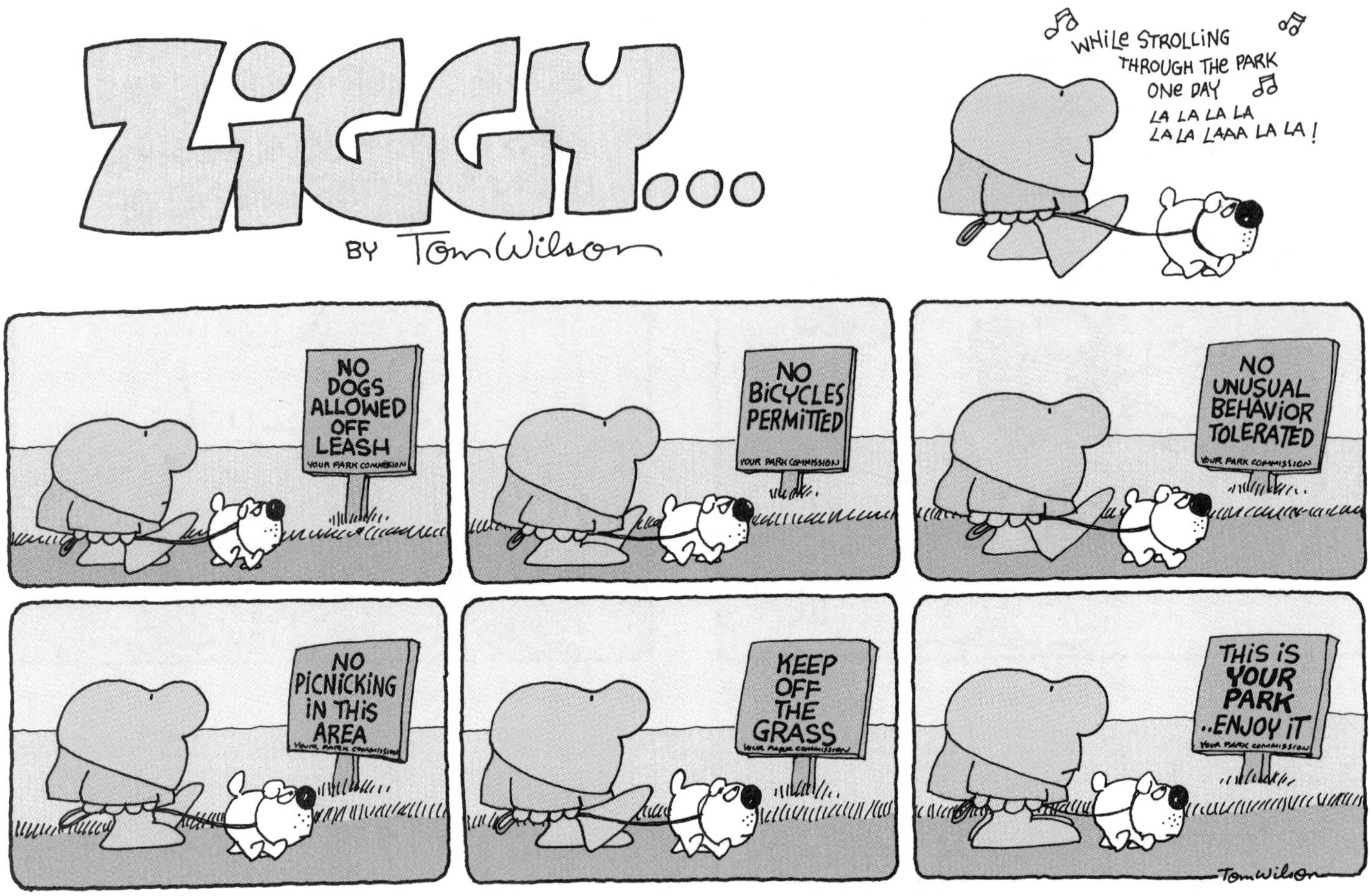
ZiGGY...
BY Tom Wilson
WHiLe STROLLiNG THROUGH THe PARK ONe DAY
LA LA LA LA LA LA LAAA LA LA!
NO DOGS ALLOWED OFF LEASH
YOUR PARK COMMISSION
NO BiCYCLES PERMiTTED
YOUR PARK COMMISSION
NO UNUSUAL BEHAViOR TOLERATED
YOUR PARK COMMISSION
NO PiCNiCKiNG iN THiS AREA
KEEP OFF THE GRASS
THiS iS YOUR PARK ..ENJOY iT
YOUR PARK COMMISSION
Tom Wilson

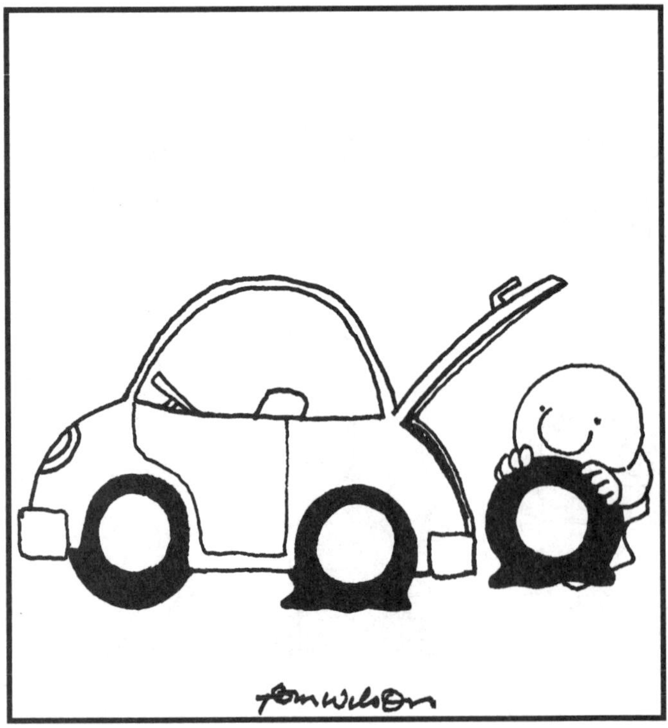
Tom Wilson

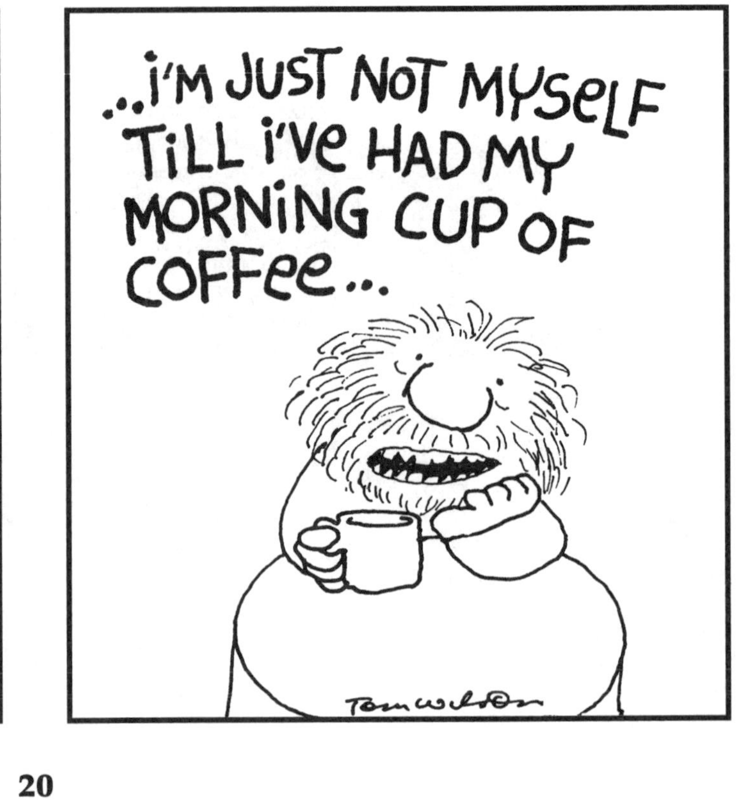
...i'M JUST NOT MYSeLF TiLL i'Ve HAD MY MORNiNG CUP OF COFFee...
Tom Wilson

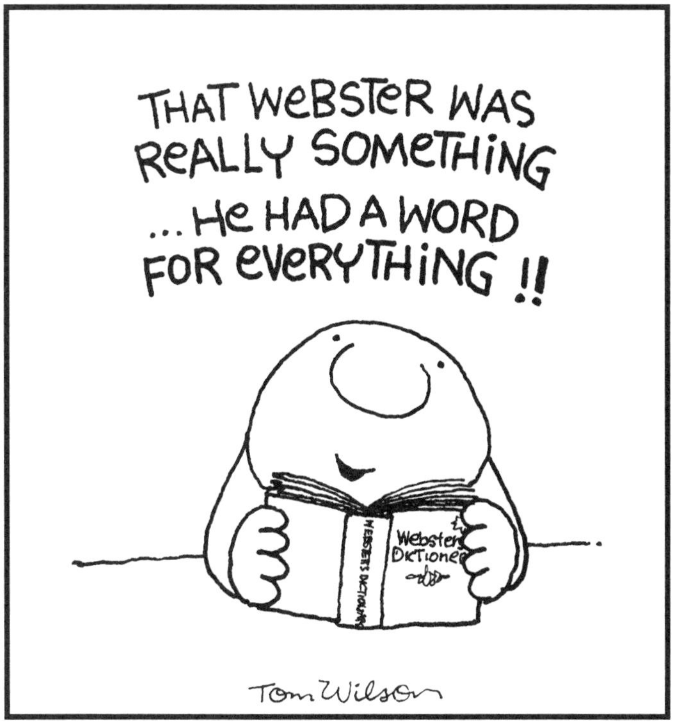
THAT WEBSTER WAS REALLY SOMETHING ...HE HAD A WORD FOR EVERYTHING !!
Webster Dictionary
WEBSTER'S DICTIONARY
Tom Wilson

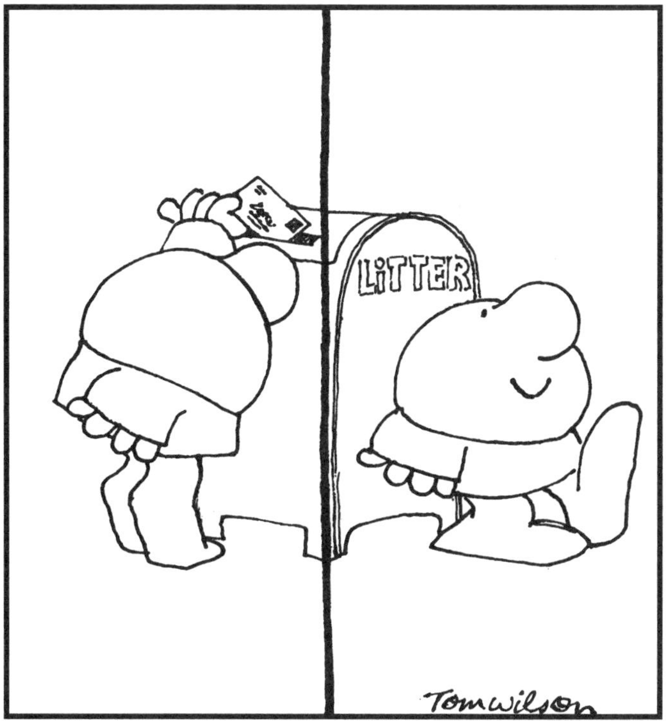
LITTER
Tom Wilson

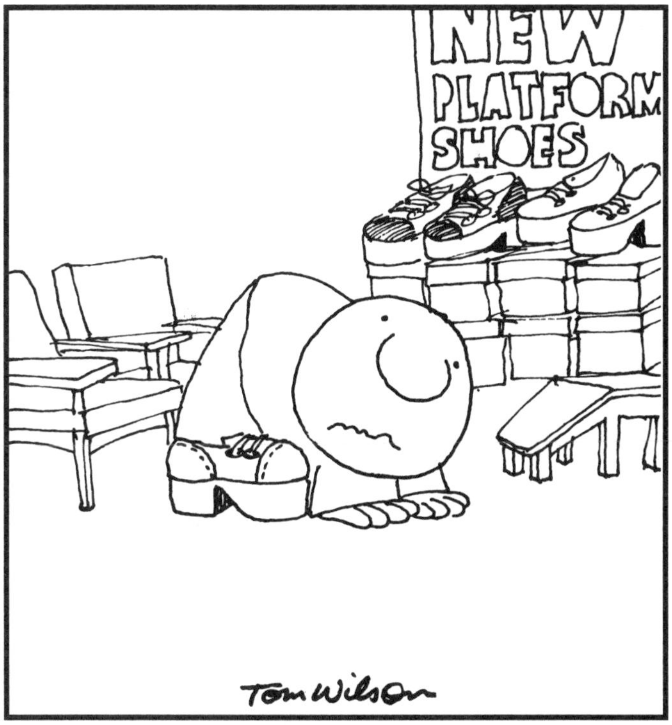
NEW PLATFORM SHOES
Tom Wilson

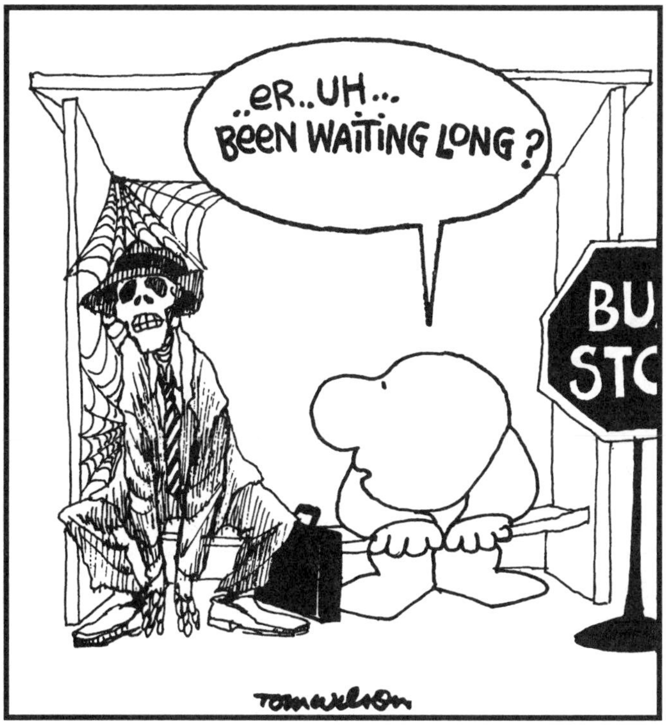
..ER..UH... BEEN WAITING LONG?
Tom Wilson

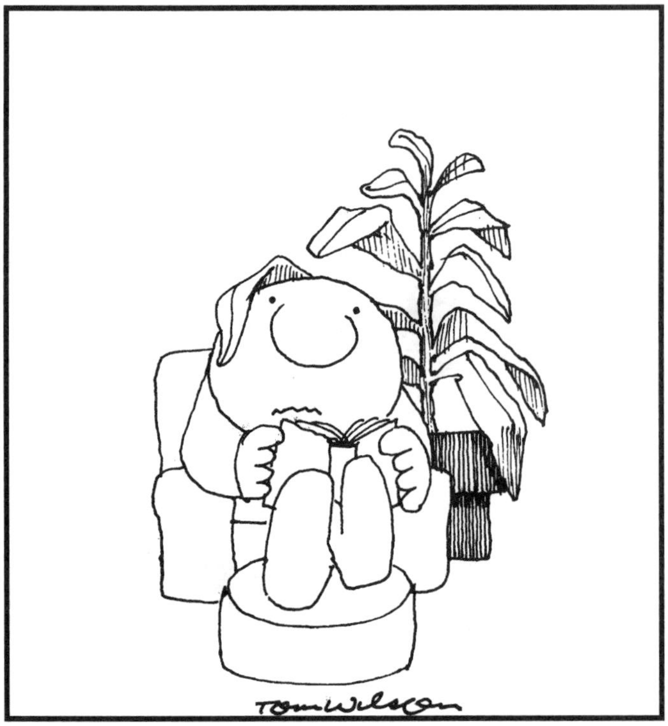

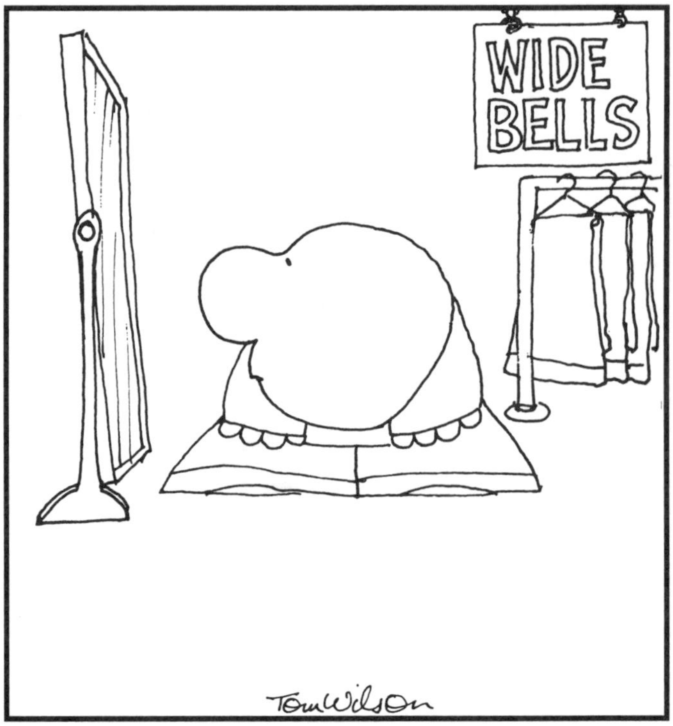
WIDE BELLS

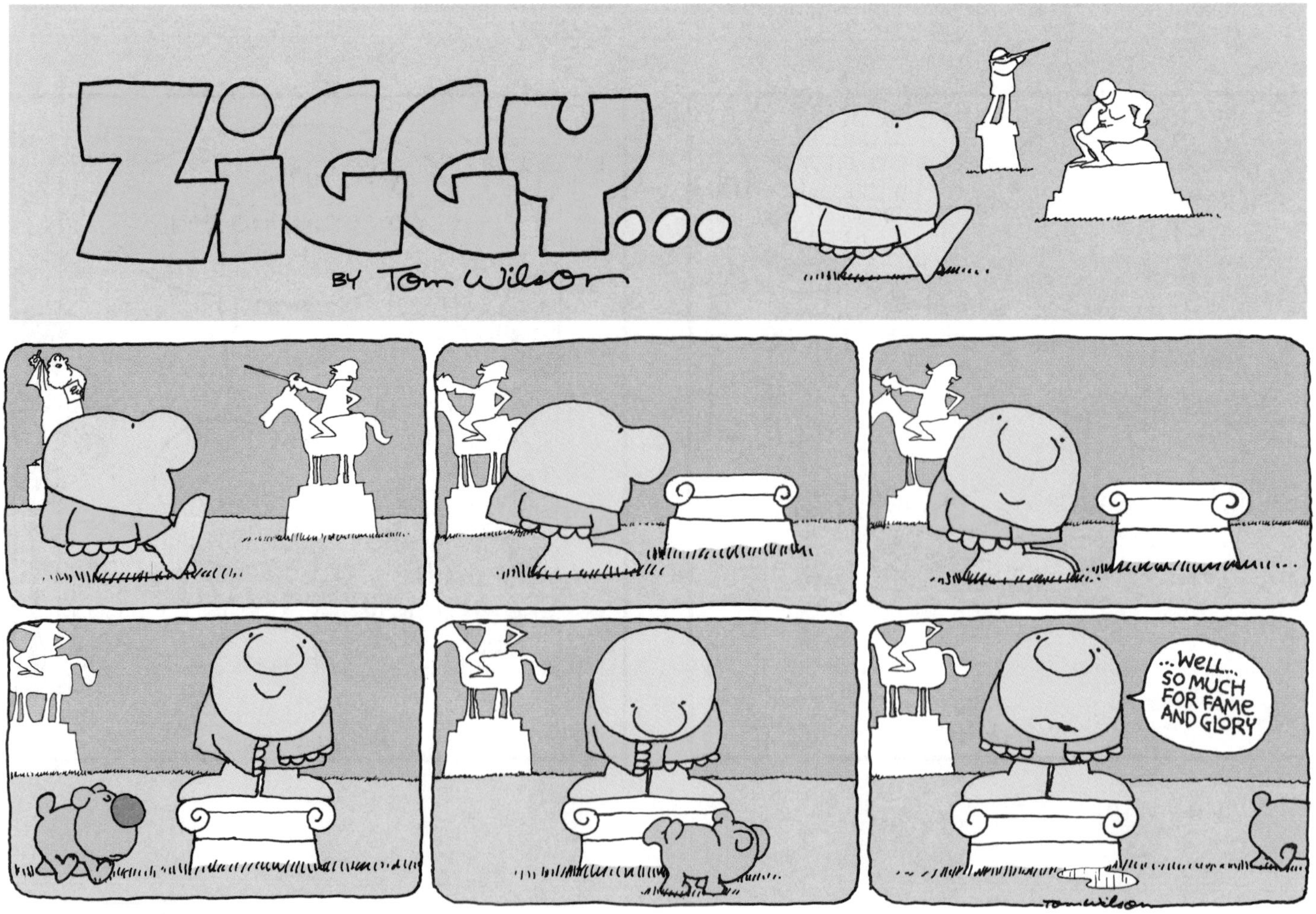
ZIGGY...
BY TOM WILSON
...WELL... SO MUCH FOR FAME AND GLORY

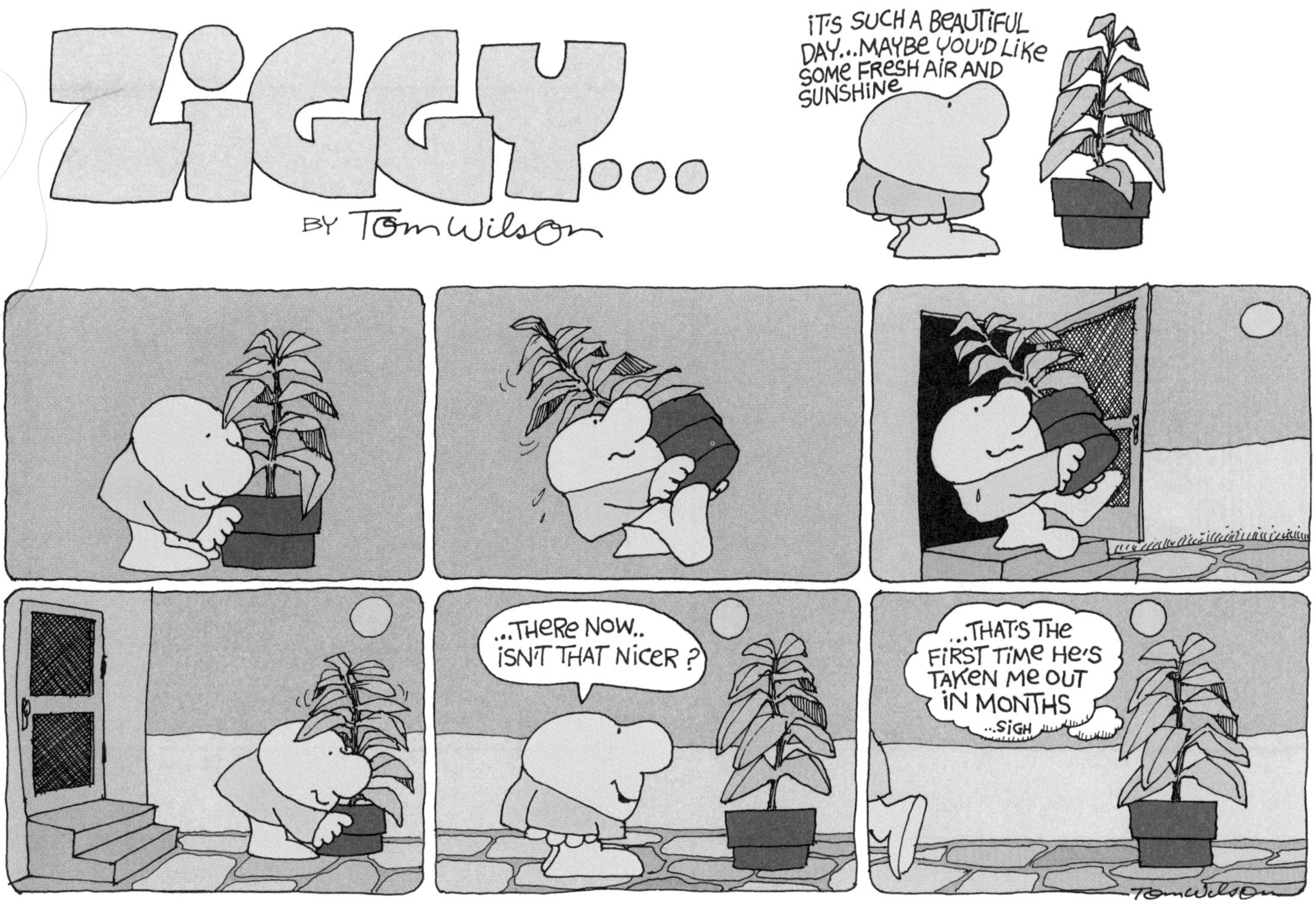
ZIGGY...
BY Tom Wilson
IT'S SUCH A BEAUTIFUL DAY...MAYBE YOU'D LIKE SOME FRESH AIR AND SUNSHINE
..THERE NOW.. ISN'T THAT NICER ?
..THAT'S THE FIRST TIME HE'S TAKEN ME OUT IN MONTHS
..SIGH
Tom Wilson

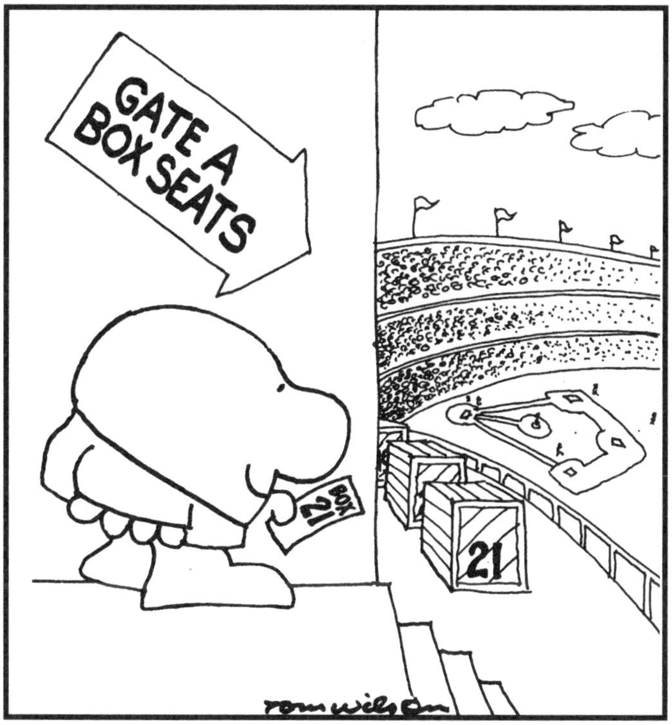
GATE A BOX SEATS
BOX 21
21
Tom Wilson

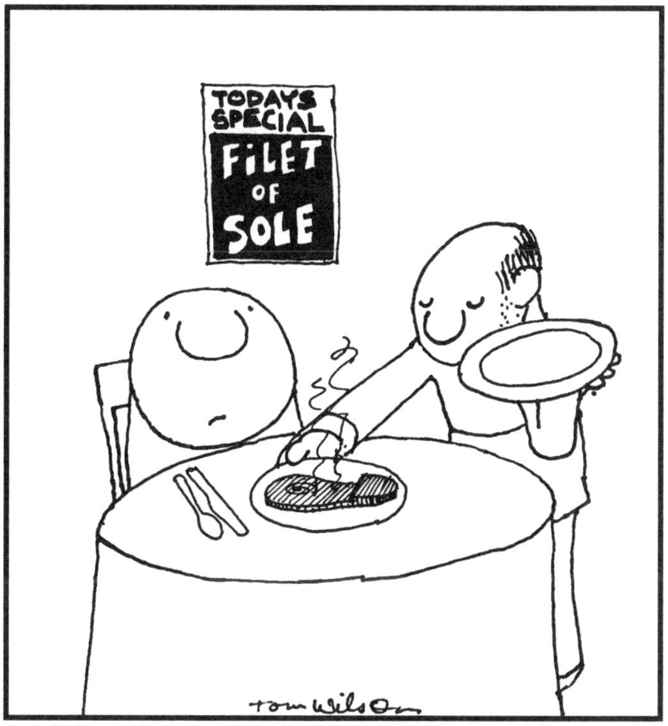
TODAYS SPECIAL
FILET OF SOLE
Tom Wilson

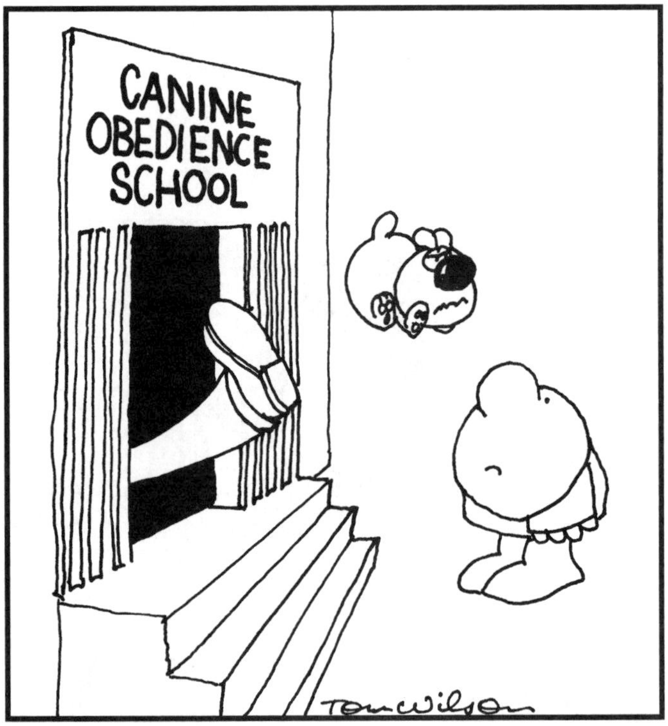
CANINE
OBEDIENCE
SCHOOL
TOM WILSON

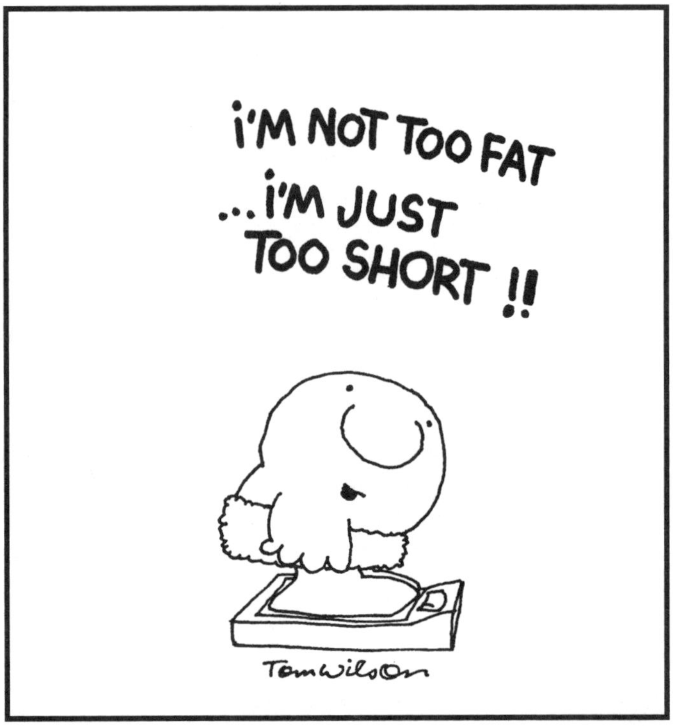
I'M NOT TOO FAT
...I'M JUST
TOO SHORT !!
TOM WILSON

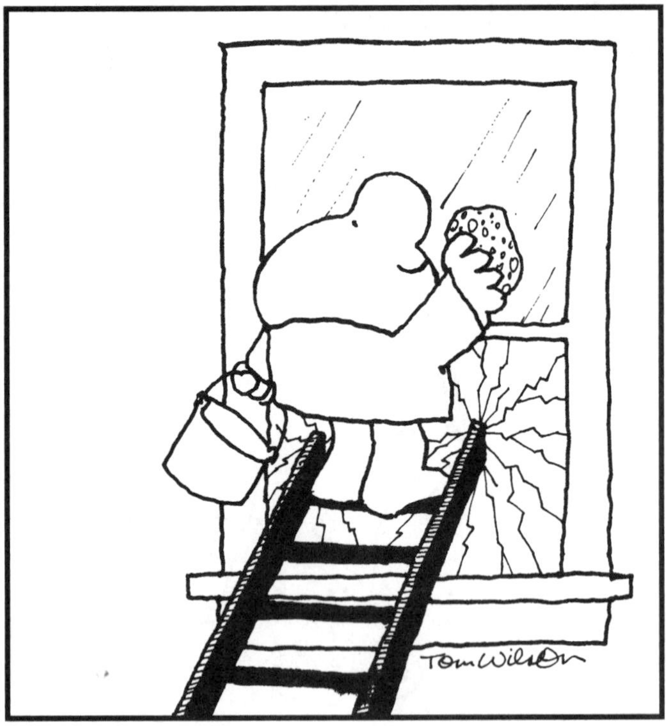
TOM WILSON

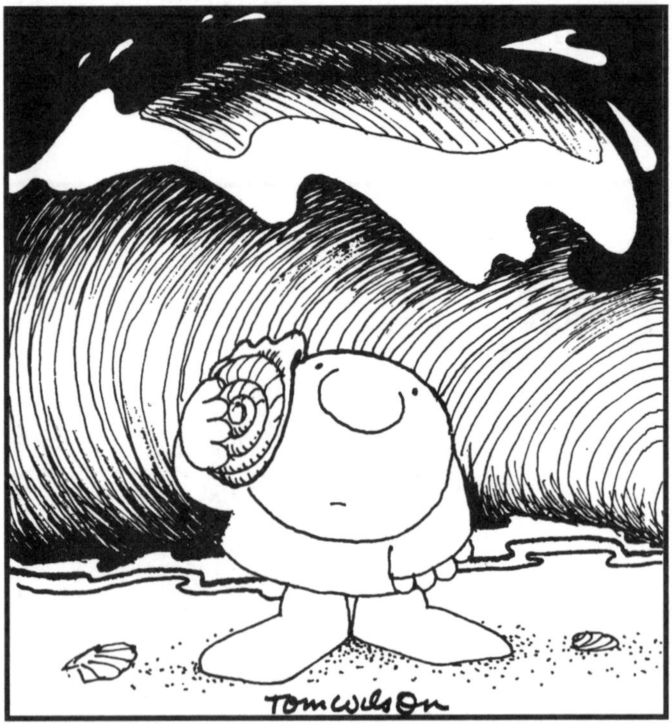
TOM WILSON

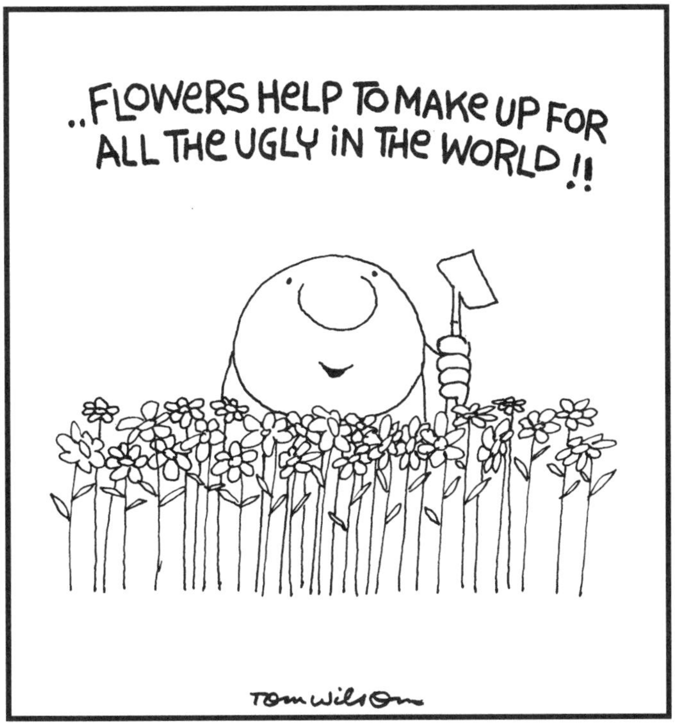
..FLOWERS HELP TO MAKE UP FOR ALL THE UGLY IN THE WORLD !!
TOM WILSON

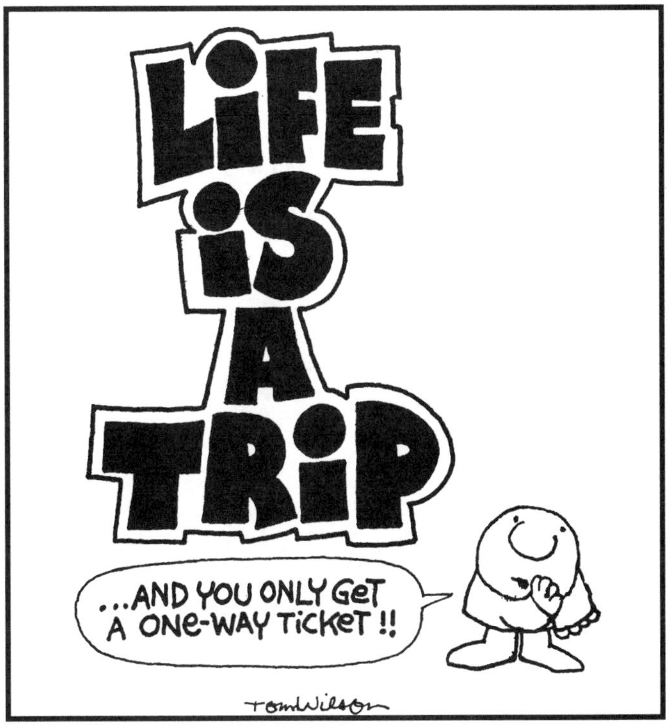
LIFE IS A TRIP
...AND YOU ONLY GET A ONE-WAY TICKET !!
TOM WILSON

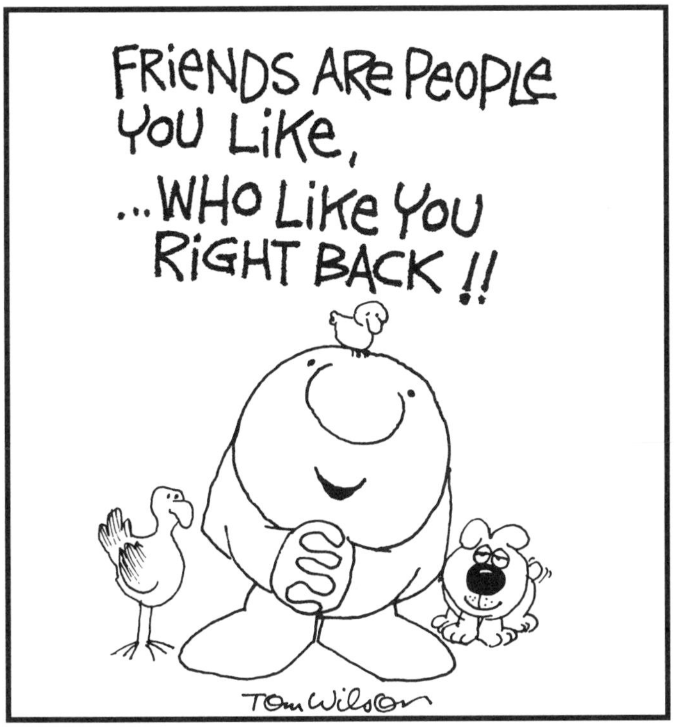
FRIENDS ARE PEOPLE YOU LIKE,
...WHO LIKE YOU RIGHT BACK !!
TOM WILSON

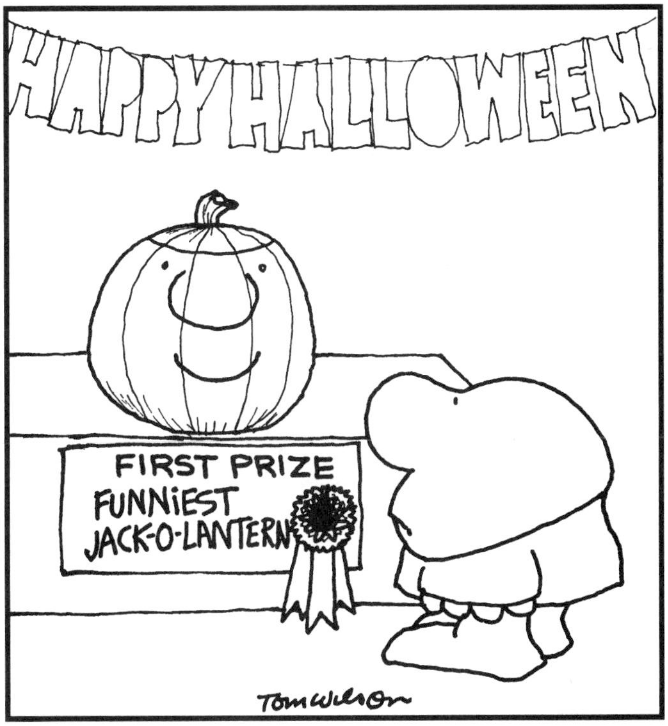
HAPPY HALLOWEEN
FIRST PRIZE
FUNNIEST
JACK-O-LANTERN
TOM WILSON

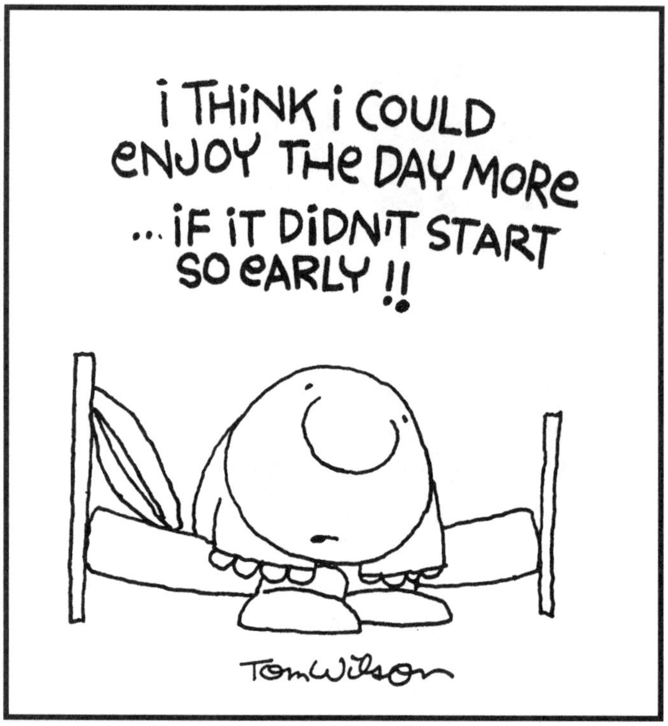
i THiNK i COULD enJOY THe DAY MORe ...iF iT DiDN'T START SO eARLY !!
Tom Wilson

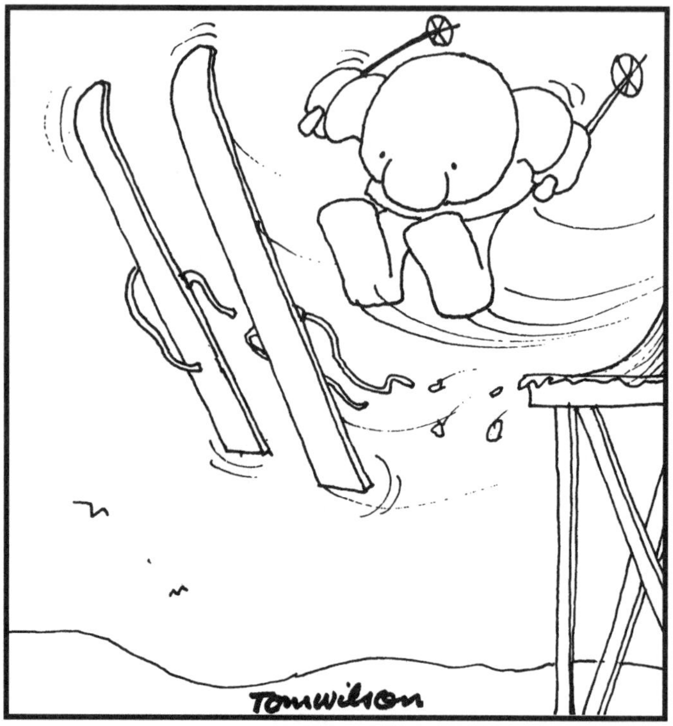
Tom Wilson

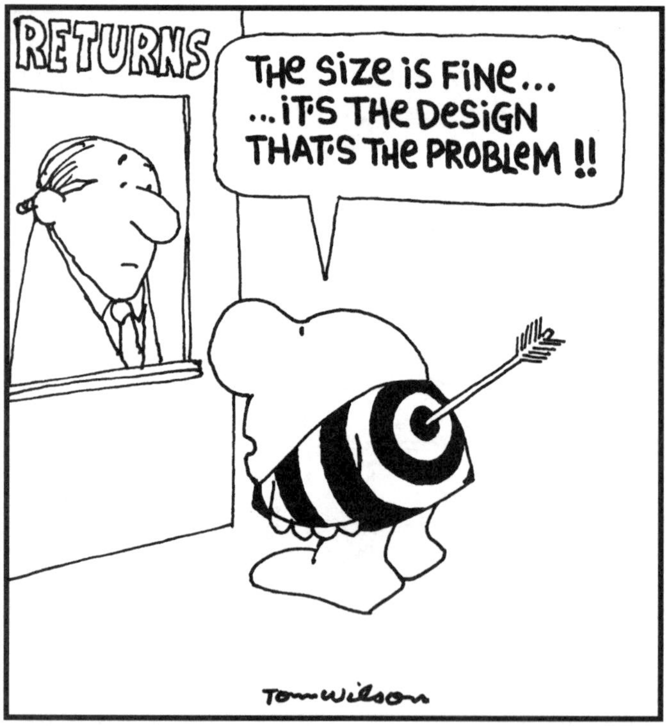
RETURNS
THe Size is FiNe... ...iT'S THe DeSiGN THAT'S THe PROBLeM !!
Tom Wilson

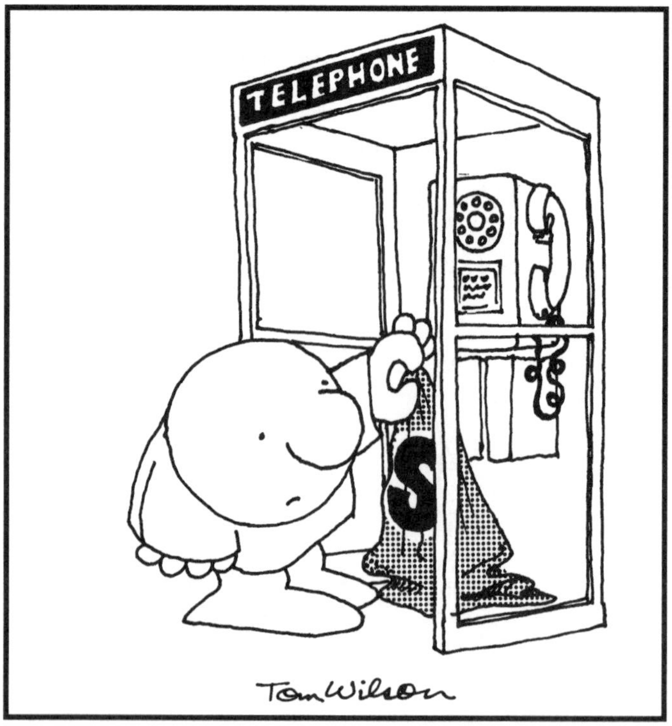
TELEPHONE
S
Tom Wilson

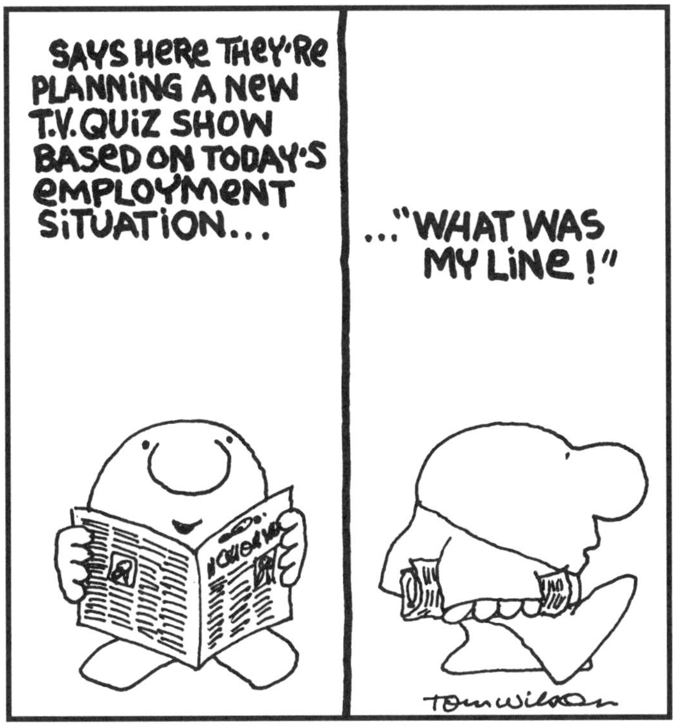
SAYS HERE THEY'RE PLANNING A NEW T.V. QUIZ SHOW BASED ON TODAY'S EMPLOYMENT SITUATION...
..."WHAT WAS MY LINE!"
Tom Wilson

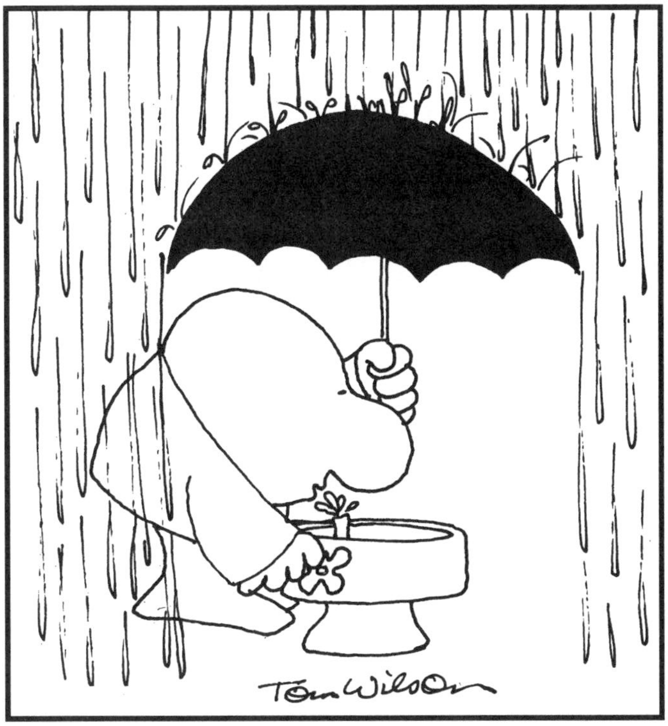
Tom Wilson

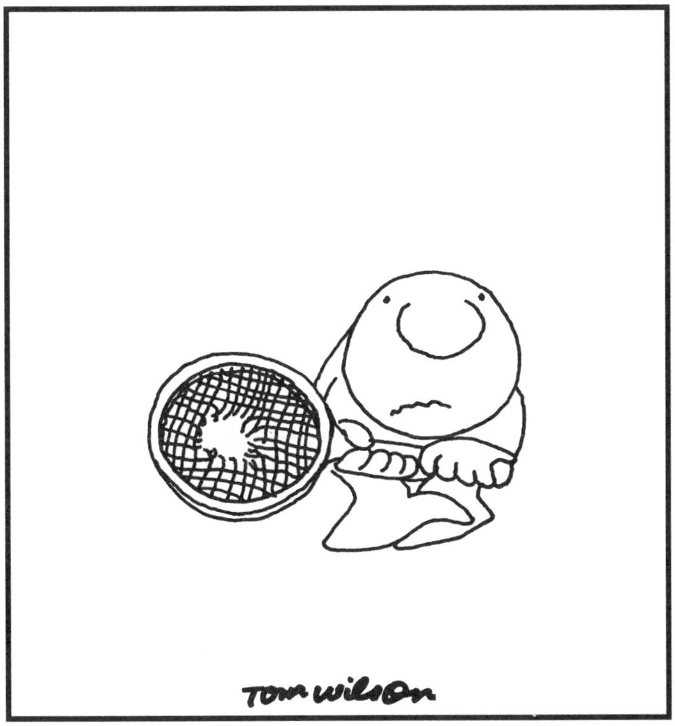
Tom Wilson

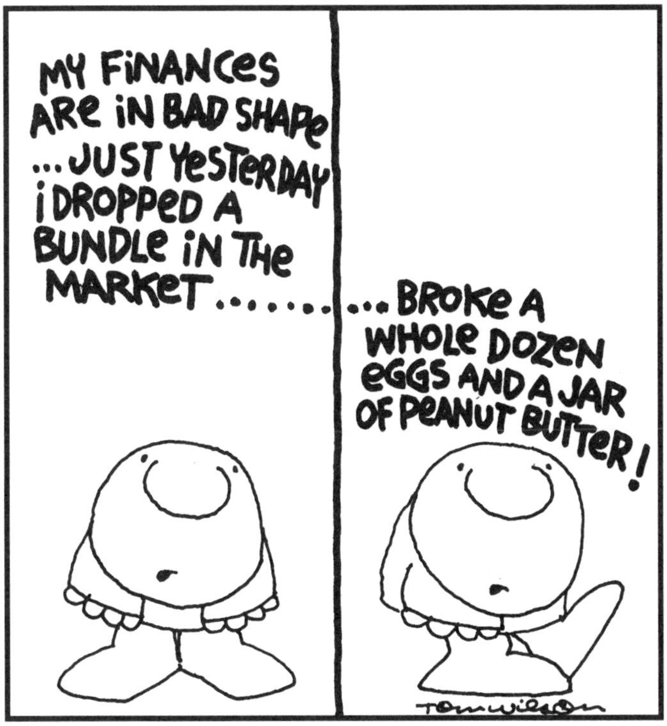
MY FINANCES ARE IN BAD SHAPE ...JUST YESTERDAY I DROPPED A BUNDLE IN THE MARKET........
...BROKE A WHOLE DOZEN EGGS AND A JAR OF PEANUT BUTTER!
Tom Wilson

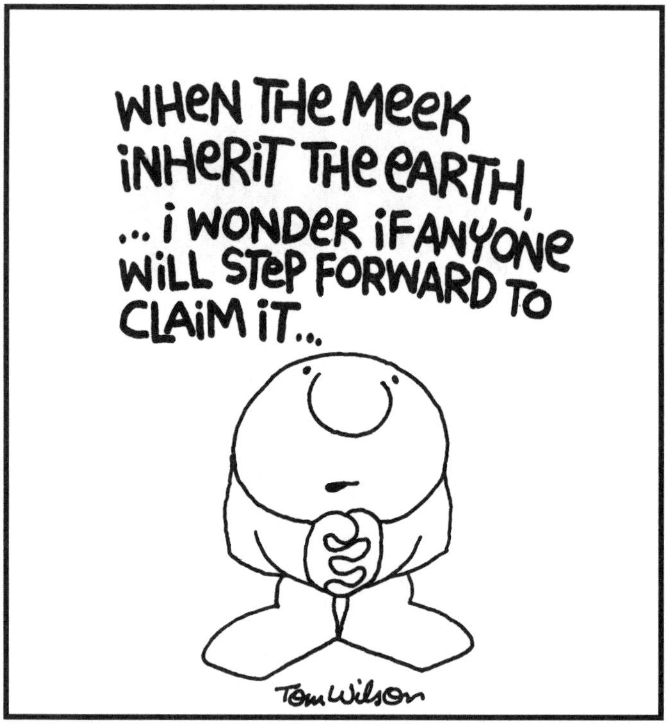
WHEN THE MEEK INHERIT THE EARTH, ... i WONDER iF ANYONE WILL STEP FORWARD TO CLAiM iT...

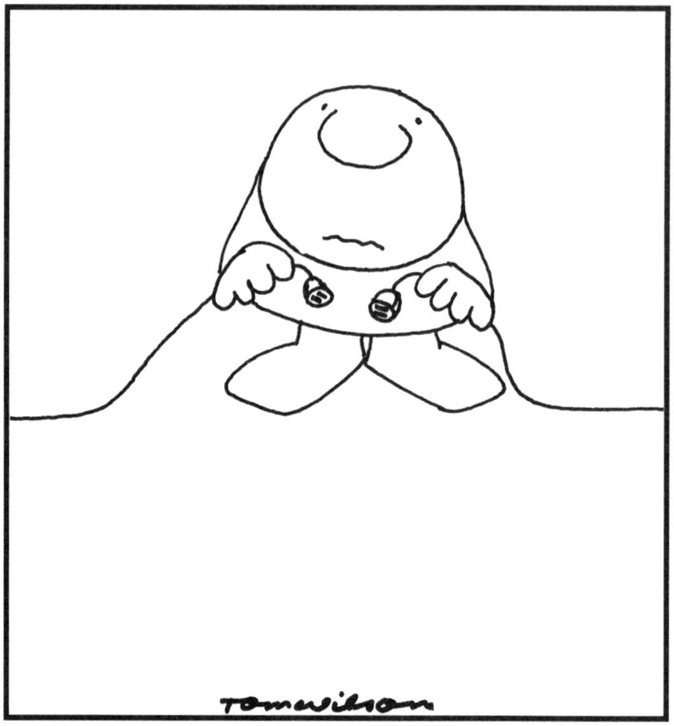

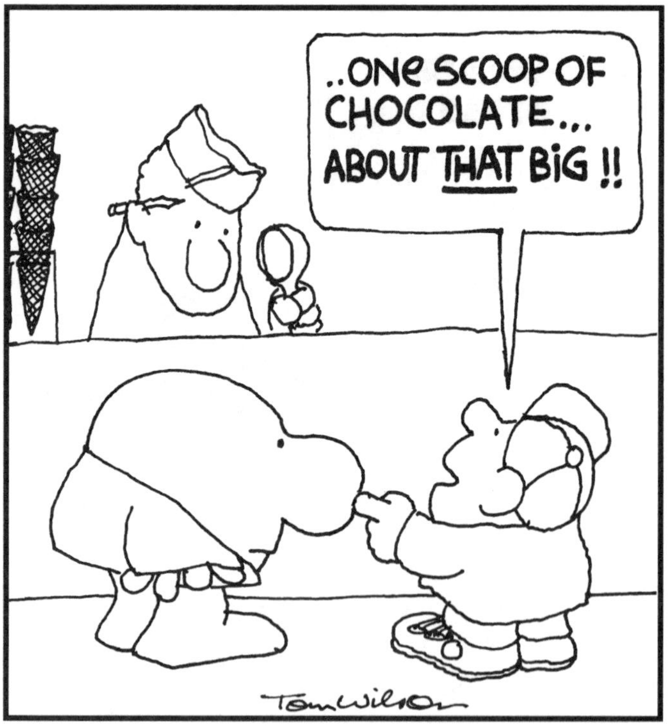
..ONE SCOOP OF CHOCOLATE... ABOUT THAT BiG !!

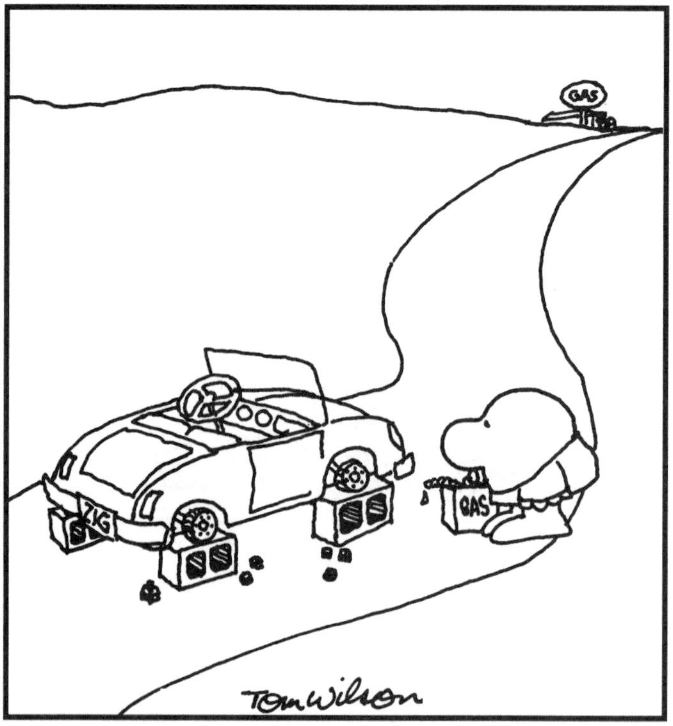
GAS
GAS

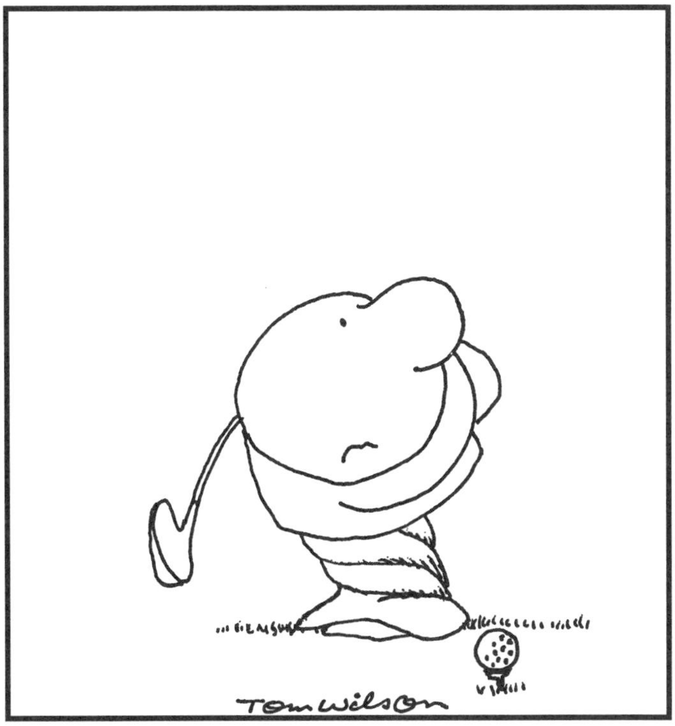
TOM WILSON

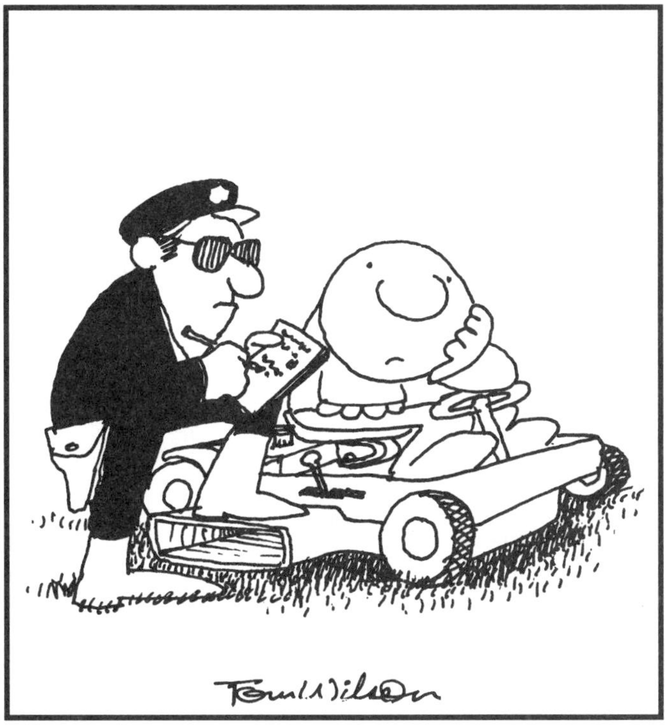
TOM WILSON

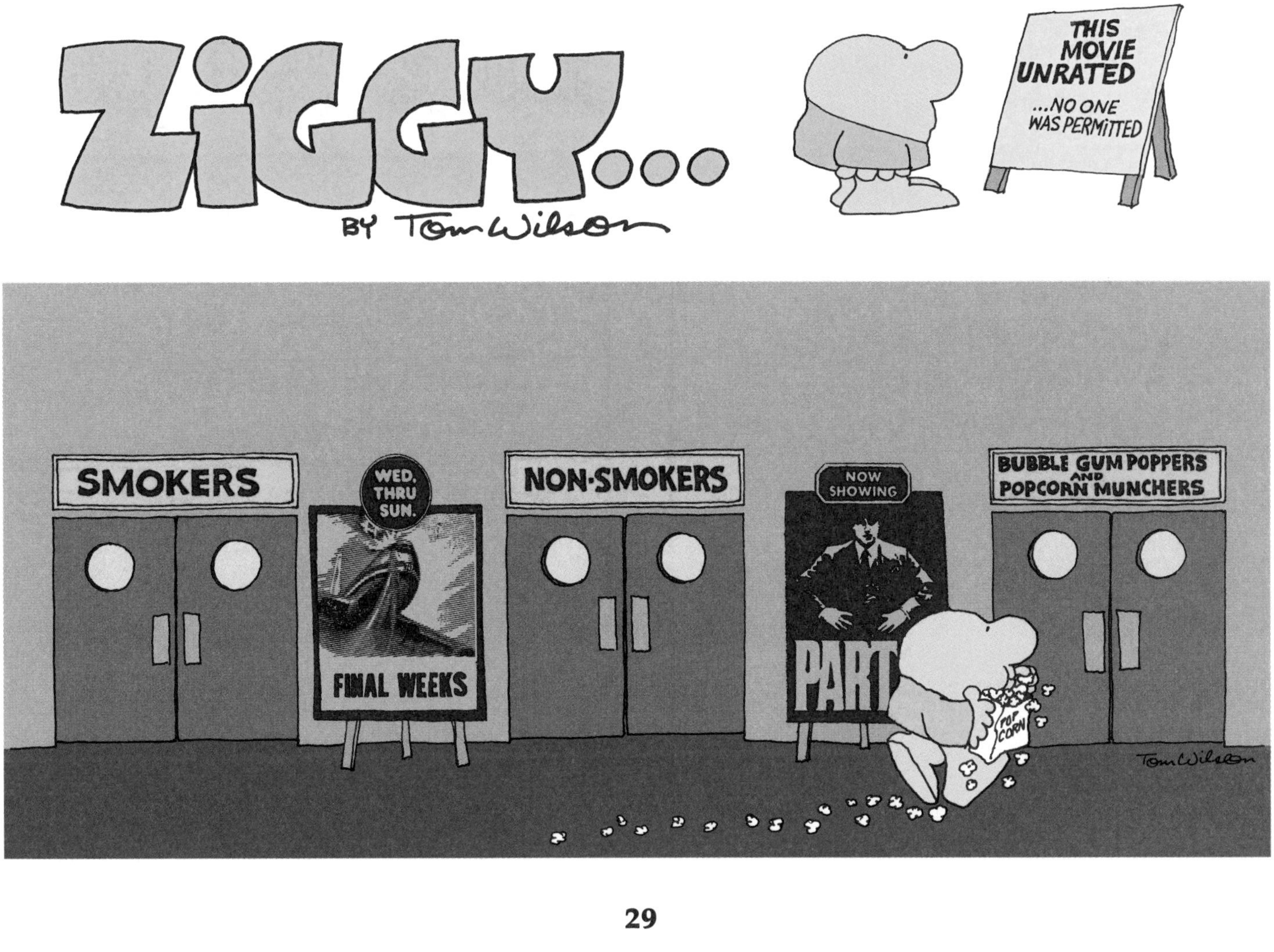
ZIGGY...
BY TOM WILSON
THIS MOVIE UNRATED
...NO ONE WAS PERMITTED
SMOKERS
WED. THRU SUN.
FINAL WEEKS
NON-SMOKERS
NOW SHOWING
PART
BUBBLE GUM POPPERS AND POPCORN MUNCHERS
POP CORN
TOM WILSON

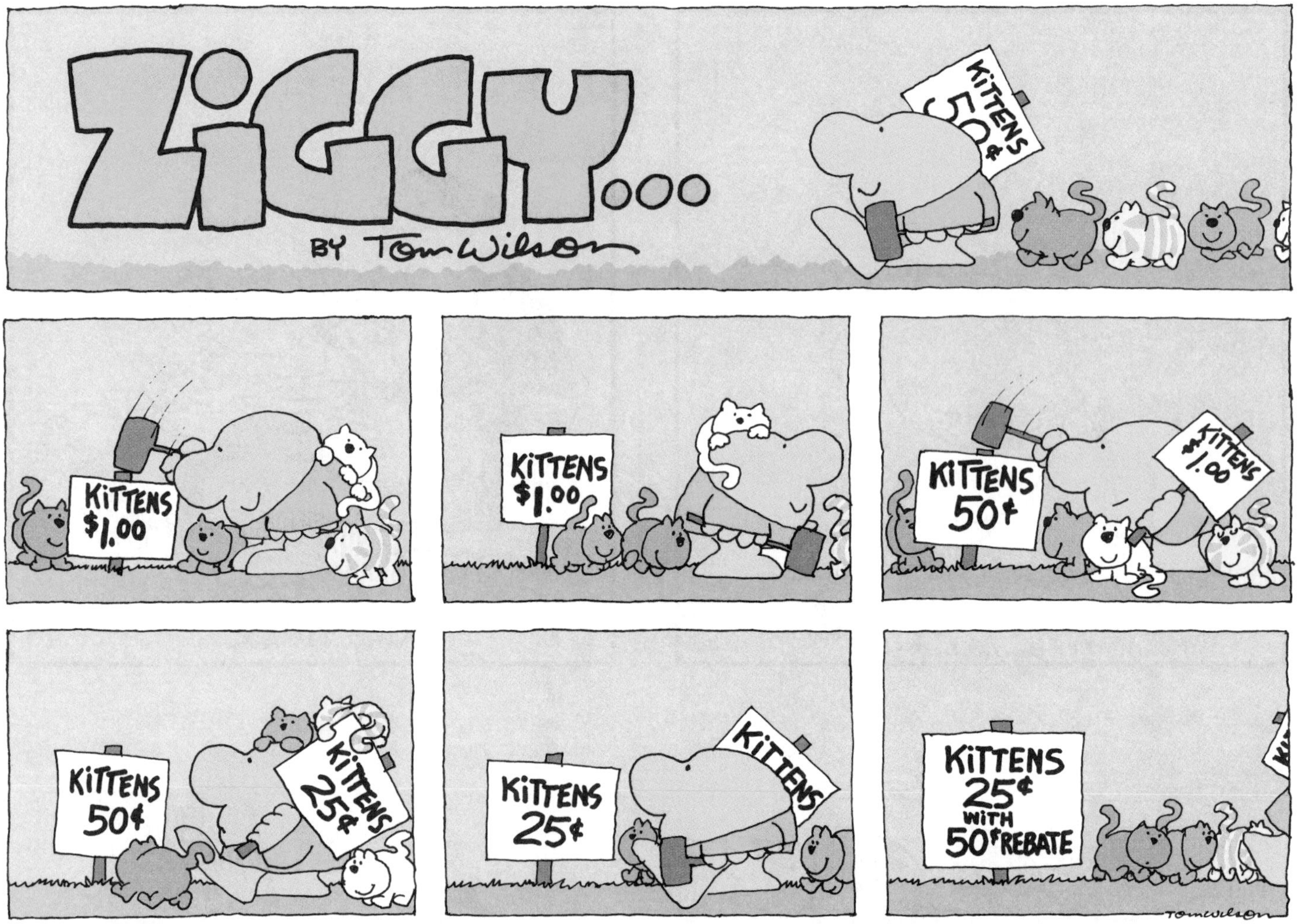
ZiGGY...
BY Tom Wilson
KiTTENS 50¢
KiTTENS $1.00
KiTTENS $1.00
KiTTENS 50¢
KiTTENS $1.00
KiTTENS 50¢
KiTTENS 25¢
KiTTENS 25¢
KiTTENS
KiTTENS 25¢ WITH 50¢ REBATE
Tom Wilson

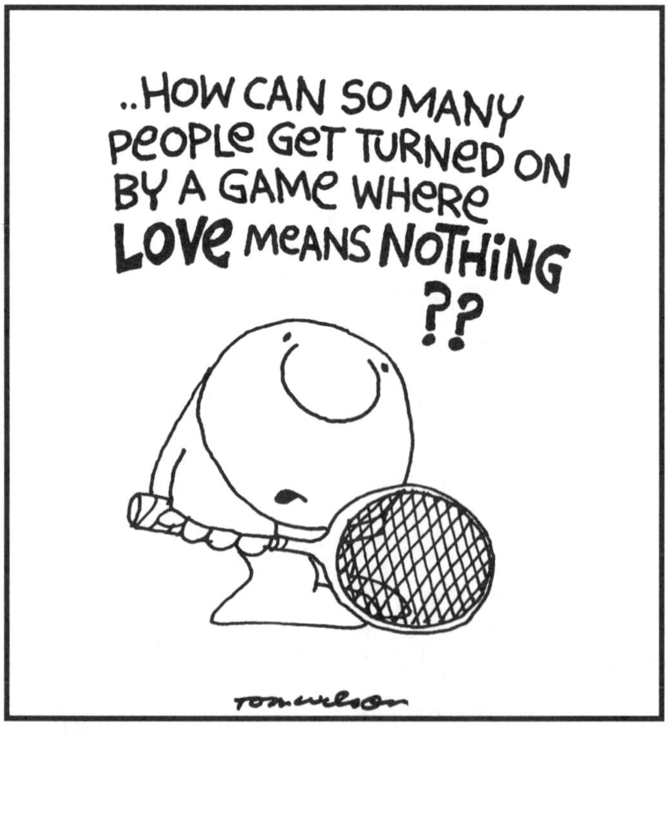
..HOW CAN SO MANY PEOPLE GET TURNED ON BY A GAME WHERE LOVE MEANS NOTHING ??
Tom Wilson

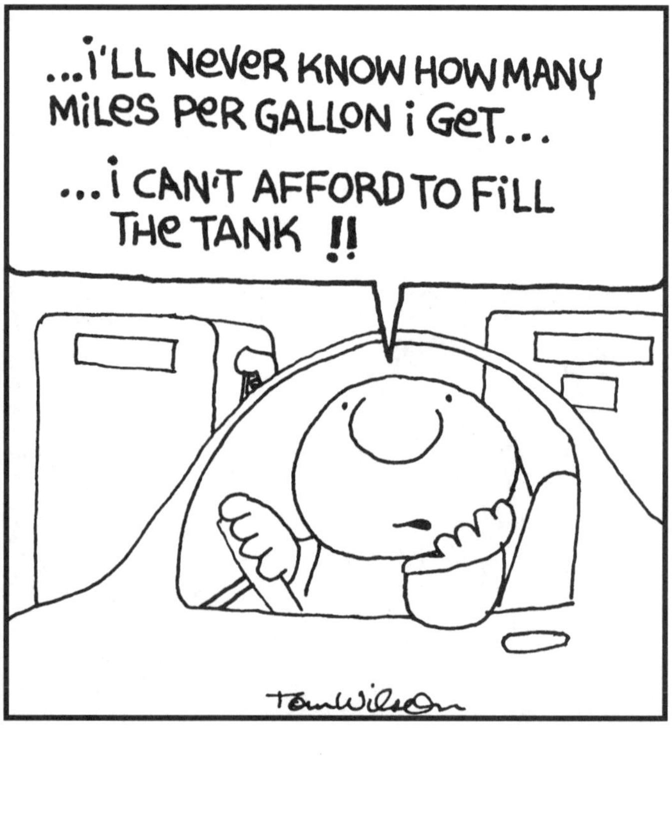
...i'LL NEVER KNOW HOW MANY MiLES PER GALLON i GET...
...i CAN'T AFFORD TO FiLL THE TANK !!
Tom Wilson

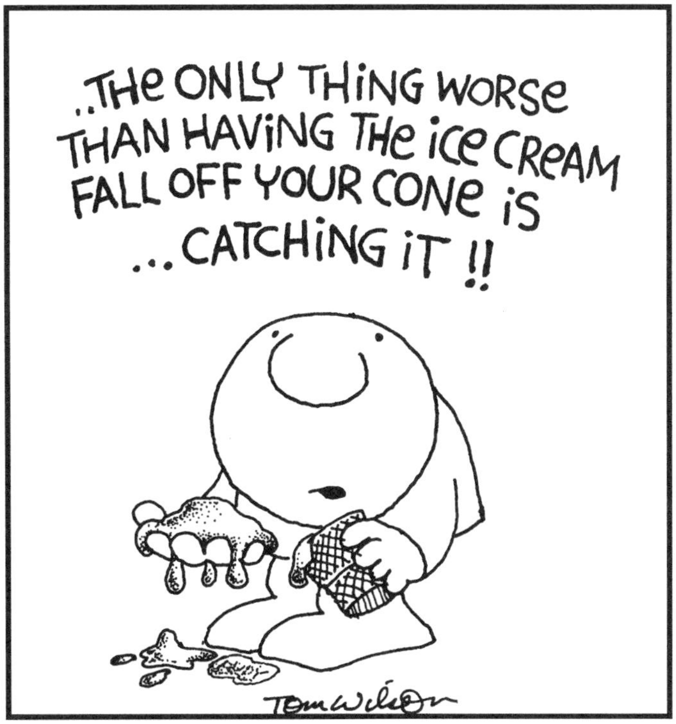
..THE ONLY THING WORSE THAN HAVING THE ice CREAM FALL OFF YOUR CONE is ...CATCHING iT !!

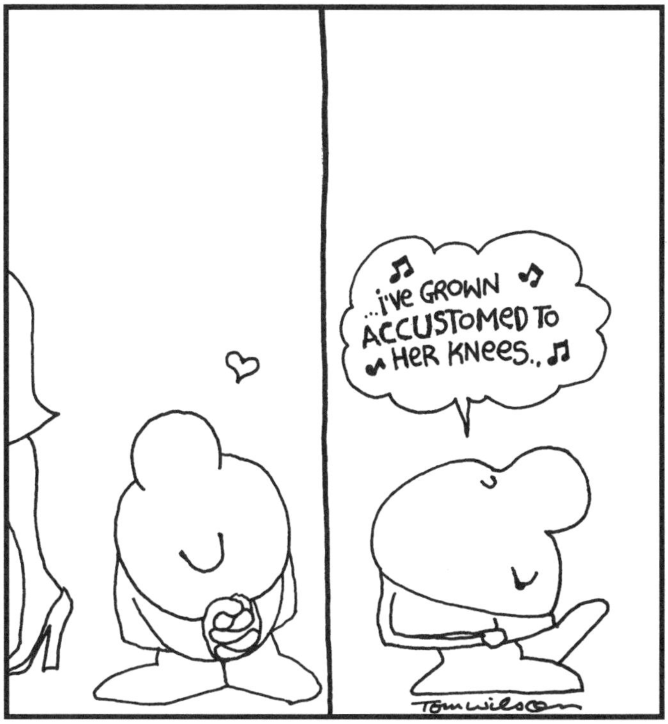
...i've GROWN ACCUSTOMED TO HER KNEES..

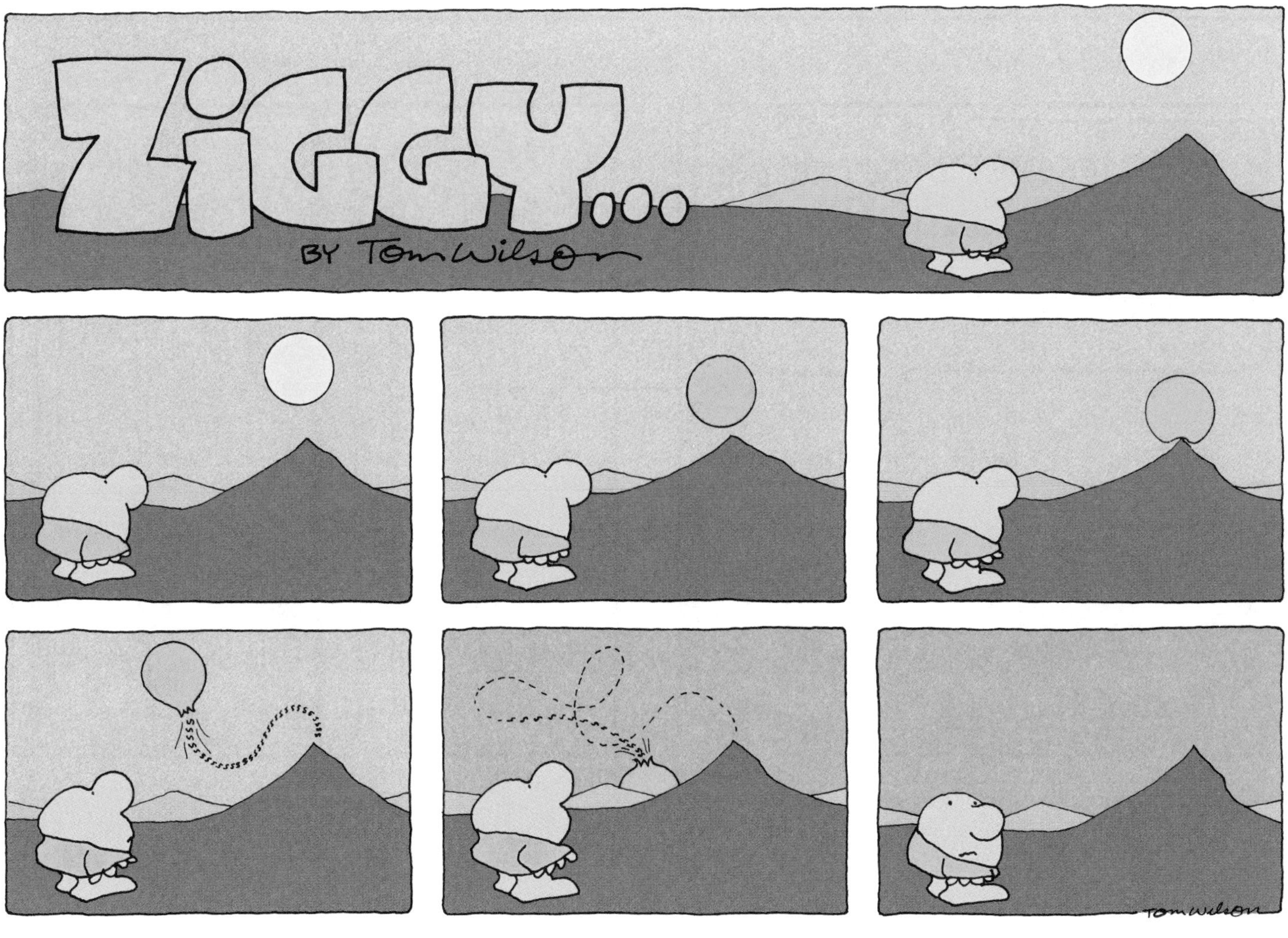
ZiGGY...
BY TOM WILSON

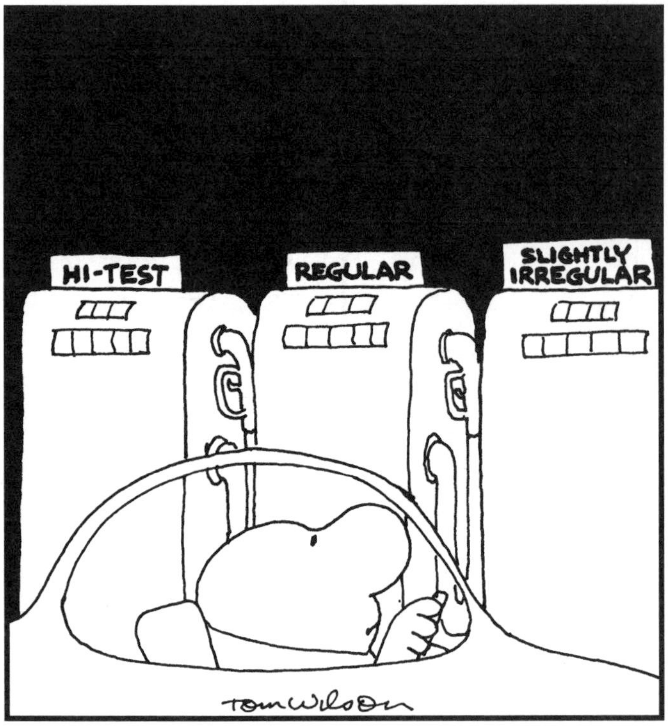
HI-TEST
REGULAR
SLIGHTLY IRREGULAR
TOM WILSON

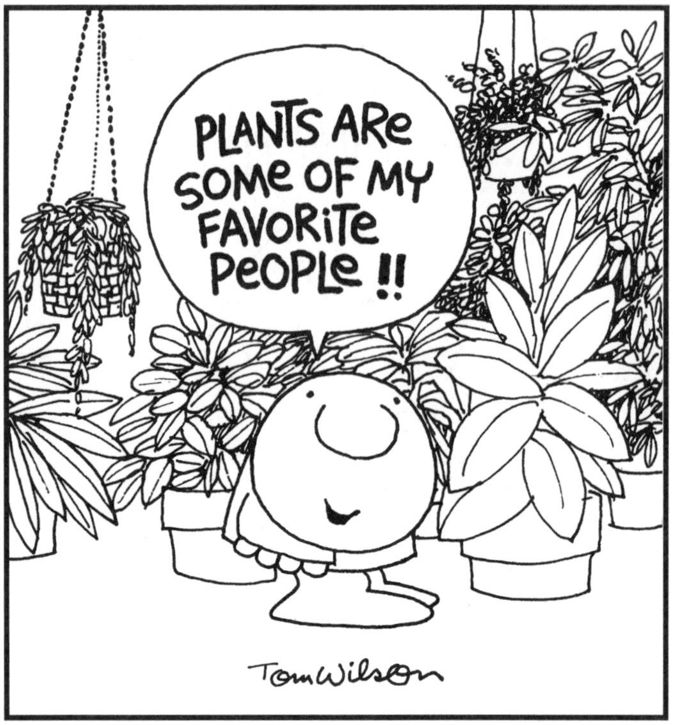
PLANTS ARE SOME OF MY FAVORITE PEOPLE !!
TOM WILSON

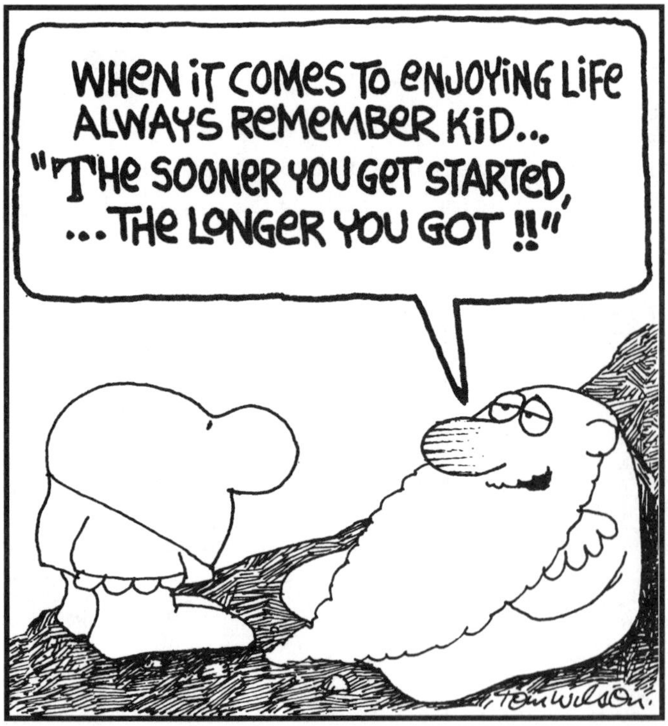
WHEN IT COMES TO ENJOYING LIFE ALWAYS REMEMBER KID... "THE SOONER YOU GET STARTED, ...THE LONGER YOU GOT !!"
TOM WILSON

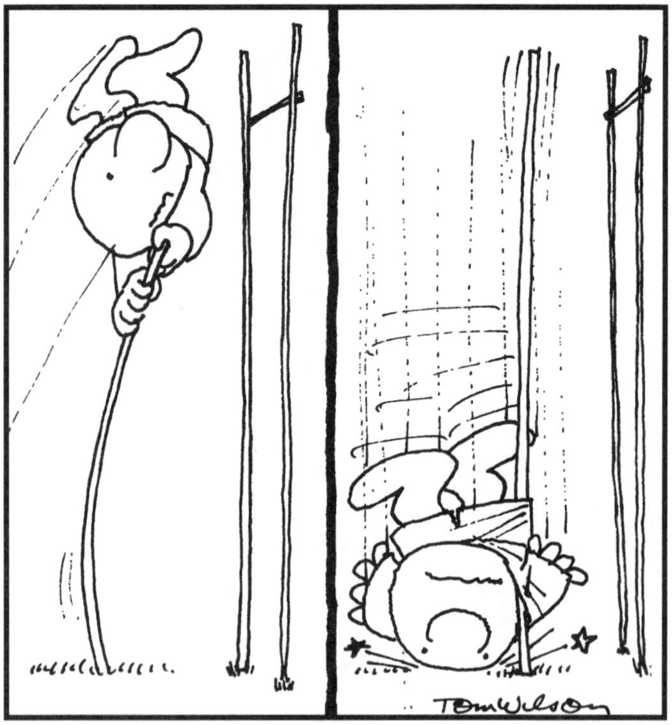
TOM WILSON

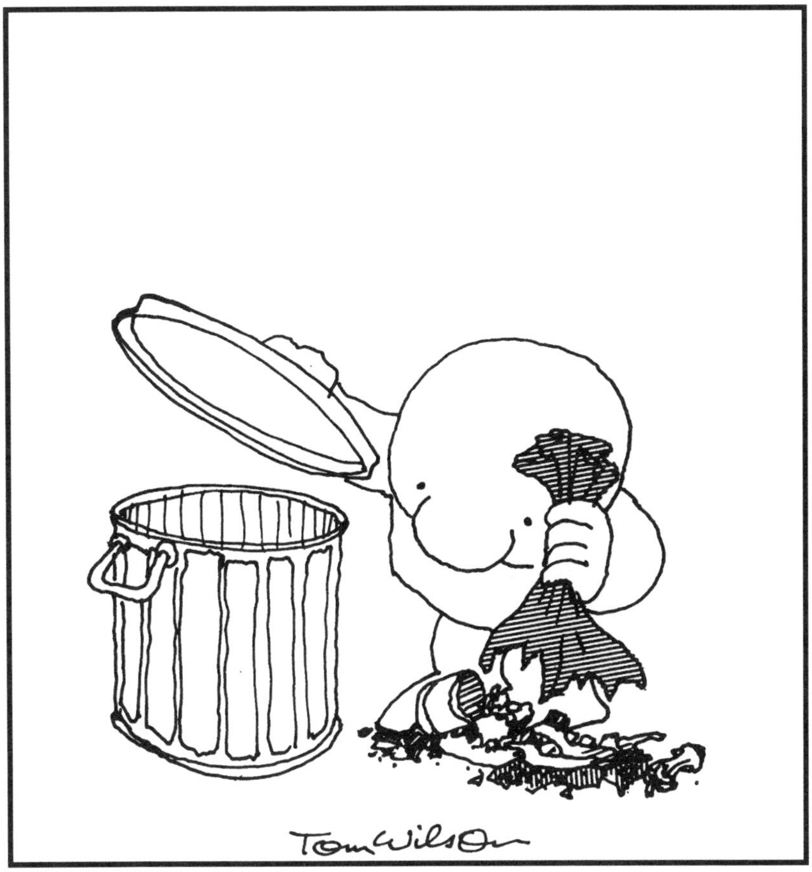
Tom Wilson

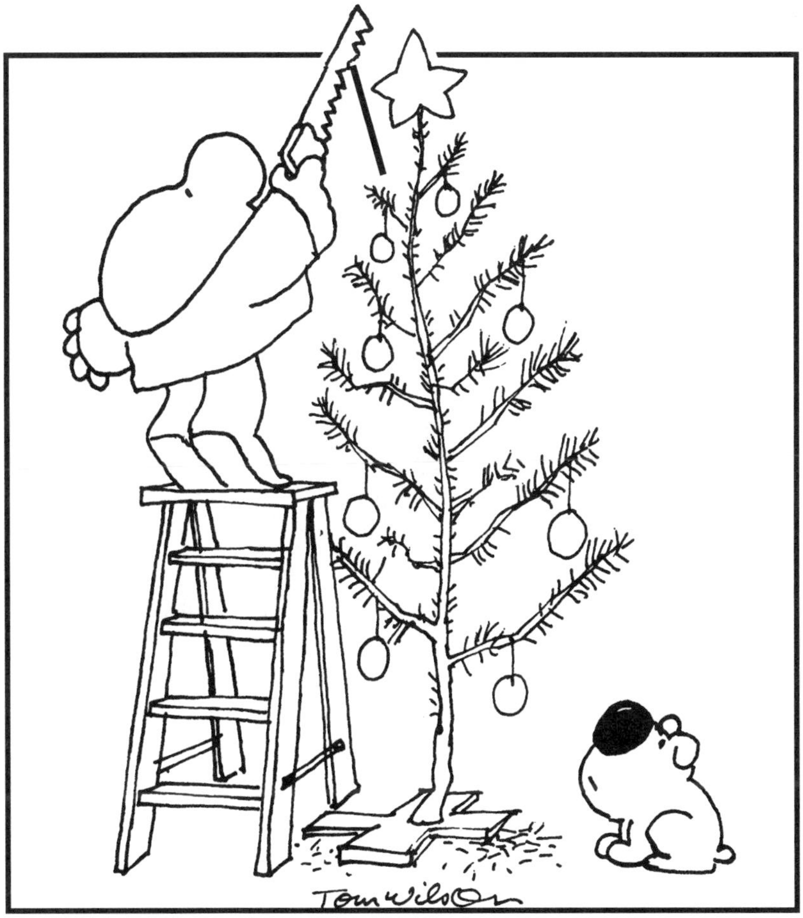
Tom Wilson

Chapter II
1976–1980

One of the best acquisitions that Universal has made is the comic panel *Ziggy*. When the late Jim Andrews asked me to help him find our first panel for syndication, I brought him a special little book called *From Me to You* and it featured this character Ziggy going through life with everything going wrong no matter what he touched. If he hung a picture on the wall, the whole wall came tumbling down. If he carried a bag of groceries, for sure the milk bottle would fall through and break, etc. Jim really liked this character and developed it with Tom Wilson for national syndication. It gave a real jump start to our company. Happy 35th Anniversary, Tom and Ziggy.

—Kathy Andrews, vice chairman, Andrews McMeel Universal

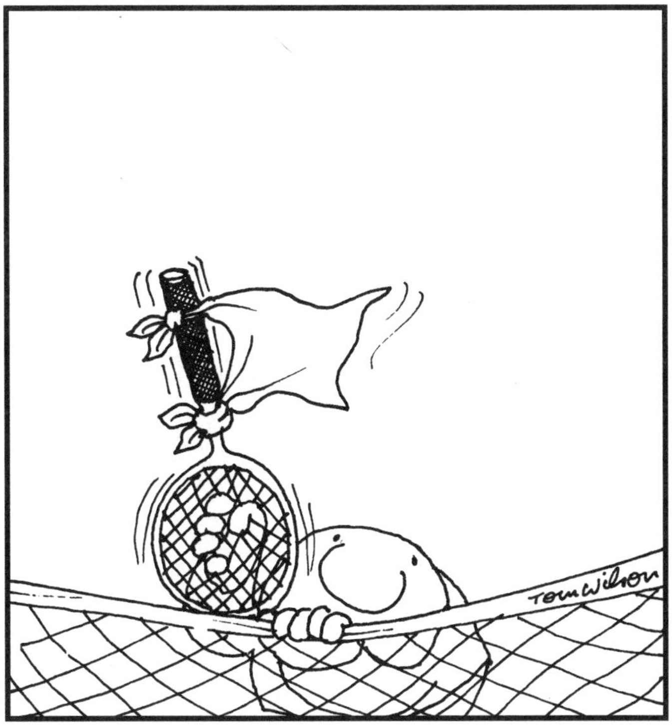
Tom Wilson

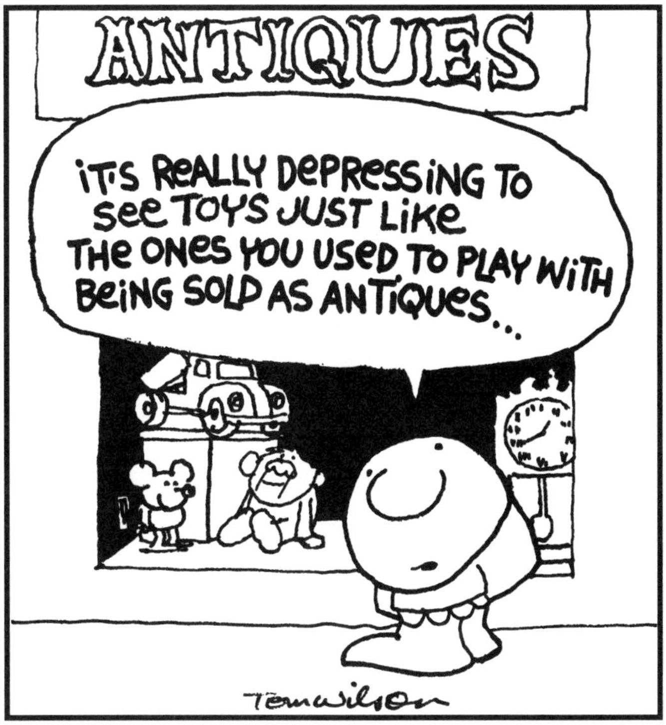
ANTIQUES
IT'S REALLY DEPRESSING TO SEE TOYS JUST LIKE THE ONES YOU USED TO PLAY WITH BEING SOLD AS ANTIQUES...
Tom Wilson

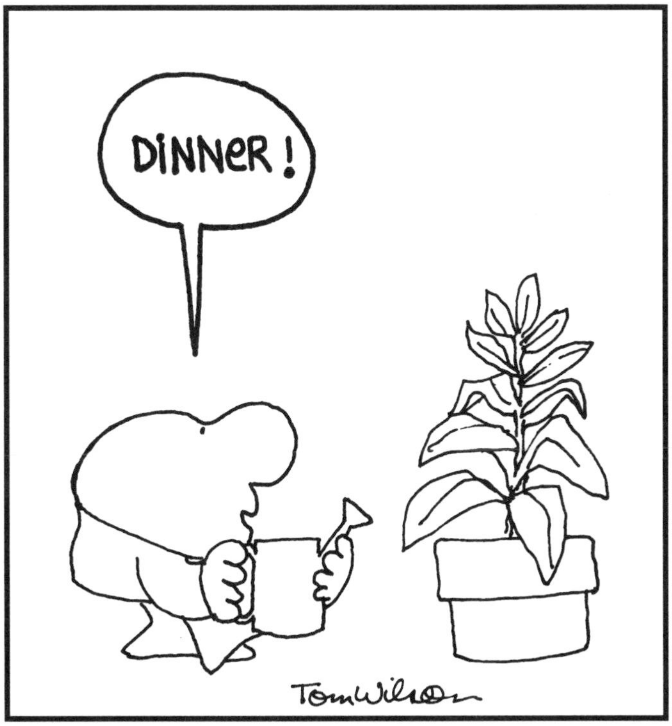
DINNER!
Tom Wilson

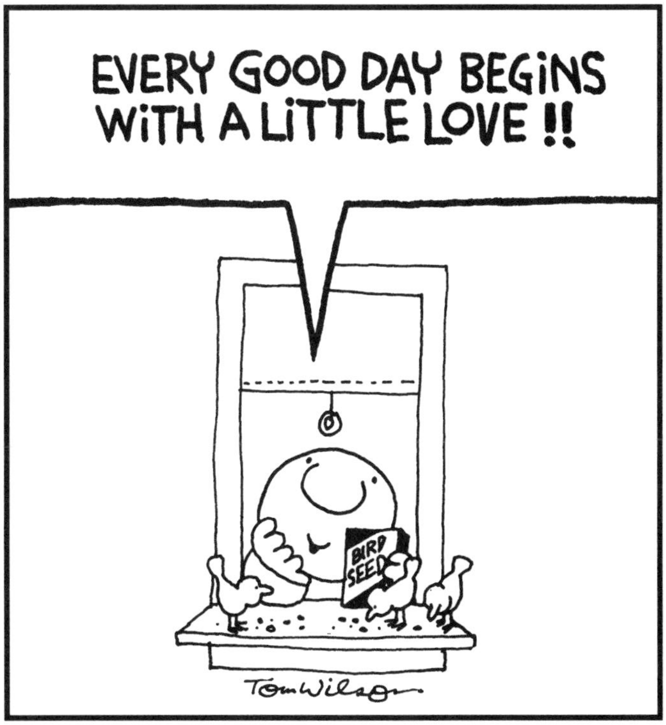
EVERY GOOD DAY BEGINS WITH A LITTLE LOVE !!
BIRD SEED
Tom Wilson

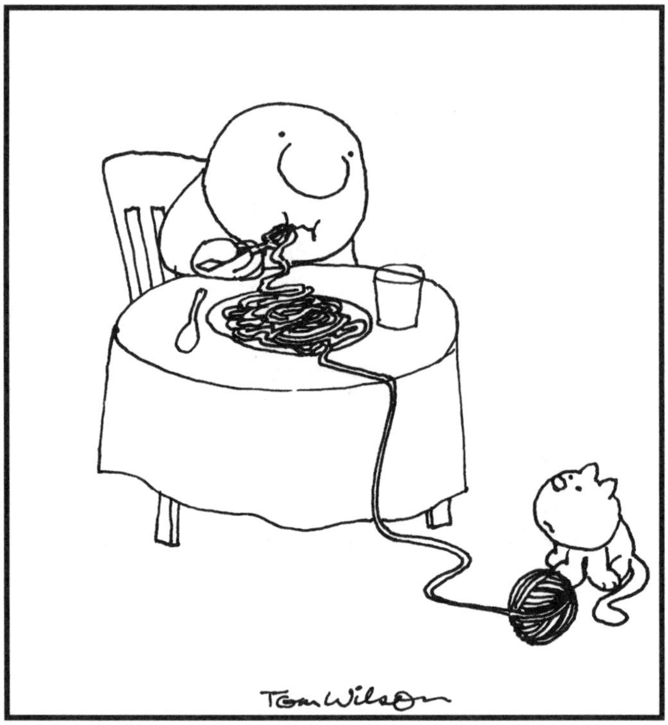
Tom Wilson

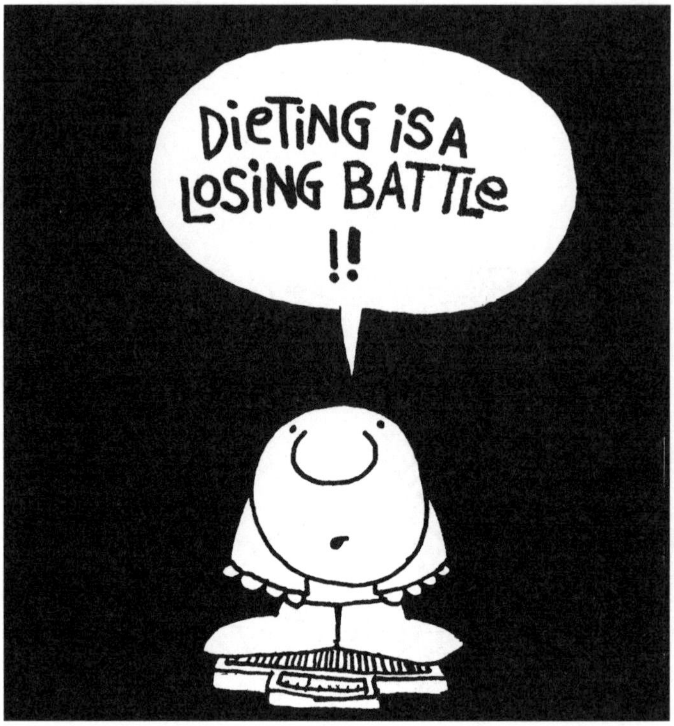
DIETING IS A LOSING BATTLE !!

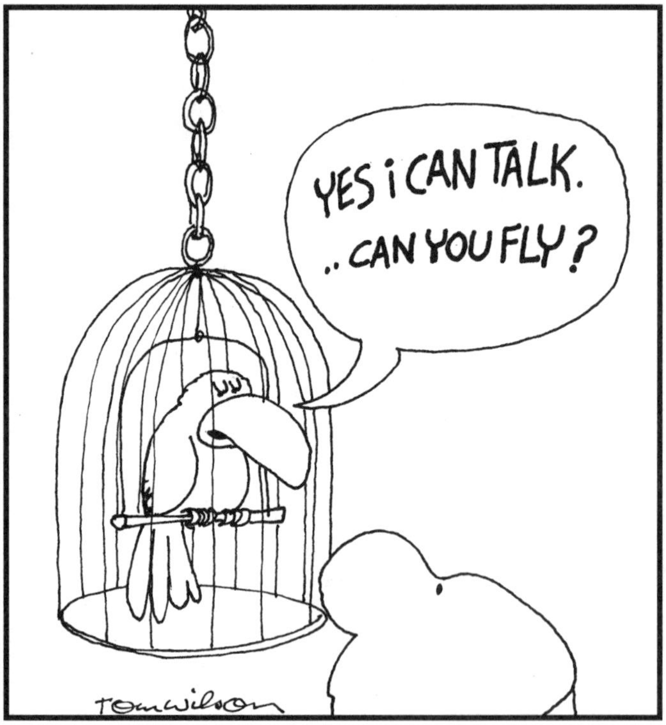
YES I CAN TALK. ..CAN YOU FLY?
Tom Wilson

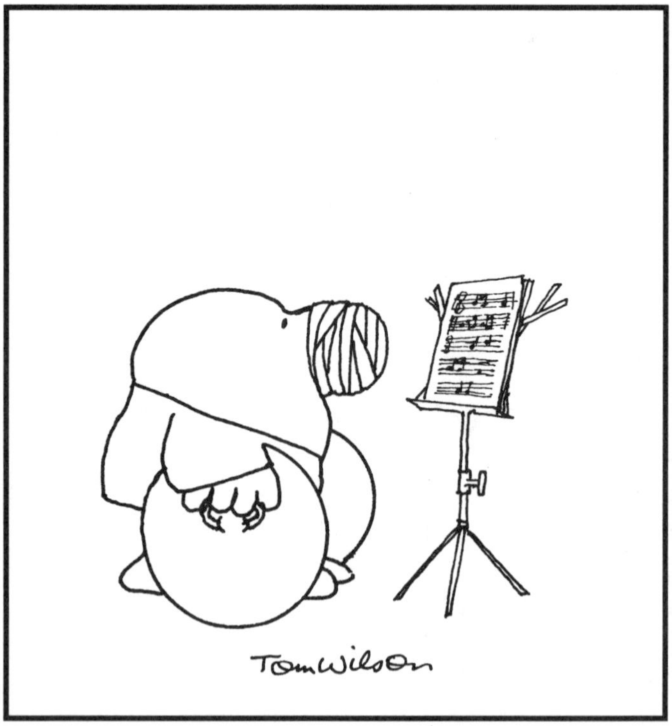
Tom Wilson

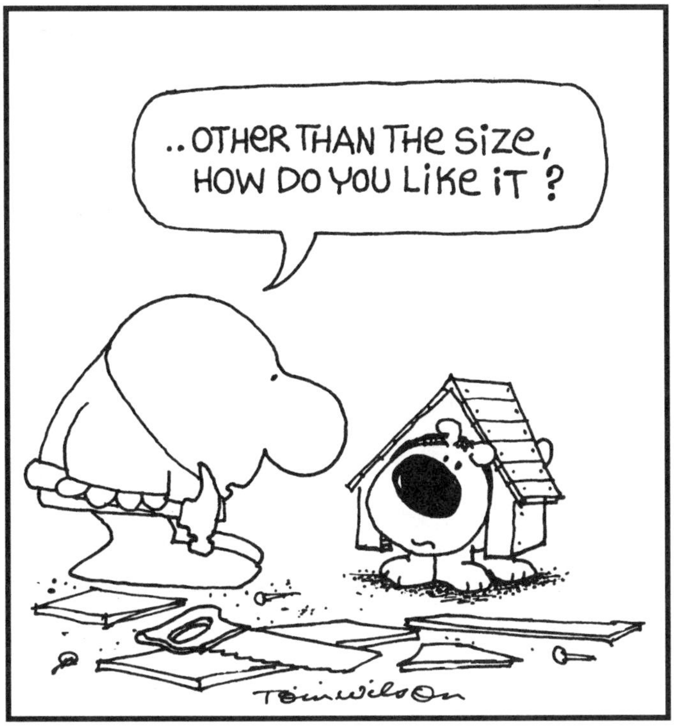
..OTHER THAN THE SIZE, HOW DO YOU LIKE IT ?
Tom Wilson

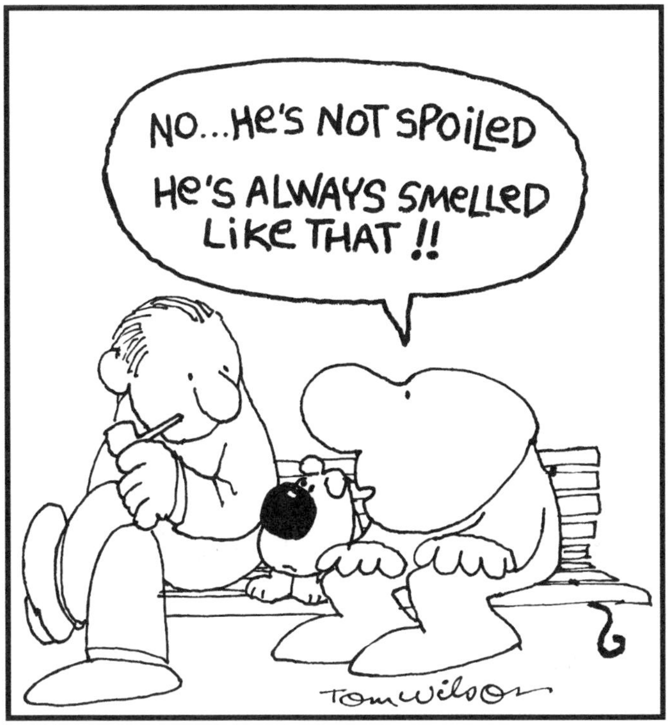
NO...HE'S NOT SPOILED
HE'S ALWAYS SMELLED LIKE THAT !!
Tom Wilson

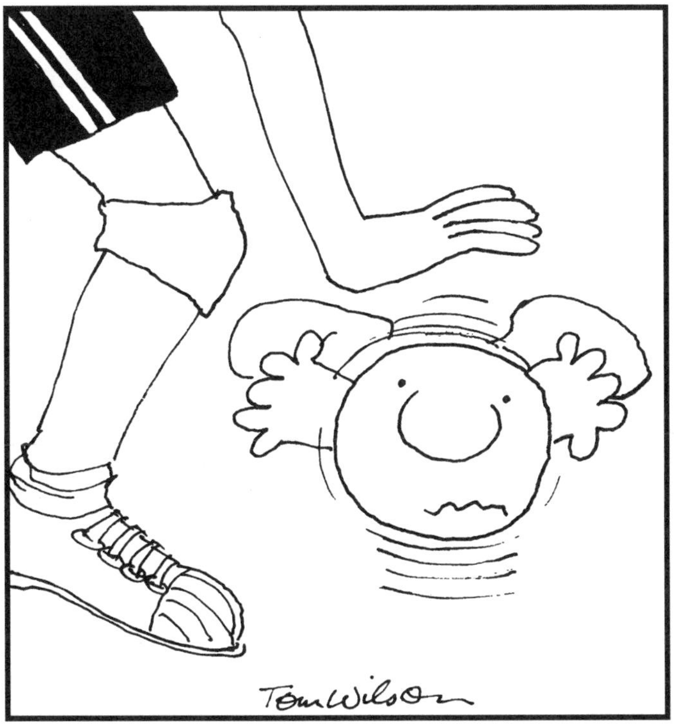
Tom Wilson

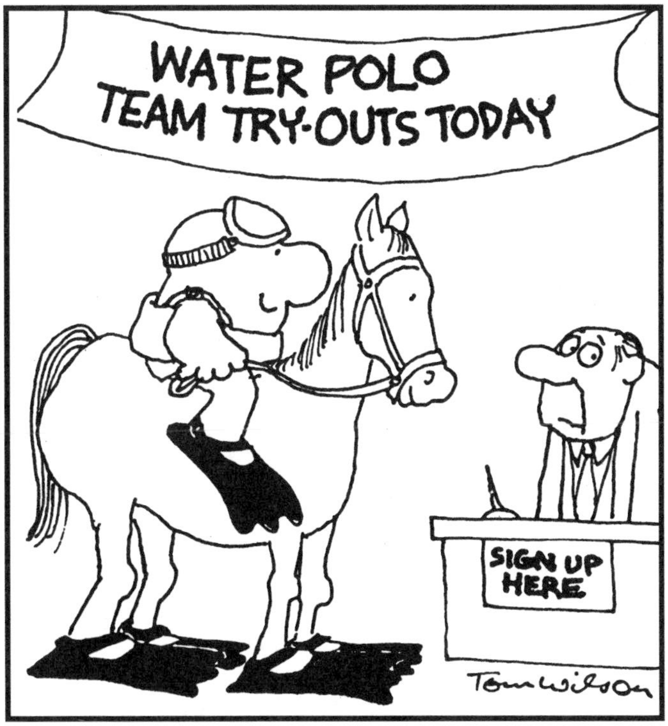
WATER POLO TEAM TRY-OUTS TODAY
SIGN UP HERE
Tom Wilson

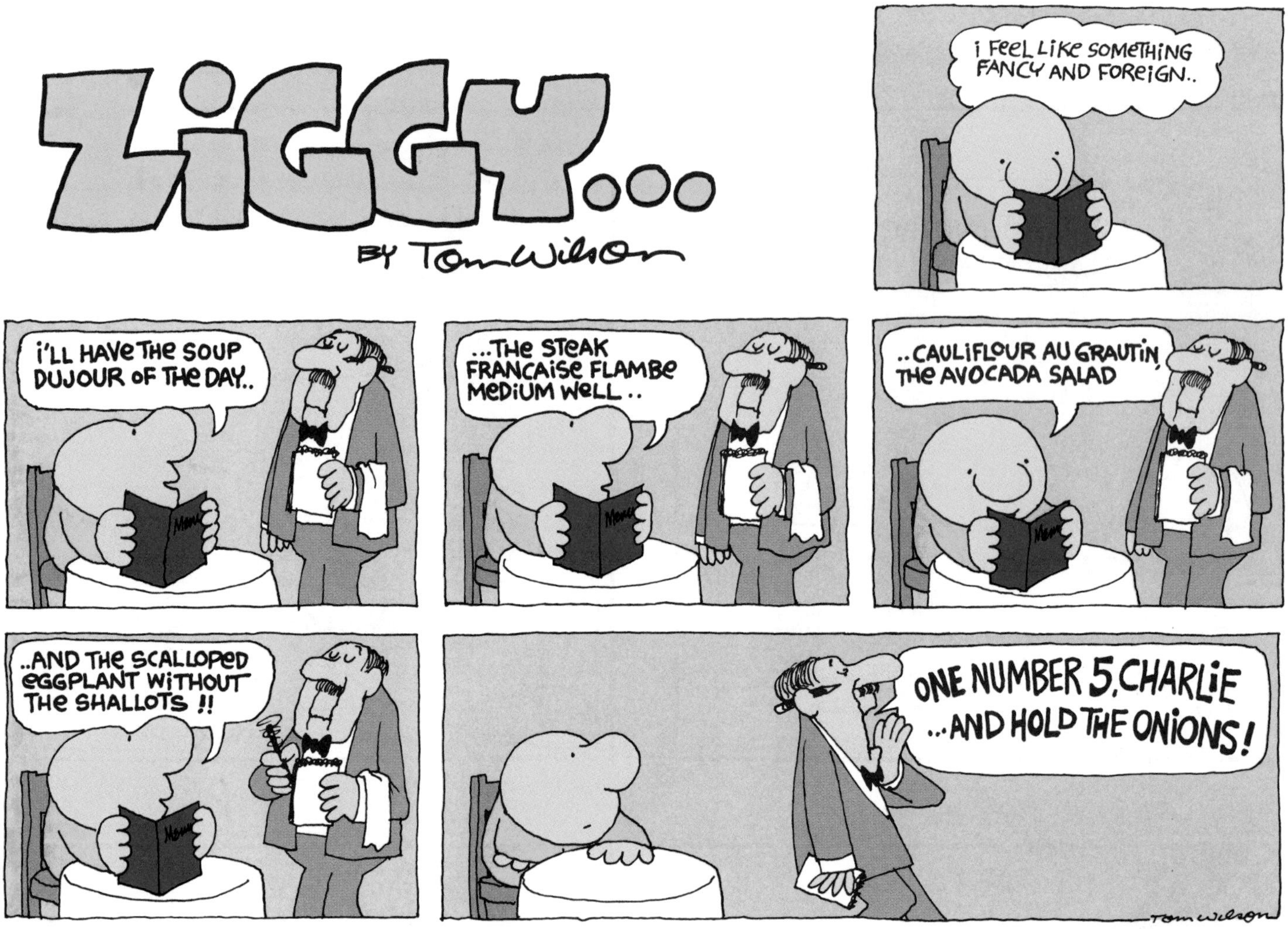
ZiGGY...
BY Tom Wilson
i FEEL LiKE SOMETHiNG FANCY AND FOReiGN..
i'LL HAVE THE SOUP DUJOUR OF THE DAY..
...THE STEAK FRANCAiSE FLAMBE MEDiUM WELL..
..CAULiFLOUR AU GRAUTiN, THE AVOCADA SALAD
..AND THE SCALLOPED EGGPLANT WiTHOUT THE SHALLOTS !!
ONE NUMBER 5, CHARLiE ...AND HOLD THE ONiONS!
Tom Wilson

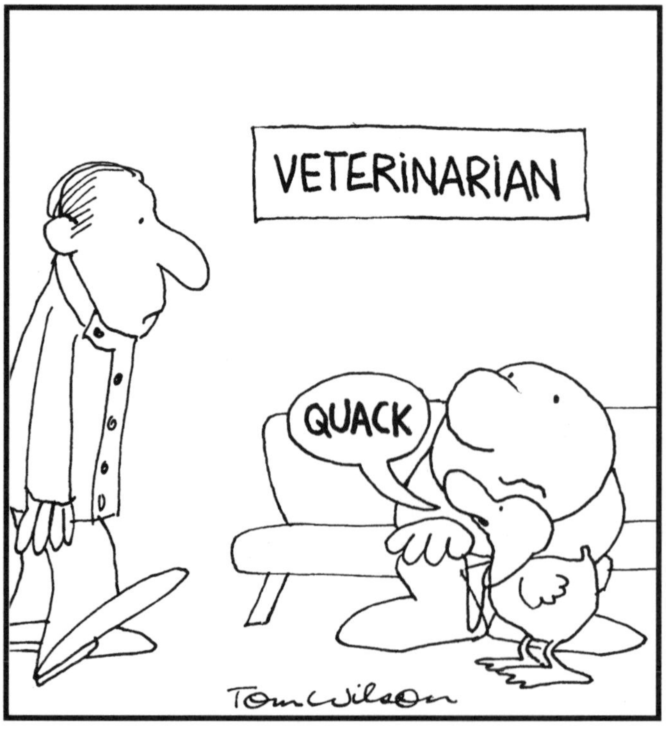
VETERiNARiAN
QUACK
Tom Wilson

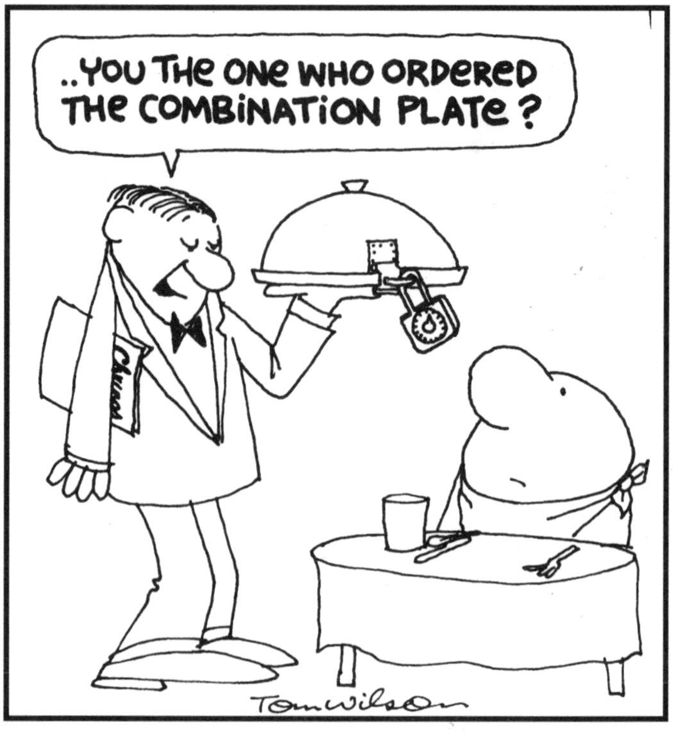
..YOU THE ONE WHO ORDERED THE COMBiNATiON PLATE?
Tom Wilson

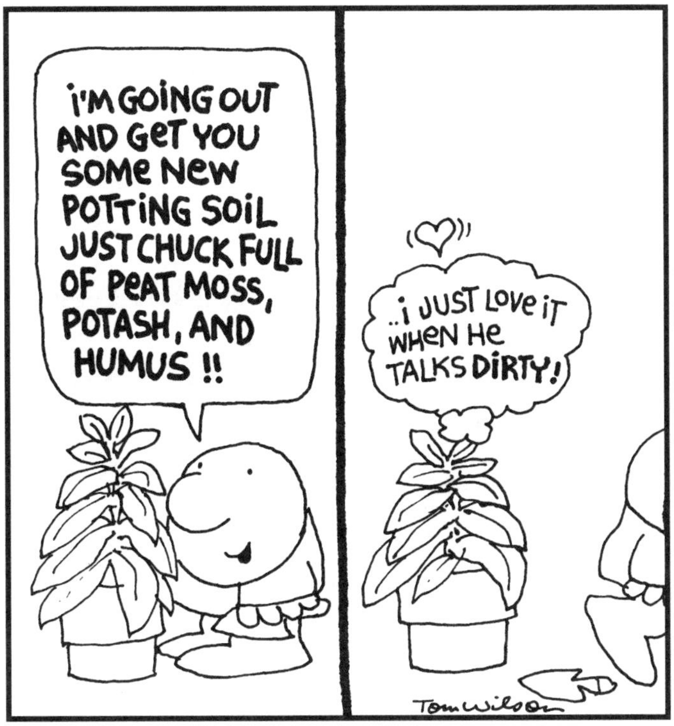
I'M GOING OUT AND GET YOU SOME NEW POTTING SOIL JUST CHUCK FULL OF PEAT MOSS, POTASH, AND HUMUS !!
..I JUST LOVE IT WHEN HE TALKS DIRTY!

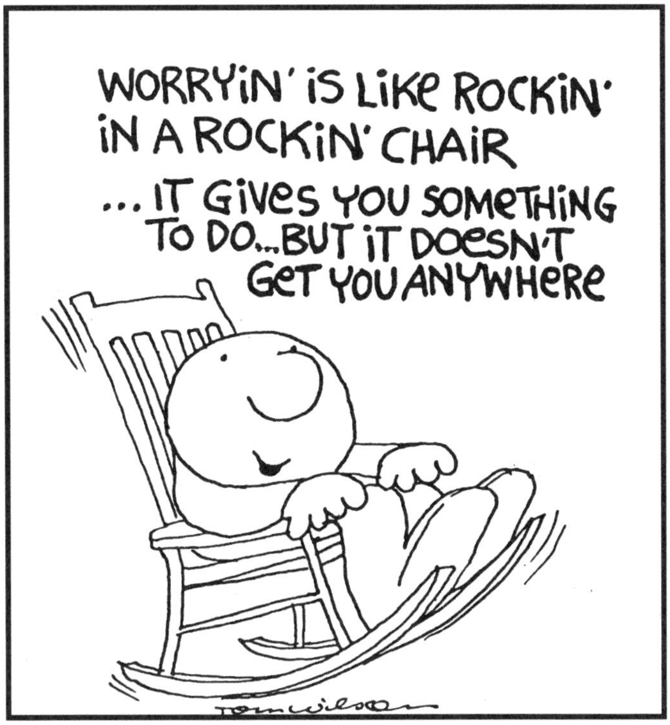
WORRYIN' IS LIKE ROCKIN' IN A ROCKIN' CHAIR
... IT GIVES YOU SOMETHING TO DO...BUT IT DOESN'T GET YOU ANYWHERE

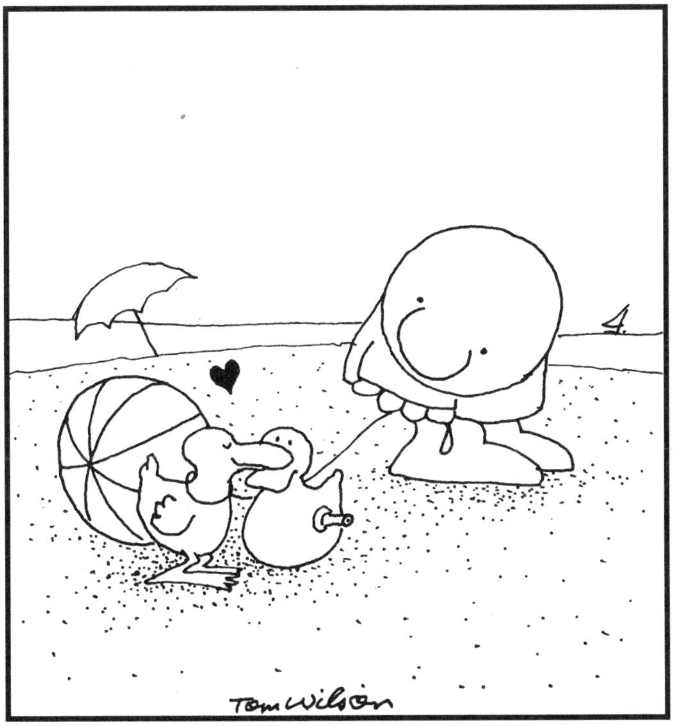

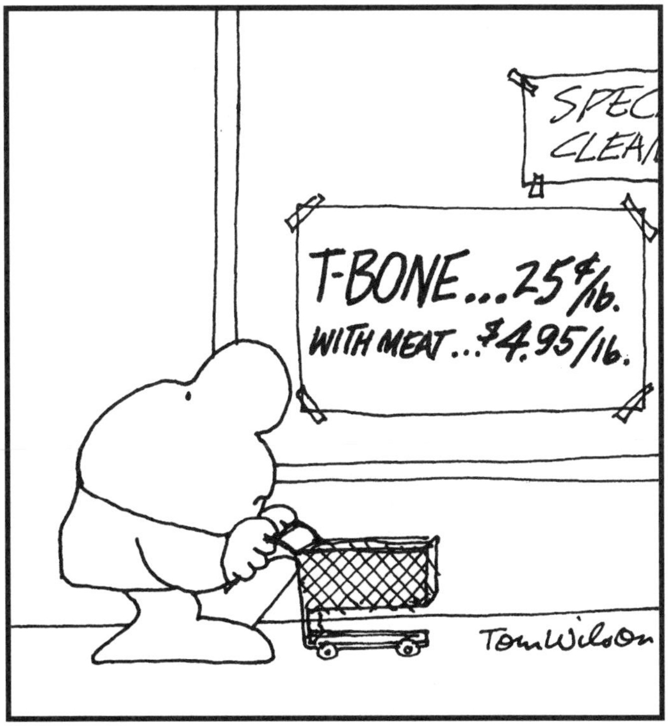
T-BONE...25¢/lb.
WITH MEAT...$4.95/lb.

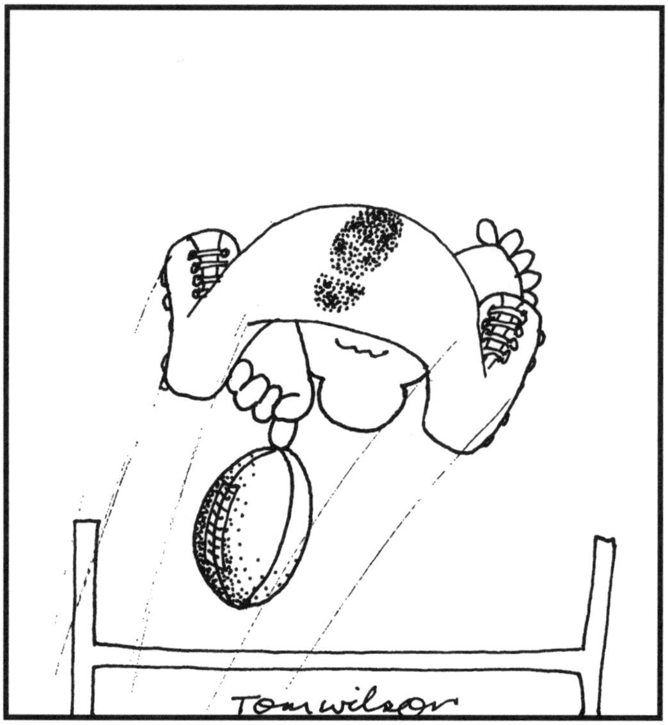
Tom Wilson

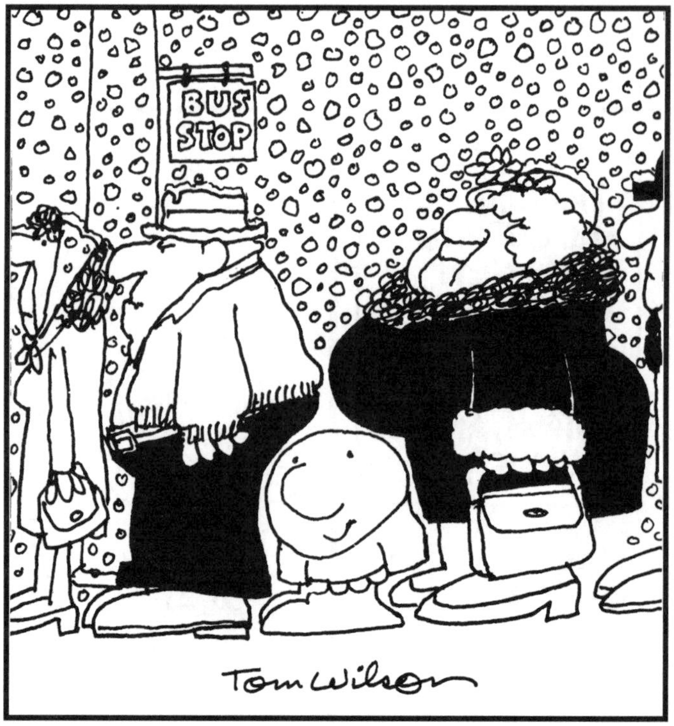
BUS STOP
Tom Wilson

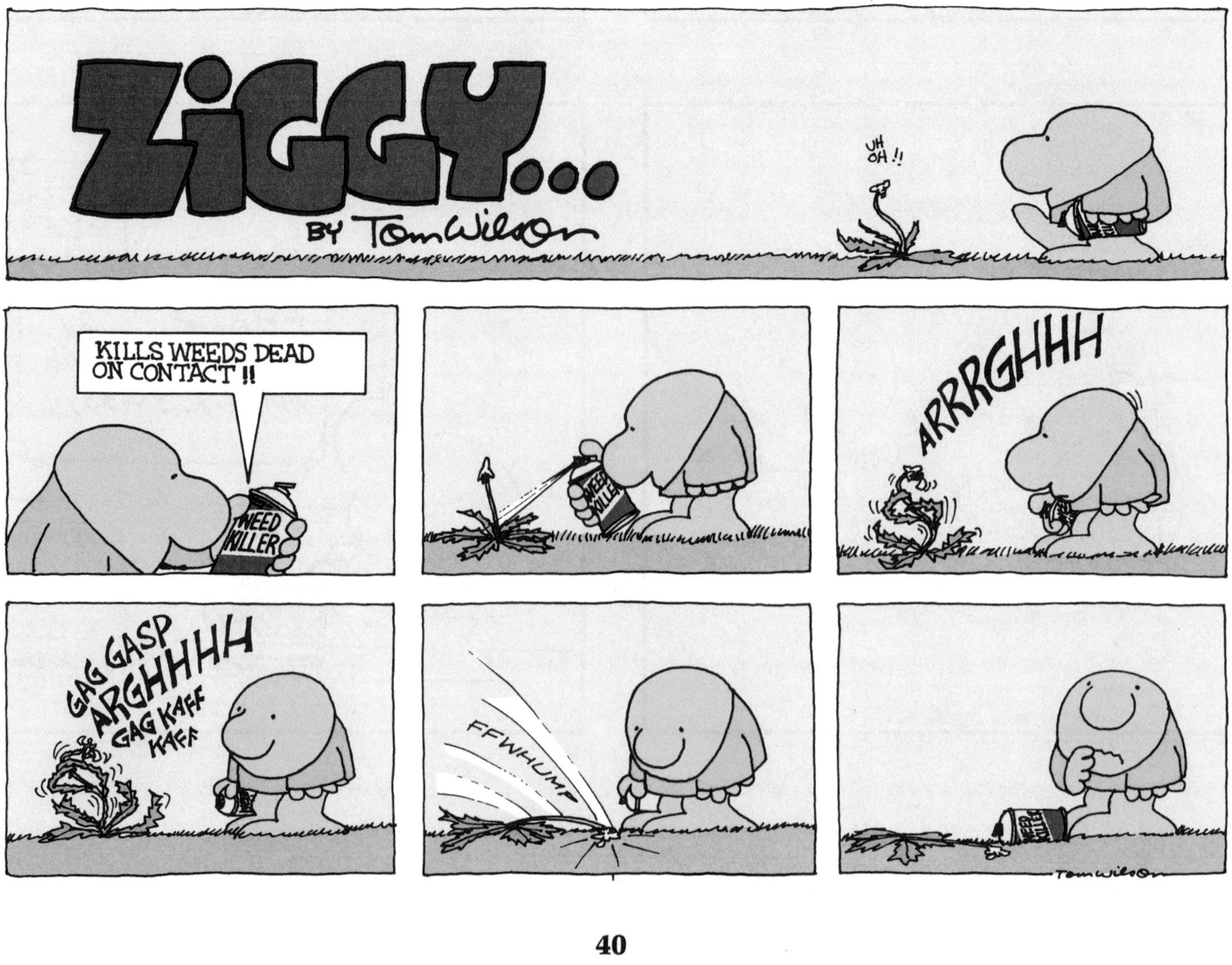
ZiGGY...
BY Tom Wilson
UH OH !!
KILLS WEEDS DEAD ON CONTACT !!
WEED KILLER
ARRRGHHH
GAG GASP
ARGHHHH
GAG KAFF
KAFF
FFWHUMP
Tom Wilson

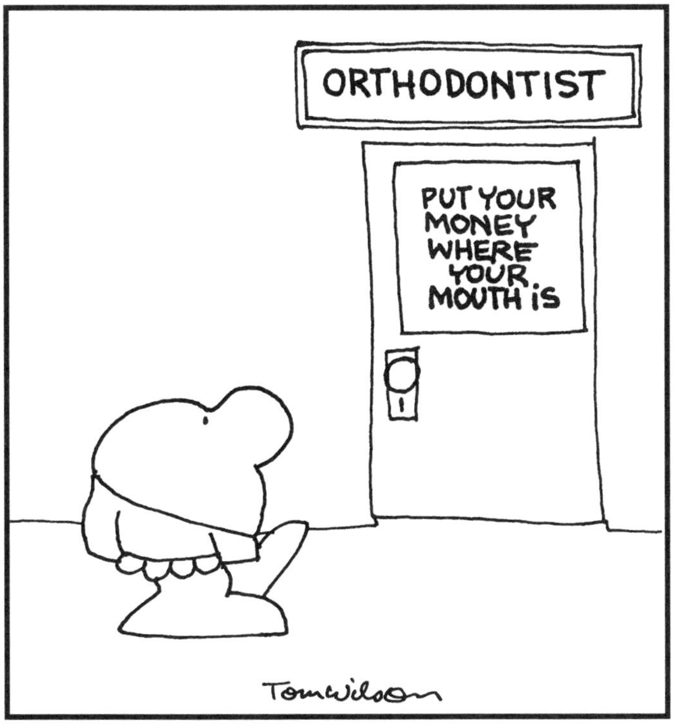
ORTHODONTIST
PUT YOUR MONEY WHERE YOUR MOUTH IS
Tom Wilson

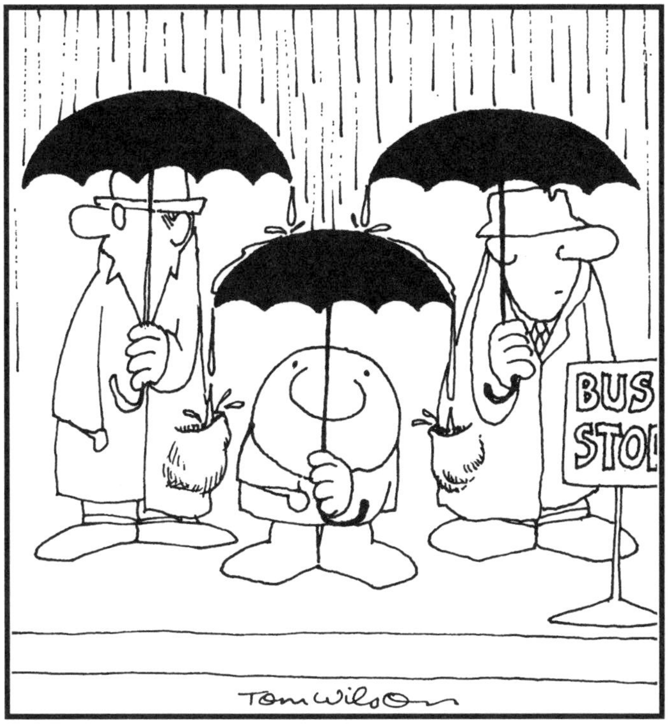
BUS
Tom Wilson

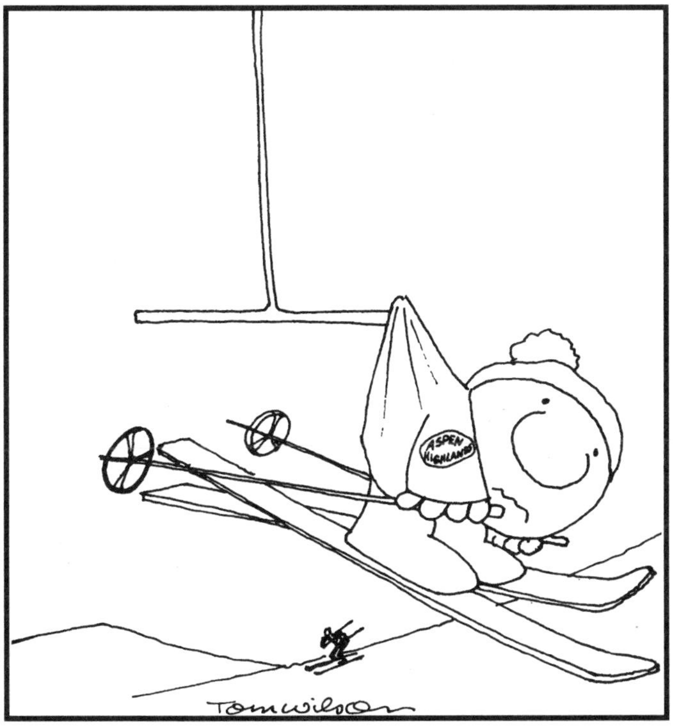
Tom Wilson

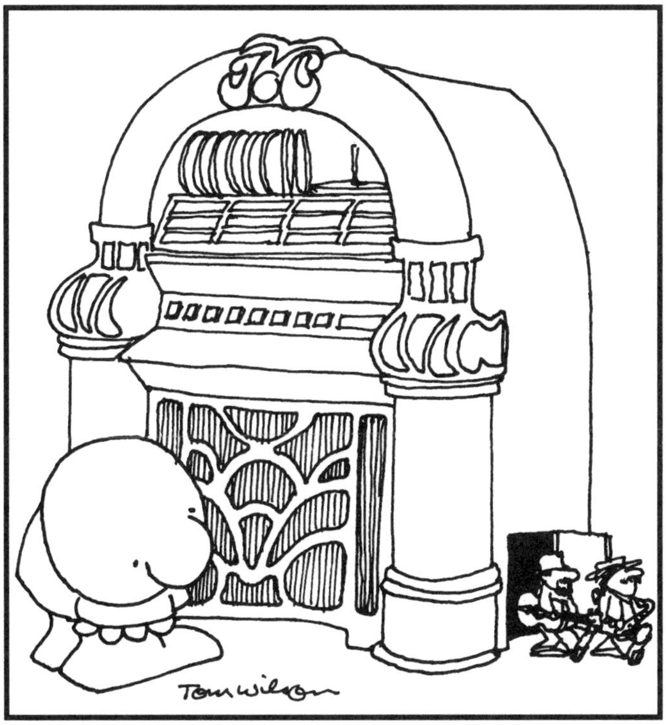
Tom Wilson

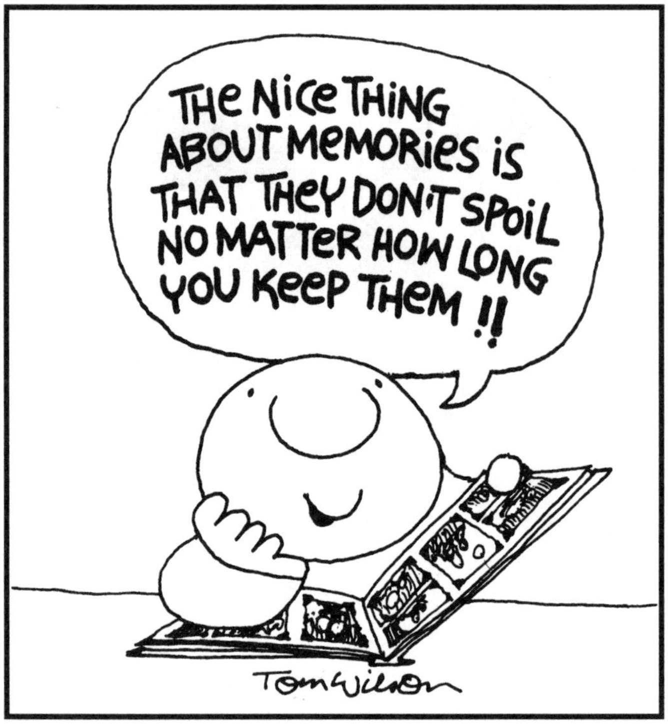
THE NICE THING ABOUT MEMORIES IS THAT THEY DON'T SPOIL NO MATTER HOW LONG YOU KEEP THEM !!
Tom Wilson

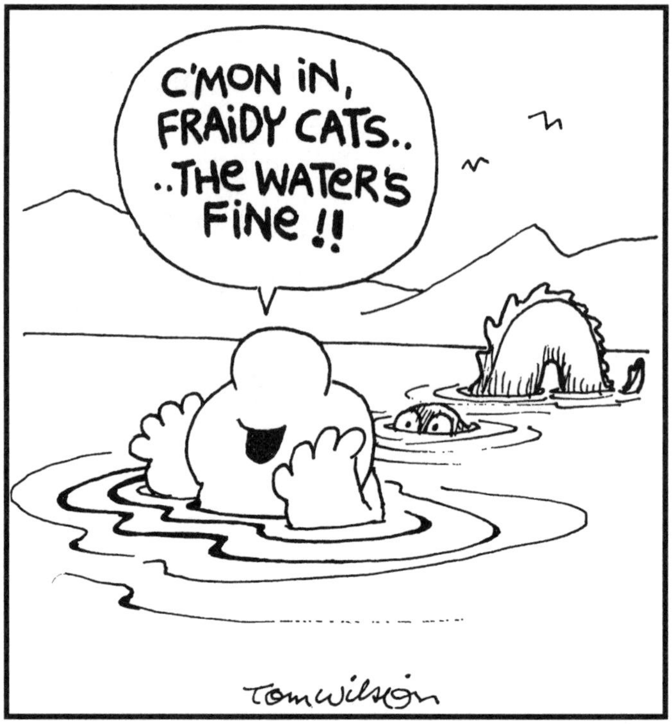
C'MON IN, FRAIDY CATS.. ..THE WATER'S FINE !!
Tom Wilson

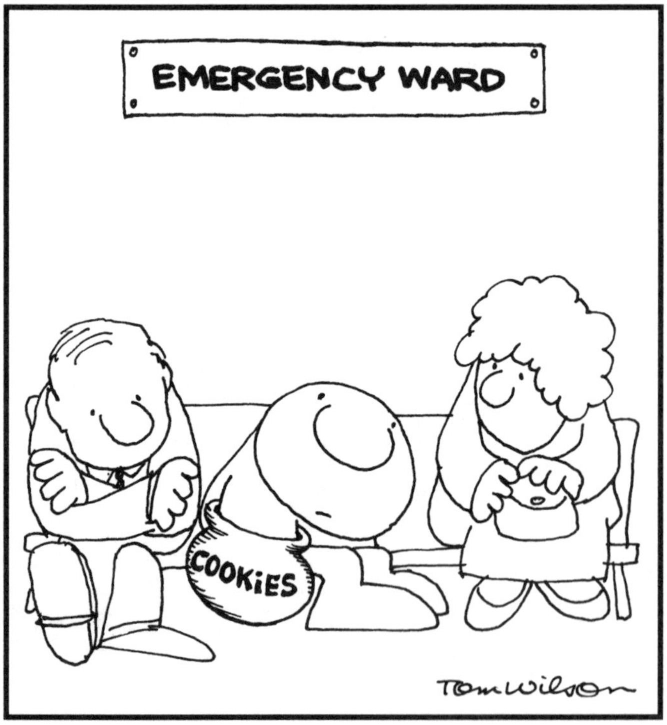
EMERGENCY WARD
COOKIES
Tom Wilson

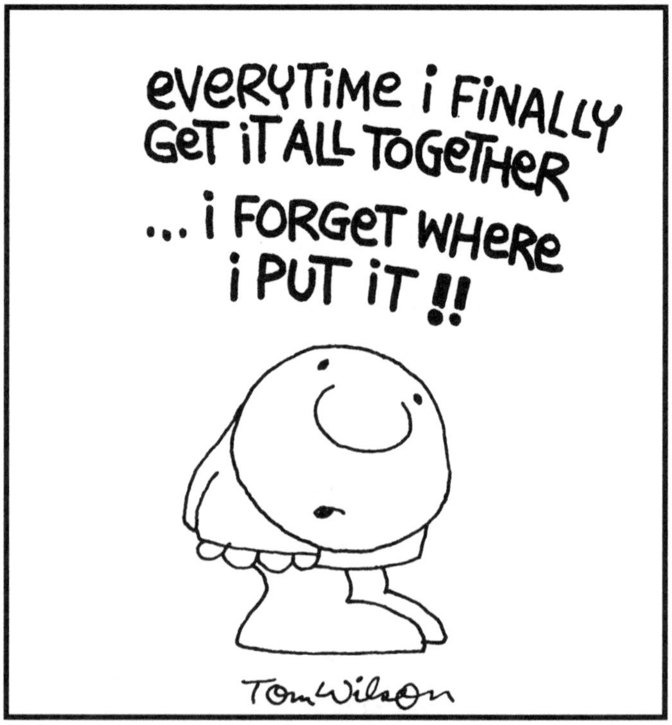
EVERYTIME I FINALLY GET IT ALL TOGETHER
... I FORGET WHERE I PUT IT !!
Tom Wilson

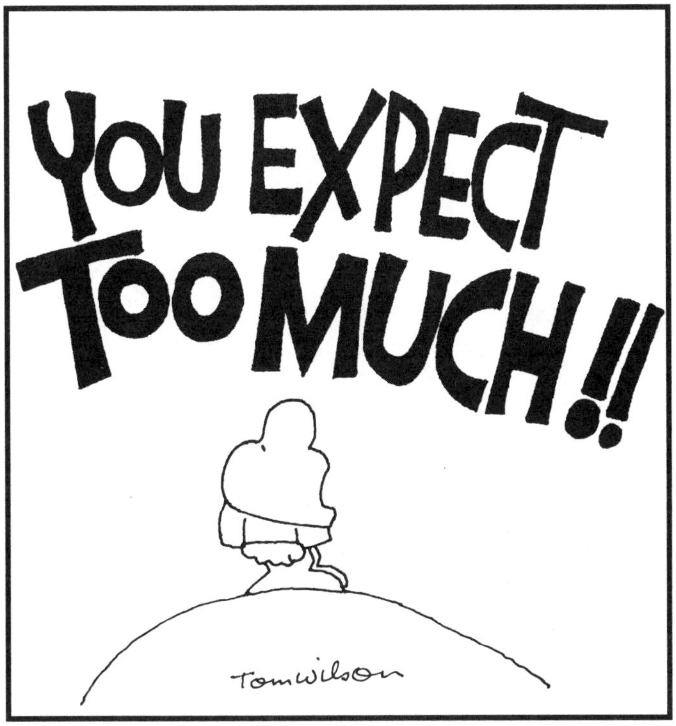
YOU EXPECT TOO MUCH!!
Tom Wilson

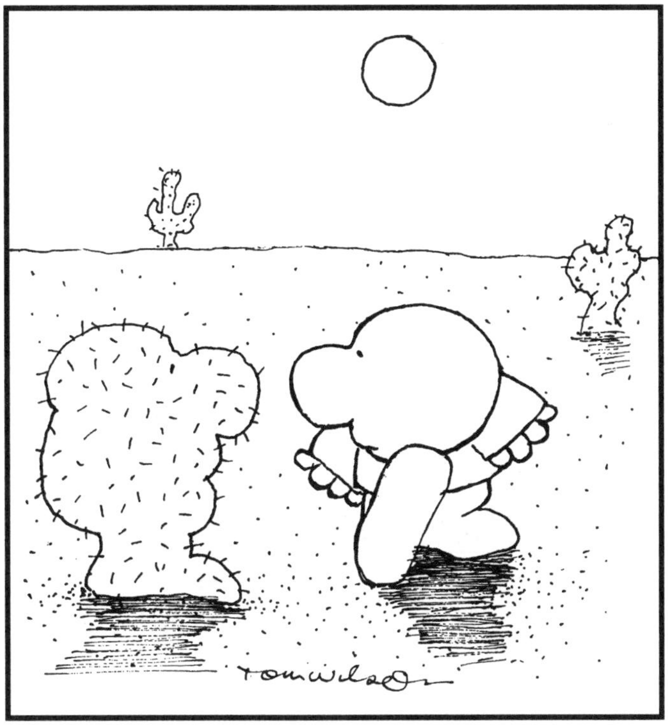
Tom Wilson

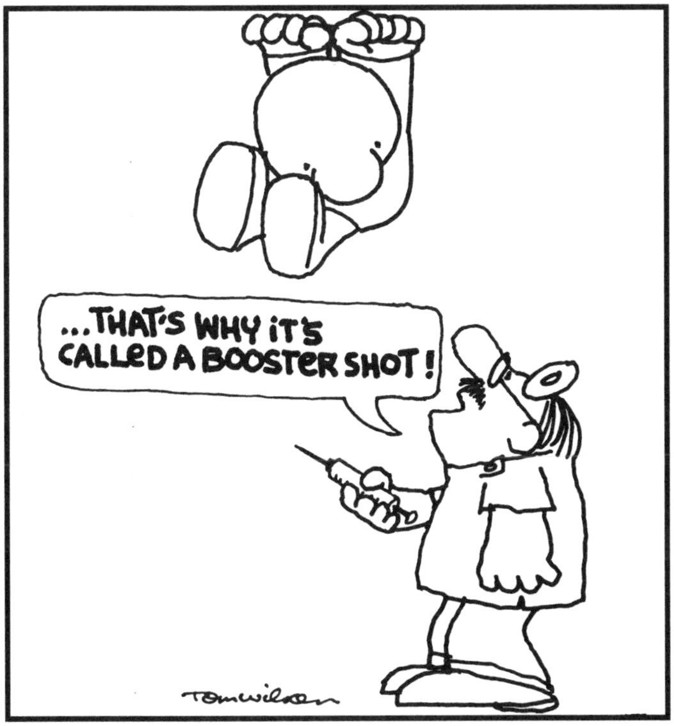
...THAT'S WHY IT'S CALLED A BOOSTER SHOT!
Tom Wilson

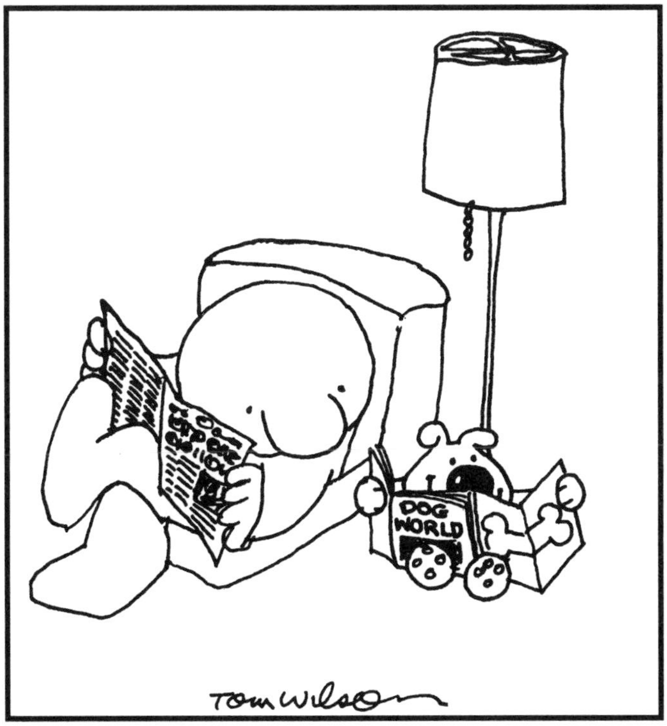
DOG WORLD
Tom Wilson

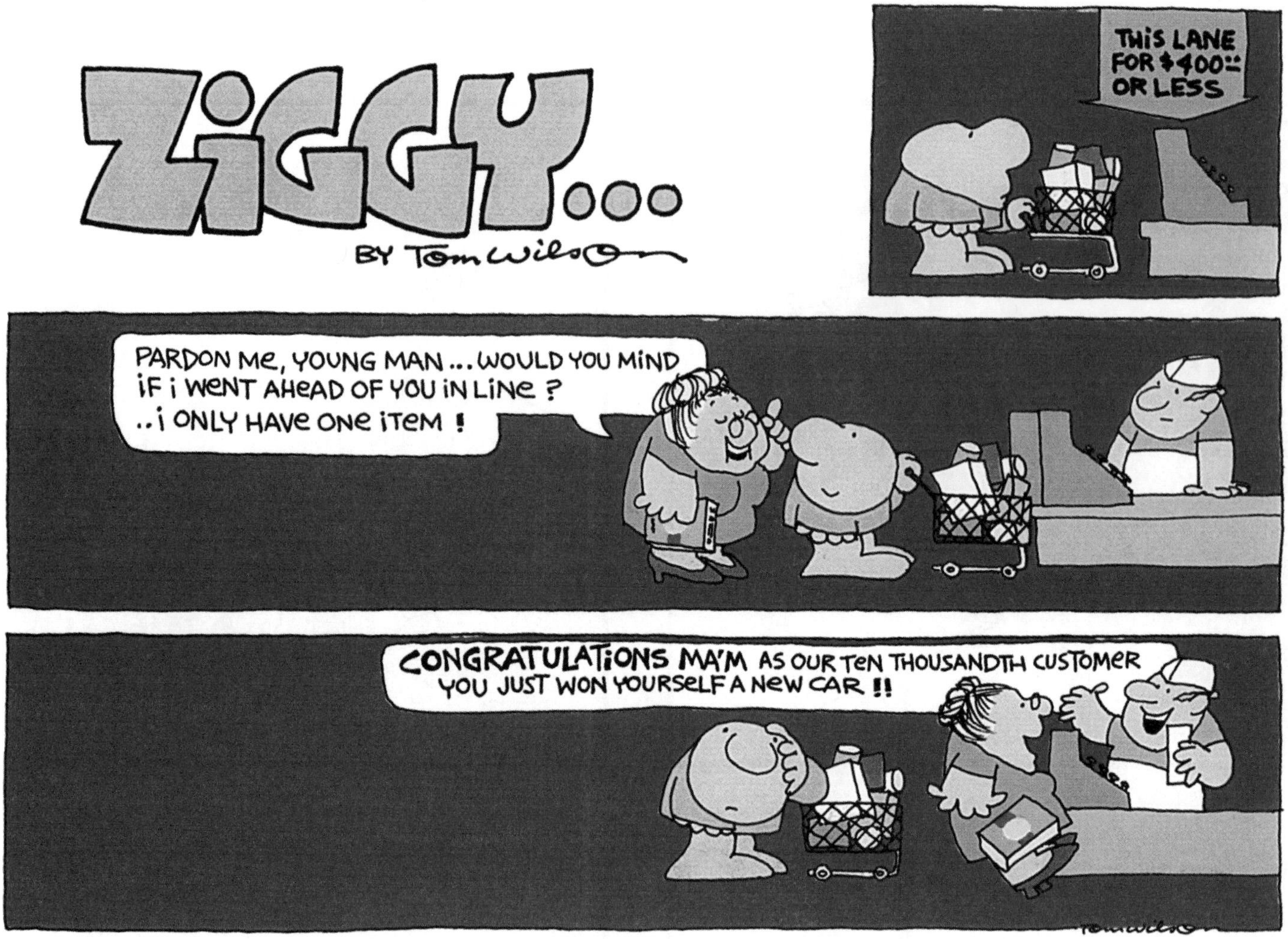
ZIGGY...
BY Tom Wilson
THIS LANE FOR $400.00 OR LESS
PARDON ME, YOUNG MAN ... WOULD YOU MIND IF I WENT AHEAD OF YOU IN LINE ? .. I ONLY HAVE ONE ITEM !
CONGRATULATIONS MA'M AS OUR TEN THOUSANDTH CUSTOMER YOU JUST WON YOURSELF A NEW CAR !!
Tom Wilson

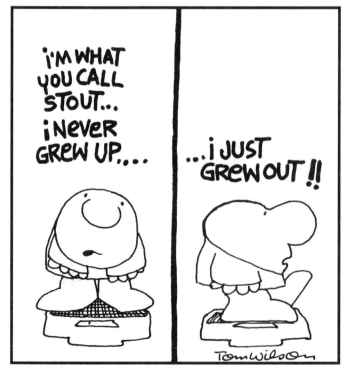

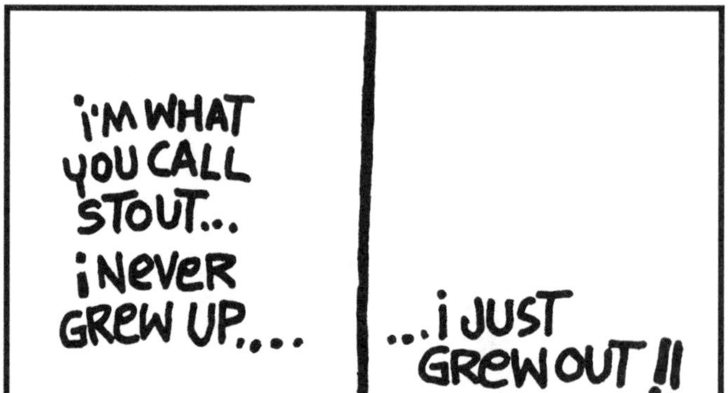
I'M WHAT YOU CALL STOUT... I NEVER GREW UP,...
...I JUST GREW OUT !!
Tom Wilson

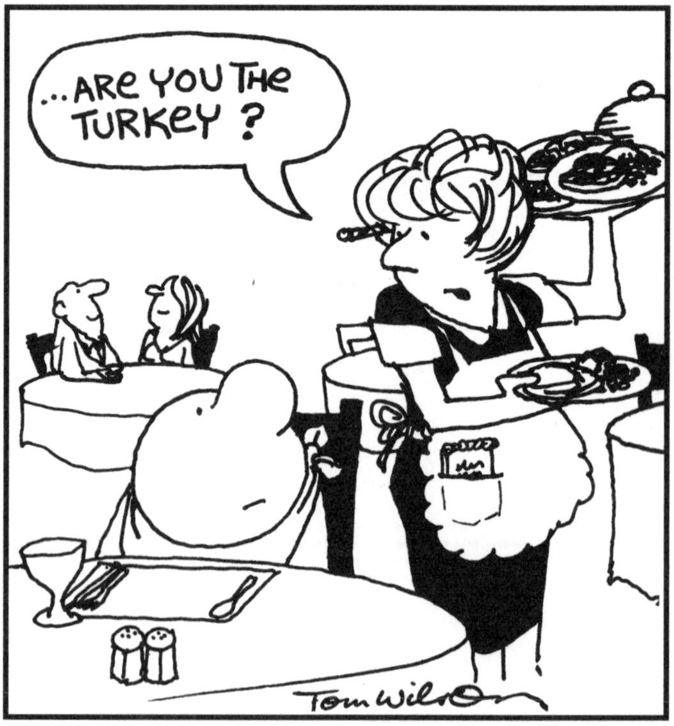
...ARE YOU THE TURKEY ?
Tom Wilson

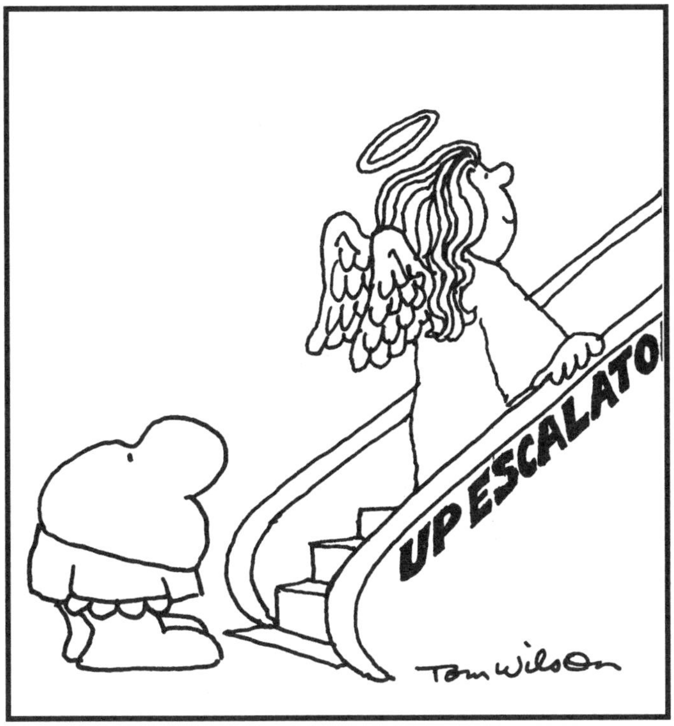
UP ESCALATO
Tom Wilson

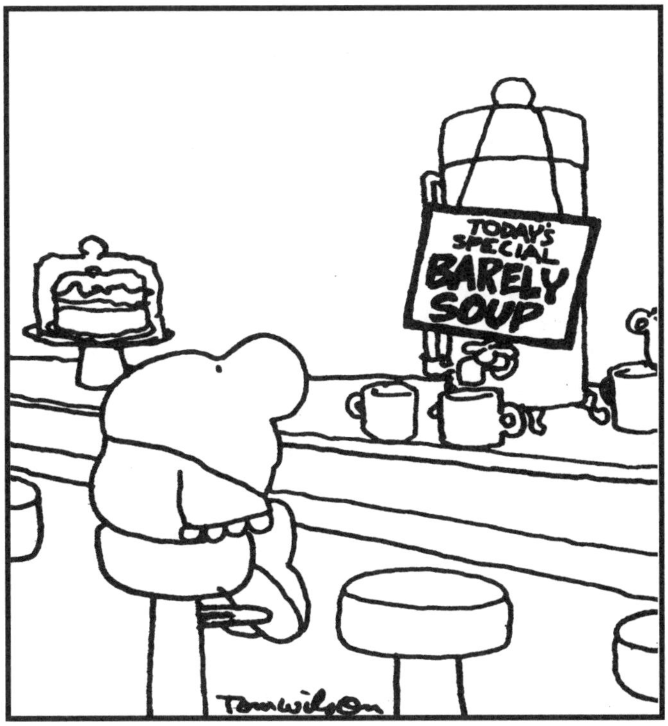
TODAY'S SPECIAL
BARELY SOUP
Tom Wilson

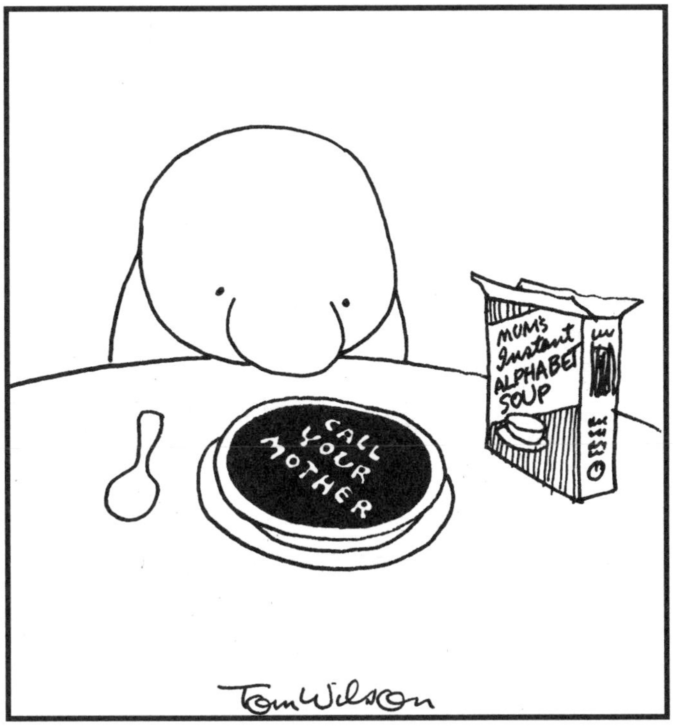
MUM'S Instant ALPHABET SOUP
CALL YOUR MOTHER
Tom Wilson

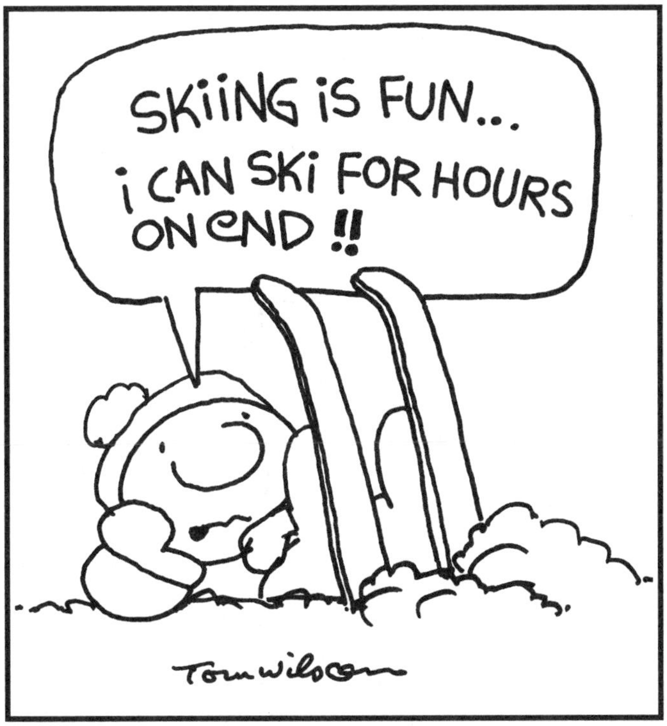
SKiiNG iS FUN...
i CAN SKi FOR HOURS ON eND !!
Tom Wilson

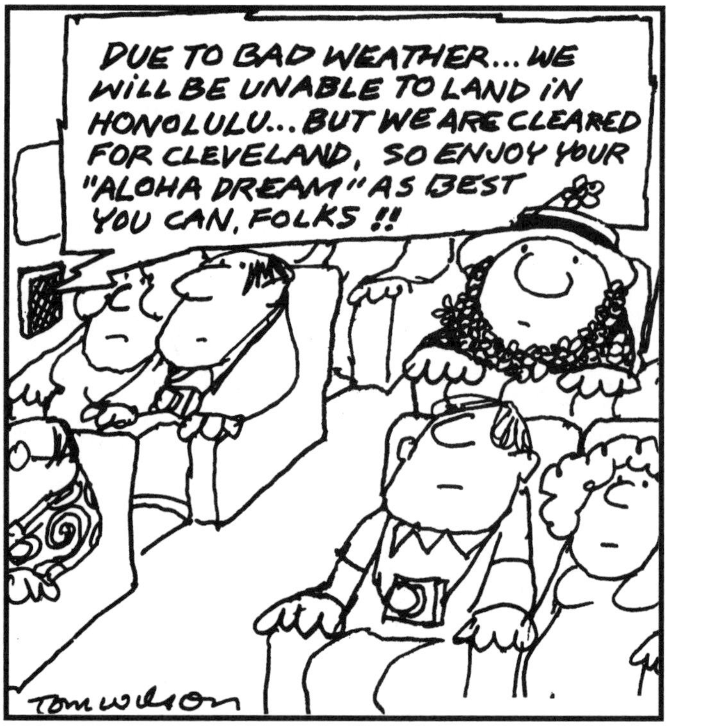
DUE TO BAD WEATHER... WE WILL BE UNABLE TO LAND IN HONOLULU... BUT WE ARE CLEARED FOR CLEVELAND, SO ENJOY YOUR "ALOHA DREAM" AS BEST YOU CAN, FOLKS !!
TOM WILSON

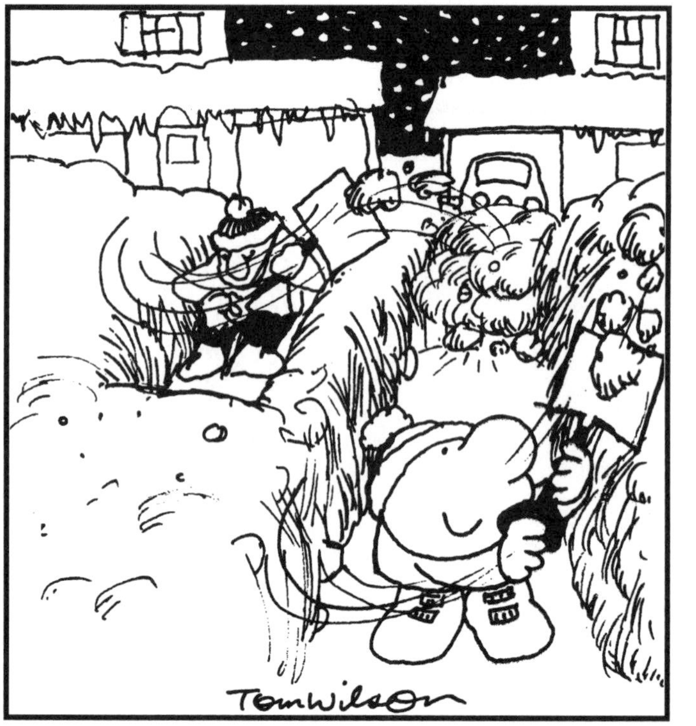
TOM WILSON

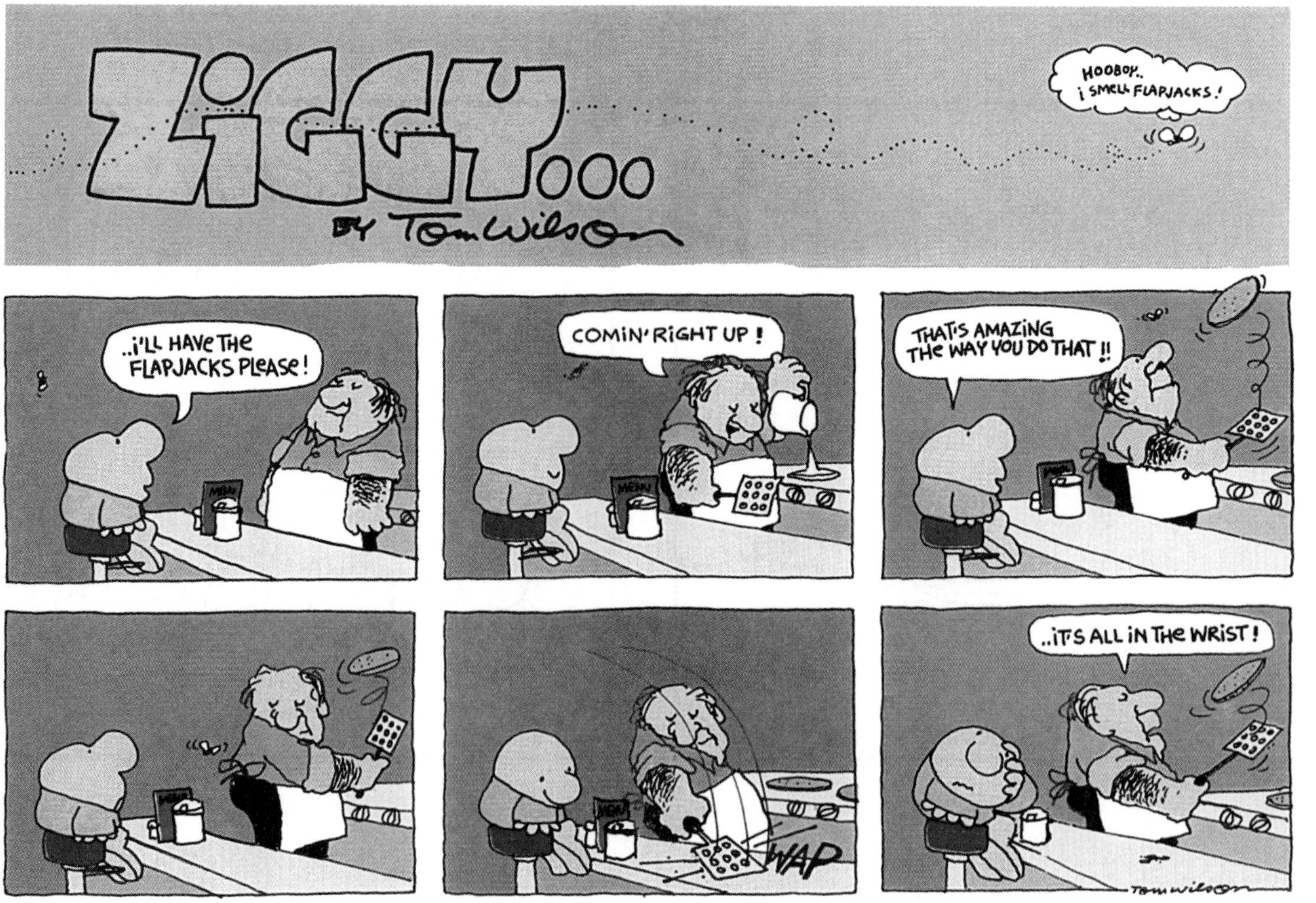
ZIGGY
BY TOM WILSON
HOOBOY.. I SMELL FLAPJACKS!
..I'LL HAVE THE FLAPJACKS PLEASE!
MENU
COMIN' RIGHT UP!
THAT'S AMAZING THE WAY YOU DO THAT!!
WAP
..IT'S ALL IN THE WRIST!
TOM WILSON

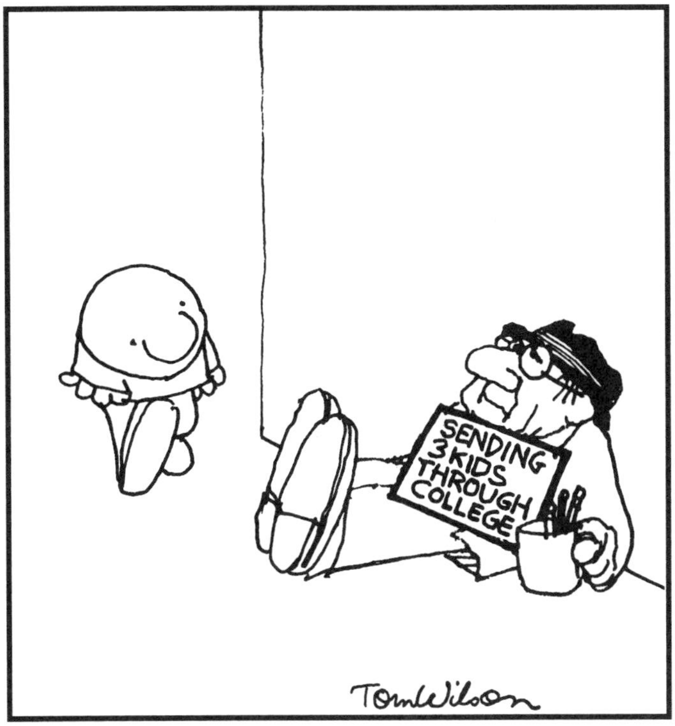
SENDING 3 KIDS THROUGH COLLEGE
Tom Wilson

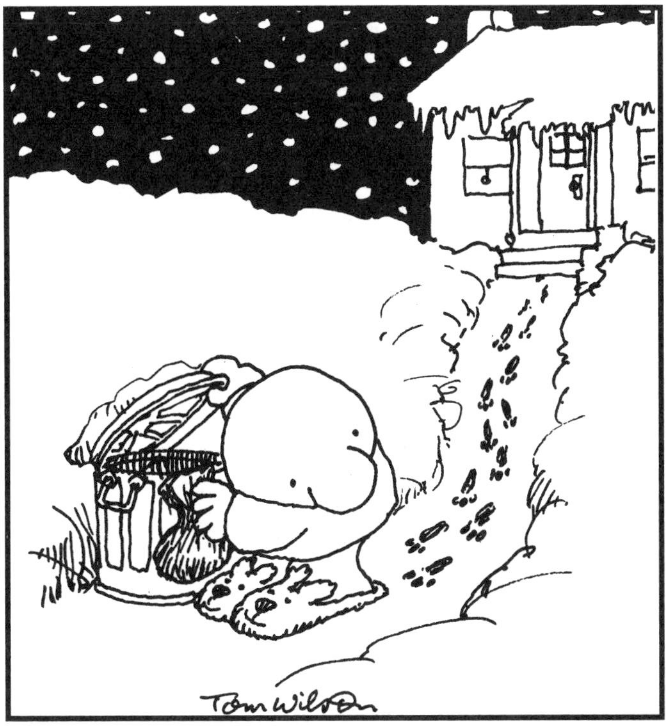
Tom Wilson

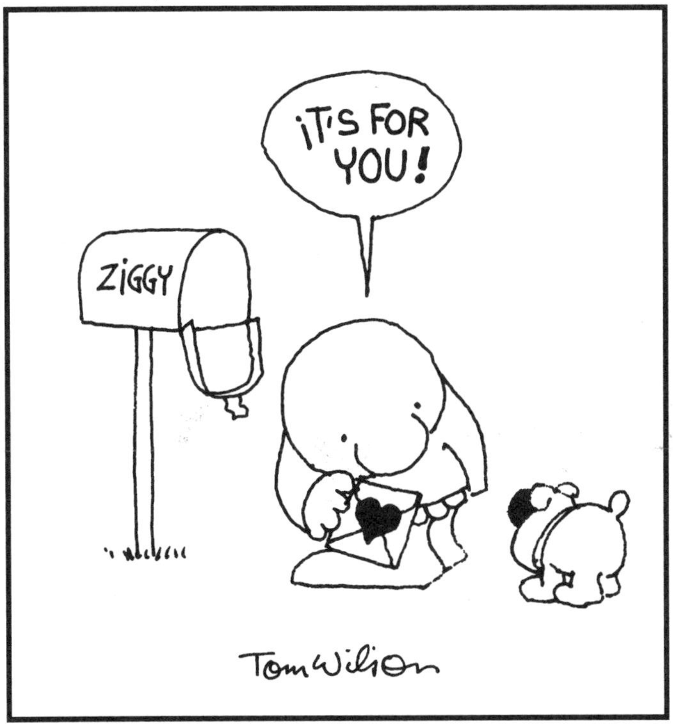
iT'S FOR YOU!
ZiGGY
Tom Wilson

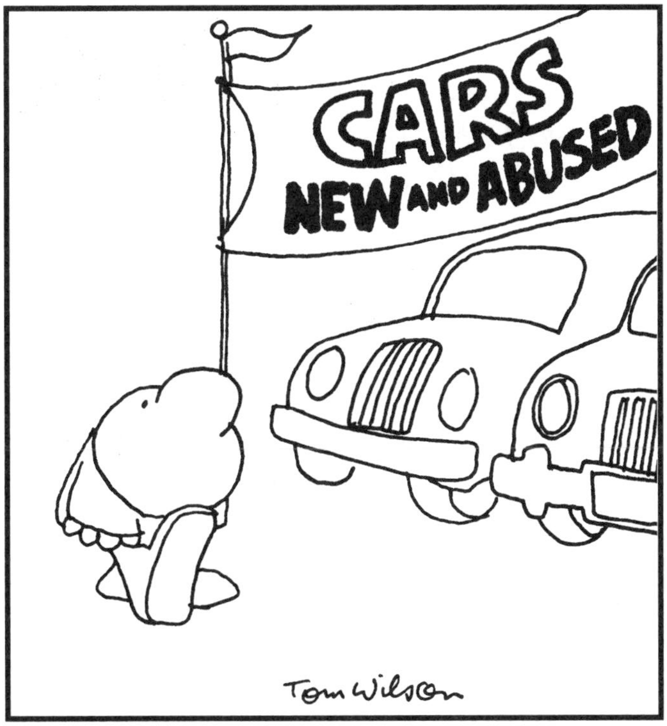
CARS
NEW AND ABUSED
Tom Wilson

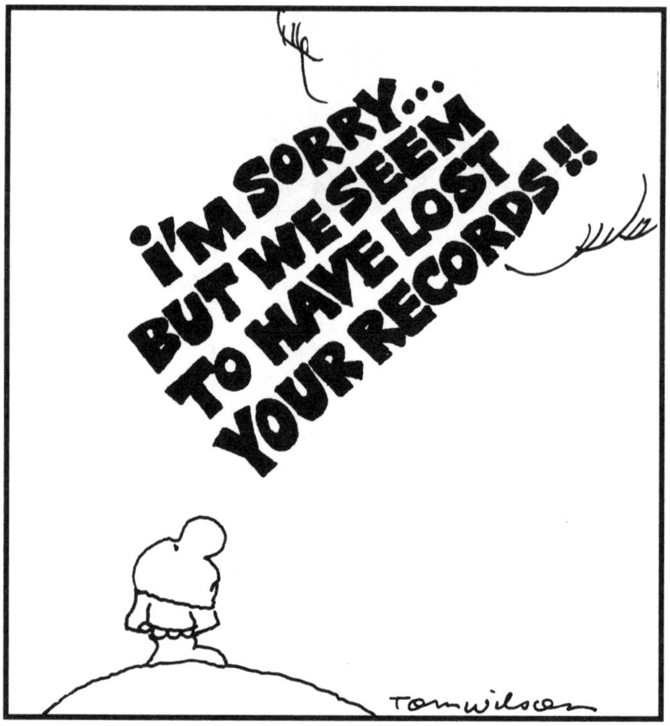
i'M SORRY... BUT WE SEEM TO HAVE LOST YOUR RECORDS!!
Tom Wilson

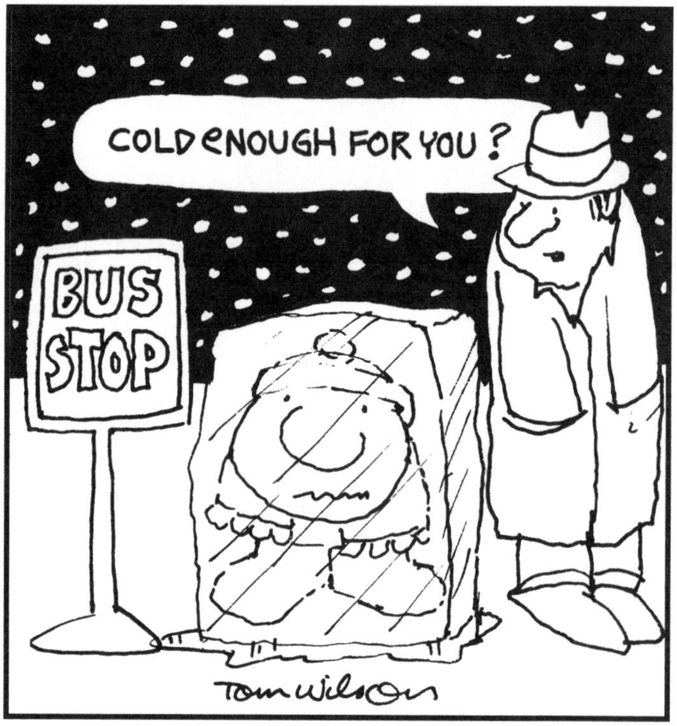
COLD ENOUGH FOR YOU?
BUS STOP
Tom Wilson

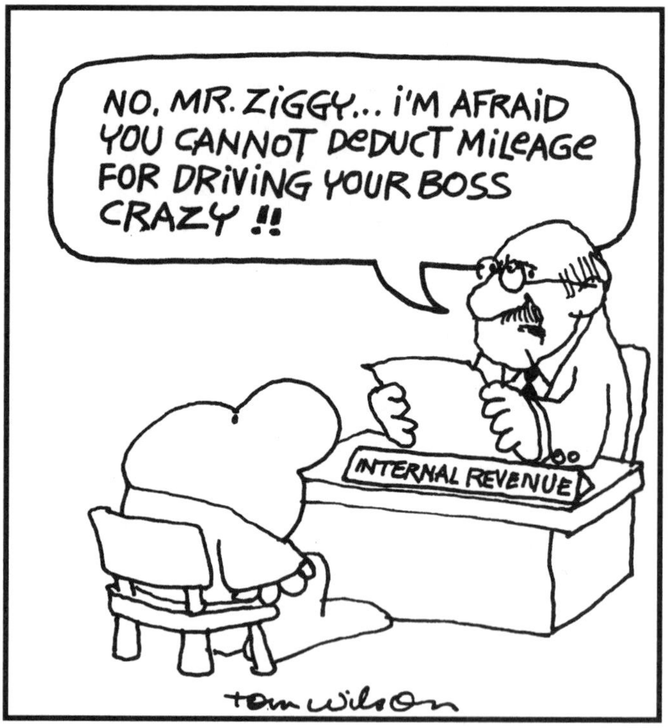
NO, MR. ZIGGY... i'M AFRAID YOU CANNOT DEDUCT MILEAGE FOR DRIVING YOUR BOSS CRAZY!!
INTERNAL REVENUE
Tom Wilson

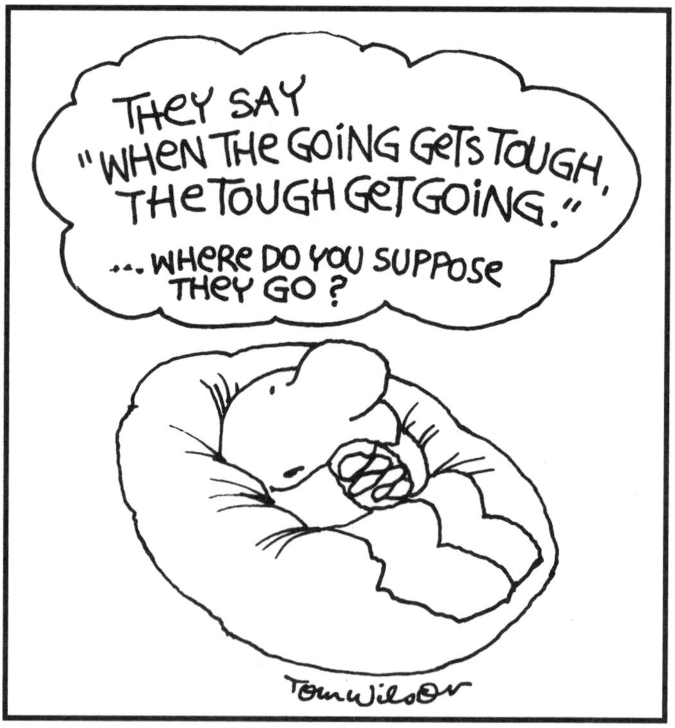
THEY SAY "WHEN THE GOING GETS TOUGH, THE TOUGH GET GOING."
...WHERE DO YOU SUPPOSE THEY GO?
Tom Wilson

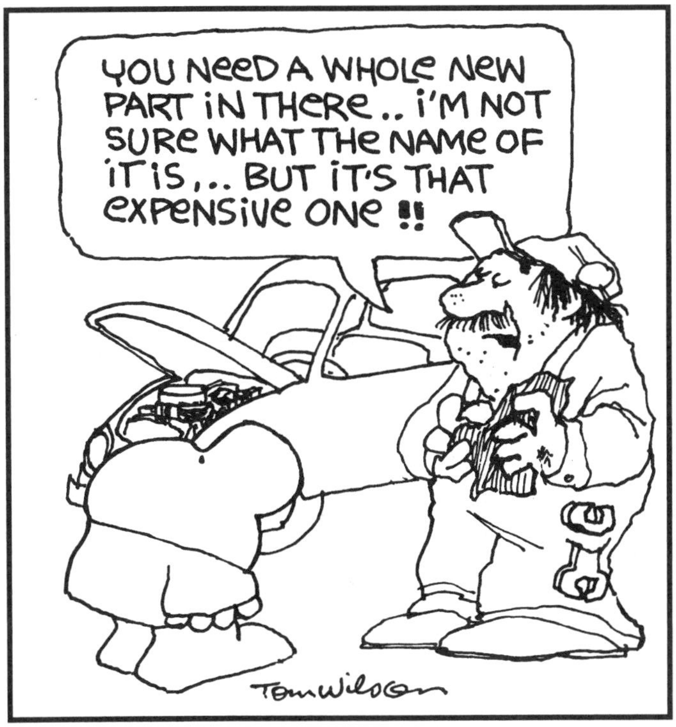
YOU NEED A WHOLE NEW PART IN THERE .. I'M NOT SURE WHAT THE NAME OF IT IS ,.. BUT IT'S THAT EXPENSIVE ONE !!
Tom Wilson

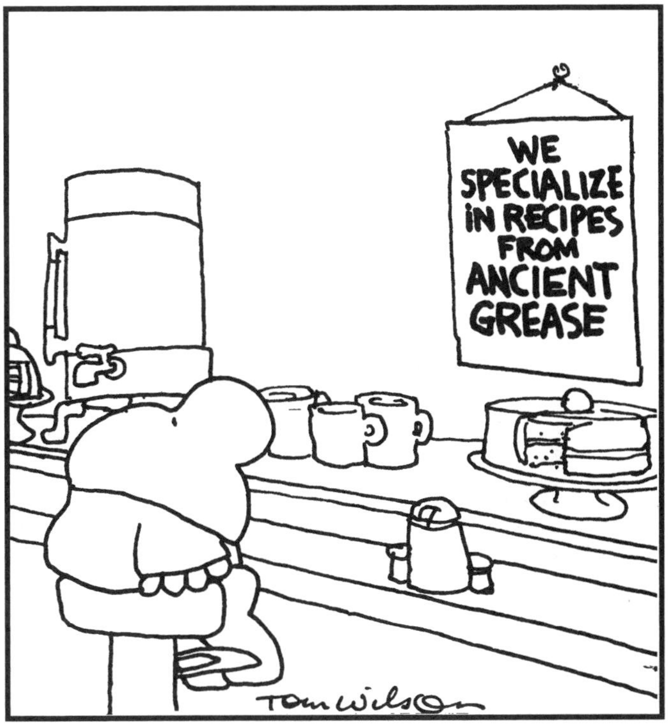
WE SPECIALIZE IN RECIPES FROM ANCIENT GREASE
Tom Wilson

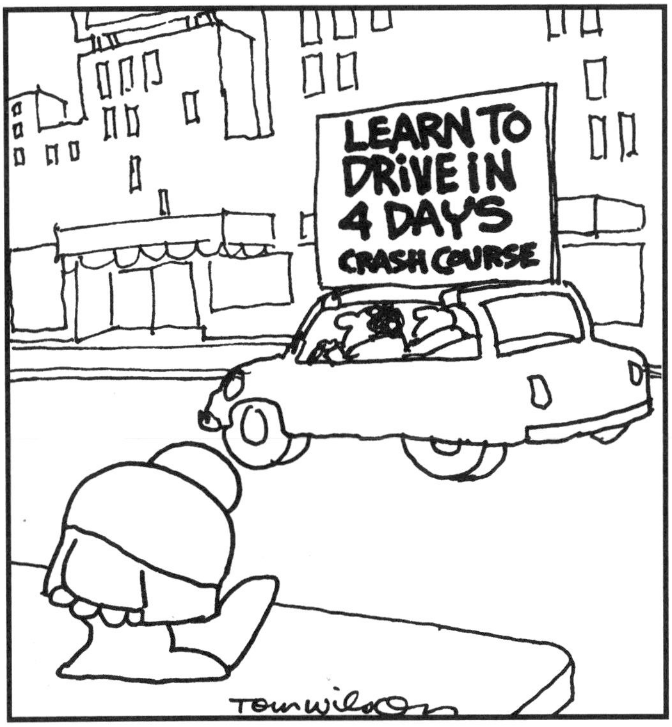
LEARN TO DRIVE IN 4 DAYS CRASH COURSE
Tom Wilson

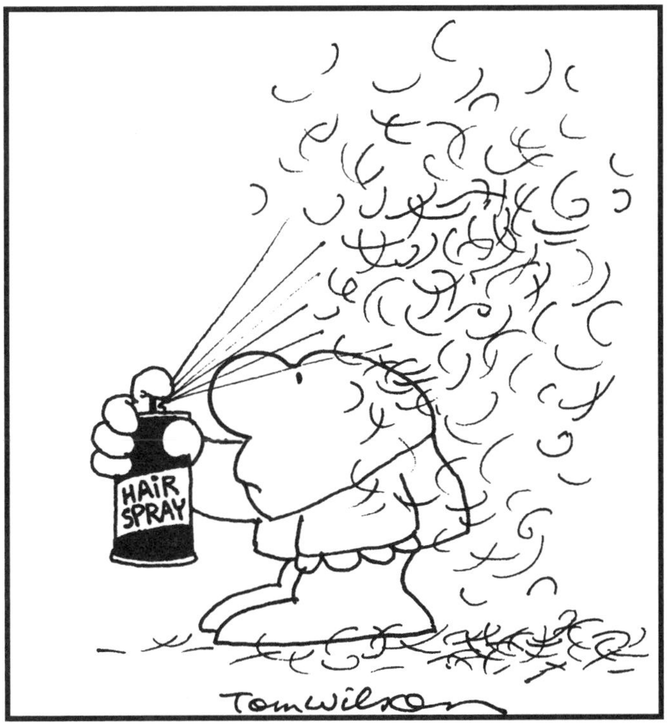
HAIR SPRAY
Tom Wilson

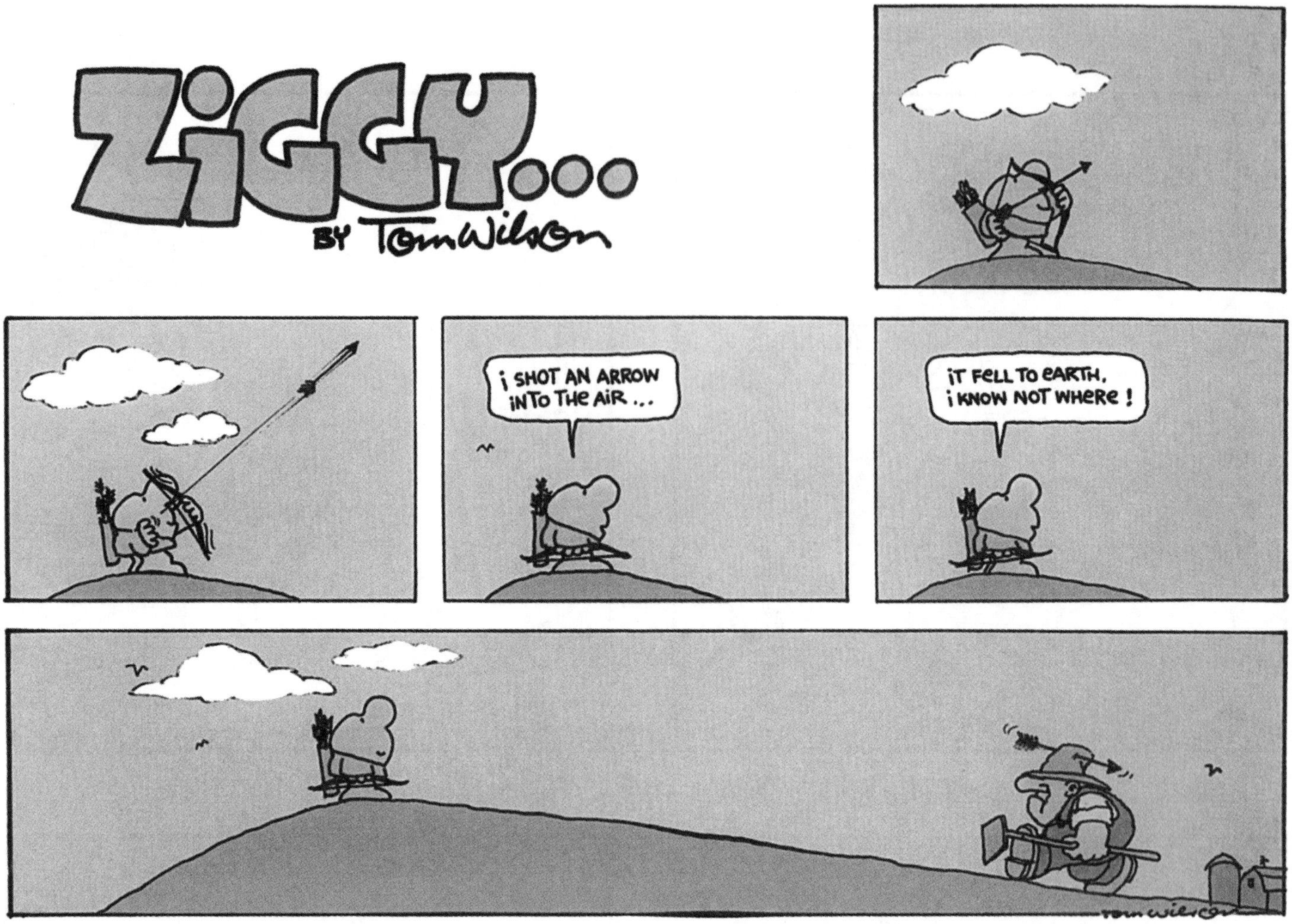
ZIGGY...
BY TOM WILSON
i SHOT AN ARROW INTO THE AIR ...
iT FELL TO EARTH, i KNOW NOT WHERE !
TOM WILSON

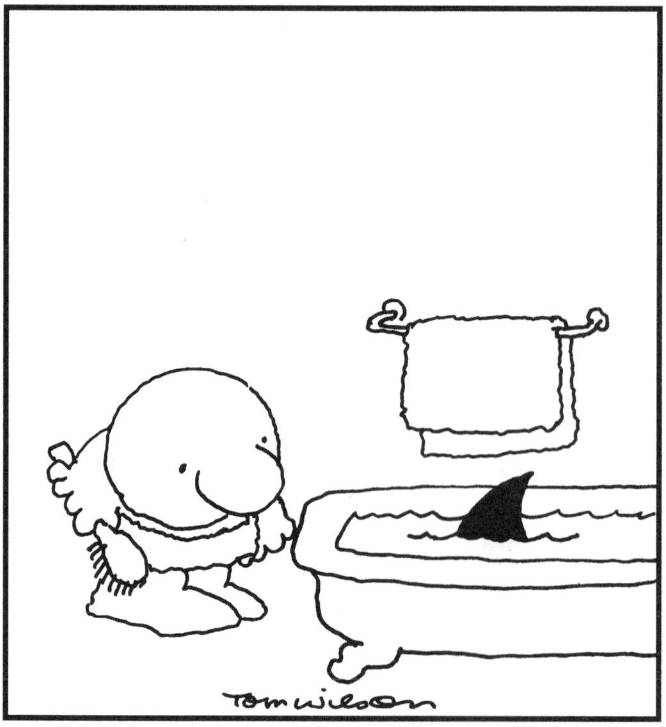
TOM WILSON

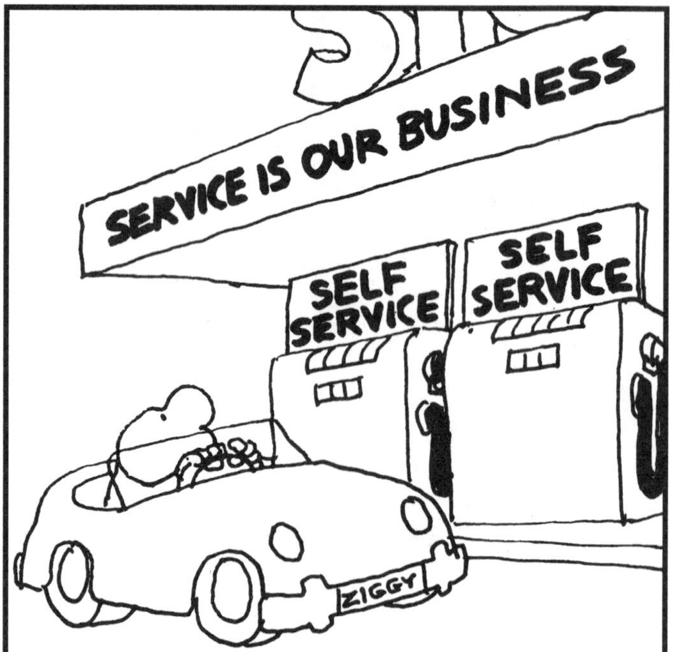
SERVICE IS OUR BUSINESS
SELF SERVICE
SELF SERVICE
ZIGGY
TOM WILSON

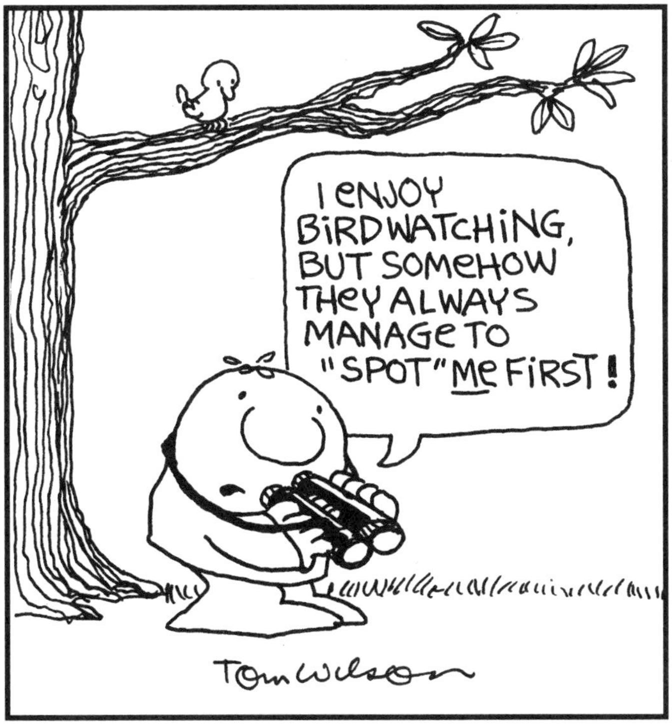
I ENJOY BIRDWATCHING, BUT SOMEHOW THEY ALWAYS MANAGE TO "SPOT" ME FIRST!
Tom Wilson

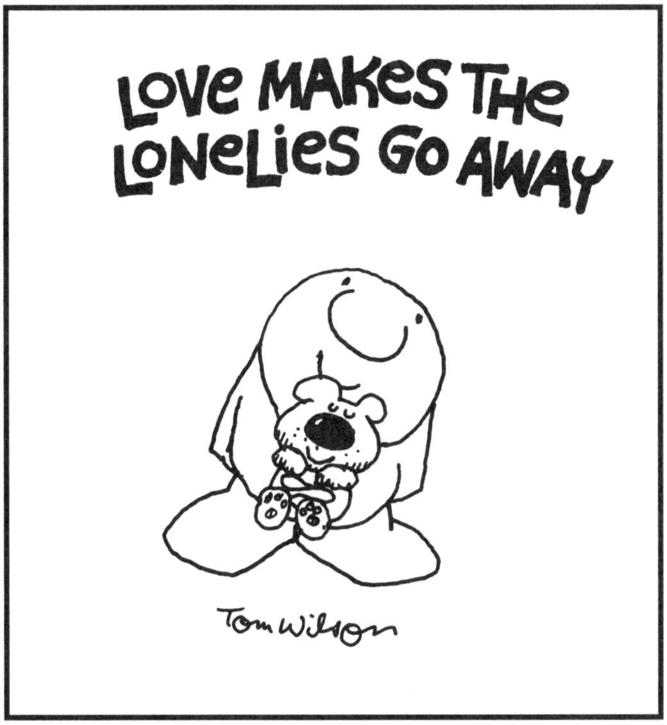
LOVE MAKES THE LONELIES GO AWAY
Tom Wilson

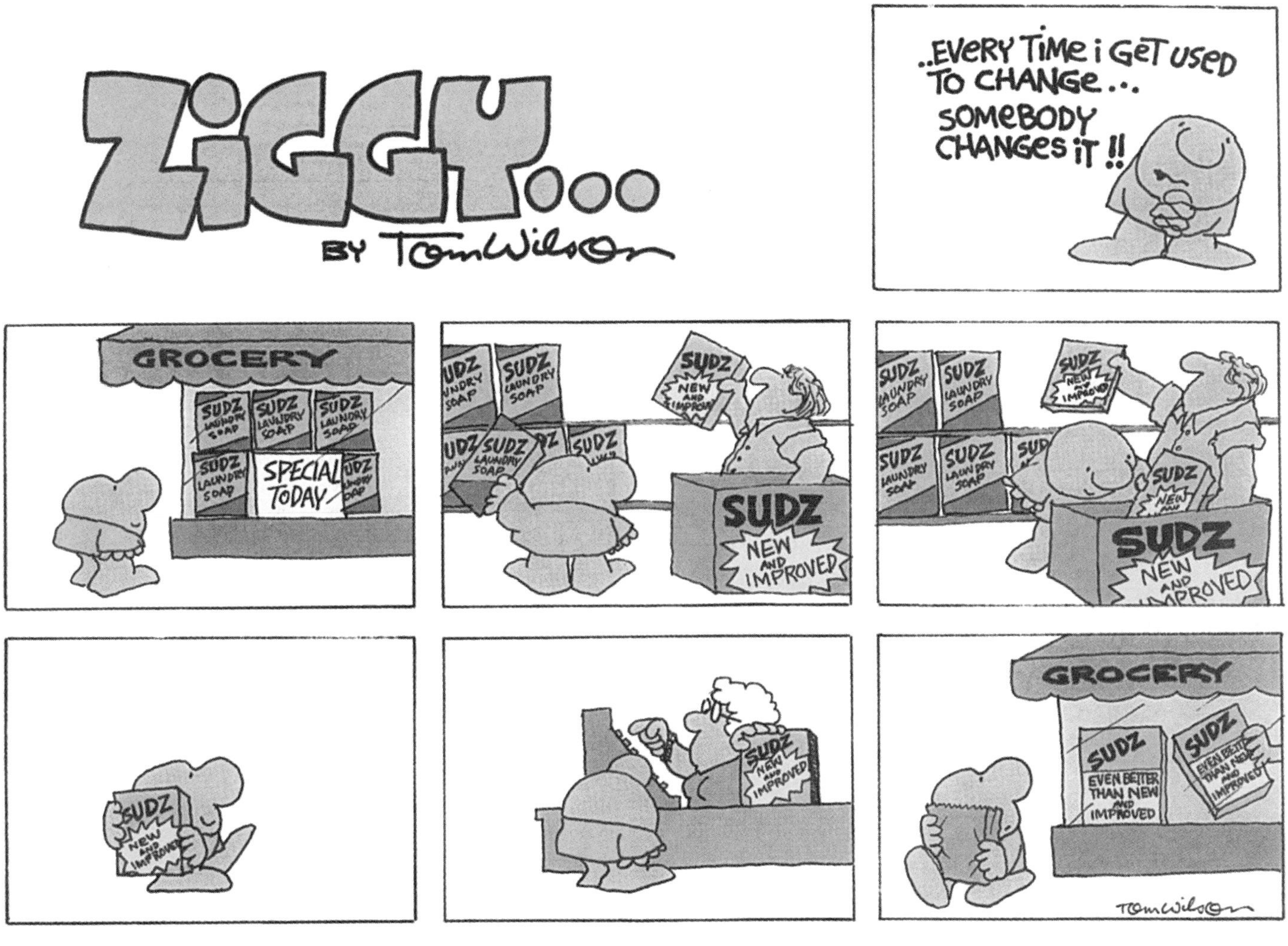
ZIGGY...
BY Tom Wilson
..EVERY TIME I GET USED TO CHANGE... SOMEBODY CHANGES IT !!
GROCERY
SUDZ LAUNDRY SOAP
SPECIAL TODAY
SUDZ NEW AND IMPROVED
SUDZ EVEN BETTER THAN NEW AND IMPROVED
Tom Wilson

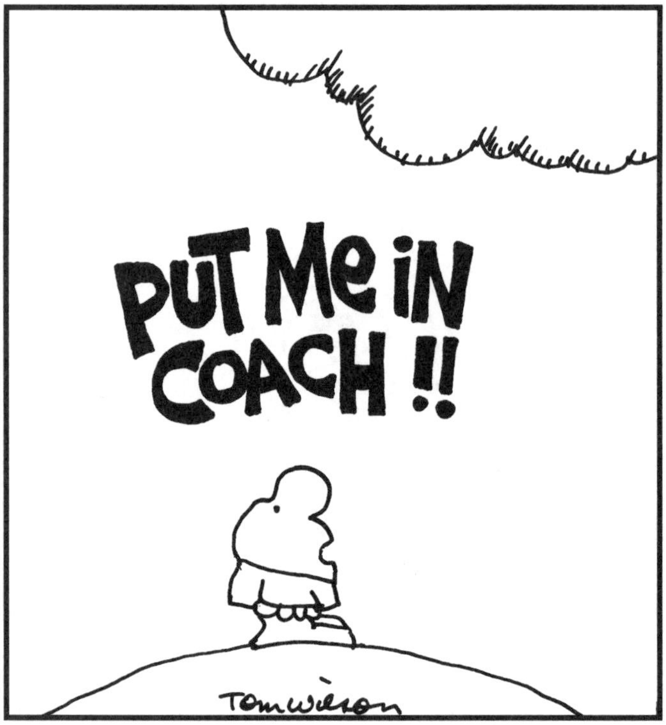
PUT ME IN
COACH !!
Tom Wilson

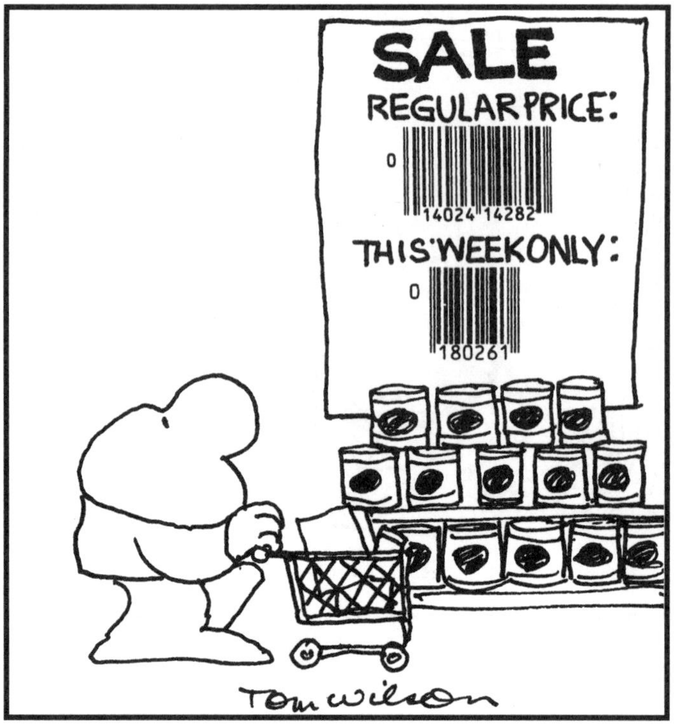
SALE
REGULAR PRICE:
0 14024 14282
THIS WEEK ONLY:
0 180261
Tom Wilson

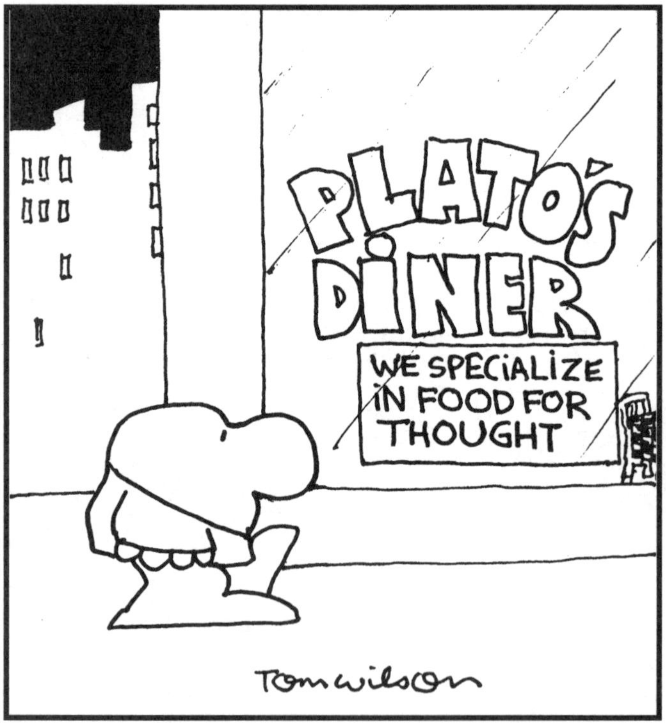
PLATO'S
DINER
WE SPECIALIZE
IN FOOD FOR
THOUGHT
Tom Wilson

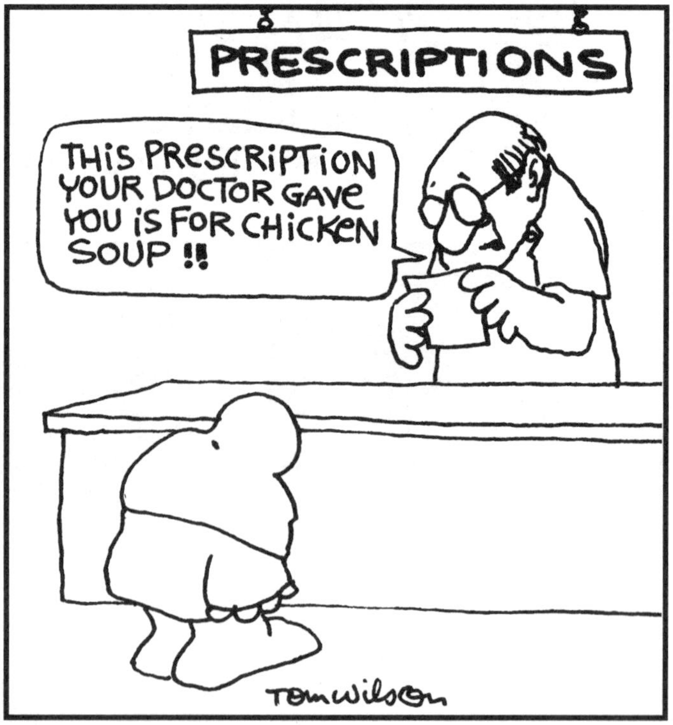
PRESCRIPTIONS
THIS PRESCRIPTION YOUR DOCTOR GAVE YOU IS FOR CHICKEN SOUP !!
Tom Wilson

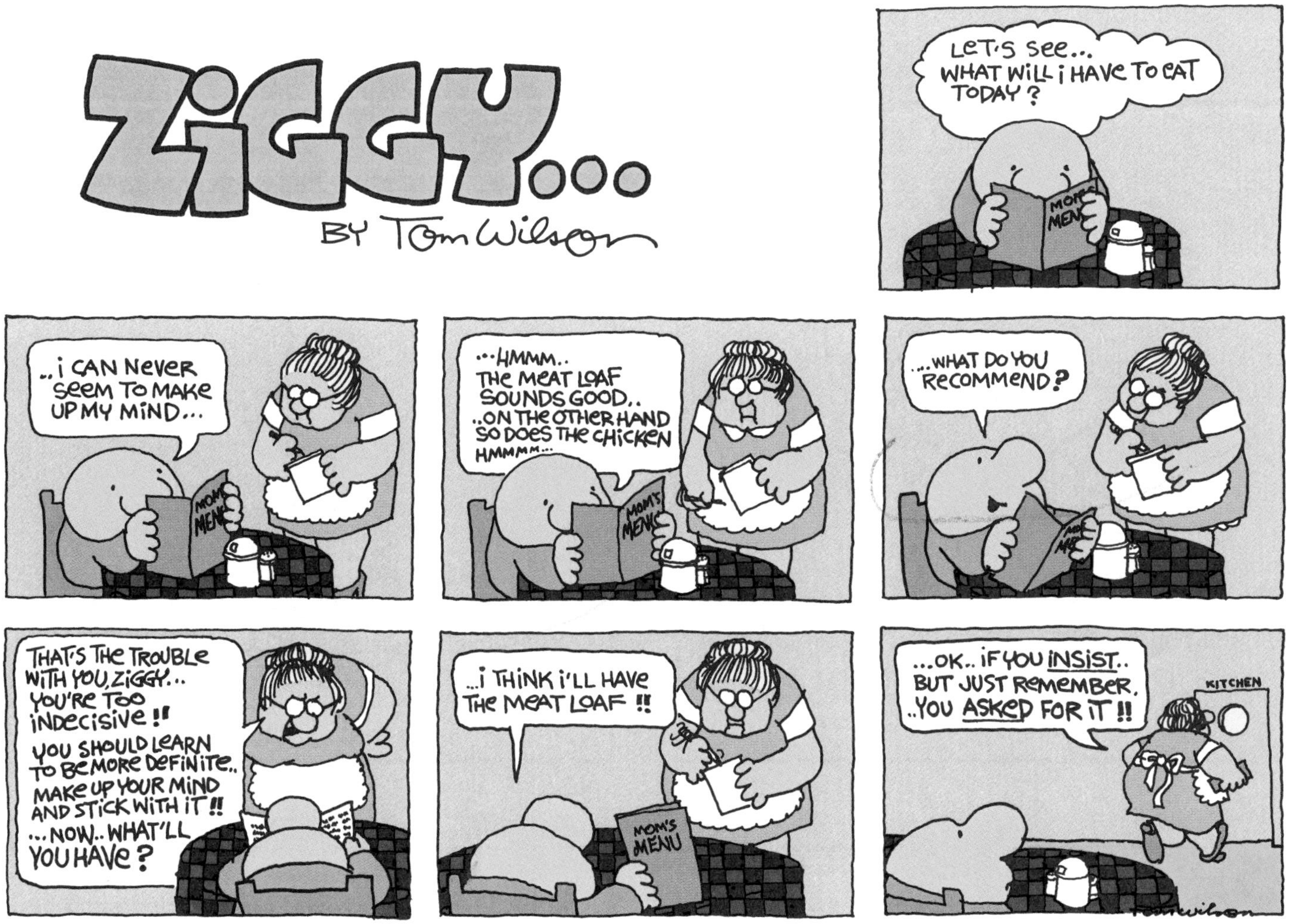
ZIGGY...
BY Tom Wilson
LET'S SEE... WHAT WILL I HAVE TO EAT TODAY?
MOM'S MENU
..I CAN NEVER SEEM TO MAKE UP MY MIND...
...HMMM.. THE MEAT LOAF SOUNDS GOOD.. ..ON THE OTHER HAND SO DOES THE CHICKEN HMMMM...
....WHAT DO YOU RECOMMEND?
THAT'S THE TROUBLE WITH YOU, ZIGGY... YOU'RE TOO INDECISIVE!! YOU SHOULD LEARN TO BE MORE DEFINITE.. MAKE UP YOUR MIND AND STICK WITH IT!! ...NOW.. WHAT'LL YOU HAVE?
...I THINK I'LL HAVE THE MEAT LOAF!!
...OK.. IF YOU INSIST.. BUT JUST REMEMBER. ..YOU ASKED FOR IT!!
KITCHEN
Tom Wilson

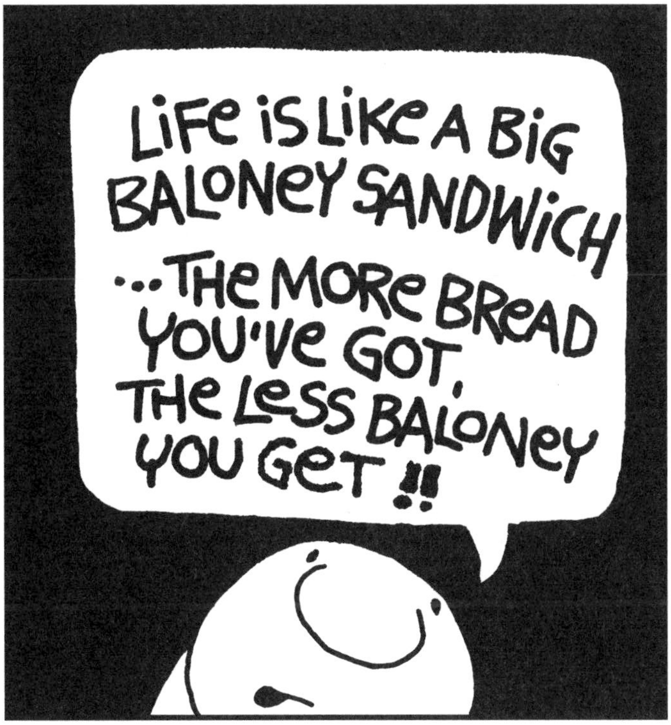
LIFE IS LIKE A BIG BALONEY SANDWICH ...THE MORE BREAD YOU'VE GOT, THE LESS BALONEY YOU GET!!

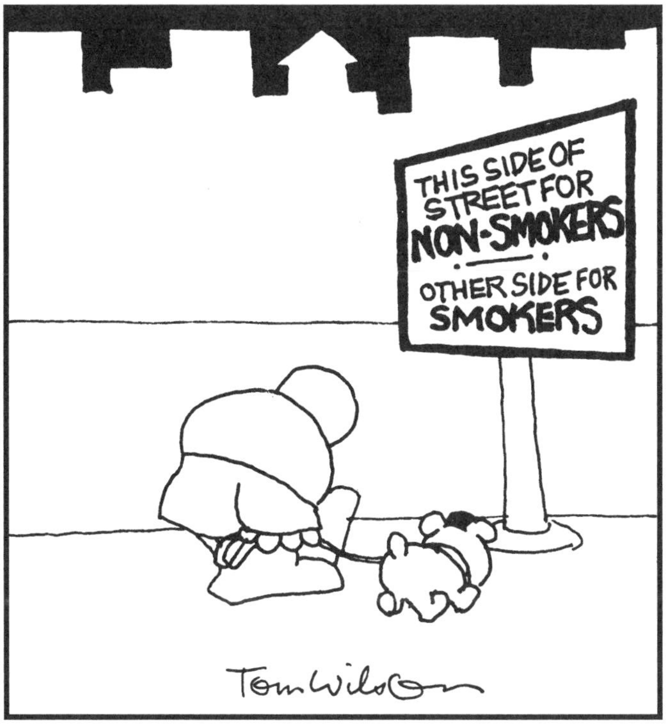
THIS SIDE OF STREET FOR NON-SMOKERS
OTHER SIDE FOR SMOKERS
Tom Wilson

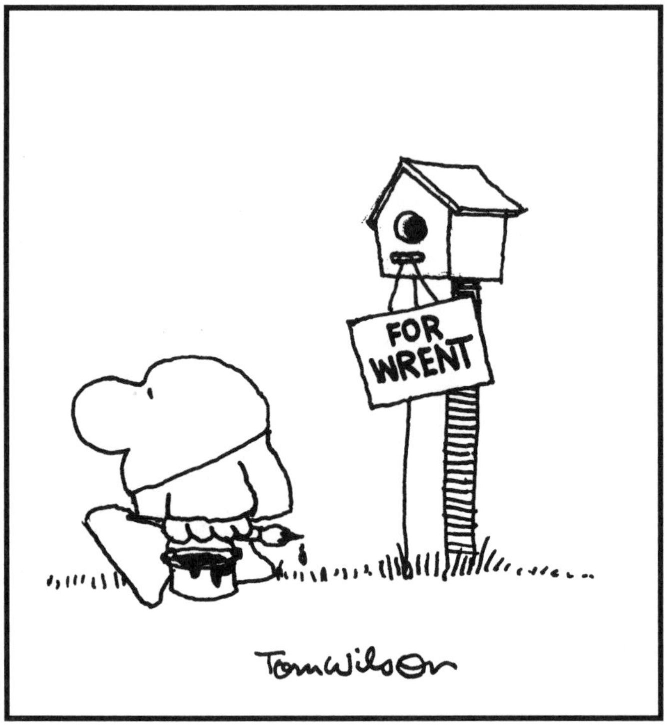
FOR WRENT
Tom Wilson

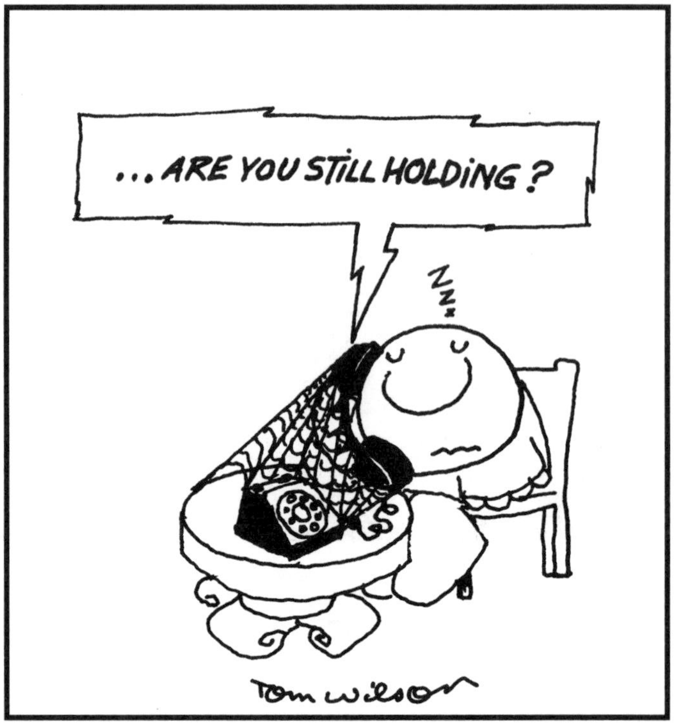
...ARE YOU STILL HOLDING?
Z Z Z
Tom Wilson

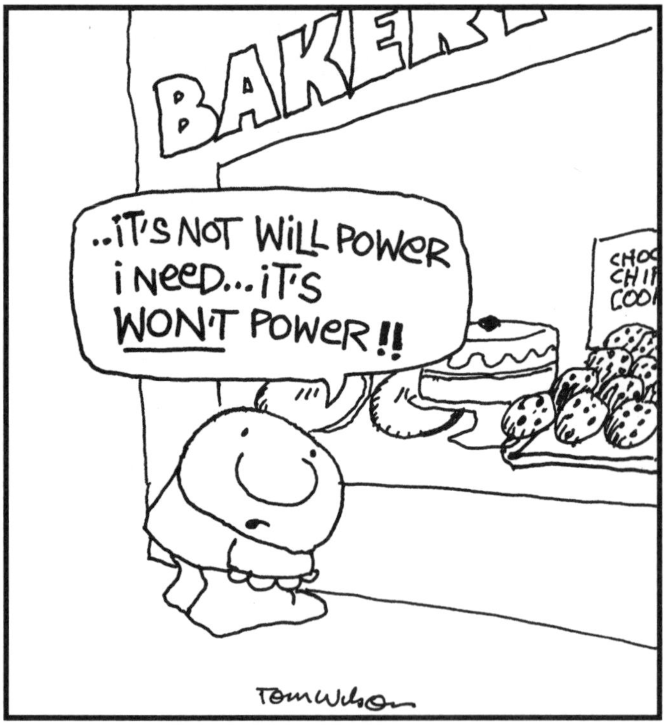
BAKER
..IT'S NOT WILL POWER I NEED...IT'S WON'T POWER!!
Tom Wilson

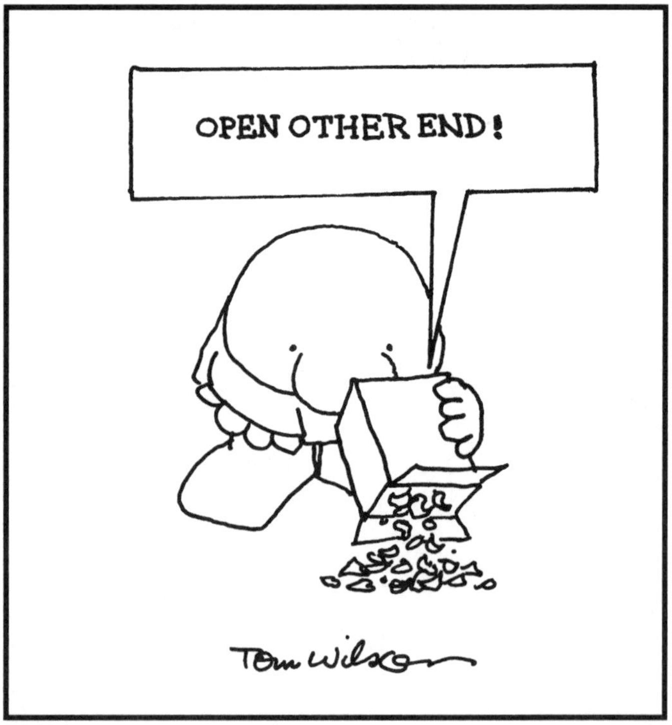
OPEN OTHER END!
Tom Wilson

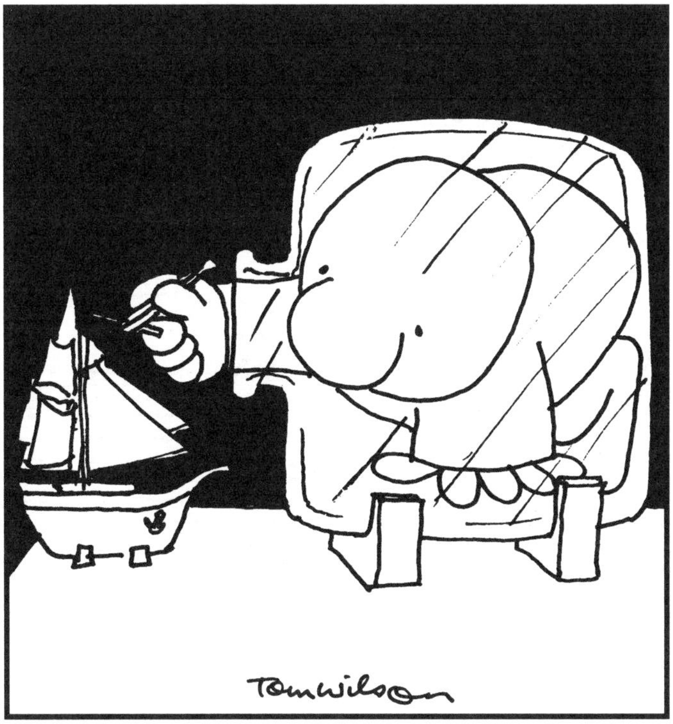
Tom Wilson

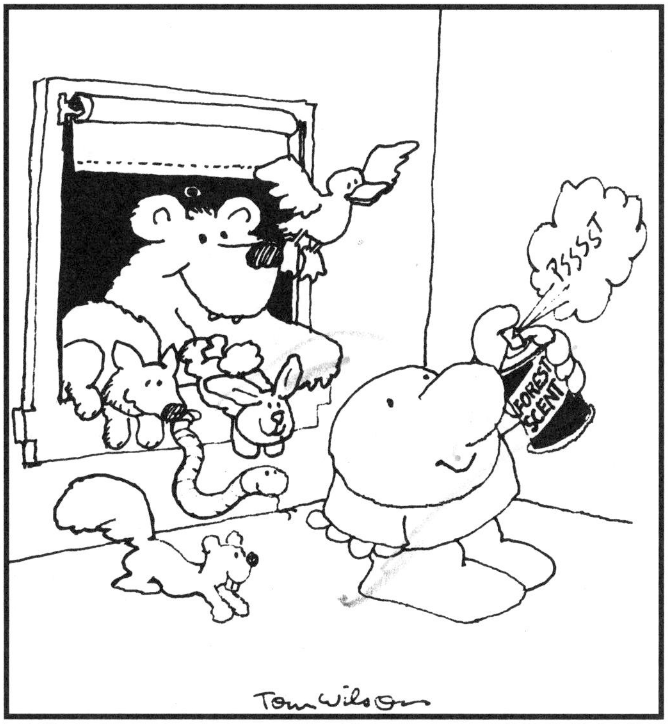
PSSSST
FOREST SCENT
Tom Wilson

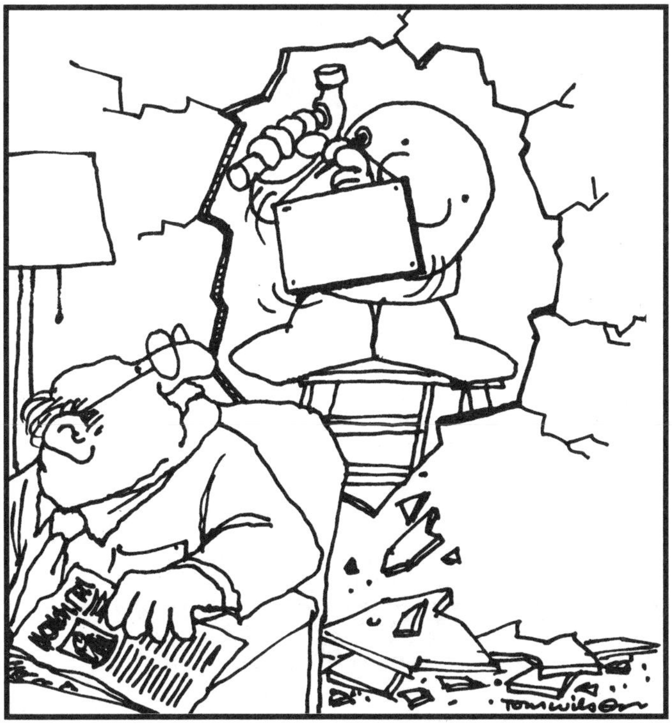
Tom Wilson

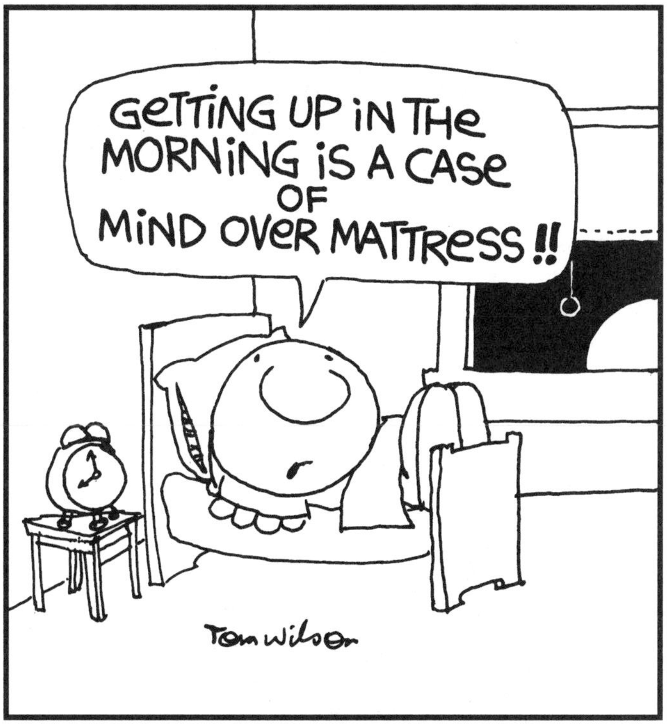
GETTING UP IN THE MORNING IS A CASE OF MIND OVER MATTRESS !!
Tom Wilson

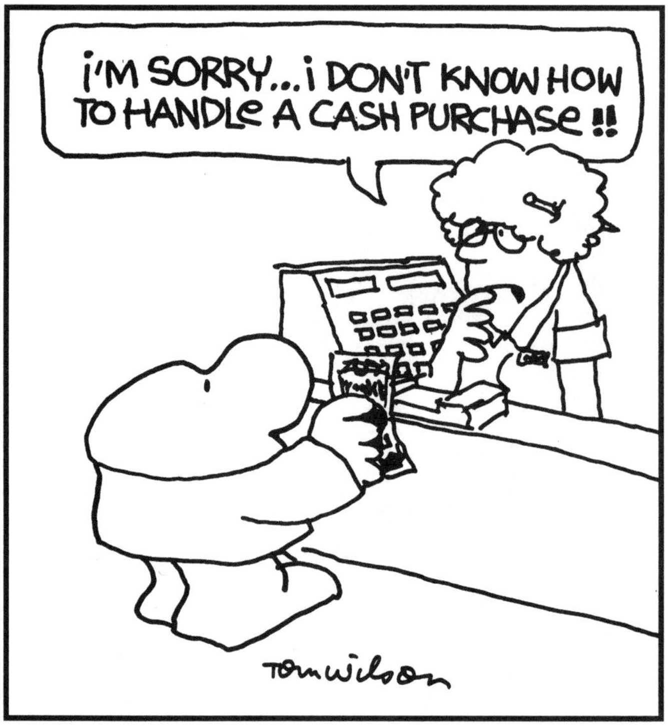
i'M SORRY...i DON'T KNOW HOW TO HANDLE A CASH PURCHASE !!
TOM WILSON

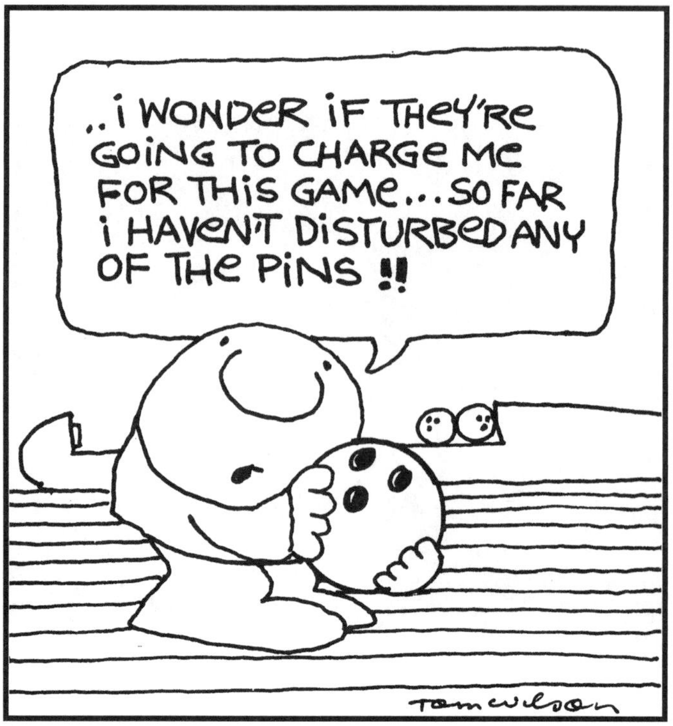
..i WONDER iF THEY'RE GOING TO CHARGE ME FOR THIS GAME...SO FAR i HAVEN'T DISTURBED ANY OF THE PINS !!
TOM WILSON

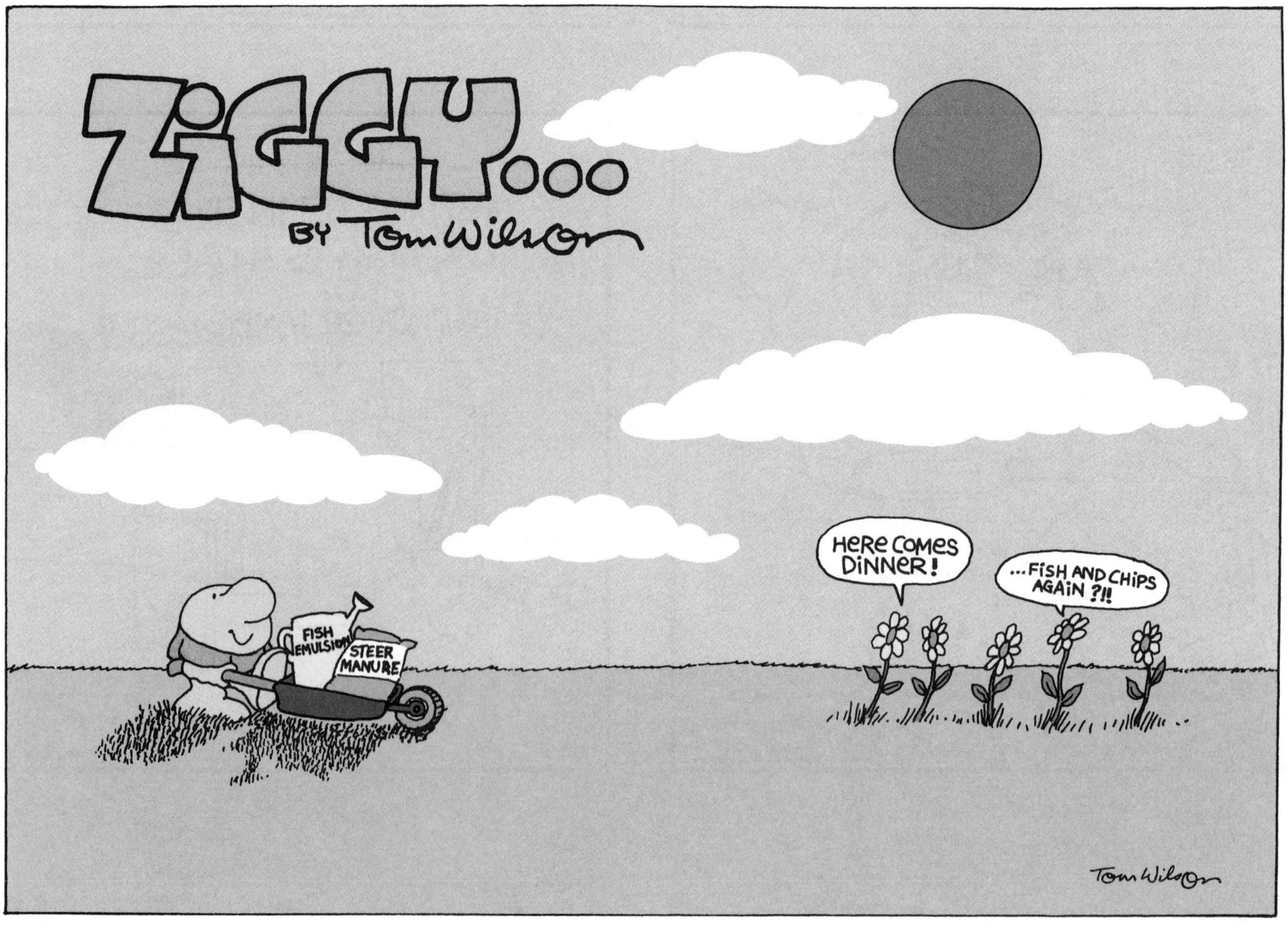
ZiGGY...
BY TOM WILSON
HERE COMES DINNER!
...FISH AND CHIPS AGAIN ?!!
FISH EMULSION
STEER MANURE
TOM WILSON

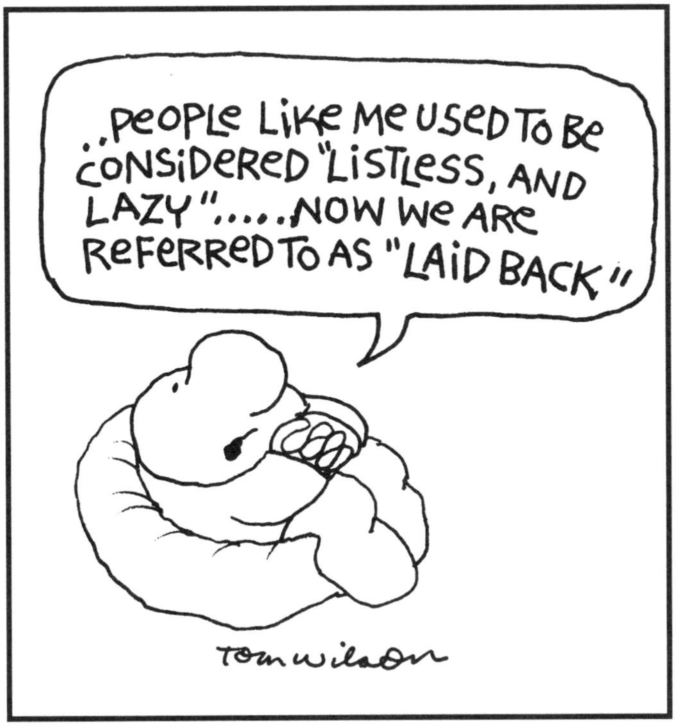
..PEOPLE LIKE ME USED TO BE CONSIDERED "LISTLESS, AND LAZY"......NOW WE ARE REFERRED TO AS "LAID BACK"

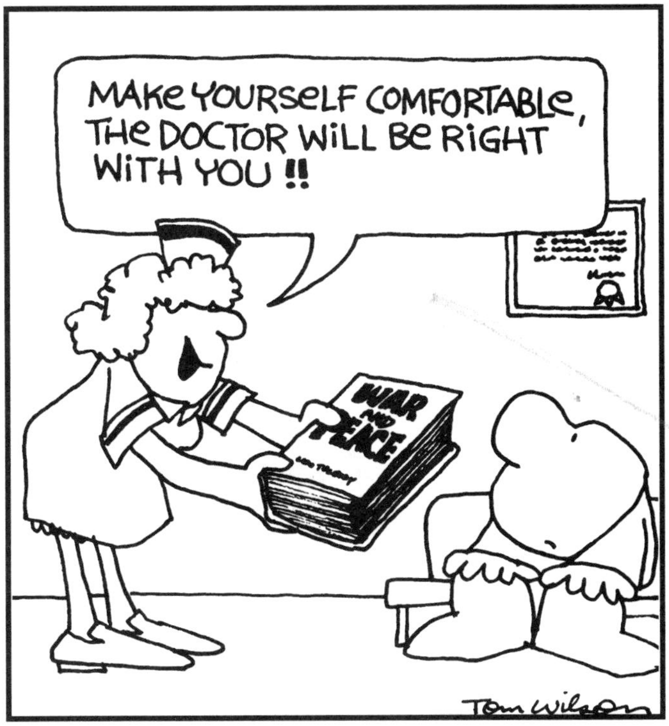
MAKE YOURSELF COMFORTABLE, THE DOCTOR WILL BE RIGHT WITH YOU !!
WAR
PEACE

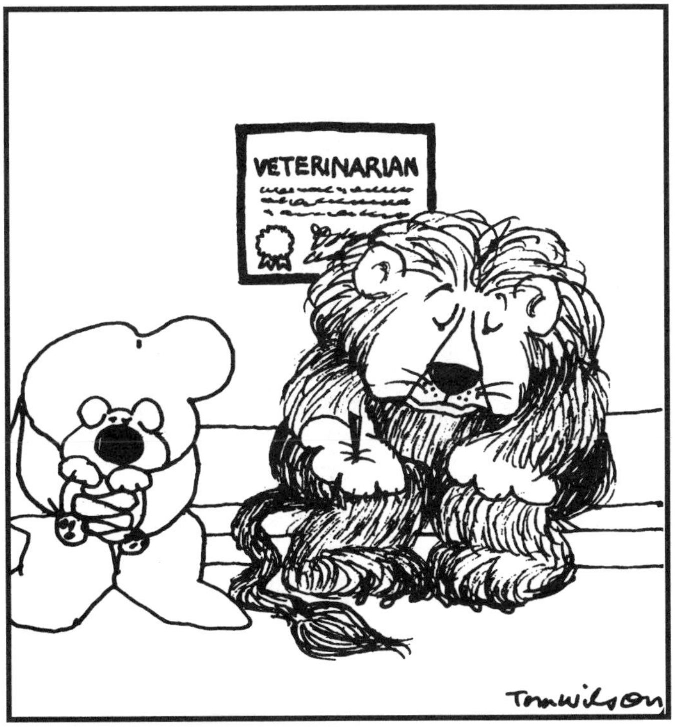
VETERINARIAN

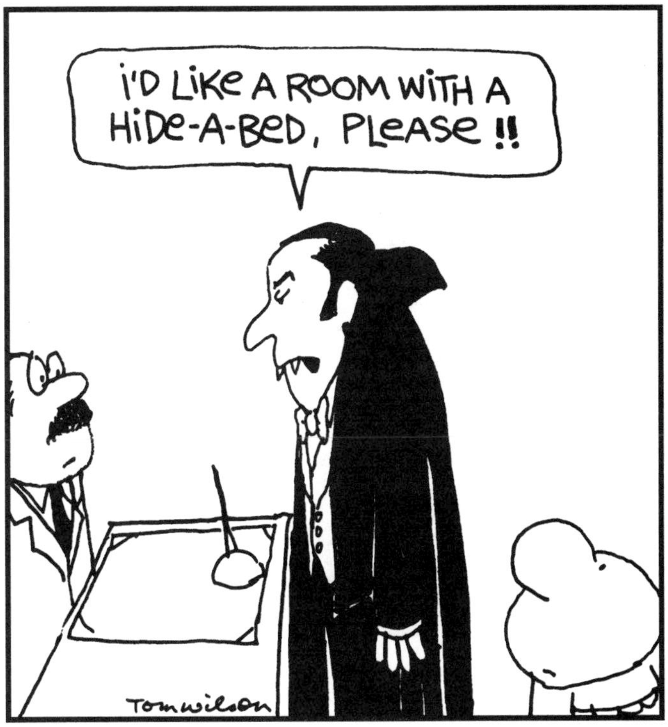
I'D LIKE A ROOM WITH A HIDE-A-BED, PLEASE !!

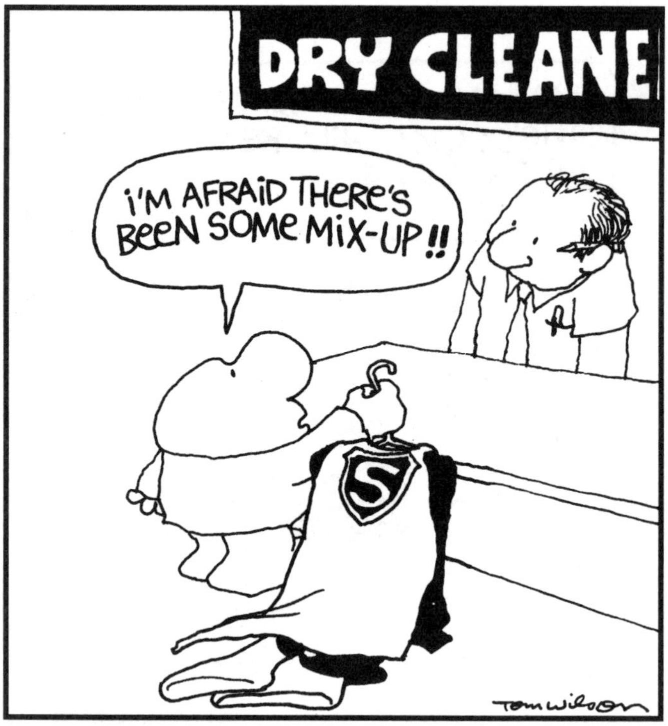
DRY CLEANE
i'M AFRAID THERE'S BEEN SOME MIX-UP !!
TOM WILSON

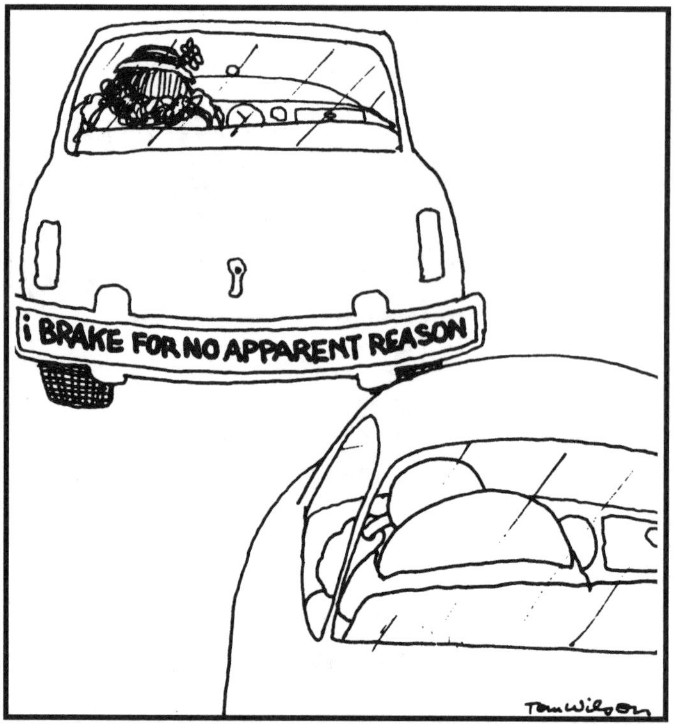
i BRAKE FOR NO APPARENT REASON
TOM WILSON

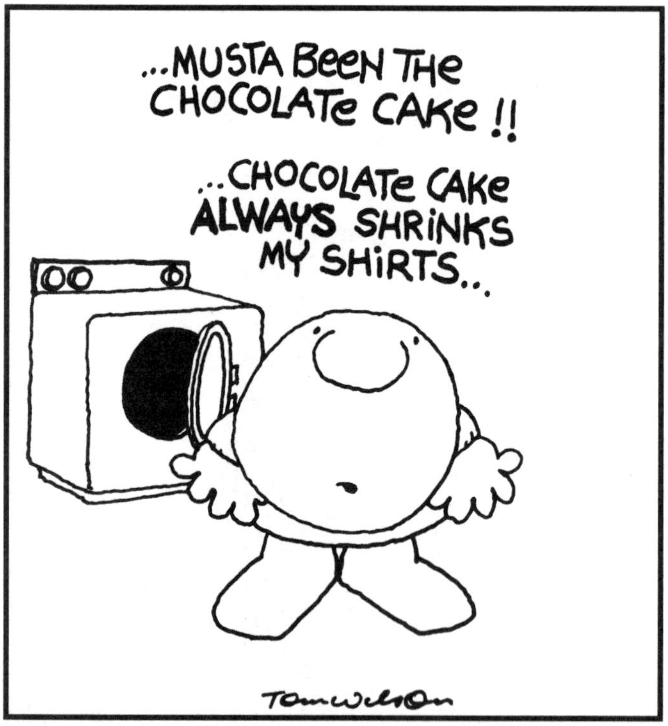
...MUSTA BEEN THE CHOCOLATE CAKE !!
...CHOCOLATE CAKE ALWAYS SHRINKS MY SHIRTS...
TOM WILSON

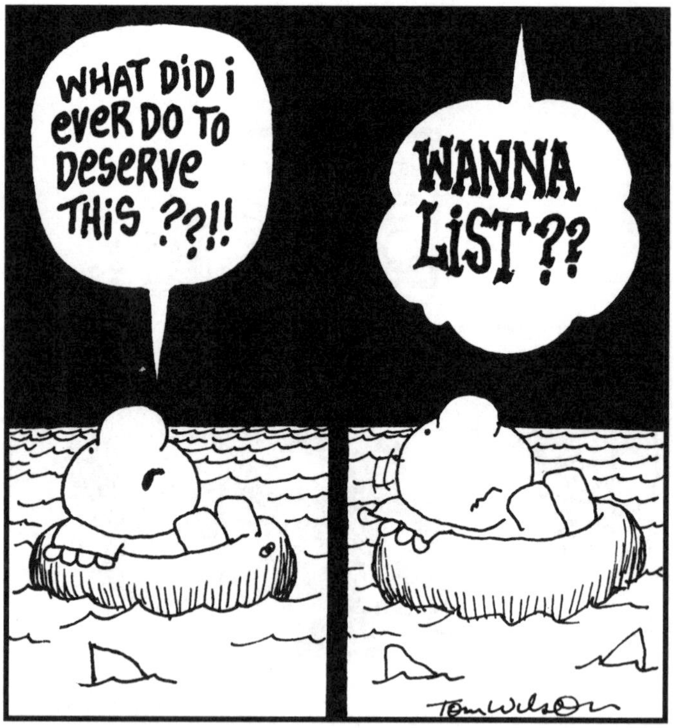
WHAT DID i EVER DO TO DESERVE THIS ??!!
WANNA LIST ??
TOM WILSON

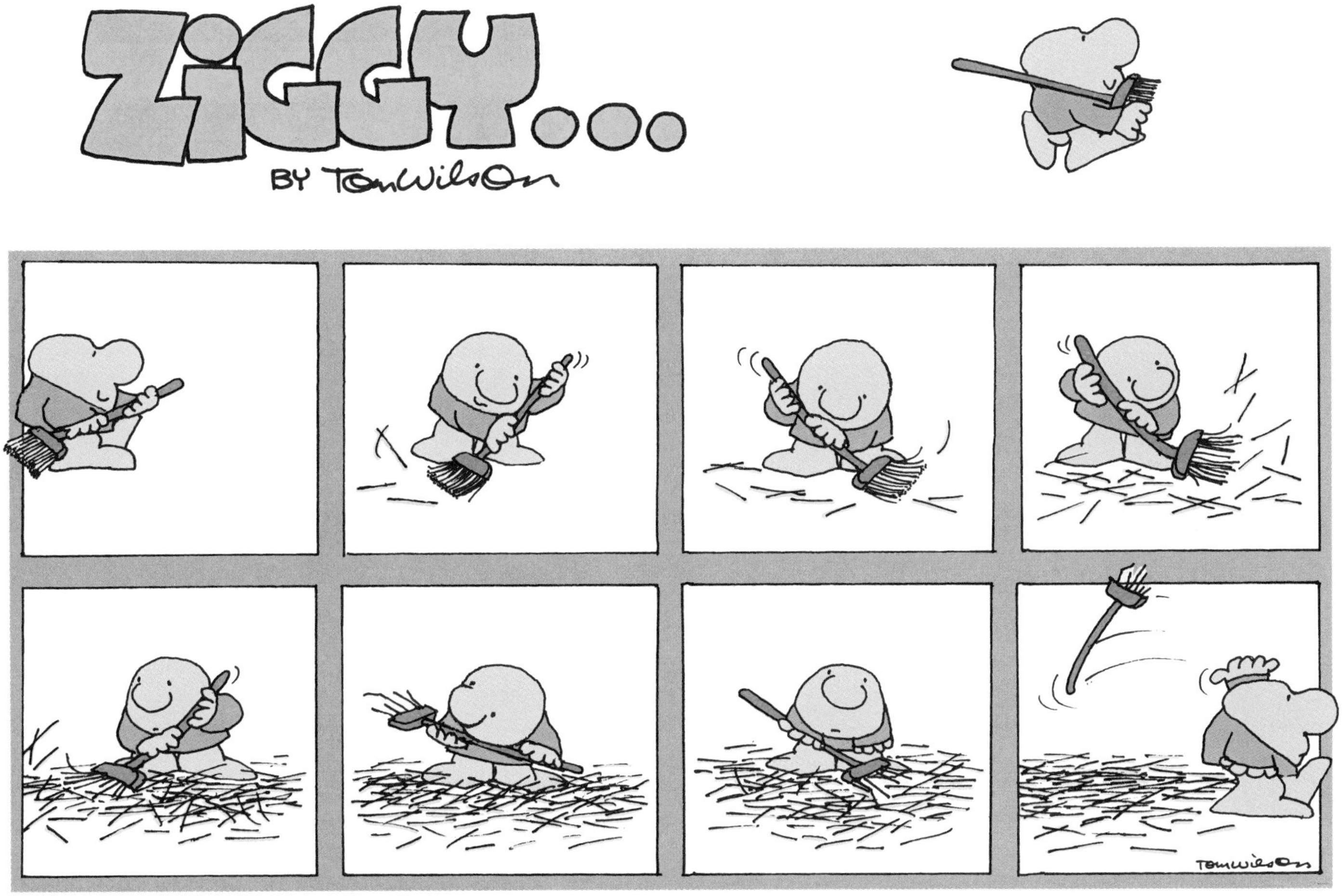
ZIGGY...
BY TOM WILSON
TOM WILSON

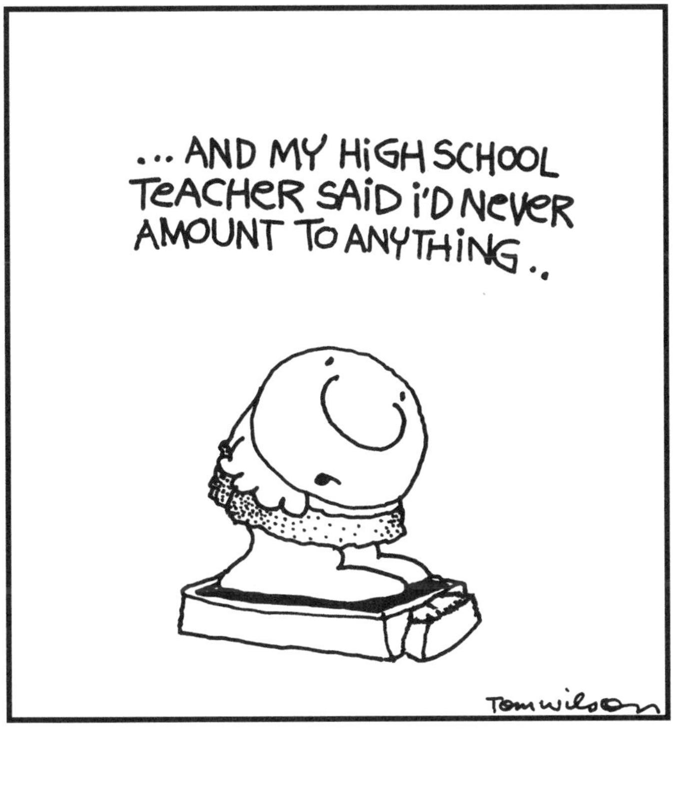
... AND MY HIGH SCHOOL TEACHER SAID I'D NEVER AMOUNT TO ANYTHING ..
TOM WILSON

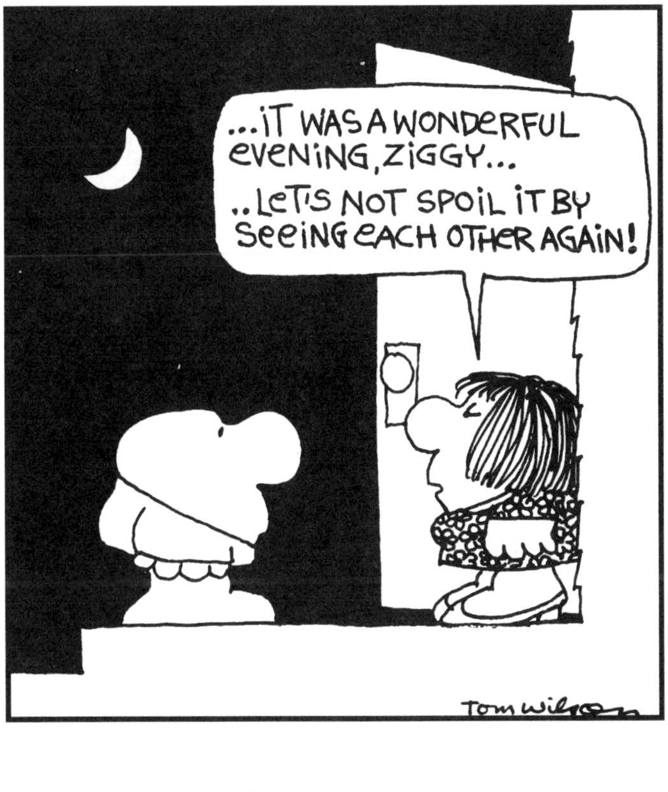
...IT WAS A WONDERFUL EVENING, ZIGGY... ..LET'S NOT SPOIL IT BY SEEING EACH OTHER AGAIN!
TOM WILSON

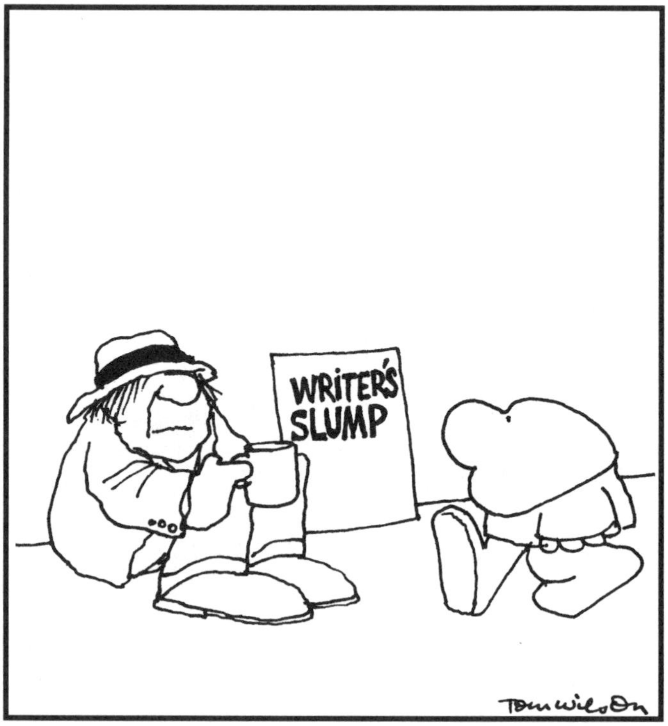
WRITER'S SLUMP
Tom Wilson

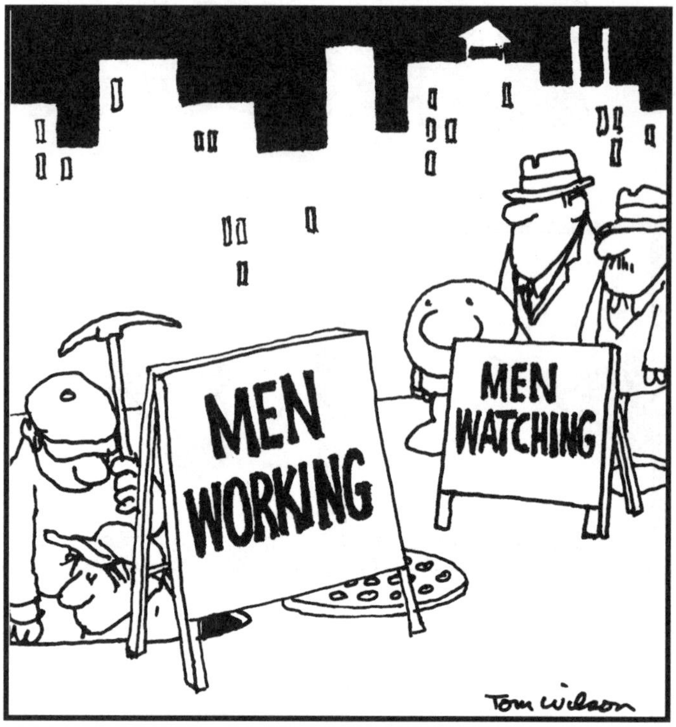
MEN WORKING
MEN WATCHING
Tom Wilson

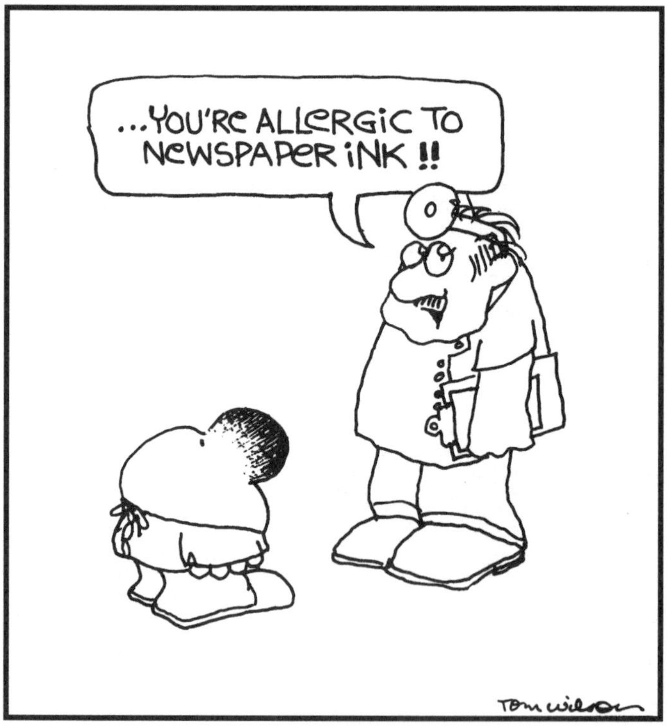
...YOU'RE ALLERGIC TO NEWSPAPER INK !!
Tom Wilson

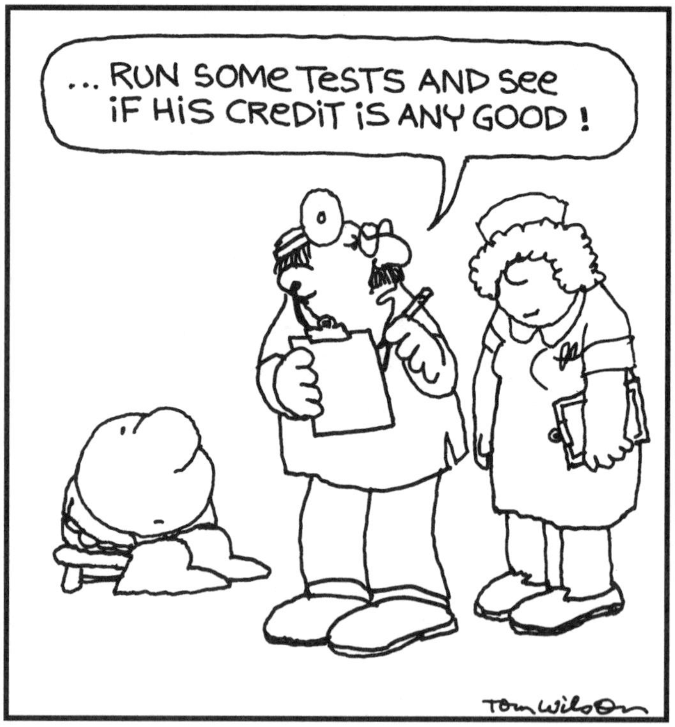
... RUN SOME TESTS AND SEE IF HIS CREDIT IS ANY GOOD !
Tom Wilson

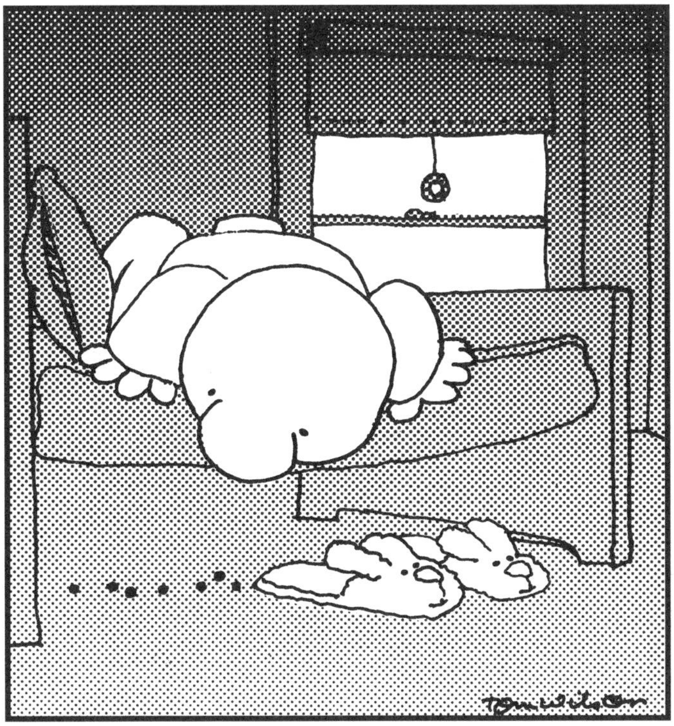
Tom Wilson

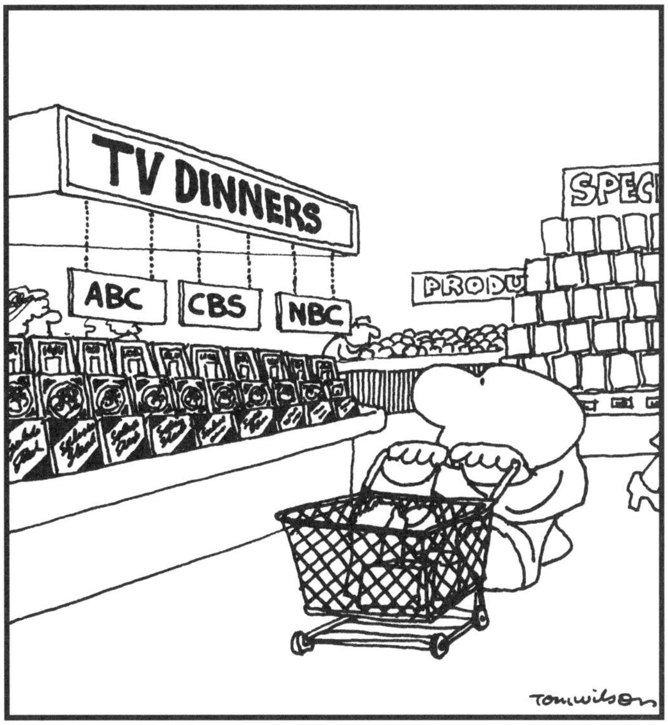
TV DINNERS
ABC
CBS
NBC
Tom Wilson

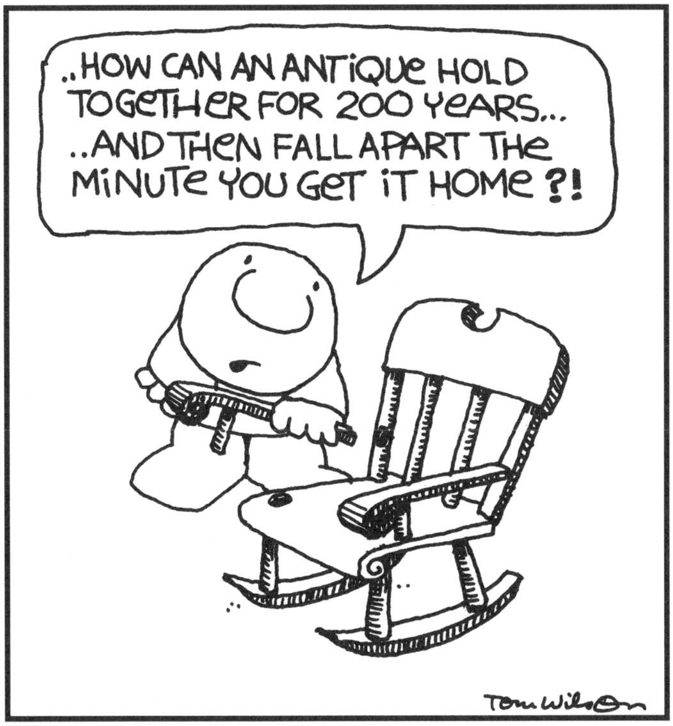
..HOW CAN AN ANTIQUE HOLD TOGETHER FOR 200 YEARS... ..AND THEN FALL APART THE MINUTE YOU GET IT HOME ?!
Tom Wilson

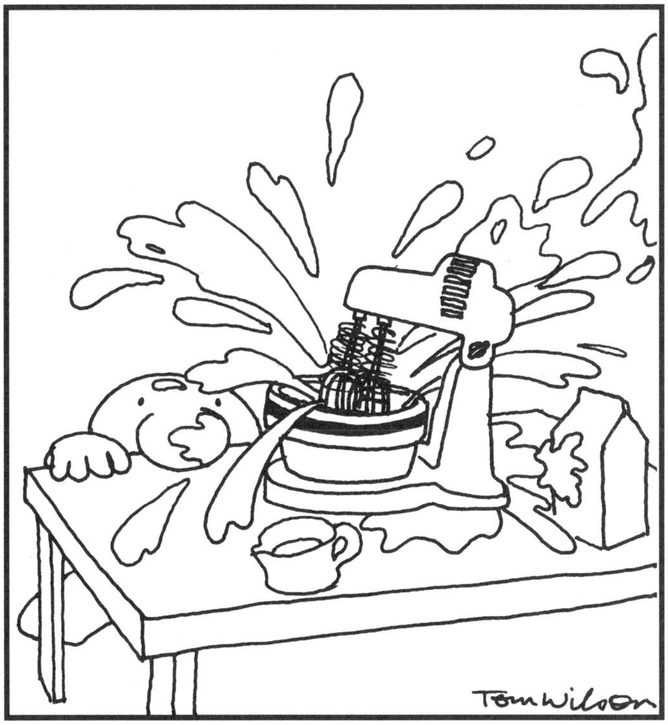
Tom Wilson

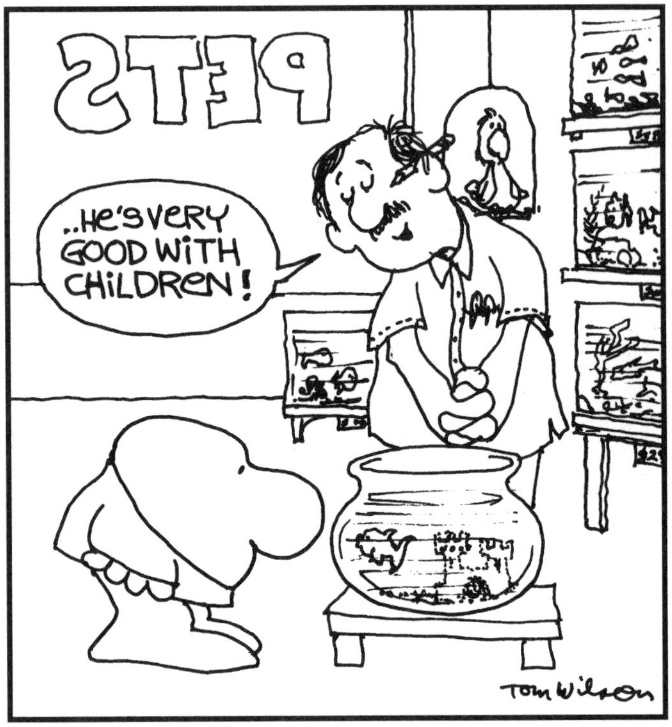
PETS
..He'S VeRY GOOD WiTH CHiLDRen!
Tom Wilson

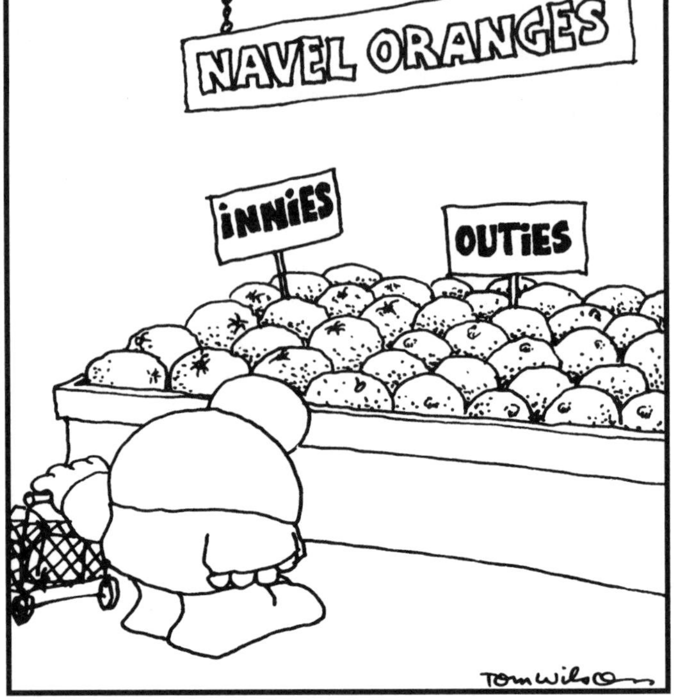
NAVEL ORANGES
iNNiES
OUTiES
Tom Wilson

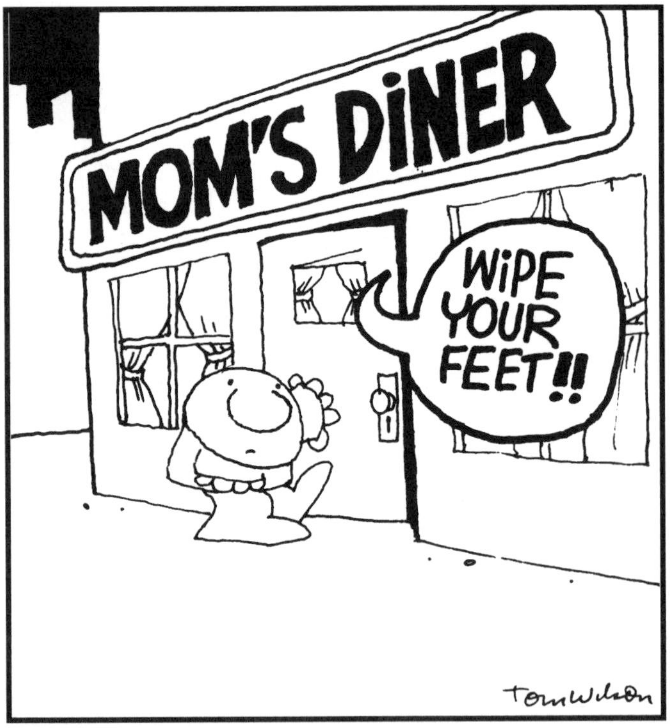
MOM'S DiNER
WiPE YOUR FEET!!
Tom Wilson

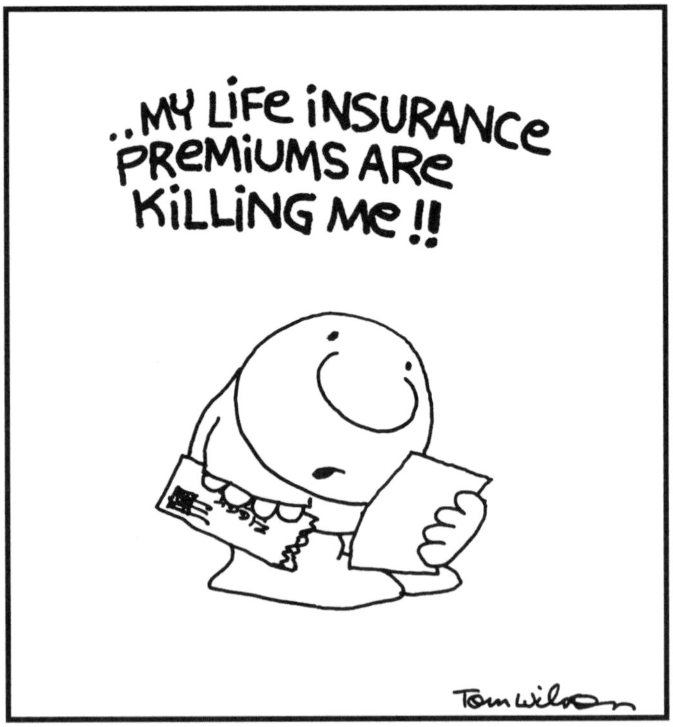
..MY LiFe iNSURANCe PReMiUMS ARe KiLLiNG Me!!
Tom Wilson

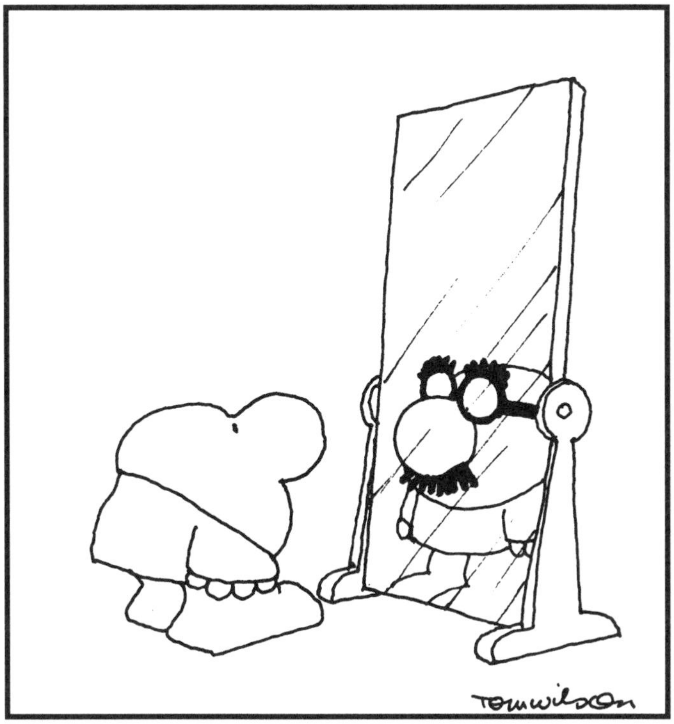

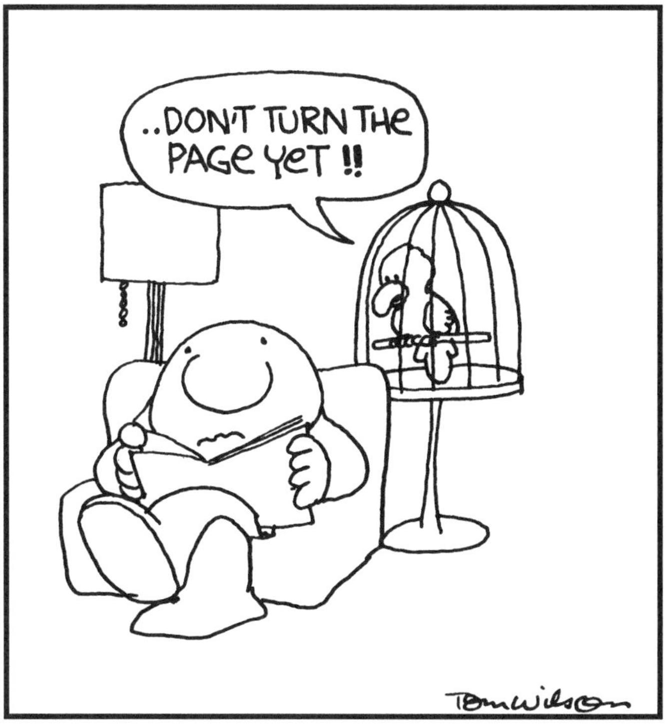
..DON'T TURN THE PAGE YET !!

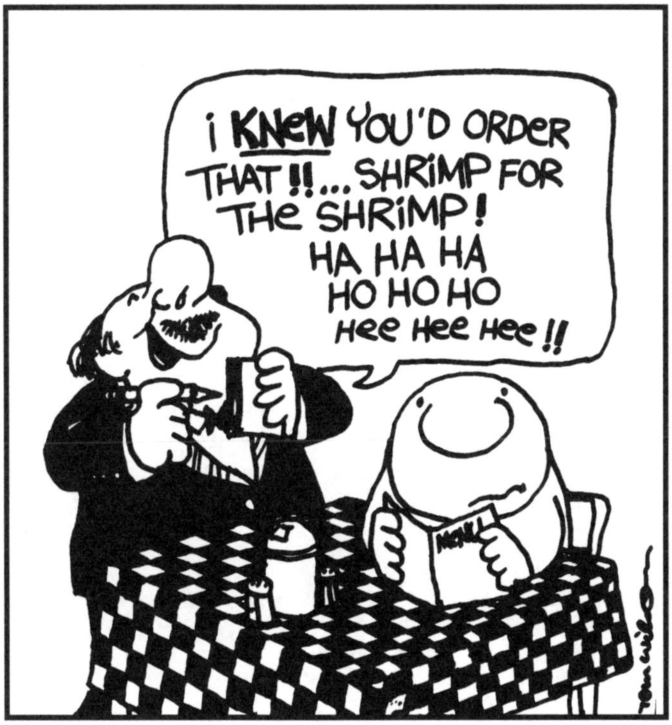
i KNEW YOU'D ORDER THAT !!... SHRIMP FOR THE SHRIMP! HA HA HA HO HO HO Hee Hee Hee !!

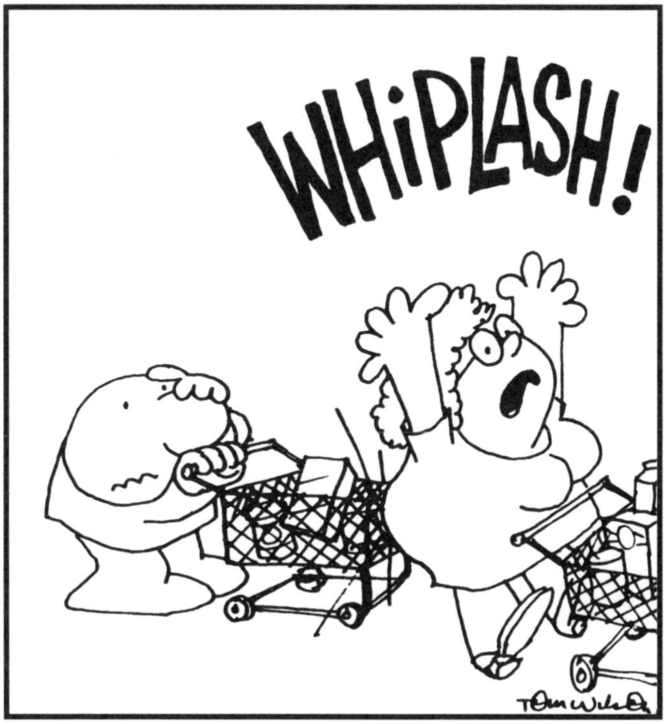
WHiPLASH!

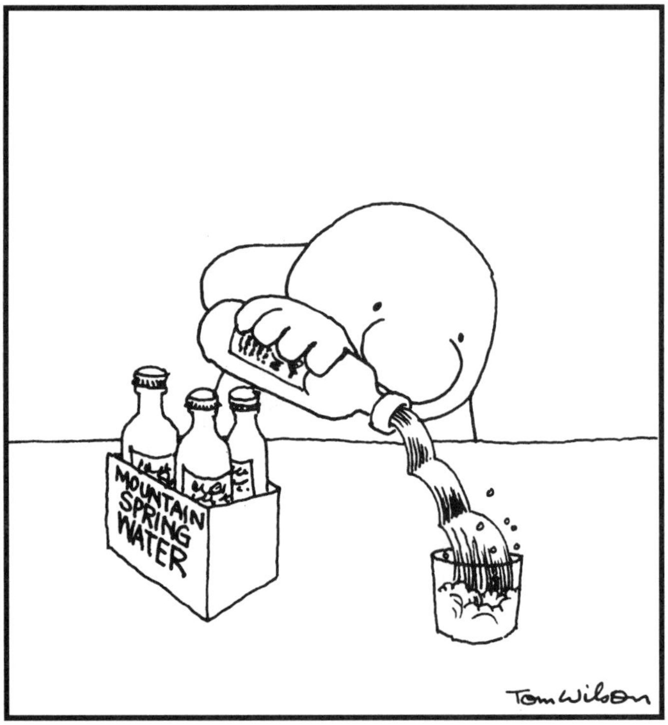
MOUNTAIN SPRING WATER
Tom Wilson

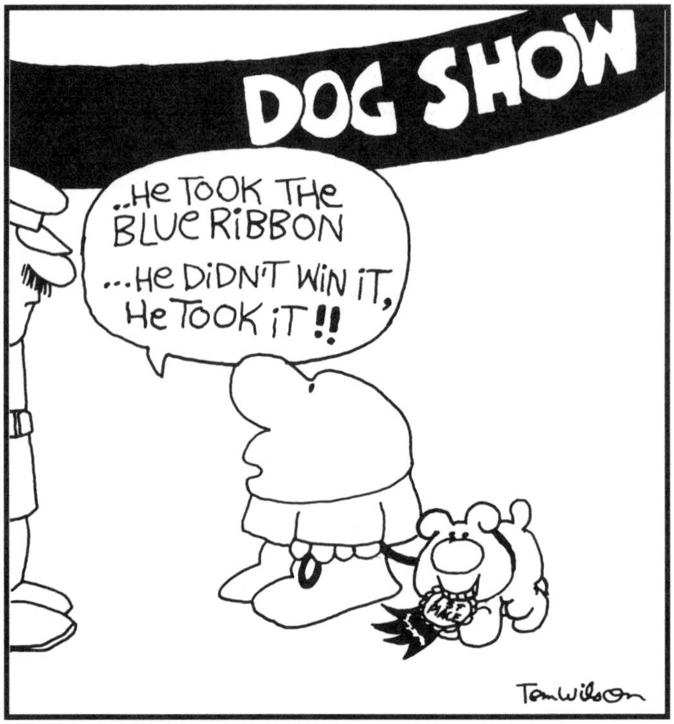
DOG SHOW
..He TOOK THE BLUE RIBBON ...He DIDN'T WIN IT, He TOOK IT !!
Tom Wilson

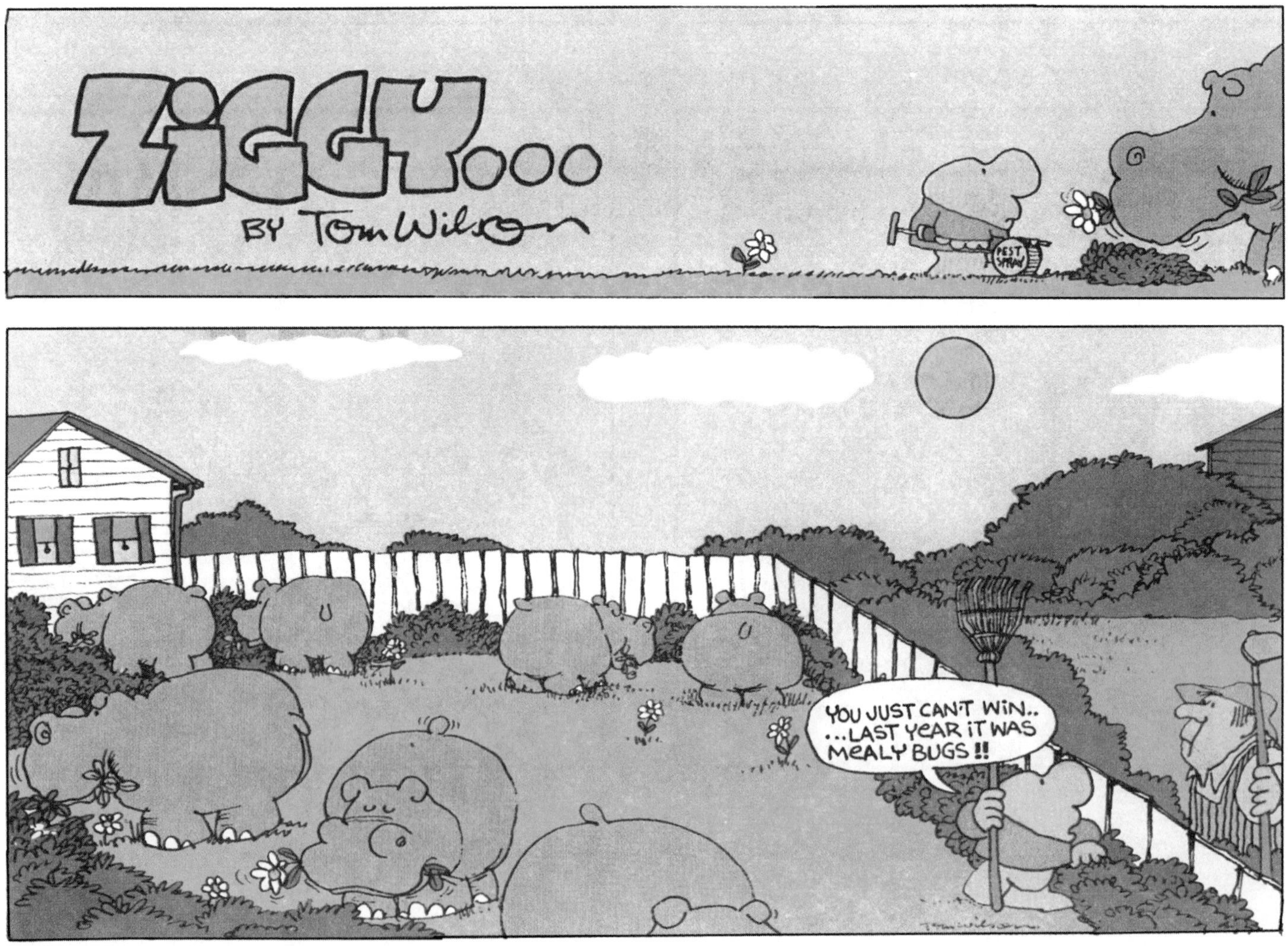
ZIGGY ooo
BY Tom Wilson
PEST SPRAY
YOU JUST CAN'T WIN.. ...LAST YEAR IT WAS MEALY BUGS !!

Chapter III
1981–1985

Ziggy made his Universal Press Syndicate (UPS) debut on June 28, 1971, but we knew the lovable genius behind this fabulous character before then. Tom Wilson came into our lives with a grin as big as Minnesota and a heart the same size. He could walk into a room and the atmosphere would become electric, charged with this giant of a man's energy. His smile could turn from soft and shy to mischievous in a matter of minutes, especially when good friends would come together for toasts and remembrances. *Ziggy* would not have existed without Tom, and there is a great likelihood that UPS would have met the same fate if there not had been a Tom Wilson on the scene. It is no secret that the revenues from *Ziggy*'s licensing sustained us in those perilous early times. The impact of the newspaper feature bolstered Universal's young status in a mature industry and helped us to be taken seriously as a competitive force.

Tom has been more than just a creator but a true and loyal friend to Jim and Kathy Andrews and Susan and me. When Jim died, Tom was one of the first people to call with words of encouragement and strength. "Stay the course," he said. "Jim would have wanted that." He is an exceptional person, and we are the beneficiaries of his vision, creativity, and most of all his loyalty and friendship. Tom is one of a kind and thank God he was ours.

Thank you, Tom, from the bottom of our hearts.

—John McMeel, chairman and president, Andrews McMeel Universal

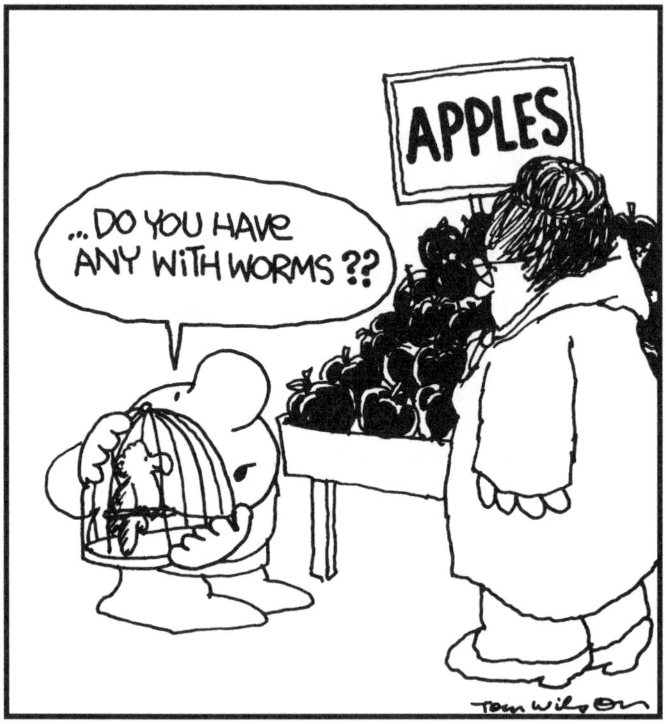
APPLES
...DO YOU HAVE ANY WITH WORMS ??
Tom Wilson

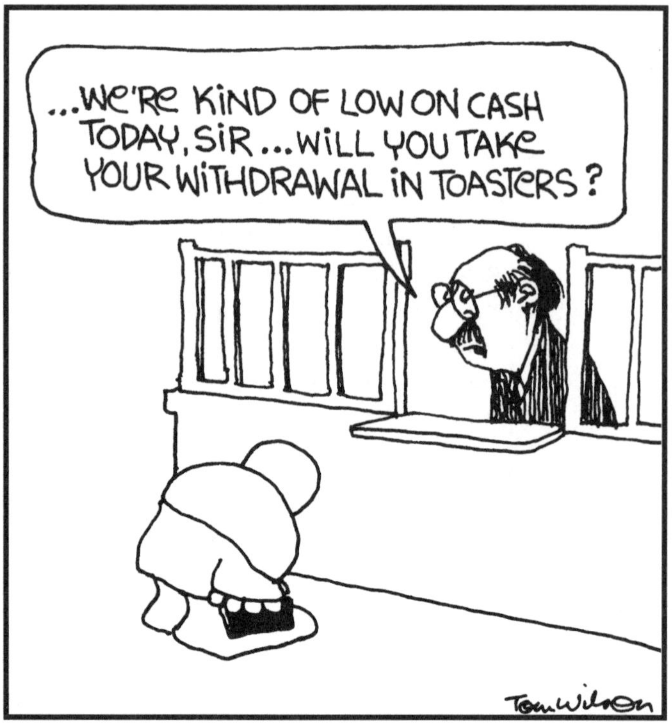
...WE'RE KIND OF LOW ON CASH TODAY, SIR ... WILL YOU TAKE YOUR WITHDRAWAL IN TOASTERS ?
Tom Wilson

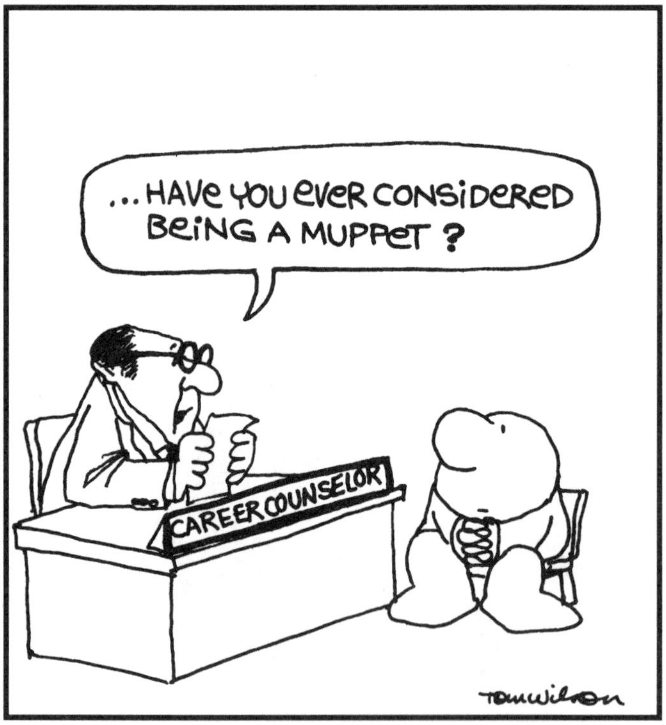
...HAVE YOU EVER CONSIDERED BEING A MUPPET ?
CAREER COUNSELOR
Tom Wilson

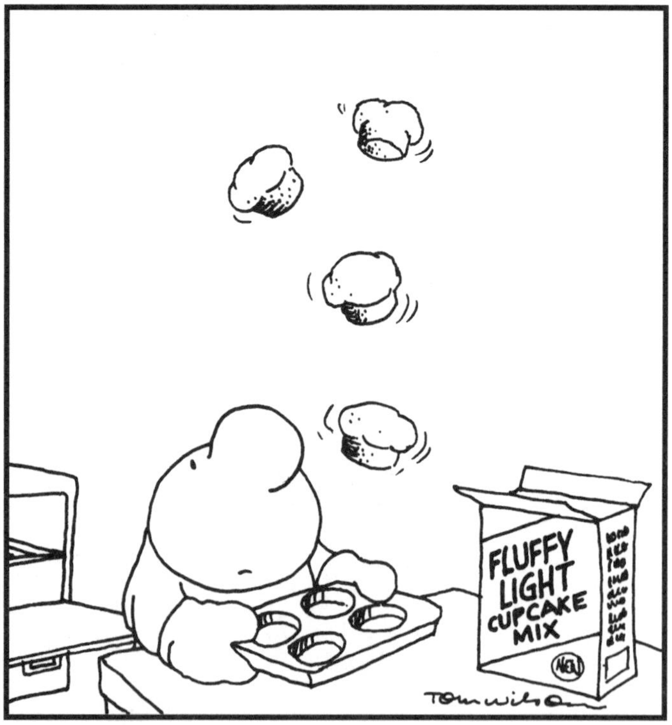
FLUFFY LIGHT CUPCAKE MIX
NEW
Tom Wilson

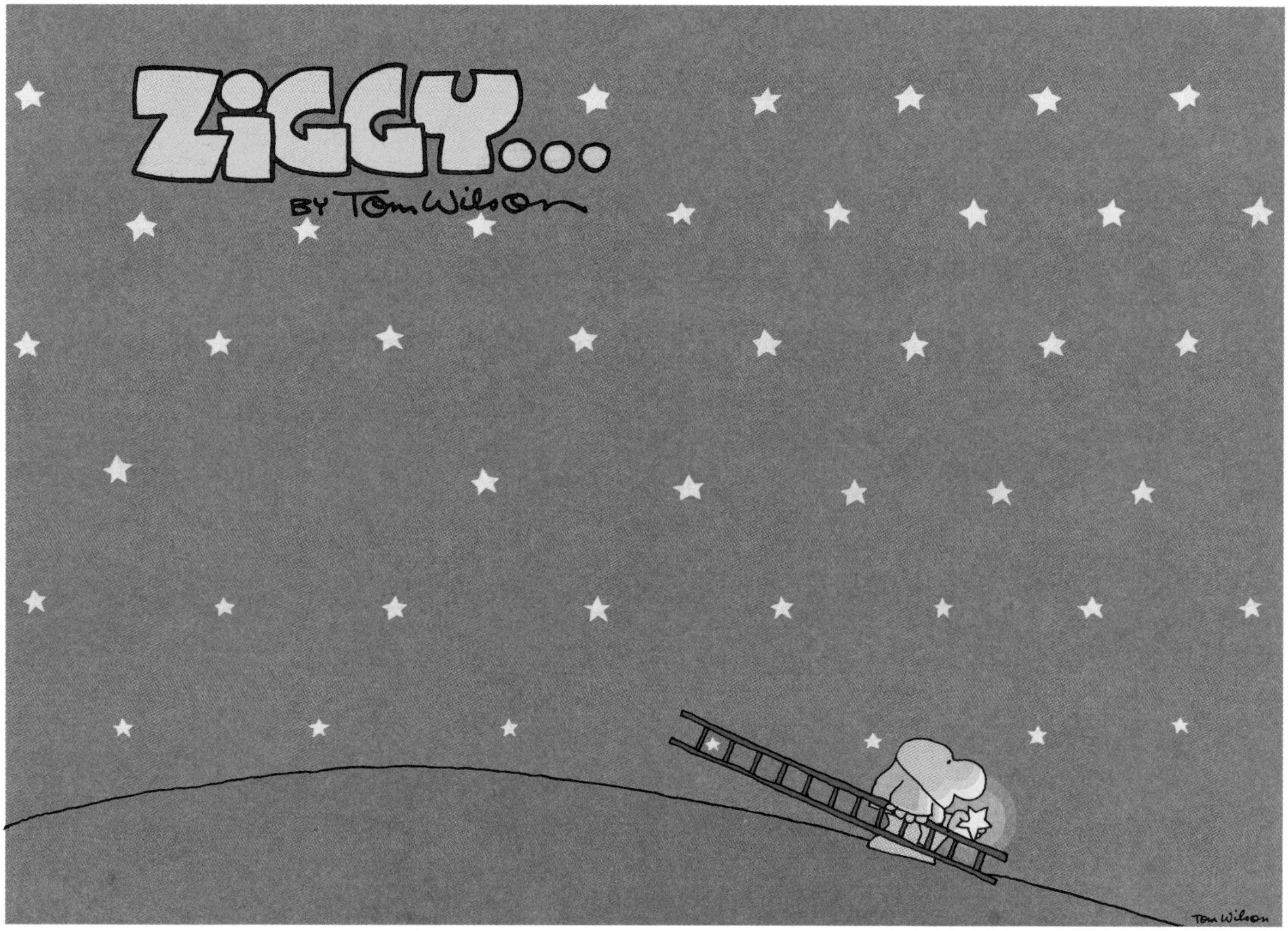
ZIGGY...
BY TOM WILSON
TOM WILSON

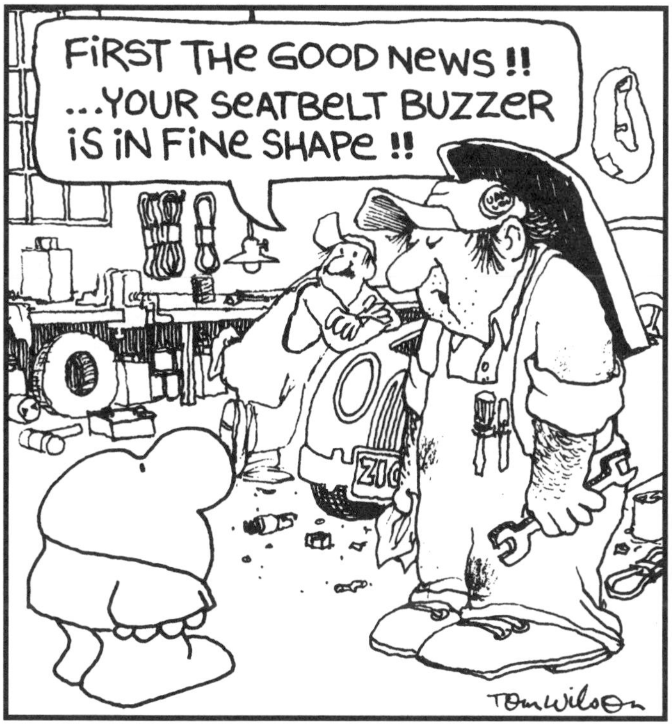
FIRST THE GOOD NEWS !!
...YOUR SEATBELT BUZZER
IS IN FINE SHAPE !!
TOM WILSON

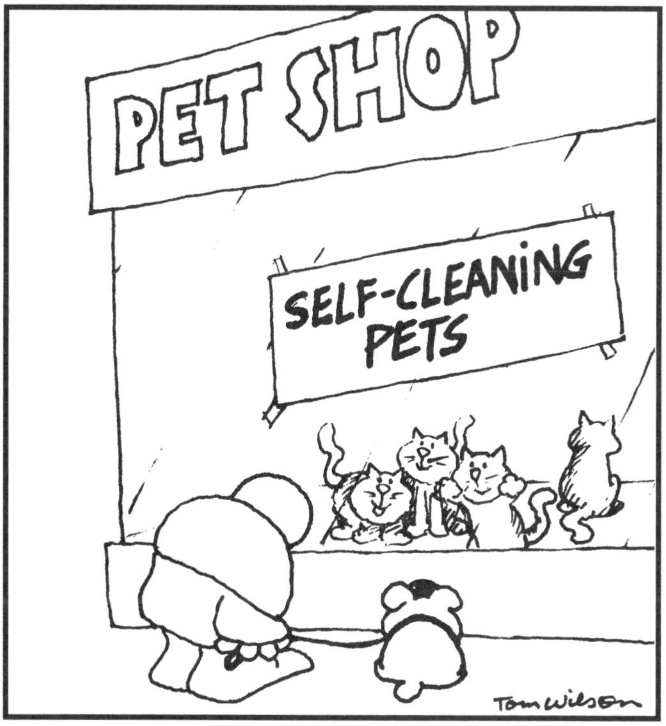
PET SHOP
SELF-CLEANING
PETS
TOM WILSON

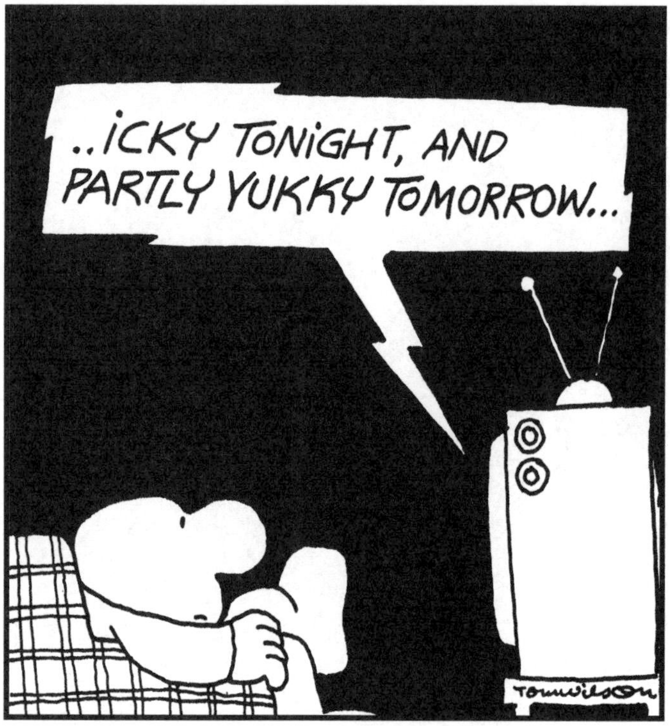
..ICKY TONIGHT, AND PARTLY YUKKY TOMORROW...

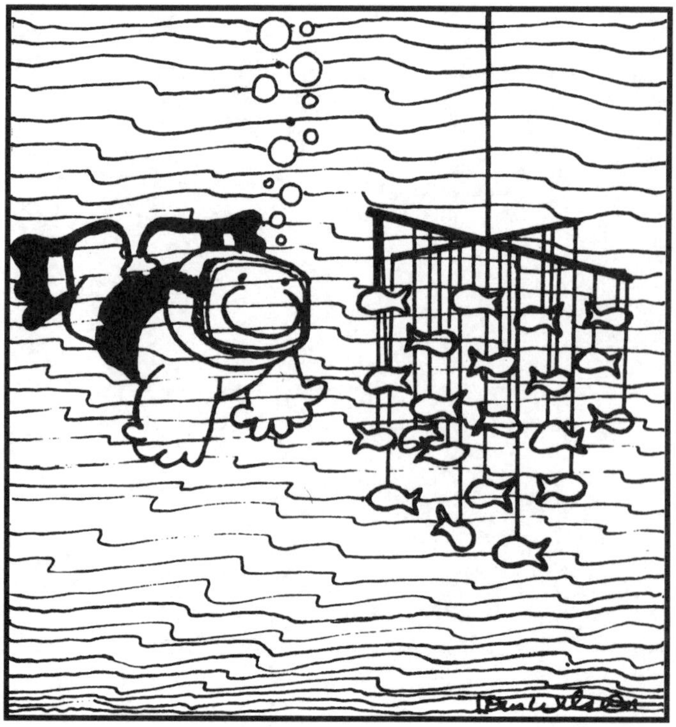

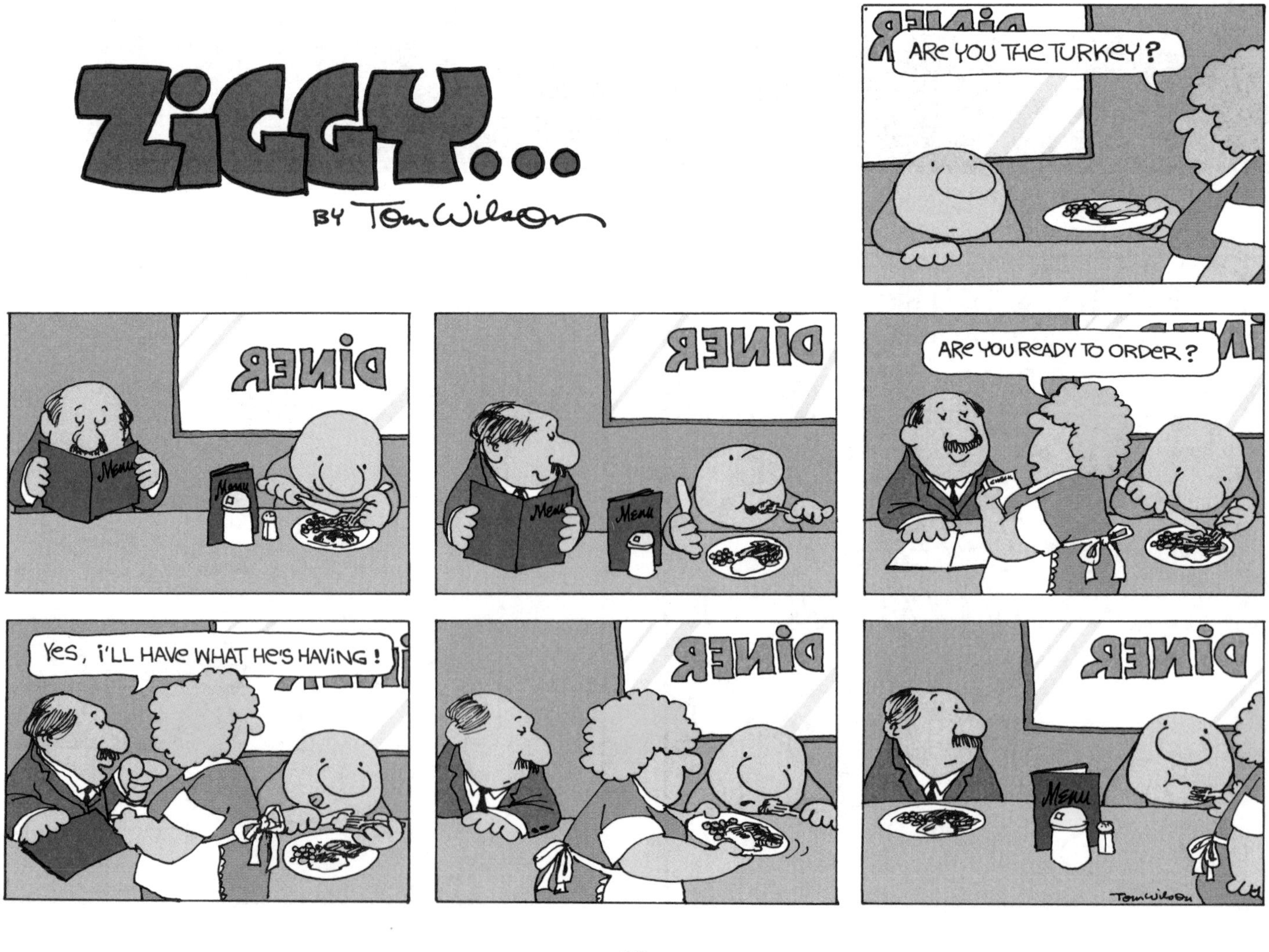
ZIGGY...
BY Tom Wilson
ARE YOU THE TURKEY?
DINER
ARE YOU READY TO ORDER?
YES, I'LL HAVE WHAT HE'S HAVING!

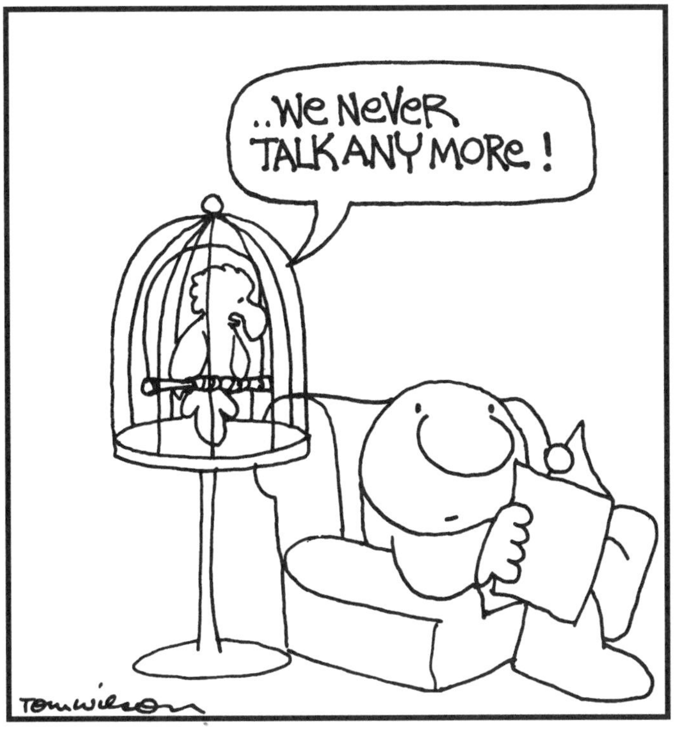
..We NeVeR TALK ANY MORe !
TOM WILSON

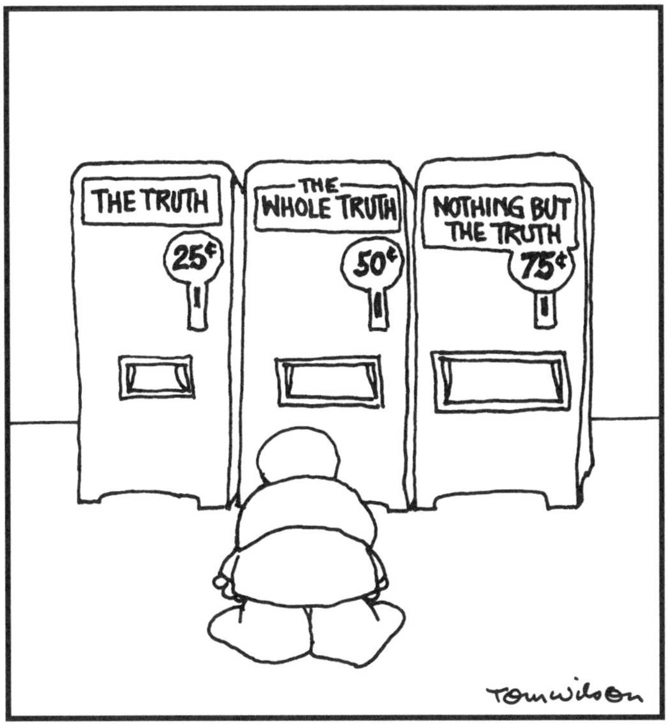
THE TRUTH
25¢
THE WHOLE TRUTH
50¢
NOTHING BUT THE TRUTH
75¢
TOM WILSON

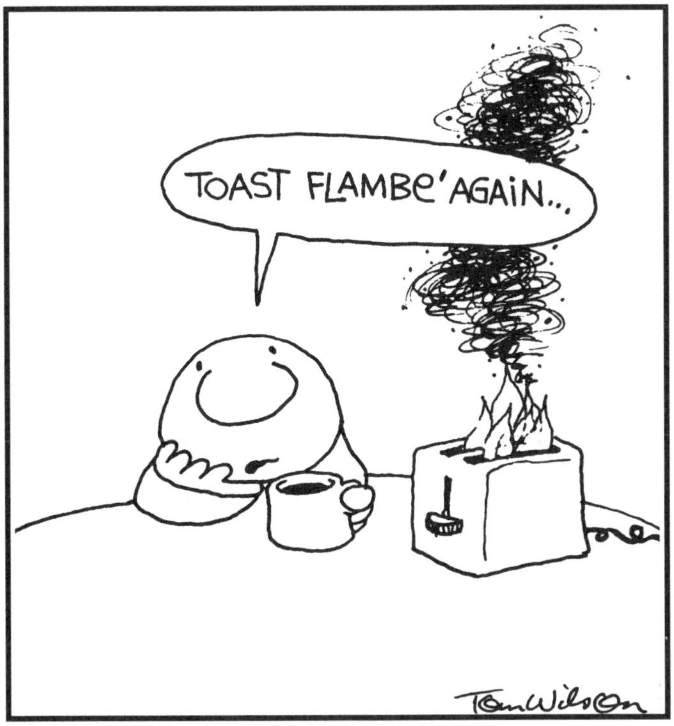
TOAST FLAMBe' AGAIN...
TOM WILSON

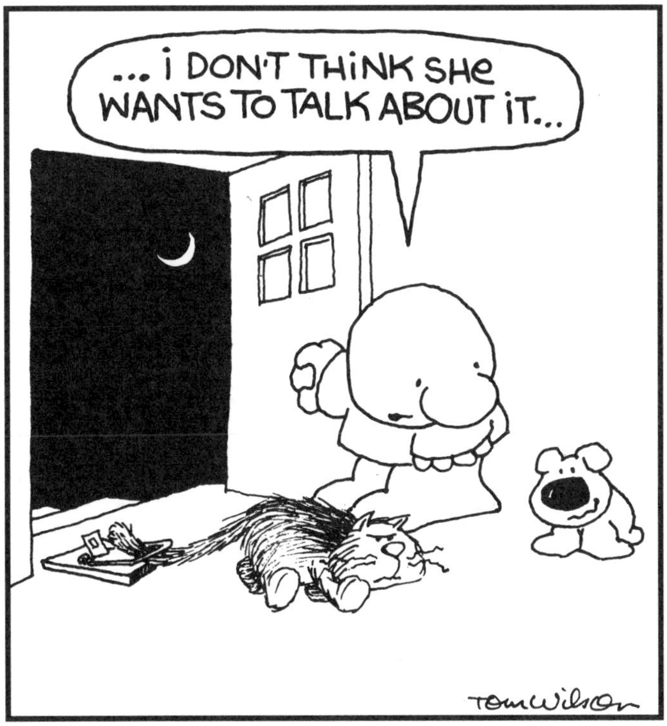
... i DON'T THINK SHe WANTS TO TALK ABOUT iT...
TOM WILSON

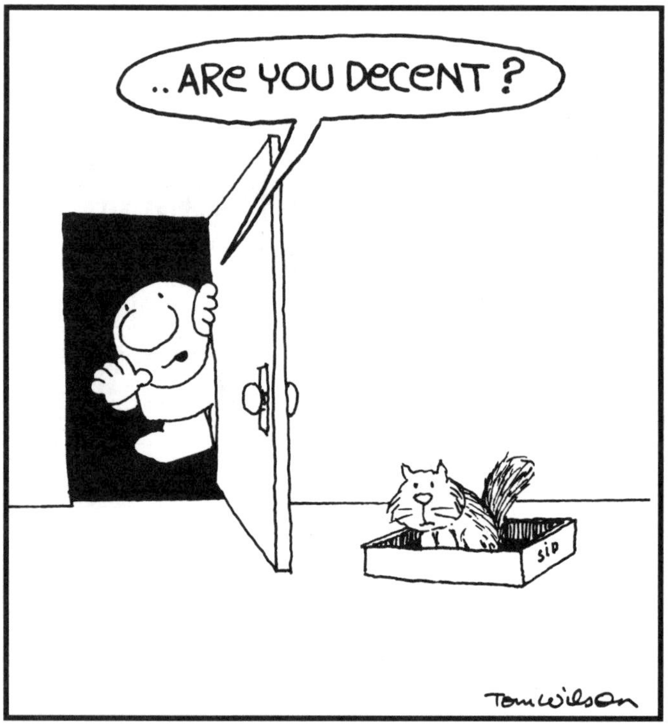
..ARE YOU DECENT ?
SID

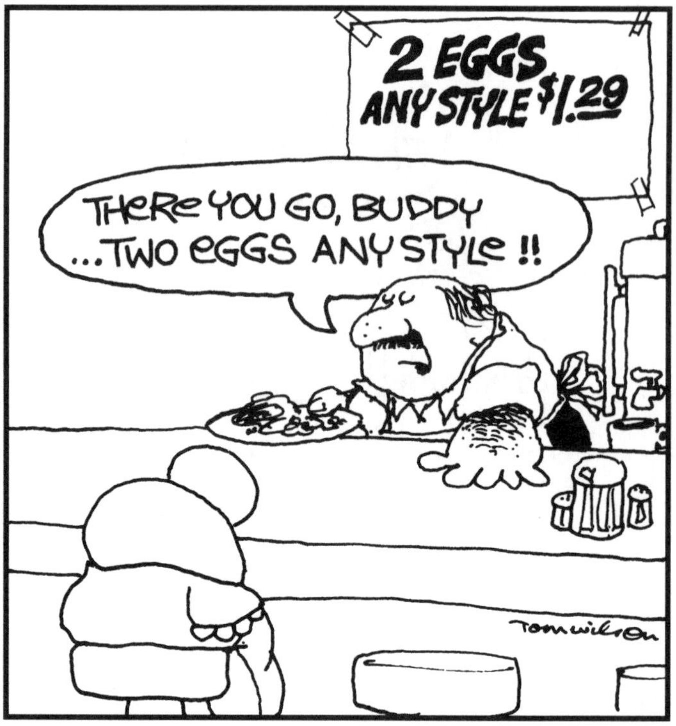
2 EGGS ANY STYLE $1.29
THERE YOU GO, BUDDY ...TWO EGGS ANY STYLE !!

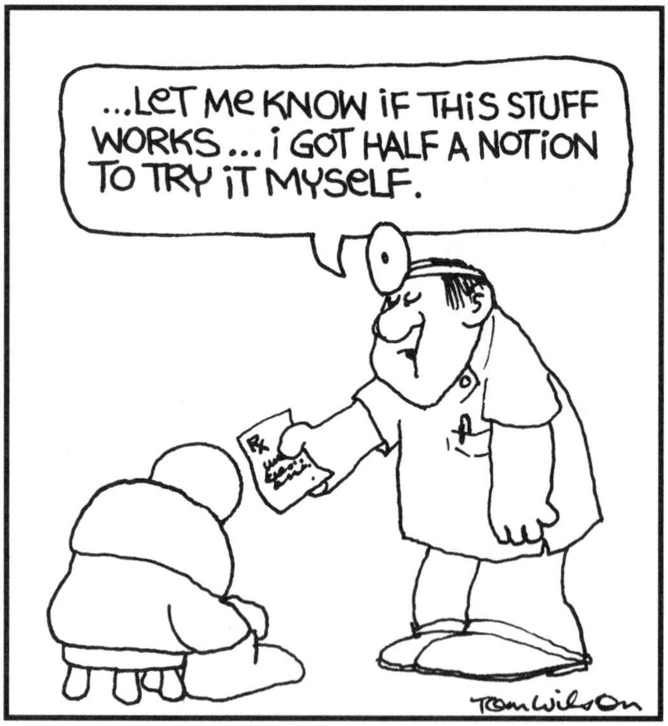
...LET ME KNOW IF THIS STUFF WORKS... I GOT HALF A NOTION TO TRY IT MYSELF.

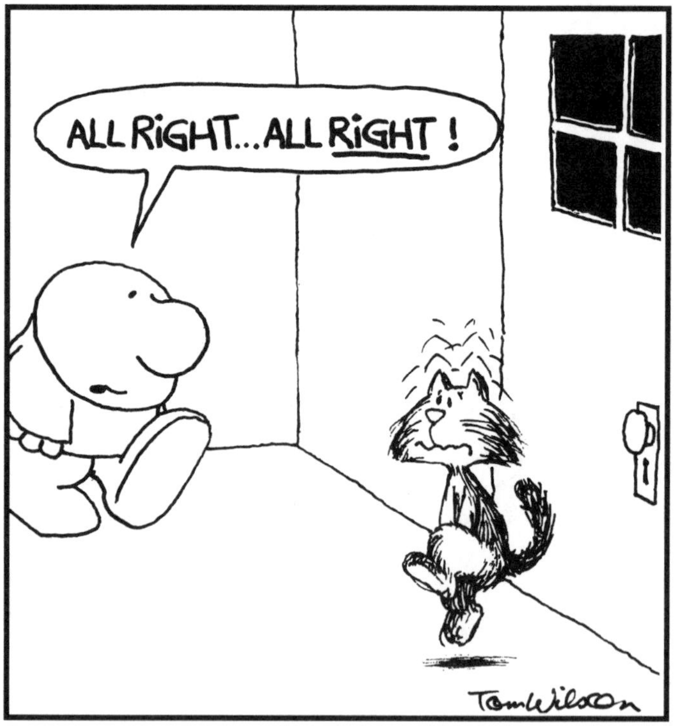
ALL RIGHT...ALL RIGHT !

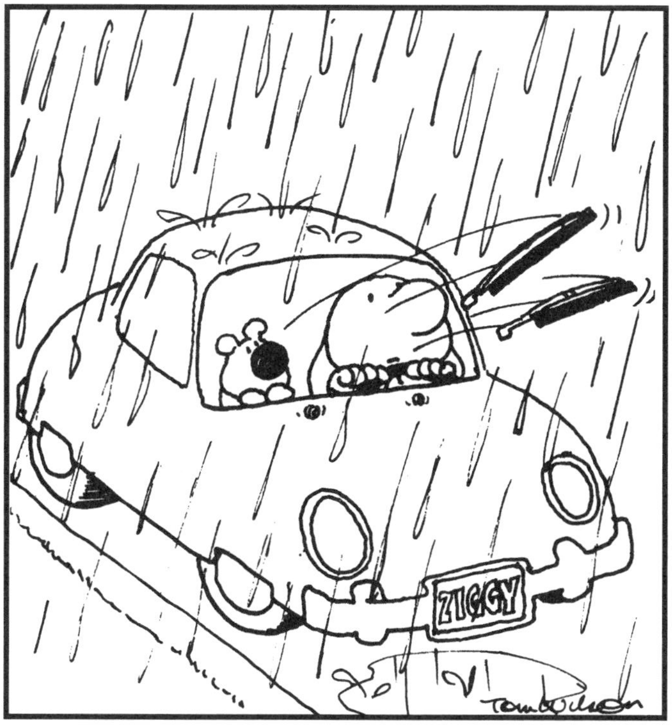
ZIGGY
TOM WILSON

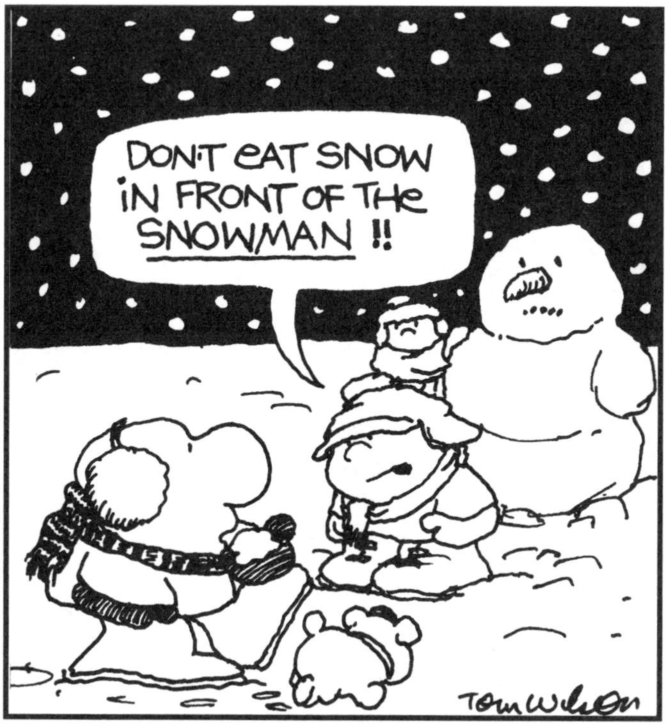
DON'T EAT SNOW IN FRONT OF THE SNOWMAN !!
TOM WILSON

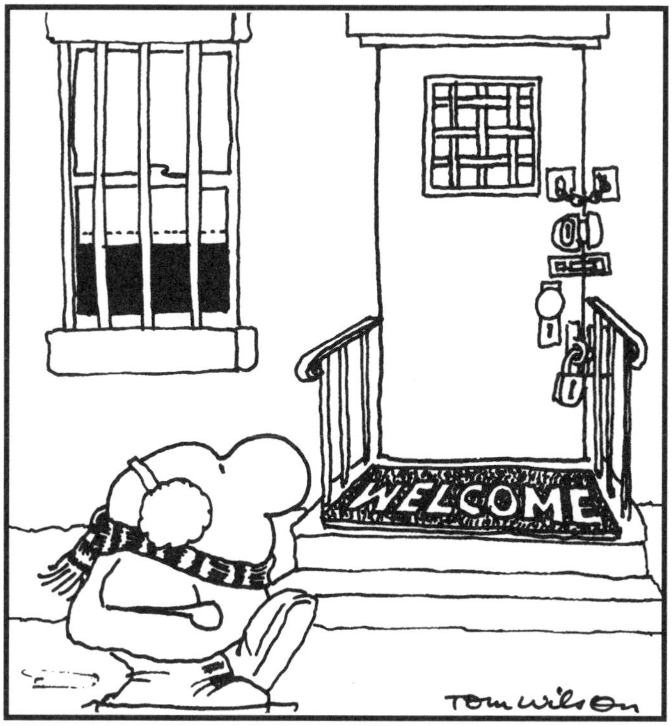
WELCOME
TOM WILSON

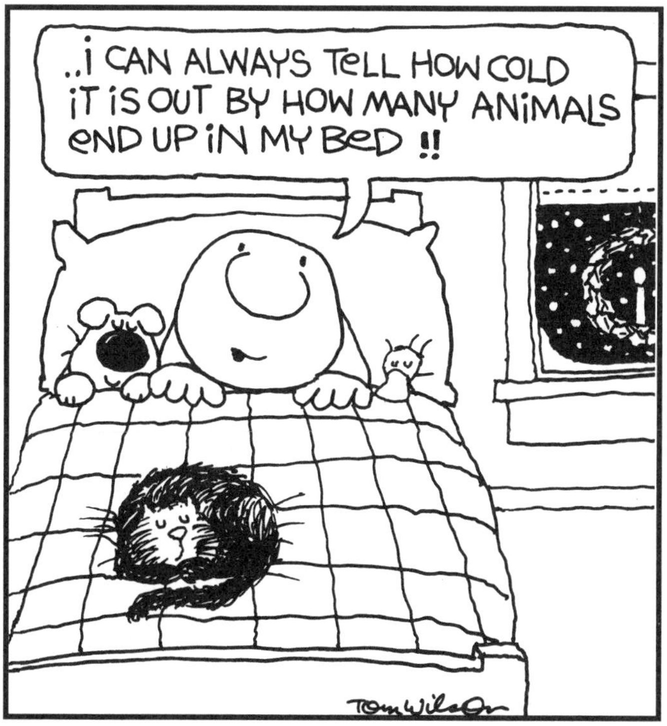
..I CAN ALWAYS TELL HOW COLD IT IS OUT BY HOW MANY ANIMALS END UP IN MY BED !!
TOM WILSON

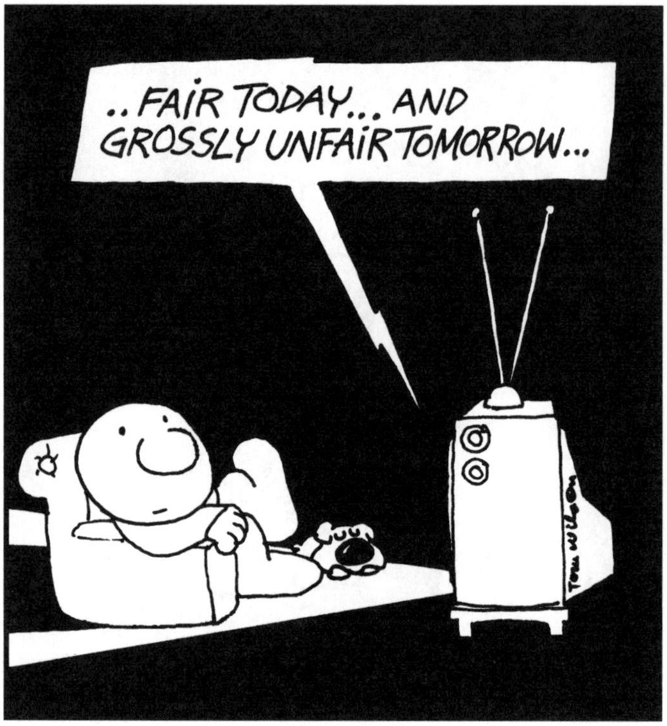
..FAIR TODAY... AND GROSSLY UNFAIR TOMORROW...
DOG BISCUITS

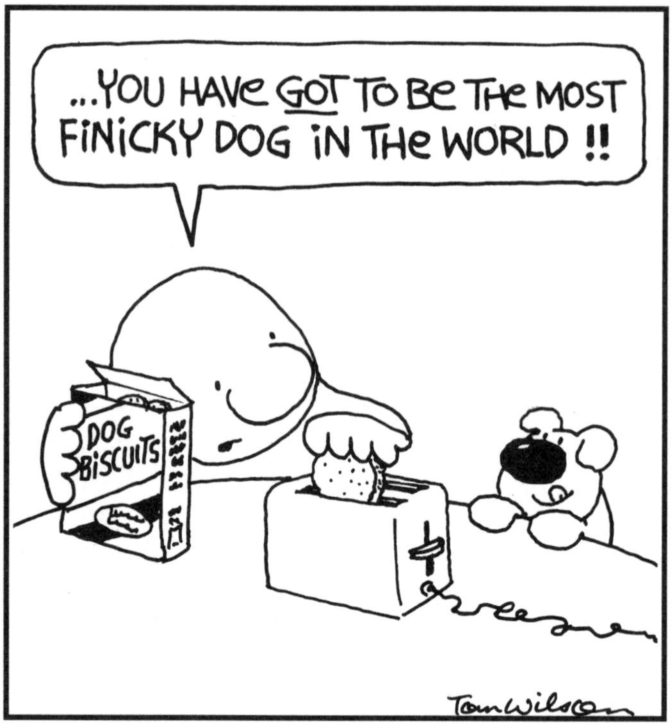
...YOU HAVE GOT TO BE THE MOST FINICKY DOG IN THE WORLD !!
DOG BISCUITS
Tom Wilson

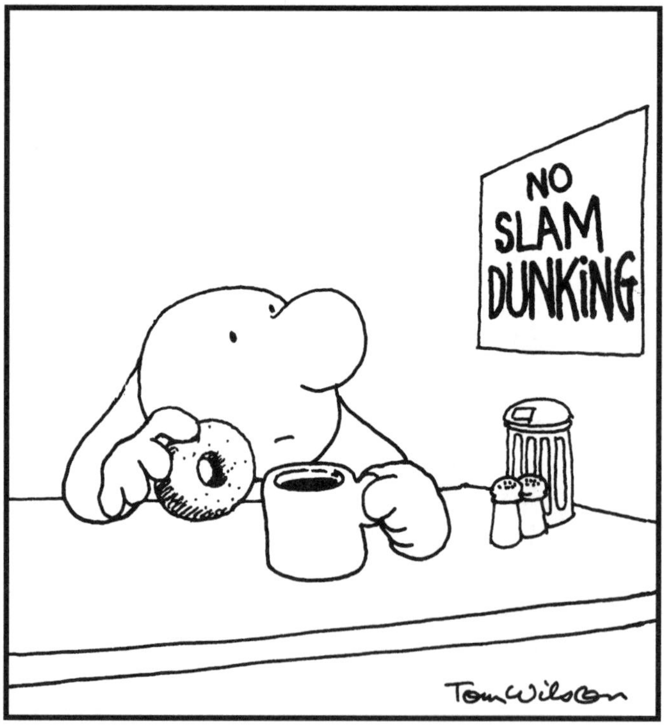
NO SLAM DUNKING
Tom Wilson

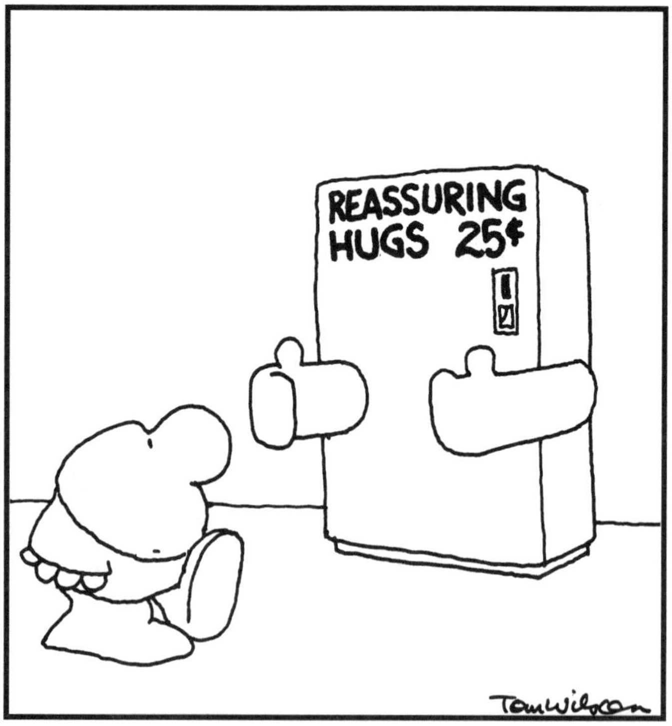
REASSURING HUGS 25¢
Tom Wilson

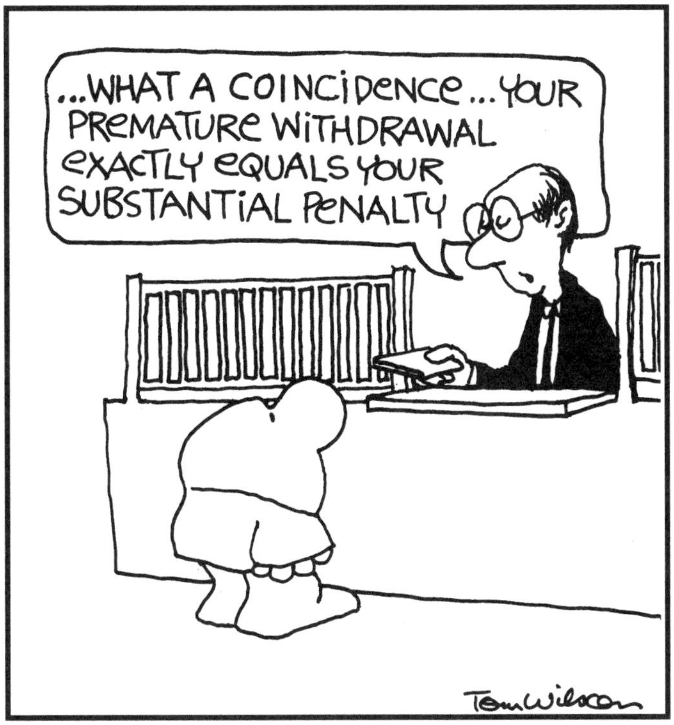
...WHAT A COINCIDENCE...YOUR PREMATURE WITHDRAWAL EXACTLY EQUALS YOUR SUBSTANTIAL PENALTY
Tom Wilson

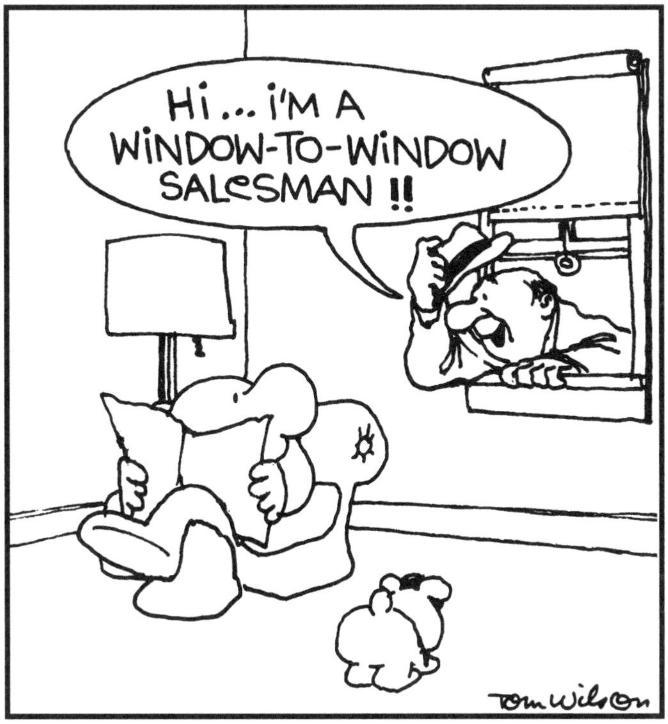
Hi... I'M A WINDOW-TO-WINDOW SALESMAN !!
Tom Wilson

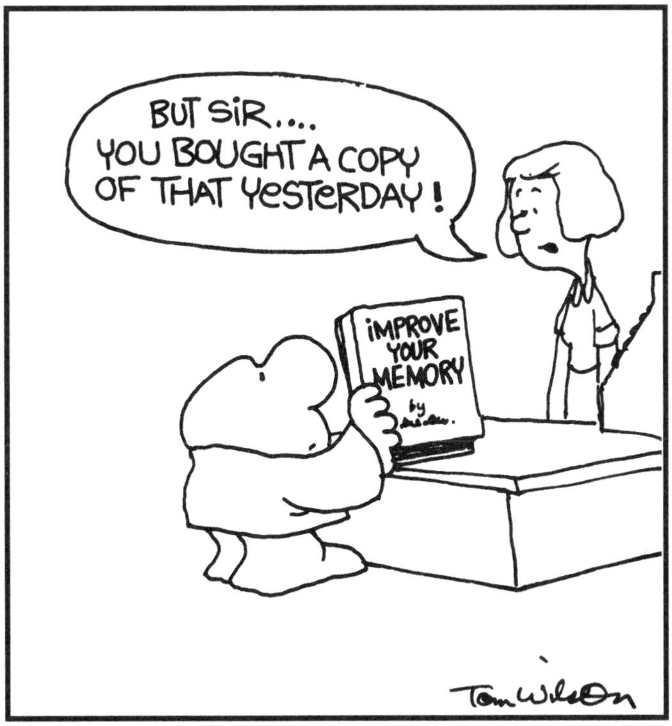
BUT SIR....
YOU BOUGHT A COPY OF THAT YESTERDAY !
IMPROVE YOUR MEMORY
by
Tom Wilson

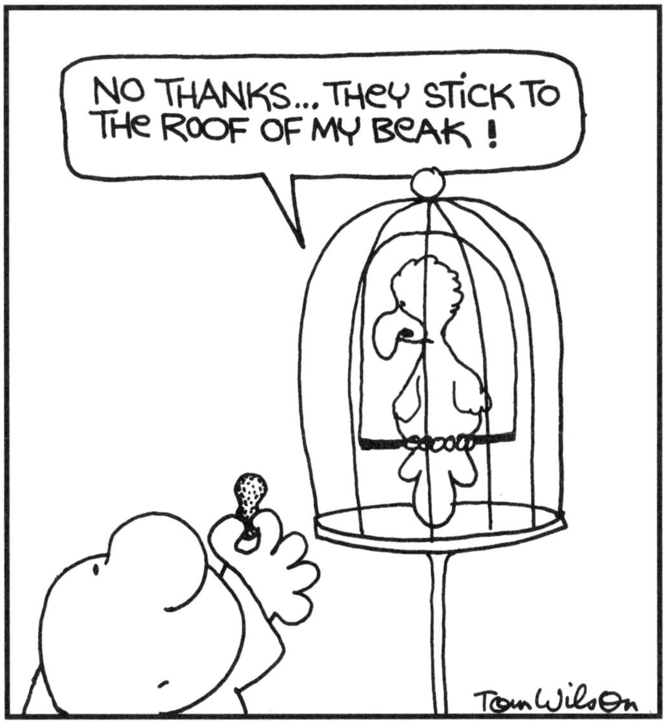
NO THANKS... THEY STICK TO THE ROOF OF MY BEAK !
Tom Wilson

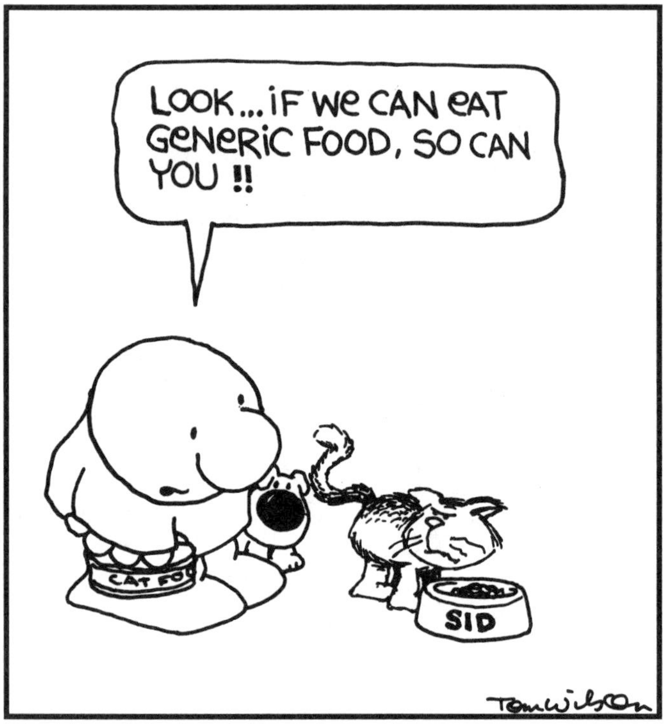
LOOK... IF WE CAN EAT GENERIC FOOD, SO CAN YOU !!
SID

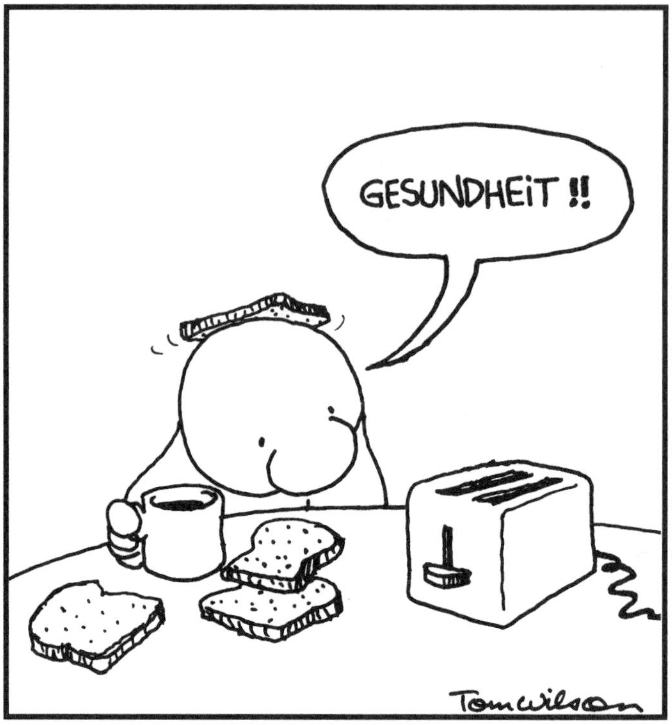
GESUNDHEIT !!

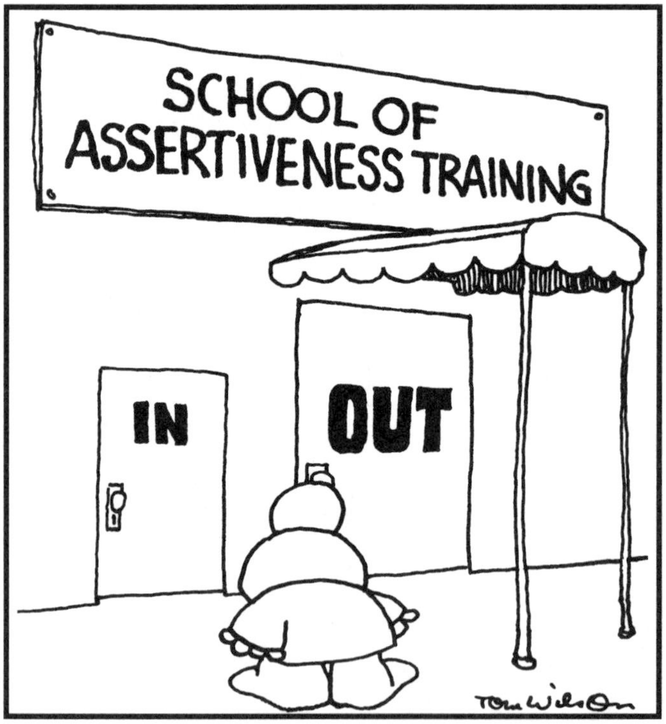
SCHOOL OF ASSERTIVENESS TRAINING
IN
OUT

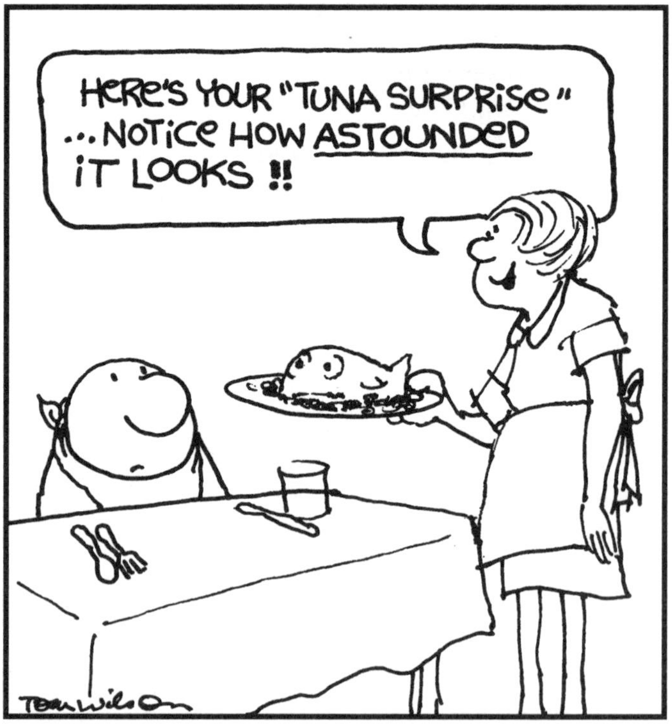
HERE'S YOUR "TUNA SURPRISE" ...NOTICE HOW ASTOUNDED IT LOOKS !!

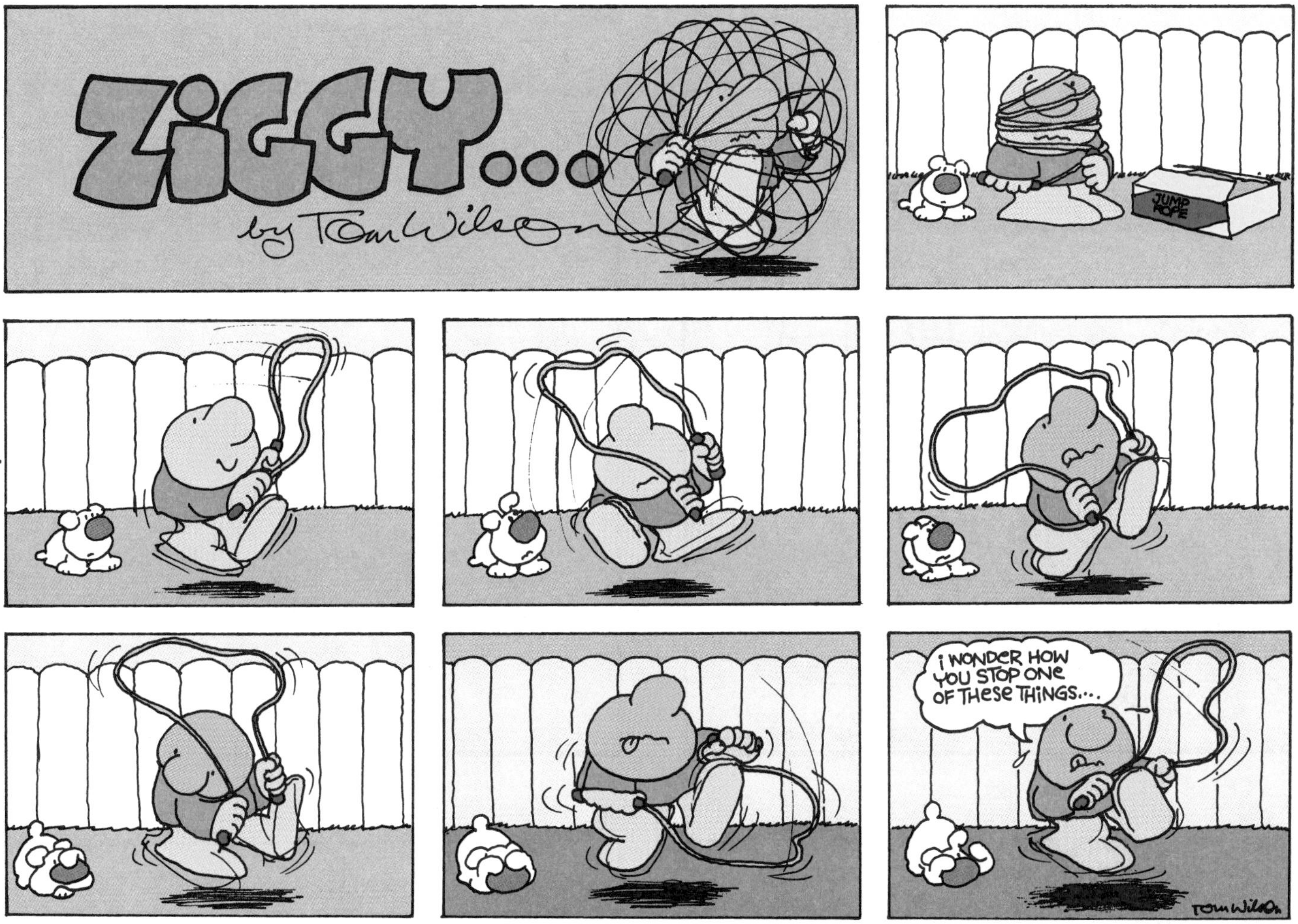
ZiGGY...
by Tom Wilson
JUMP ROPE
i WONDER HOW YOU STOP ONE OF THESE THINGS....
Tom Wilson

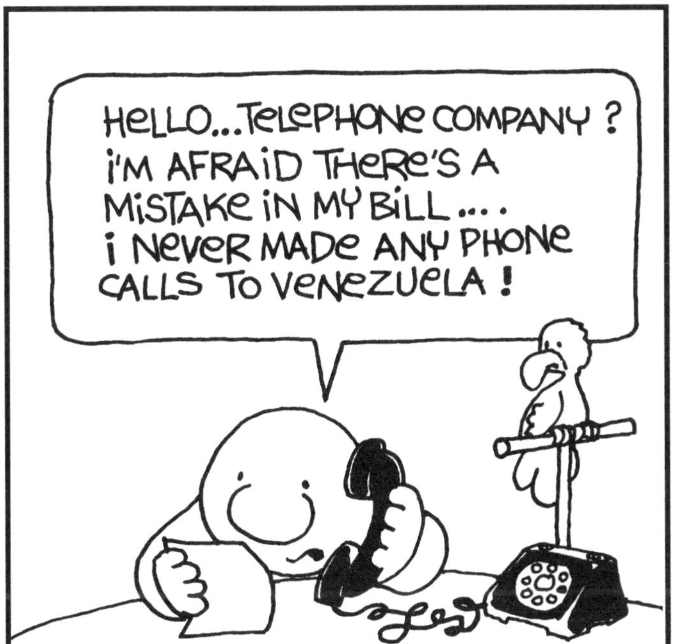
HELLO...TELEPHONE COMPANY ? i'M AFRAID THERE'S A MISTAKE iN MY BiLL .... i NEVER MADE ANY PHONE CALLS TO VENEZUELA !
Tom Wilson

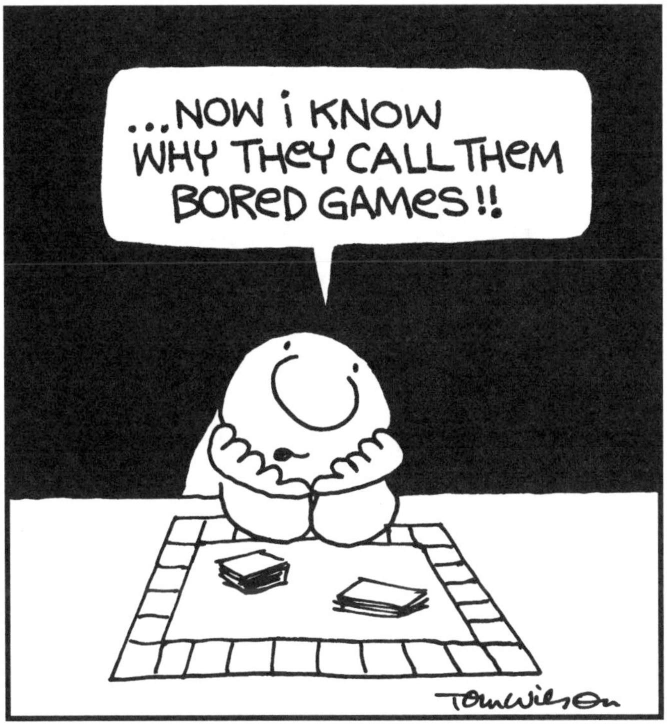
...NOW i KNOW WHY THEY CALL THEM BORED GAMES !!
Tom Wilson

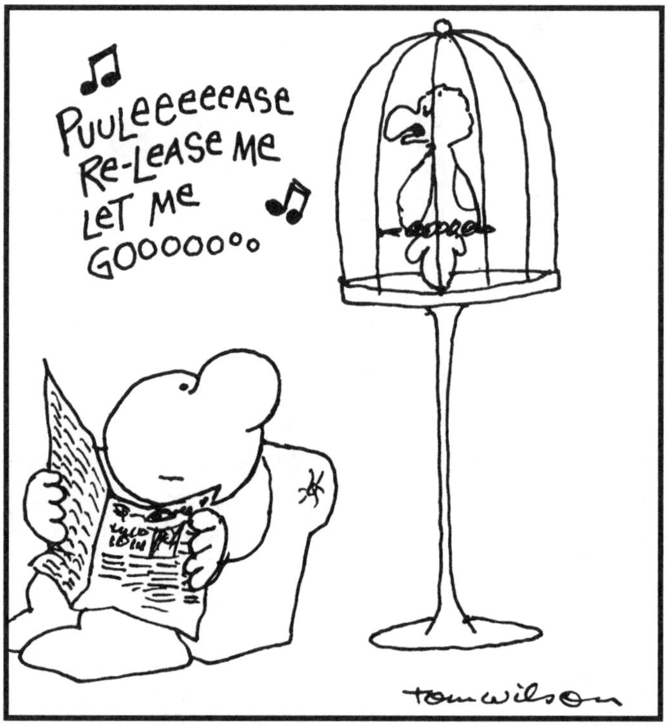
PUULEEEEEASE
RE-LEASE ME
LET ME
GOOOOOOo

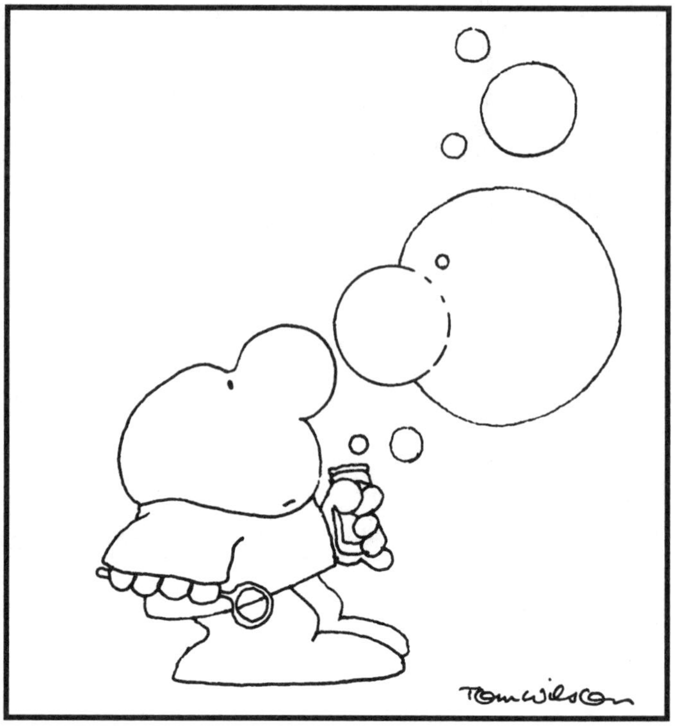

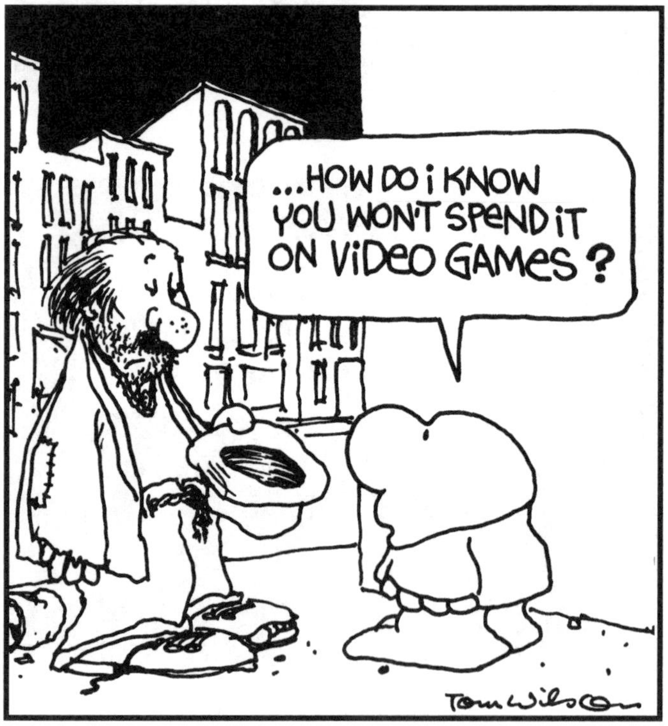
...HOW DO I KNOW YOU WON'T SPEND IT ON VIDEO GAMES?

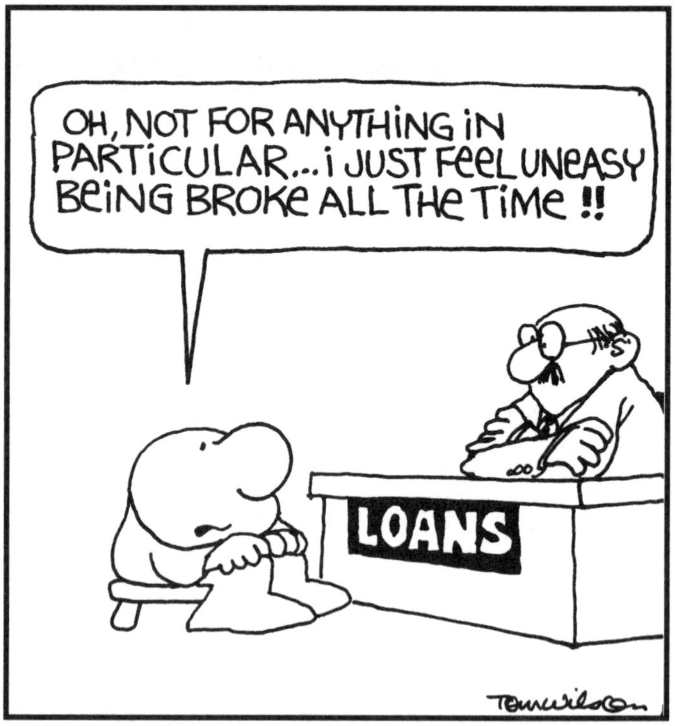
OH, NOT FOR ANYTHING IN PARTICULAR... I JUST FEEL UNEASY BEING BROKE ALL THE TIME !!
LOANS

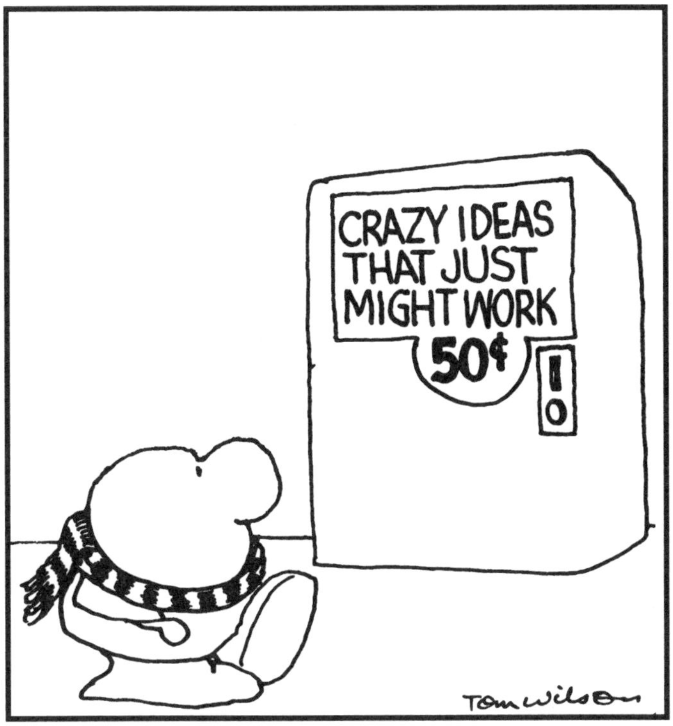
CRAZY IDEAS THAT JUST MIGHT WORK
50¢

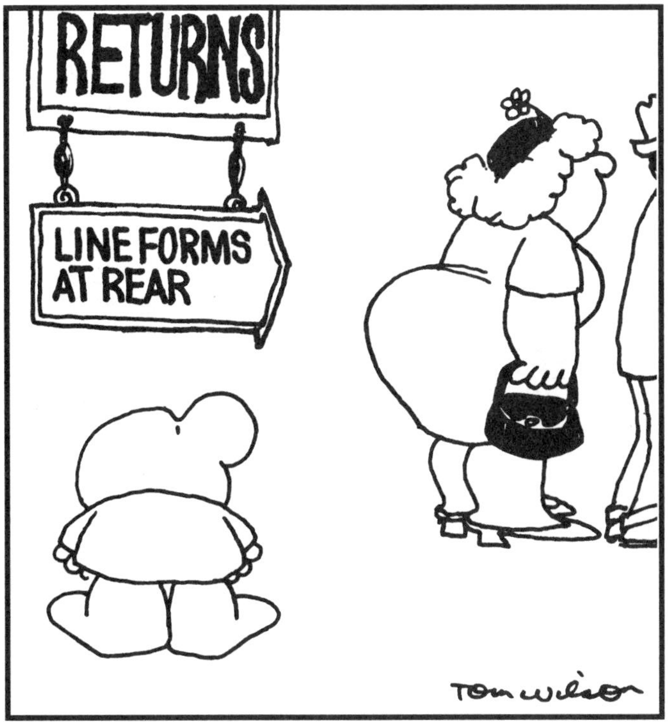
RETURNS
LINE FORMS AT REAR

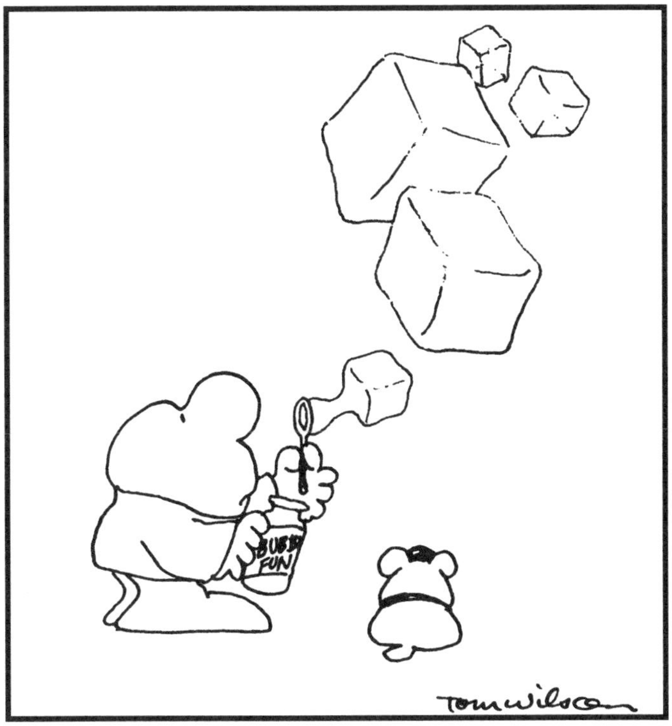

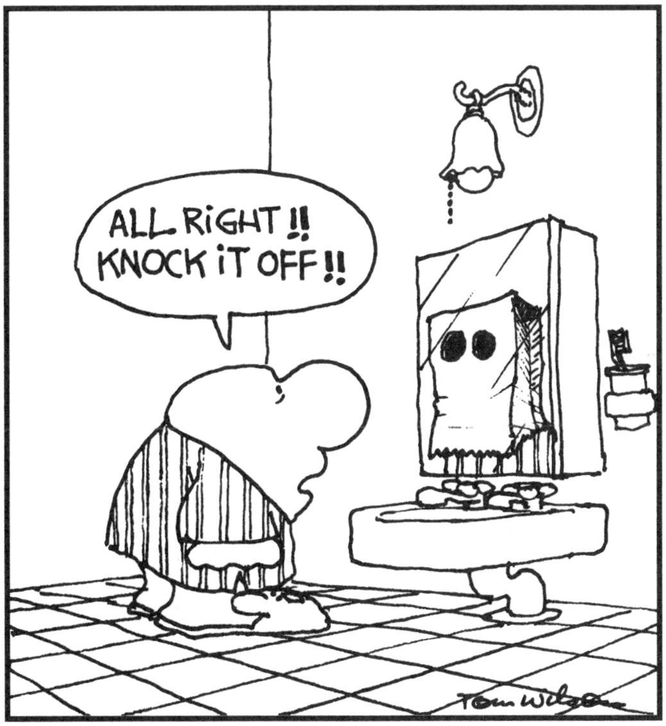
ALL RIGHT !! KNOCK IT OFF !!

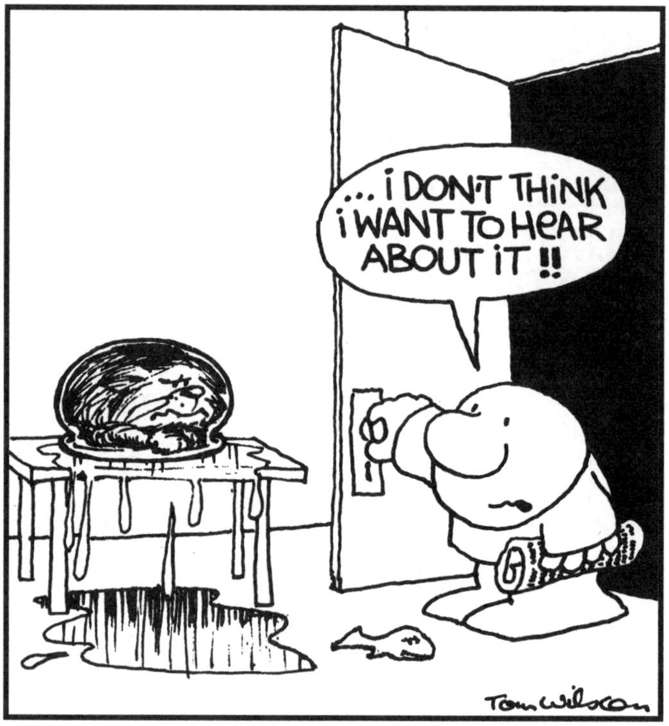
...i DON'T THiNK i WANT TO HeAR ABOUT iT !!
Tom Wilson

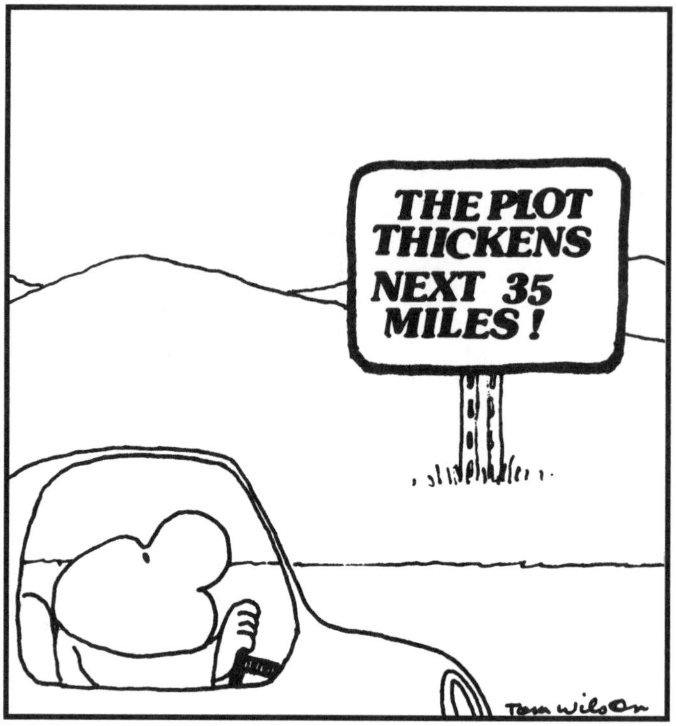
THE PLOT THICKENS NEXT 35 MILES!
Tom Wilson

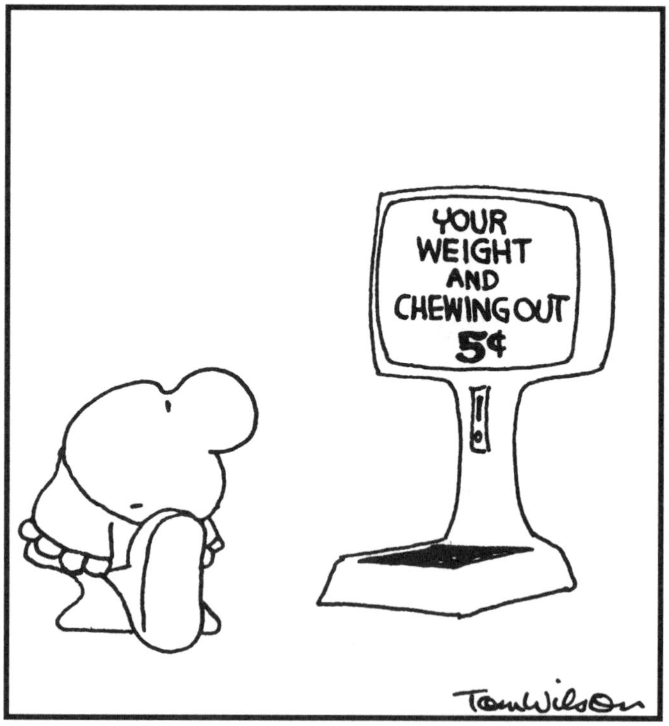
YOUR WEIGHT AND CHEWING OUT 5¢
Tom Wilson

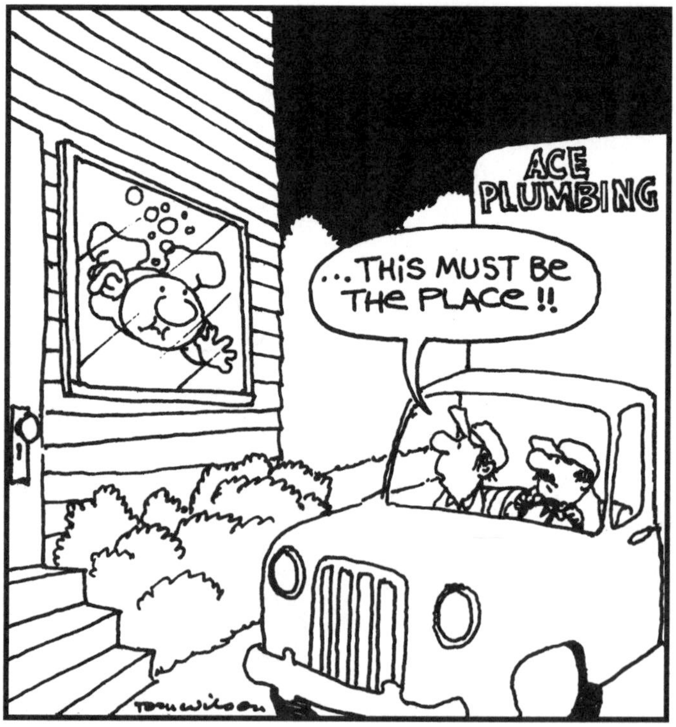
ACE PLUMBING
...THiS MUST Be THe PLACe !!
Tom Wilson

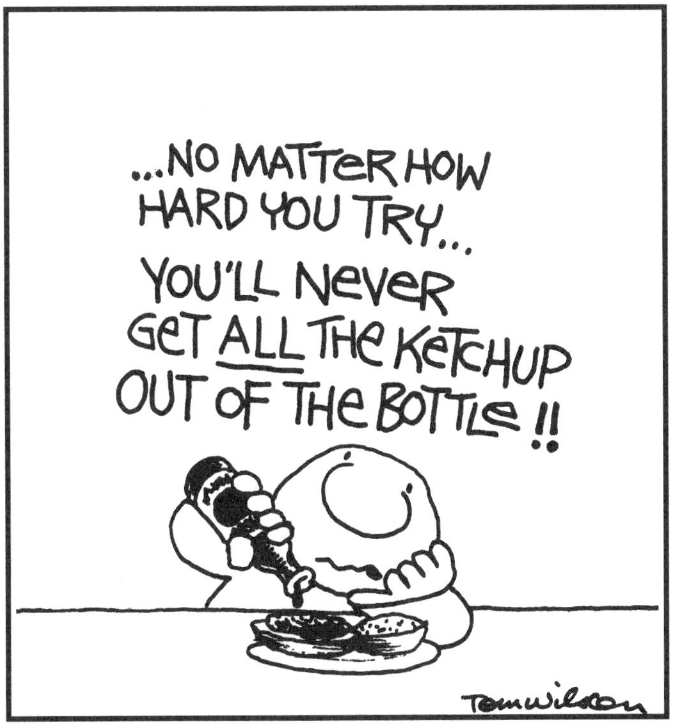
...NO MATTER HOW HARD YOU TRY... YOU'LL NEVER GET ALL THE KETCHUP OUT OF THE BOTTLE !!
Tom Wilson

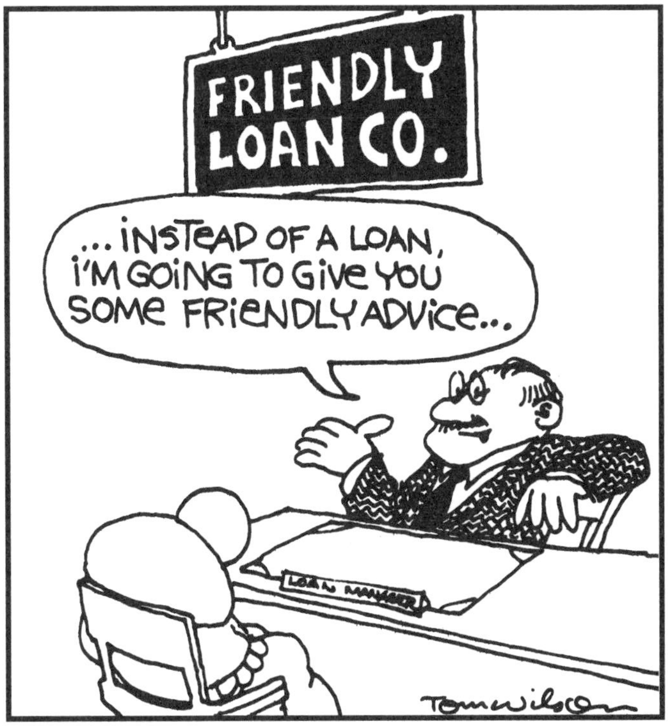
FRIENDLY LOAN CO.
...INSTEAD OF A LOAN, I'M GOING TO GIVE YOU SOME FRIENDLY ADVICE...
LOAN MANAGER
Tom Wilson

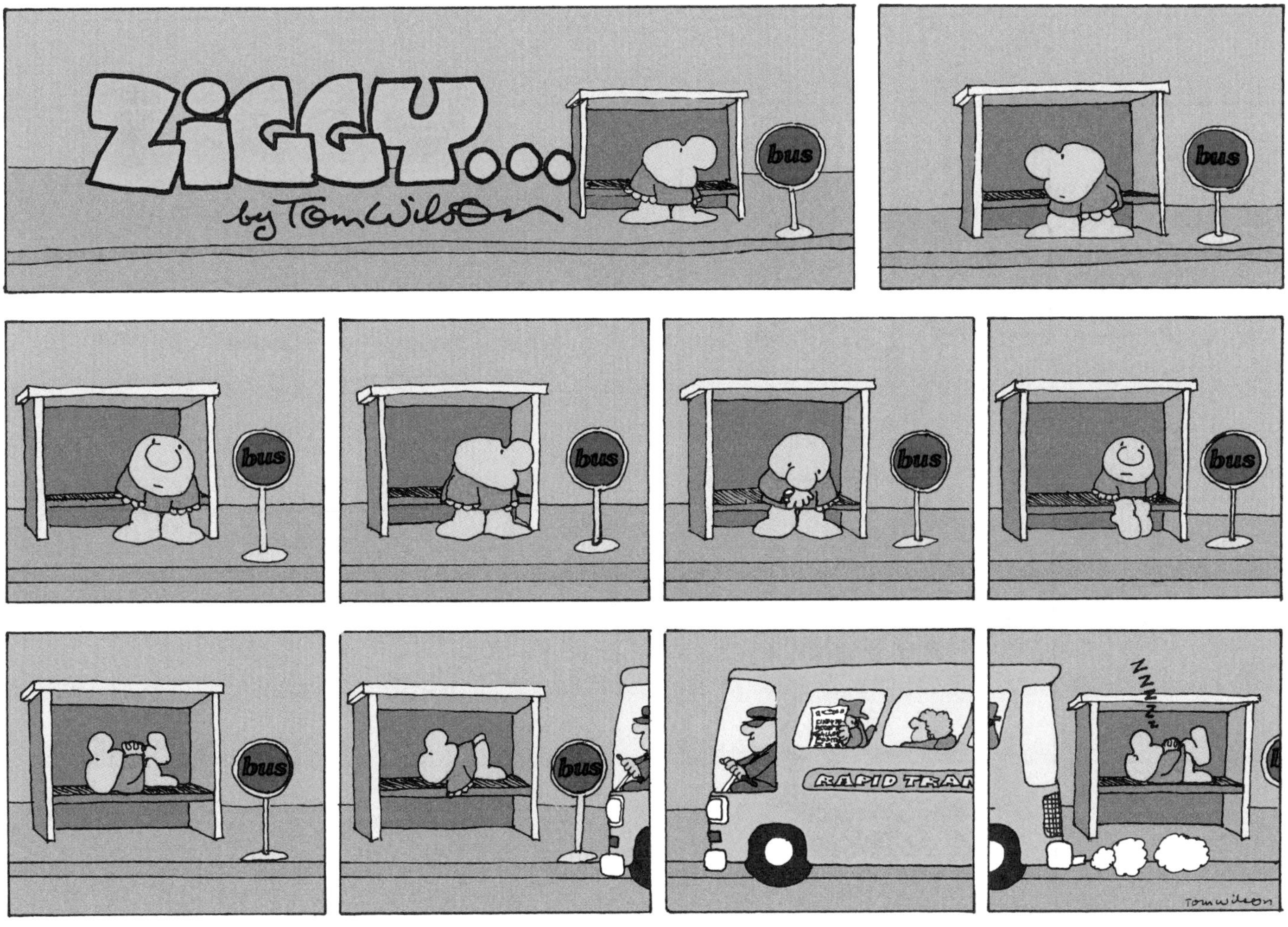
ZIGGY...
by Tom Wilson
bus
RAPID TRAN
Z Z Z Z
Tom Wilson

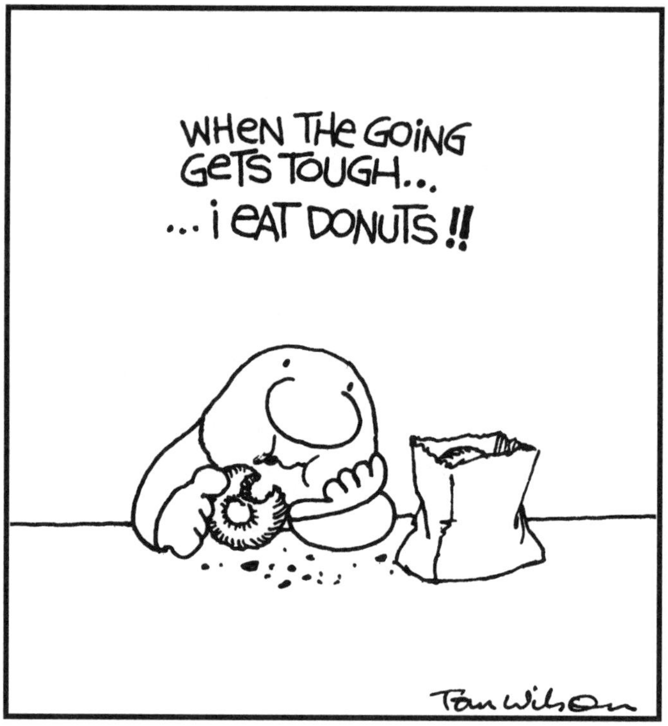
WHEN THE GOING GETS TOUGH...
... i EAT DONUTS !!
Tom Wilson

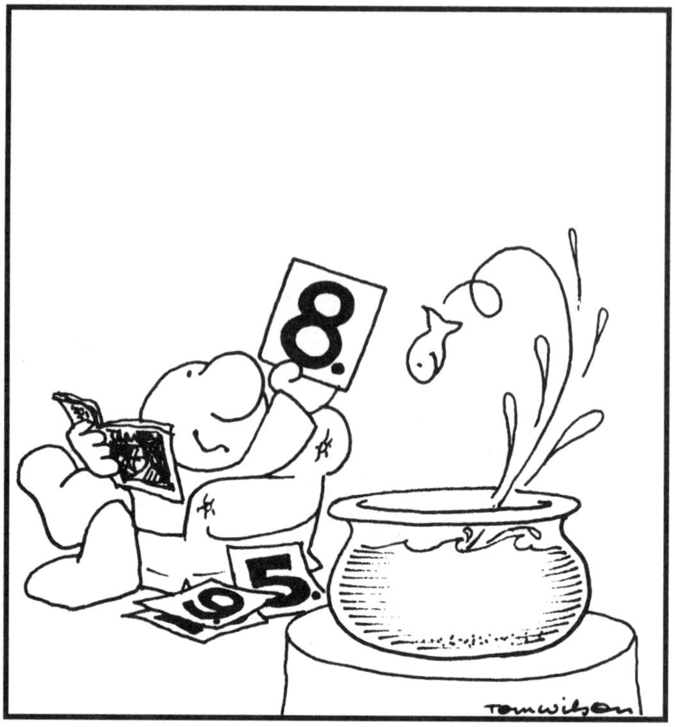
8.
5.
9.
Tom Wilson

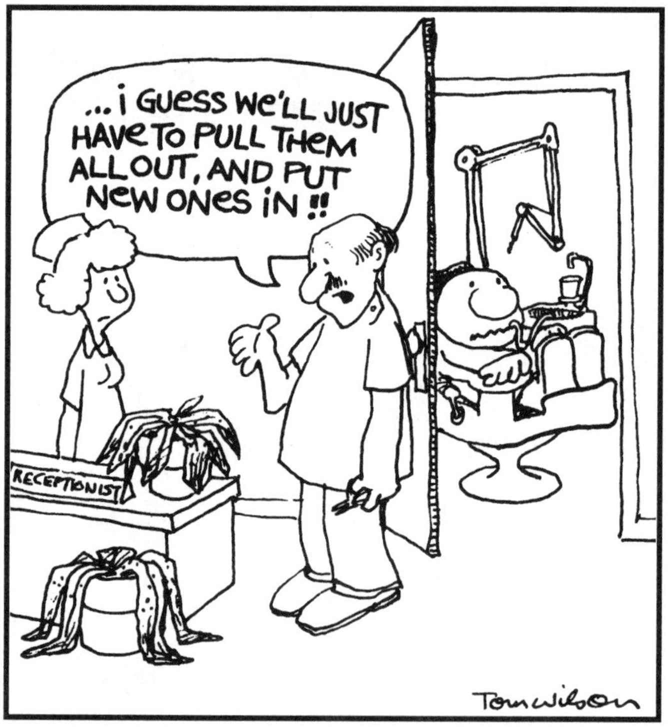
... i GUESS WE'LL JUST HAVE TO PULL THEM ALL OUT, AND PUT NEW ONES iN !!
RECEPTIONIST
Tom Wilson

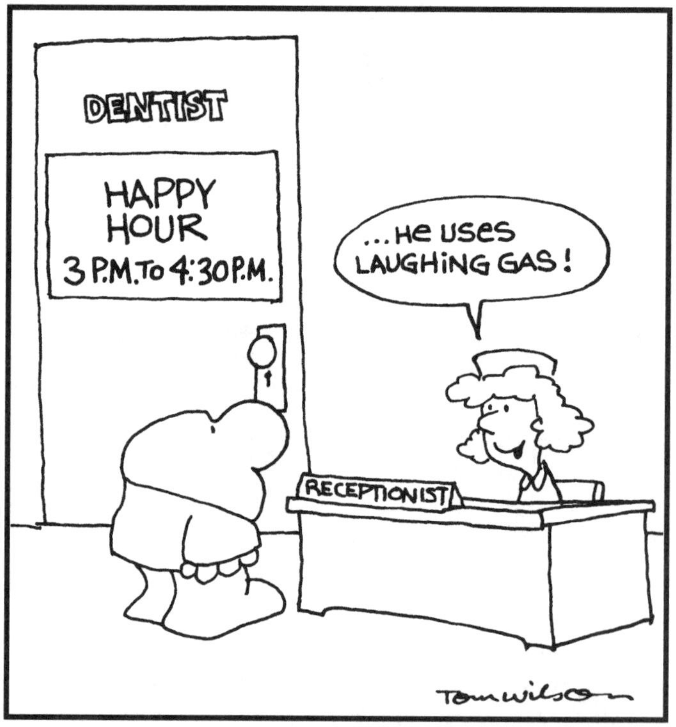
DENTIST
HAPPY HOUR
3 P.M. TO 4:30 P.M.
... HE USES LAUGHING GAS!
RECEPTIONIST
Tom Wilson

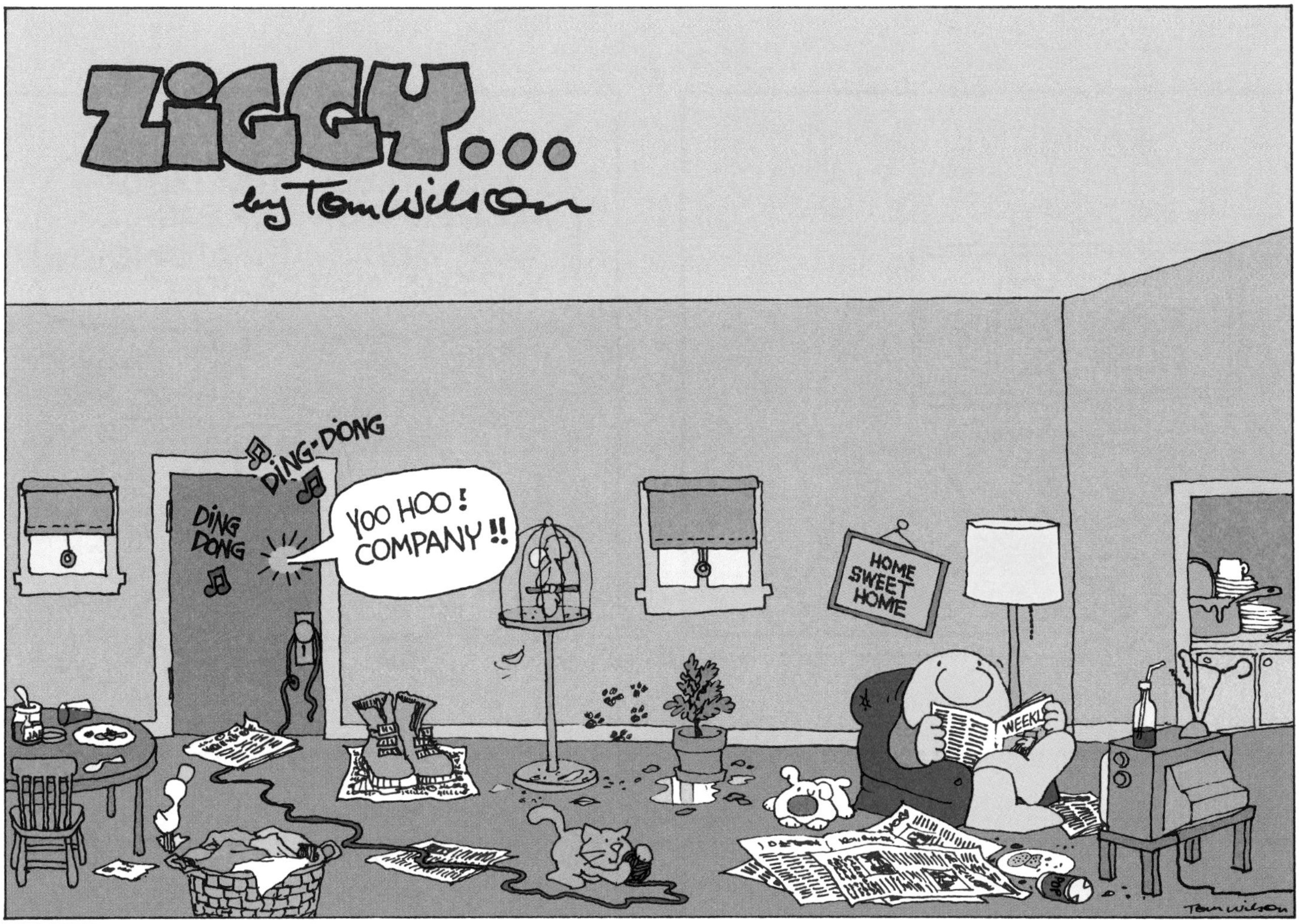
ZIGGY...
by Tom Wilson
DING-DONG
DING DONG
YOO HOO! COMPANY!!
HOME SWEET HOME
WEEKLY
Tom Wilson

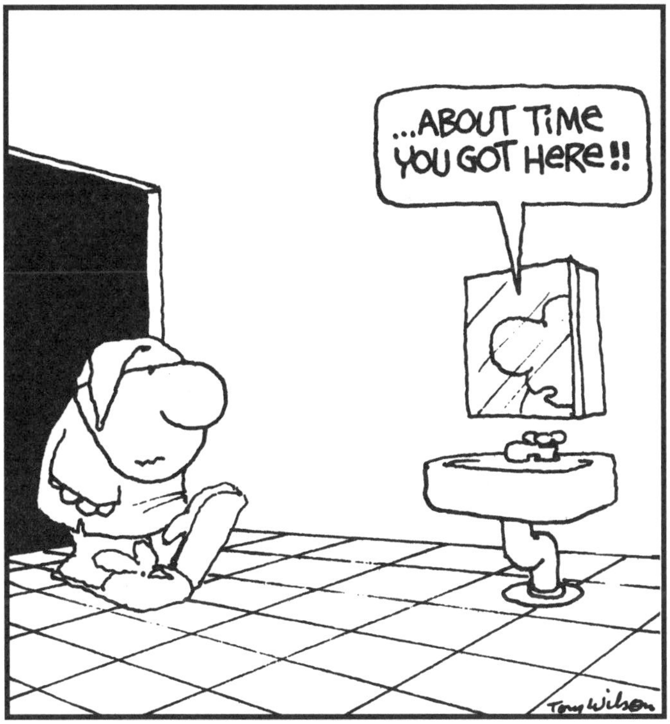
...ABOUT TIME YOU GOT HERE!!
Tom Wilson

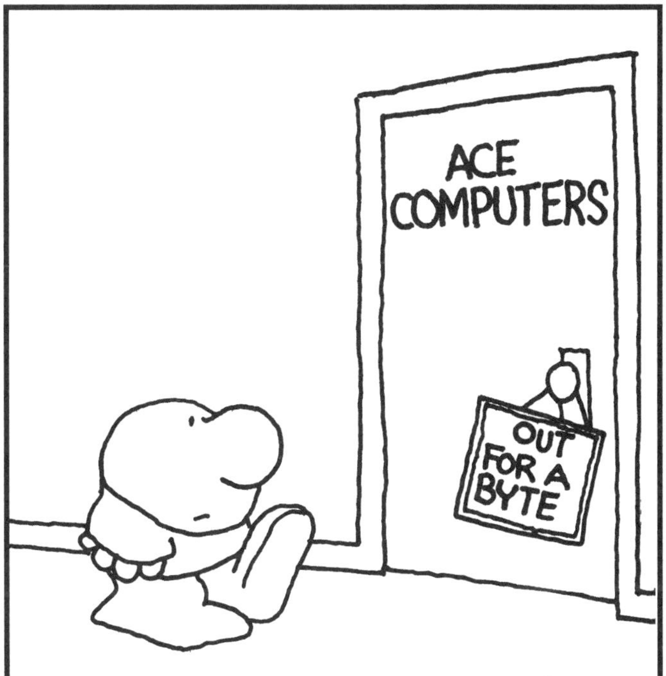
ACE COMPUTERS
OUT FOR A BYTE
Tom Wilson

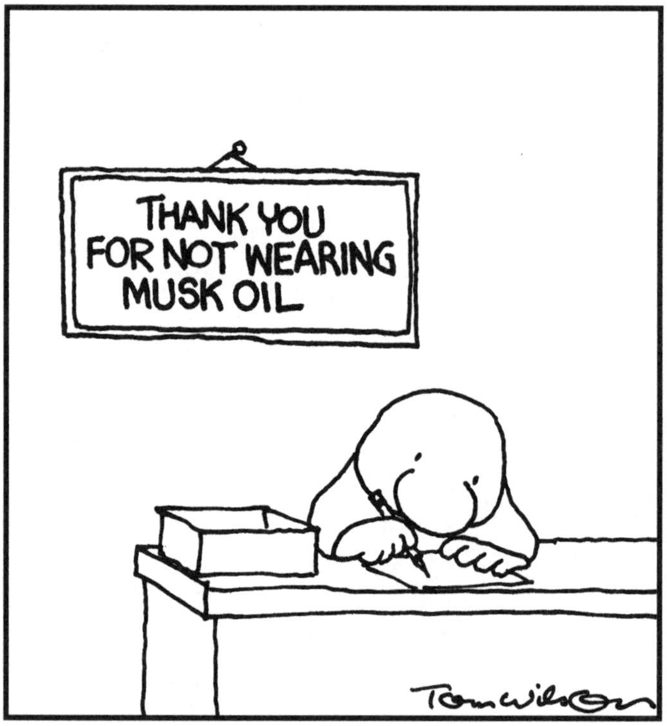
THANK YOU FOR NOT WEARING MUSK OIL
Tom Wilson

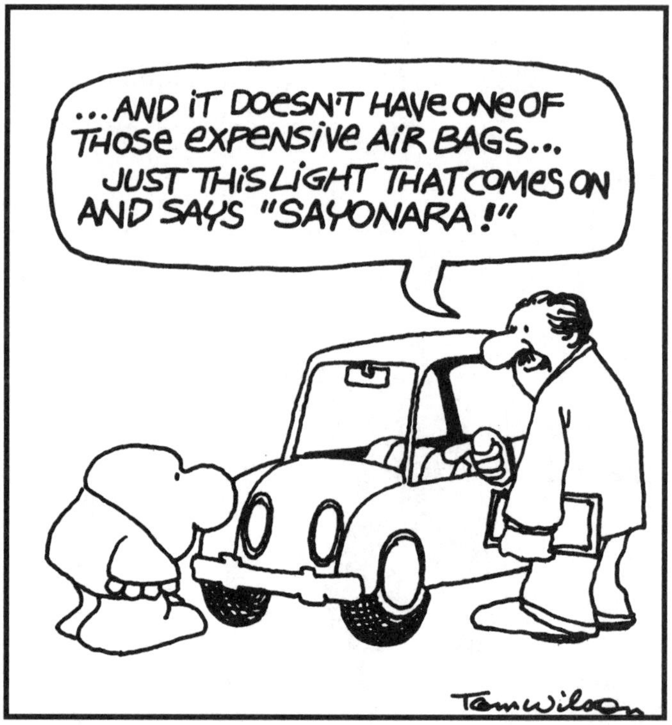
...AND IT DOESN'T HAVE ONE OF THOSE EXPENSIVE AIR BAGS... JUST THIS LIGHT THAT COMES ON AND SAYS "SAYONARA!"
Tom Wilson

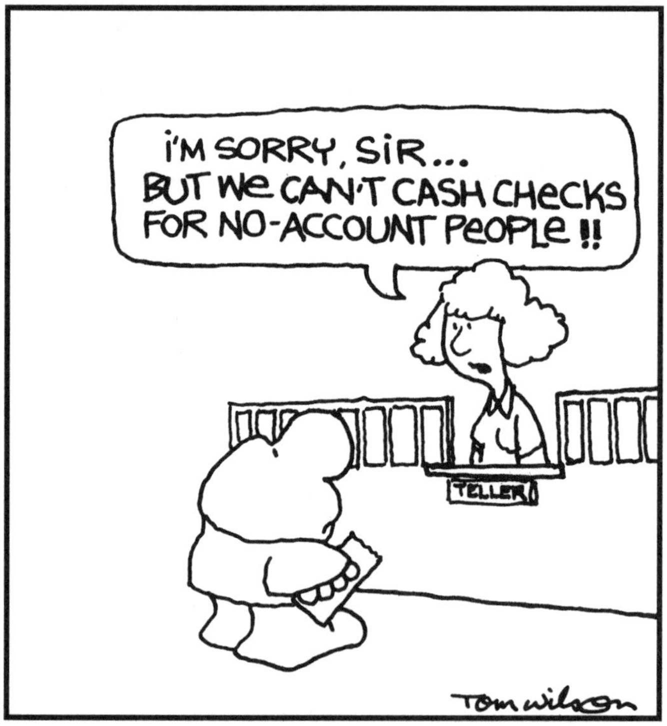
I'M SORRY, SIR... BUT WE CAN'T CASH CHECKS FOR NO-ACCOUNT PEOPLE!!
TELLER
Tom Wilson

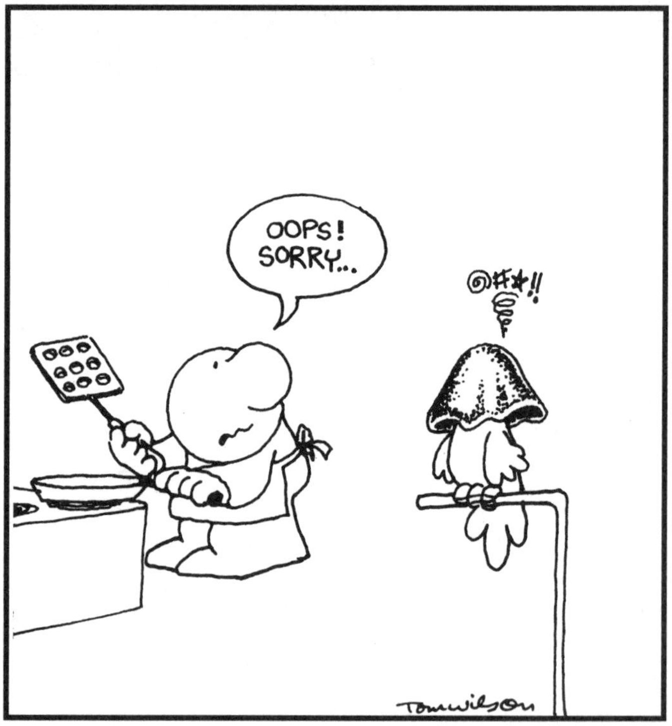
OOPS! SORRY...
@#*!!
Tom Wilson

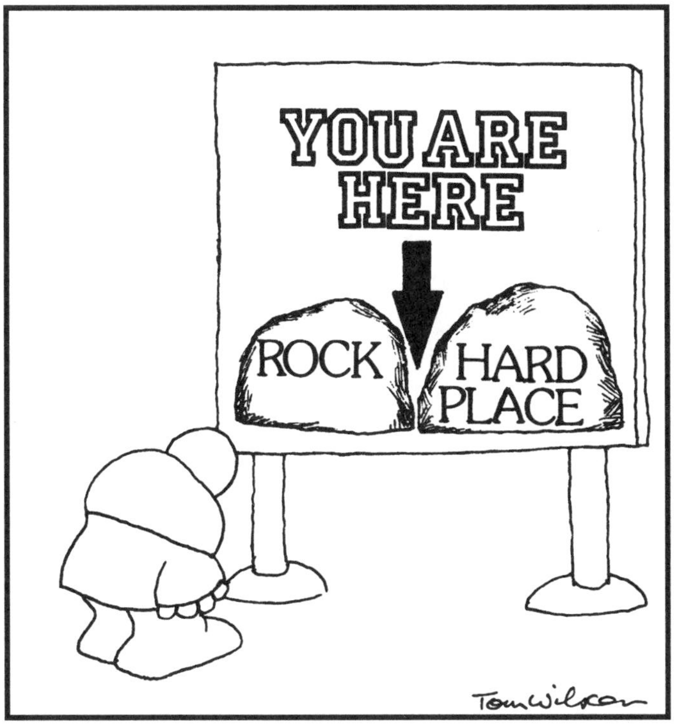
YOU ARE HERE
ROCK
HARD PLACE
Tom Wilson

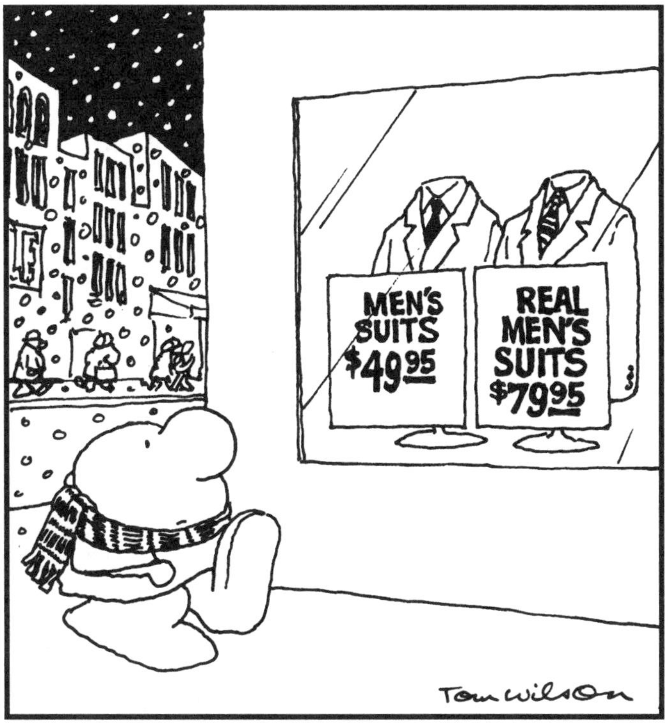
MEN'S SUITS $49.95
REAL MEN'S SUITS $79.95
Tom Wilson

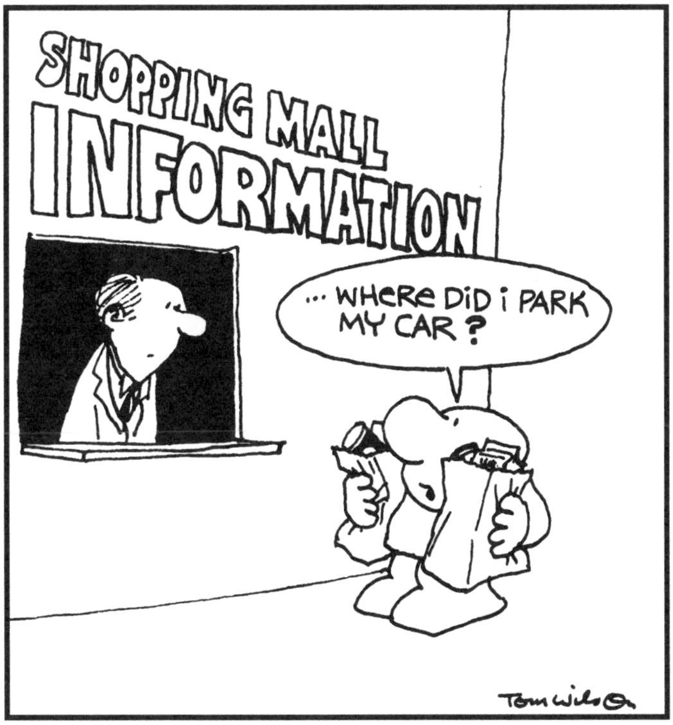
SHOPPING MALL INFORMATION
... WHERE DID I PARK MY CAR?
Tom Wilson

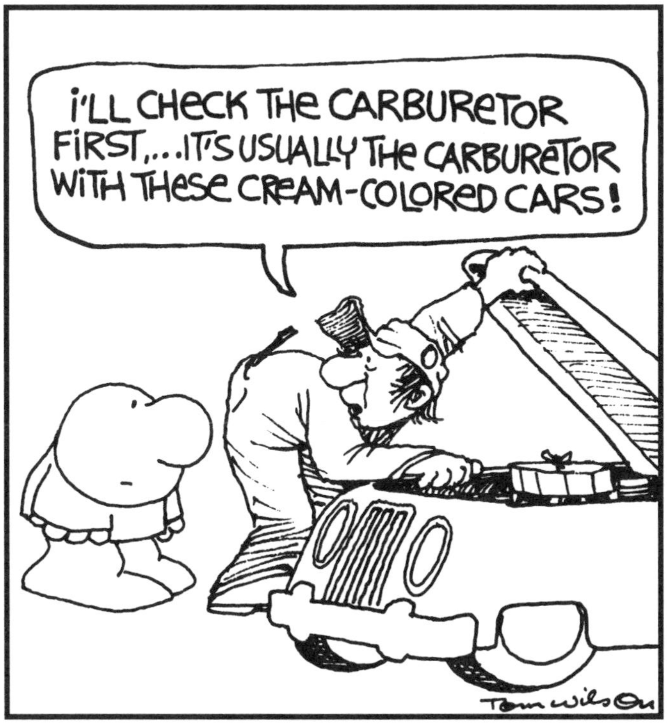
I'LL CHECK THE CARBURETOR FIRST,...IT'S USUALLY THE CARBURETOR WITH THESE CREAM-COLORED CARS!
Tom Wilson

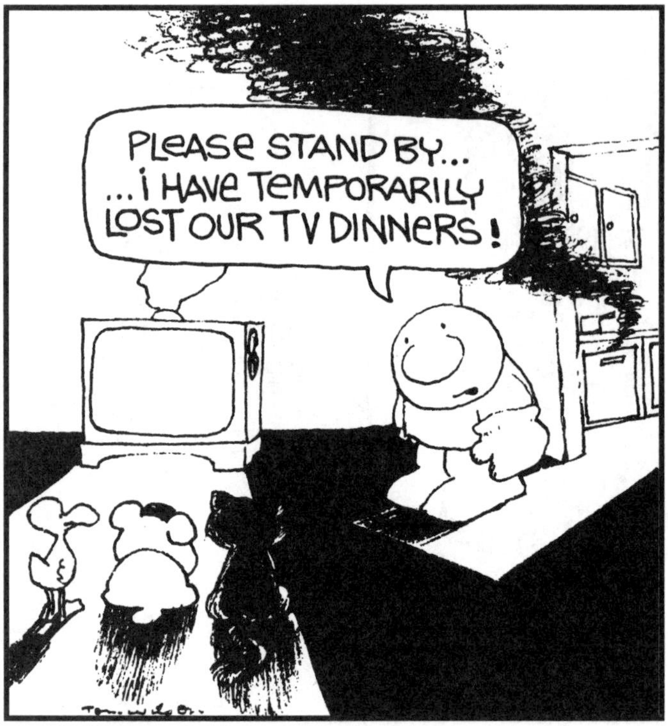
PLEASE STAND BY... ...I HAVE TEMPORARILY LOST OUR TV DINNERS!

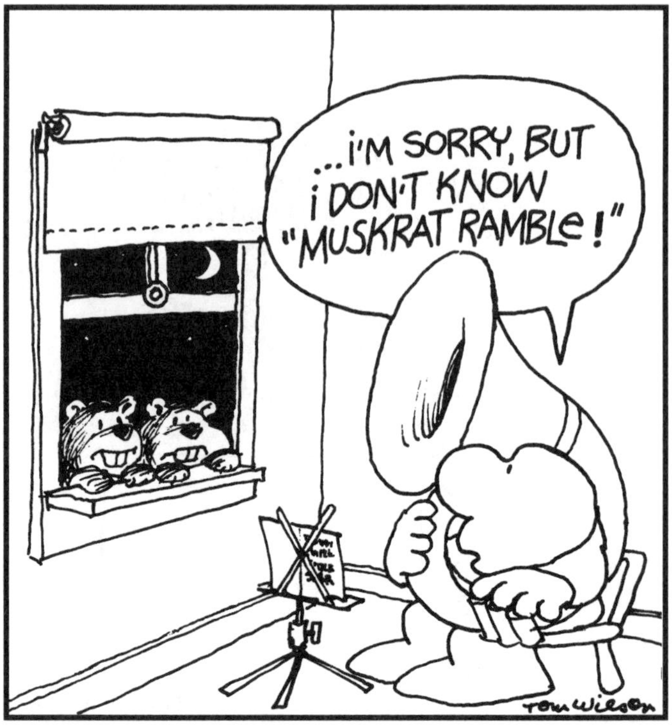
...I'M SORRY, BUT I DON'T KNOW "MUSKRAT RAMBLE!"
Tom Wilson

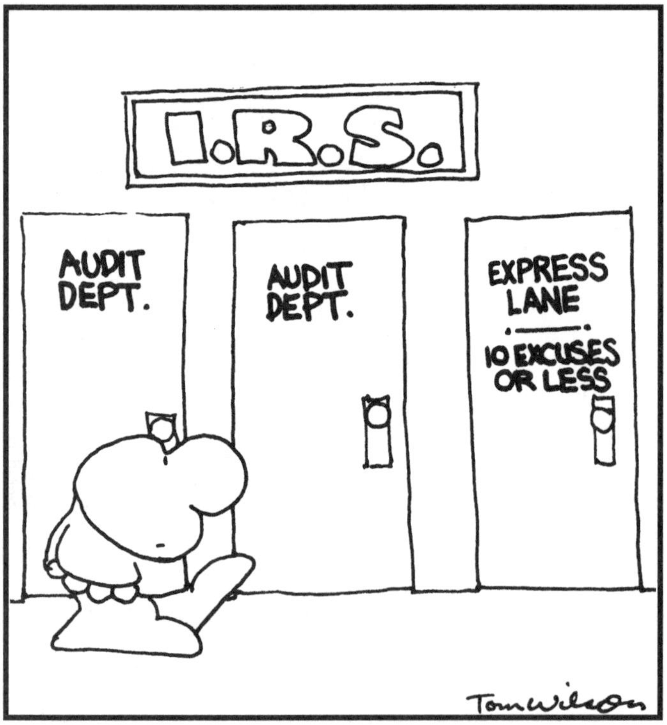
I.R.S.
AUDIT DEPT.
AUDIT DEPT.
EXPRESS LANE
10 EXCUSES OR LESS
Tom Wilson

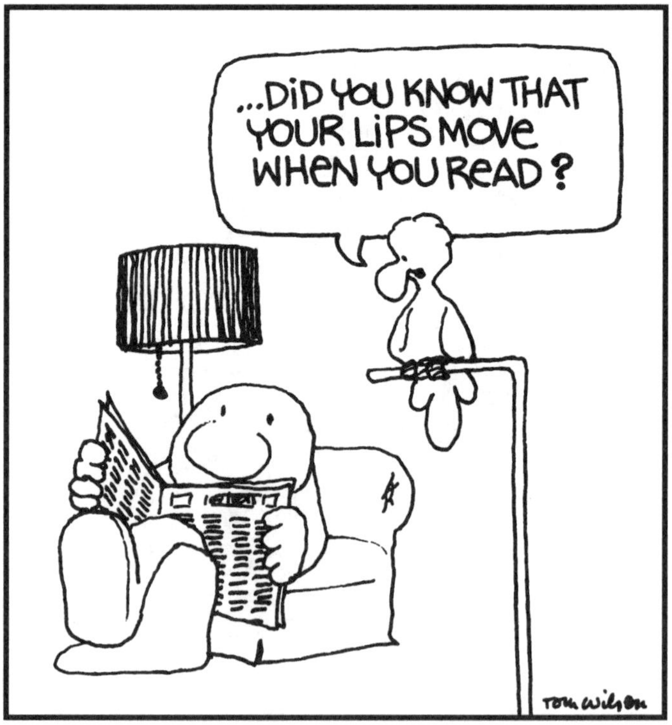
...DID YOU KNOW THAT YOUR LIPS MOVE WHEN YOU READ?
Tom Wilson

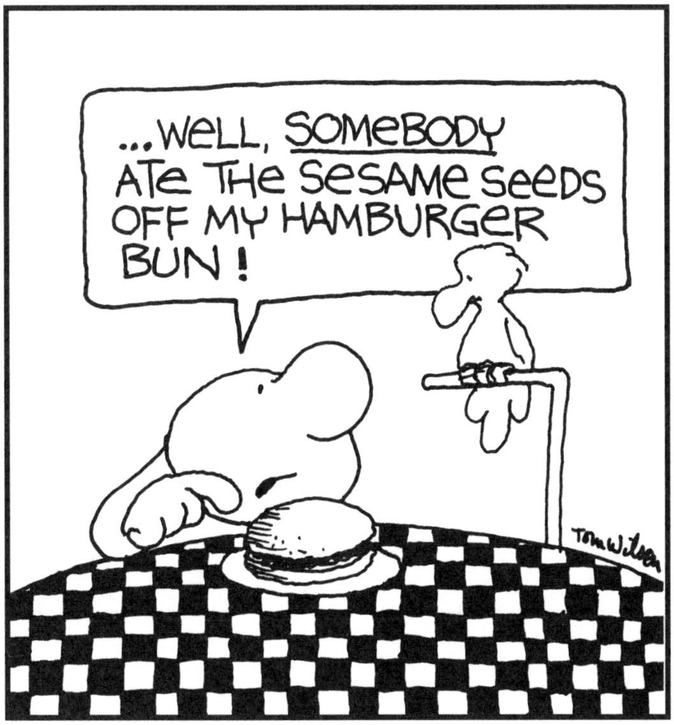
...WELL, SOMEBODY ATE THE SESAME SEEDS OFF MY HAMBURGER BUN!
Tom Wilson

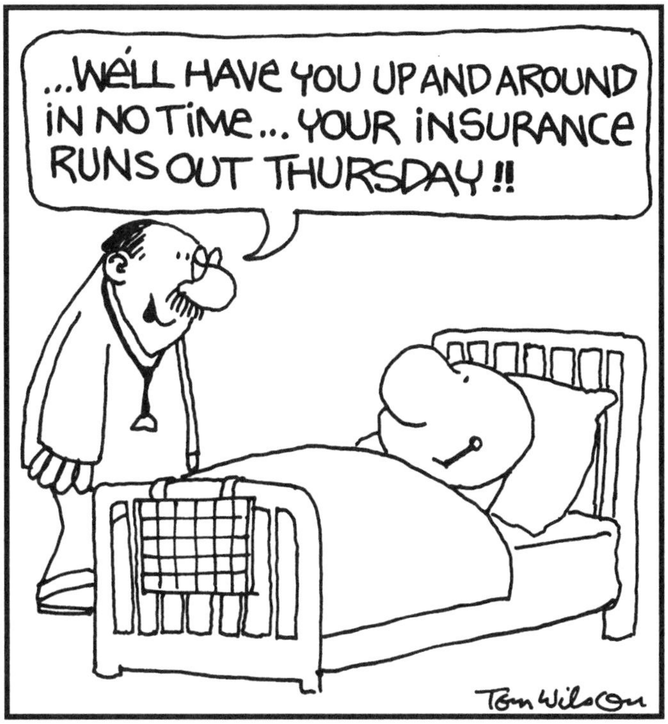
...WE'LL HAVE YOU UP AND AROUND IN NO TIME... YOUR INSURANCE RUNS OUT THURSDAY!!
Tom Wilson

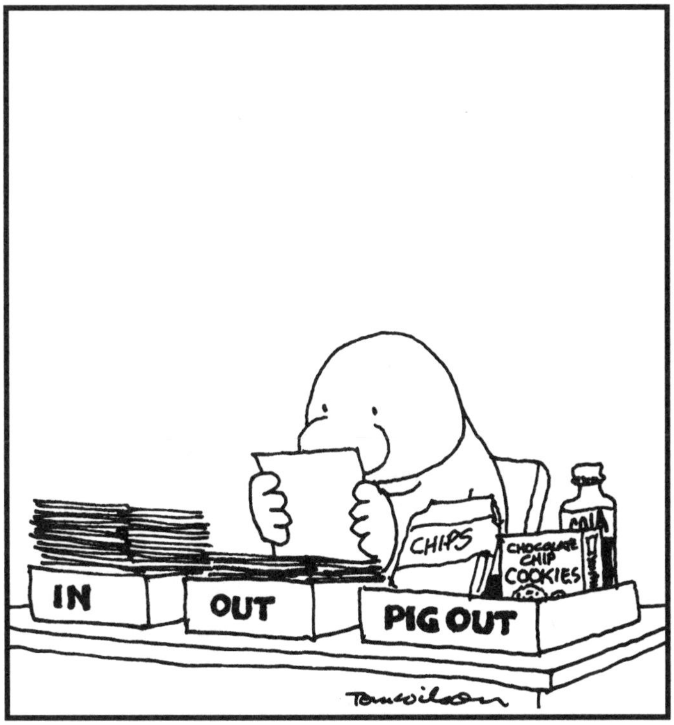
IN
OUT
PIG OUT
CHIPS
CHOCOLATE CHIP COOKIES
COLA
Tom Wilson

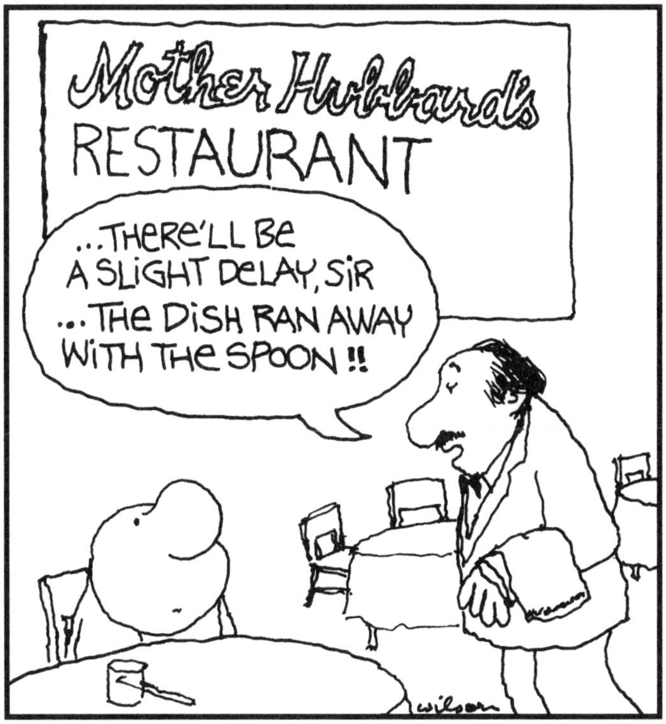
Mother Hubbard's RESTAURANT
...THERE'LL BE A SLIGHT DELAY, SIR ...THE DISH RAN AWAY WITH THE SPOON!!
Wilson

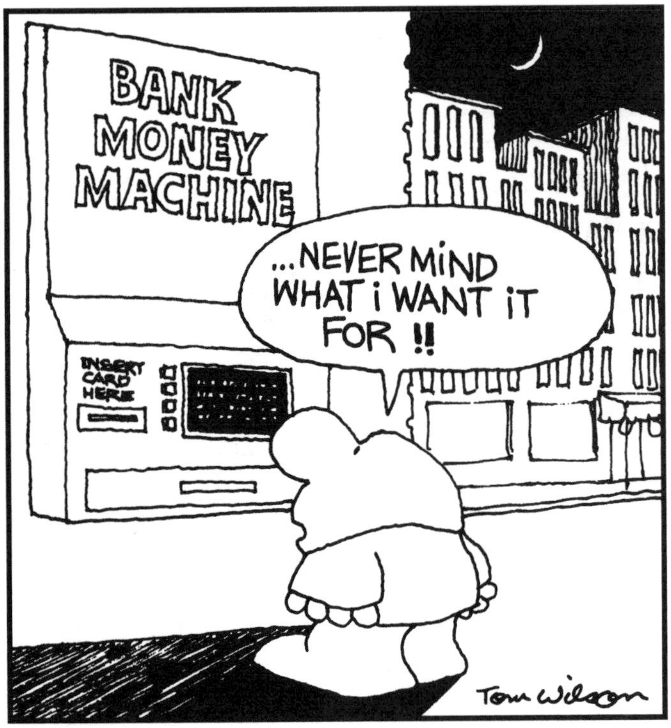
BANK
MONEY
MACHINE
INSERT CARD HERE
...NEVER MIND WHAT i WANT iT FOR !!
Tom Wilson

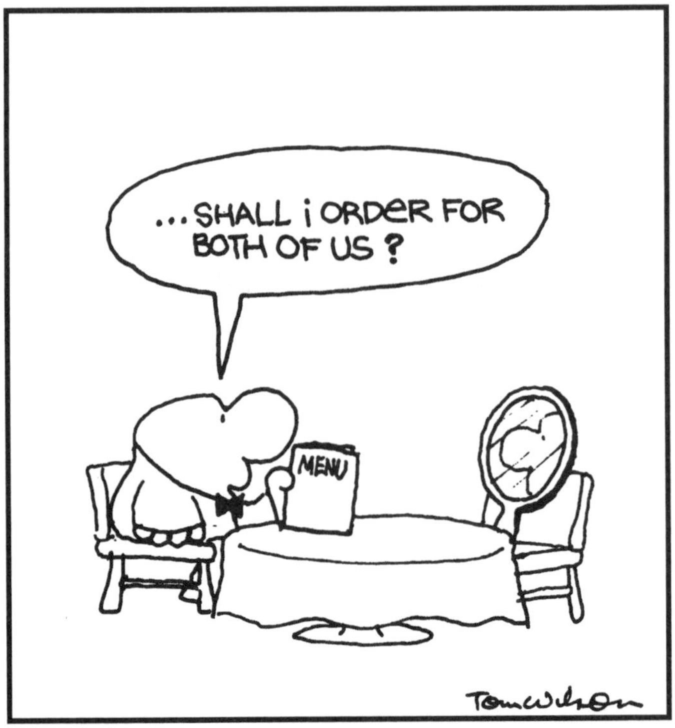
...SHALL i ORDER FOR BOTH OF US ?
MENU
Tom Wilson

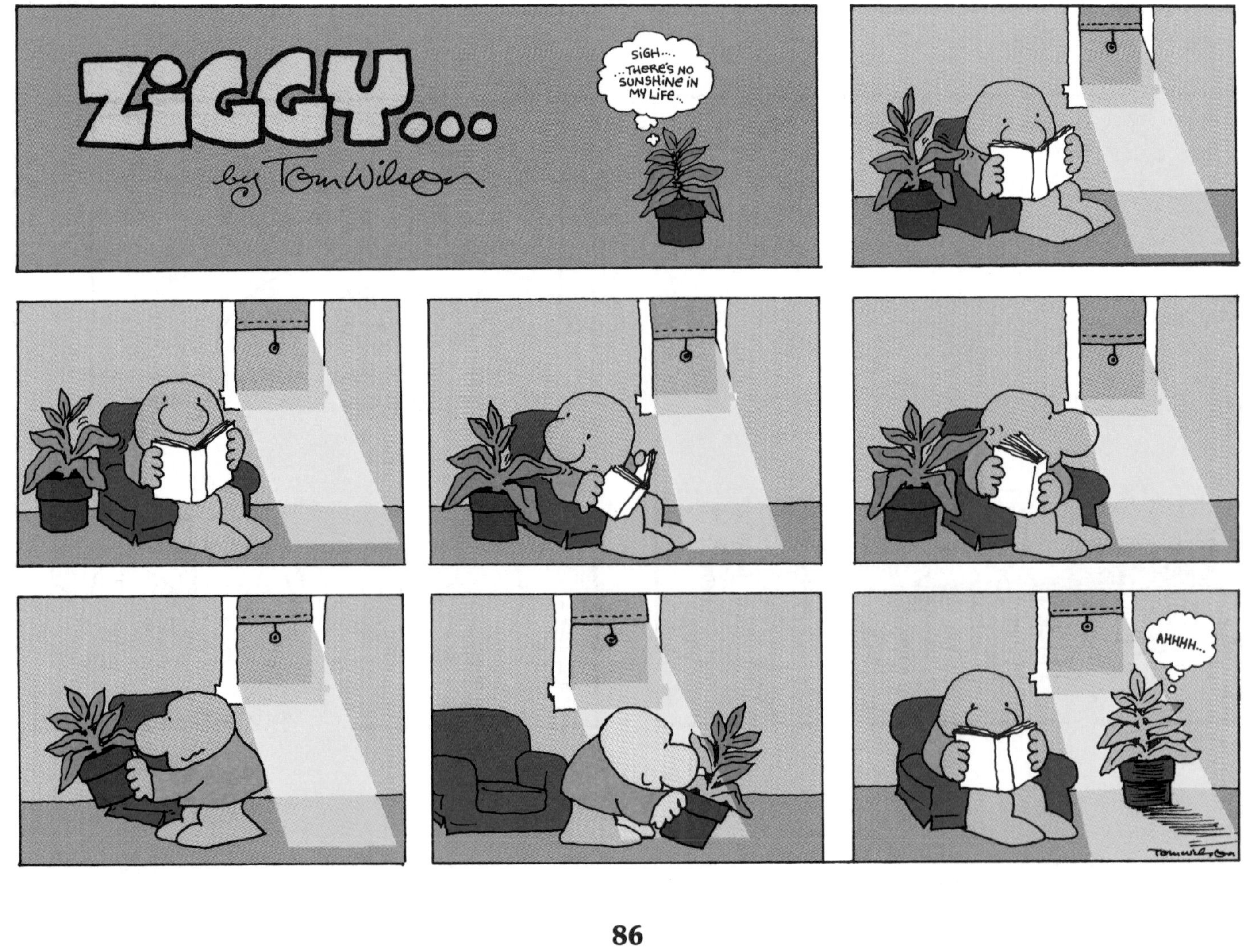
ZiGGY...
by Tom Wilson
SiGH.... ...THERE'S NO SUNSHiNE iN MY LiFE..
AHHHH...

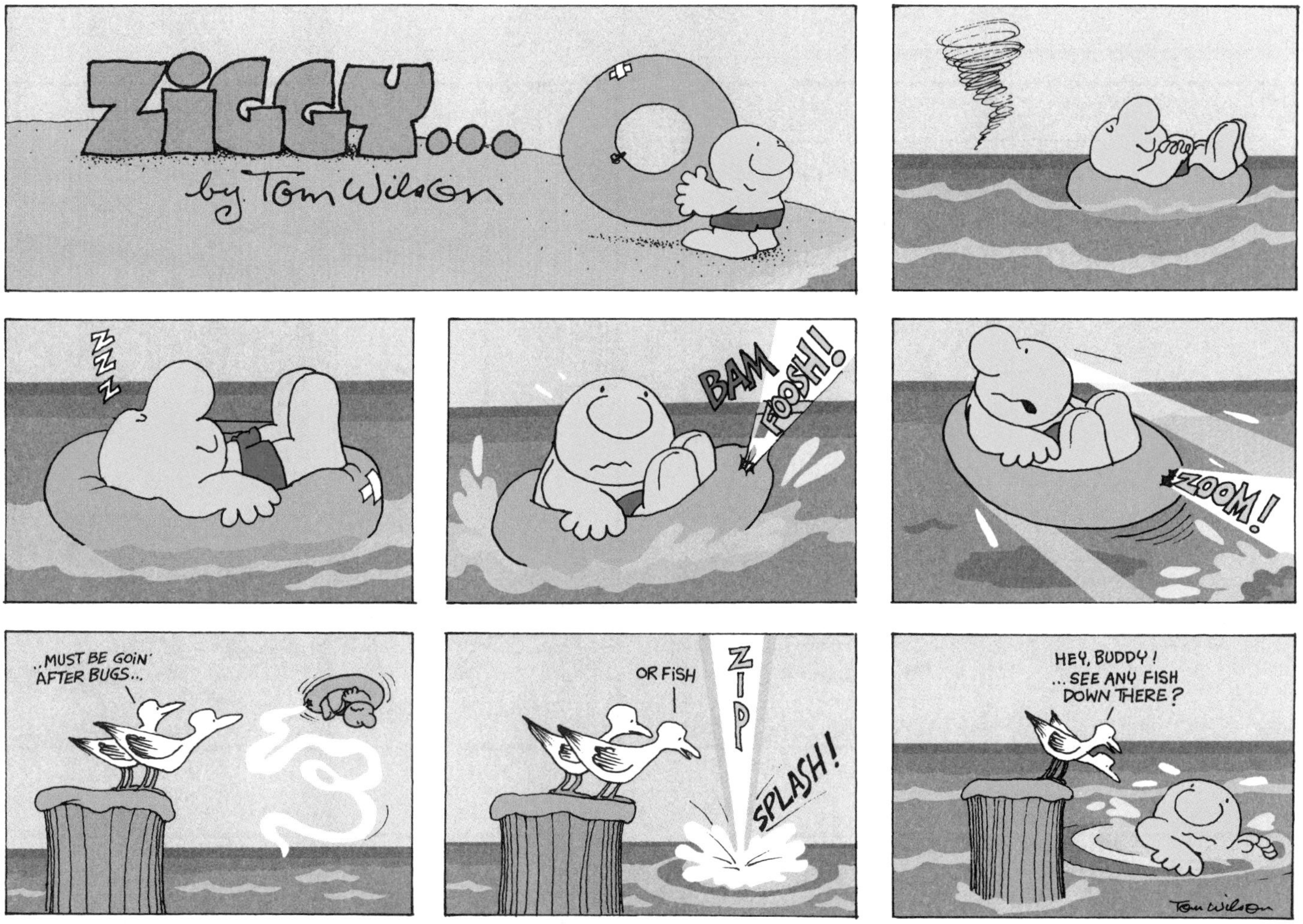
ZIGGY...
by Tom Wilson
ZZZ
BAM
FOOSH!
ZOOM!
..MUST BE GOIN' AFTER BUGS...
OR FISH
ZIP
SPLASH!
HEY, BUDDY! ...SEE ANY FISH DOWN THERE?
Tom Wilson

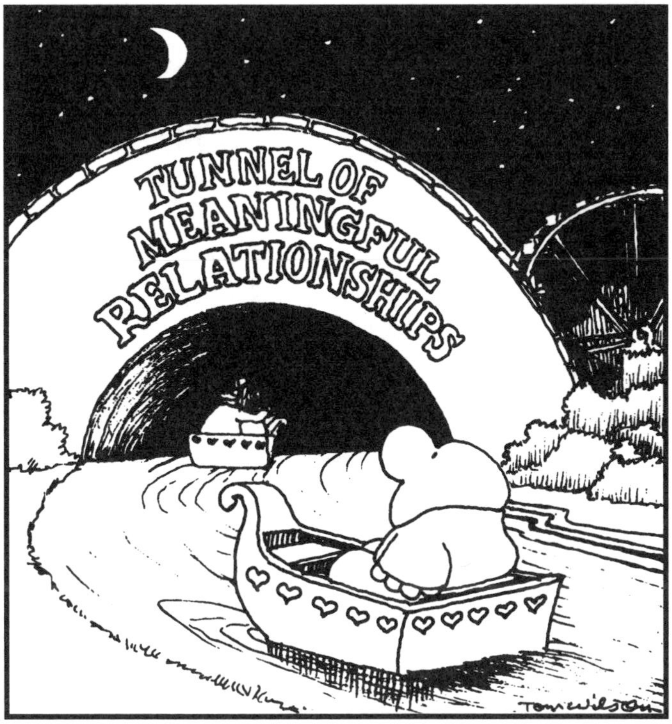
TUNNEL OF MEANINGFUL RELATIONSHIPS
Tom Wilson

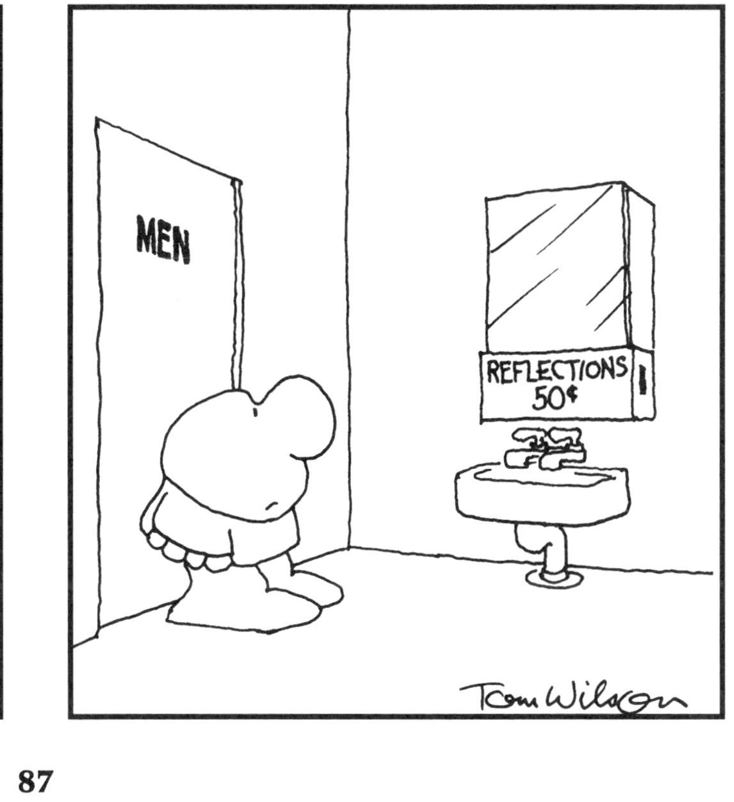
MEN
REFLECTIONS 50¢
Tom Wilson

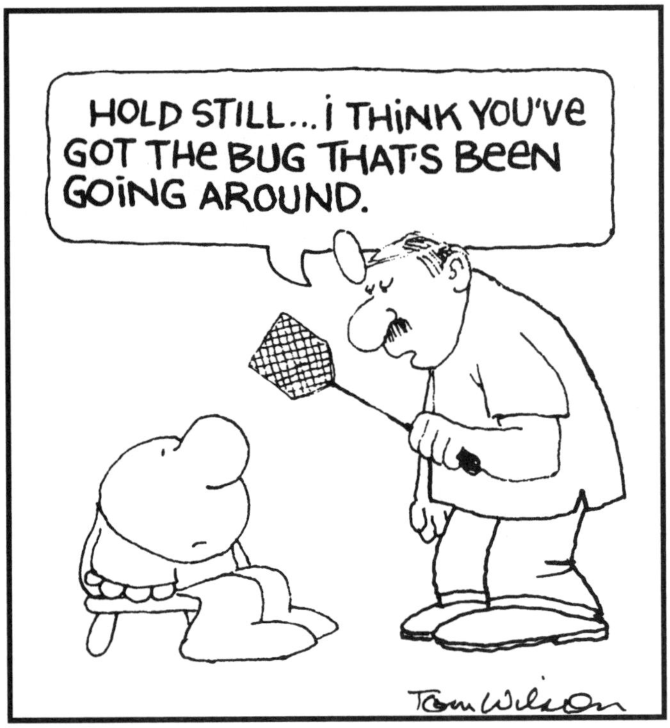
HOLD STILL... I THINK YOU'VE GOT THE BUG THAT'S BEEN GOING AROUND.
Tom Wilson

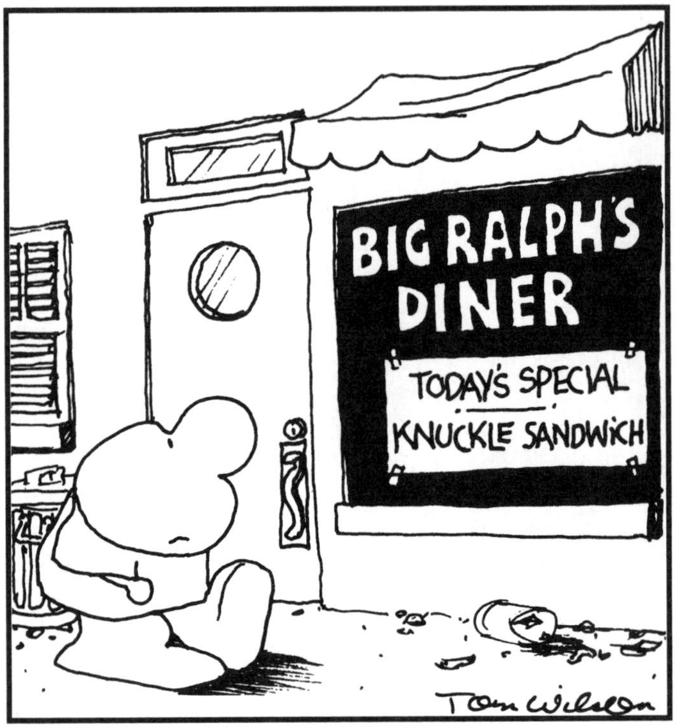
BIG RALPH'S DINER
TODAY'S SPECIAL
KNUCKLE SANDWICH
Tom Wilson

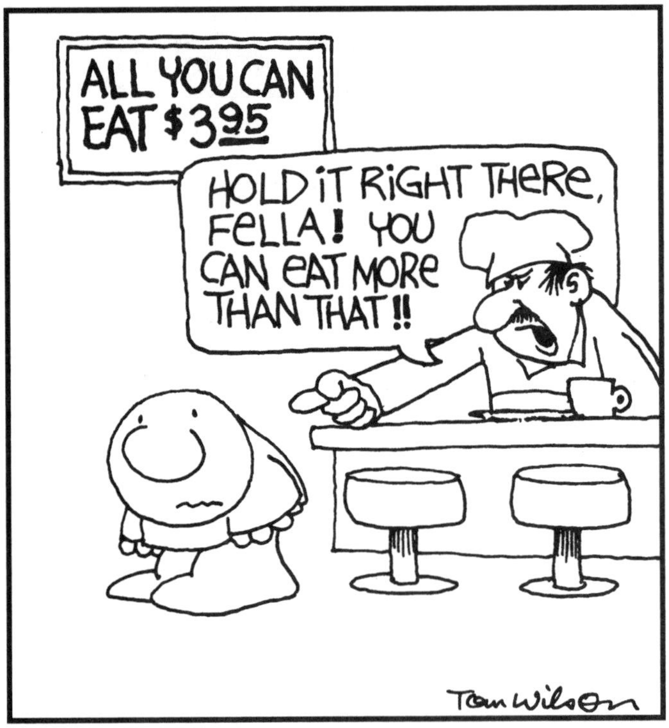
ALL YOU CAN EAT $3.95
HOLD IT RIGHT THERE, FELLA! YOU CAN EAT MORE THAN THAT!!
Tom Wilson

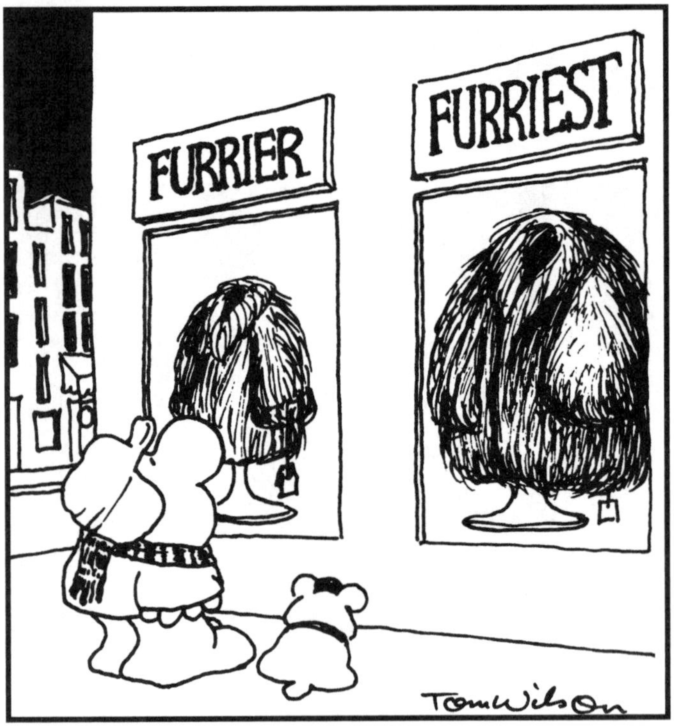
FURRIER
FURRIEST
Tom Wilson

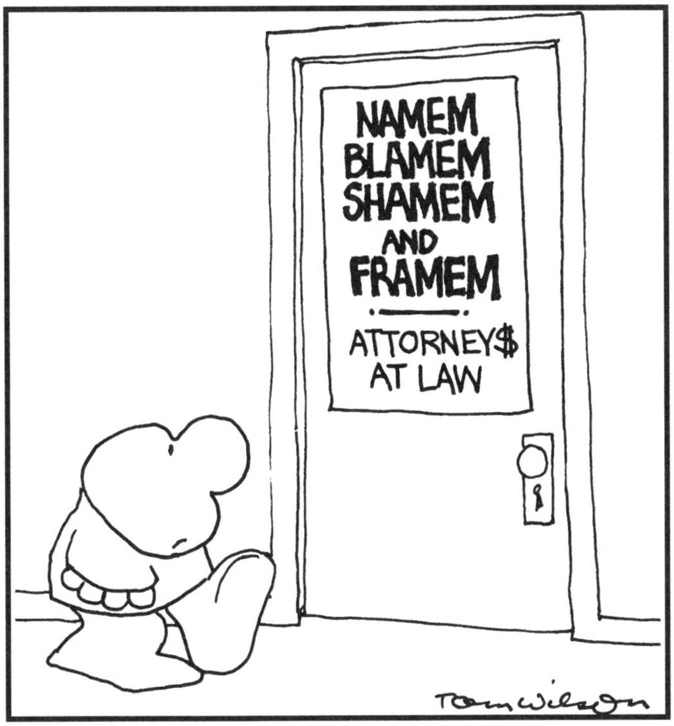
NAMEM BLAMEM SHAMEM AND FRAMEM
ATTORNEY$ AT LAW

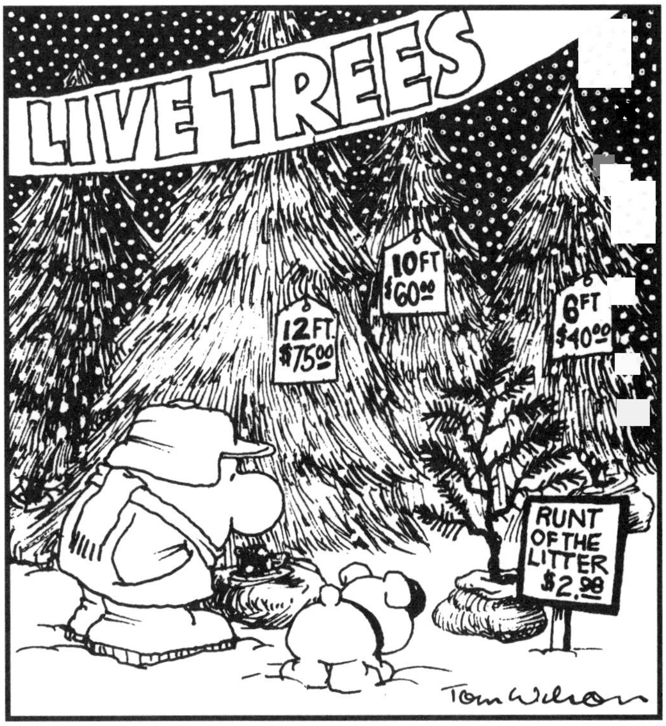
LIVE TREES
12 FT. $75.00
10 FT $60.00
6 FT $40.00
RUNT OF THE LITTER $2.98

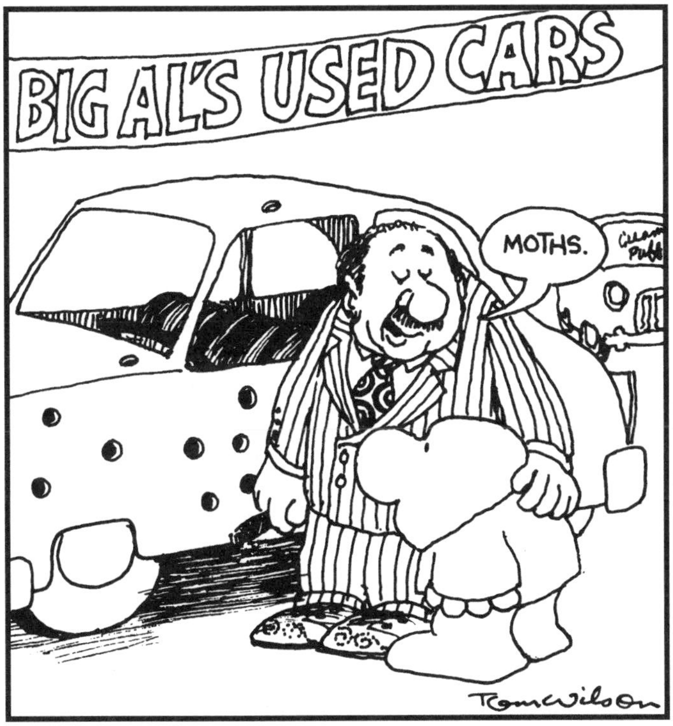
BIG AL'S USED CARS
MOTHS.

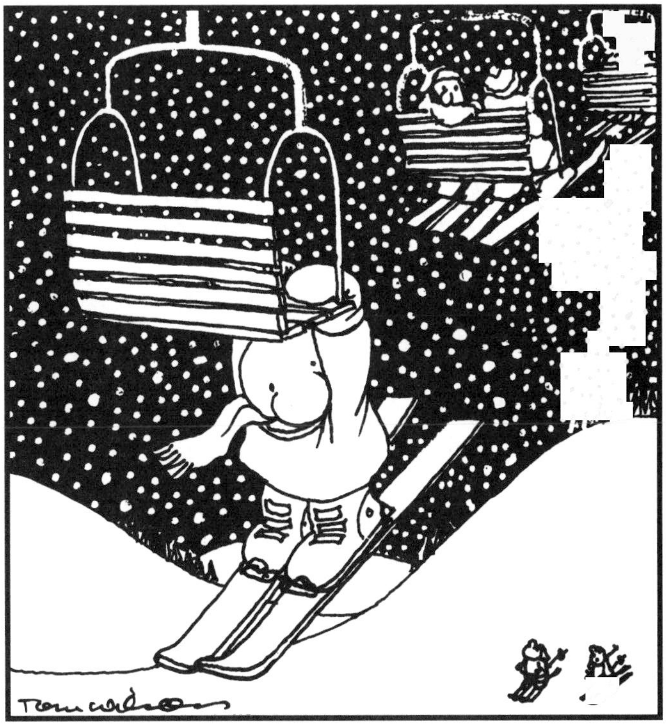

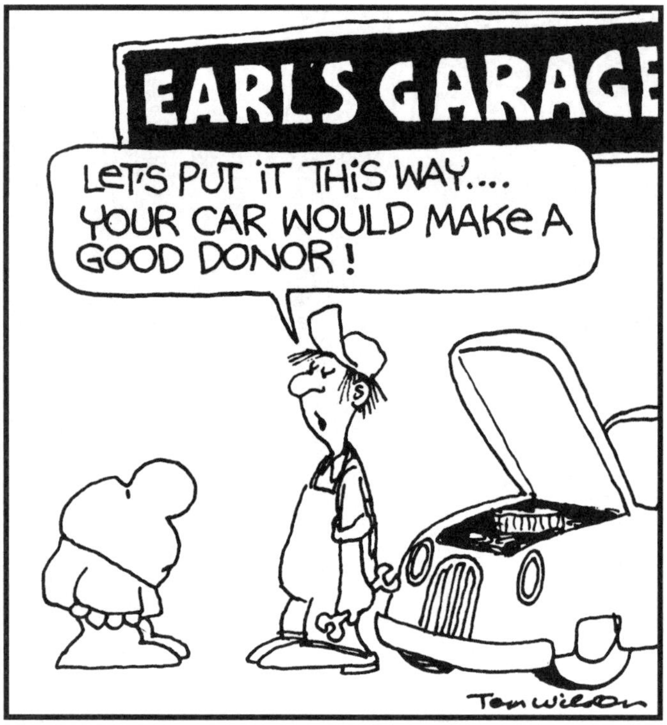
EARL'S GARAGE
LET'S PUT IT THIS WAY.... YOUR CAR WOULD MAKE A GOOD DONOR!
Tom Wilson

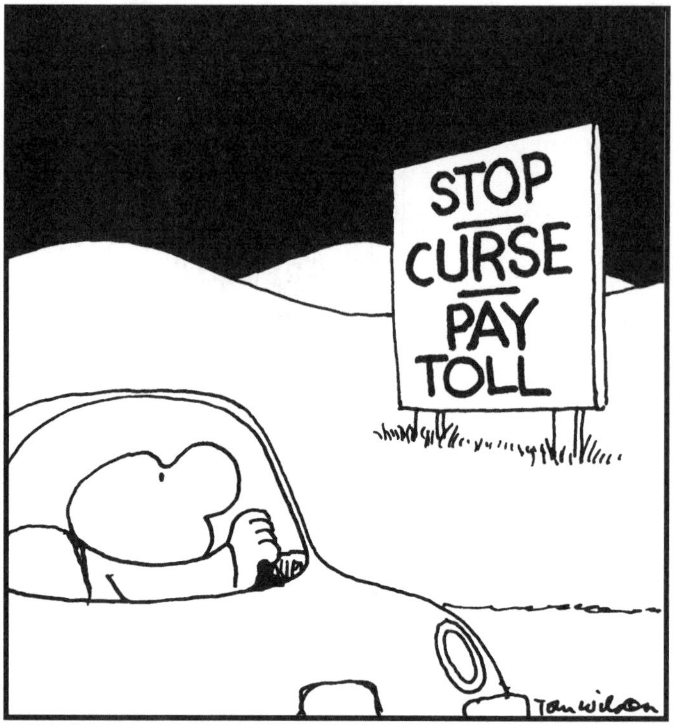
STOP
CURSE
PAY TOLL
Tom Wilson

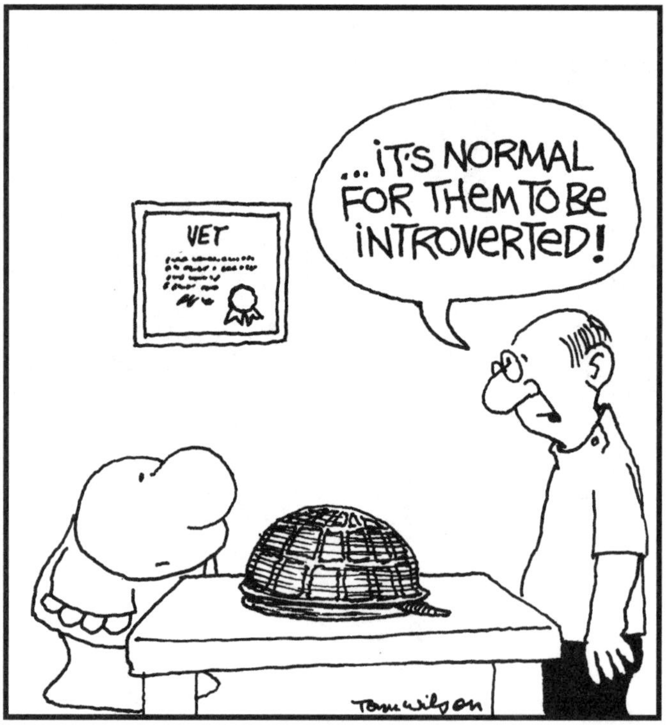
VET
...IT'S NORMAL FOR THEM TO BE INTROVERTED!
Tom Wilson

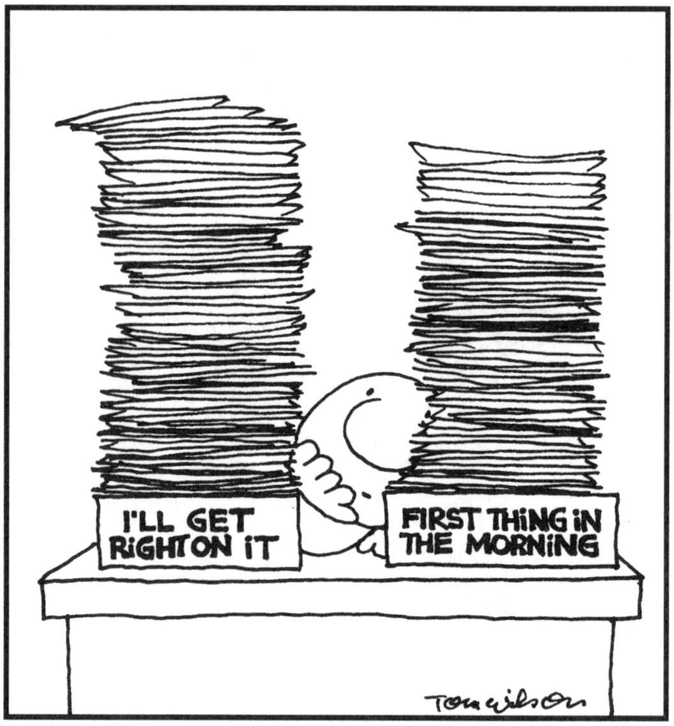
I'LL GET RIGHT ON IT
FIRST THING IN THE MORNING
Tom Wilson

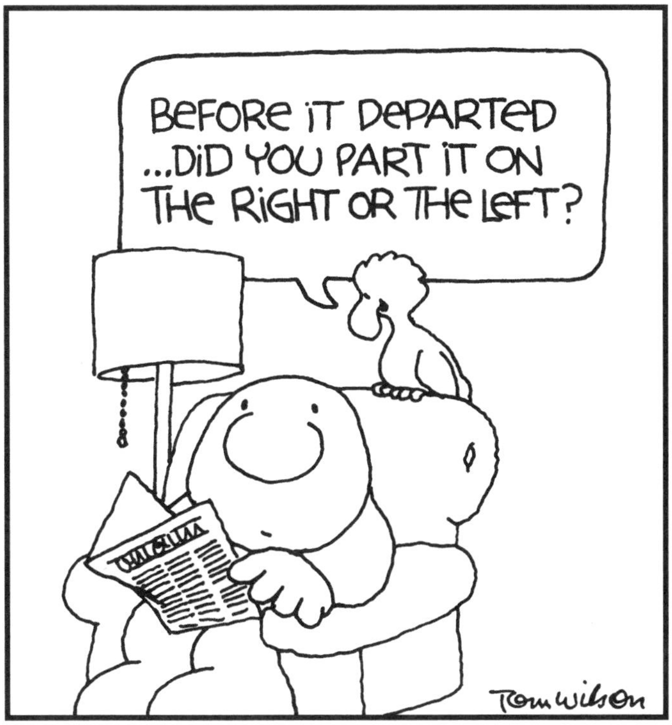
BEFORE IT DEPARTED ...DID YOU PART IT ON THE RIGHT OR THE LEFT?
Tom Wilson

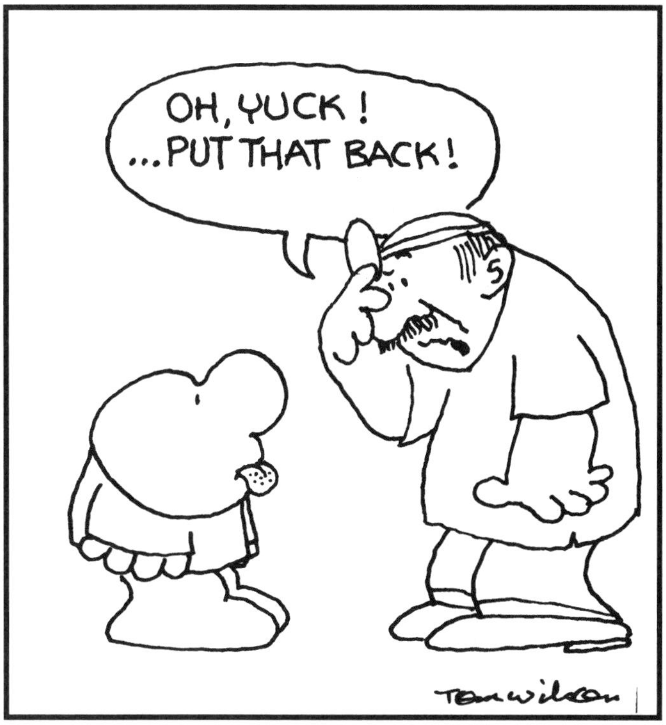
OH, YUCK! ...PUT THAT BACK!
Tom Wilson

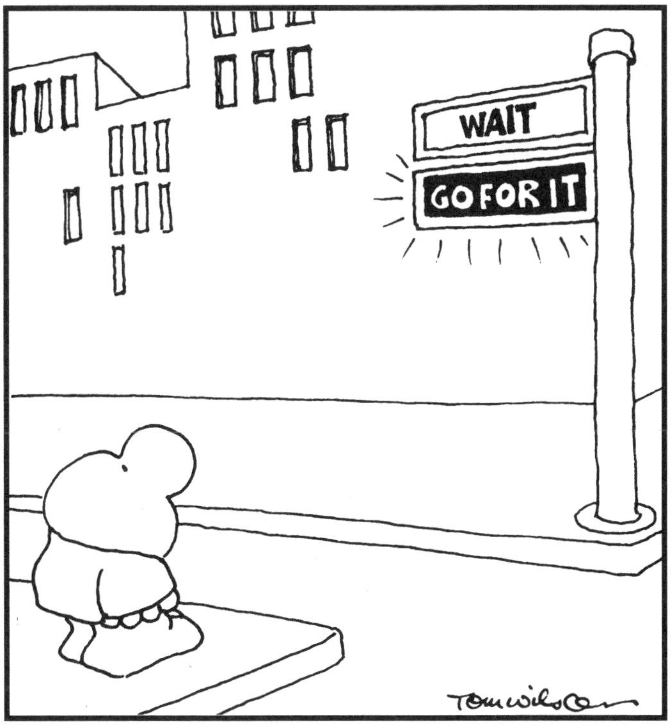
WAIT
GO FOR IT
Tom Wilson

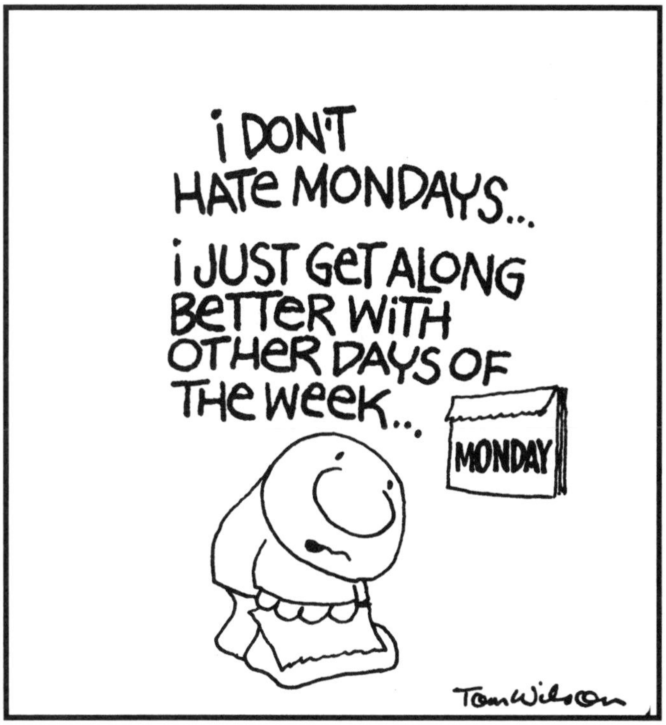
I DON'T HATE MONDAYS... I JUST GET ALONG BETTER WITH OTHER DAYS OF THE WEEK...
MONDAY
Tom Wilson

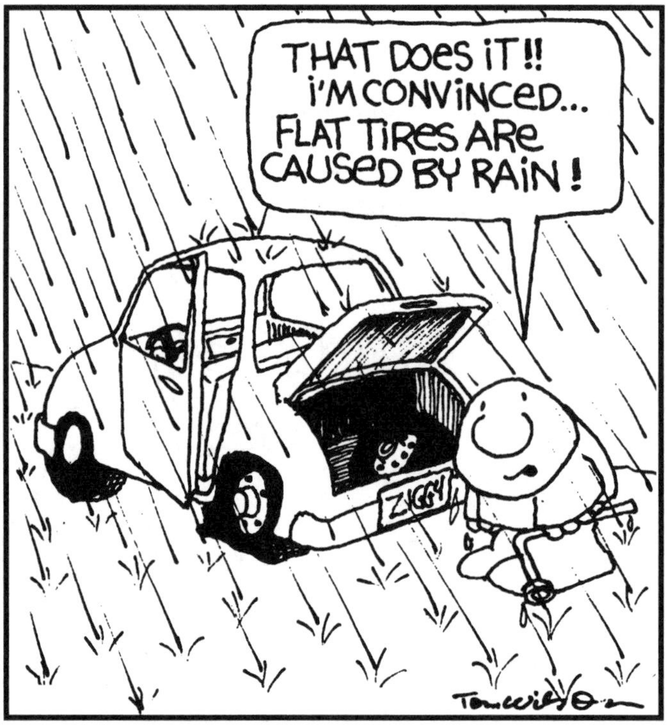
THAT DOES iT!! i'M CONVINCED... FLAT TIRES ARE CAUSED BY RAIN!
ZIGGY
Tom Wilson

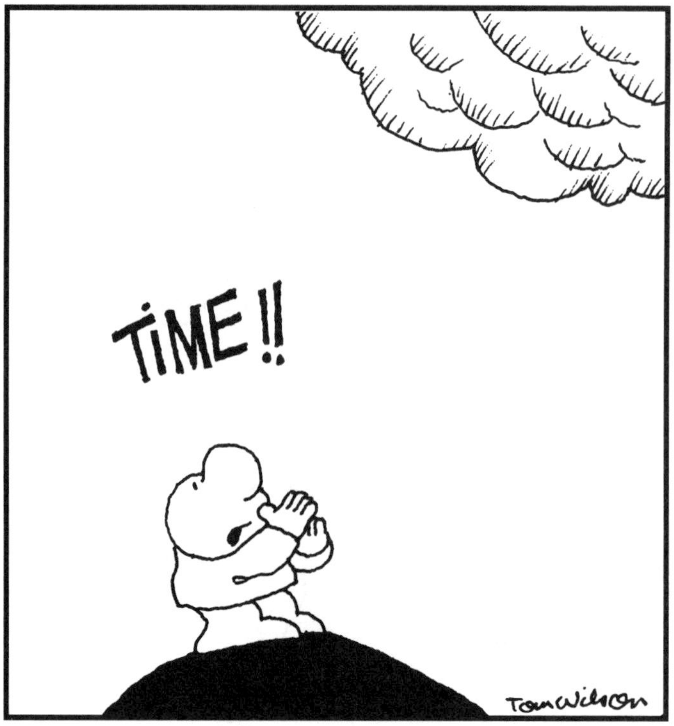
TiME!!
Tom Wilson

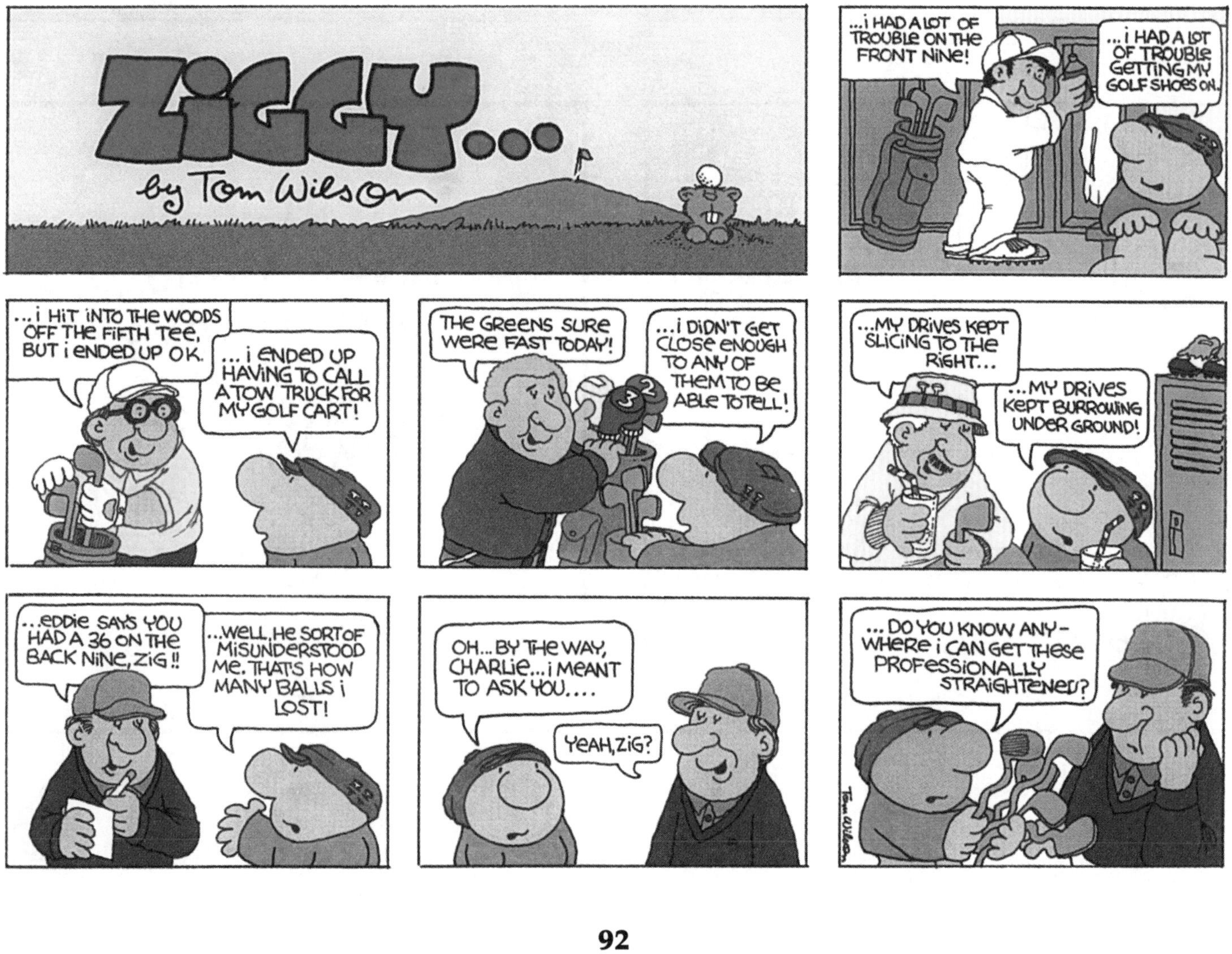
ZiGGY...
by Tom Wilson
...i HAD A LOT OF TROUBLE ON THE FRONT NiNE!
...i HAD A LOT OF TROUBLE GETTING MY GOLF SHOES ON.
...i HiT iNTO THE WOODS OFF THE FiFTH TEE, BUT i ENDED UP O.K.
...i ENDED UP HAVING TO CALL A TOW TRUCK FOR MY GOLF CART!
THE GREENS SURE WERE FAST TODAY!
...i DIDN'T GET CLOSE ENOUGH TO ANY OF THEM TO BE ABLE TO TELL!
...MY DRiVES KEPT SLiCiNG TO THE RiGHT...
...MY DRiVES KEPT BURROWiNG UNDER GROUND!
...EDDiE SAYS YOU HAD A 36 ON THE BACK NiNE, ZiG!!
...WELL, HE SORT OF MiSUNDERSTOOD ME. THAT'S HOW MANY BALLS i LOST!
OH... BY THE WAY, CHARLiE...i MEANT TO ASK YOU....
YEAH, ZiG?
... DO YOU KNOW ANY-WHERE i CAN GET THESE PROFESSIONALLY STRAiGHTENED?
Tom Wilson

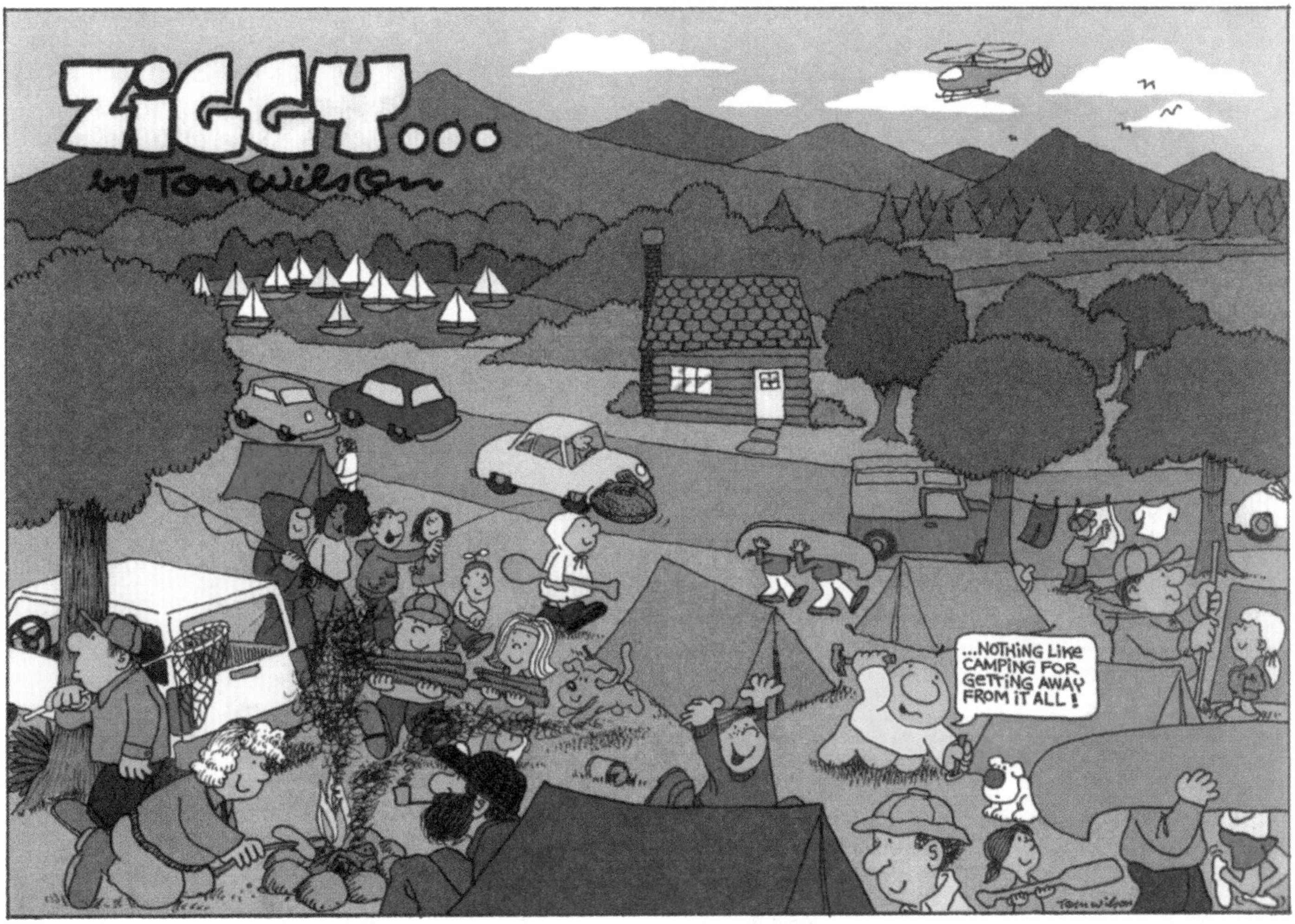
ZIGGY...
by Tom Wilson
...NOTHING LIKE CAMPING FOR GETTING AWAY FROM IT ALL!
Tom Wilson

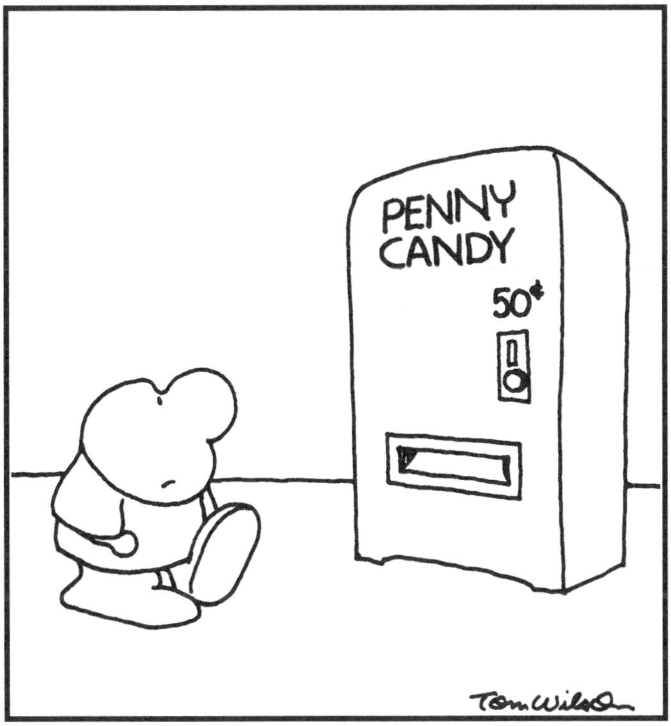
PENNY CANDY
50¢
Tom Wilson

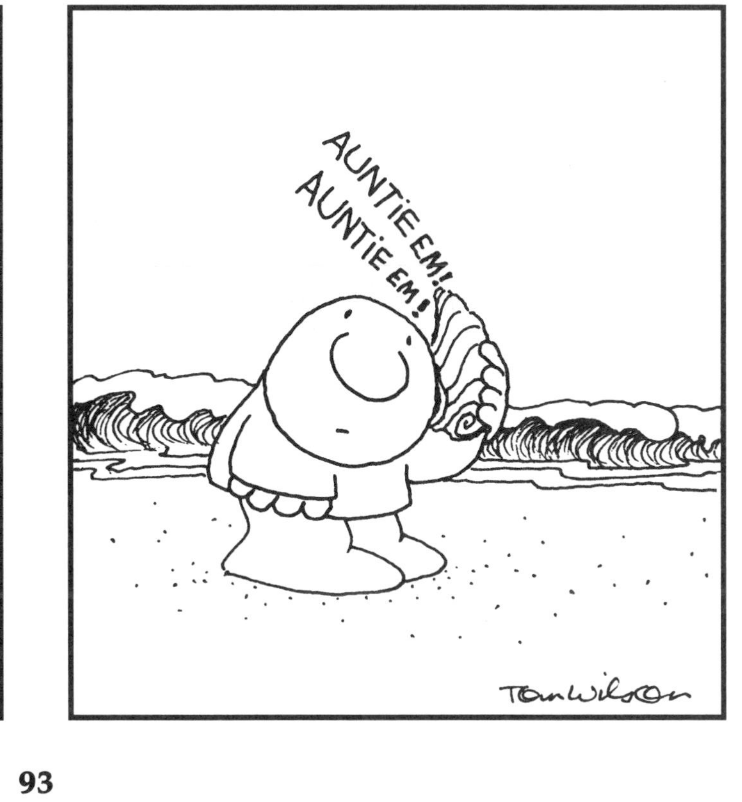
AUNTIE EM!
AUNTIE EM!
Tom Wilson

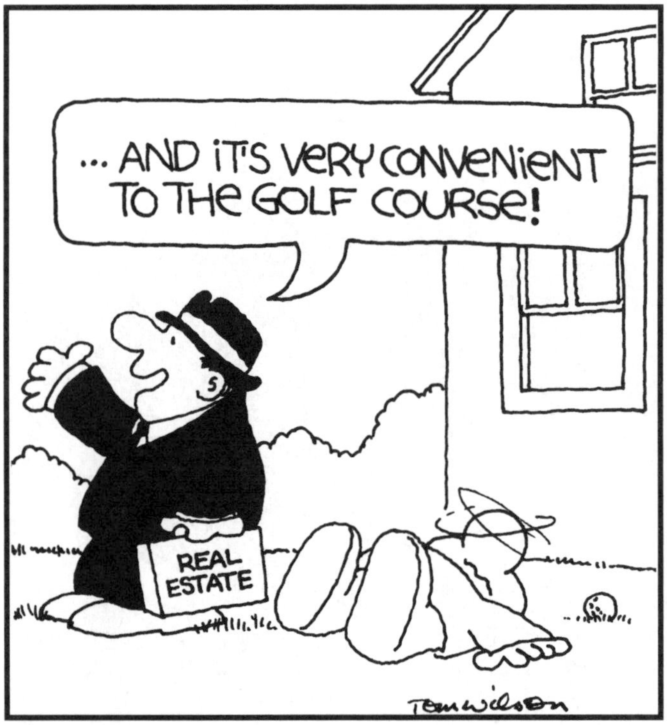
... AND IT'S VERY CONVENIENT TO THE GOLF COURSE!
REAL ESTATE
TOM WILSON

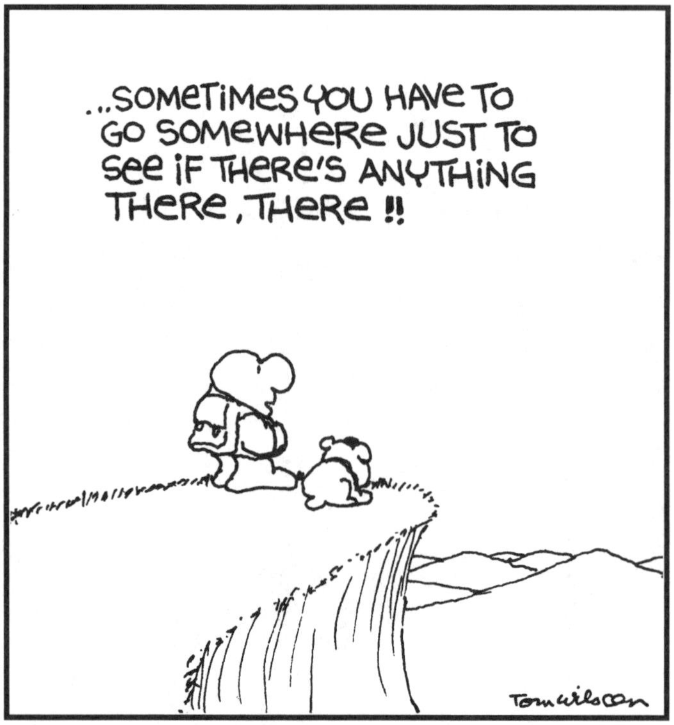
...SOMETIMES YOU HAVE TO GO SOMEWHERE JUST TO SEE IF THERE'S ANYTHING THERE, THERE !!
TOM WILSON

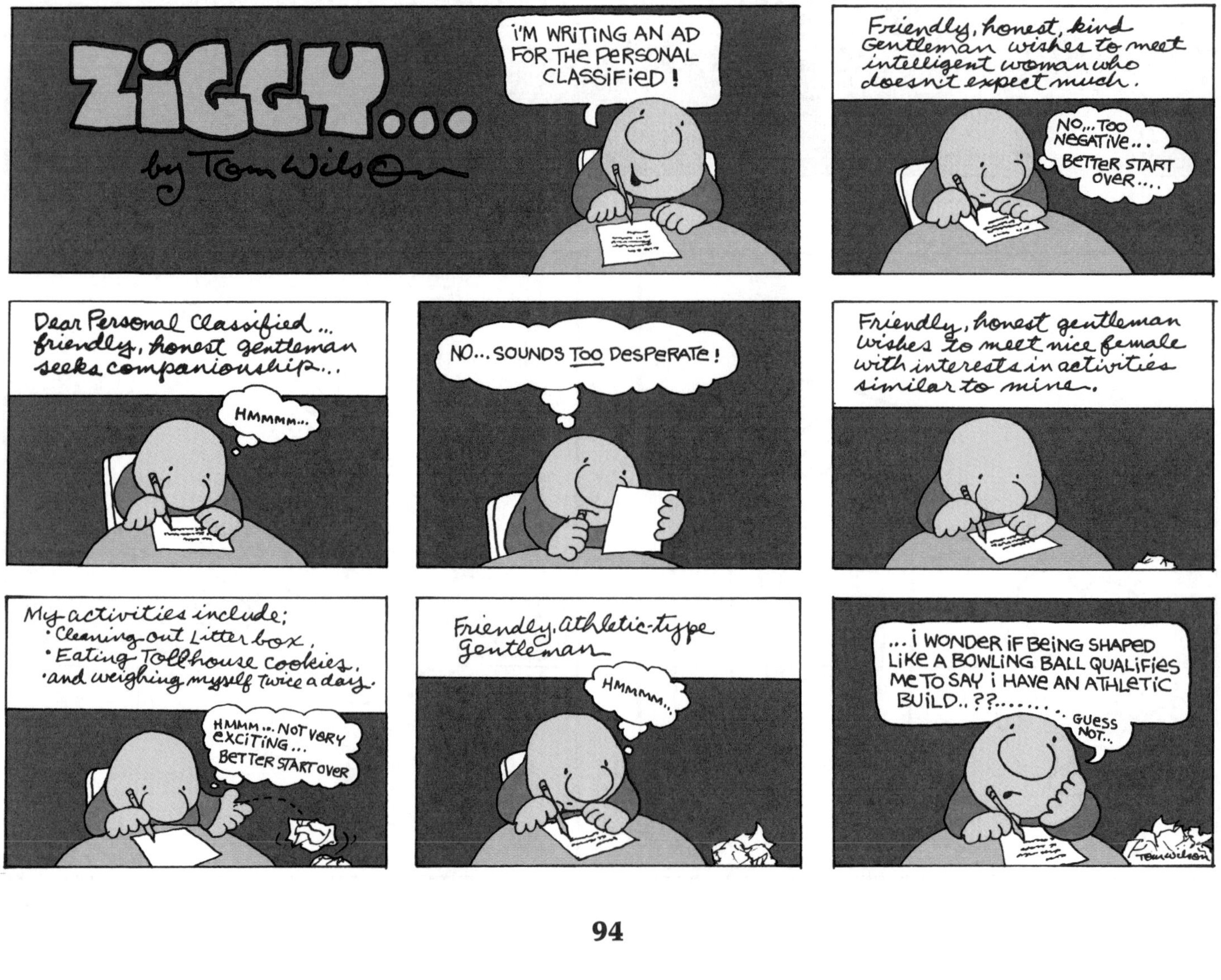
ZIGGY...
by Tom Wilson
I'M WRITING AN AD FOR THE PERSONAL CLASSIFIED!
Friendly, honest, kind Gentleman wishes to meet intelligent woman who doesn't expect much.
NO... TOO NEGATIVE... BETTER START OVER....
Dear Personal Classified... friendly, honest gentleman seeks companionship...
HMMMM...
NO... SOUNDS TOO DESPERATE!
Friendly, honest gentleman wishes to meet nice female with interests in activities similar to mine.
My activities include: • Cleaning out Litter box, • Eating Tollhouse cookies, • and weighing myself twice a day.
HMMM... NOT VERY EXCITING... BETTER START OVER
Friendly, athletic-type Gentleman
HMMMM...
... I WONDER IF BEING SHAPED LIKE A BOWLING BALL QUALIFIES ME TO SAY I HAVE AN ATHLETIC BUILD..??......... GUESS NOT...

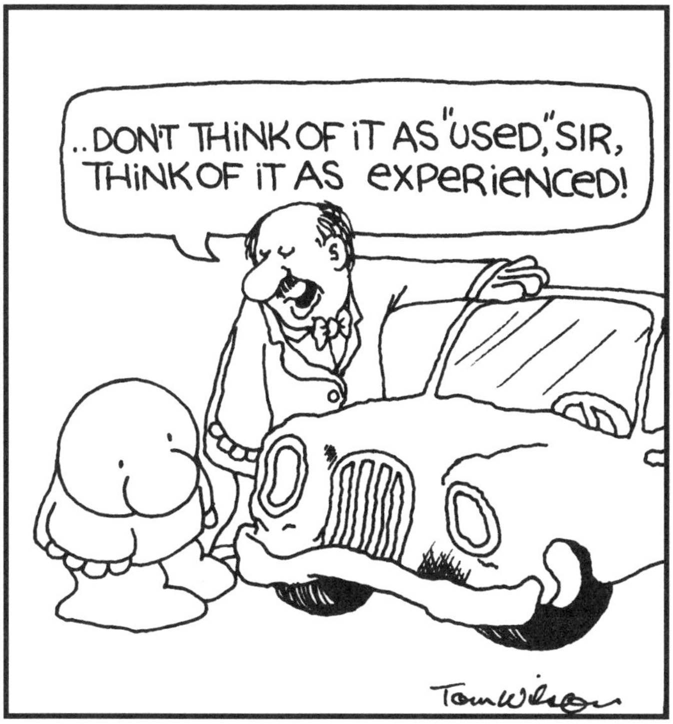
..DON'T THINK OF IT AS "USED," SIR, THINK OF IT AS EXPERIENCED!
TomWilson

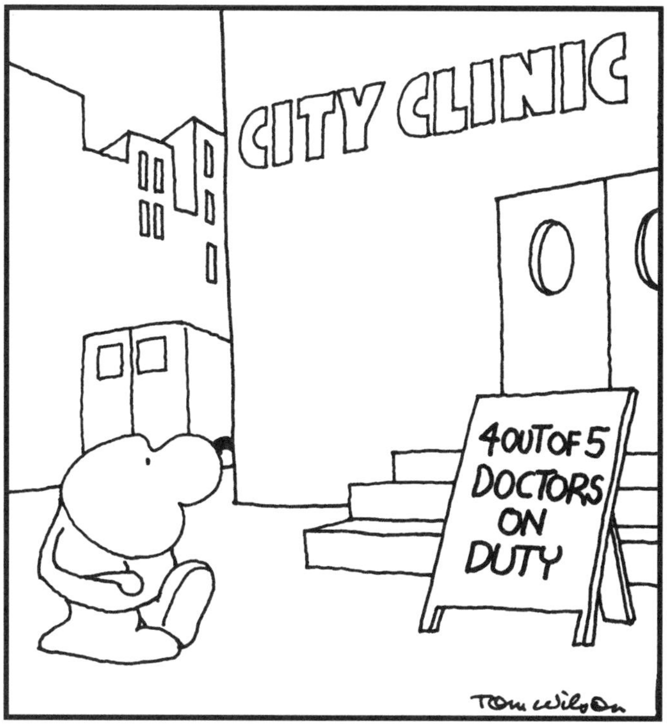
CITY CLINIC
4 OUT OF 5 DOCTORS ON DUTY
TomWilson

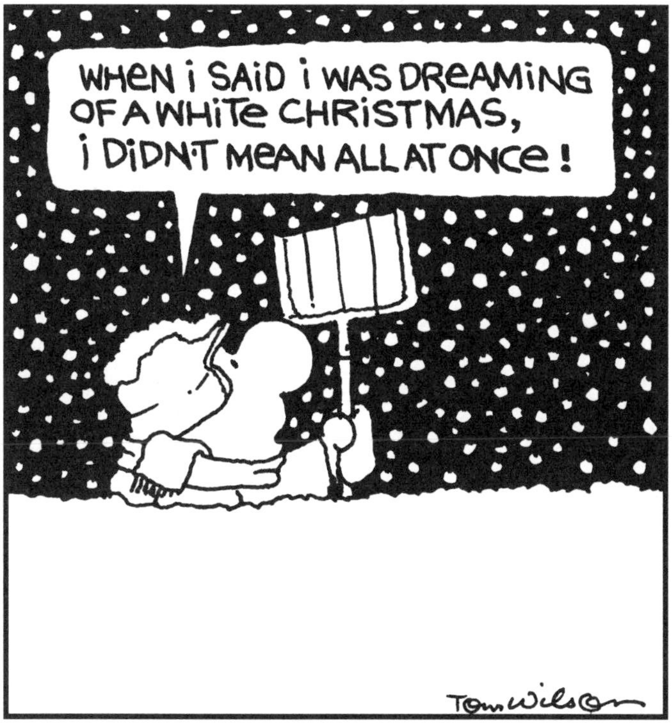
WHEN I SAID I WAS DREAMING OF A WHITE CHRISTMAS, I DIDN'T MEAN ALL AT ONCE!
TomWilson

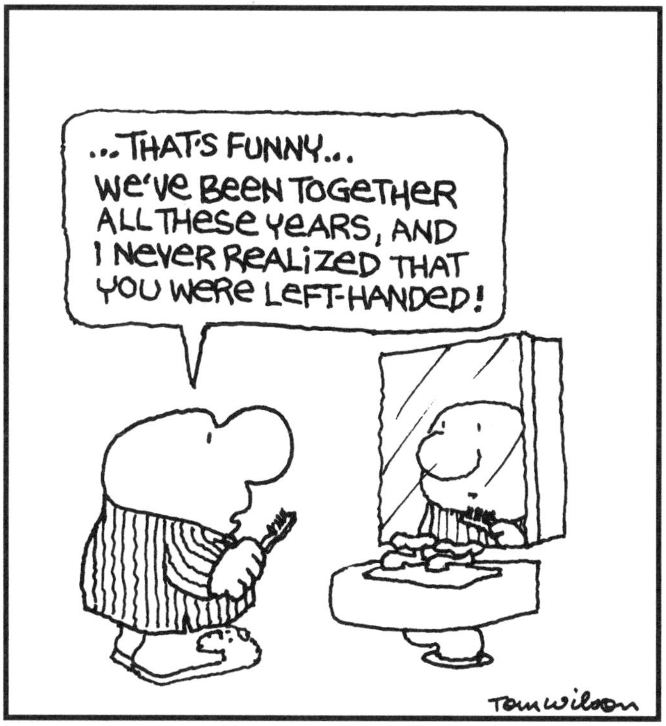
...THAT'S FUNNY... WE'VE BEEN TOGETHER ALL THESE YEARS, AND I NEVER REALIZED THAT YOU WERE LEFT-HANDED!
TomWilson

Chapter IV
1986–1990

When I first started at Universal Press in 1989, I was thrilled to be editing *Ziggy*—a cartoon panel that was featured in hundreds of newspapers and had products all over the world! Nearly seventeen years later, it is still my pleasure to work with Tom Wilson on the world's favorite "everyman." We take great pride in being the syndicate that offers *Ziggy*, and I take personal pride in being *Ziggy*'s editor. Congratulations, Tom, Tom II, and Ziggy!
—Lisa Tarry, associate editor, Universal Press Syndicate

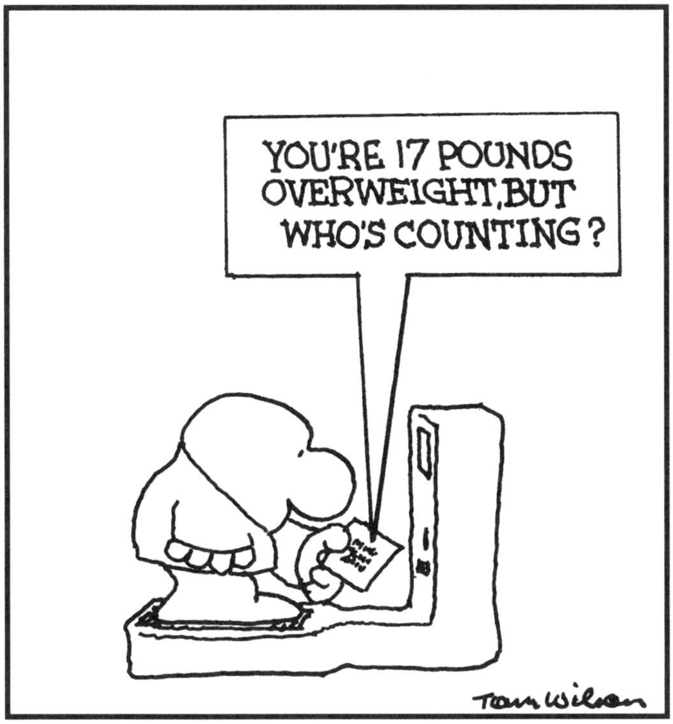
YOU'RE 17 POUNDS OVERWEIGHT, BUT WHO'S COUNTING?

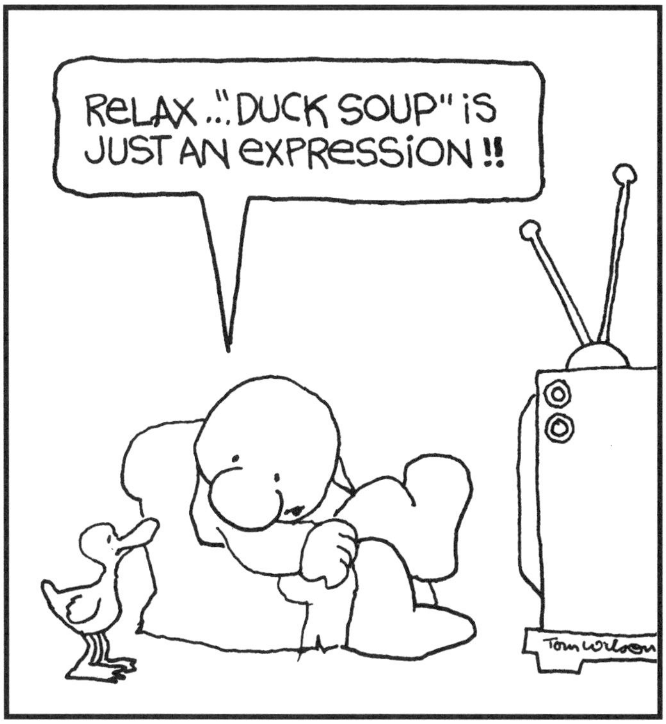
RELAX ... "DUCK SOUP" IS JUST AN EXPRESSION !!

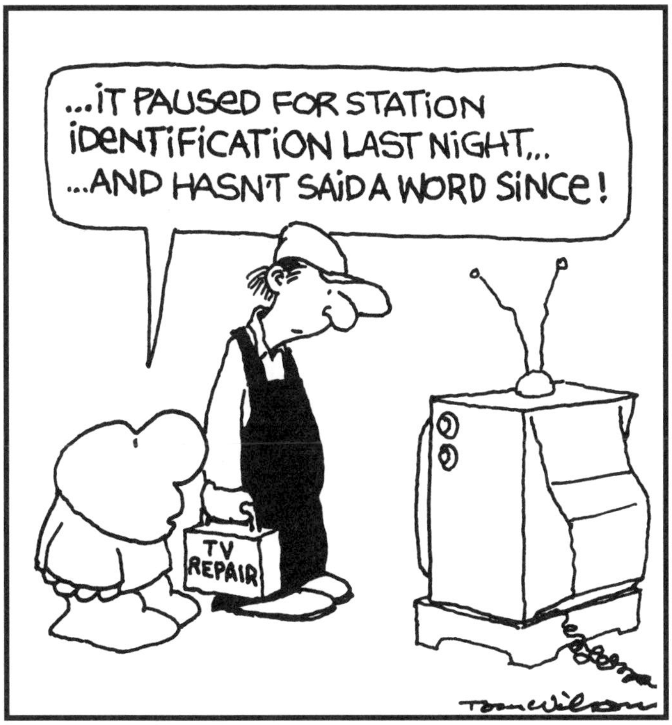
...IT PAUSED FOR STATION IDENTIFICATION LAST NIGHT,... ...AND HASN'T SAID A WORD SINCE!
TV REPAIR

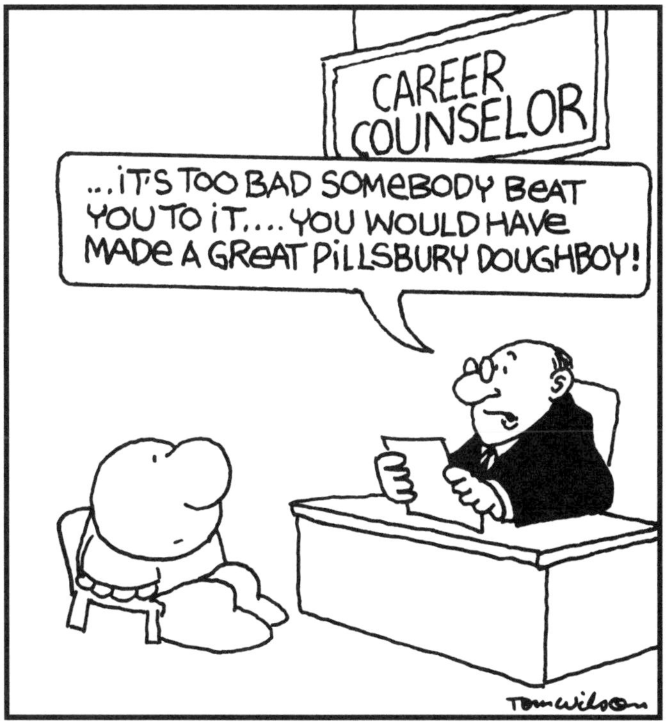
CAREER COUNSELOR
...IT'S TOO BAD SOMEBODY BEAT YOU TO IT.... YOU WOULD HAVE MADE A GREAT PILLSBURY DOUGHBOY!

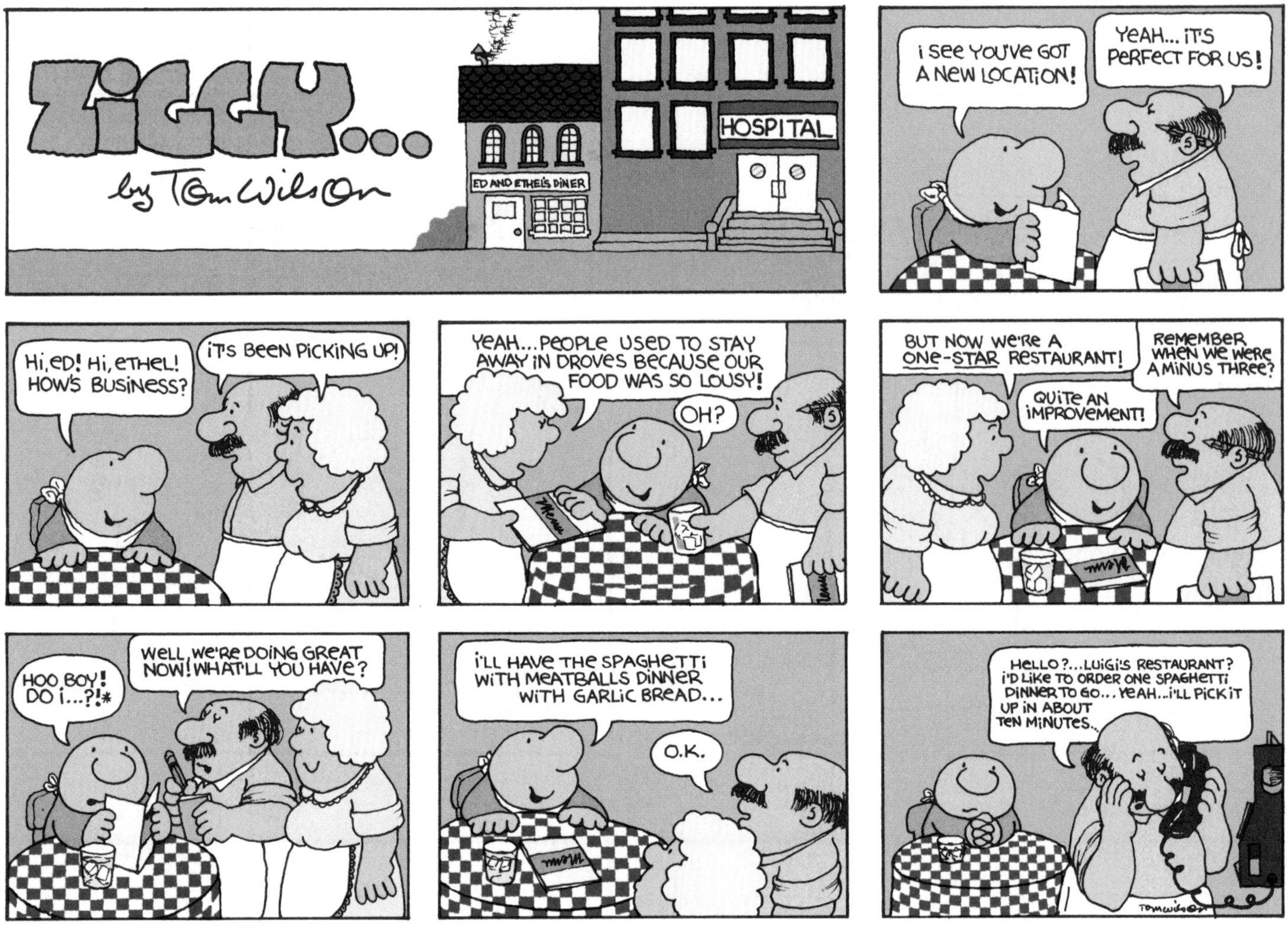
ZIGGY...
by Tom Wilson
ED AND ETHEL'S DINER
HOSPITAL
I SEE YOU'VE GOT A NEW LOCATION!
YEAH... IT'S PERFECT FOR US!
HI, ED! HI, ETHEL! HOW'S BUSINESS?
IT'S BEEN PICKING UP!
YEAH...PEOPLE USED TO STAY AWAY IN DROVES BECAUSE OUR FOOD WAS SO LOUSY!
OH?
BUT NOW WE'RE A ONE-STAR RESTAURANT!
REMEMBER WHEN WE WERE A MINUS THREE?
QUITE AN IMPROVEMENT!
HOO BOY! DO I...?!*
WELL, WE'RE DOING GREAT NOW! WHAT'LL YOU HAVE?
I'LL HAVE THE SPAGHETTI WITH MEATBALLS DINNER WITH GARLIC BREAD...
O.K.
HELLO?...LUIGI'S RESTAURANT? I'D LIKE TO ORDER ONE SPAGHETTI DINNER TO GO... YEAH...I'LL PICK IT UP IN ABOUT TEN MINUTES..
Tom Wilson

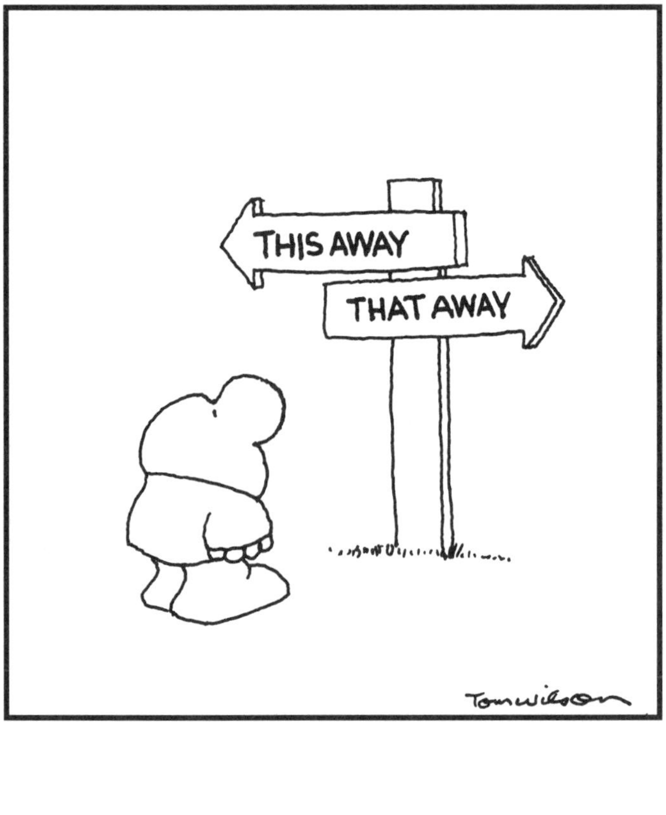
THIS AWAY
THAT AWAY
Tom Wilson

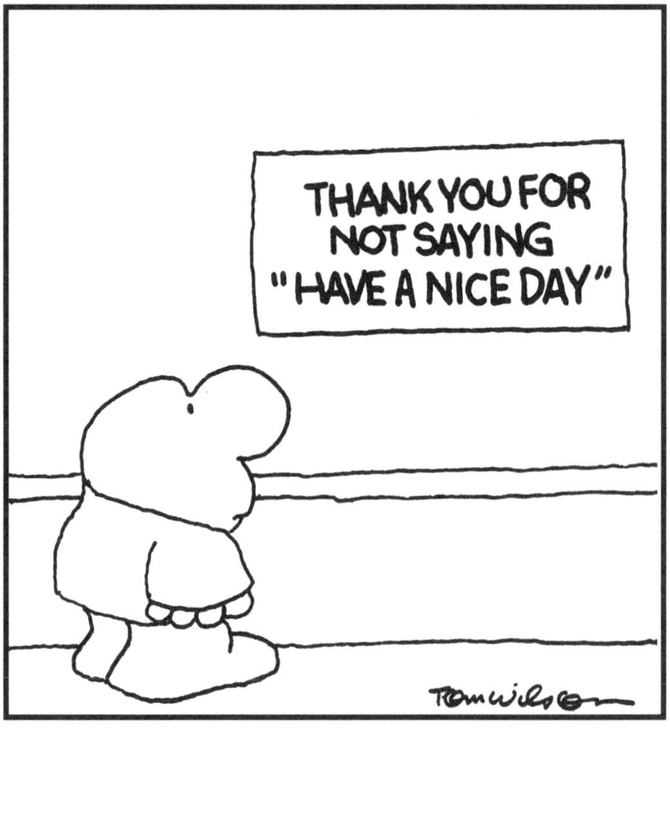
THANK YOU FOR NOT SAYING "HAVE A NICE DAY"
Tom Wilson

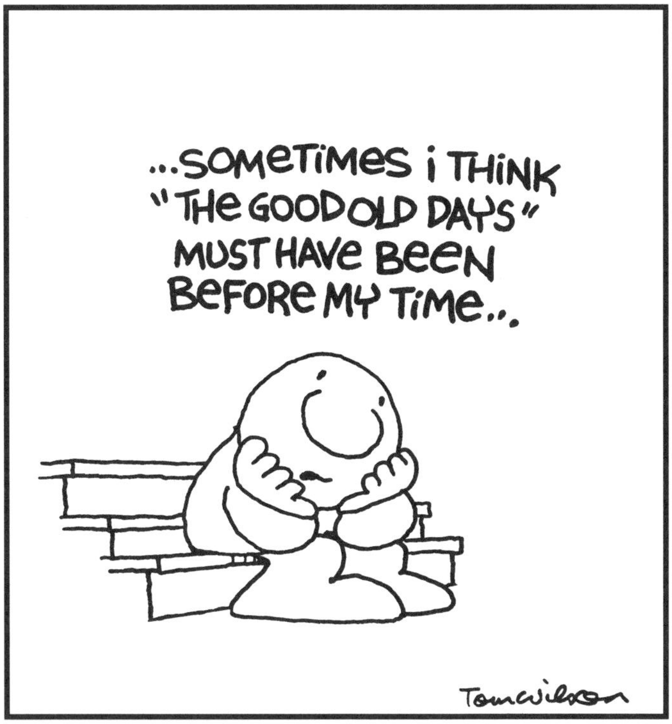
...SOMETIMES I THINK "THE GOOD OLD DAYS" MUST HAVE BEEN BEFORE MY TIME...

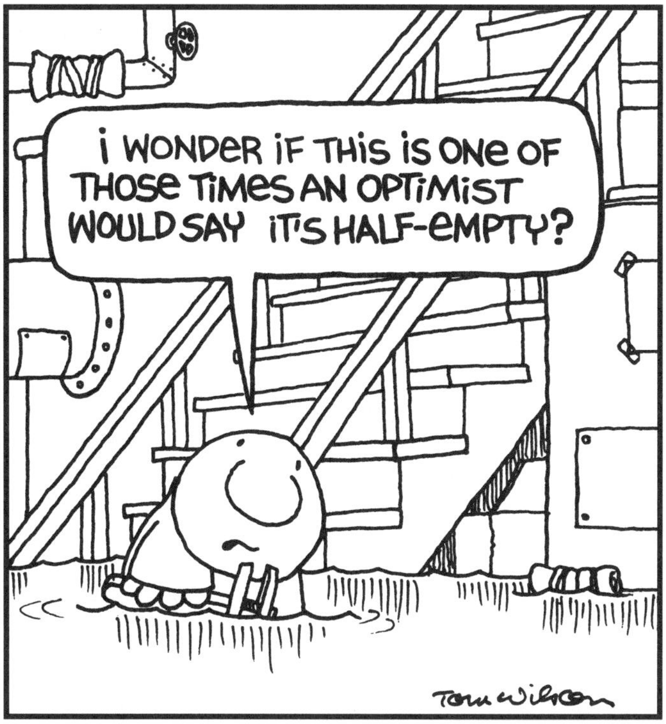
I WONDER IF THIS IS ONE OF THOSE TIMES AN OPTIMIST WOULD SAY IT'S HALF-EMPTY?

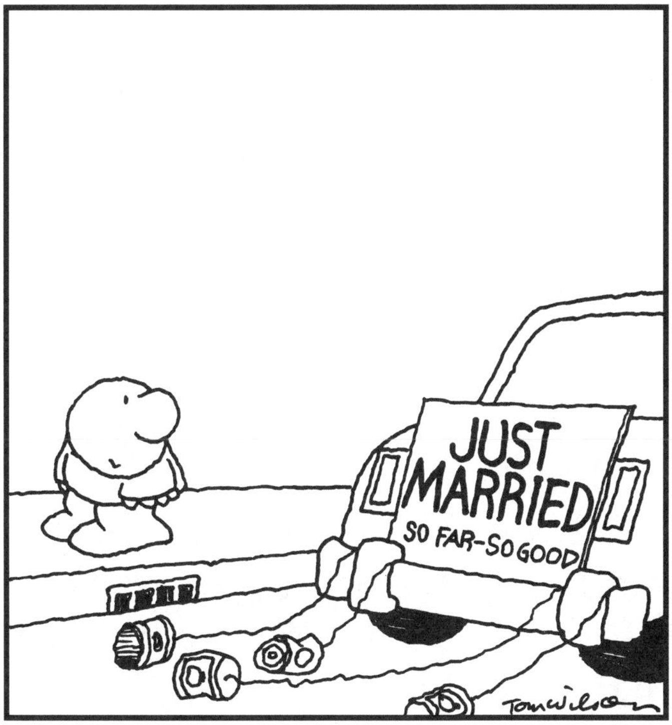
JUST MARRIED
SO FAR-SO GOOD

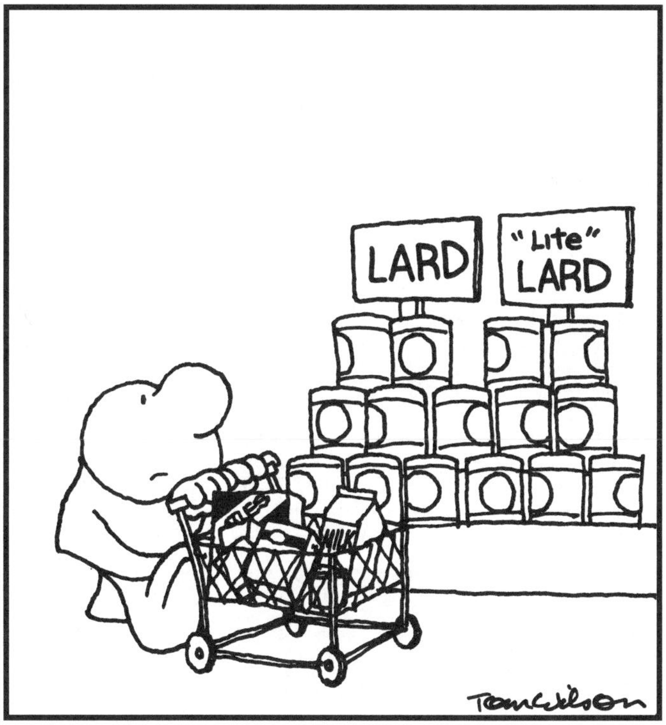
LARD
"Lite" LARD

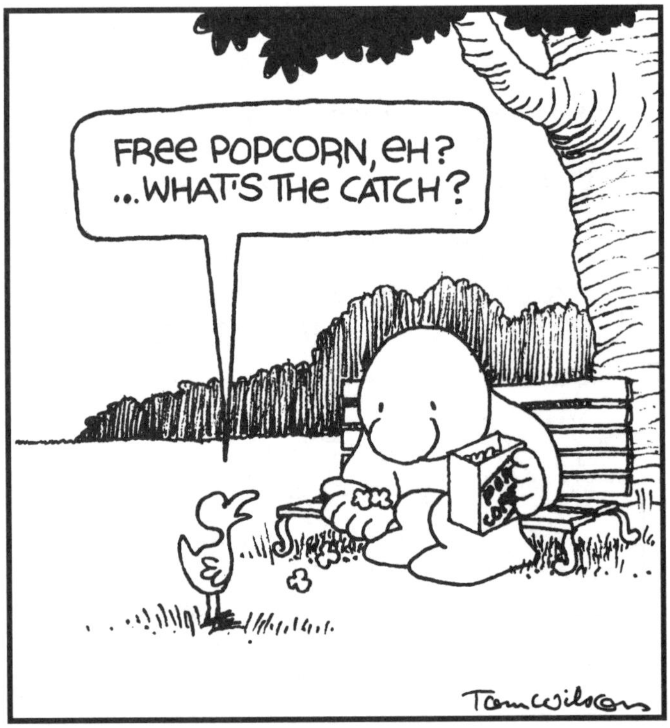
FREE POPCORN, EH?
...WHAT'S THE CATCH?

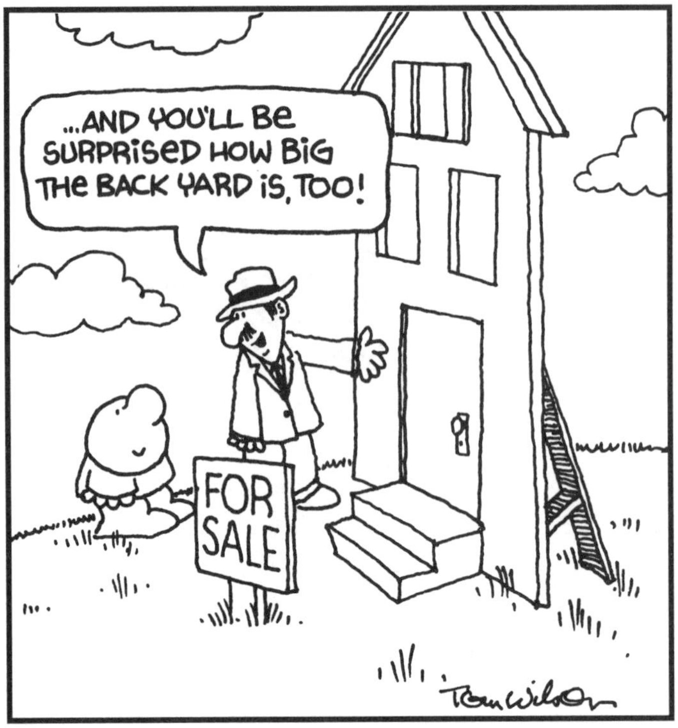
...AND YOU'LL BE SURPRISED HOW BIG THE BACK YARD IS, TOO!
FOR SALE

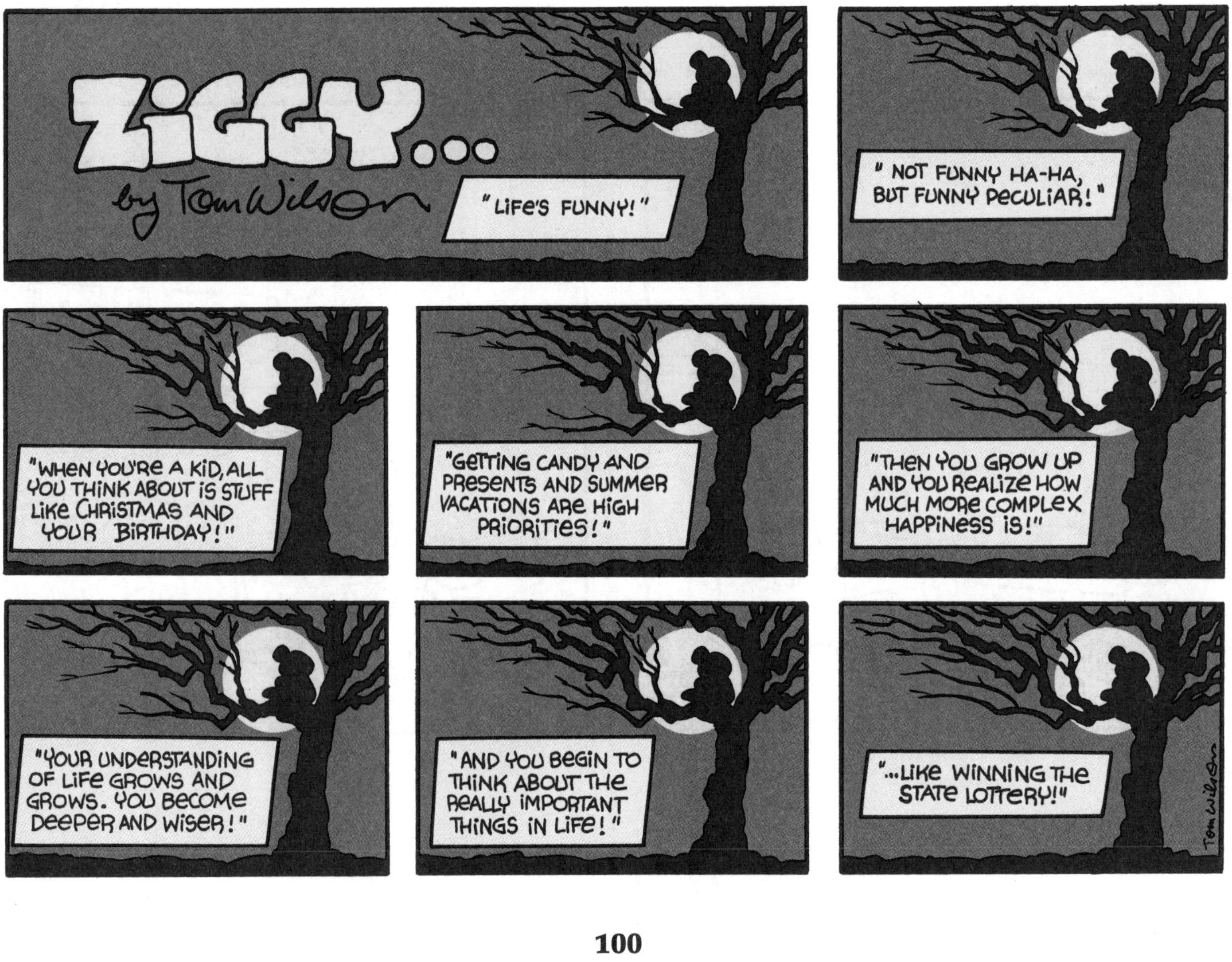
ZIGGY...
by Tom Wilson
"LIFE'S FUNNY!"
" NOT FUNNY HA-HA, BUT FUNNY PECULIAR!"
"WHEN YOU'RE A KID, ALL YOU THINK ABOUT IS STUFF LIKE CHRISTMAS AND YOUR BIRTHDAY!"
"GETTING CANDY AND PRESENTS AND SUMMER VACATIONS ARE HIGH PRIORITIES!"
"THEN YOU GROW UP AND YOU REALIZE HOW MUCH MORE COMPLEX HAPPINESS IS!"
"YOUR UNDERSTANDING OF LIFE GROWS AND GROWS. YOU BECOME DEEPER AND WISER!"
"AND YOU BEGIN TO THINK ABOUT THE REALLY IMPORTANT THINGS IN LIFE!"
"...LIKE WINNING THE STATE LOTTERY!"

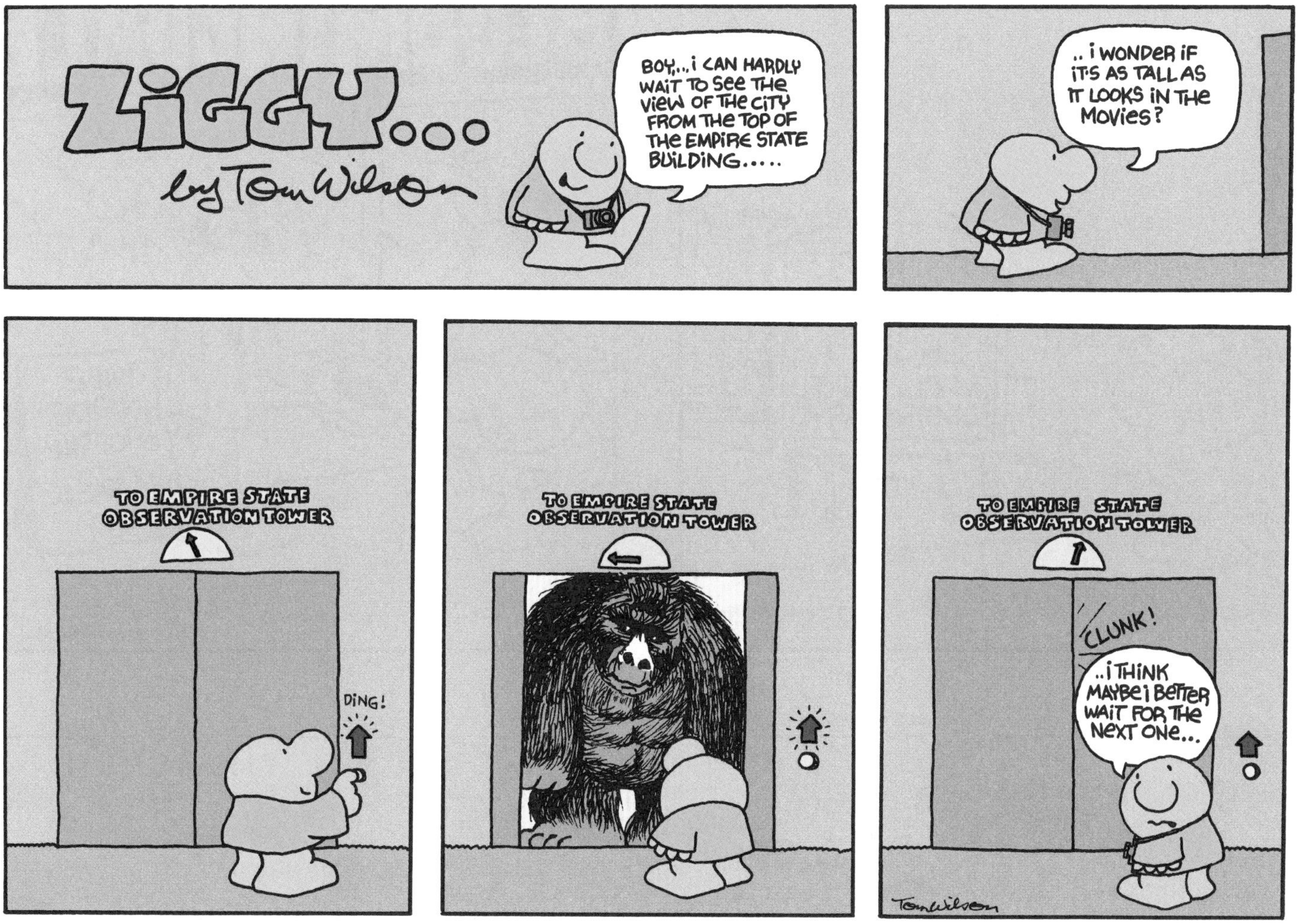
ZiGGY...
by Tom Wilson
BOY,...i CAN HARDLY WAIT TO SEE THE VIEW OF THE CITY FROM THE TOP OF THE EMPIRE STATE BUILDING.....
.. i WONDER iF IT'S AS TALL AS IT LOOKS IN THE MOVIES?
TO EMPIRE STATE OBSERVATION TOWER
DING!
TO EMPIRE STATE OBSERVATION TOWER
TO EMPIRE STATE OBSERVATION TOWER
CLUNK!
..i THINK MAYBE i BETTER WAIT FOR THE NEXT ONE...
Tom Wilson

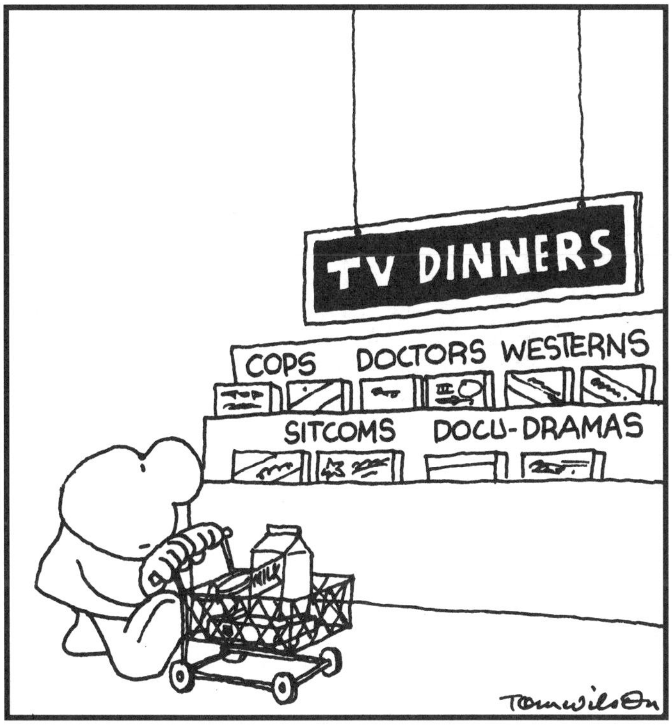
TV DINNERS
COPS
DOCTORS
WESTERNS
SITCOMS
DOCU-DRAMAS
MILK
Tom Wilson

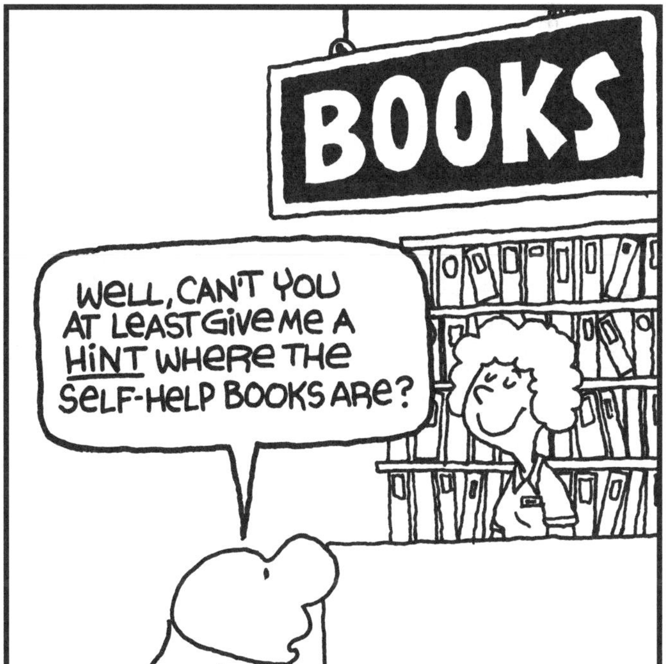
BOOKS
WELL, CAN'T YOU AT LEAST GIVE ME A HINT WHERE THE SELF-HELP BOOKS ARE?
Tom Wilson

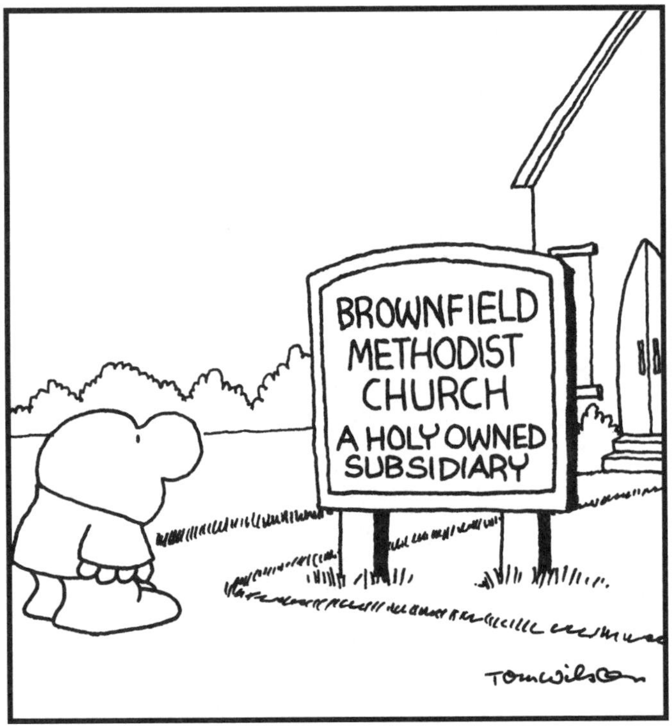
BROWNFIELD METHODIST CHURCH
A HOLY OWNED SUBSIDIARY
TOM WILSON

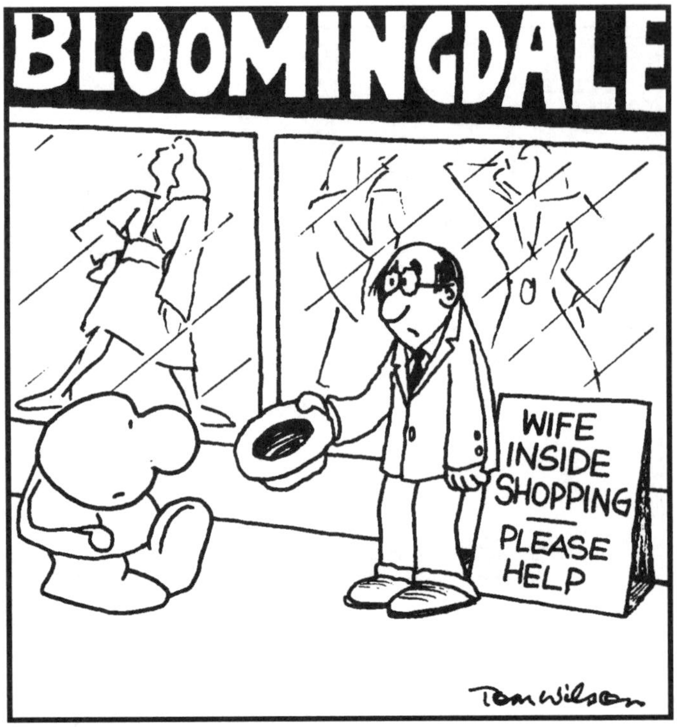
BLOOMINGDALE
WIFE INSIDE SHOPPING
PLEASE HELP
TOM WILSON

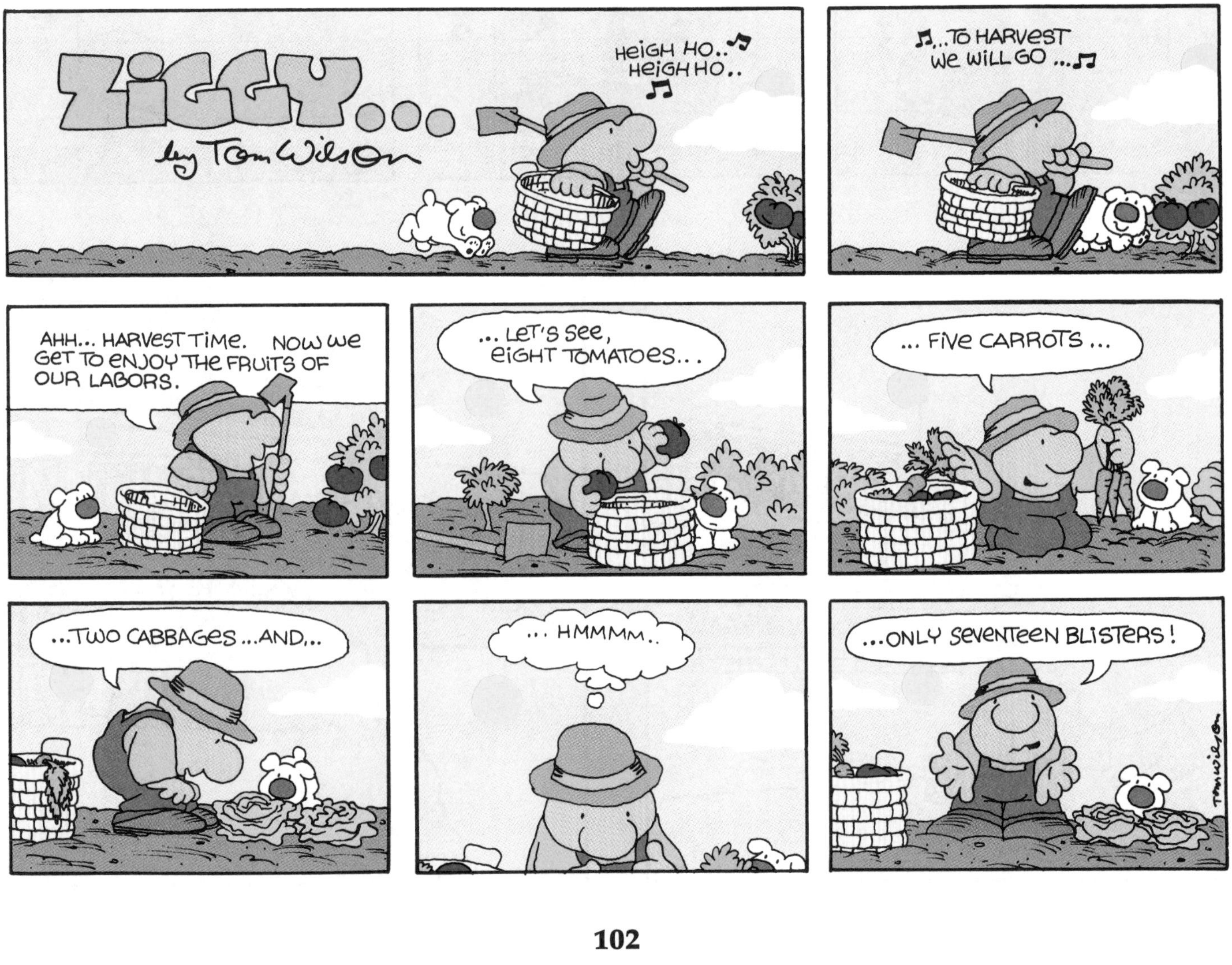
ZIGGY...
by Tom Wilson
HEIGH HO.. HEIGH HO..
...TO HARVEST WE WILL GO ...
AHH... HARVEST TIME. NOW WE GET TO ENJOY THE FRUITS OF OUR LABORS.
... LET'S SEE, EIGHT TOMATOES...
... FIVE CARROTS ...
...TWO CABBAGES ...AND,...
... HMMMM..
...ONLY SEVENTEEN BLISTERS!

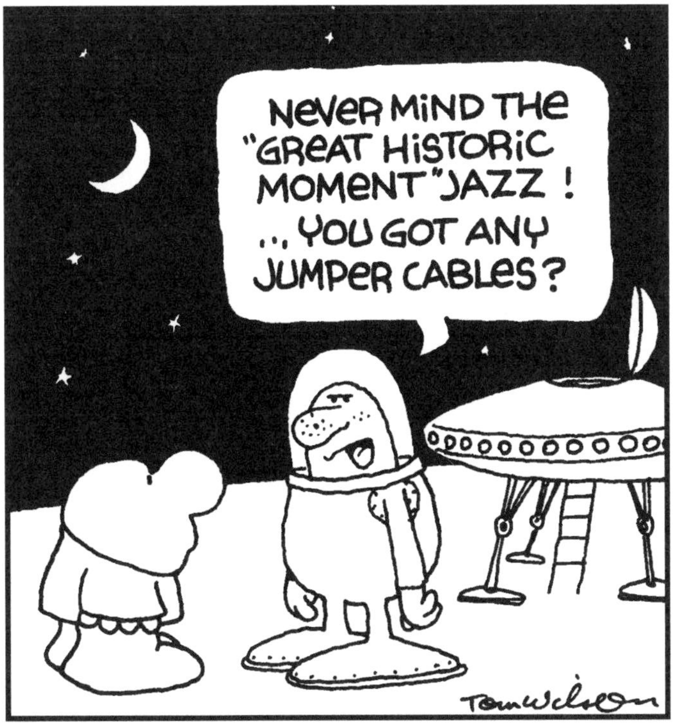
NEVER MIND THE "GREAT HISTORIC MOMENT" JAZZ ! .., YOU GOT ANY JUMPER CABLES?
TomWilson

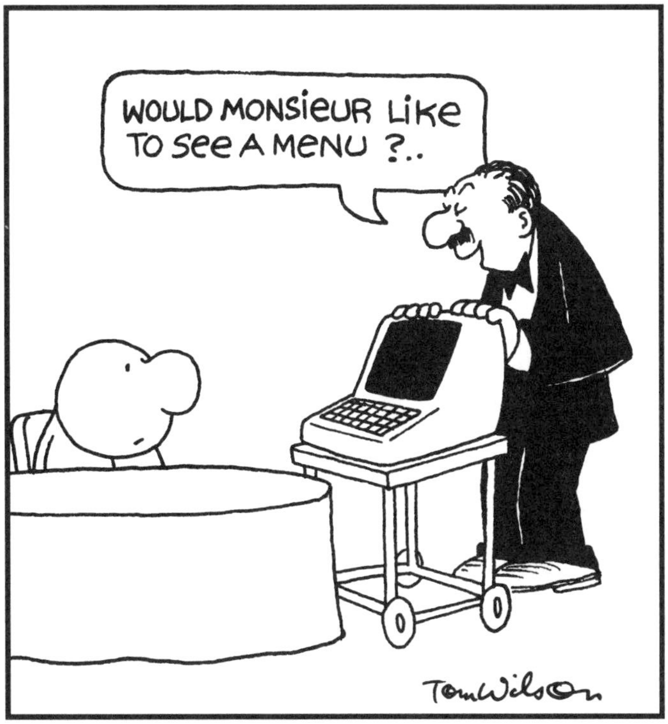
WOULD MONSIEUR LIKE TO SEE A MENU ?..
TomWilson

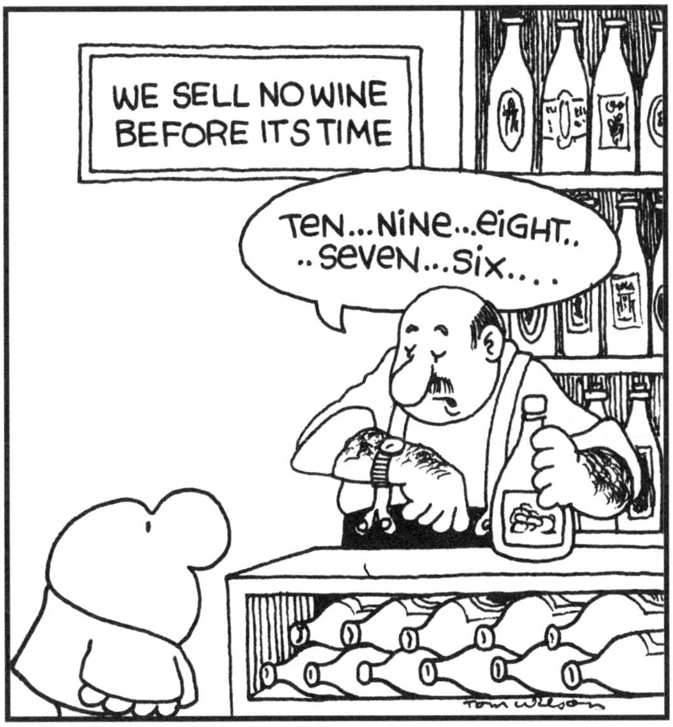
WE SELL NO WINE BEFORE ITS TIME
TEN...NINE...EIGHT.. ..SEVEN...SIX....
Tom Wilson

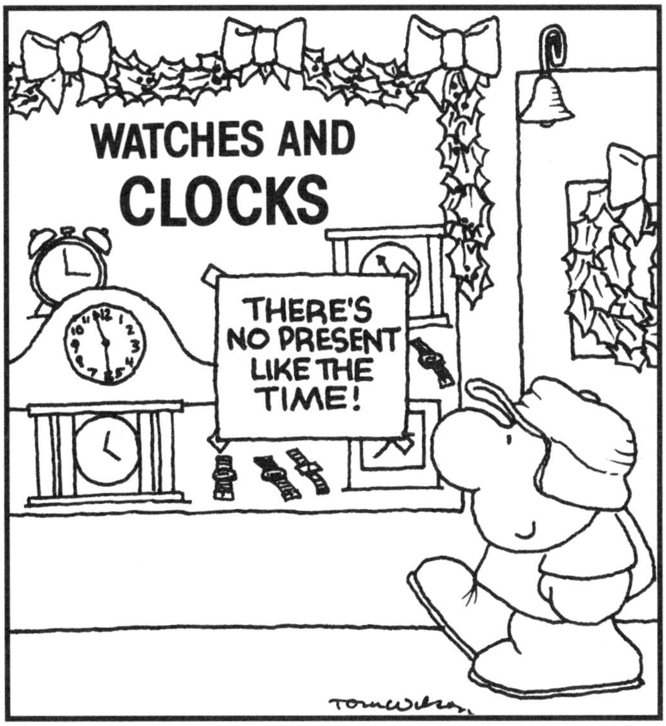
WATCHES AND CLOCKS
THERE'S NO PRESENT LIKE THE TIME!
TomWilson

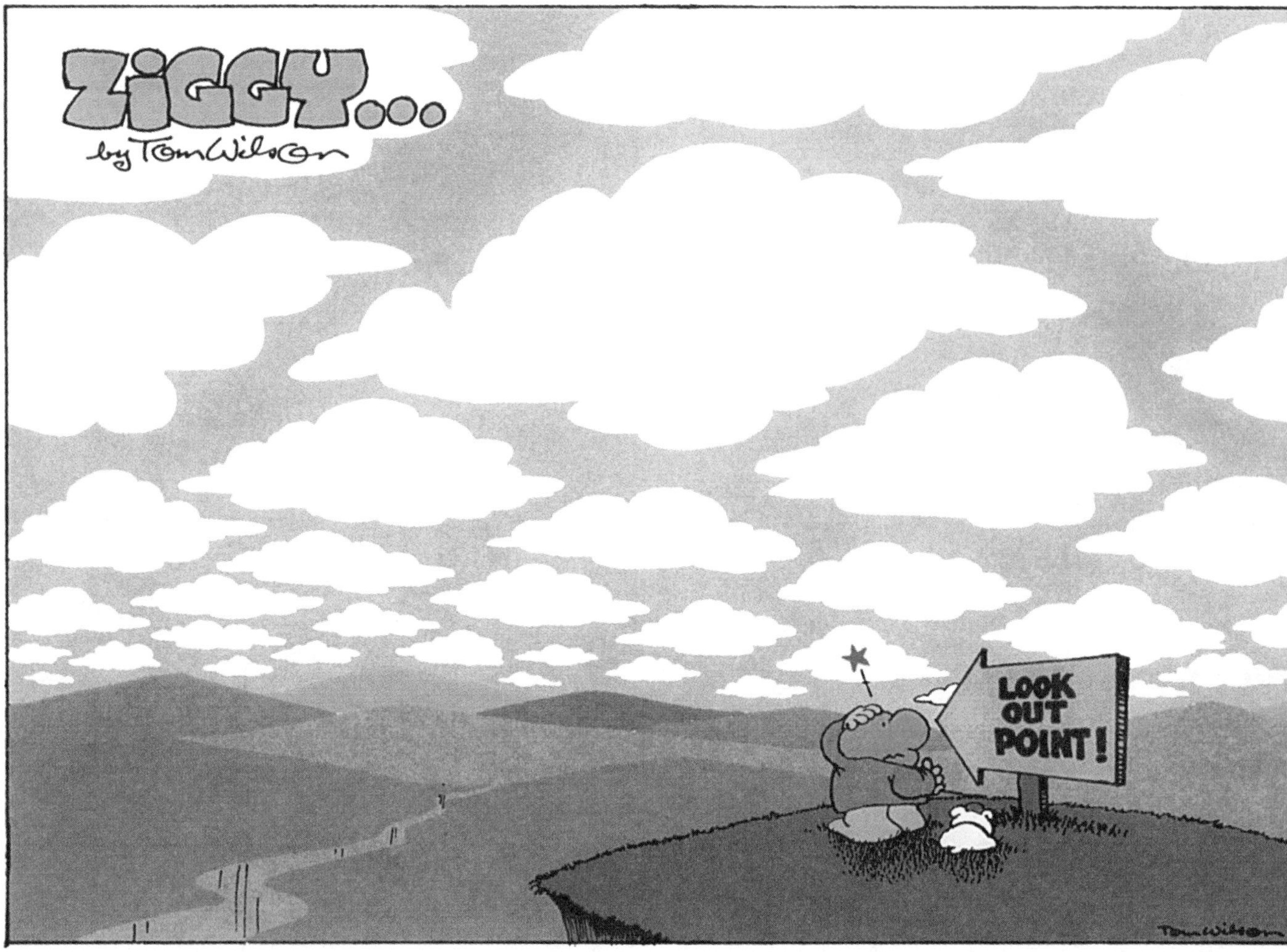
ZIGGY...
by Tom Wilson
LOOK OUT POINT!
Tom Wilson

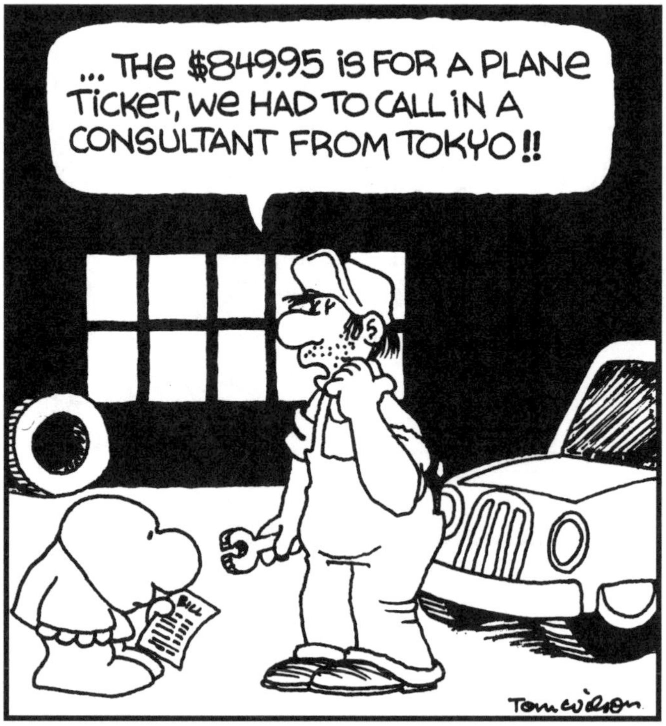
... THE $849.95 IS FOR A PLANE TICKET, WE HAD TO CALL IN A CONSULTANT FROM TOKYO!!
Tom Wilson

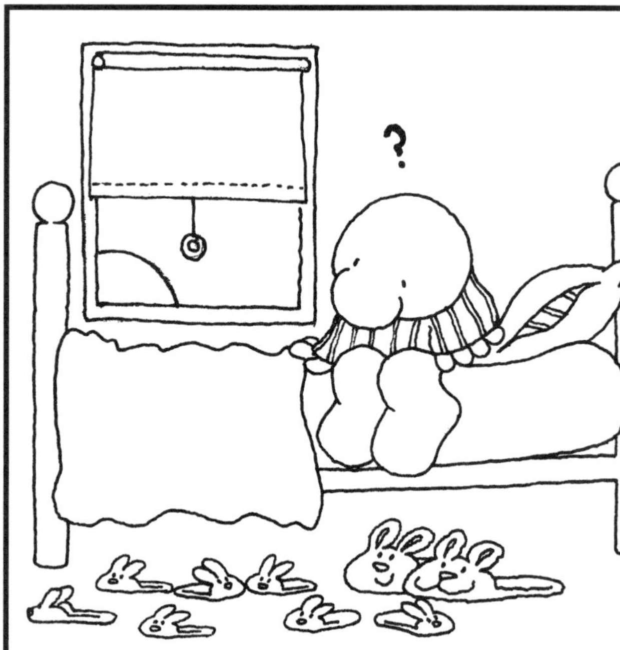
?
Tom Wilson

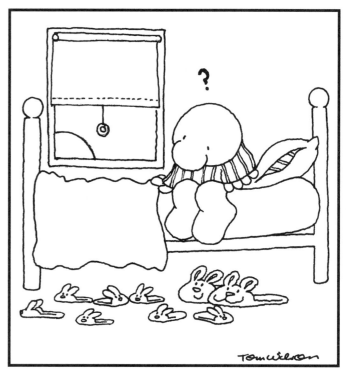

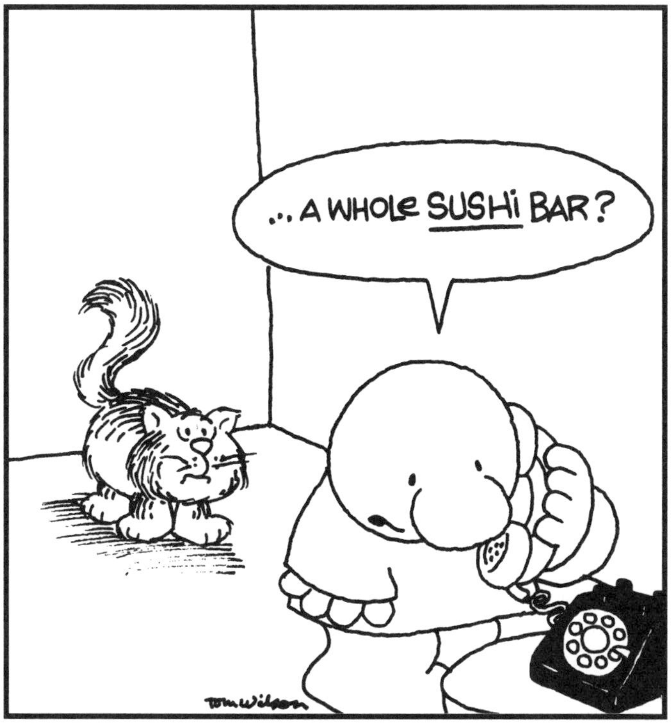
...A WHOLE SUSHI BAR?
Tom Wilson

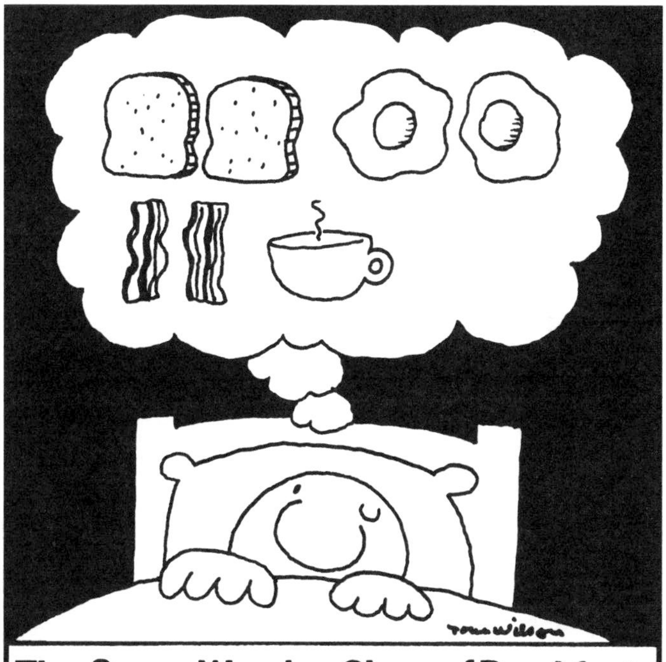
Tom Wilson

The Seven Warning Signs of Breakfast

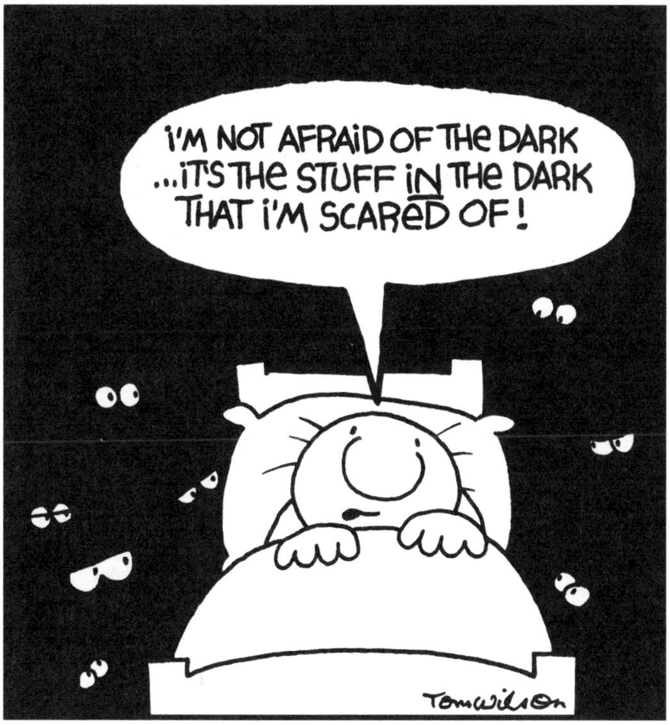
I'M NOT AFRAID OF THE DARK ...IT'S THE STUFF IN THE DARK THAT I'M SCARED OF!
Tom Wilson

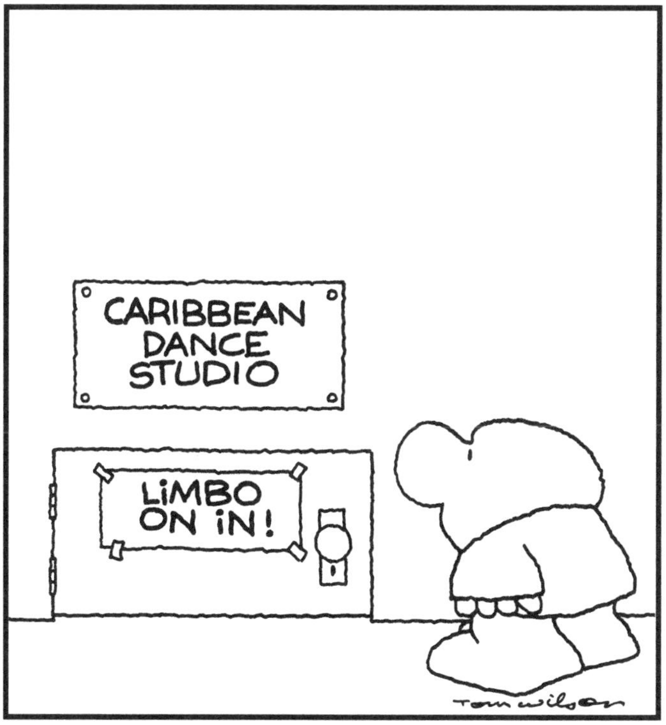
CARIBBEAN DANCE STUDIO
LIMBO ON IN!
Tom Wilson

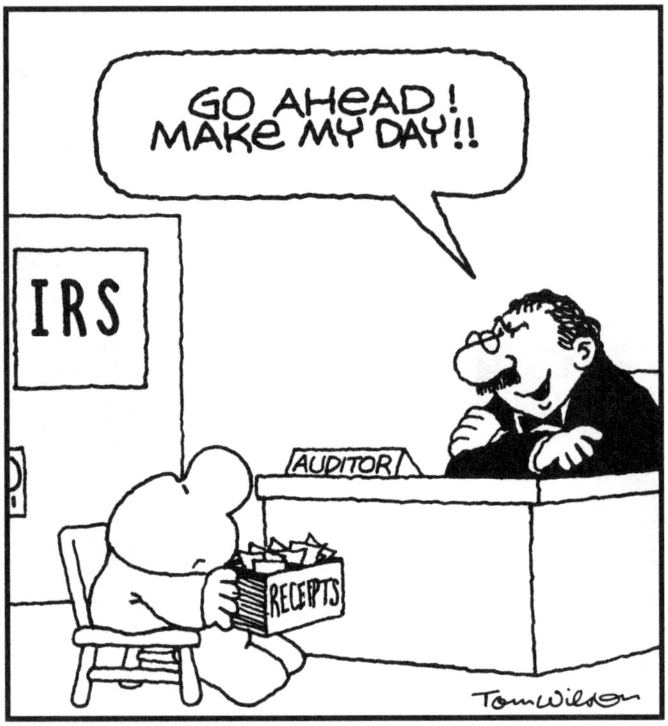
GO AHEAD! MAKE MY DAY!!
IRS
AUDITOR
RECEIPTS

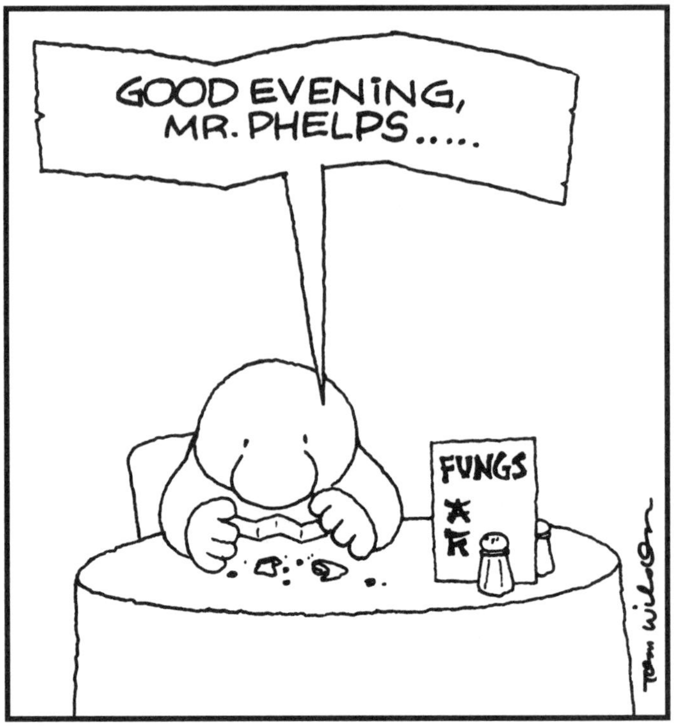
GOOD EVENING, MR. PHELPS.....
FUNGS

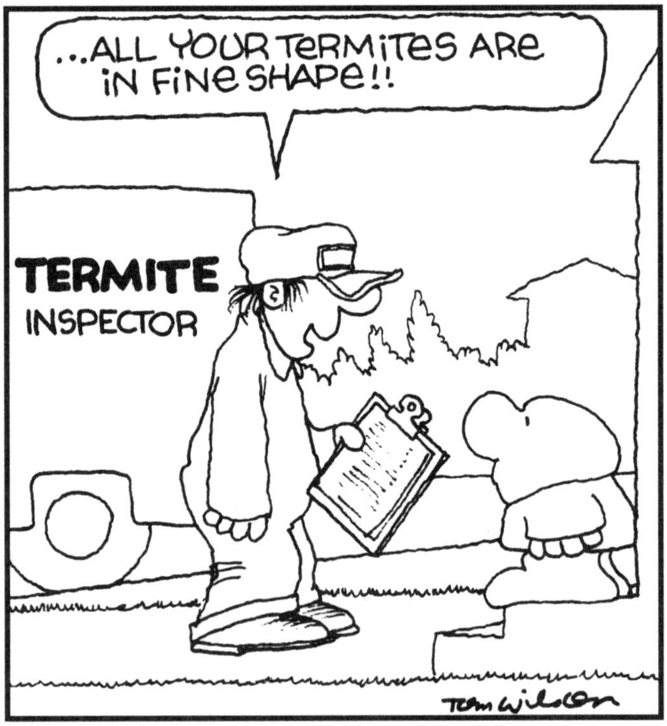
...ALL YOUR TERMITES ARE IN FINE SHAPE!!
TERMITE
INSPECTOR

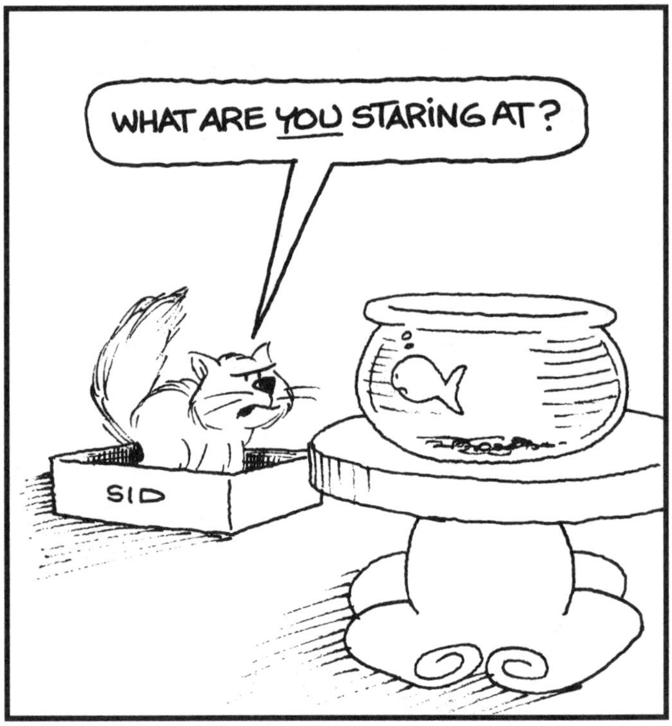
WHAT ARE YOU STARING AT?
SID

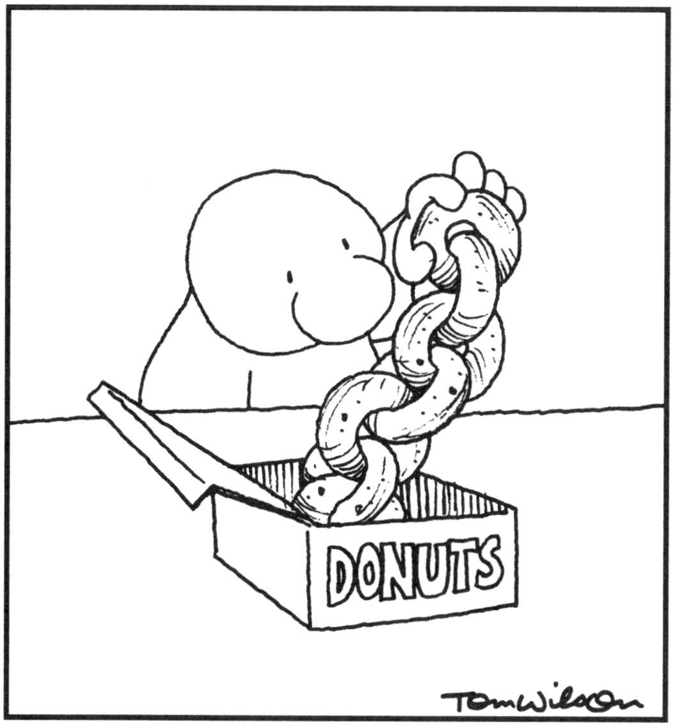
DONUTS
Tom Wilson

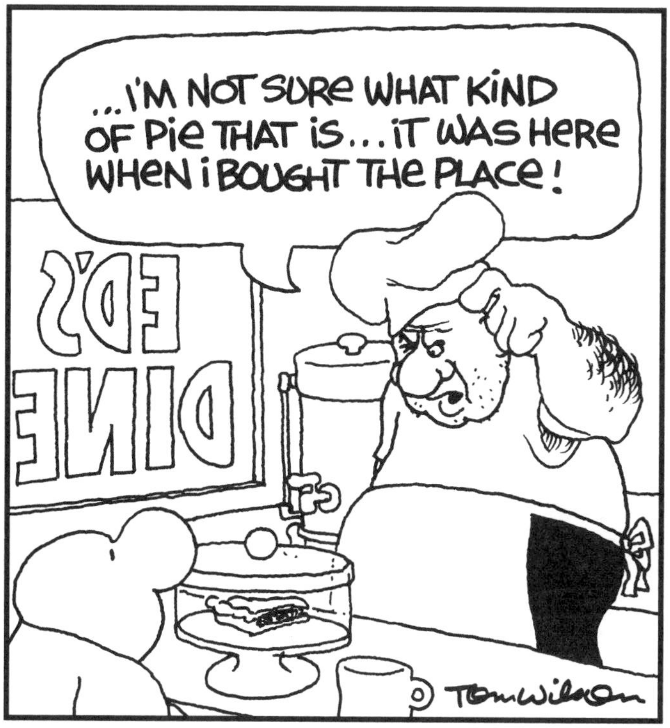
...I'M NOT SURE WHAT KIND OF PIE THAT IS... IT WAS HERE WHEN I BOUGHT THE PLACE!
ED'S DINE
Tom Wilson

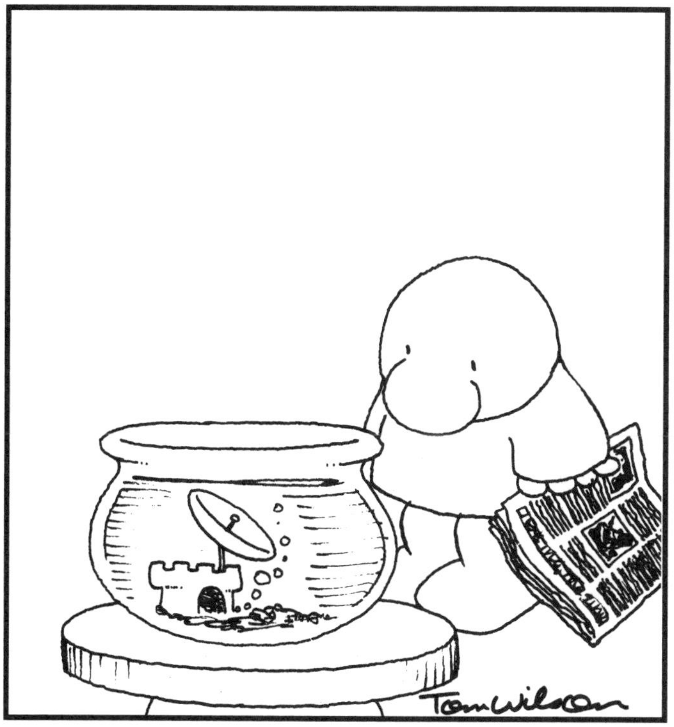
Tom Wilson

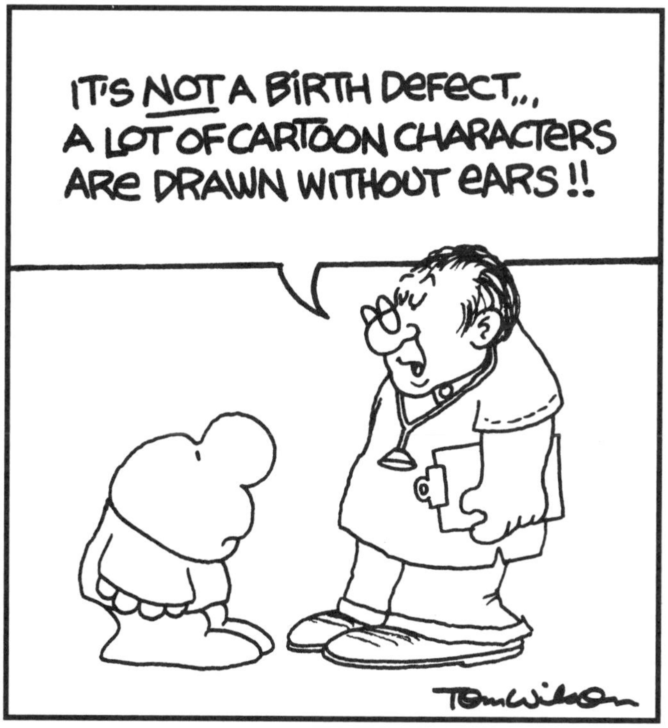
IT'S NOT A BIRTH DEFECT... A LOT OF CARTOON CHARACTERS ARE DRAWN WITHOUT EARS!!
Tom Wilson

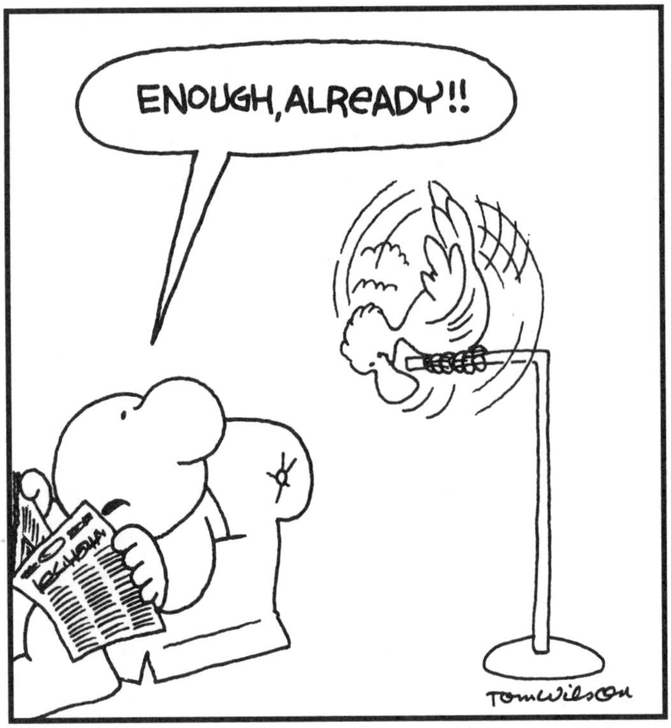
ENOUGH, ALREADY!!
Tom Wilson

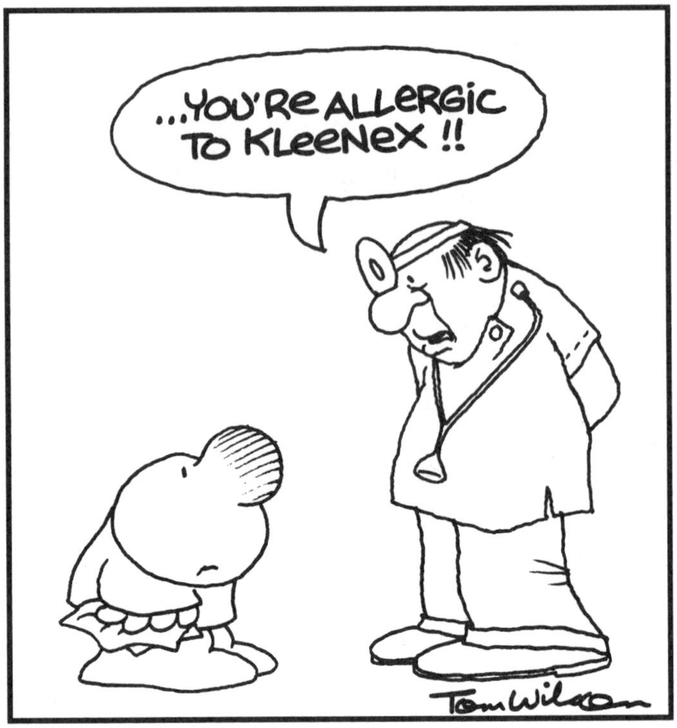
...YOU'RE ALLERGIC TO KLEENEX !!
Tom Wilson

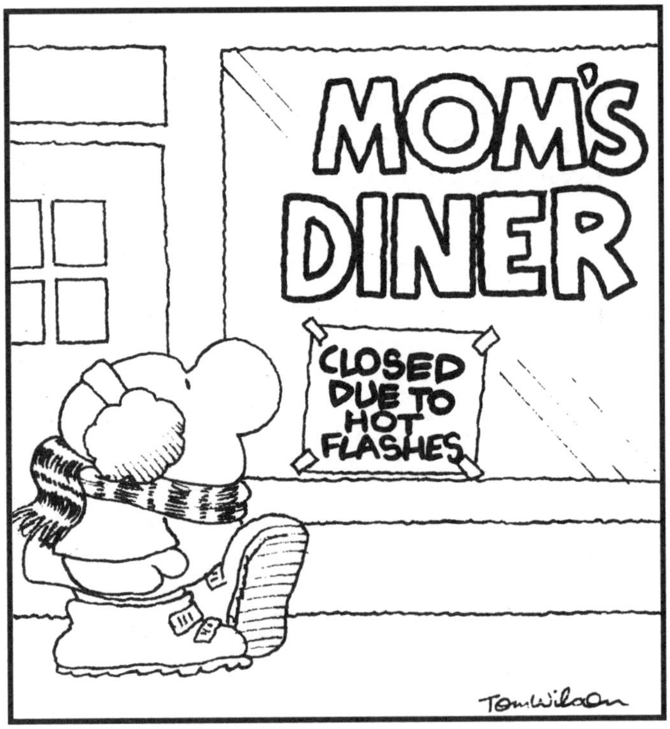
MOM'S DINER
CLOSED DUE TO HOT FLASHES
Tom Wilson

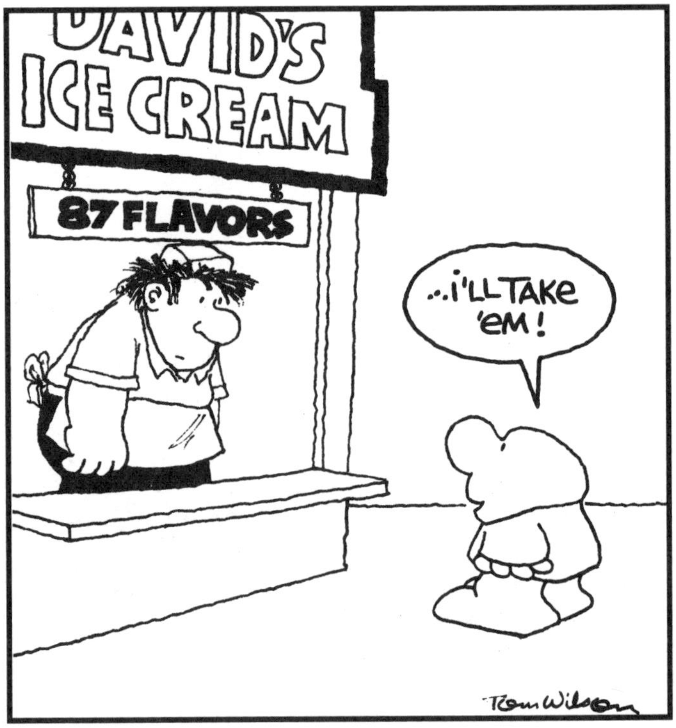
DAVID'S ICE CREAM
87 FLAVORS
..I'LL TAKE 'EM!
Tom Wilson

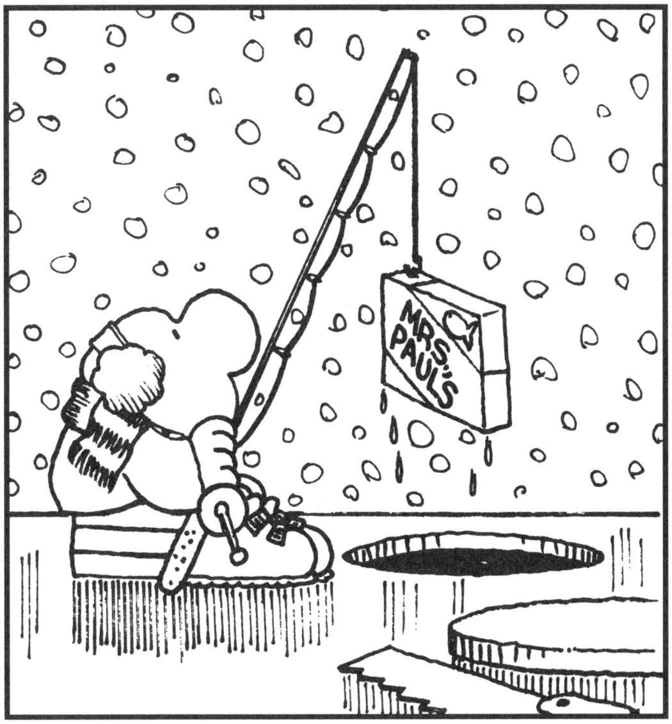
MRS. PAUL'S

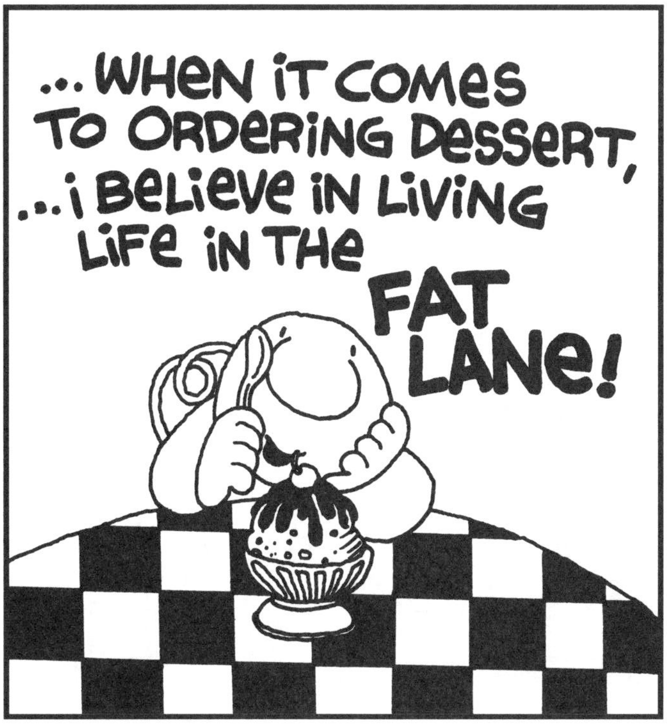
...WHEN IT COMES TO ORDERING DESSERT, ...I BELIEVE IN LIVING LIFE IN THE FAT LANE!

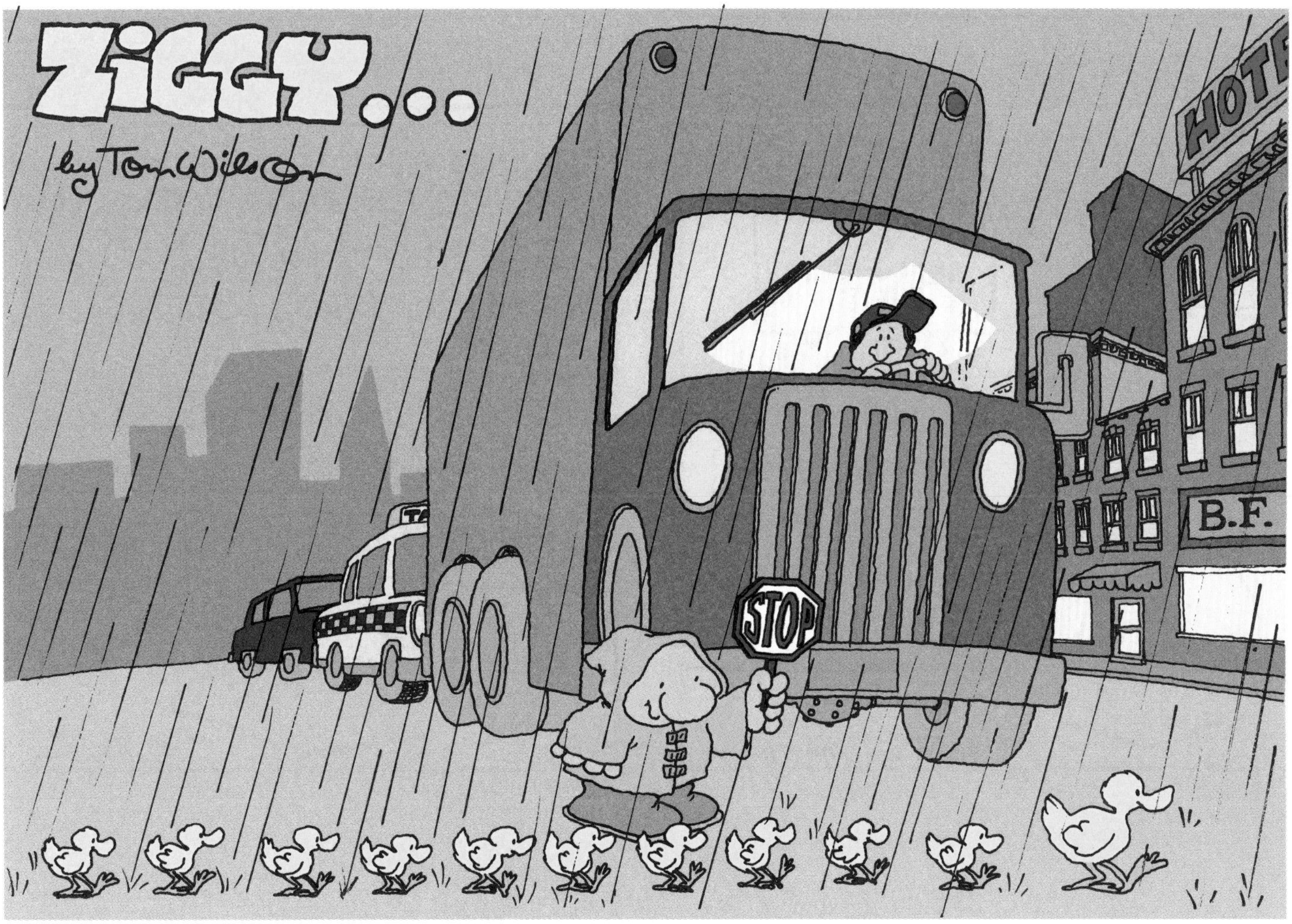
ZIGGY...
by Tom Wilson
HOTE
B.F.
STOP

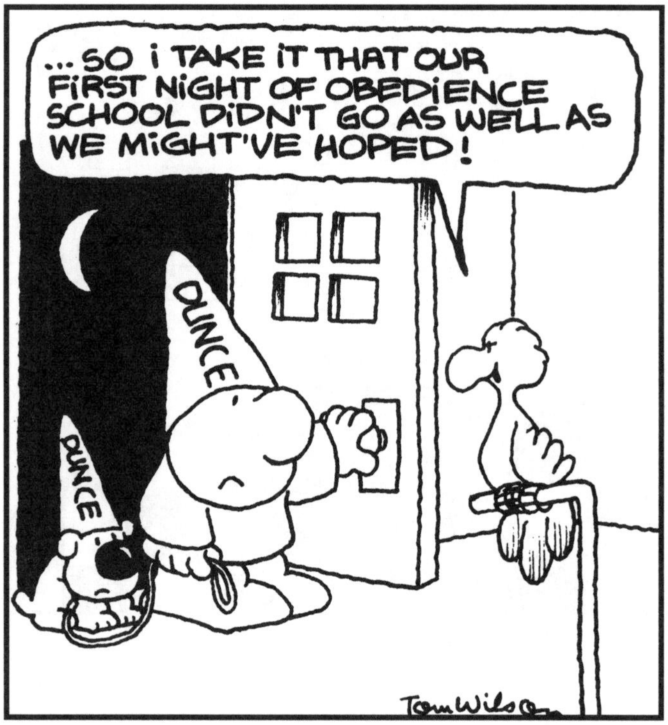
...SO I TAKE IT THAT OUR FIRST NIGHT OF OBEDIENCE SCHOOL DIDN'T GO AS WELL AS WE MIGHT'VE HOPED!
DUNCE
DUNCE
Tom Wilson

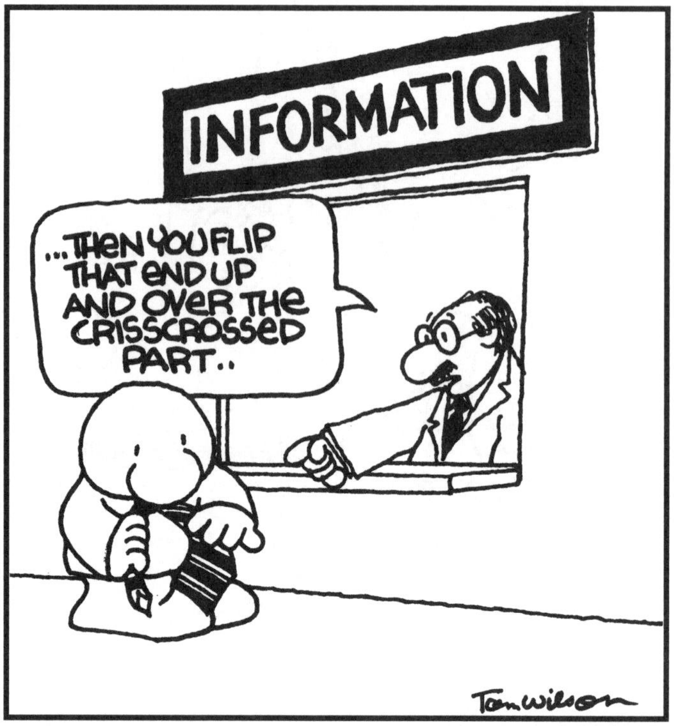
INFORMATION
...THEN YOU FLIP THAT END UP AND OVER THE CRISSCROSSED PART..
Tom Wilson

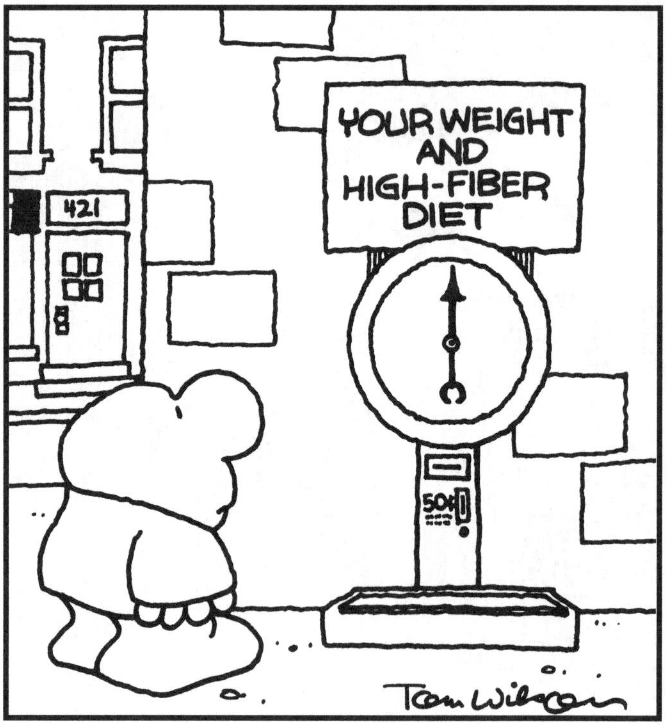
YOUR WEIGHT AND HIGH-FIBER DIET
421
50¢
Tom Wilson

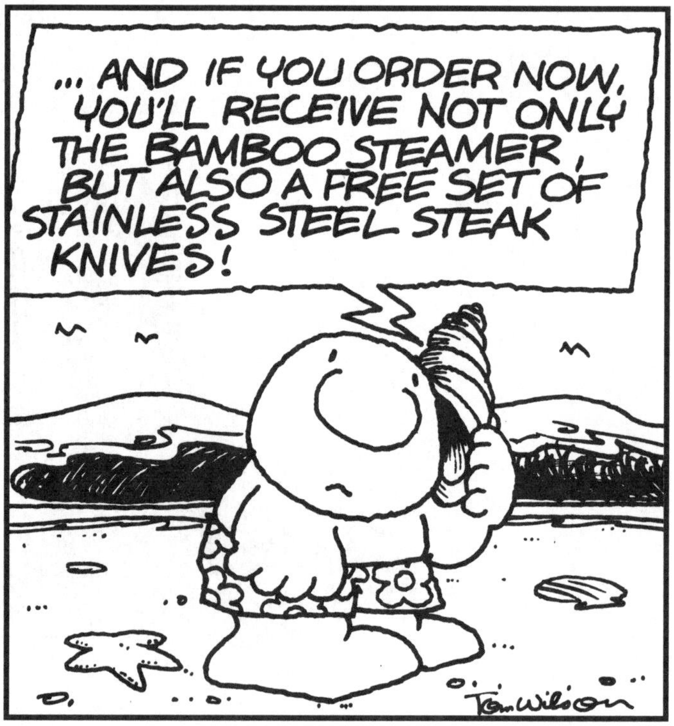
...AND IF YOU ORDER NOW, YOU'LL RECEIVE NOT ONLY THE BAMBOO STEAMER, BUT ALSO A FREE SET OF STAINLESS STEEL STEAK KNIVES!
Tom Wilson

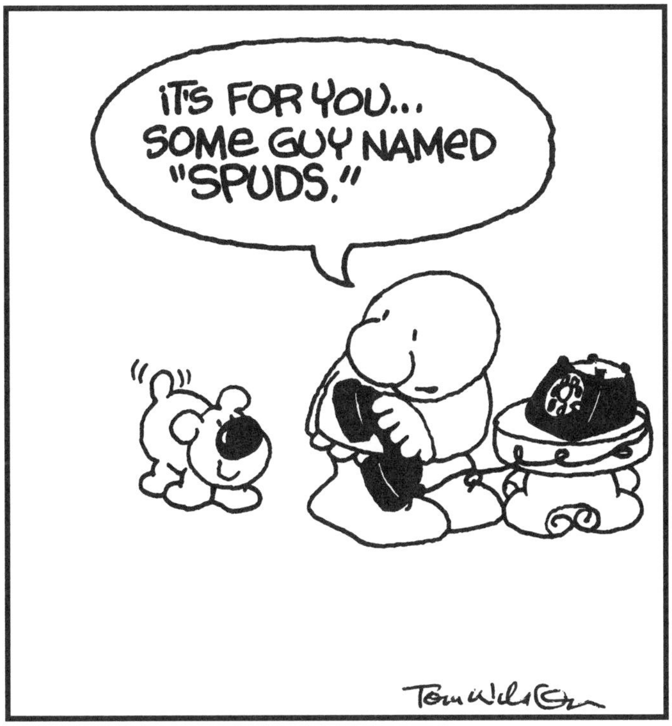
IT'S FOR YOU... SOME GUY NAMED "SPUDS."
Tom Wilson

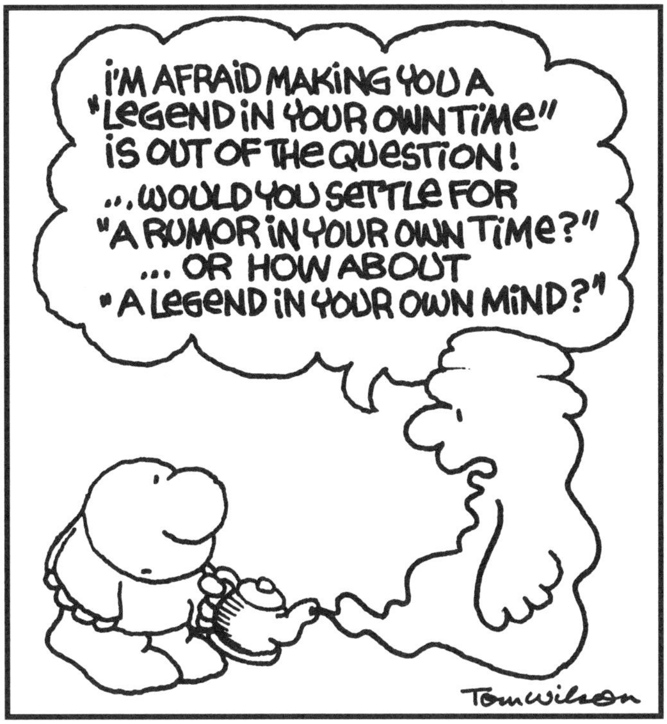
I'M AFRAID MAKING YOU A "LEGEND IN YOUR OWN TIME" IS OUT OF THE QUESTION! ...WOULD YOU SETTLE FOR "A RUMOR IN YOUR OWN TIME?" ... OR HOW ABOUT "A LEGEND IN YOUR OWN MIND?"
Tom Wilson

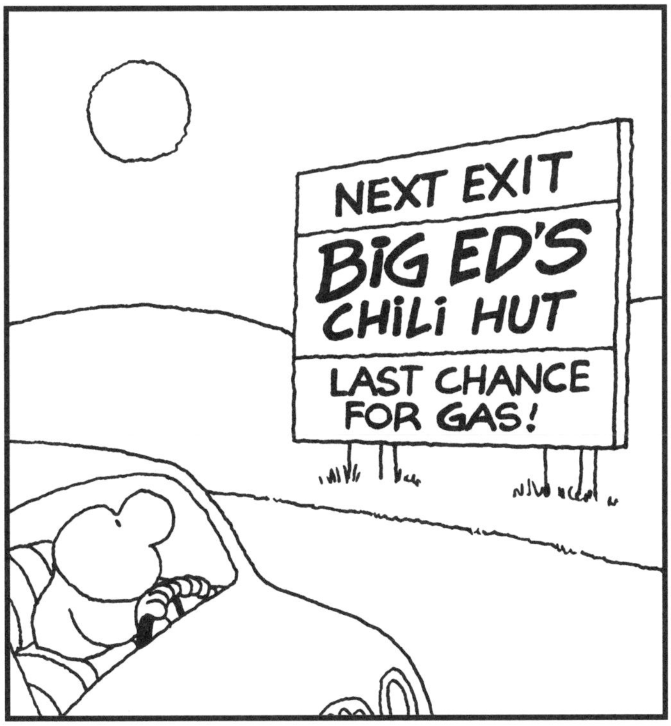
NEXT EXIT
BIG ED'S CHILI HUT
LAST CHANCE FOR GAS!

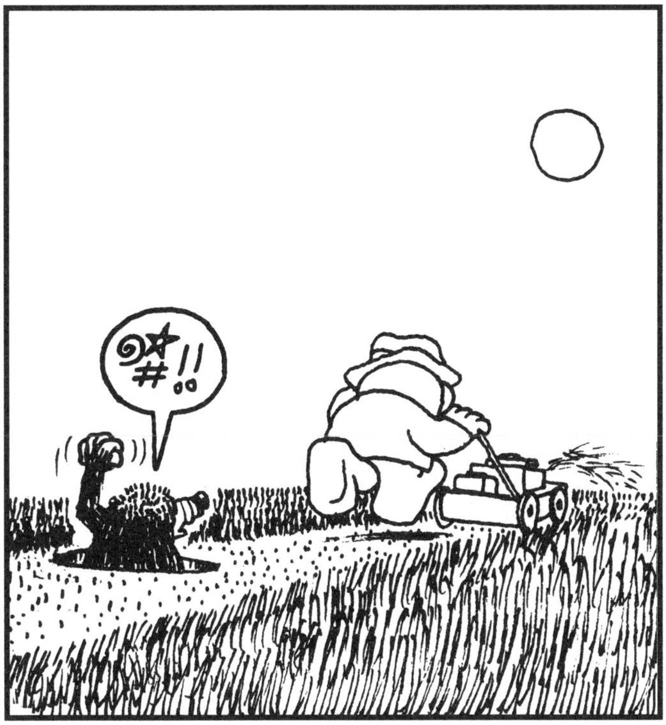

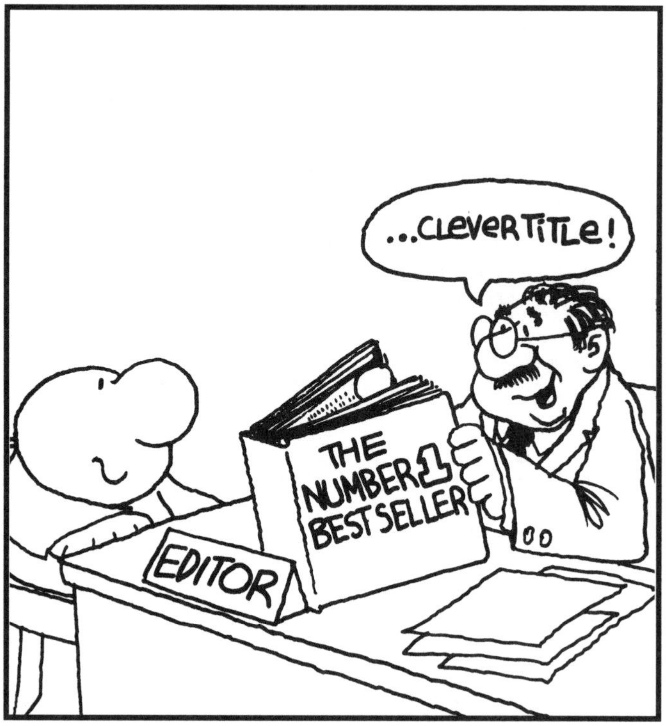
...CLEVER TITLE!
THE NUMBER 1 BEST SELLER
EDITOR

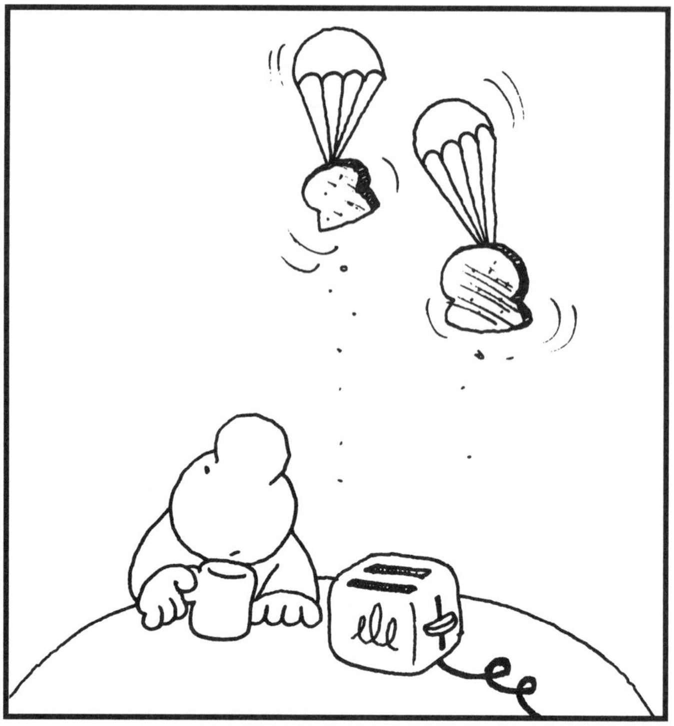

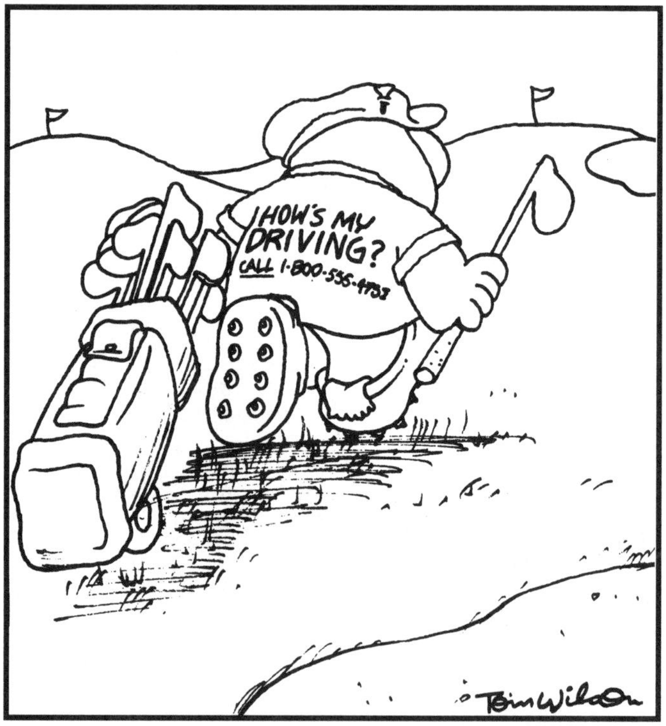
HOW'S MY DRIVING?
CALL 1-800-555-4753
Tom Wilson

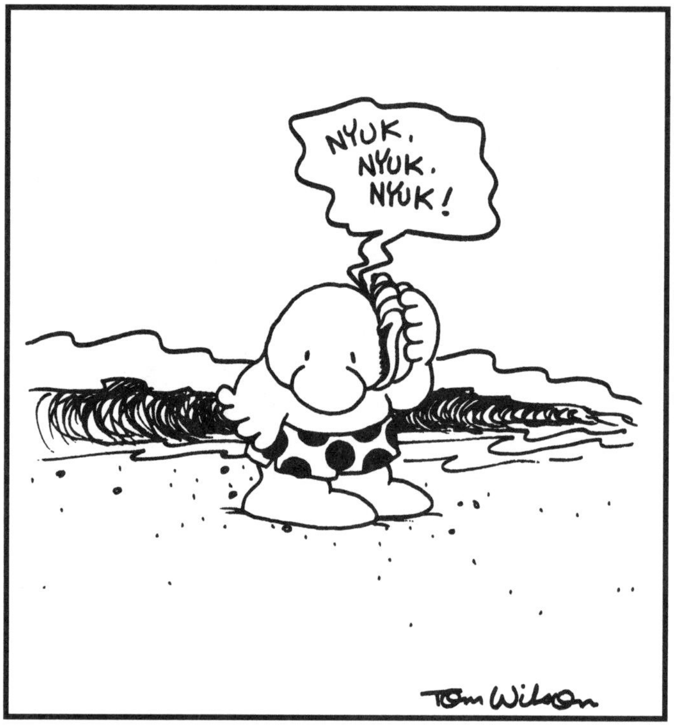
NYUK. NYUK. NYUK!
Tom Wilson

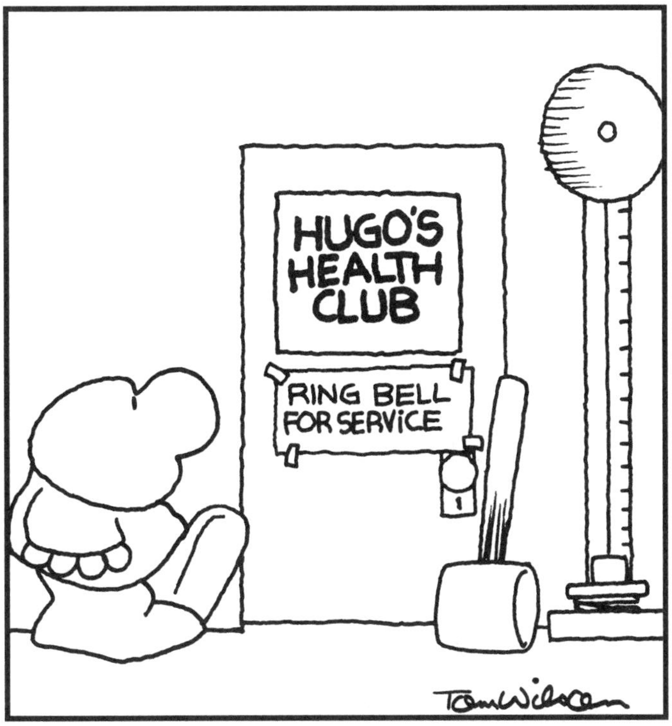
HUGO'S HEALTH CLUB
RING BELL FOR SERVICE
Tom Wilson

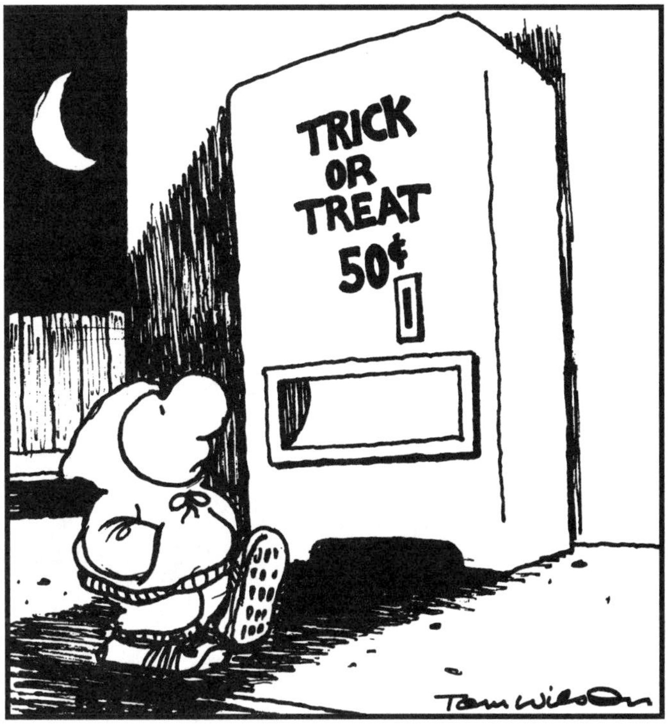
TRICK OR TREAT 50¢
Tom Wilson

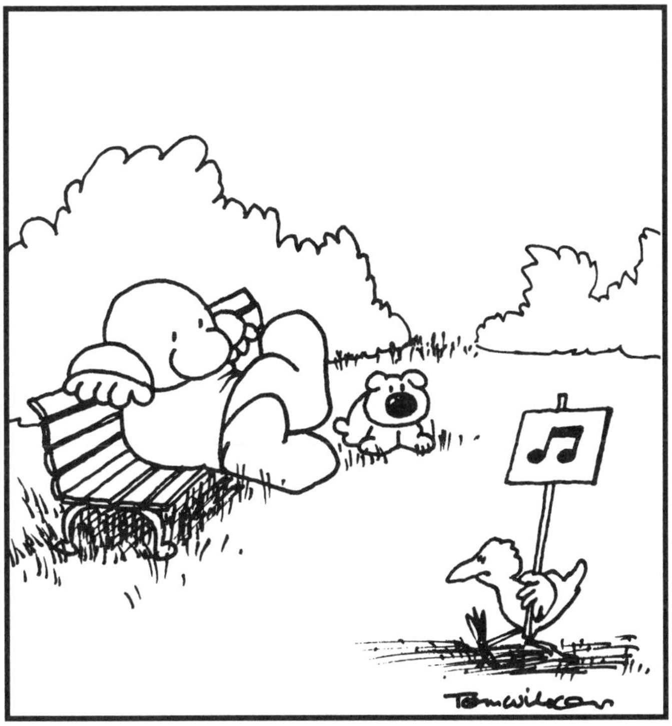
Tom Wilson

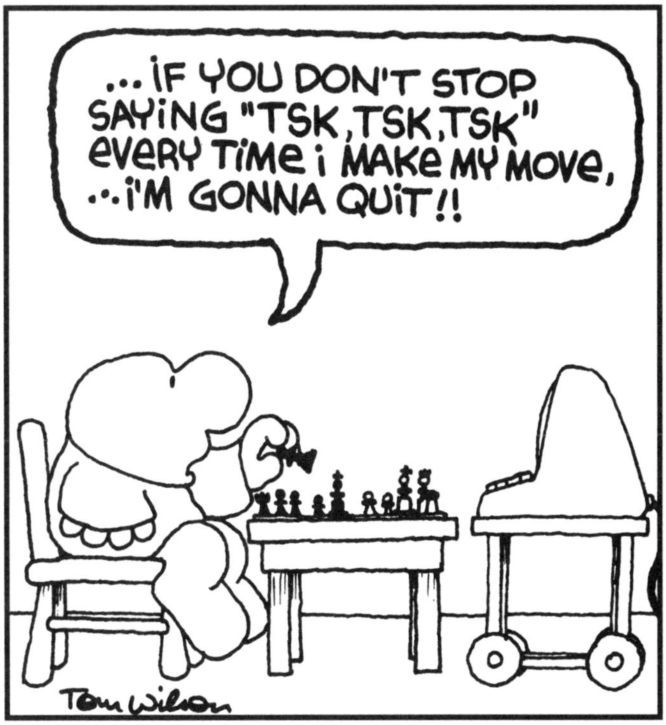
...IF YOU DON'T STOP SAYING "TSK,TSK,TSK" every TIME i MAKE MY MOVE, ...i'M GONNA QUIT!!
Tom Wilson

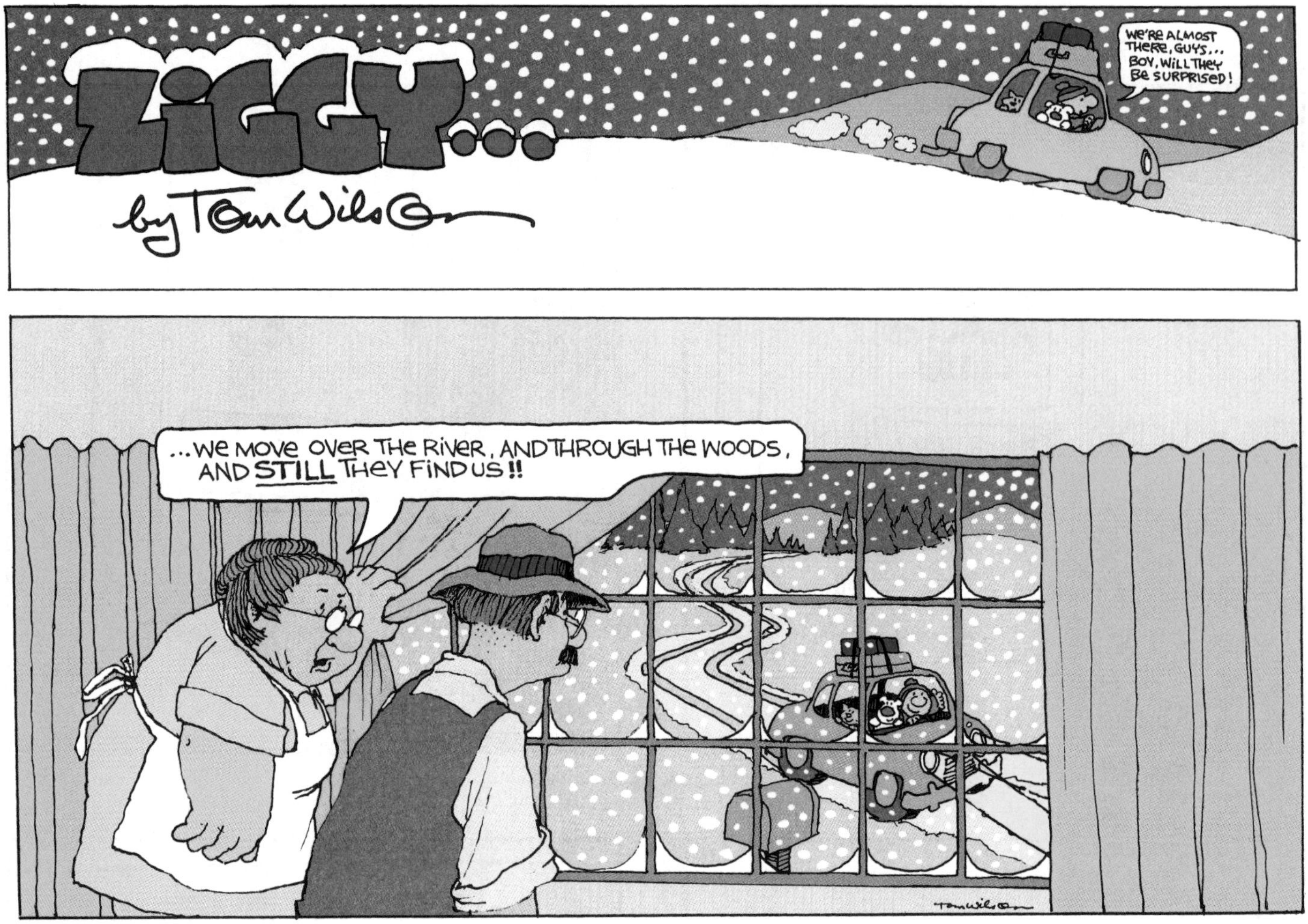
Ziggy...
by Tom Wilson
WE'RE ALMOST THERE, GUYS... BOY, WILL THEY BE SURPRISED!
...WE MOVE OVER THE RIVER, AND THROUGH THE WOODS, AND STILL THEY FIND US!!
Tom Wilson

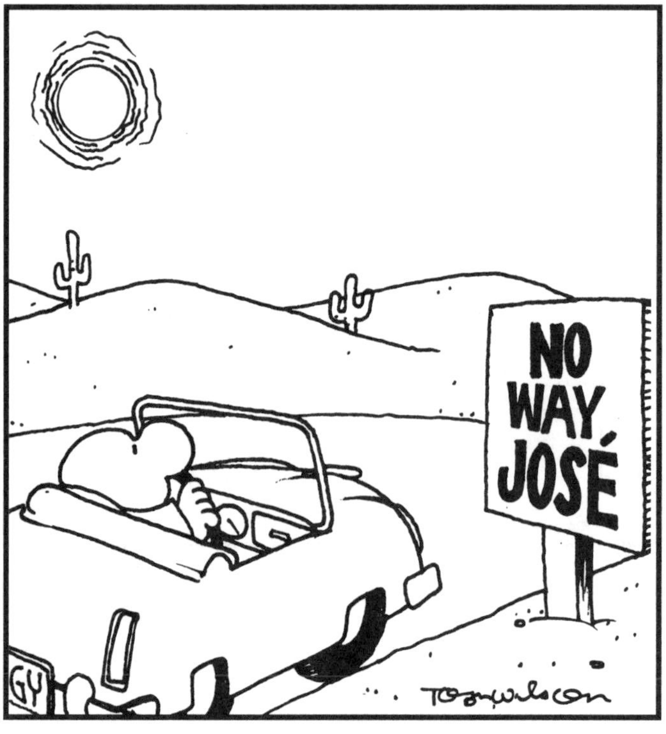
NO WAY JOSÉ
GY
Tom Wilson

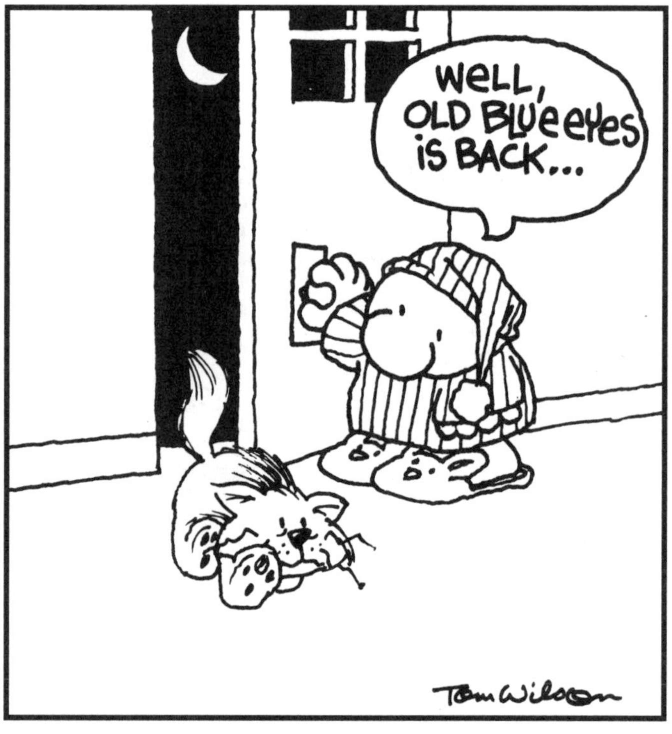
WELL, OLD BLUE EYES IS BACK...
Tom Wilson

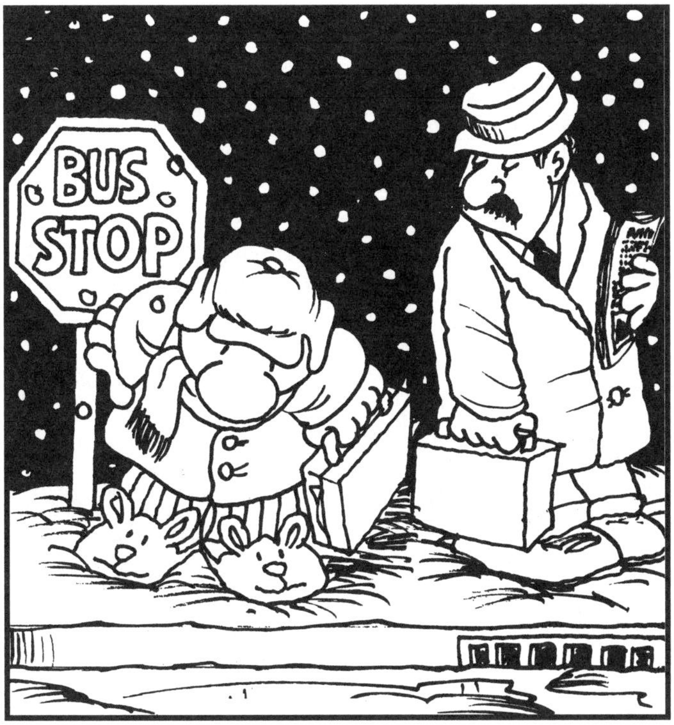
BUS STOP

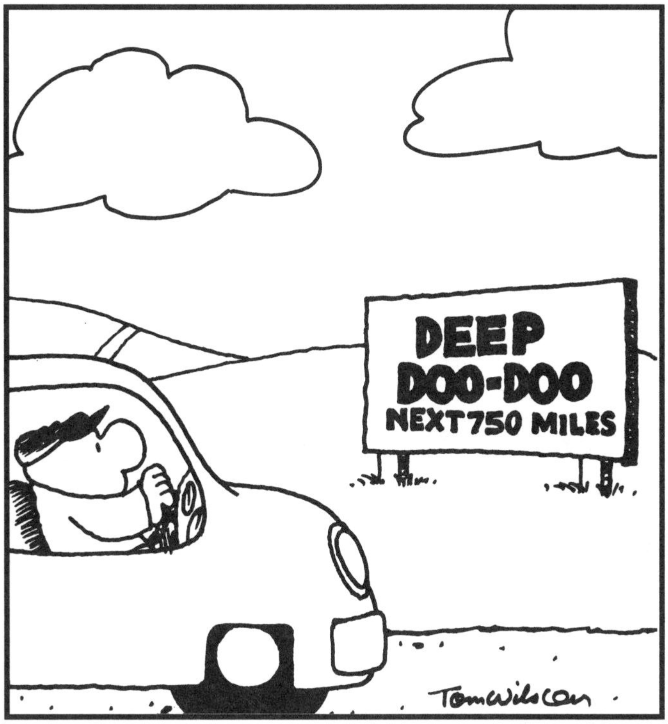
DEEP DOO-DOO NEXT 750 MILES
Tom Wilson

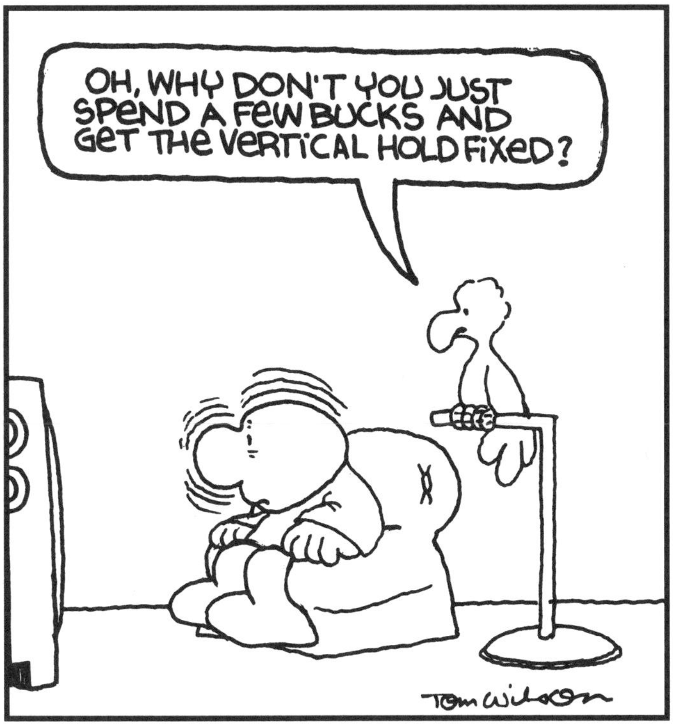
OH, WHY DON'T YOU JUST SPEND A FEW BUCKS AND GET THE VERTICAL HOLD FIXED?
Tom Wilson

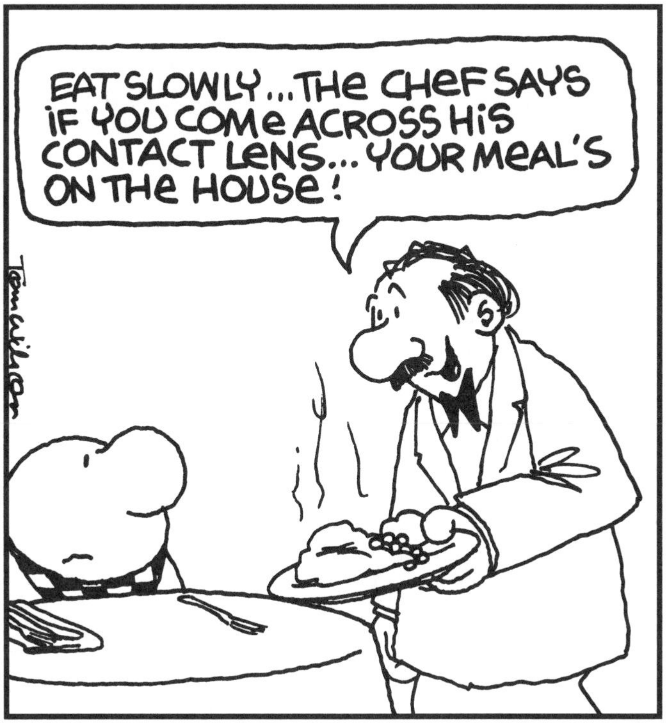
EAT SLOWLY... THE CHEF SAYS IF YOU COME ACROSS HIS CONTACT LENS... YOUR MEAL'S ON THE HOUSE!
Tom Wilson

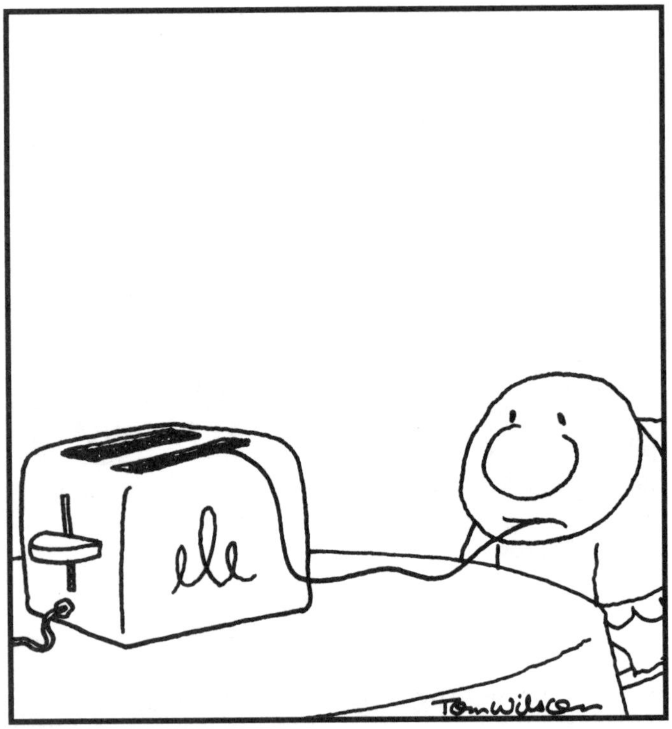

TOM WILSON

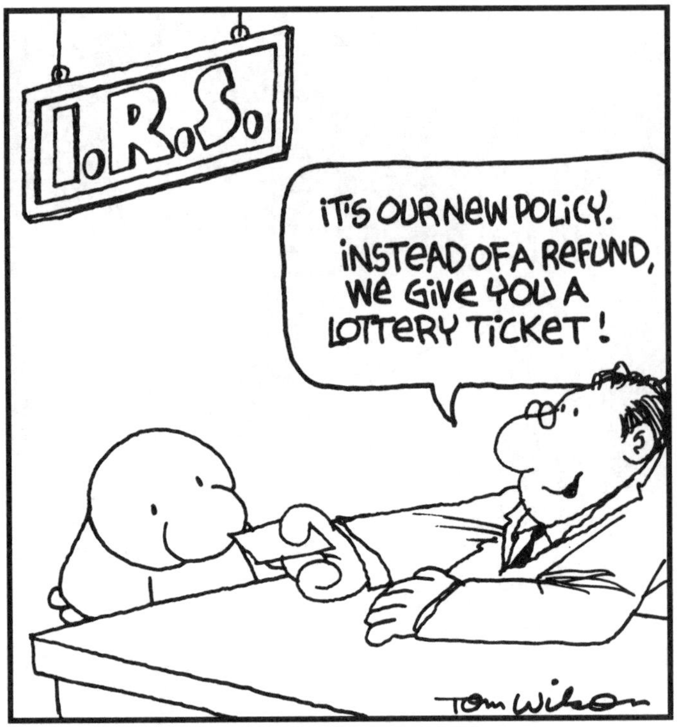

I.R.S.
IT'S OUR NEW POLICY. INSTEAD OF A REFUND, WE GIVE YOU A LOTTERY TICKET!
TOM WILSON

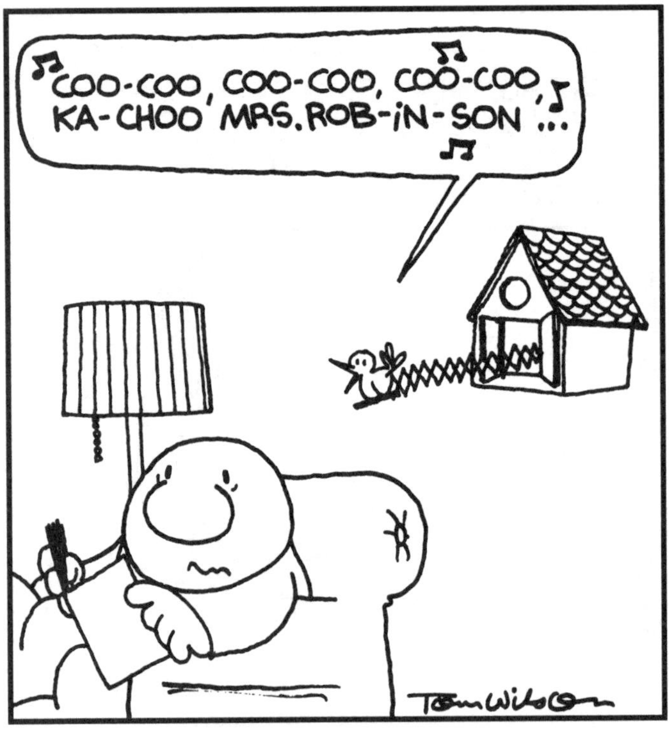

COO-COO, COO-COO, COO-COO, KA-CHOO MRS. ROB-IN-SON ...
TOM WILSON

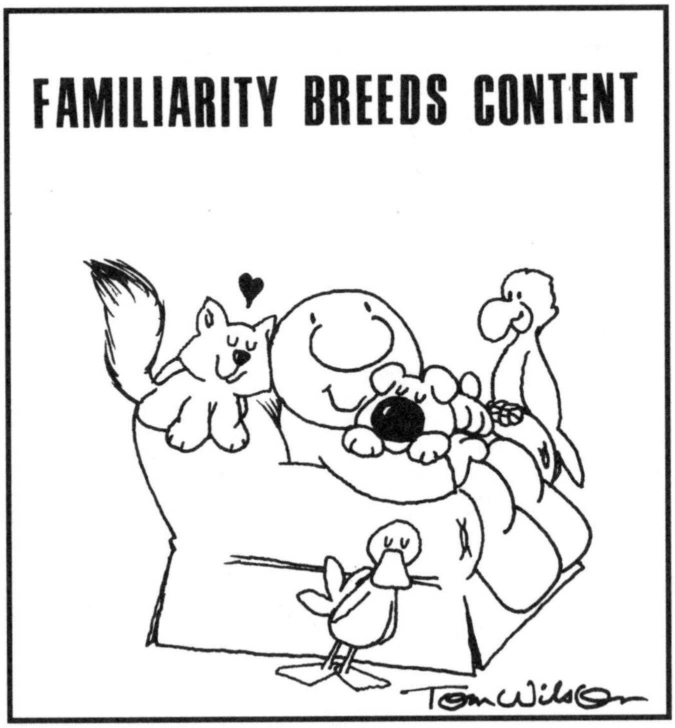

FAMILIARITY BREEDS CONTENT
TOM WILSON

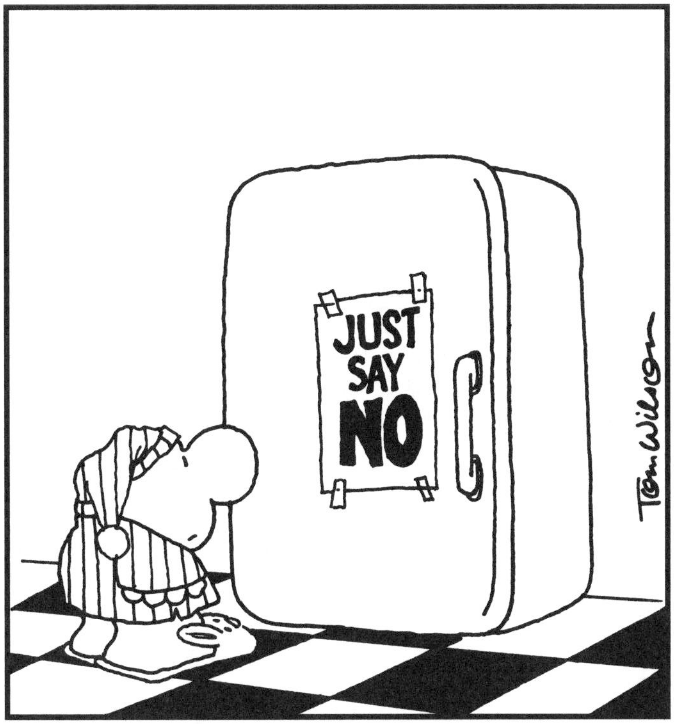
JUST SAY NO
Tom Wilson

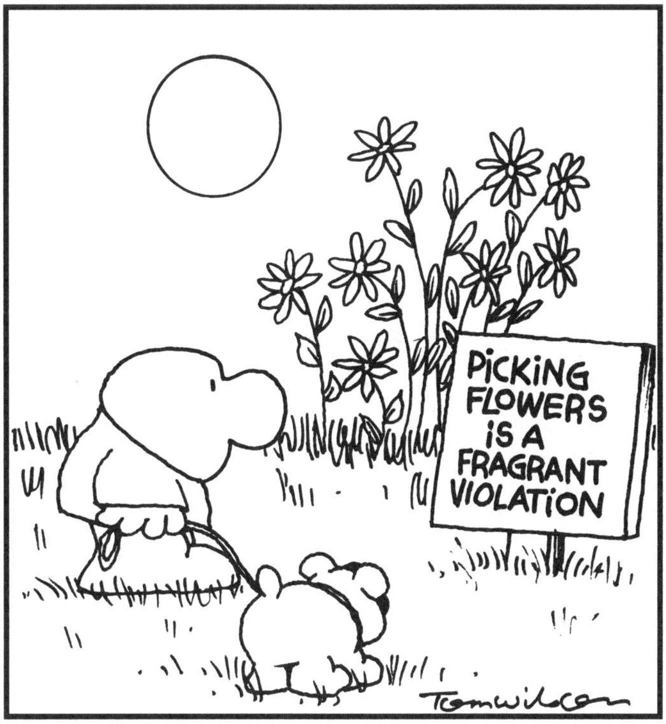
PICKING FLOWERS IS A FRAGRANT VIOLATION
Tom Wilson

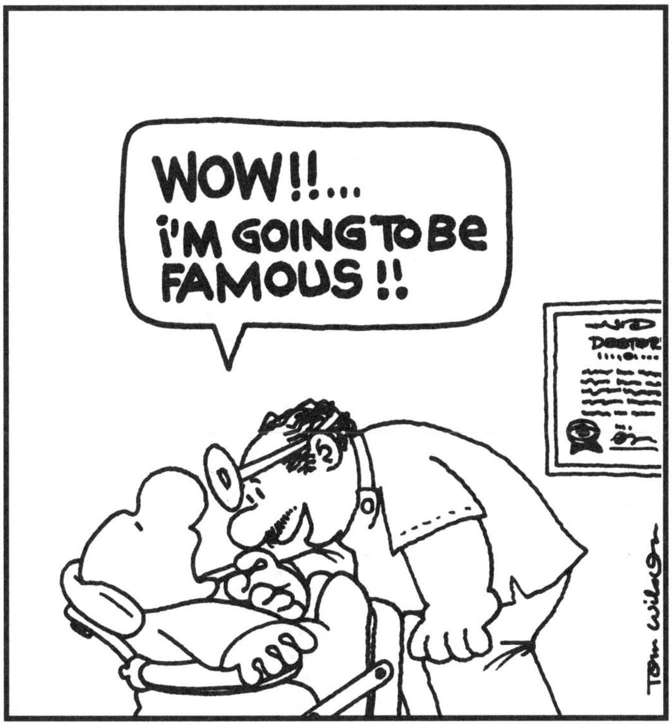
WOW!!... I'M GOING TO BE FAMOUS!!
Tom Wilson

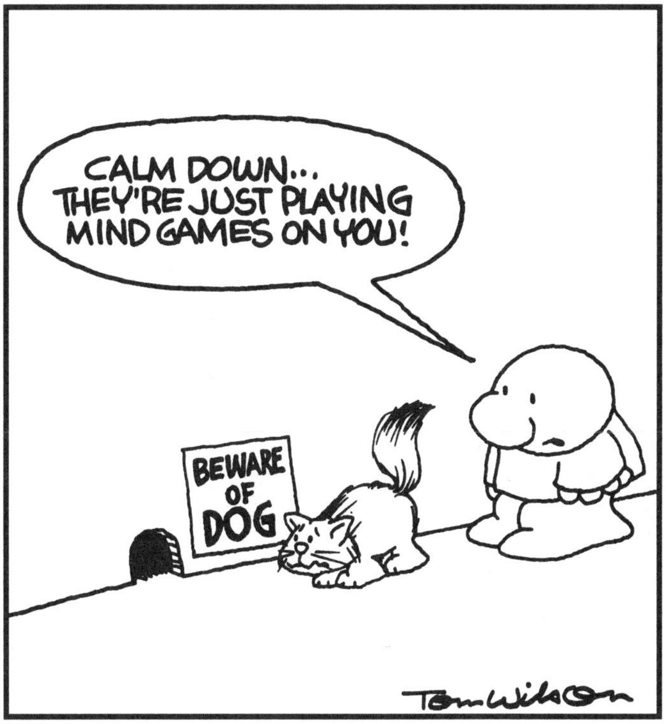
CALM DOWN... THEY'RE JUST PLAYING MIND GAMES ON YOU!
BEWARE OF DOG
Tom Wilson

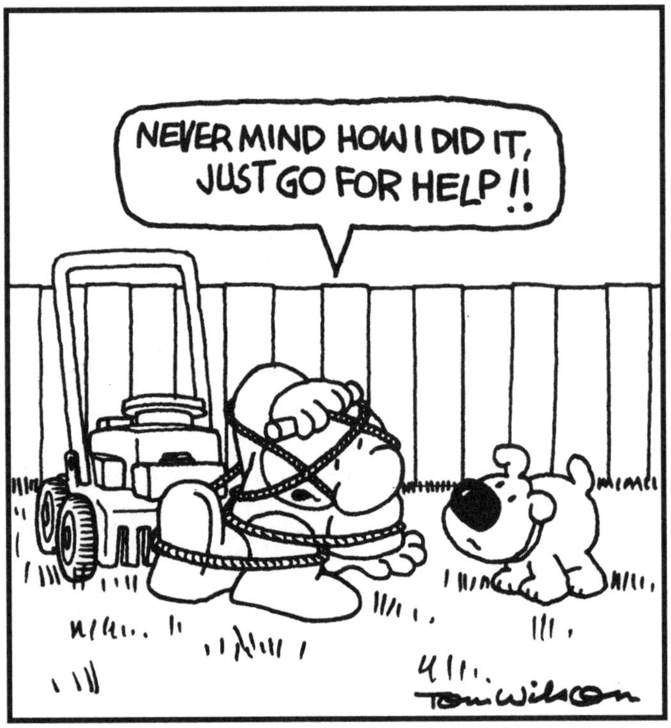
NEVER MIND HOW I DID IT, JUST GO FOR HELP!!
Tom Wilson

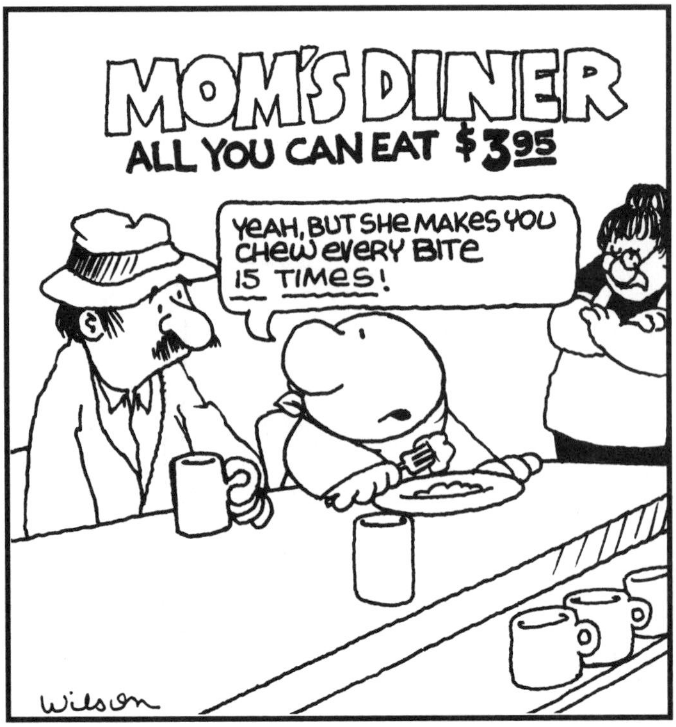
MOM'S DINER
ALL YOU CAN EAT $3.95
YEAH, BUT SHE MAKES YOU CHEW EVERY BITE 15 TIMES!
Wilson

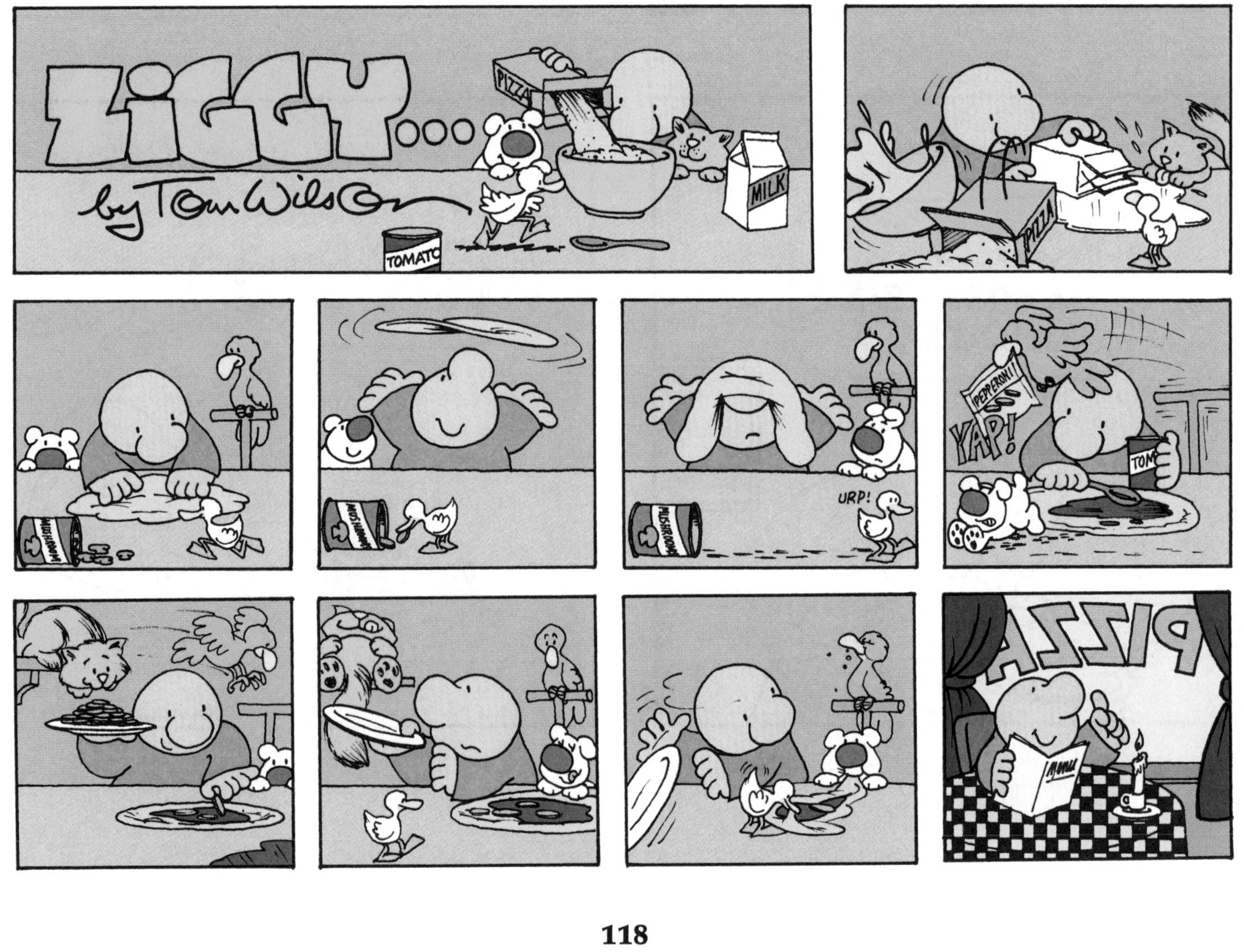
ZIGGY...
by Tom Wilson
PIZZA
MILK
TOMATO
PIZZA
URP!
PEPPERONI!
YAP!
TOM
PIZZA

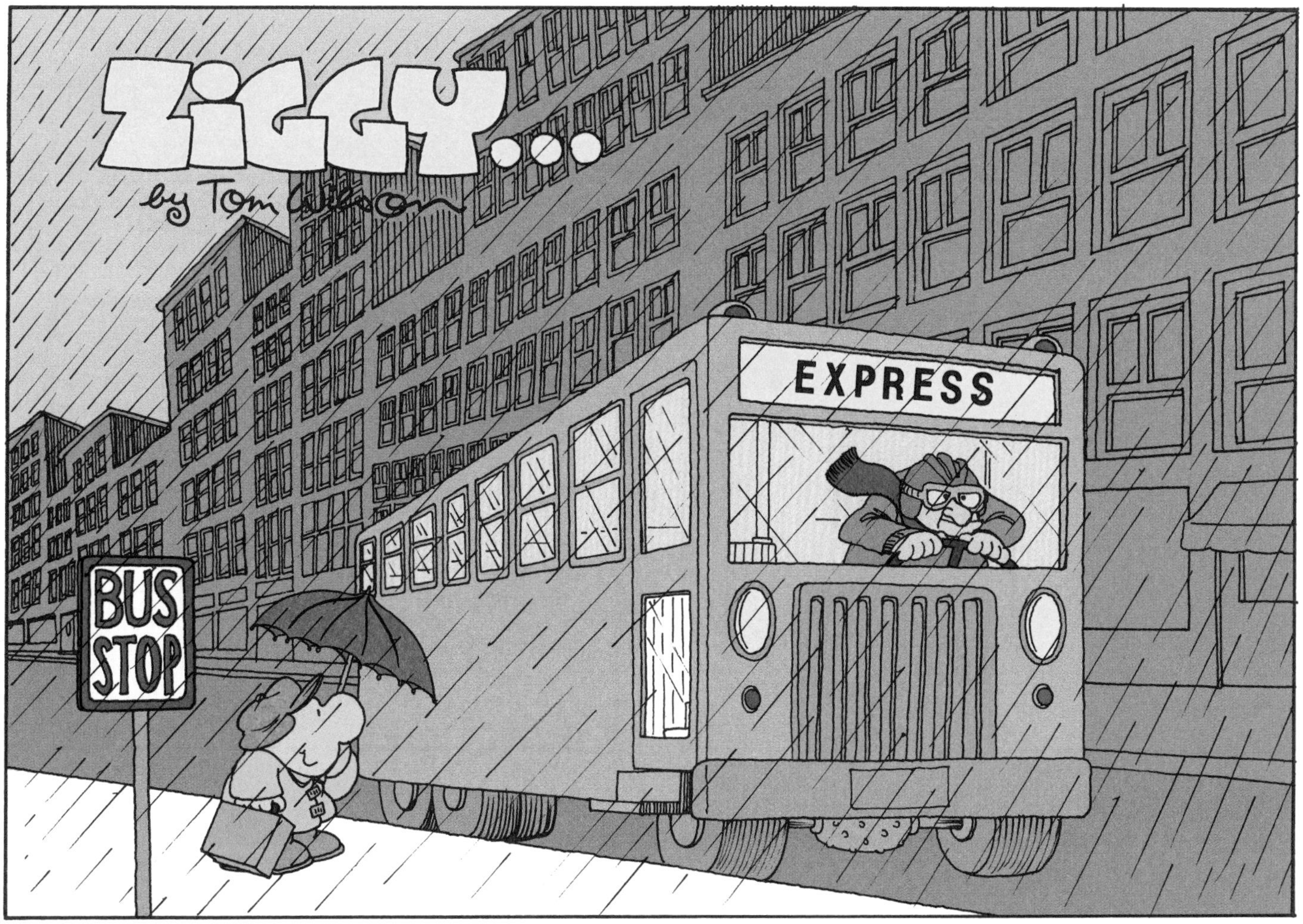
ZIGGY...
by Tom Wilson
EXPRESS
BUS STOP

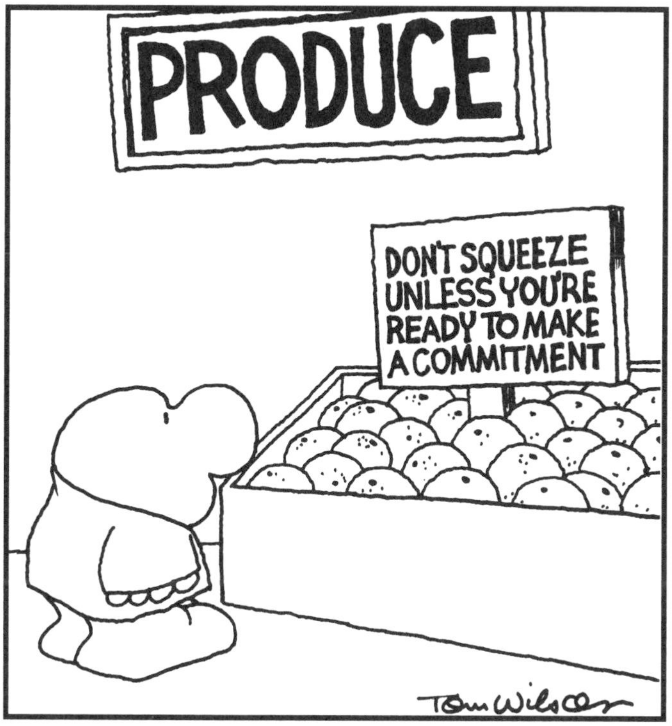
PRODUCE
DON'T SQUEEZE UNLESS YOU'RE READY TO MAKE A COMMITMENT
Tom Wilson

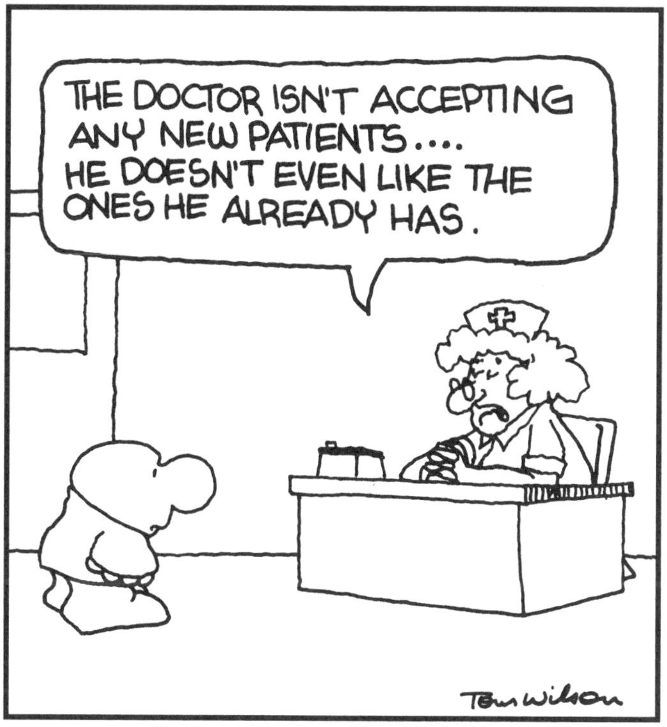
THE DOCTOR ISN'T ACCEPTING ANY NEW PATIENTS.... HE DOESN'T EVEN LIKE THE ONES HE ALREADY HAS.
Tom Wilson

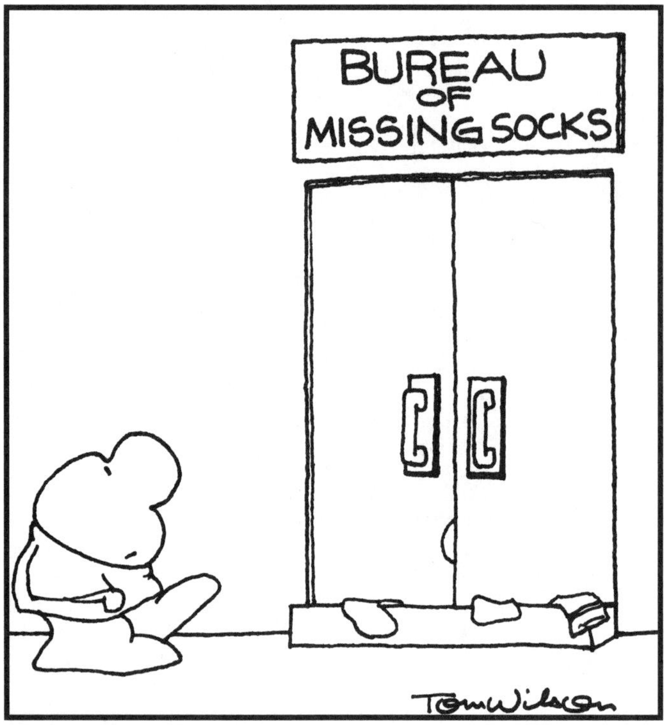
BUREAU OF MISSING SOCKS
TOM WILSON

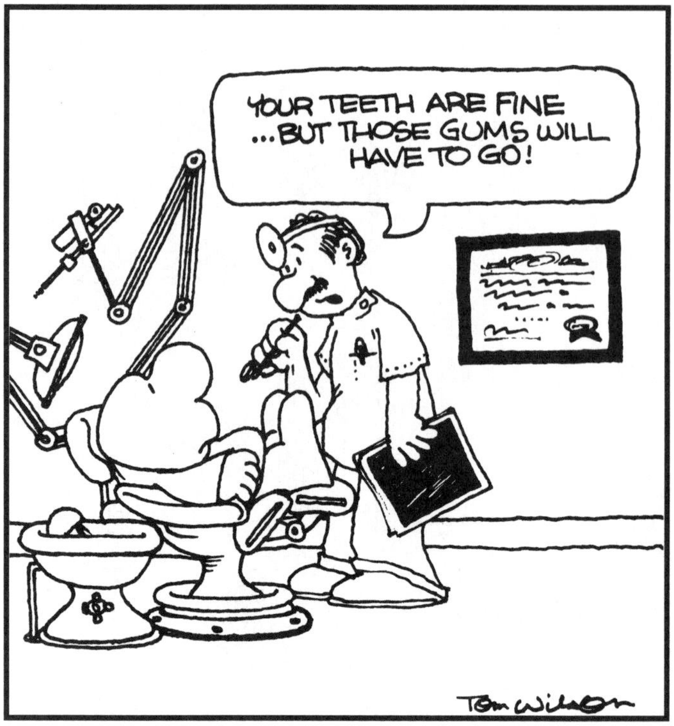
YOUR TEETH ARE FINE ...BUT THOSE GUMS WILL HAVE TO GO!
TOM WILSON

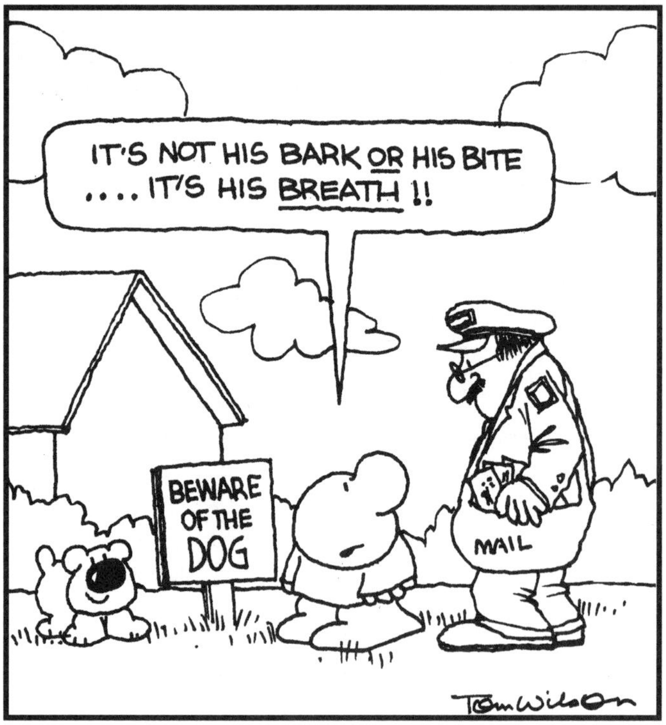
IT'S NOT HIS BARK OR HIS BITE .... IT'S HIS BREATH !!
BEWARE OF THE DOG
MAIL
TOM WILSON

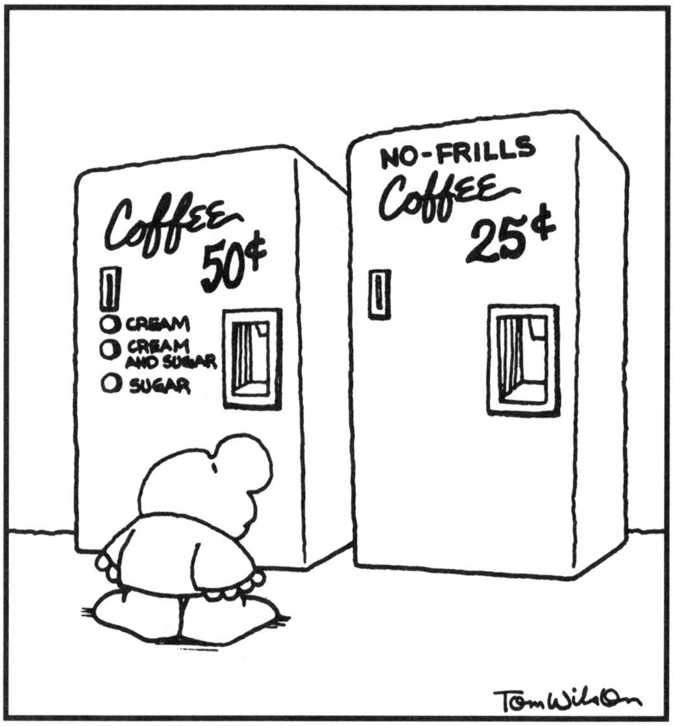
Coffee 50¢
CREAM
CREAM AND SUGAR
SUGAR
NO-FRILLS Coffee 25¢
TOM WILSON

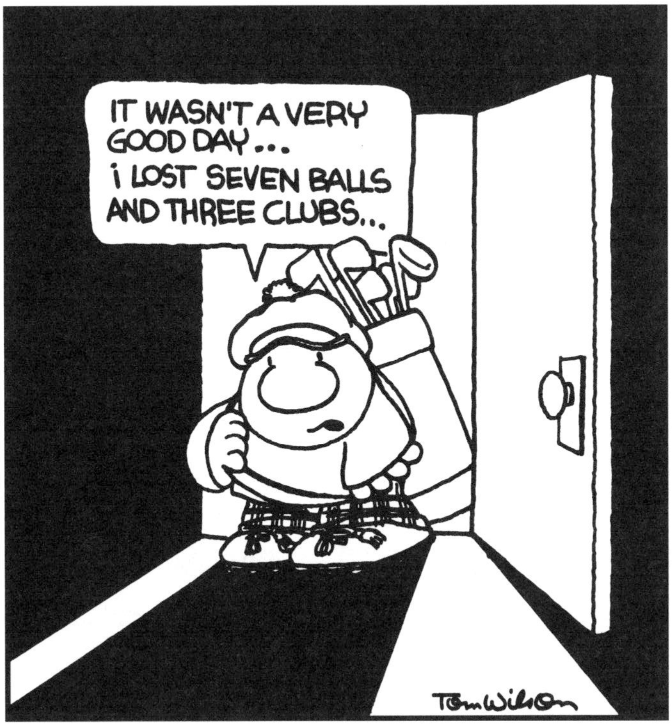
IT WASN'T A VERY GOOD DAY... i LOST SEVEN BALLS AND THREE CLUBS...
Tom Wilson

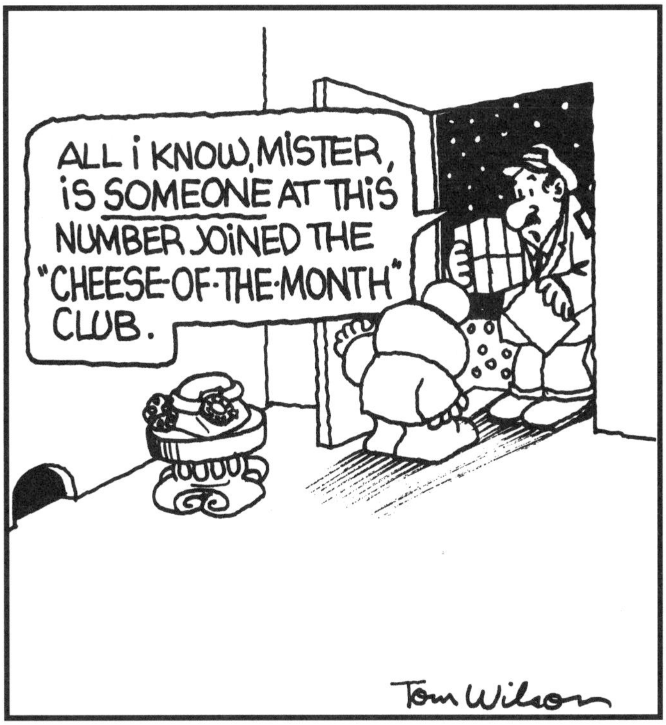
ALL i KNOW, MISTER, iS SOMEONE AT THIS NUMBER JOINED THE "CHEESE-OF-THE-MONTH" CLUB.
Tom Wilson

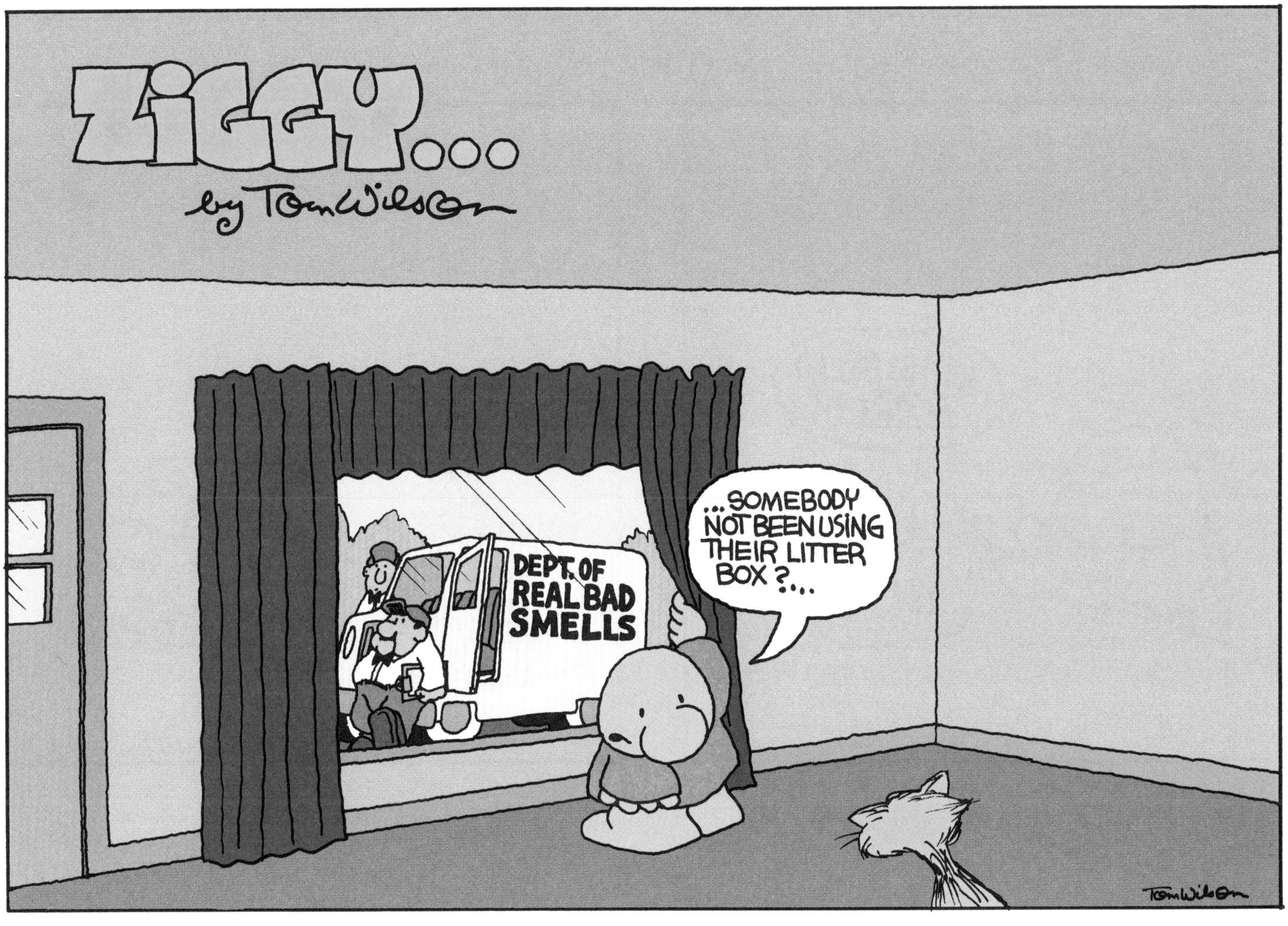
ZiGGY...
by Tom Wilson
DEPT. OF REAL BAD SMELLS
...SOMEBODY NOT BEEN USING THEIR LITTER BOX ?...
Tom Wilson

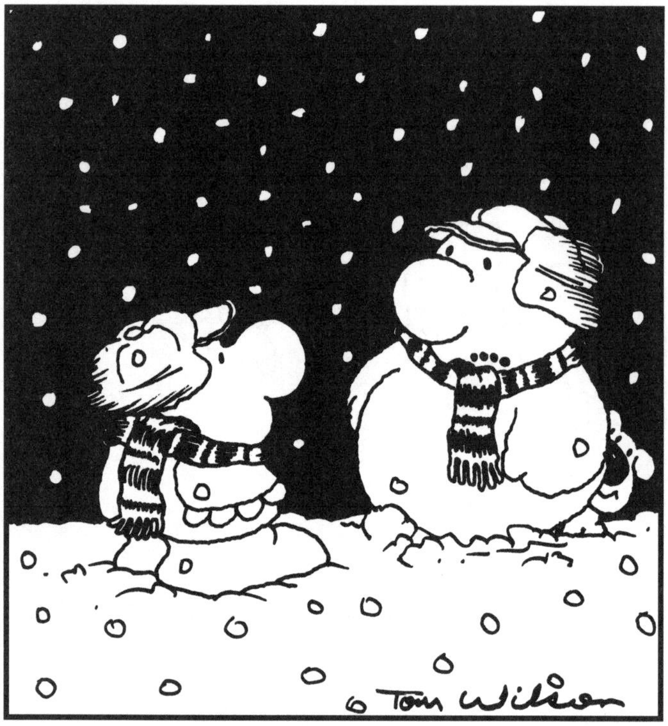

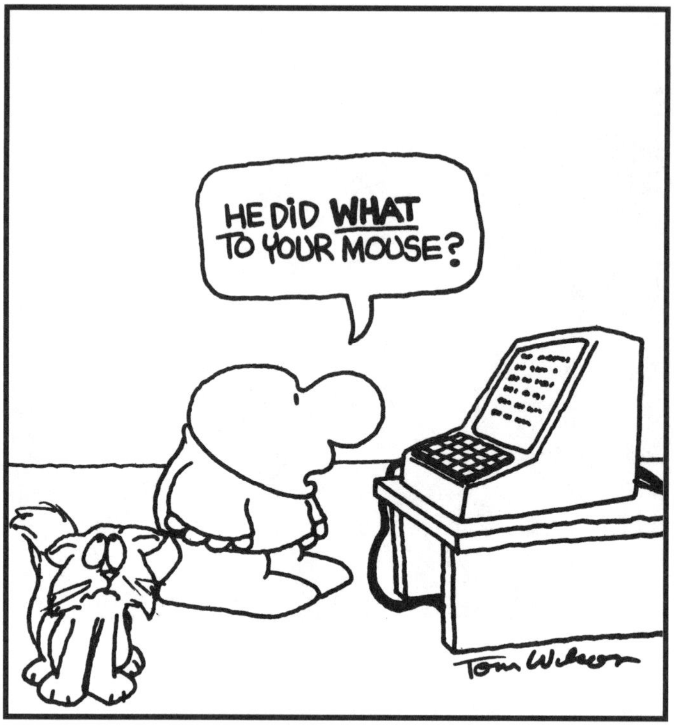
HE DID WHAT TO YOUR MOUSE?

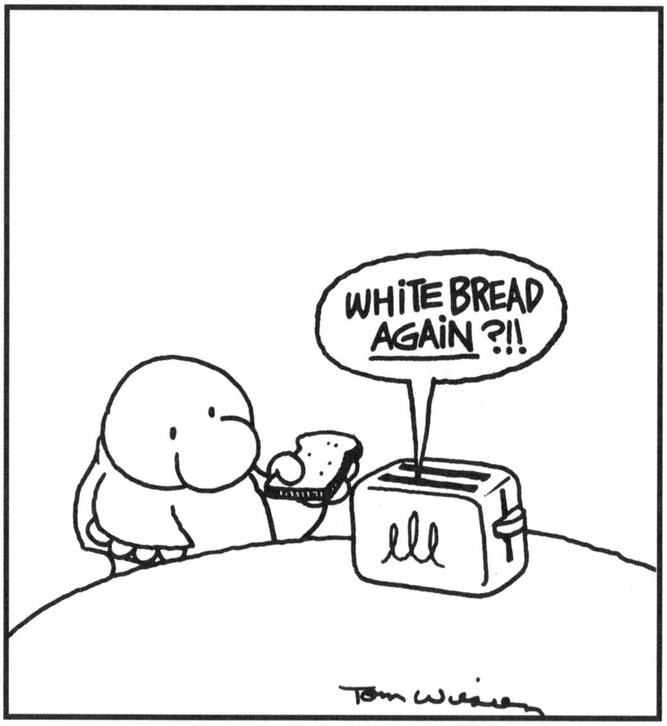
WHITE BREAD AGAIN?!!

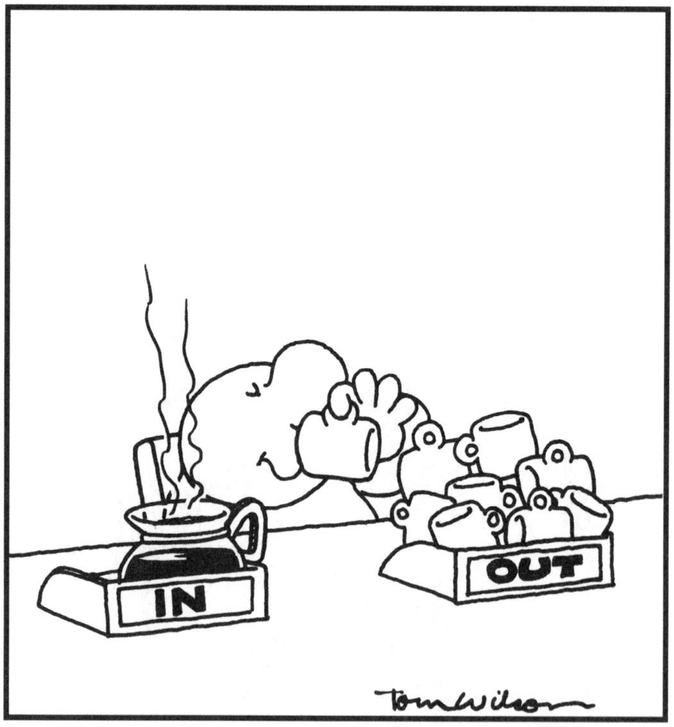
IN
OUT

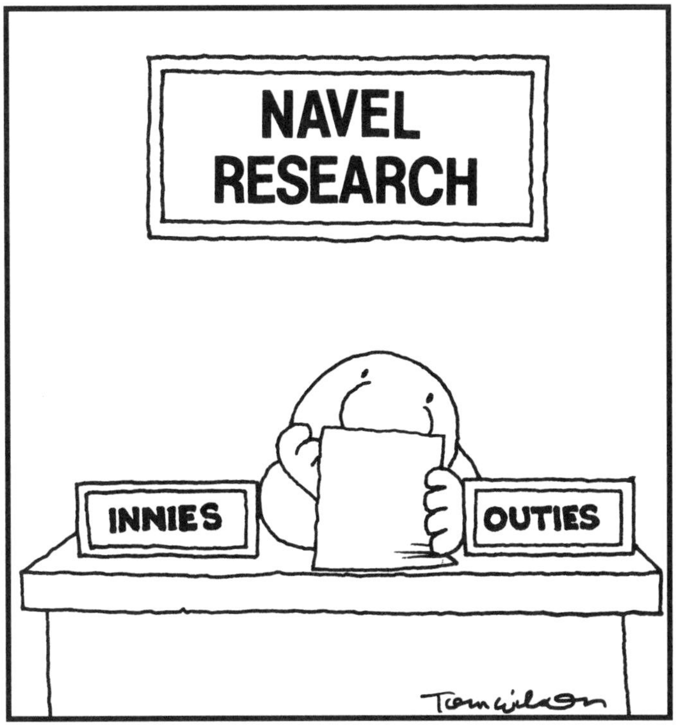
NAVEL RESEARCH
INNIES
OUTIES
Tom Wilson

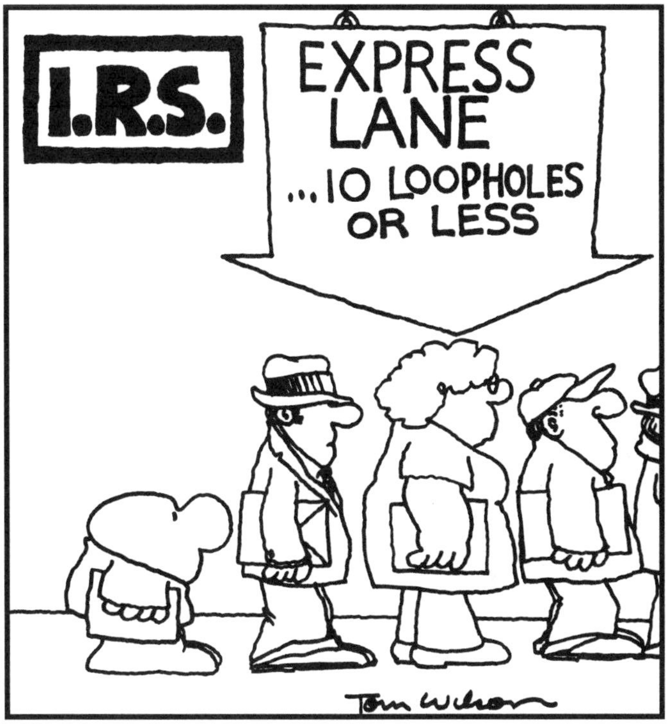
I.R.S.
EXPRESS LANE
...10 LOOPHOLES OR LESS
Tom Wilson

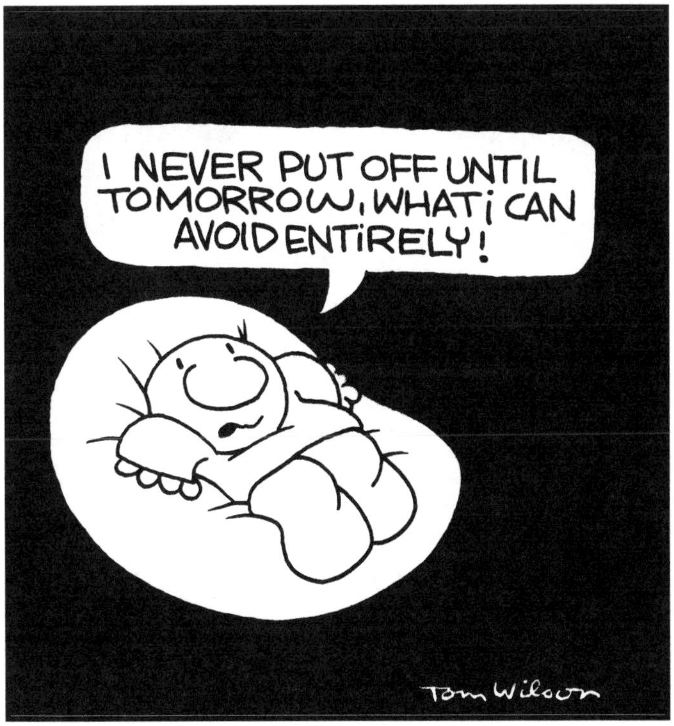
I NEVER PUT OFF UNTIL TOMORROW, WHAT I CAN AVOID ENTIRELY!
Tom Wilson

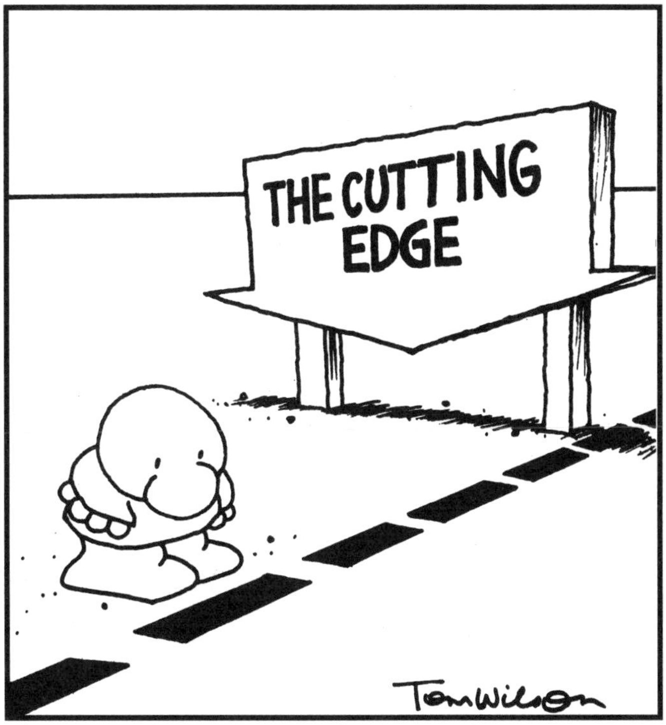
THE CUTTING EDGE
Tom Wilson

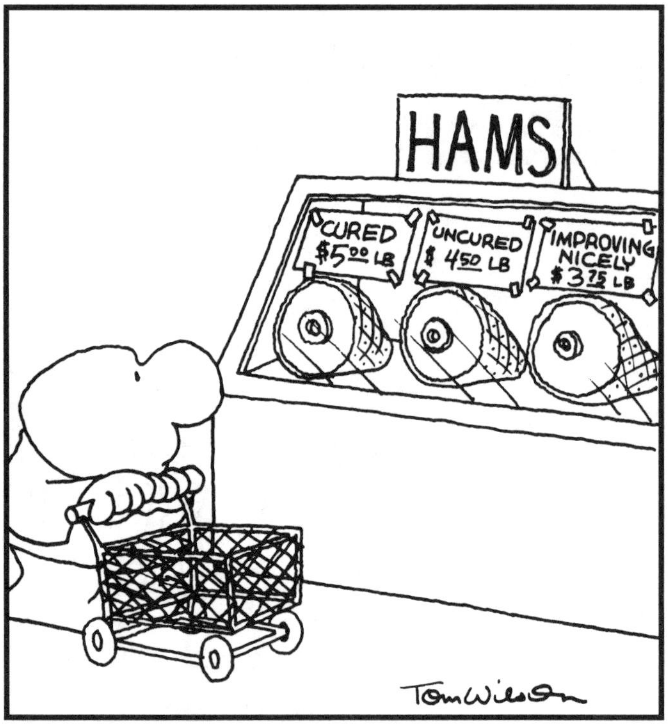
HAMS
CURED $5.00 LB
UNCURED $4.50 LB
IMPROVING NICELY $3.75 LB
Tom Wilson

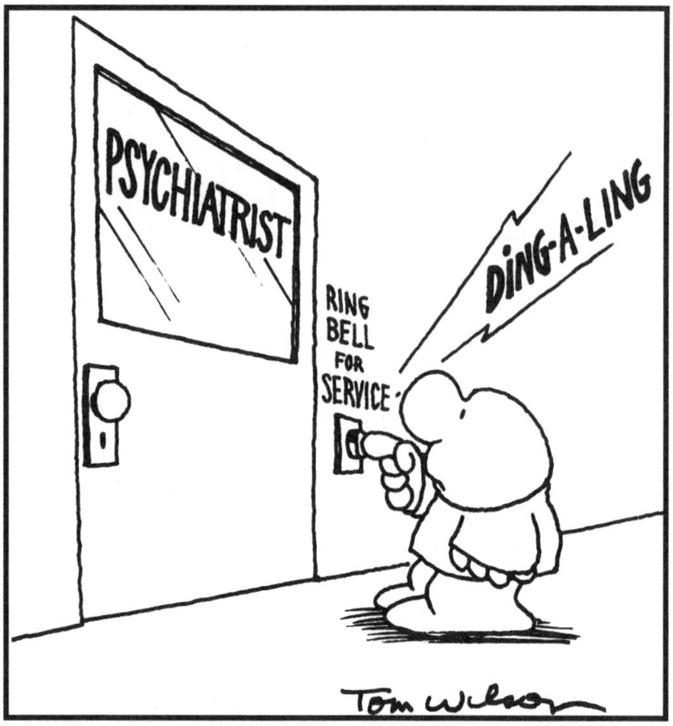
PSYCHIATRIST
RING BELL FOR SERVICE
DING-A-LING
Tom Wilson

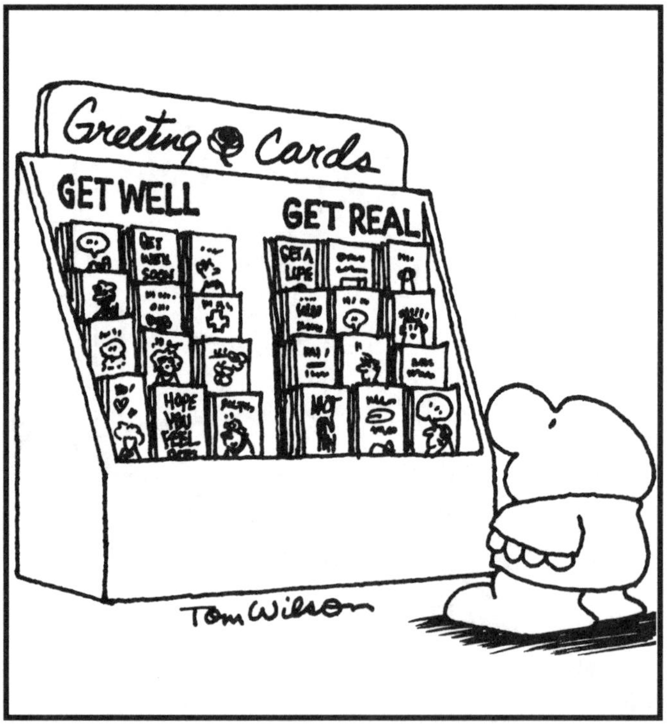
Greeting Cards
GET WELL
GET REAL
Tom Wilson

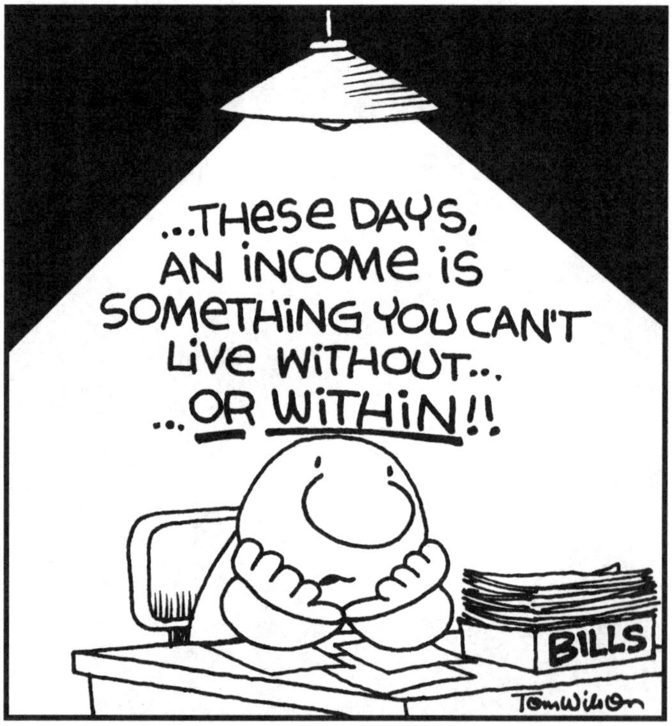
...THESE DAYS, AN INCOME IS SOMETHING YOU CAN'T LIVE WITHOUT... ...OR WITHIN!!
BILLS
Tom Wilson

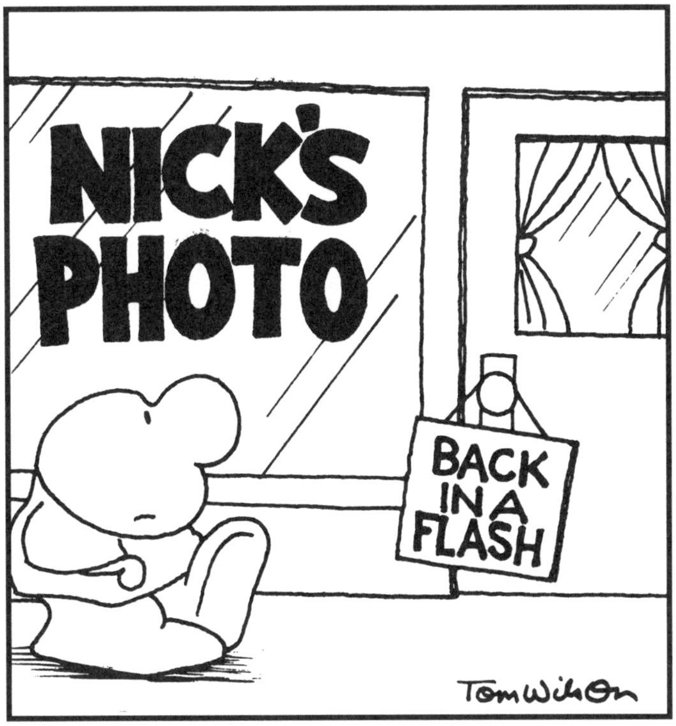
NICK'S PHOTO
BACK IN A FLASH
Tom Wilson

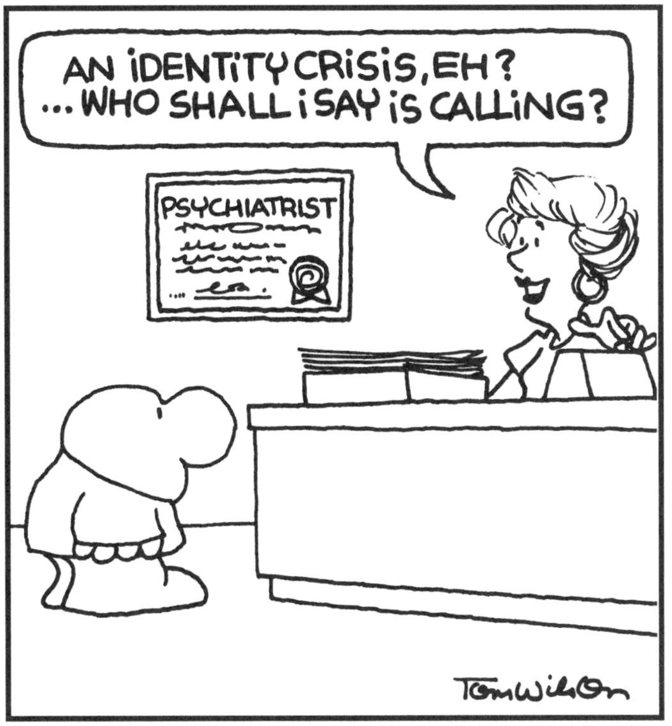
AN IDENTITY CRISIS, EH? ...WHO SHALL I SAY IS CALLING?
PSYCHIATRIST
Tom Wilson

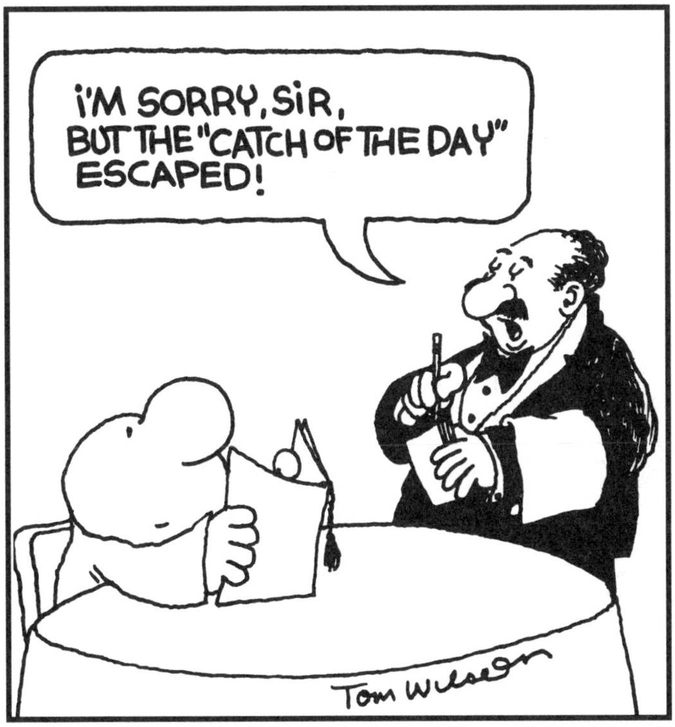
I'M SORRY, SIR, BUT THE "CATCH OF THE DAY" ESCAPED!
Tom Wilson

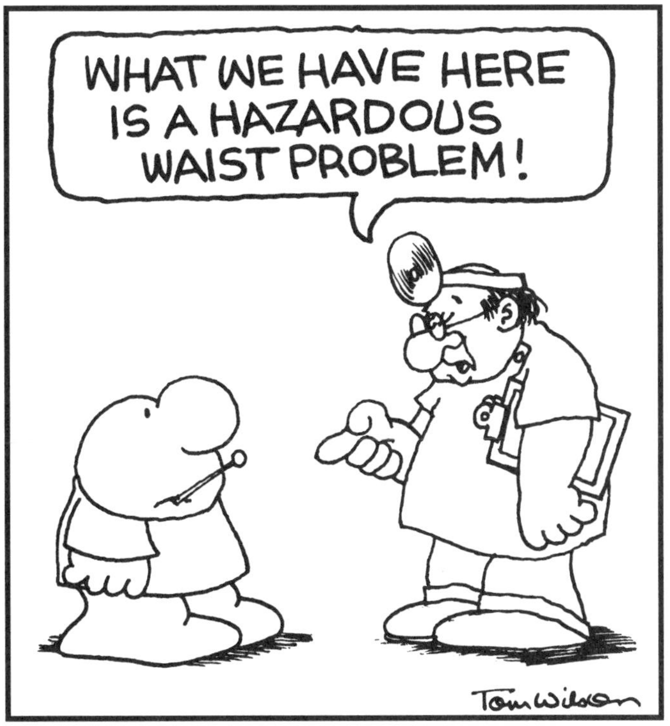
WHAT WE HAVE HERE IS A HAZARDOUS WAIST PROBLEM!
Tom Wilson

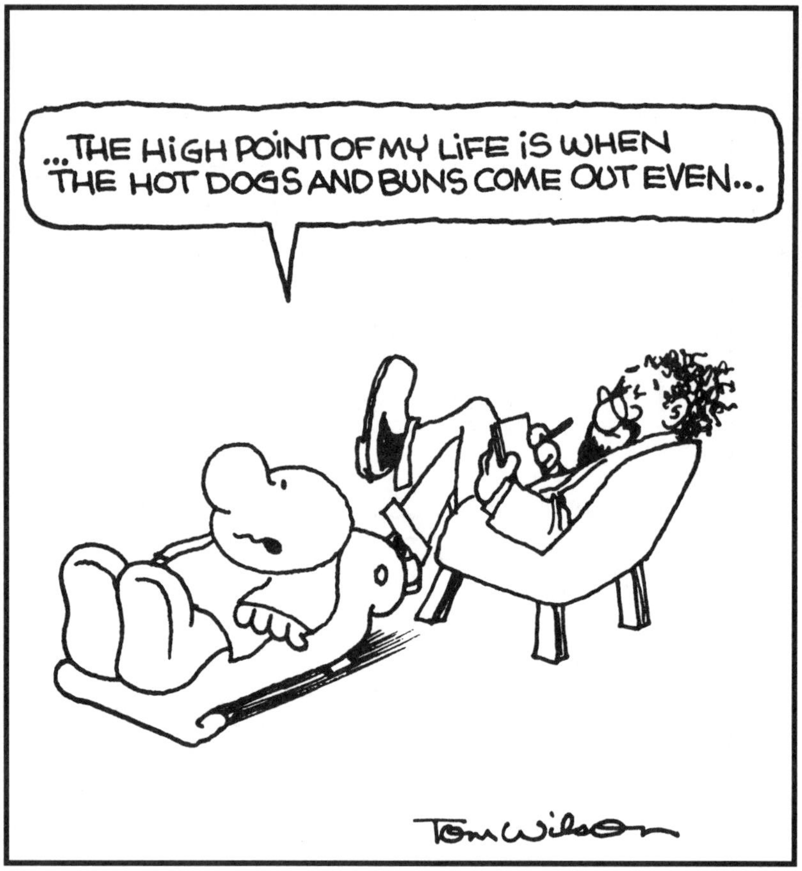
...THE HIGH POINT OF MY LIFE IS WHEN THE HOT DOGS AND BUNS COME OUT EVEN...
Tom Wilson

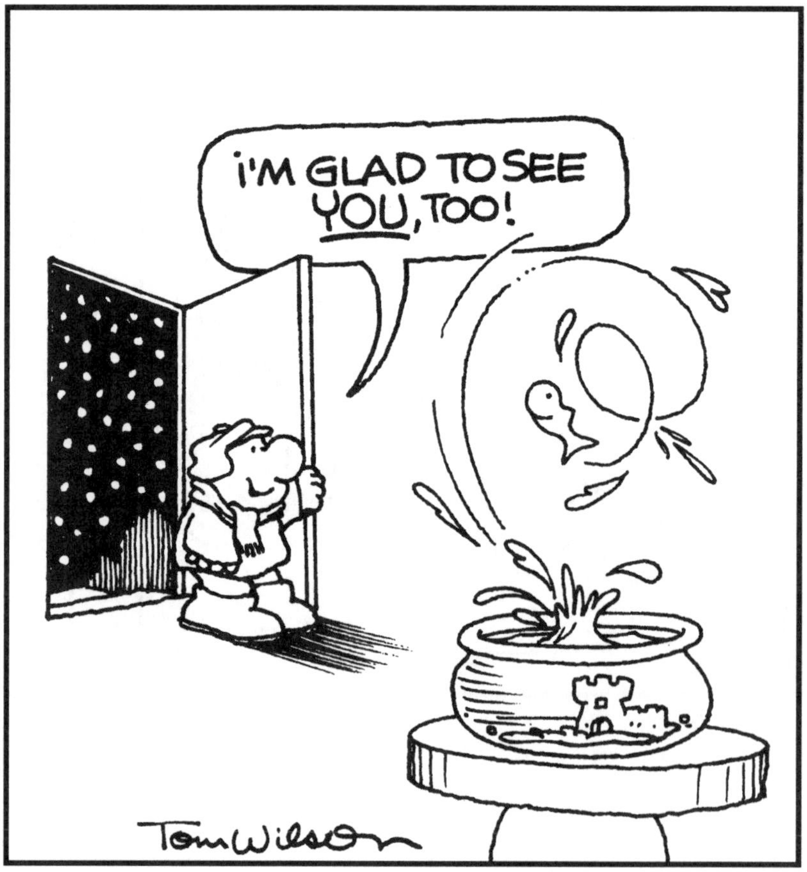
I'M GLAD TO SEE YOU, TOO!
Tom Wilson

Chapter V
1991–1995

My first thought on first meeting Tom Wilson more than thirty years ago was, "He *is* Ziggy!" And the more I got to know Tom, the more true my reaction seemed. Then I met Tom Wilson Jr. and became confused. "Wait," I thought. "*He* is Ziggy! How can that be?"

This affable, lovable character that has brought so much comfort and so many smiles to millions does accurately reflect the sensibilities and personalities of the two Toms, and that in large part explains Ziggy's enduring charm. In watching *Ziggy* in the hands (and spirit) of Tom I, then seeing both Toms work together to breathe life into the character, and, now, seeing Tom Jr. so ably shepherding the life and reactions of Ziggy, I've come to realize that there is a special Wilson quality that comes out in *Ziggy*. Call it heart, or soul, or whatever. But these two masters of the craft have both given life to the little guy. He owes everything to the two Toms.

—Lee Salem, executive vice president/editor, Universal Press Syndicate

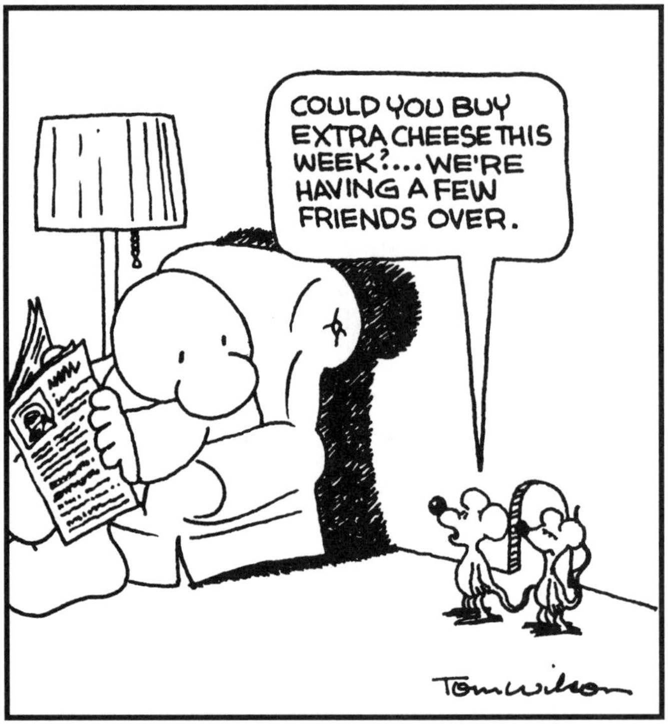
COULD YOU BUY EXTRA CHEESE THIS WEEK?... WE'RE HAVING A FEW FRIENDS OVER.
TomWilson

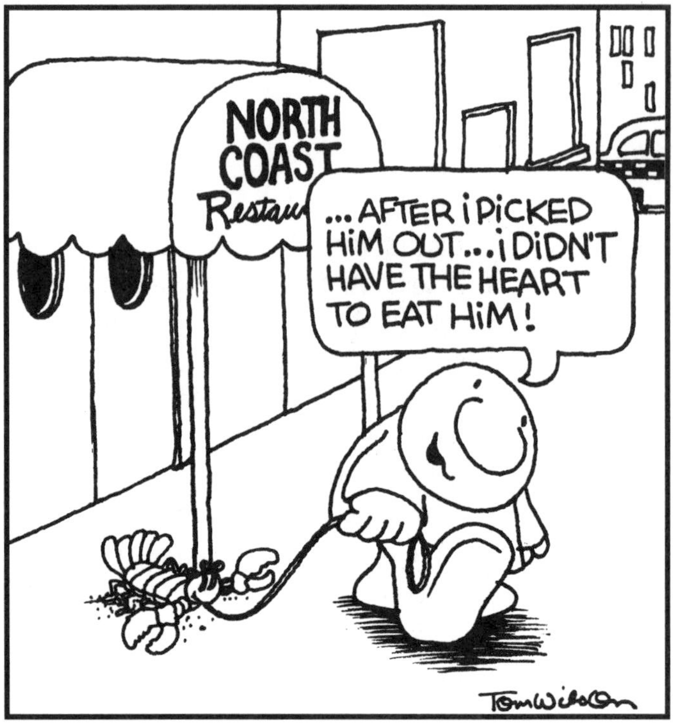
NORTH COAST
...AFTER I PICKED HIM OUT...I DIDN'T HAVE THE HEART TO EAT HIM!
TomWilson

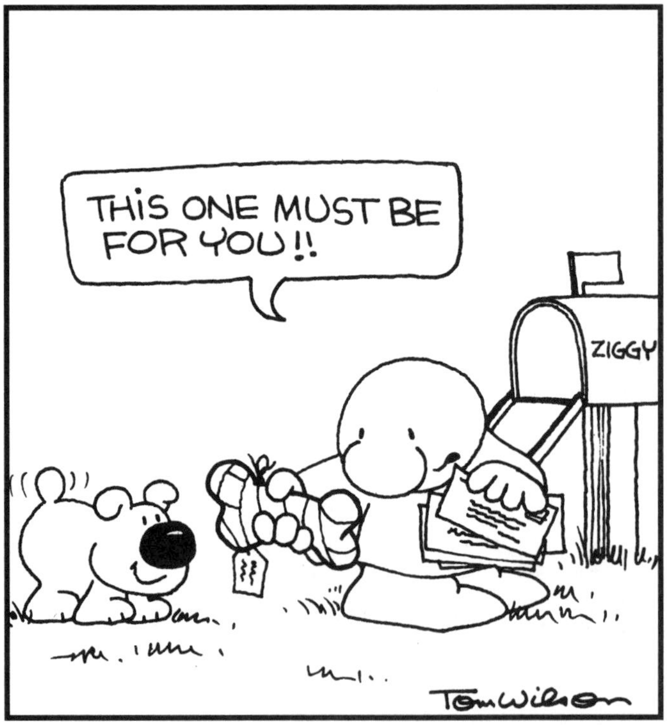
THIS ONE MUST BE FOR YOU!!
ZIGGY
TomWilson

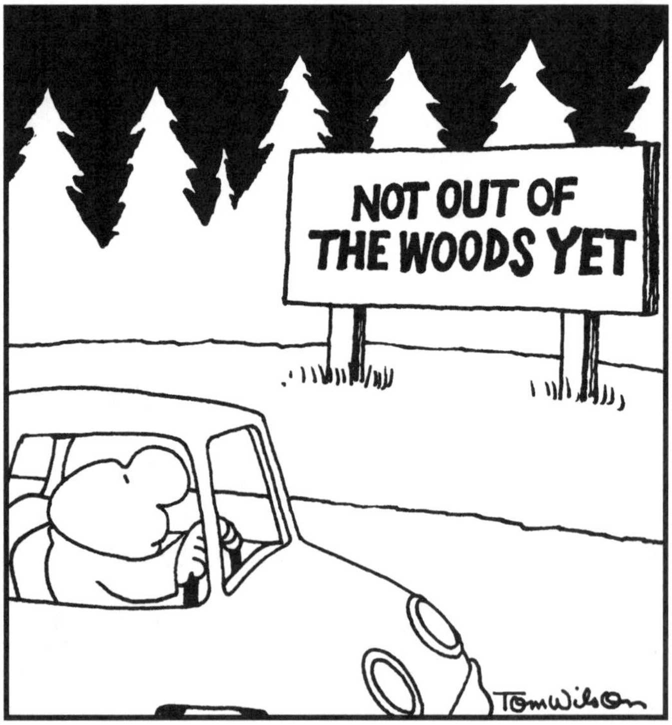
NOT OUT OF THE WOODS YET
TomWilson

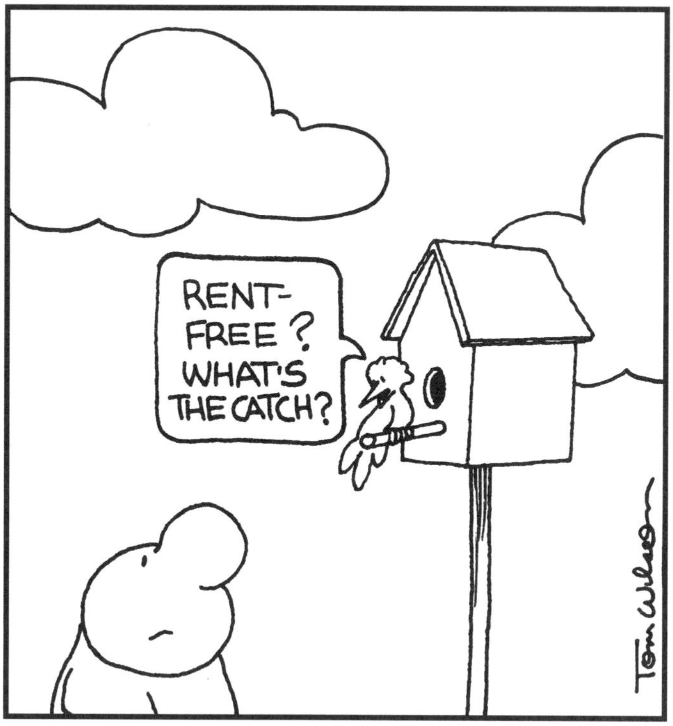
RENT-FREE? WHAT'S THE CATCH?
Tom Wilson

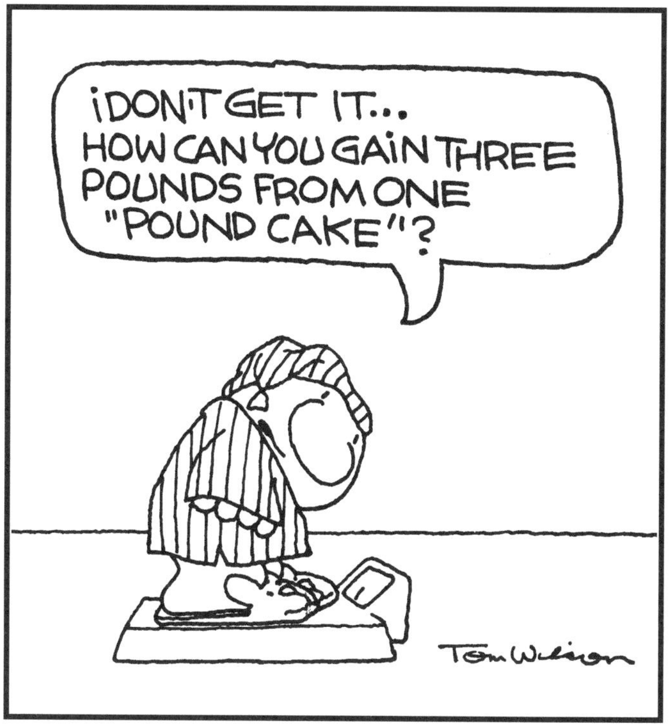
I DON'T GET IT... HOW CAN YOU GAIN THREE POUNDS FROM ONE "POUND CAKE"?
Tom Wilson

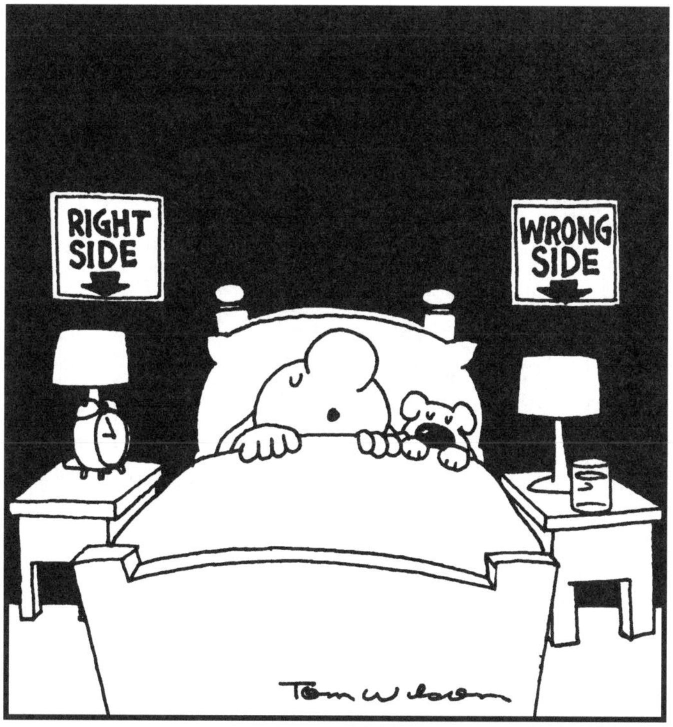
RIGHT SIDE
WRONG SIDE
Tom Wilson

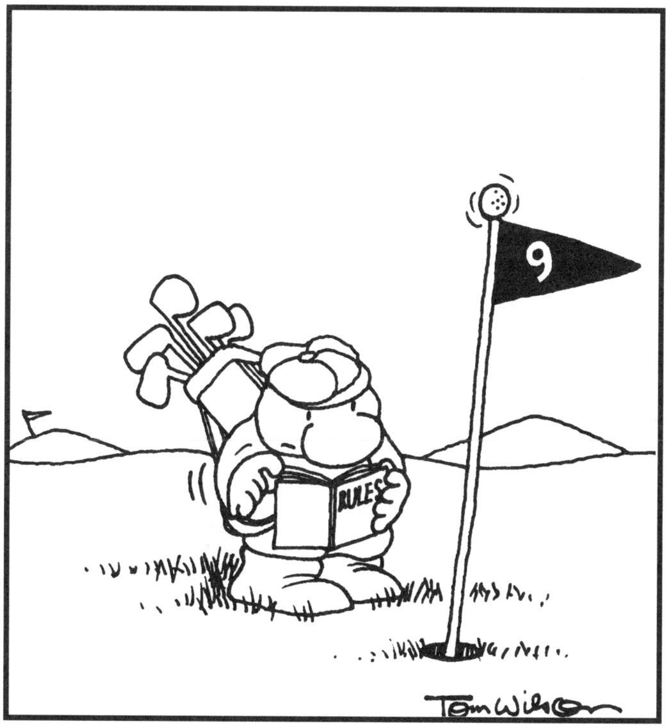
9
RULES
Tom Wilson

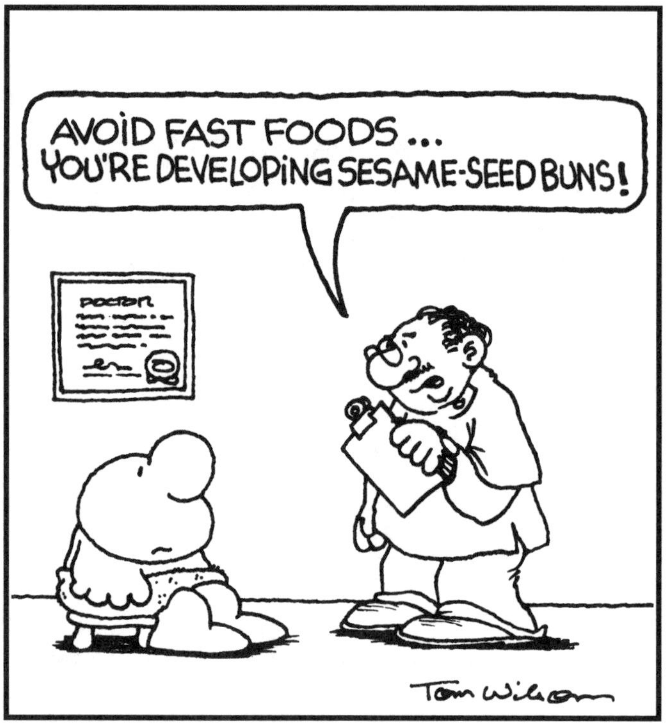
AVOID FAST FOODS...
YOU'RE DEVELOPING SESAME-SEED BUNS!
Tom Wilson

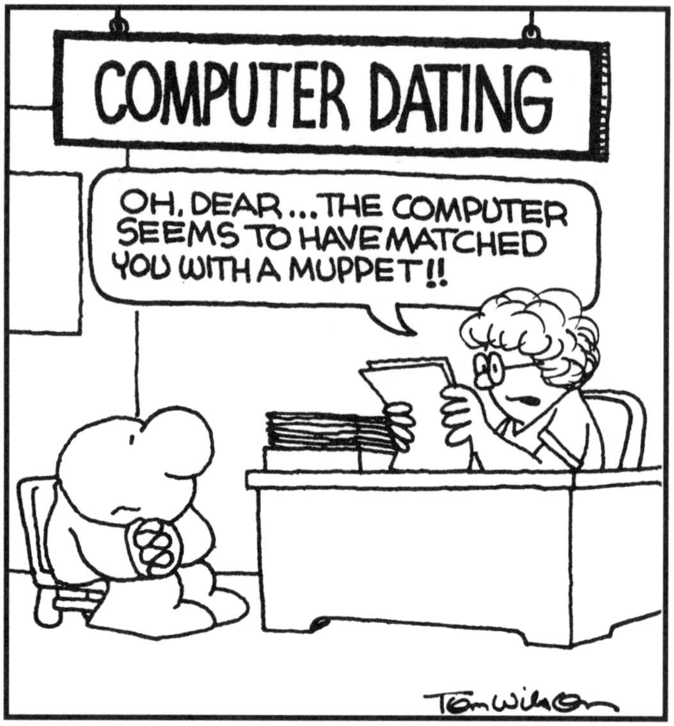
COMPUTER DATING
OH, DEAR...THE COMPUTER SEEMS TO HAVE MATCHED YOU WITH A MUPPET!!
Tom Wilson

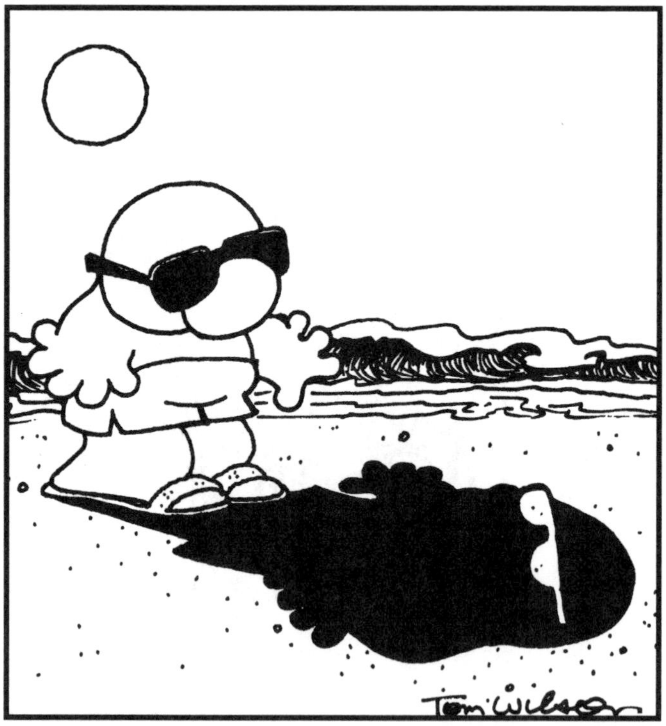
Tom Wilson

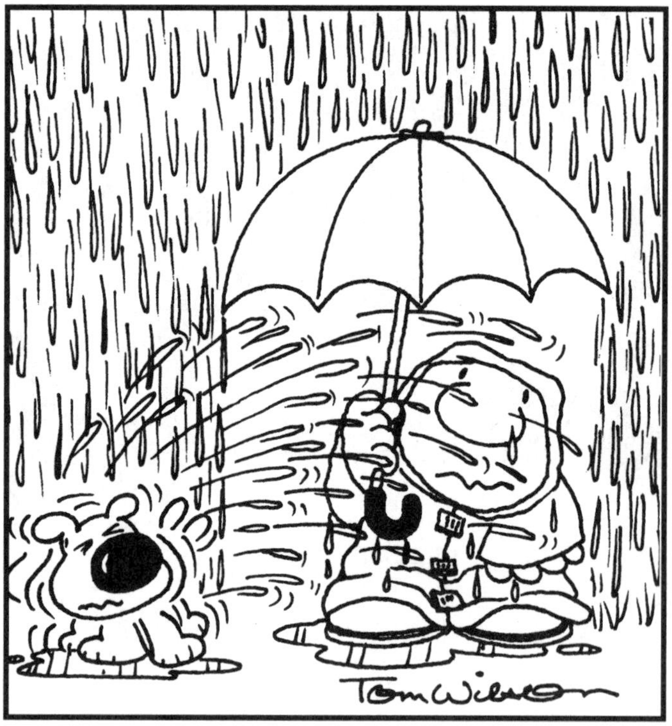
Tom Wilson

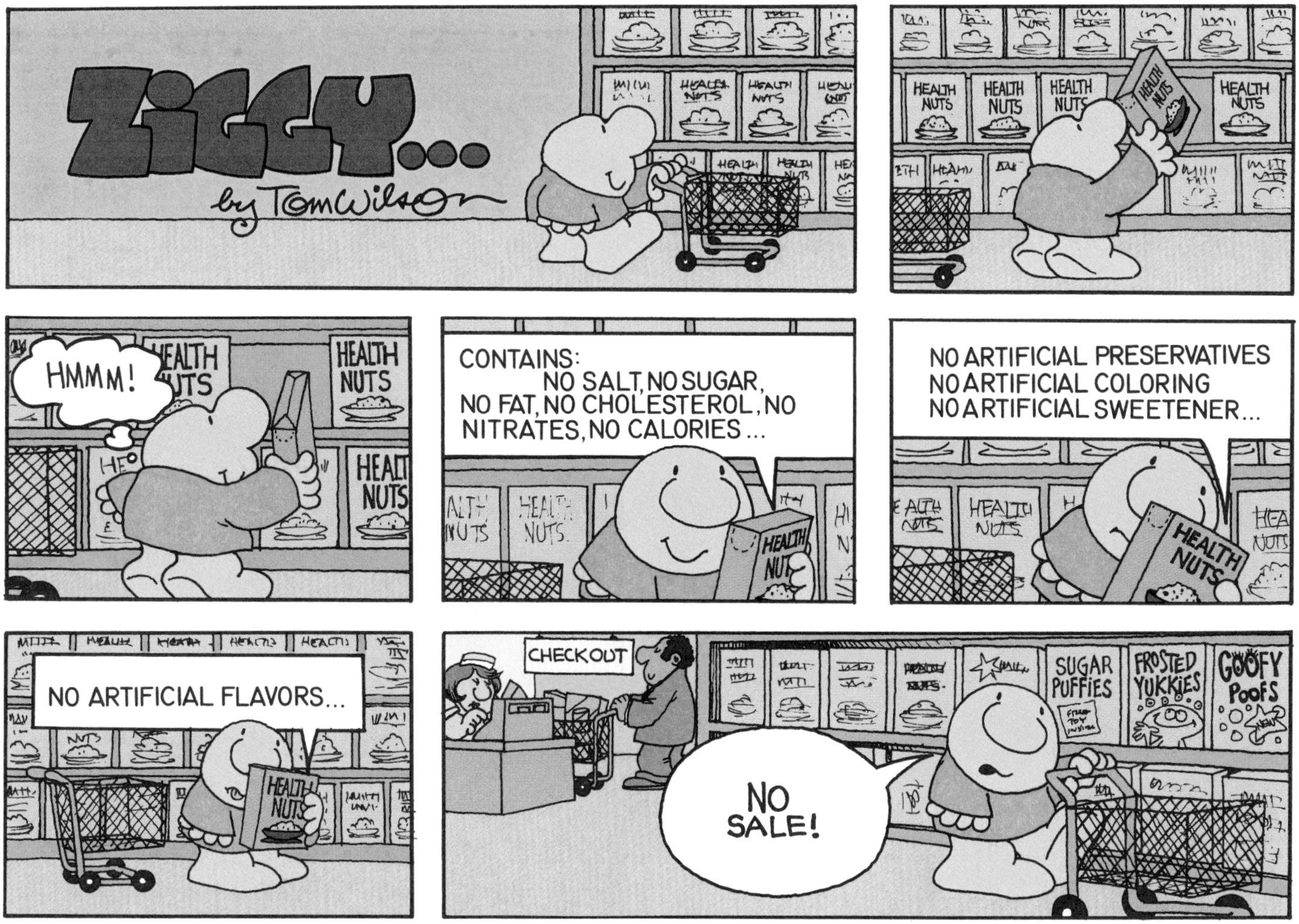
ZIGGY...
by Tom Wilson
HEALTH NUTS
HMMM!
CONTAINS:
NO SALT, NO SUGAR,
NO FAT, NO CHOLESTEROL, NO
NITRATES, NO CALORIES...
NO ARTIFICIAL PRESERVATIVES
NO ARTIFICIAL COLORING
NO ARTIFICIAL SWEETENER...
NO ARTIFICIAL FLAVORS...
CHECKOUT
SUGAR PUFFIES
FROSTED YUKKIES
GOOFY POOFS
NO SALE!

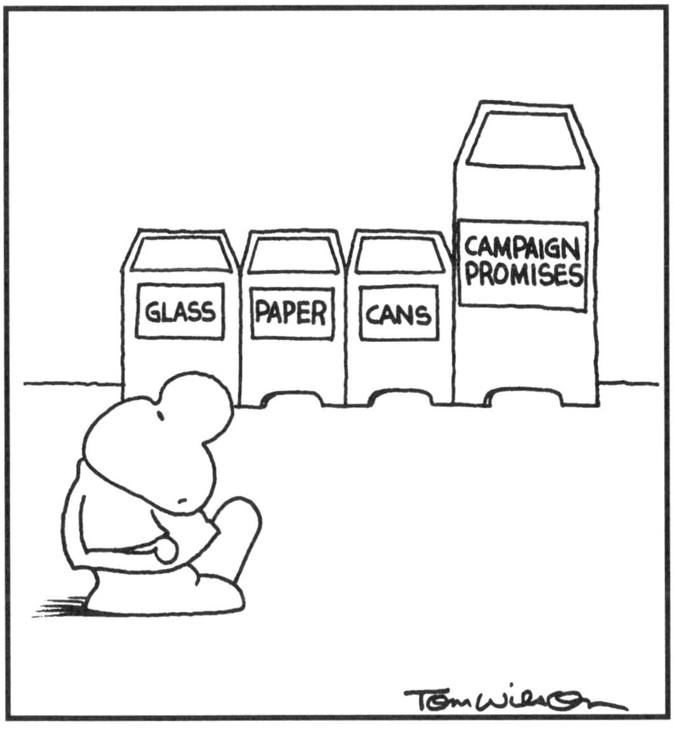
GLASS
PAPER
CANS
CAMPAIGN PROMISES
Tom Wilson

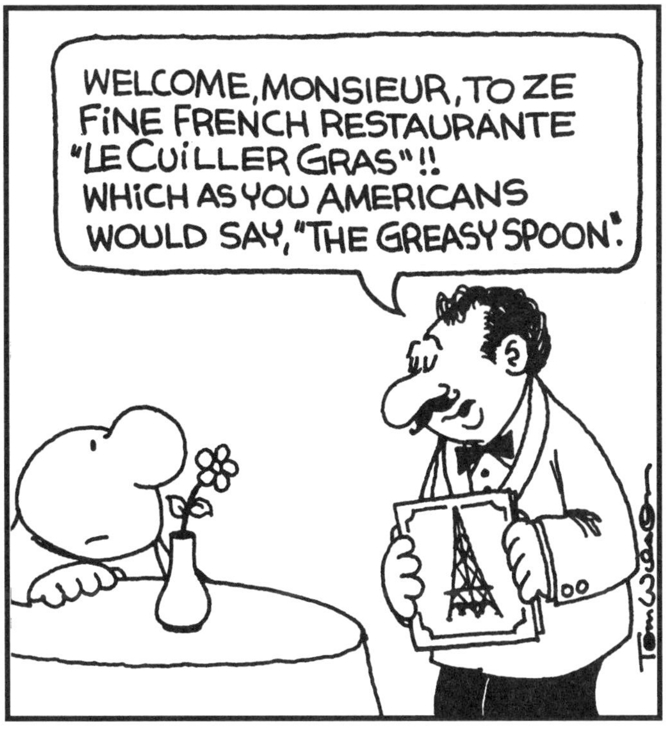
WELCOME, MONSIEUR, TO ZE FINE FRENCH RESTAURANTE "LE CUILLER GRAS"!! WHICH AS YOU AMERICANS WOULD SAY, "THE GREASY SPOON".
Tom Wilson

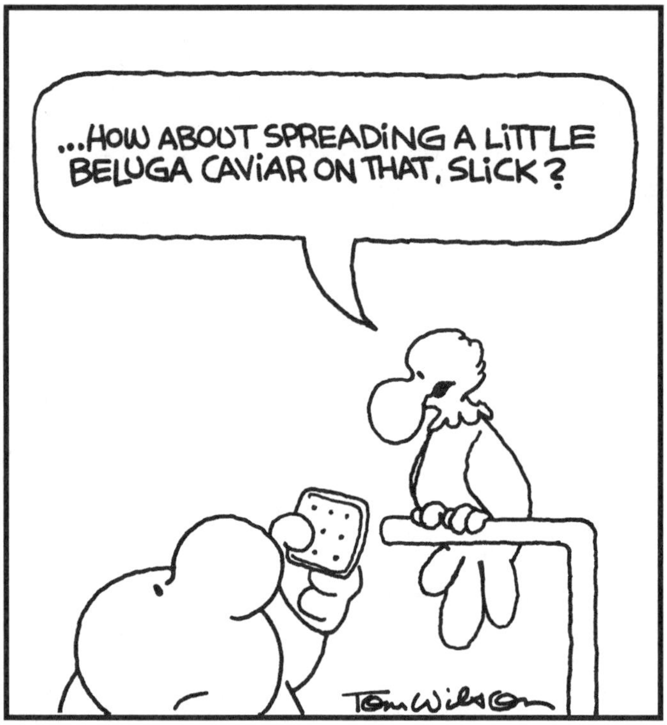
...HOW ABOUT SPREADING A LITTLE BELUGA CAVIAR ON THAT, SLICK?
Tom Wilson

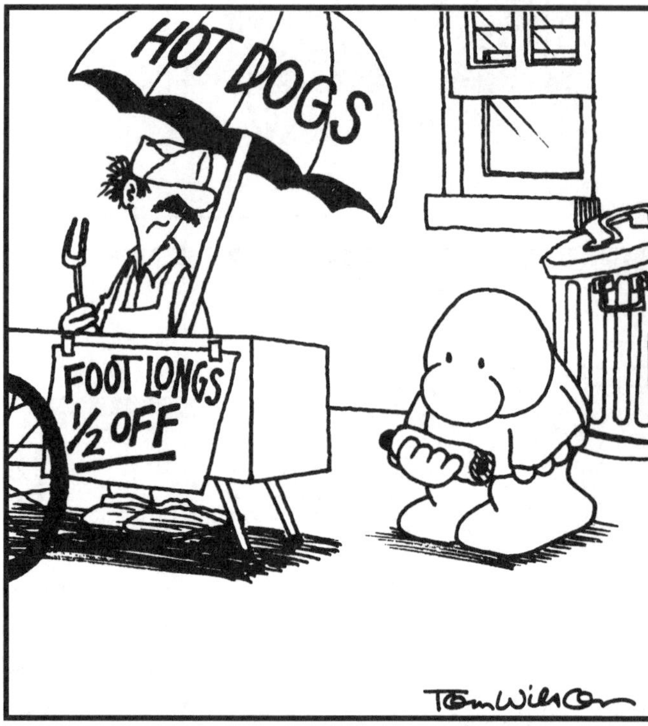
HOT DOGS
FOOT LONGS 1/2 OFF
Tom Wilson

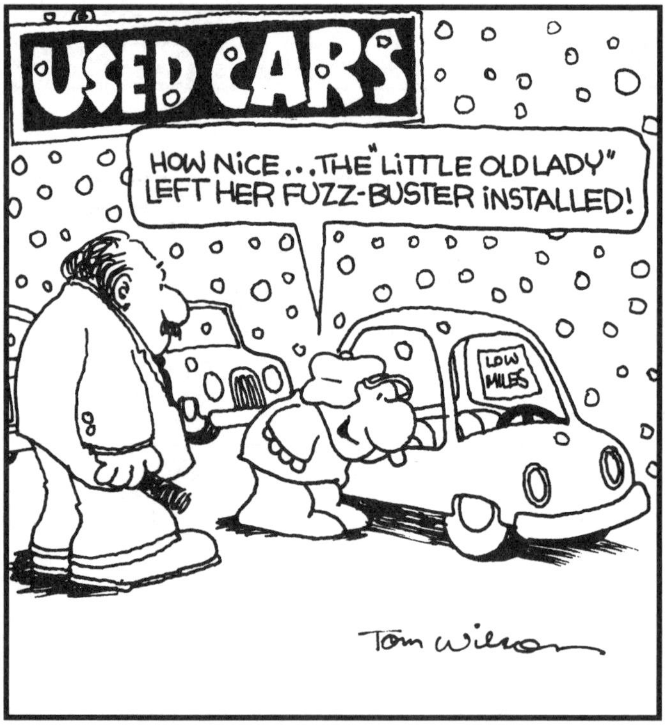
USED CARS
HOW NICE... THE "LITTLE OLD LADY" LEFT HER FUZZ-BUSTER INSTALLED!
LOW MILES
Tom Wilson

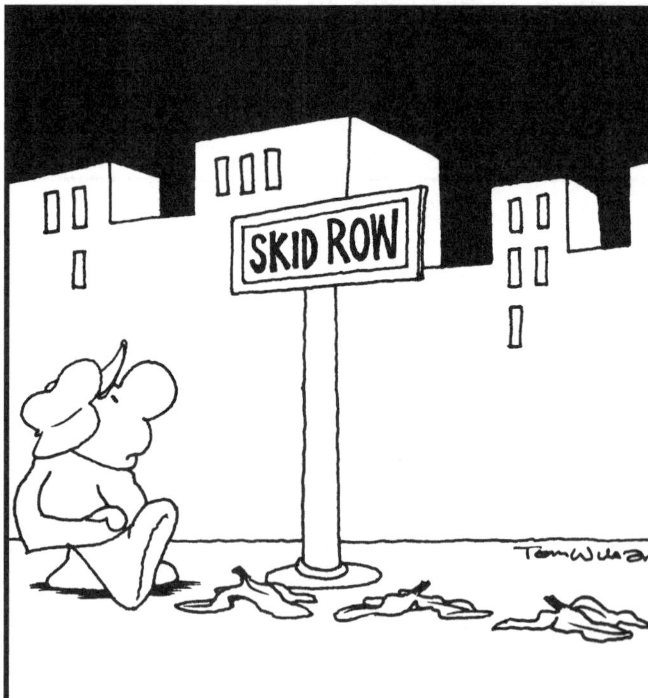
SKID ROW
Tom Wilson

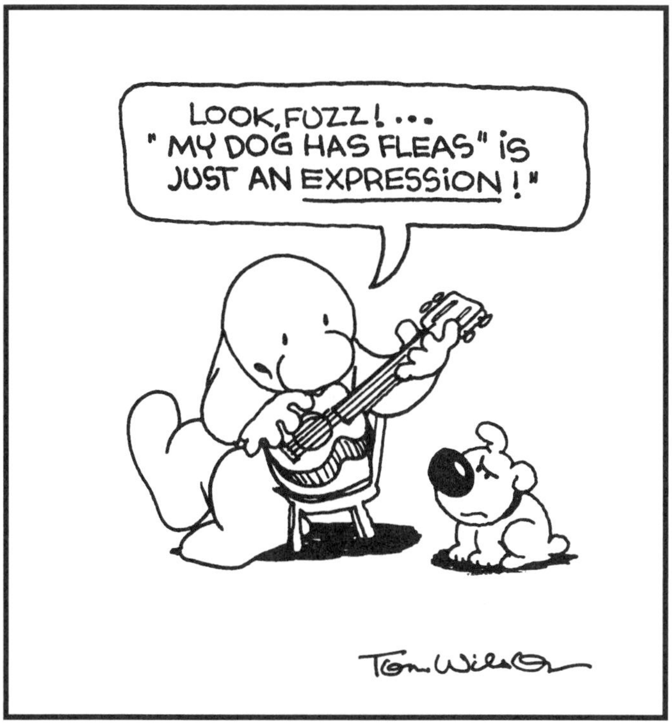
LOOK, FUZZ! ... " MY DOG HAS FLEAS" IS JUST AN EXPRESSION ! "
Tom Wilson

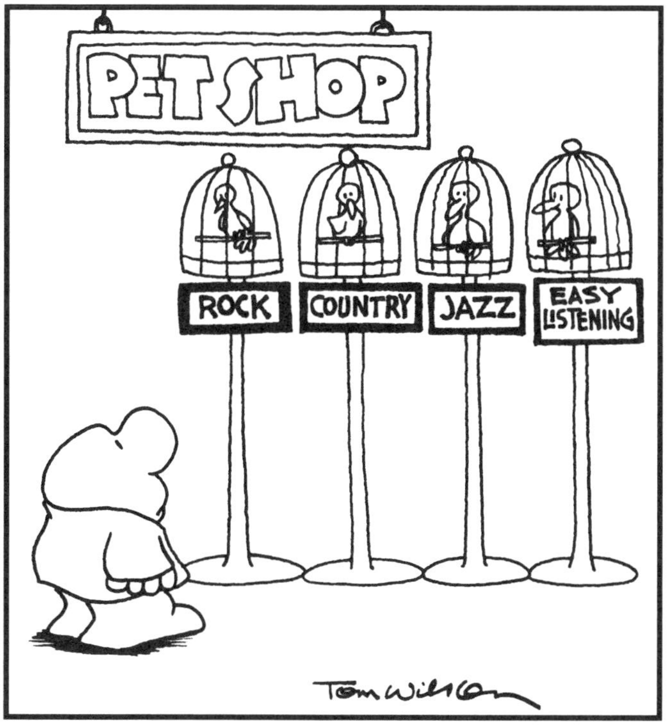
PET SHOP
ROCK
COUNTRY
JAZZ
EASY LISTENING
Tom Wilson

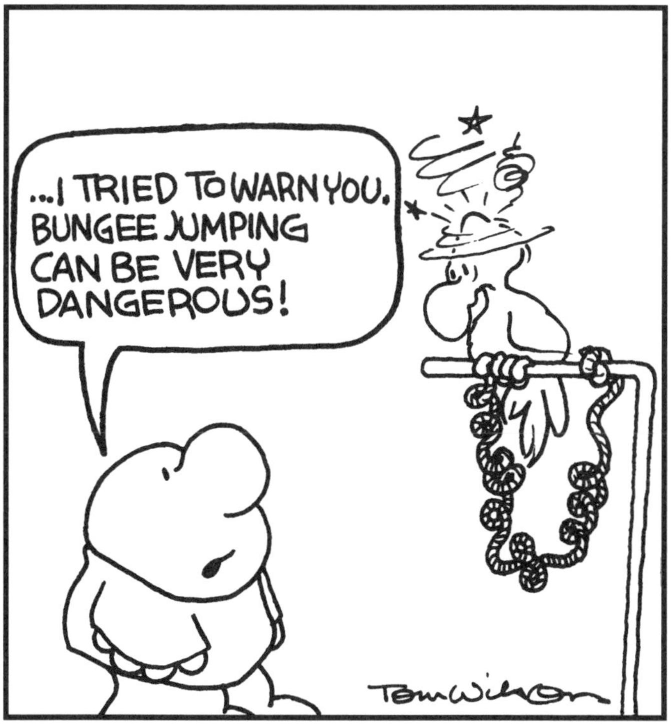
...I TRIED TO WARN YOU. BUNGEE JUMPING CAN BE VERY DANGEROUS!
Tom Wilson

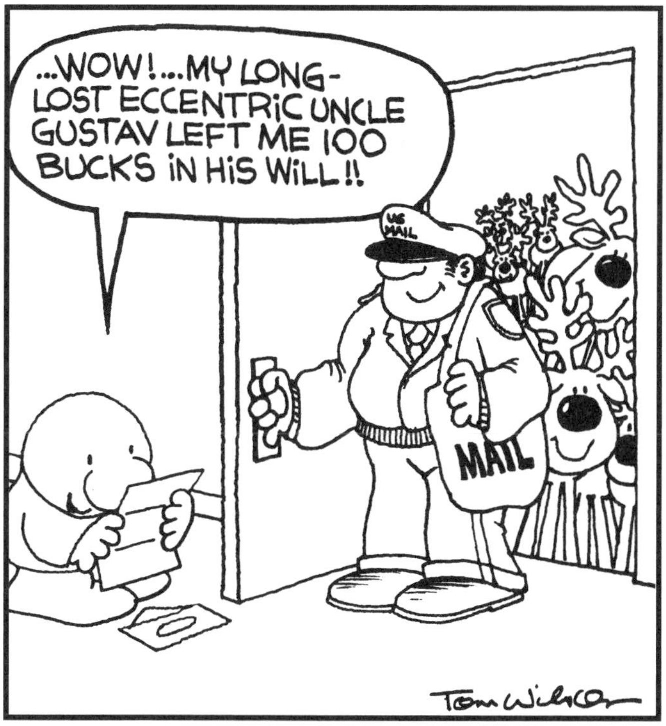
...WOW!...MY LONG-LOST ECCENTRIC UNCLE GUSTAV LEFT ME 100 BUCKS IN HIS WILL!!
MAIL
Tom Wilson

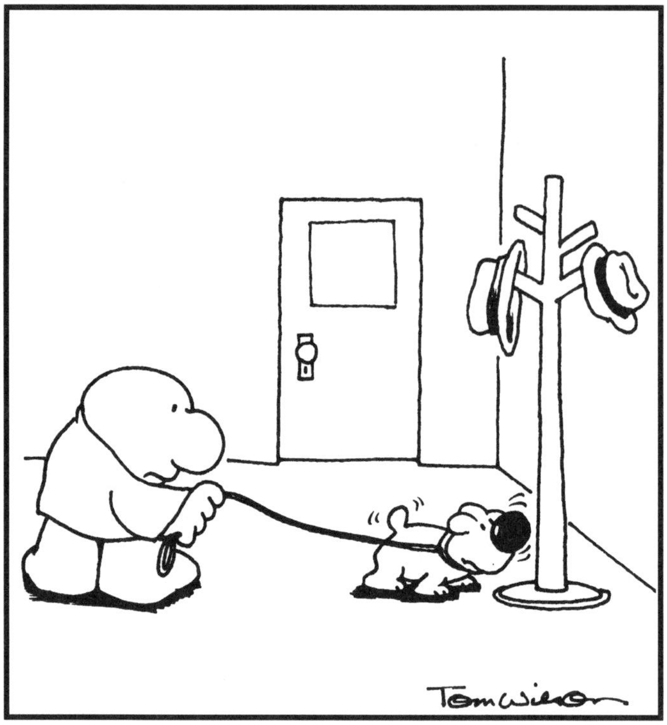
Tom Wilson

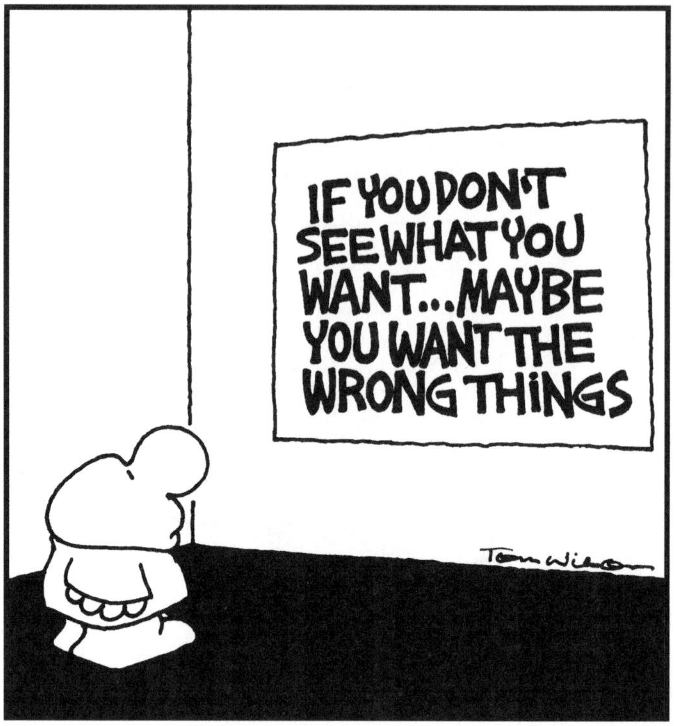
IF YOU DON'T SEE WHAT YOU WANT...MAYBE YOU WANT THE WRONG THINGS
Tom Wilson

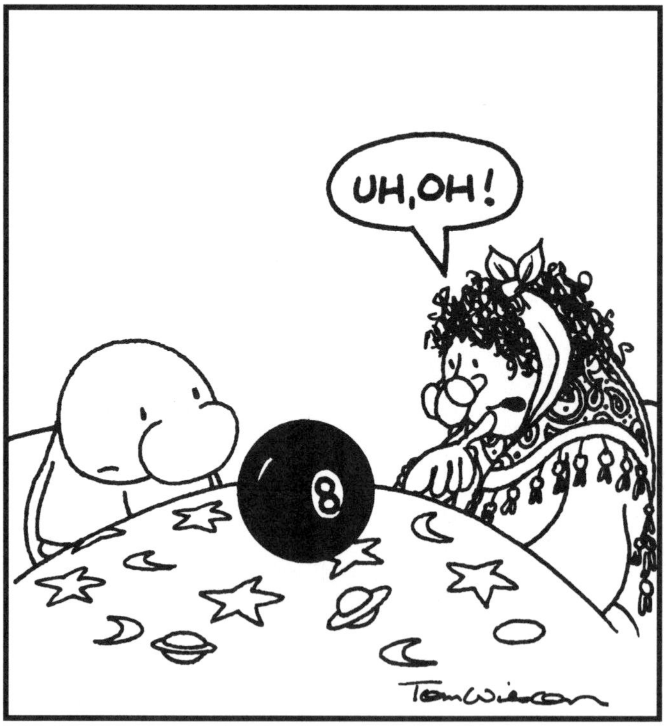
UH, OH!
8
Tom Wilson

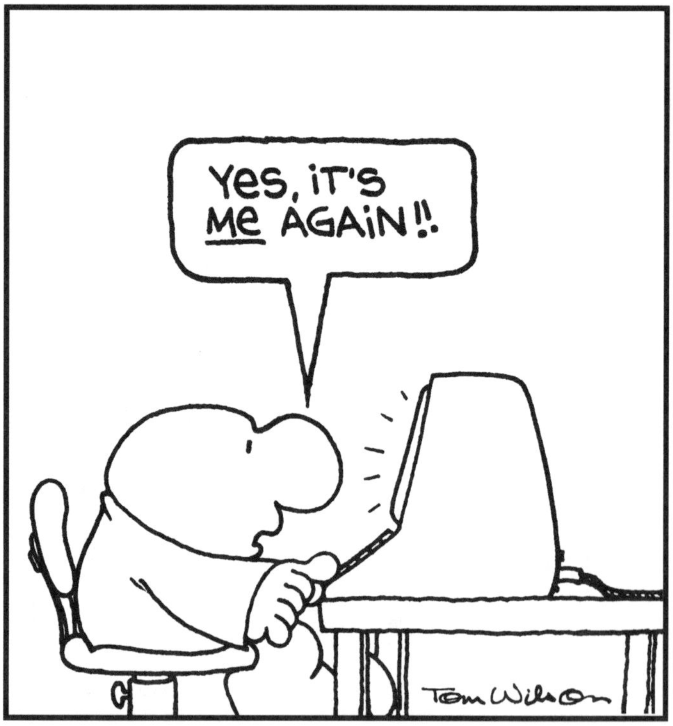
YES, IT'S ME AGAIN!!
Tom Wilson

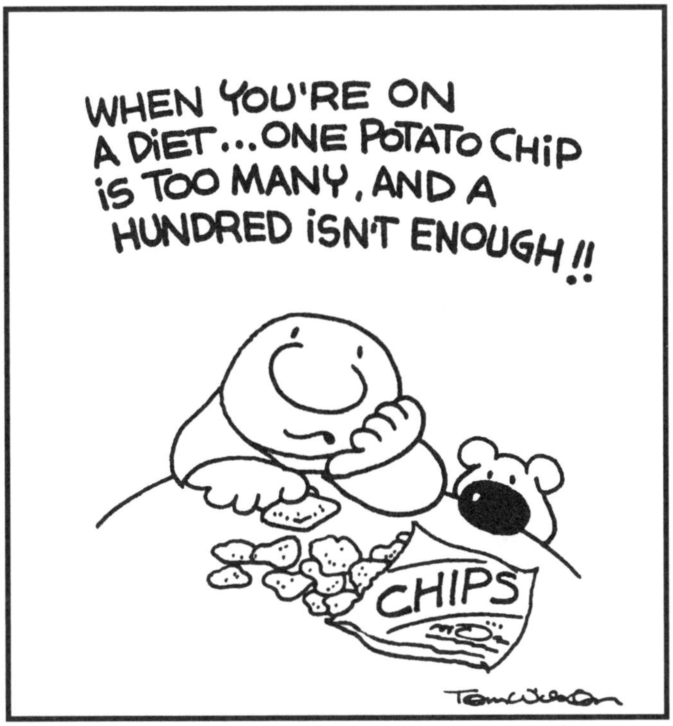
WHEN YOU'RE ON A DIET...ONE POTATO CHIP IS TOO MANY, AND A HUNDRED ISN'T ENOUGH!!
CHIPS
Tom Wilson

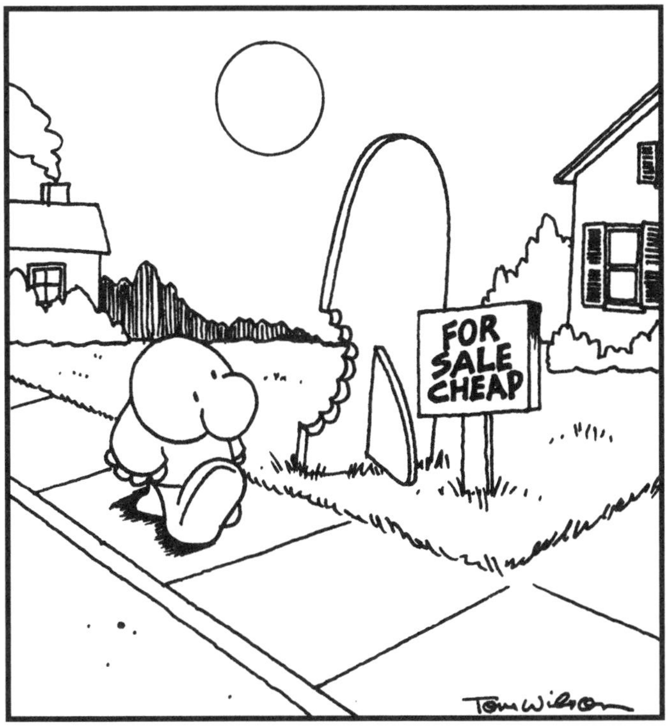
FOR SALE CHEAP
Tom Wilson

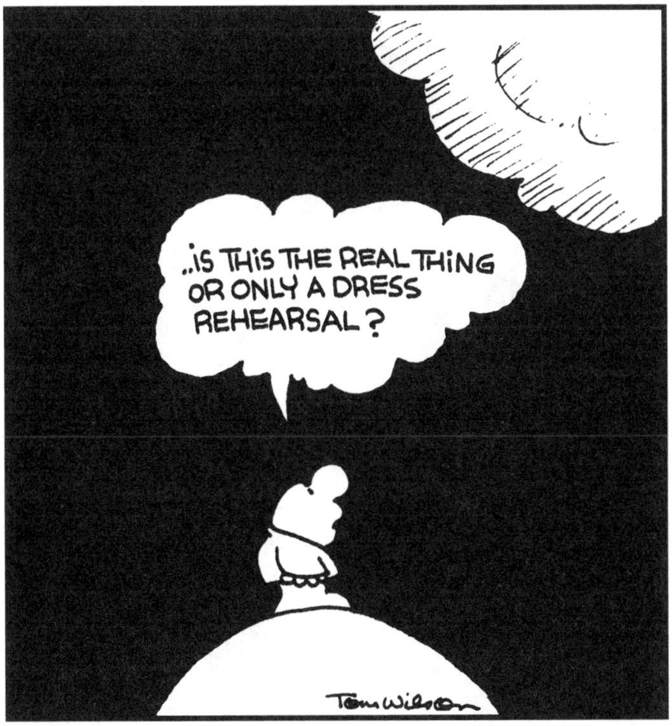
..IS THIS THE REAL THING OR ONLY A DRESS REHEARSAL?
Tom Wilson

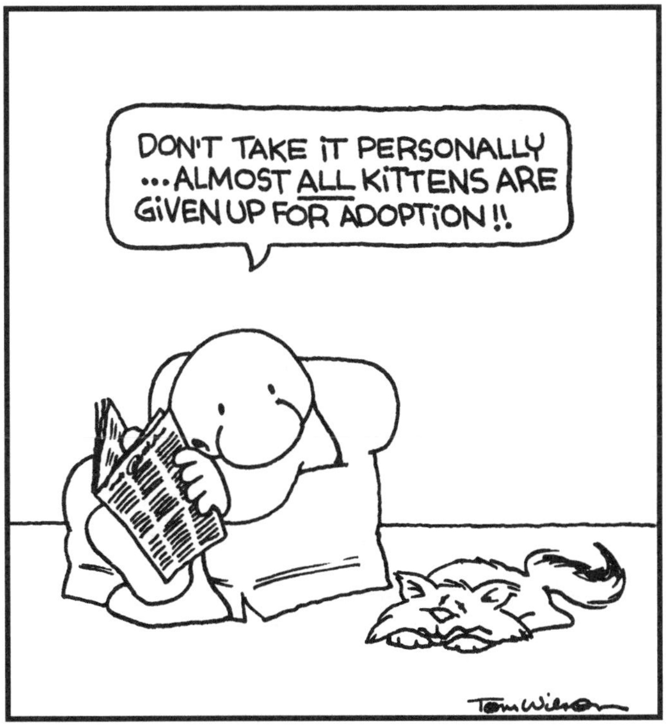
DON'T TAKE IT PERSONALLY ...ALMOST ALL KITTENS ARE GIVEN UP FOR ADOPTION!!
Tom Wilson

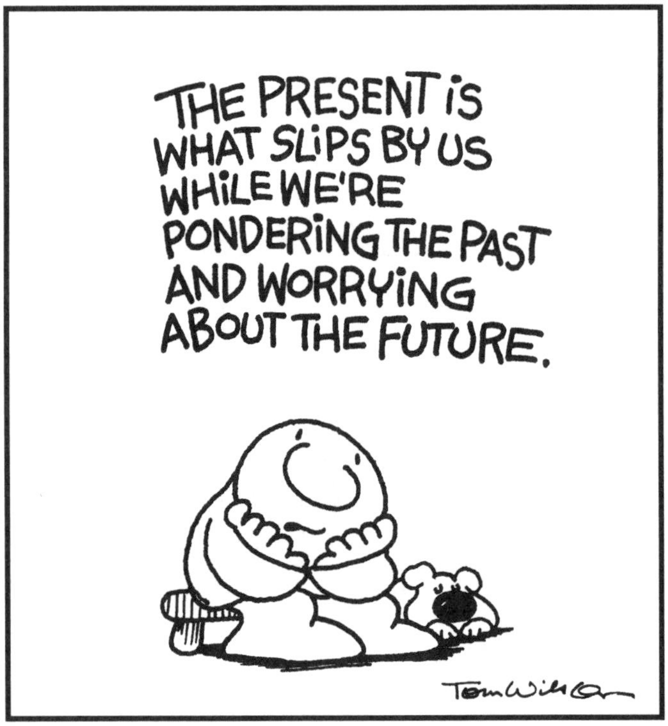
THE PRESENT IS WHAT SLIPS BY US WHILE WE'RE PONDERING THE PAST AND WORRYING ABOUT THE FUTURE.
Tom Wilson

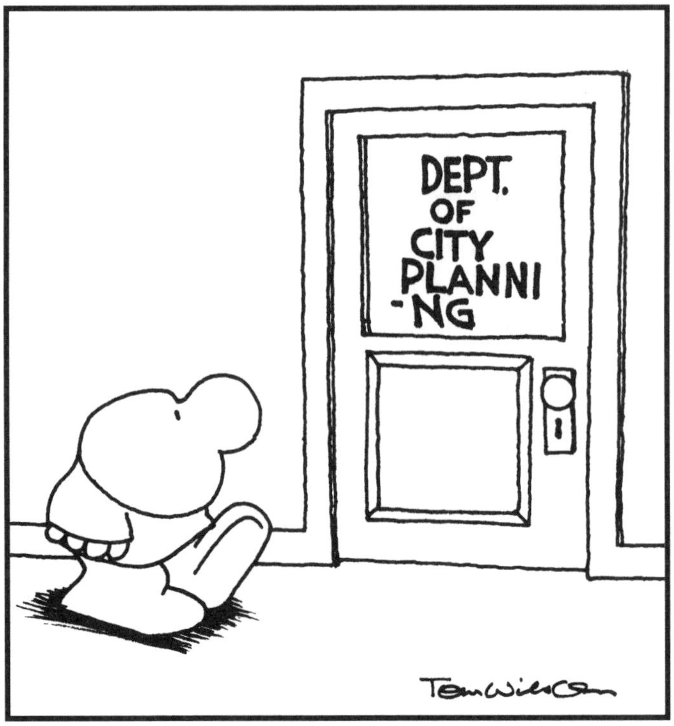
DEPT. OF CITY PLANNI -NG
Tom Wilson

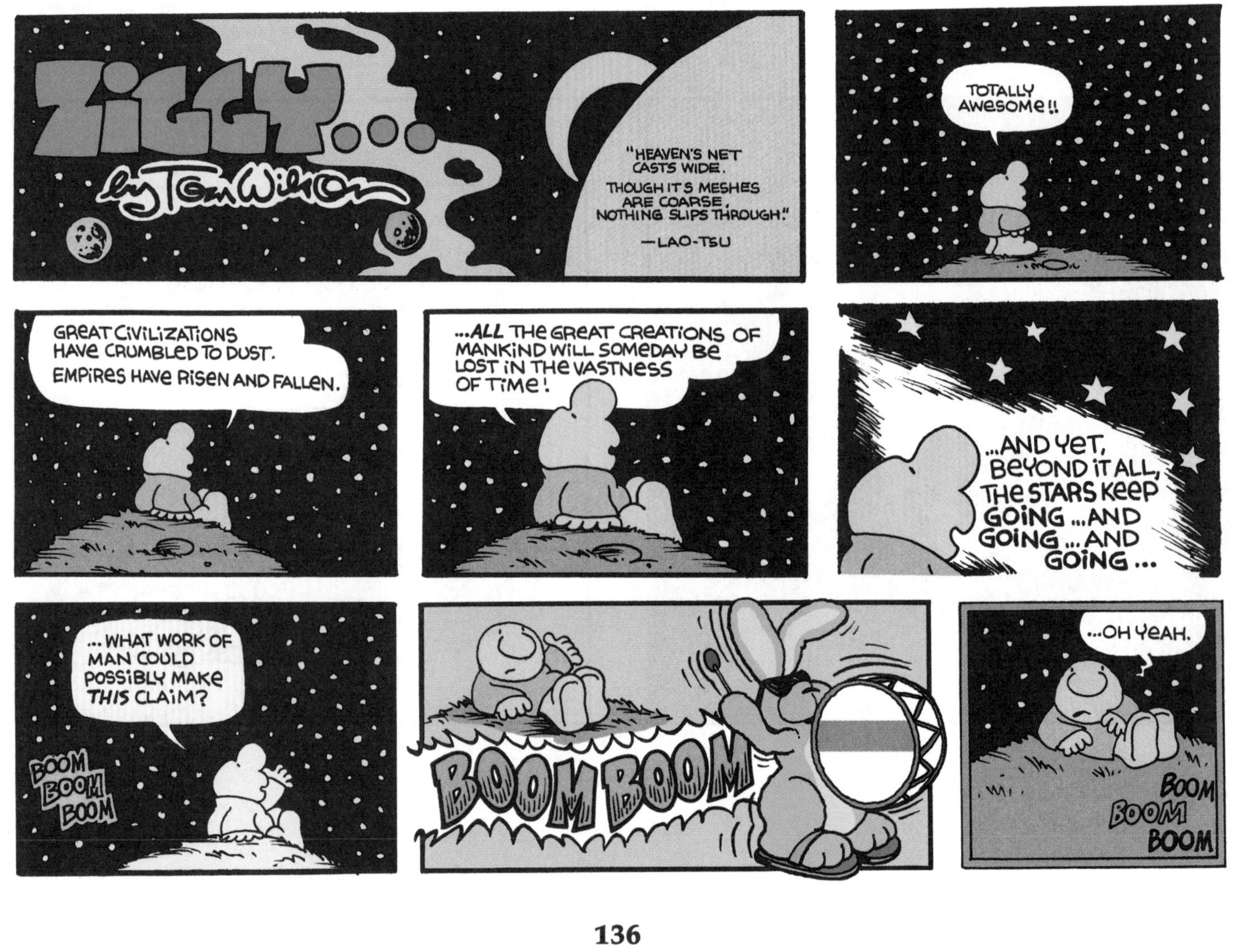
ZIGGY...
by Tom Wilson
"HEAVEN'S NET CASTS WIDE. THOUGH IT'S MESHES ARE COARSE, NOTHING SLIPS THROUGH."
—LAO-TSU
TOTALLY AWESOME!!
GREAT CIVILIZATIONS HAVE CRUMBLED TO DUST.
EMPIRES HAVE RISEN AND FALLEN.
...ALL THE GREAT CREATIONS OF MANKIND WILL SOMEDAY BE LOST IN THE VASTNESS OF TIME!
...AND YET, BEYOND IT ALL, THE STARS KEEP GOING ...AND GOING ...AND GOING ...
...WHAT WORK OF MAN COULD POSSIBLY MAKE THIS CLAIM?
BOOM BOOM BOOM
BOOM BOOM
...OH YEAH.
BOOM BOOM BOOM

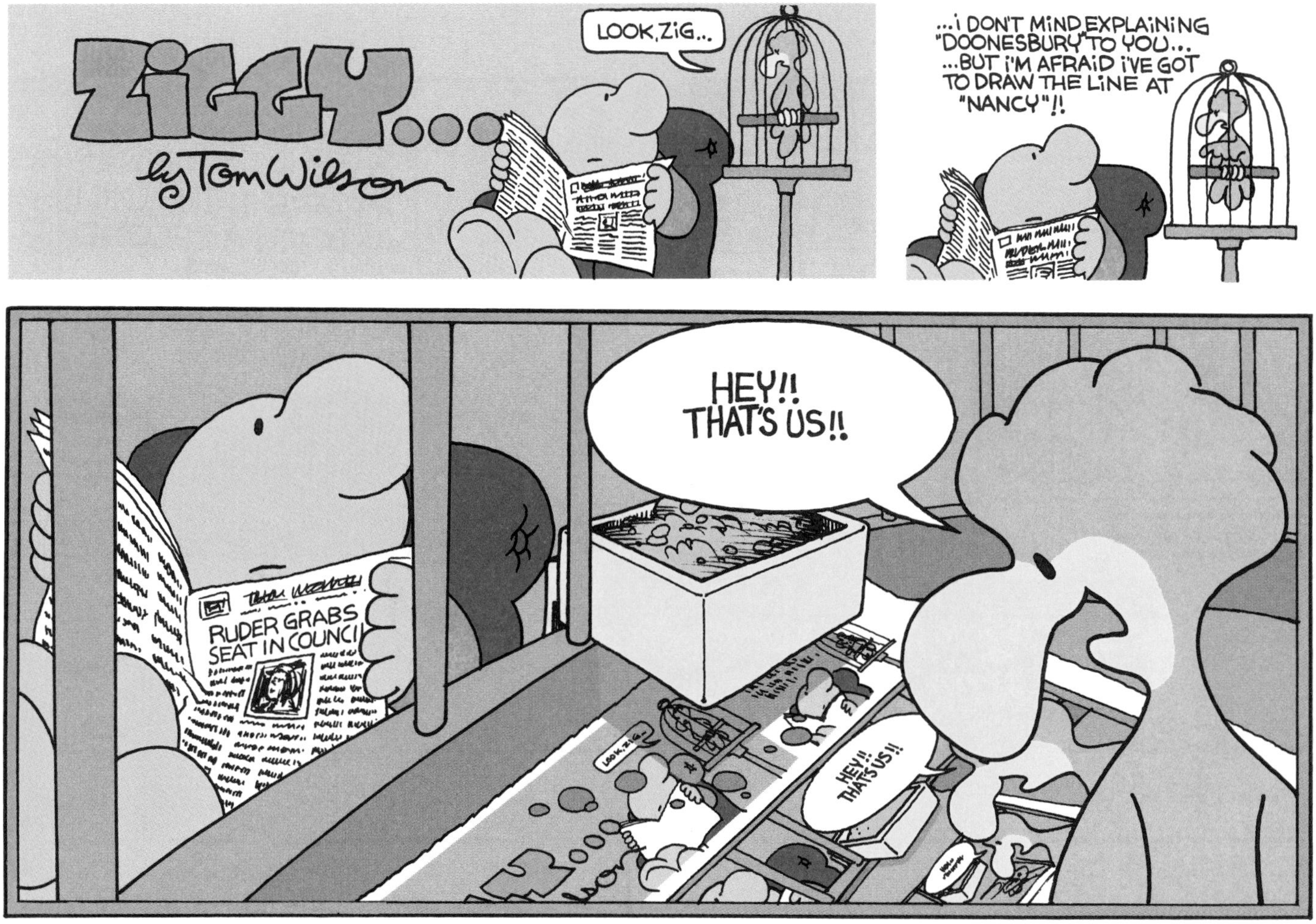
ZIGGY...
by Tom Wilson
LOOK, ZIG...
...I DON'T MIND EXPLAINING "DOONESBURY" TO YOU... ...BUT I'M AFRAID I'VE GOT TO DRAW THE LINE AT "NANCY"!!
RUDER GRABS SEAT IN COUNCI
HEY!! THAT'S US!!

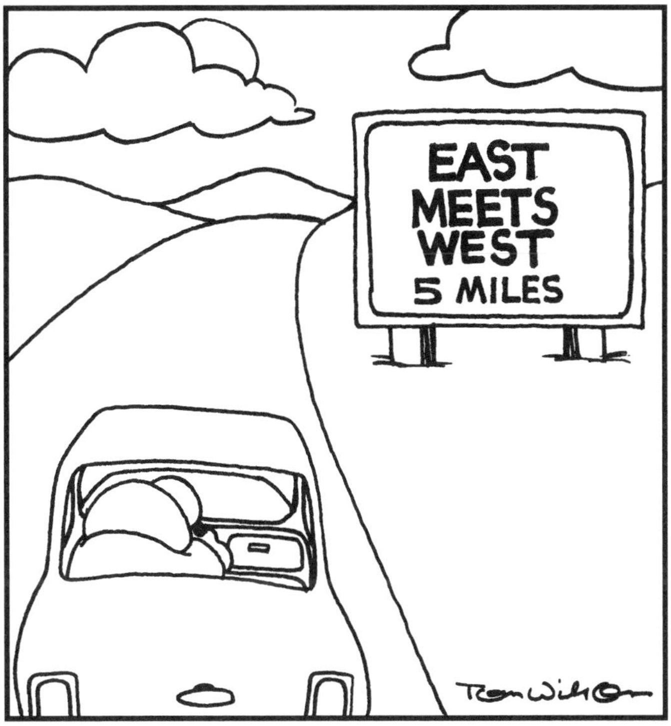
EAST MEETS WEST 5 MILES
Tom Wilson

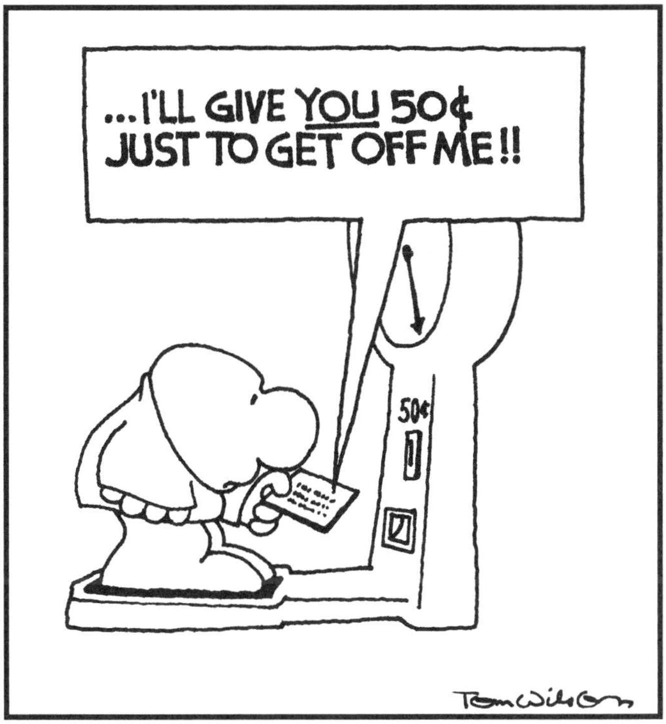
...I'LL GIVE YOU 50¢ JUST TO GET OFF ME!!
50¢
Tom Wilson

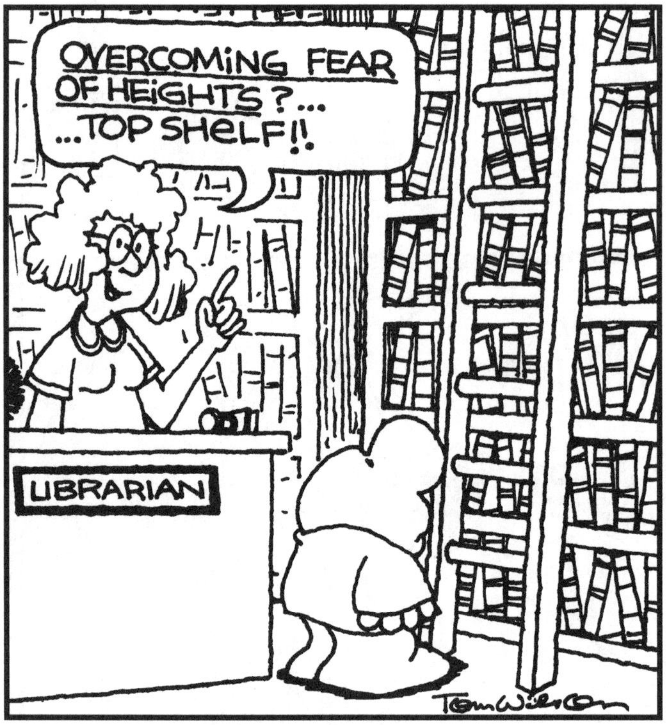
OVERCOMING FEAR OF HEIGHTS?... ...TOP SHELF!!
LIBRARIAN

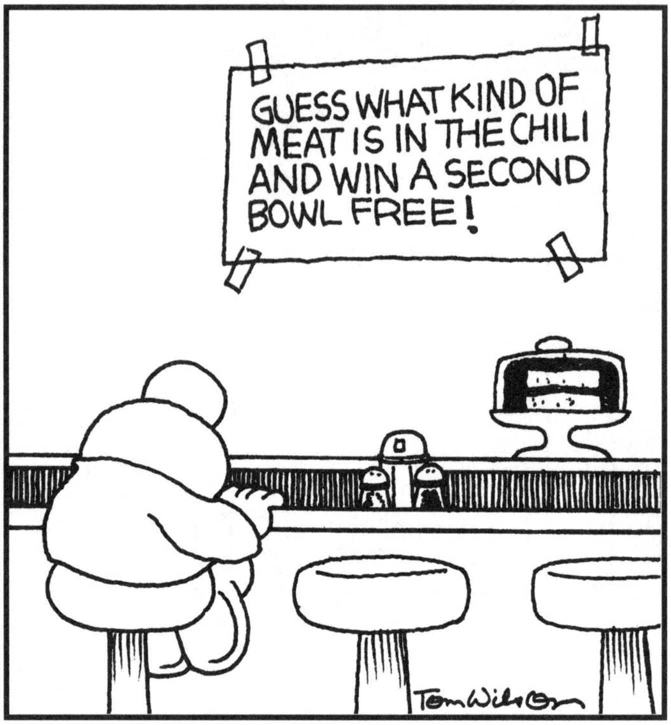
GUESS WHAT KIND OF MEAT IS IN THE CHILI AND WIN A SECOND BOWL FREE!

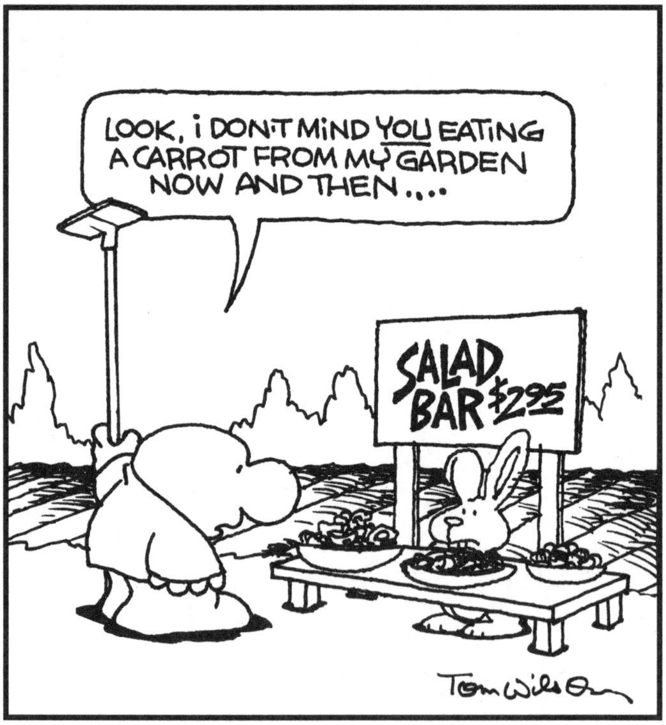
LOOK, I DON'T MIND YOU EATING A CARROT FROM MY GARDEN NOW AND THEN....
SALAD BAR $2.95

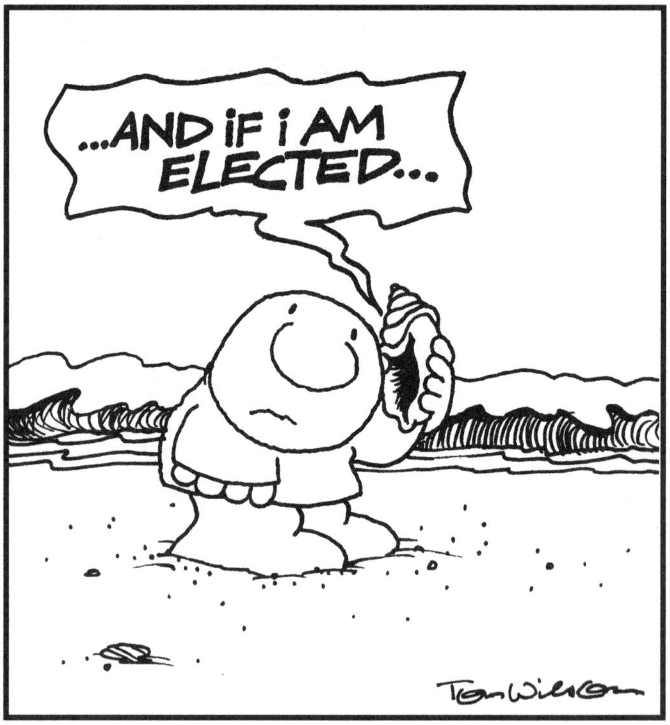
...AND IF I AM ELECTED...

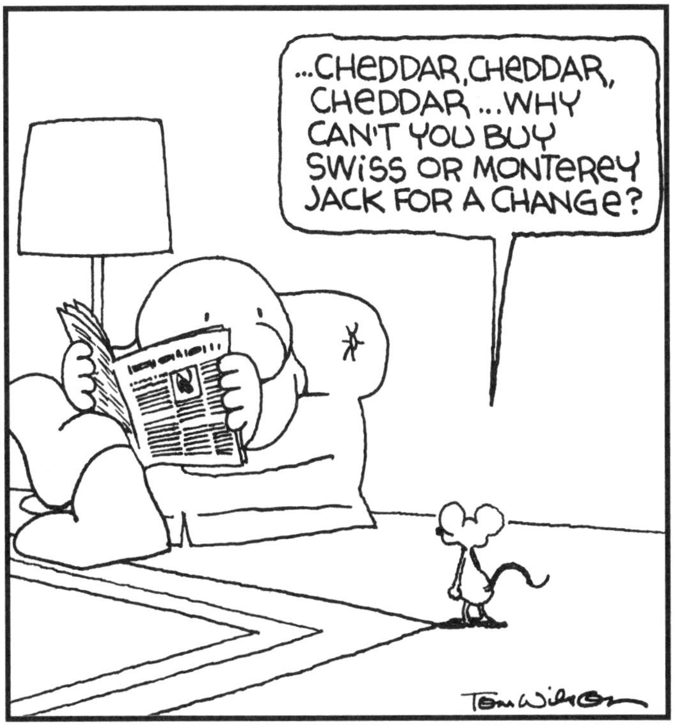
...CHEDDAR, CHEDDAR, CHEDDAR ...WHY CAN'T YOU BUY SWISS OR MONTEREY JACK FOR A CHANGE?
Tom Wilson

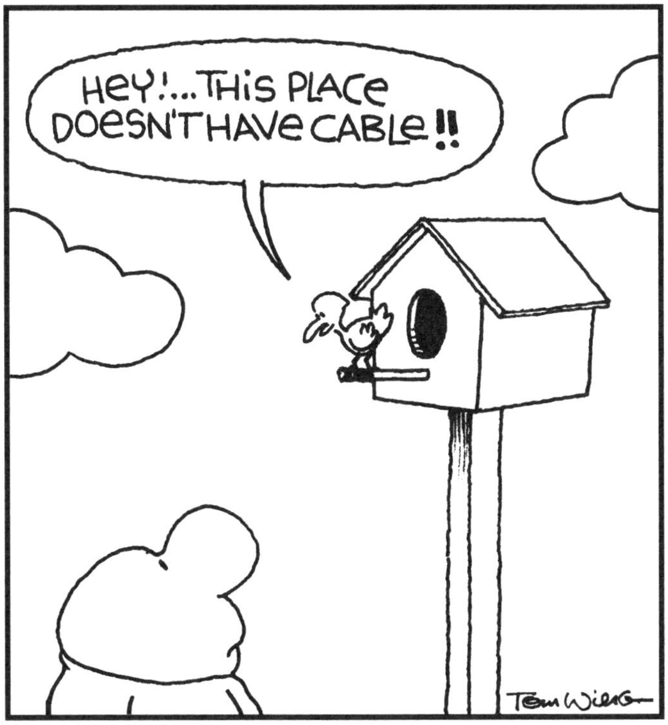
HEY!...THIS PLACE DOESN'T HAVE CABLE!!
Tom Wilson

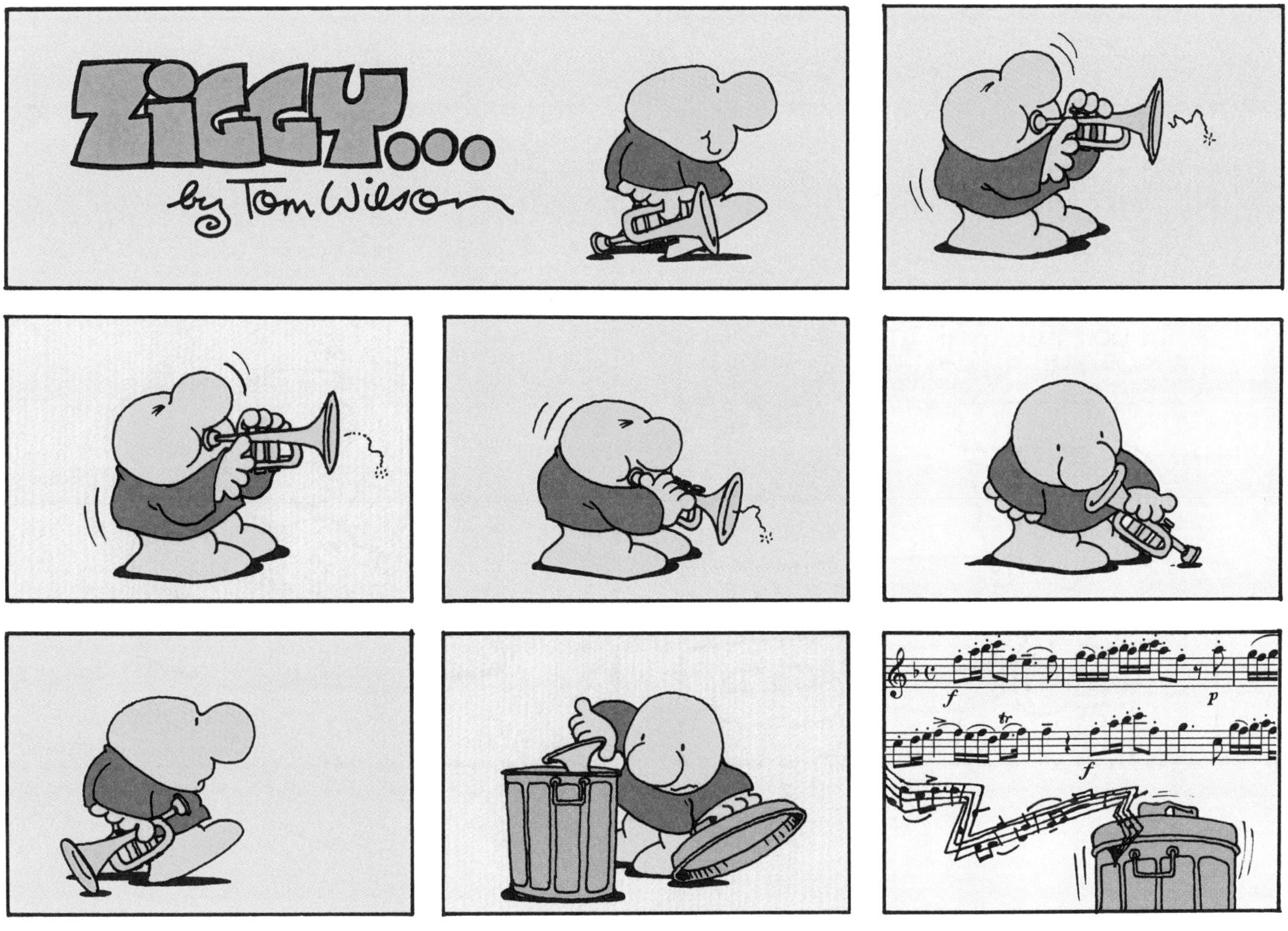
ZIGGY...
by Tom Wilson

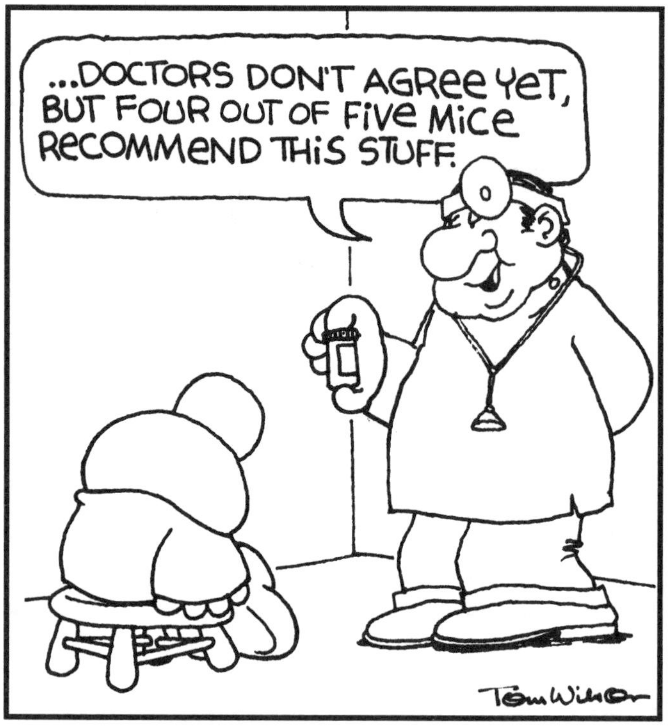
...DOCTORS DON'T AGREE YET, BUT FOUR OUT OF FIVE MICE RECOMMEND THIS STUFF.
Tom Wilson

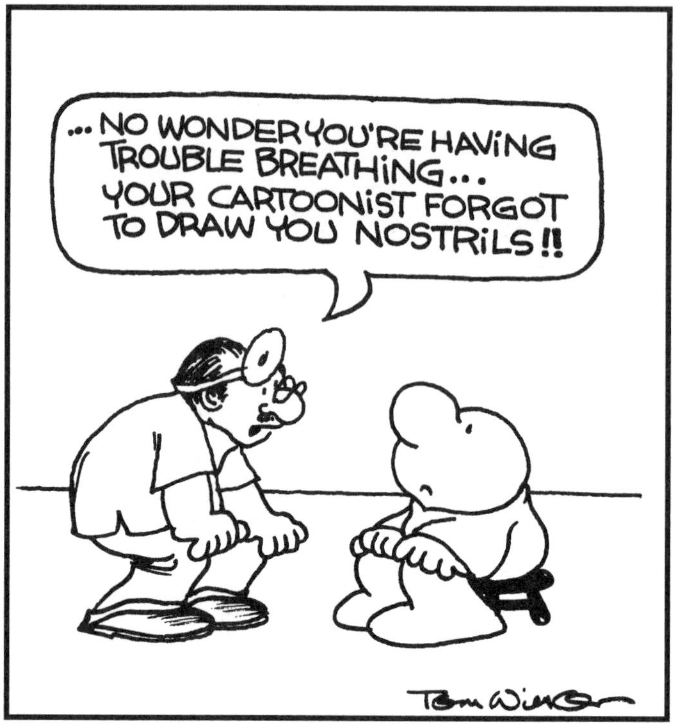
...NO WONDER YOU'RE HAVING TROUBLE BREATHING... YOUR CARTOONIST FORGOT TO DRAW YOU NOSTRILS!!
Tom Wilson

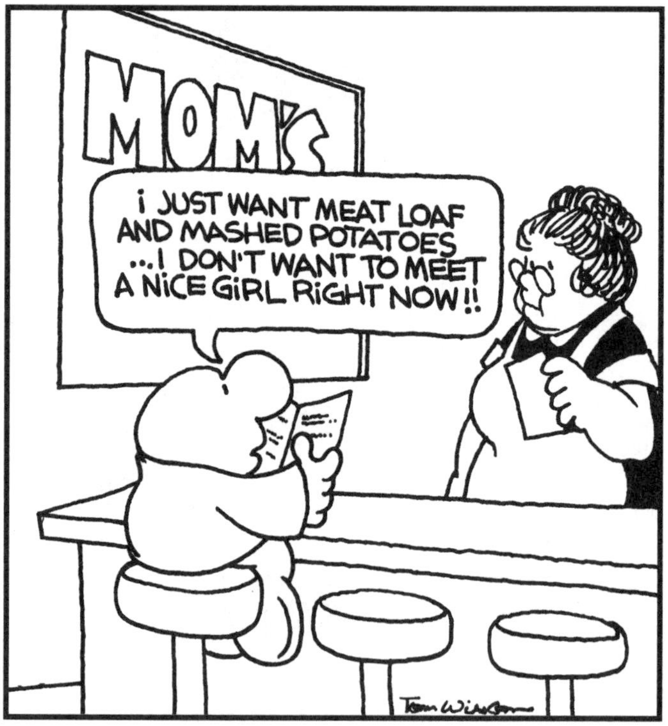
MOM'S
I JUST WANT MEAT LOAF AND MASHED POTATOES ...I DON'T WANT TO MEET A NICE GIRL RIGHT NOW!!
Tom Wilson

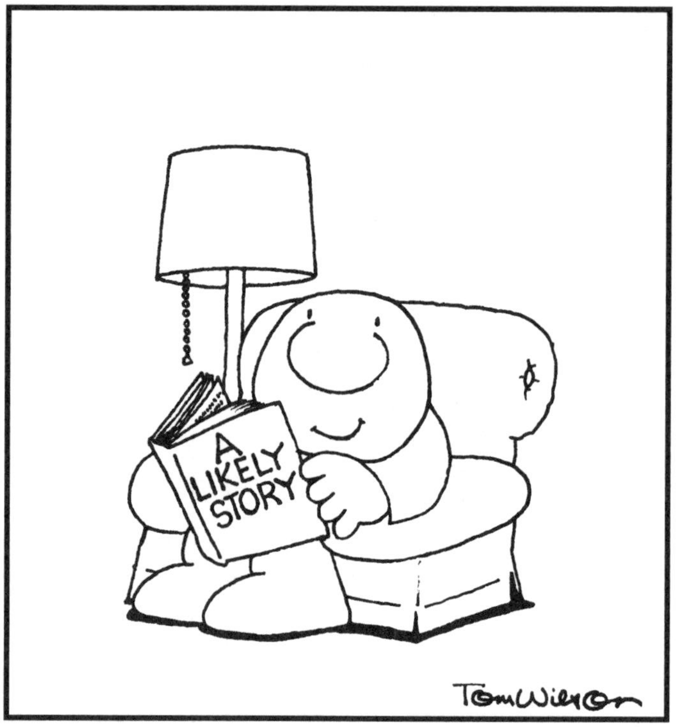
A LIKELY STORY
Tom Wilson

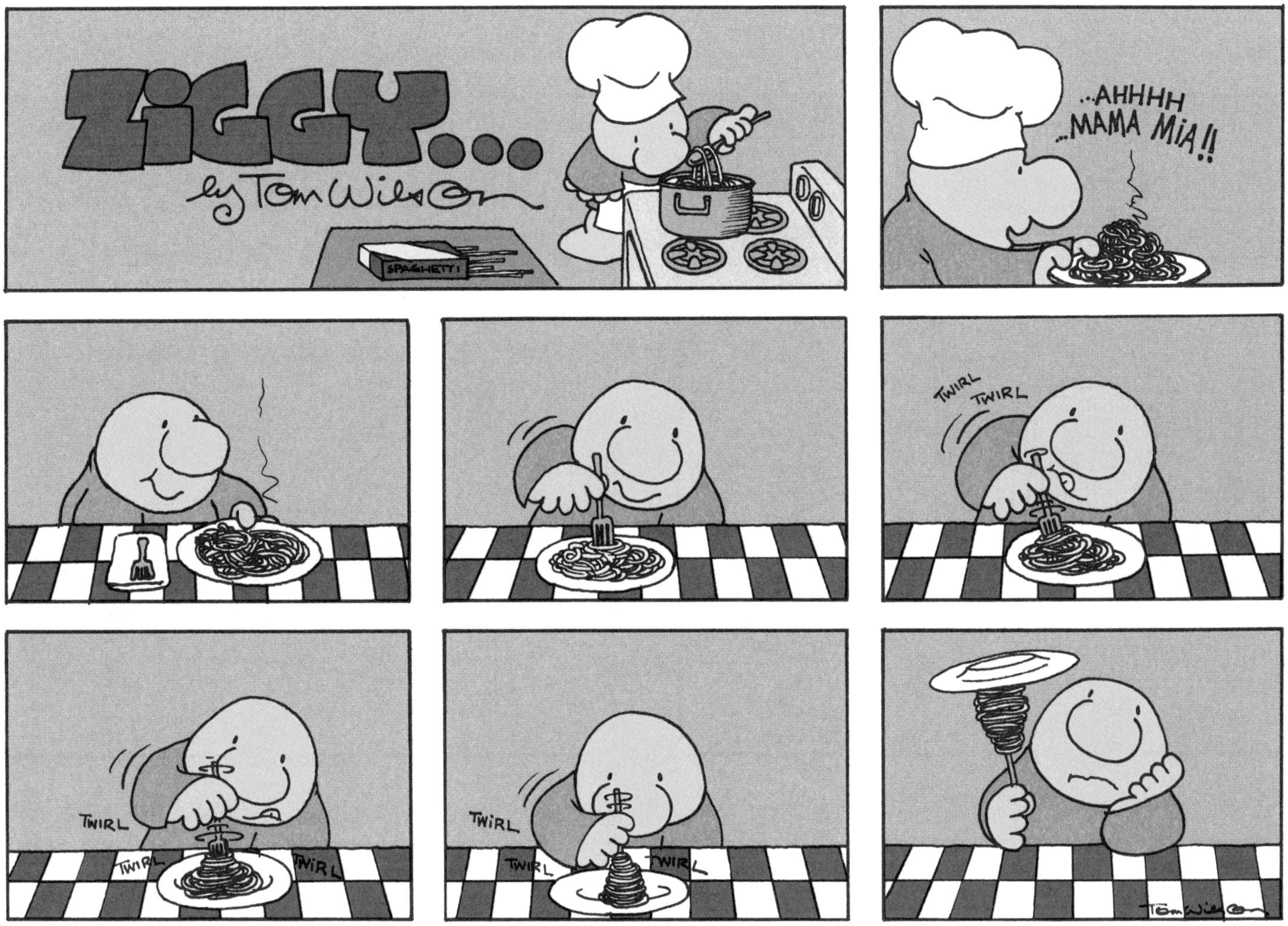
ZIGGY...
by Tom Wilson
SPAGHETTI
...AHHHH ...MAMA MIA!!
TWIRL TWIRL
TWIRL
TWIRL
TWIRL
TWIRL
TWIRL
TWIRL
Tom Wilson

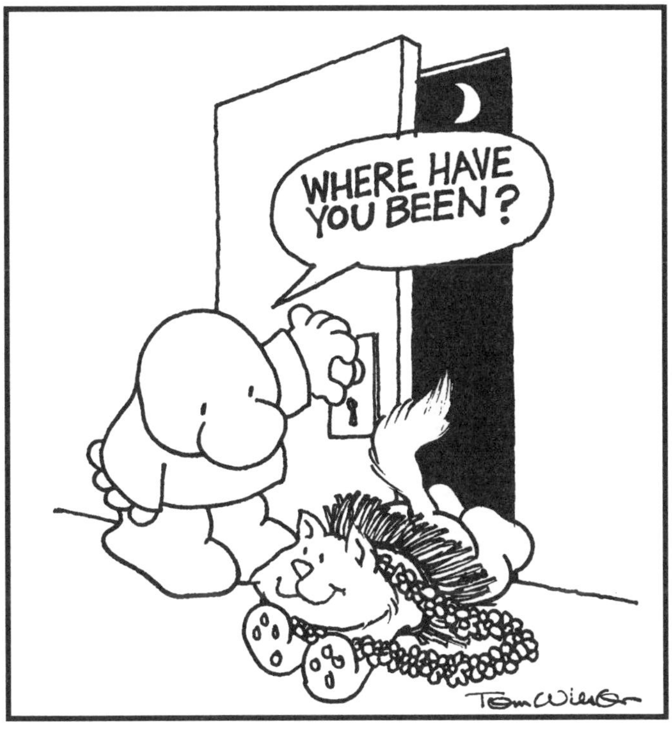
WHERE HAVE YOU BEEN?
Tom Wilson

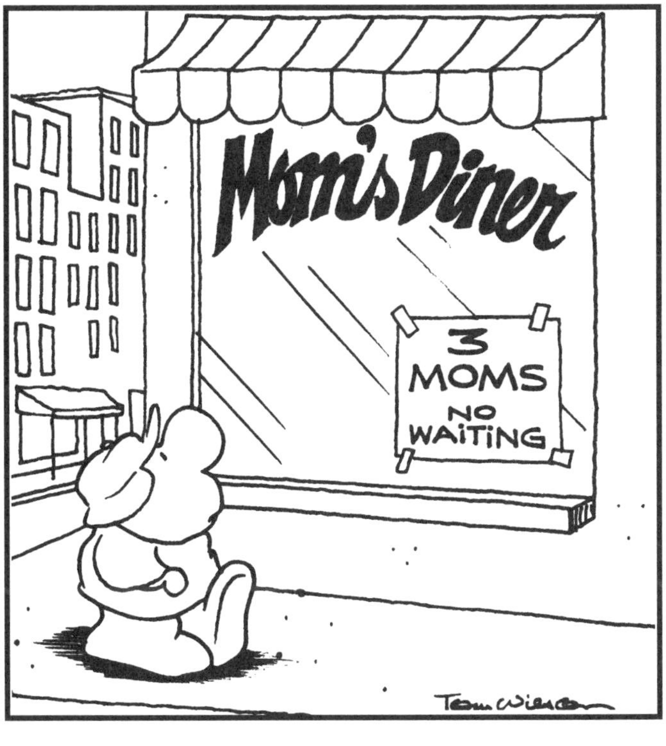
Mom's Diner
3 MOMS NO WAITING
Tom Wilson

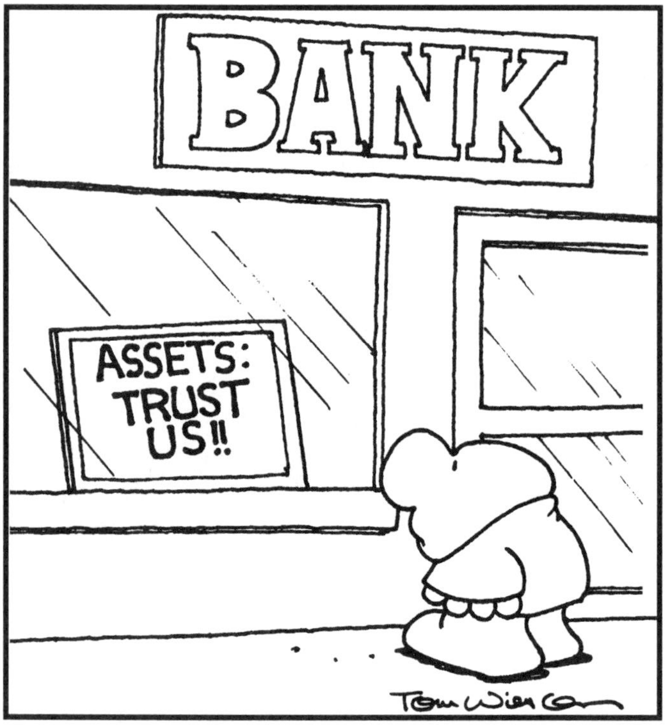
BANK
ASSETS: TRUST US!!
Tom Wilson

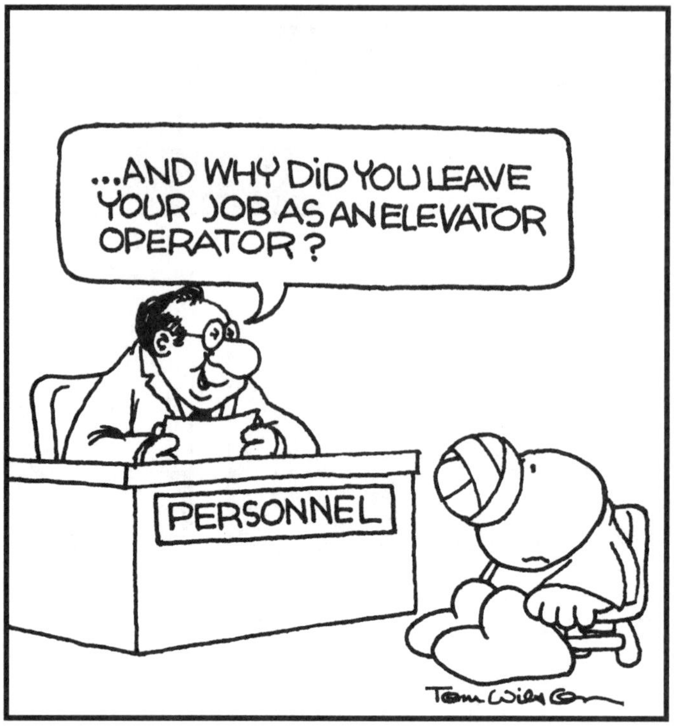
...AND WHY DID YOU LEAVE YOUR JOB AS AN ELEVATOR OPERATOR?
PERSONNEL
Tom Wilson

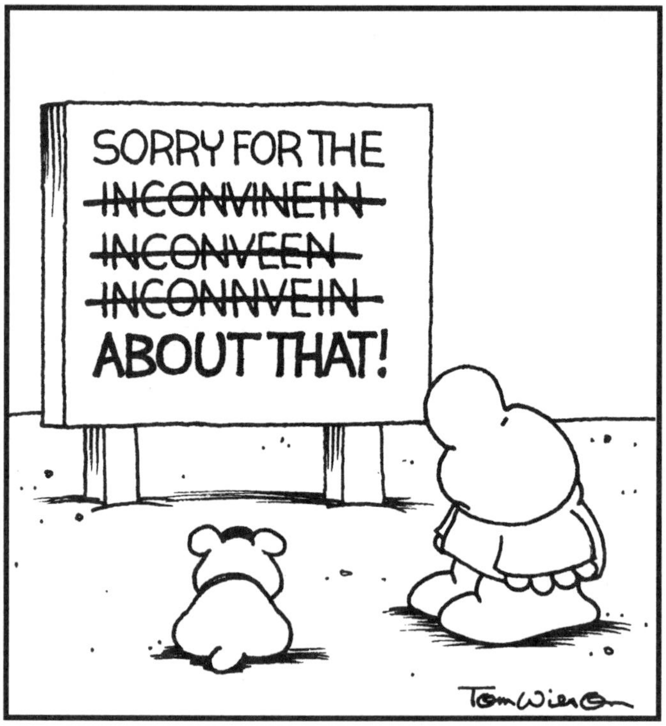
SORRY FOR THE
~~INCONVINEIN~~
~~INCONVEEN~~
~~INCONNVEIN~~
ABOUT THAT!
Tom Wilson

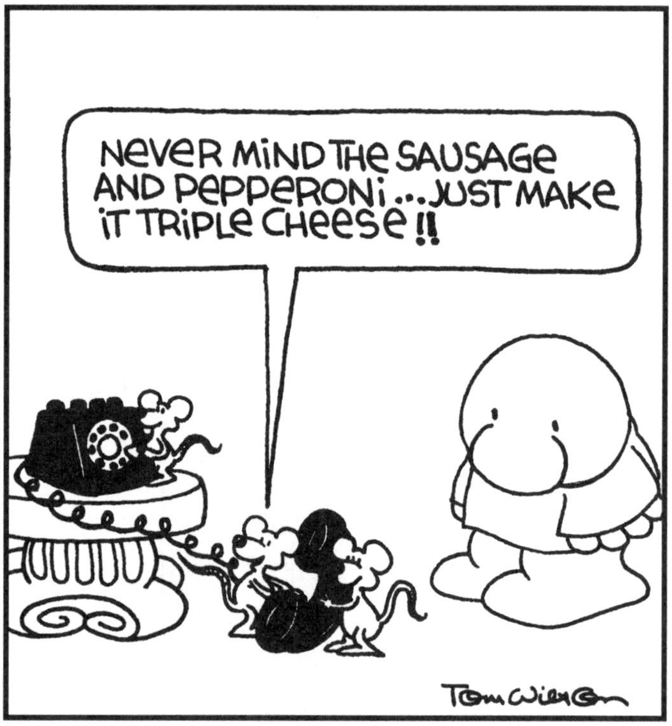
NEVER MIND THE SAUSAGE AND PEPPERONI...JUST MAKE IT TRIPLE CHEESE!!
Tom Wilson

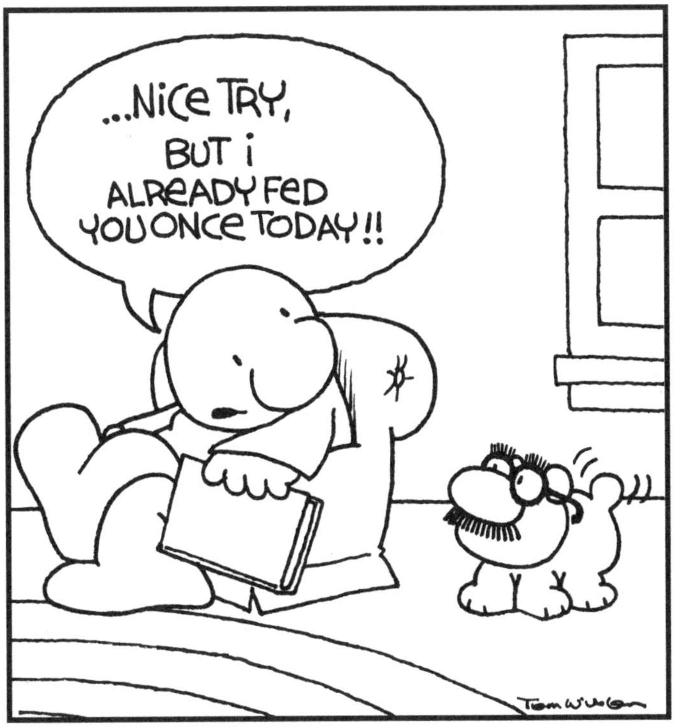
...NICE TRY, BUT I ALREADY FED YOU ONCE TODAY!!
TOM WILSON

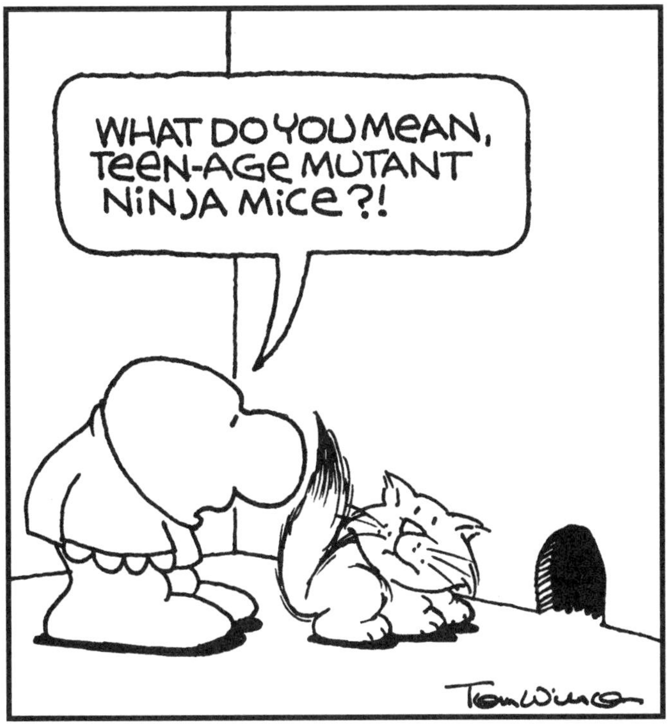
WHAT DO YOU MEAN, TEEN-AGE MUTANT NINJA MICE?!
TOM WILSON

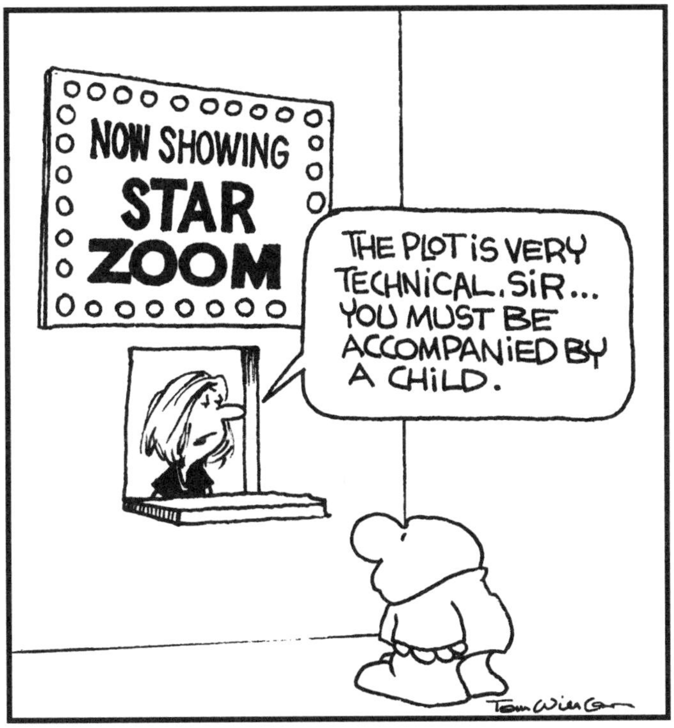
NOW SHOWING
STAR
ZOOM
THE PLOT IS VERY TECHNICAL, SIR... YOU MUST BE ACCOMPANIED BY A CHILD.
TOM WILSON

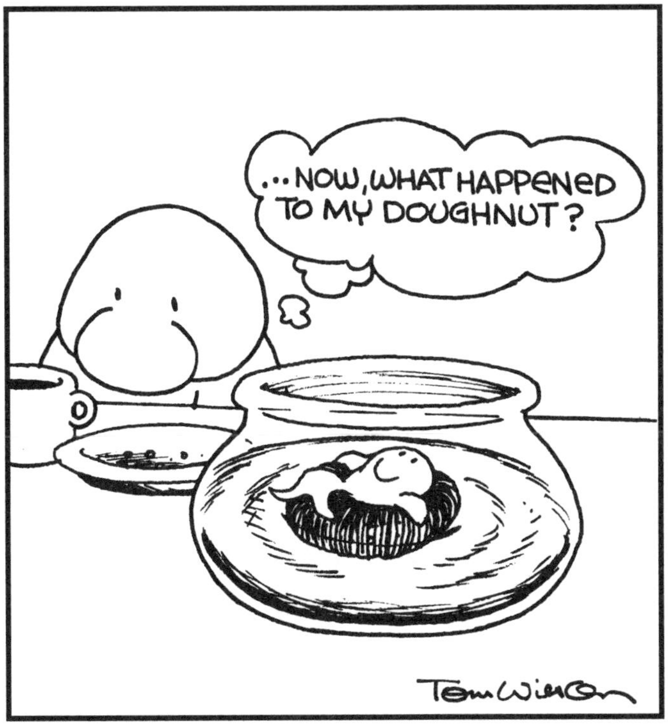
...NOW, WHAT HAPPENED TO MY DOUGHNUT?
TOM WILSON

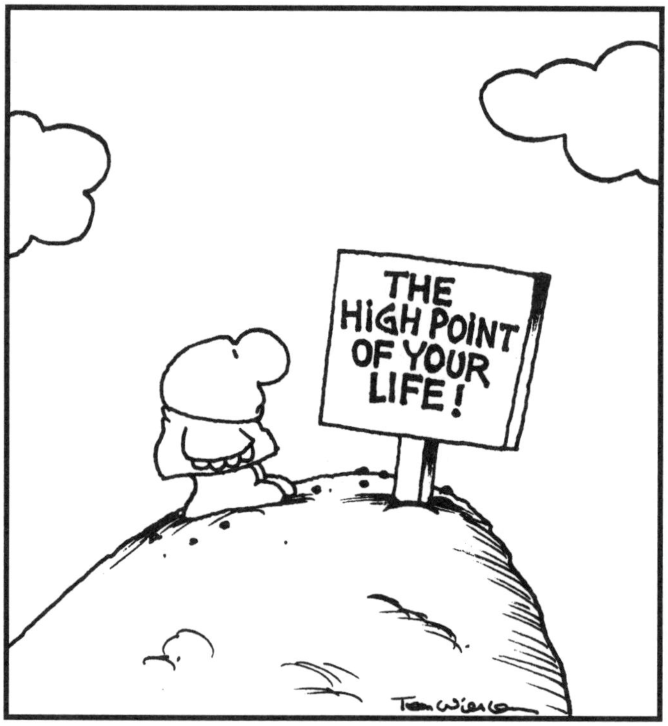
THE HIGH POINT OF YOUR LIFE!
Tom Wilson

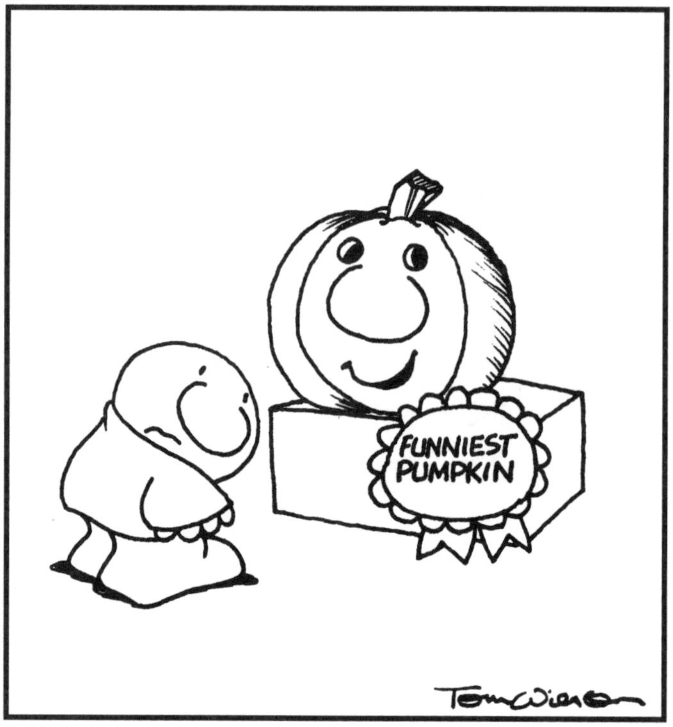
FUNNIEST PUMPKIN
Tom Wilson

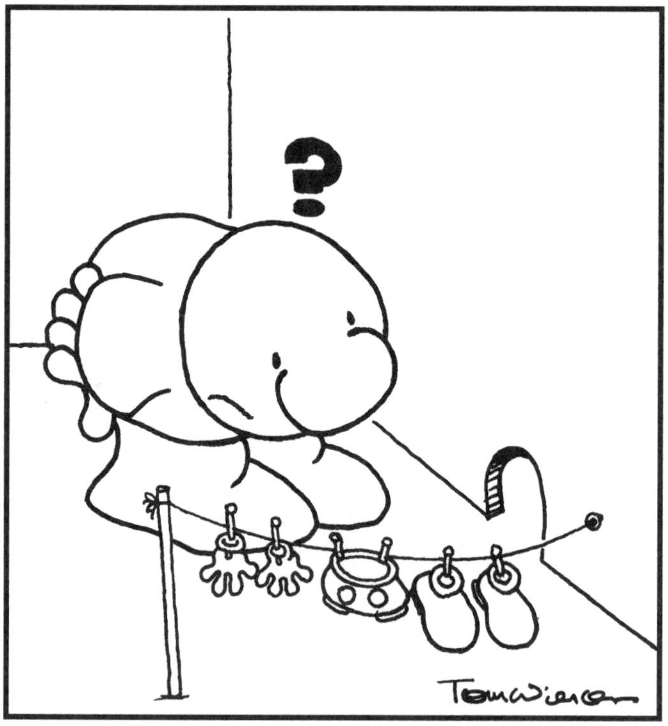
?
Tom Wilson

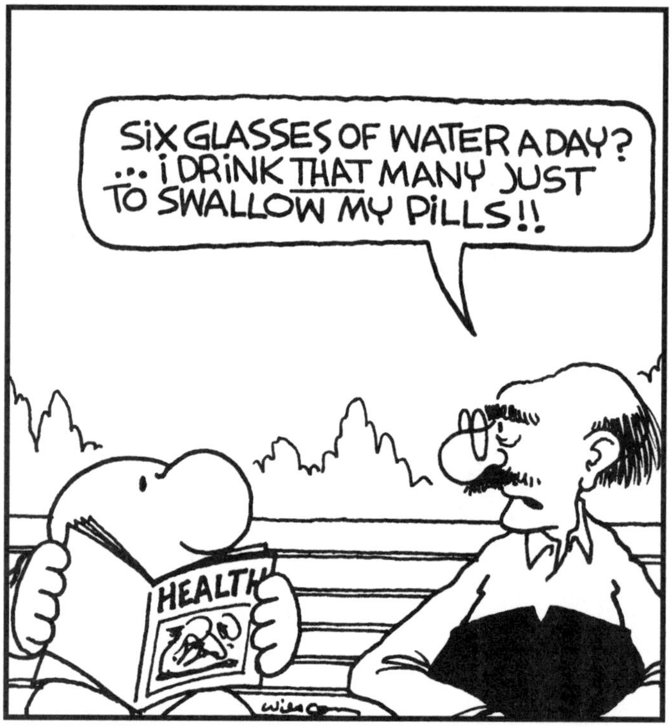
SIX GLASSES OF WATER A DAY? ... I DRINK THAT MANY JUST TO SWALLOW MY PILLS!!
HEALTH
Wilson

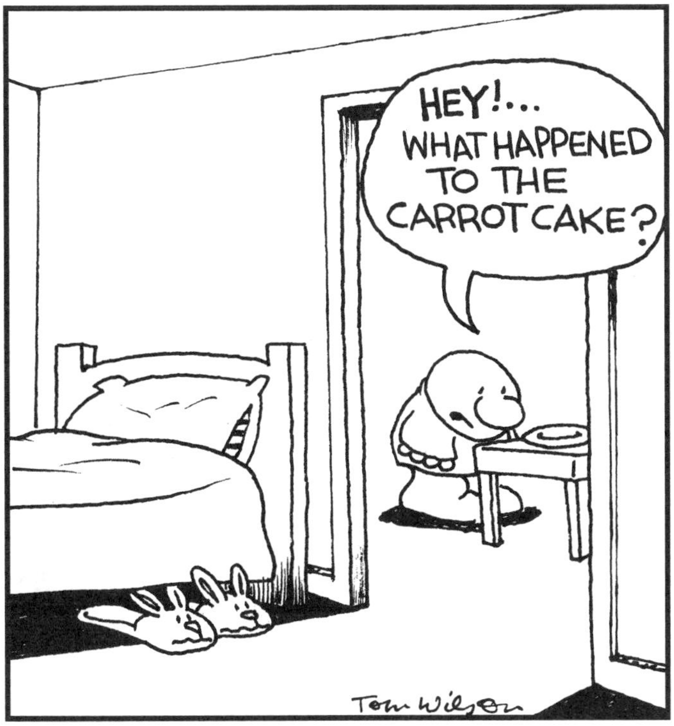
HEY!... WHAT HAPPENED TO THE CARROT CAKE?
Tom Wilson

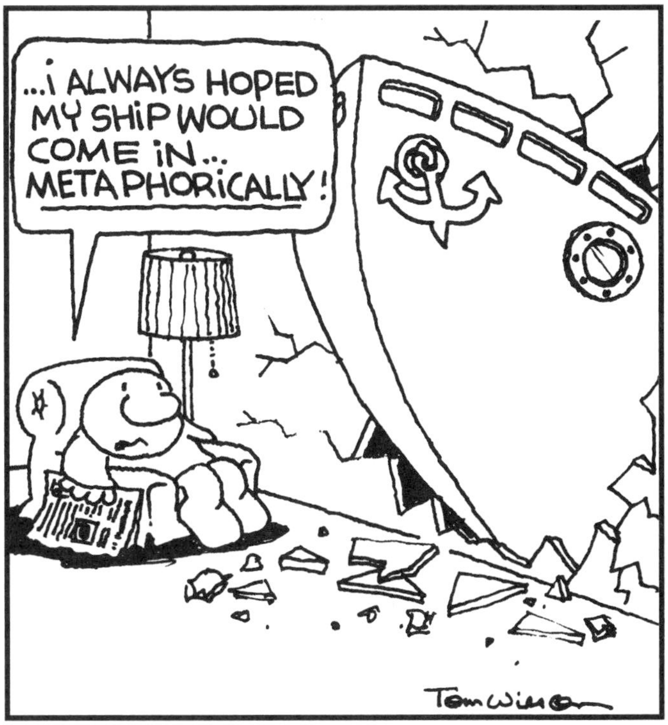
...I ALWAYS HOPED MY SHIP WOULD COME IN... METAPHORICALLY!
Tom Wilson

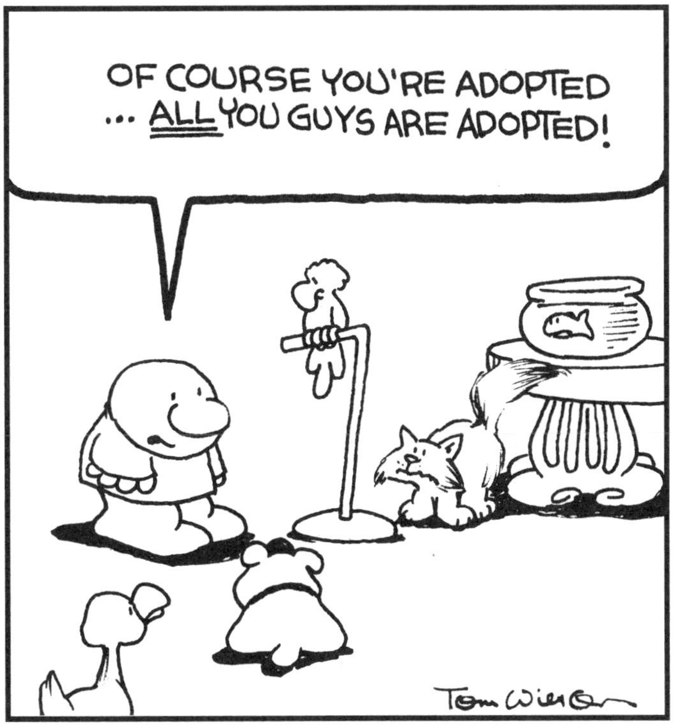
OF COURSE YOU'RE ADOPTED ... ALL YOU GUYS ARE ADOPTED!
Tom Wilson

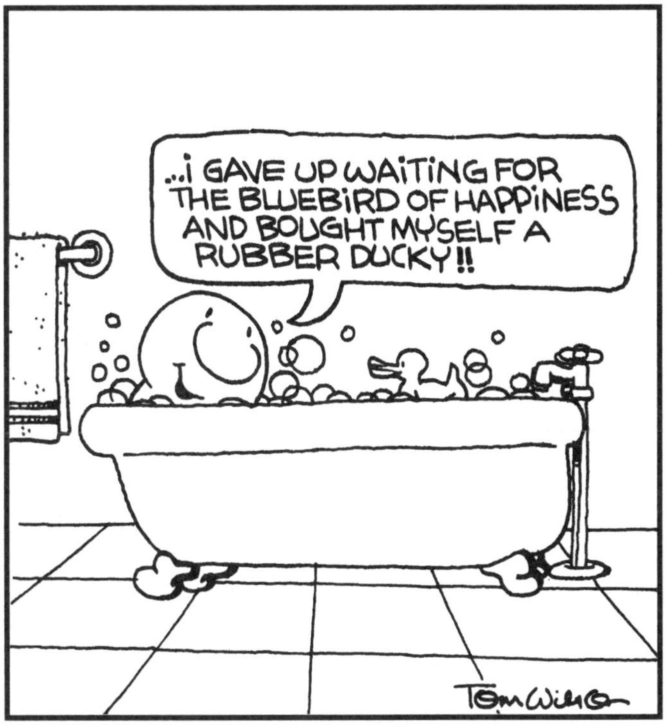
...I GAVE UP WAITING FOR THE BLUEBIRD OF HAPPINESS AND BOUGHT MYSELF A RUBBER DUCKY!!
Tom Wilson

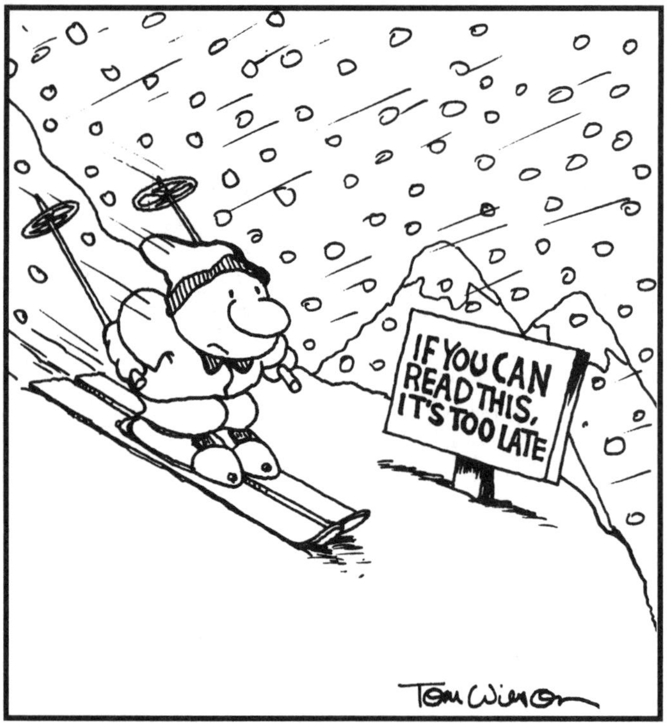
IF YOU CAN READ THIS, IT'S TOO LATE
TOM WILSON

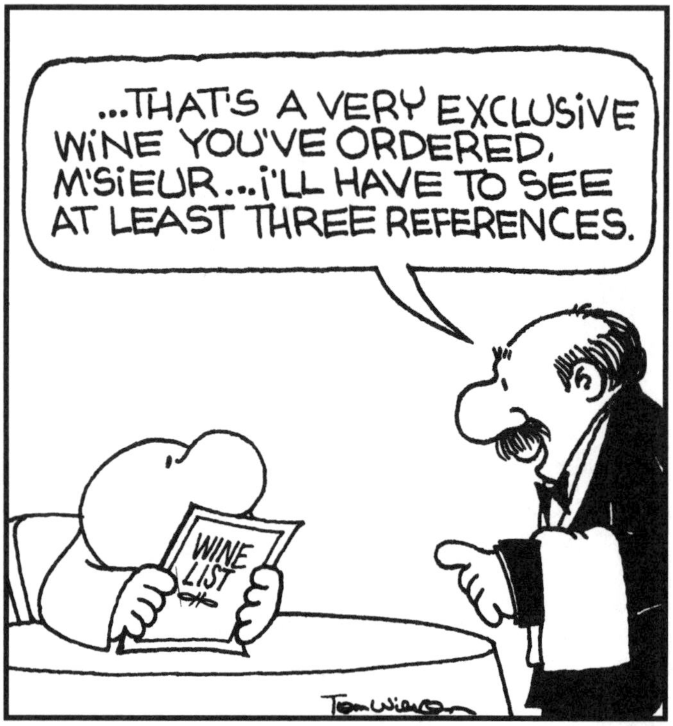
...THAT'S A VERY EXCLUSIVE WiNE YOU'VE ORDERED, M'SiEUR...i'LL HAVE TO SEE AT LEAST THREE REFERENCES.
WINE LIST
TOM WILSON

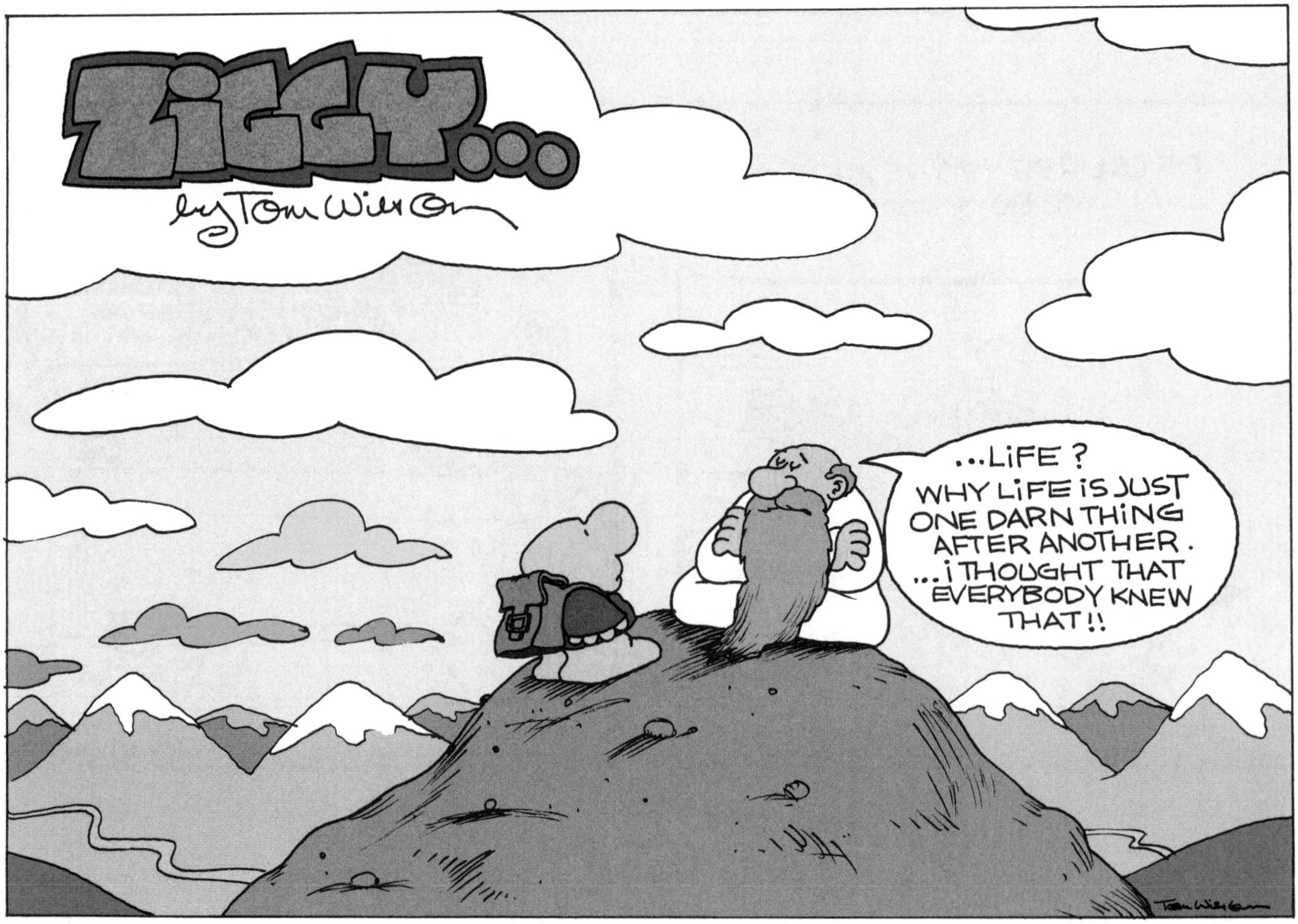
ZIGGY...
by TOM WILSON
...LiFE ?
WHY LiFE iS JUST ONE DARN THiNG AFTER ANOTHER.
...i THOUGHT THAT EVERYBODY KNEW THAT!!
TOM WILSON

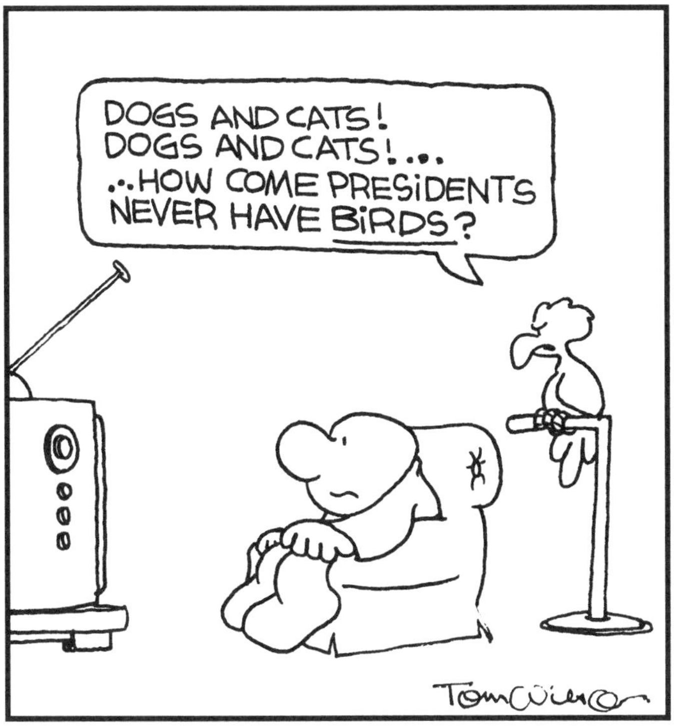
DOGS AND CATS!
DOGS AND CATS!...
...HOW COME PRESIDENTS NEVER HAVE BIRDS?
Tom Wilson

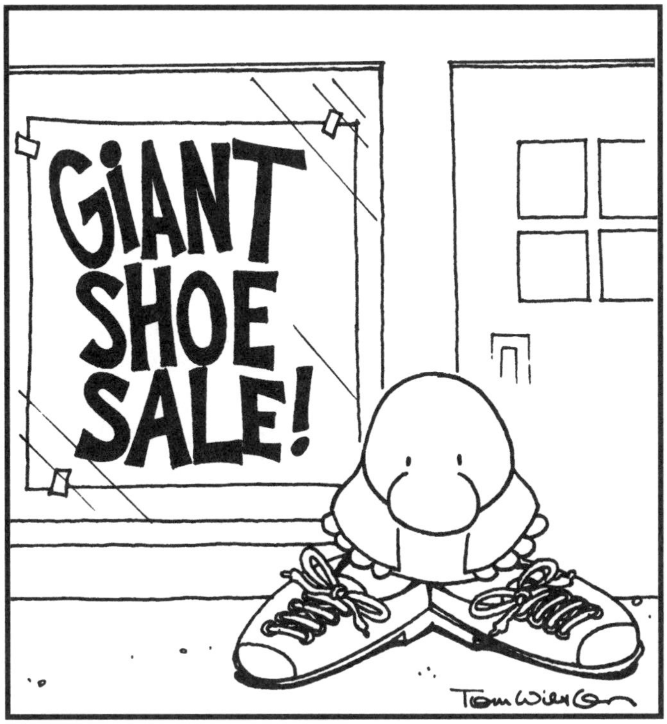
GiANT SHOE SALE!
Tom Wilson

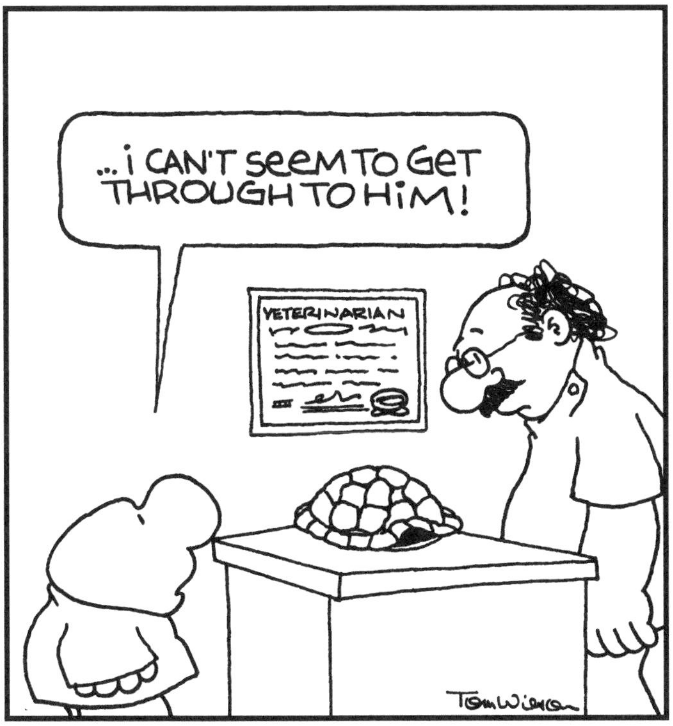
...i CAN'T seem TO GeT THROUGH TO HiM!
VETERINARIAN
Tom Wilson

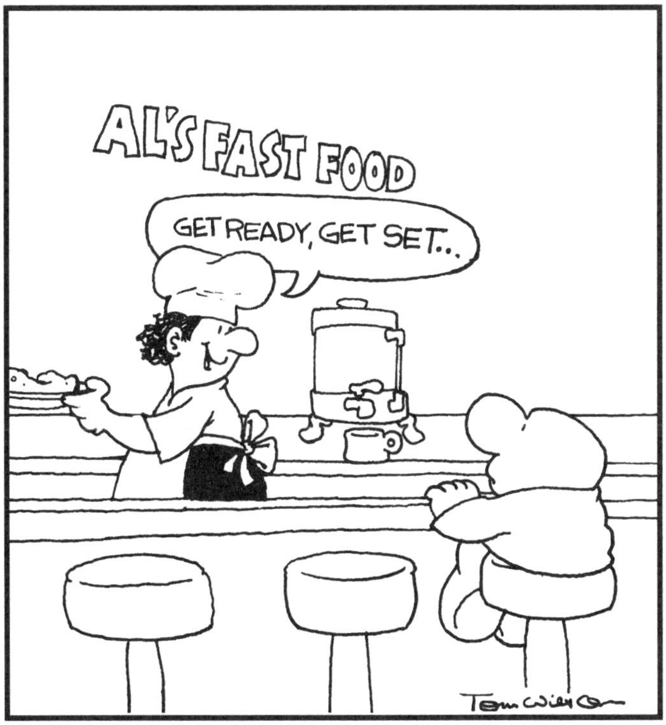
AL'S FAST FOOD
GET READY, GET SET...
Tom Wilson

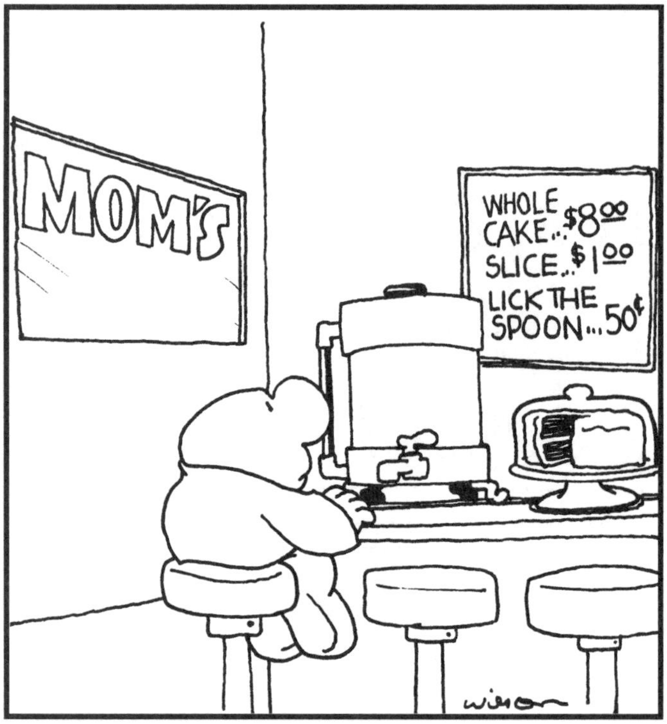
MOM'S
WHOLE CAKE..$8.00
SLICE..$1.00
LICK THE SPOON...50¢

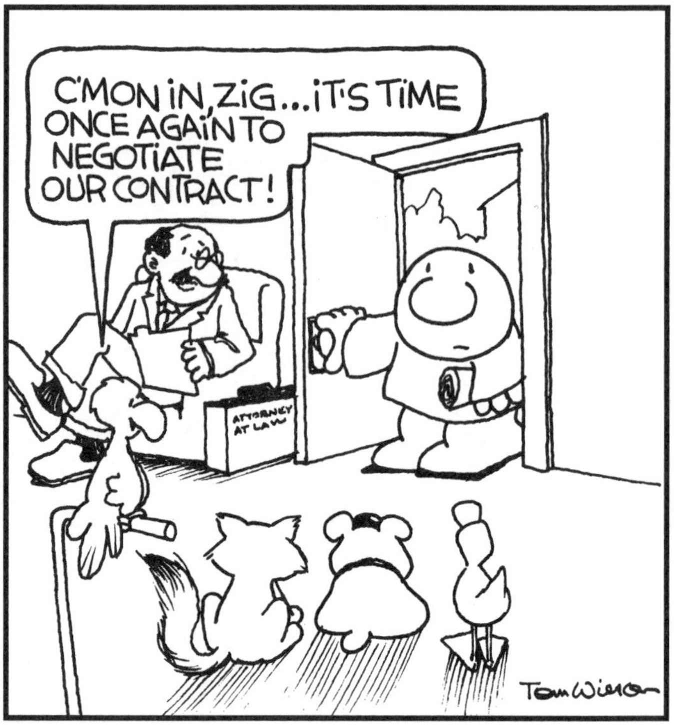
C'MON IN, ZIG...IT'S TIME ONCE AGAIN TO NEGOTIATE OUR CONTRACT!
ATTORNEY AT LAW

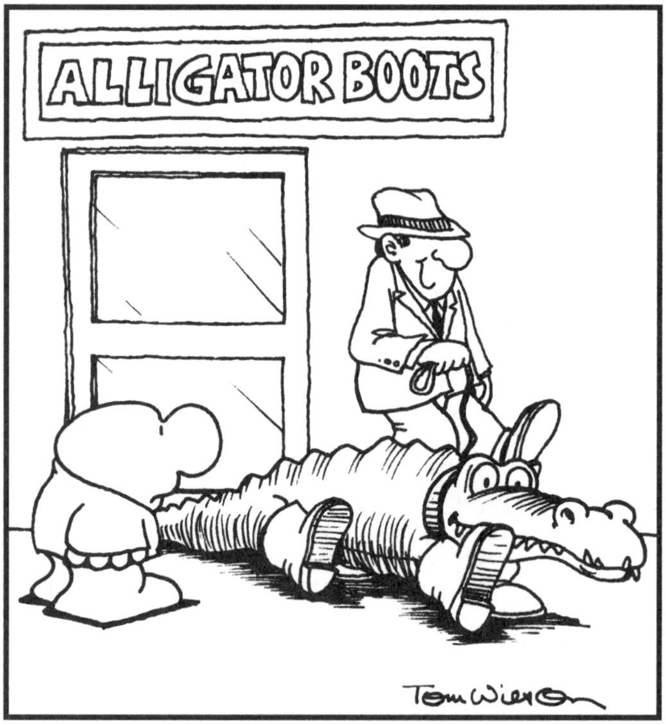
ALLIGATOR BOOTS

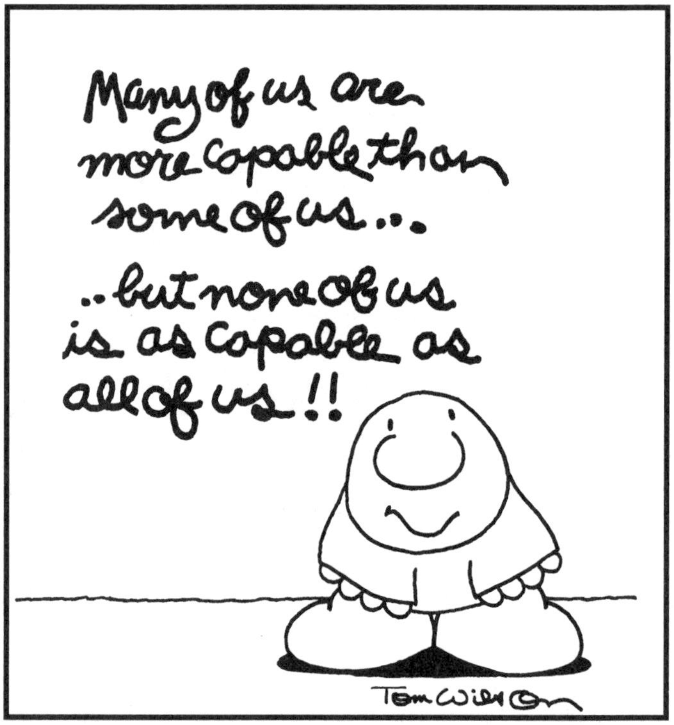
Many of us are more capable than some of us...
..but none of us is as capable as all of us!!

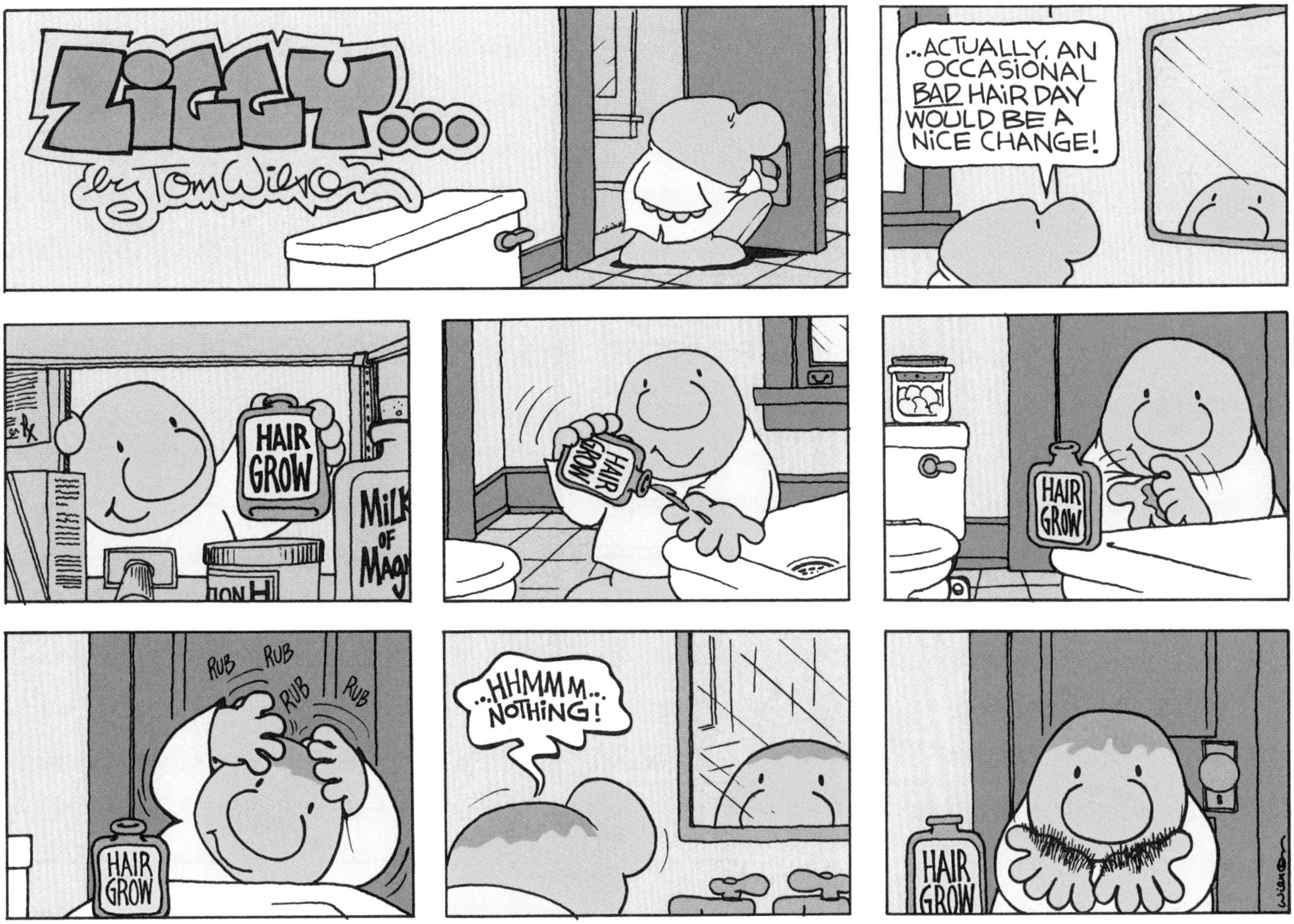
ZIGGY...
by Tom Wilson
...ACTUALLY, AN OCCASIONAL BAD HAIR DAY WOULD BE A NICE CHANGE!
HAIR GROW
HAIR GROW
HAIR GROW
RUB RUB RUB RUB
HAIR GROW
...HHMMM... NOTHING!
HAIR GROW

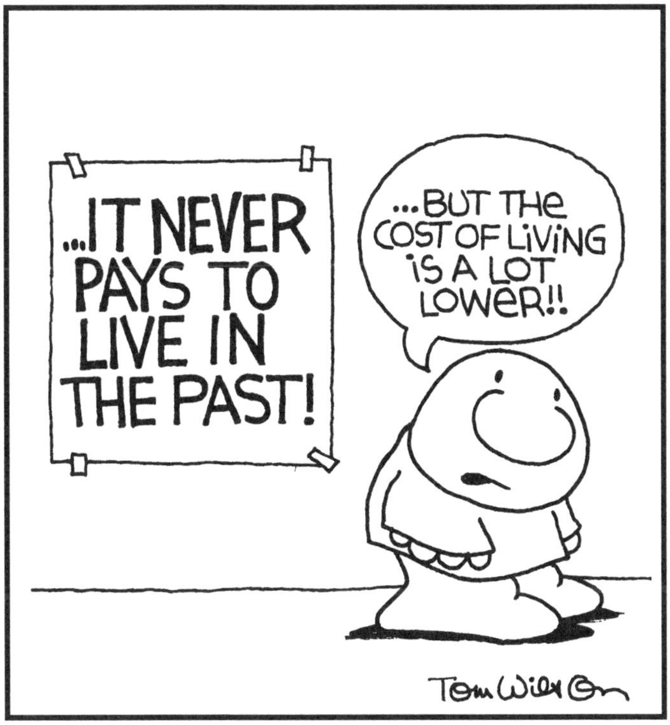
...IT NEVER PAYS TO LIVE IN THE PAST!
...BUT THE COST OF LIVING IS A LOT LOWER!!
Tom Wilson

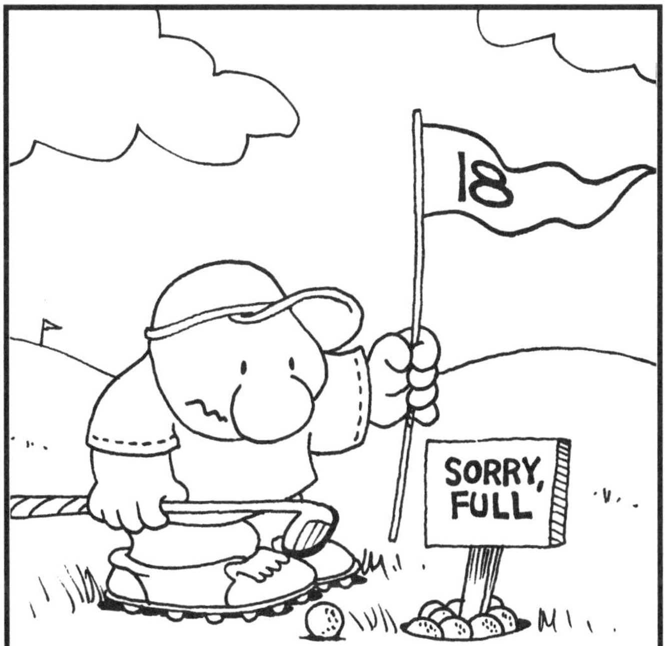
18
SORRY, FULL
Tom Wilson

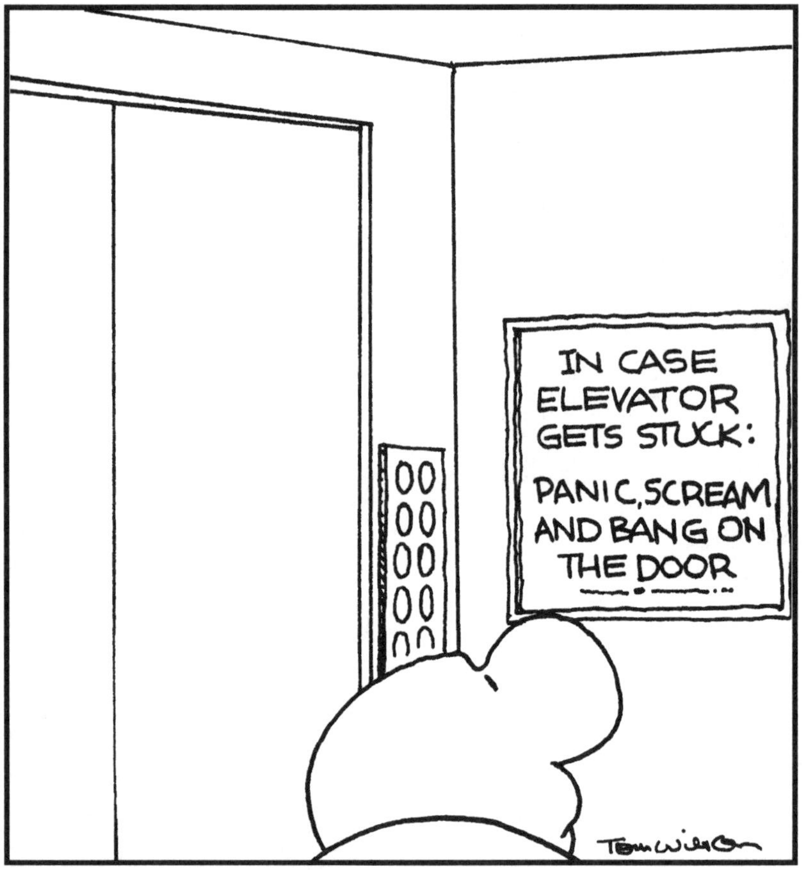
IN CASE ELEVATOR GETS STUCK:
PANIC, SCREAM AND BANG ON THE DOOR
Tom Wilson

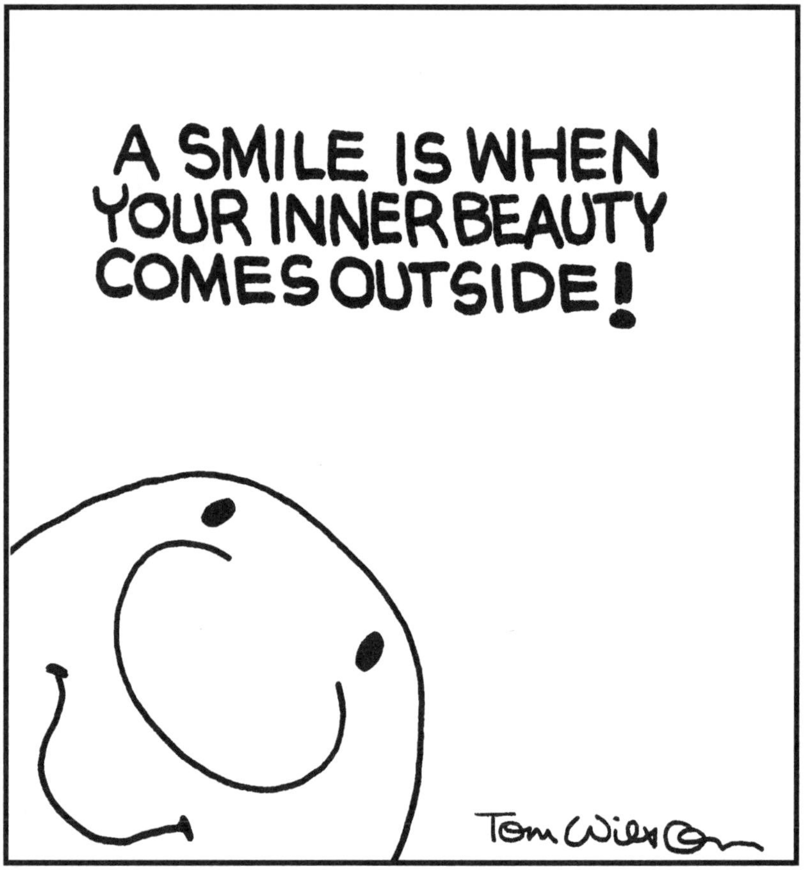
A SMILE IS WHEN YOUR INNER BEAUTY COMES OUTSIDE!
Tom Wilson

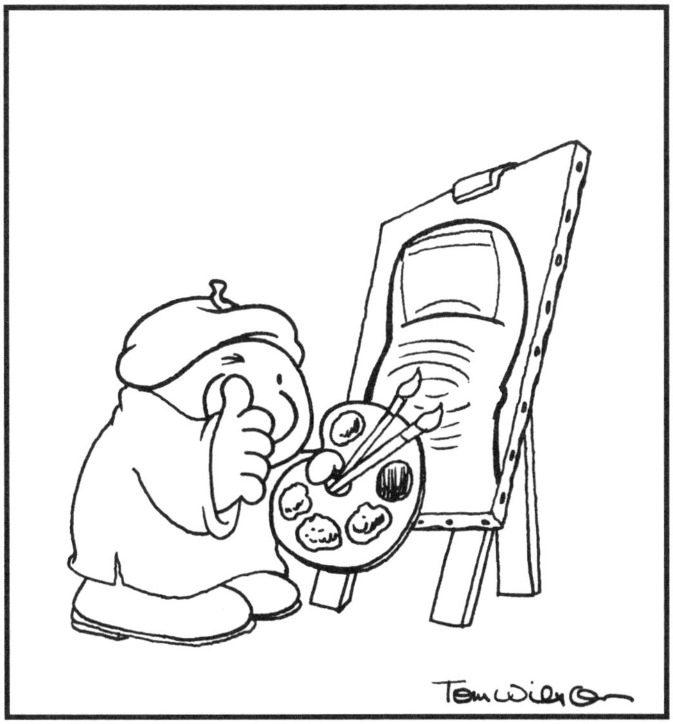

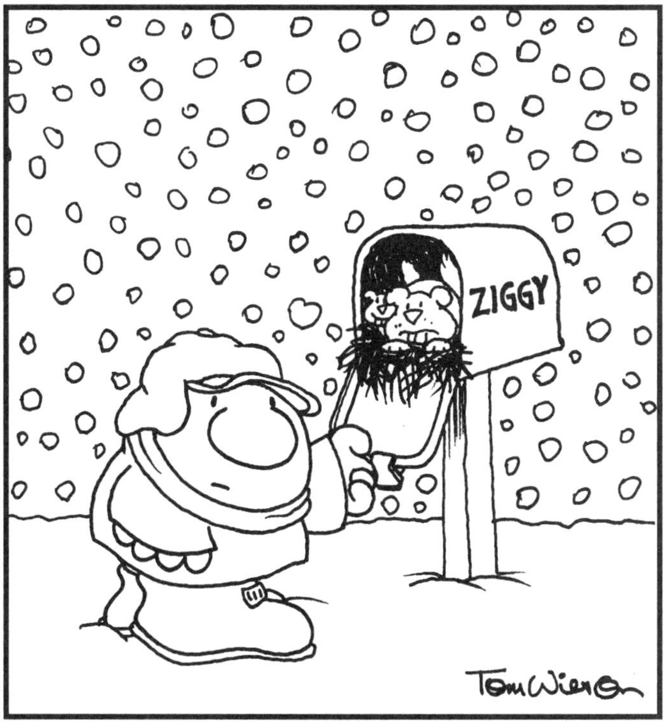
ZIGGY

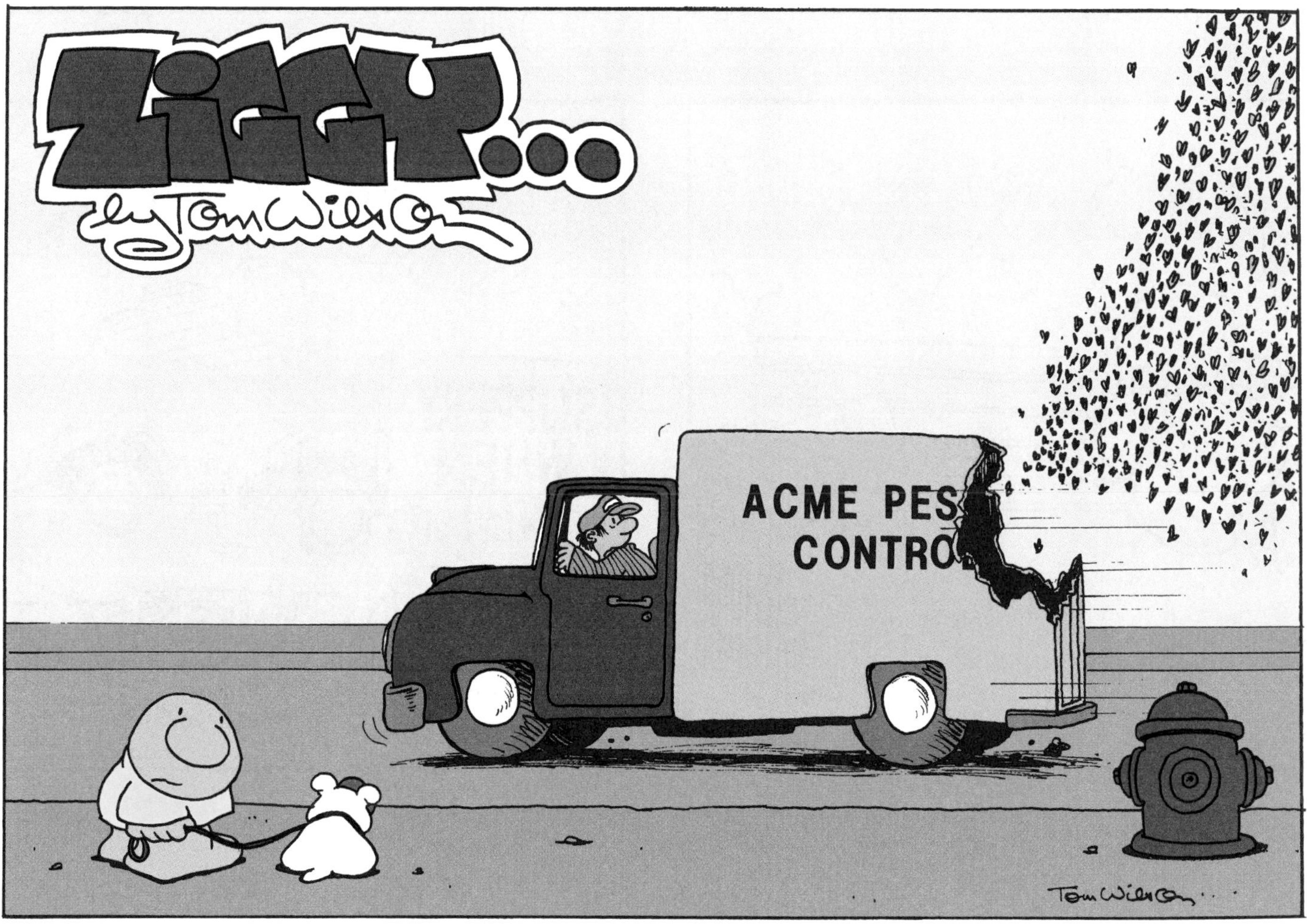
ZIGGY...
by Tom Wilson
ACME PES
CONTRO

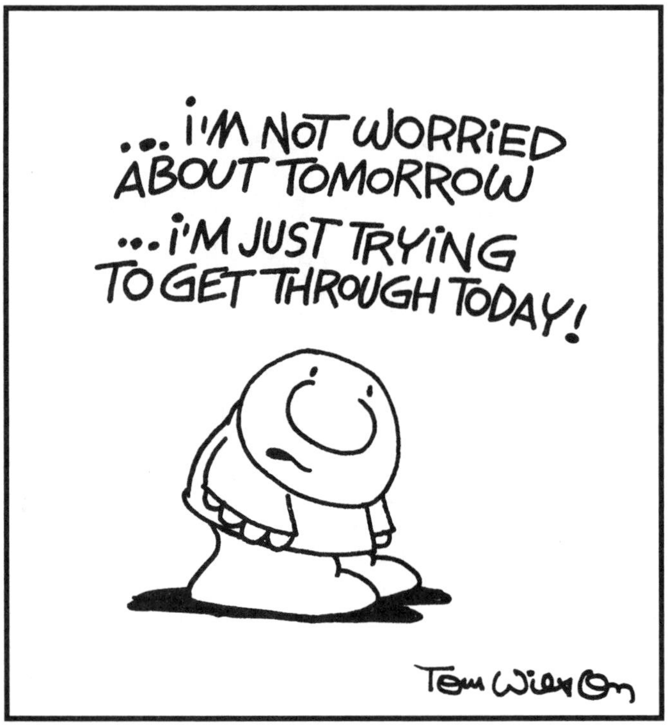
...I'M NOT WORRIED ABOUT TOMORROW ...I'M JUST TRYING TO GET THROUGH TODAY!
Tom Wilson

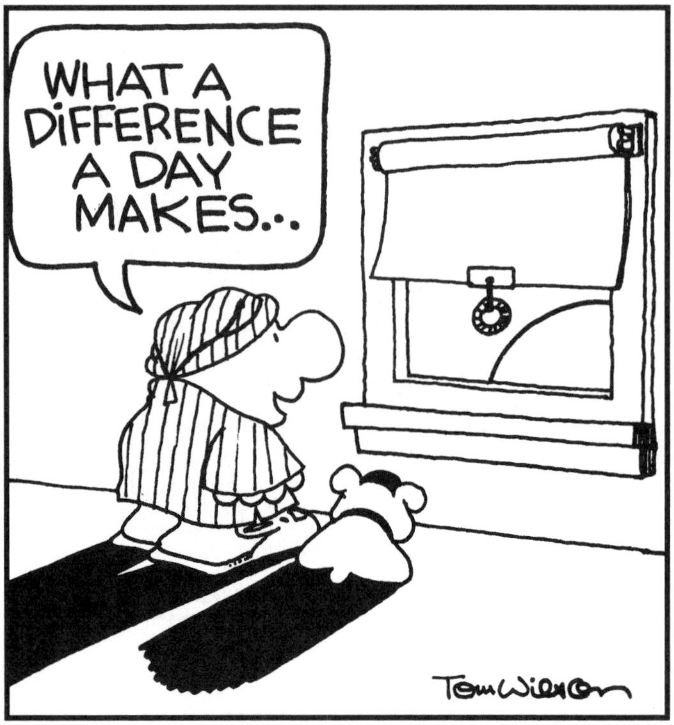
WHAT A DIFFERENCE A DAY MAKES...
Tom Wilson

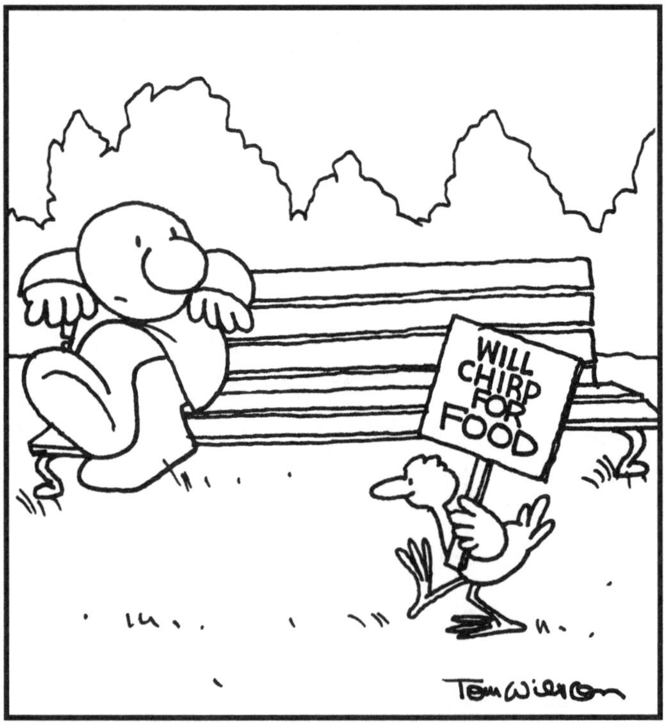
WILL CHIRP FOR FOOD
Tom Wilson

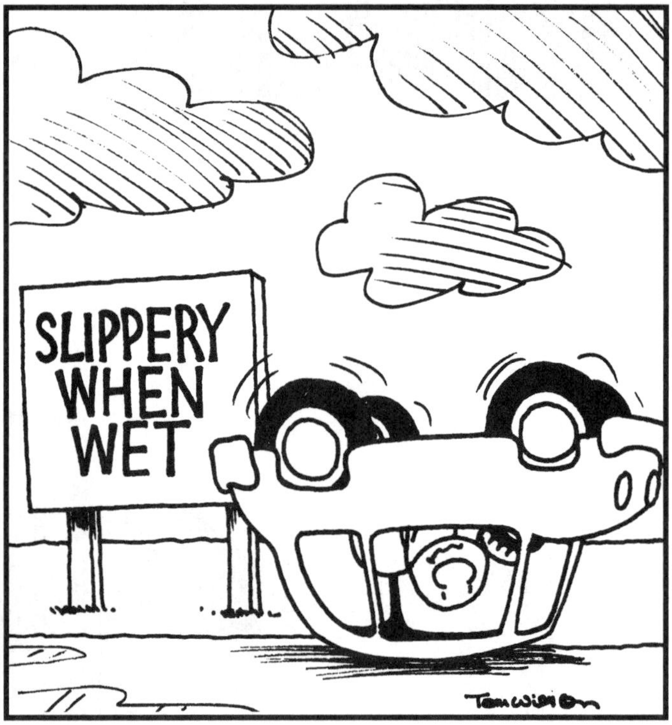
SLIPPERY WHEN WET
Tom Wilson

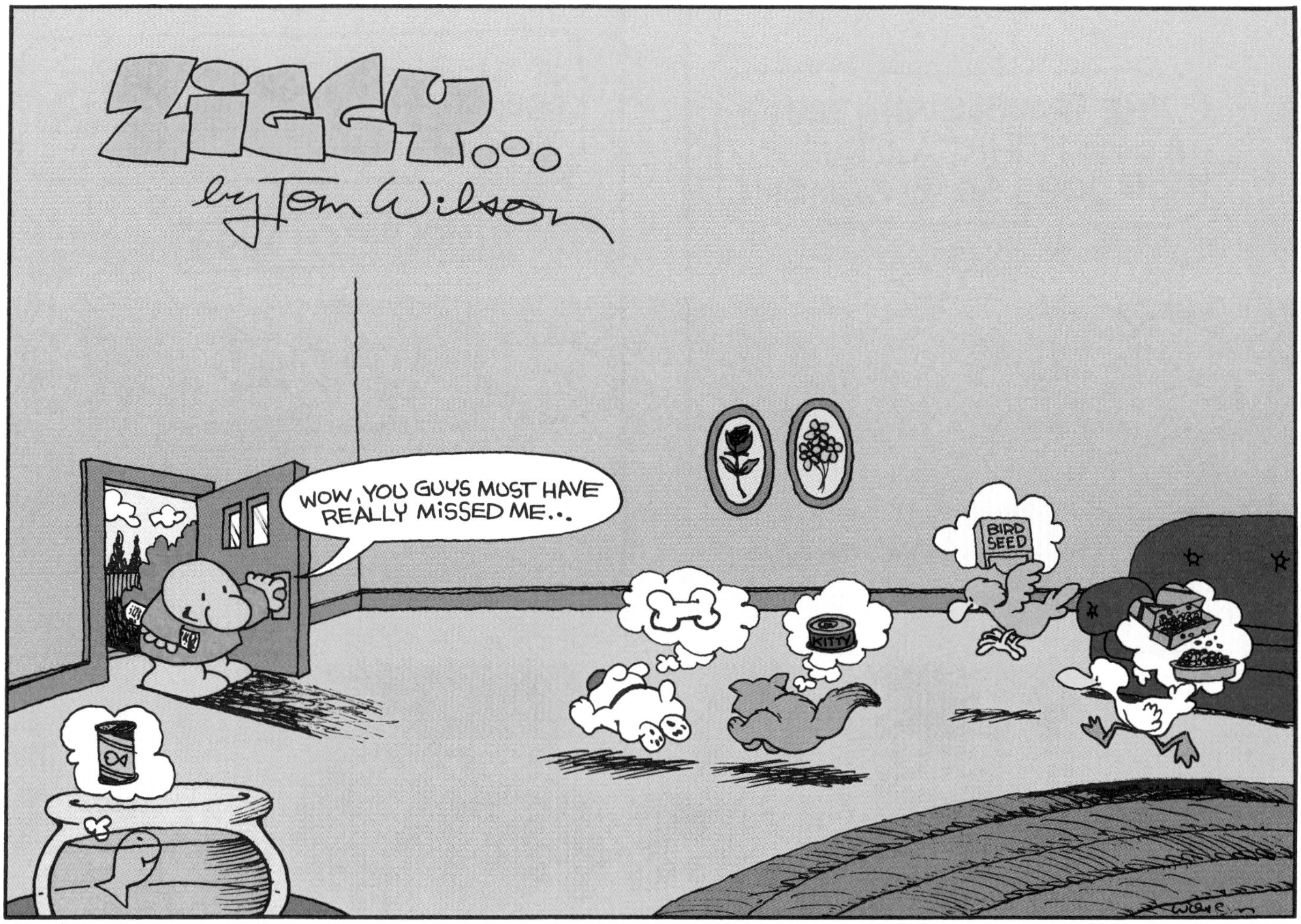
ZIGGY...
by Tom Wilson
WOW, YOU GUYS MUST HAVE REALLY MISSED ME...
BIRD SEED
KITTY
WILSON

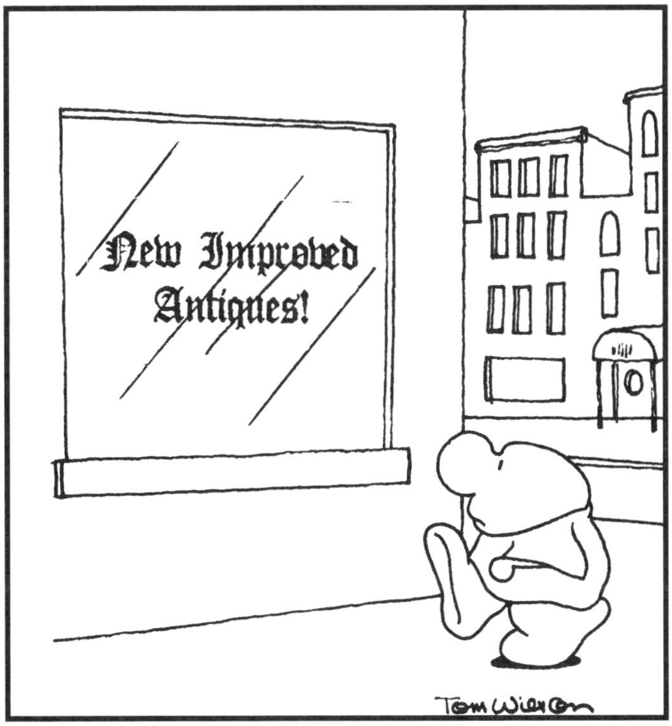
New Improved Antiques!
TOM WILSON

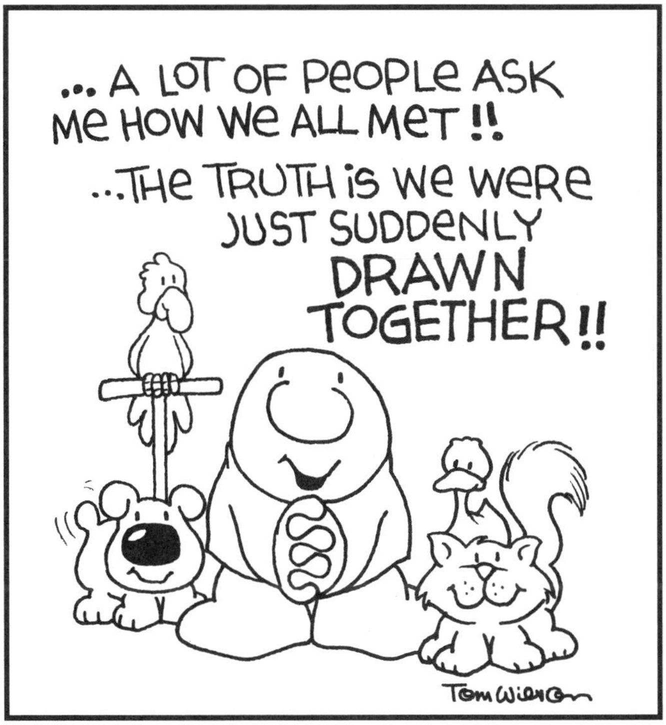
... A LOT OF PEOPLE ASK ME HOW WE ALL MET !!
...THE TRUTH IS WE WERE JUST SUDDENLY DRAWN TOGETHER !!
TOM WILSON

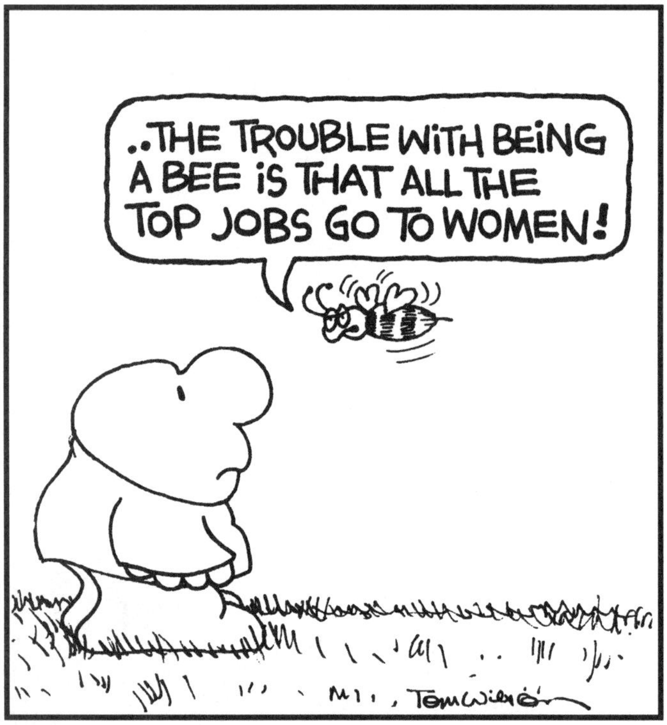
..THE TROUBLE WITH BEING A BEE IS THAT ALL THE TOP JOBS GO TO WOMEN!
Tom Wilson

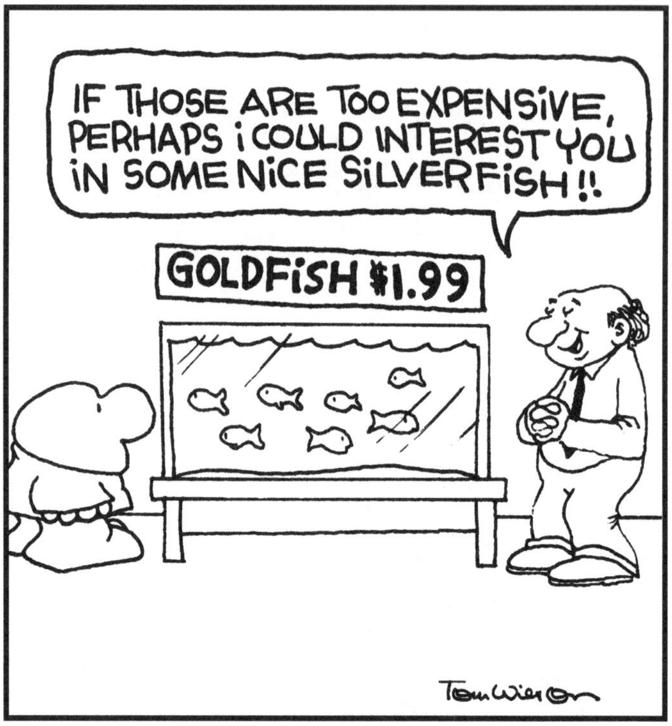
IF THOSE ARE TOO EXPENSIVE, PERHAPS I COULD INTEREST YOU IN SOME NICE SILVERFISH!!
GOLDFISH $1.99
Tom Wilson

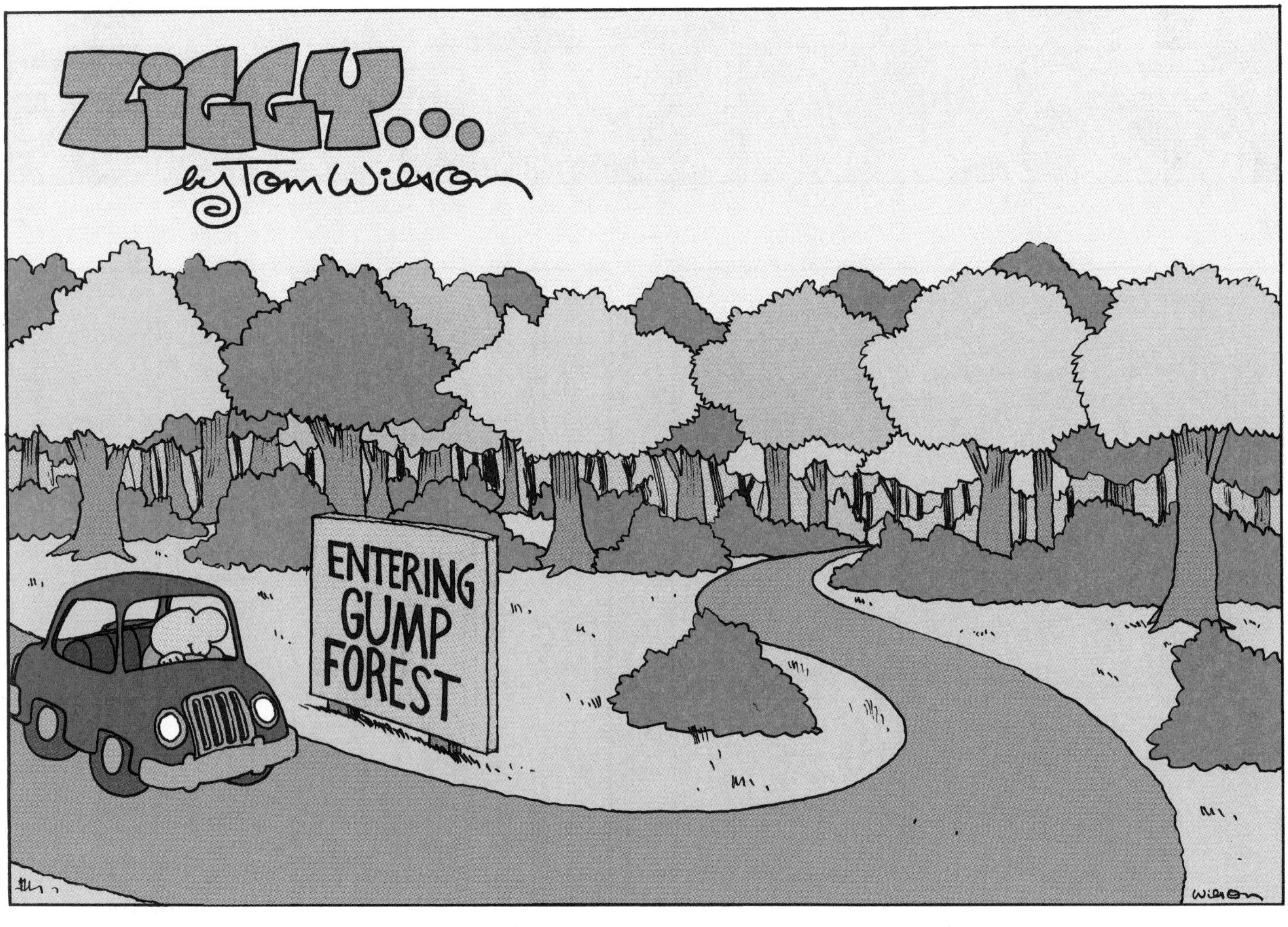
ZIGGY...
by Tom Wilson
ENTERING GUMP FOREST
Wilson

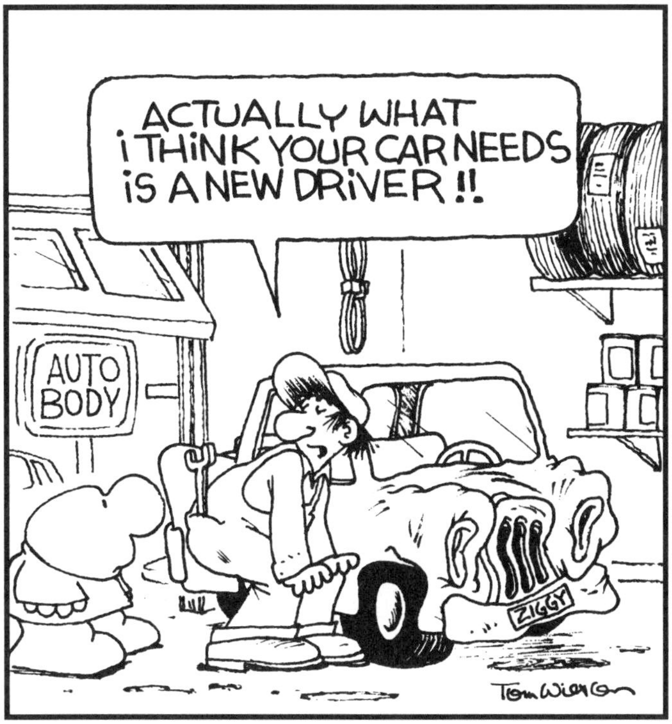
ACTUALLY WHAT i THiNK YOUR CAR NEEDS iS A NEW DRiVER !!
AUTO BODY
ZIGGY
Tom Wilson

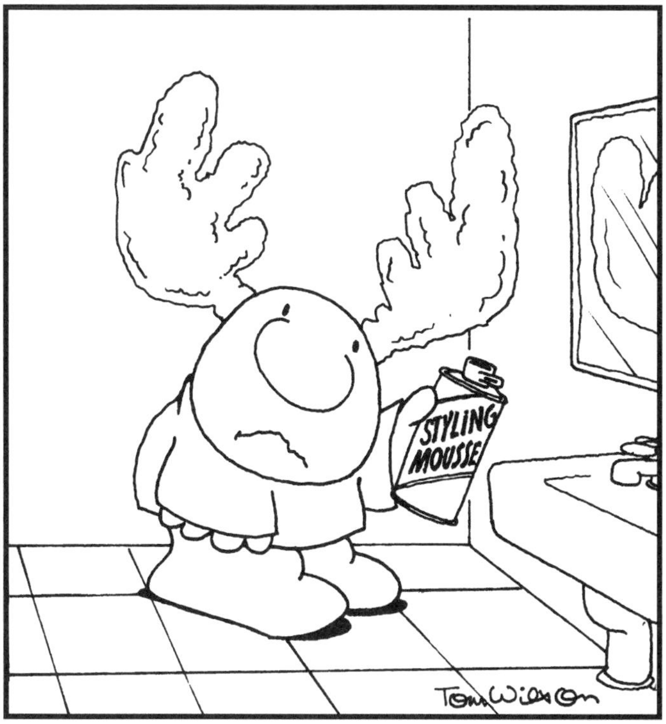
STYLING MOUSSE
Tom Wilson

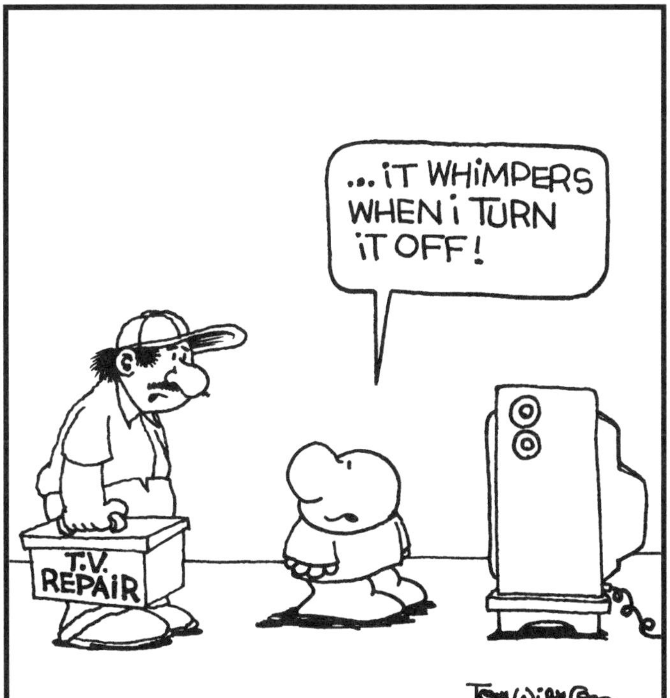
... iT WHiMPERS WHEN i TURN iT OFF!
T.V. REPAIR
Tom Wilson

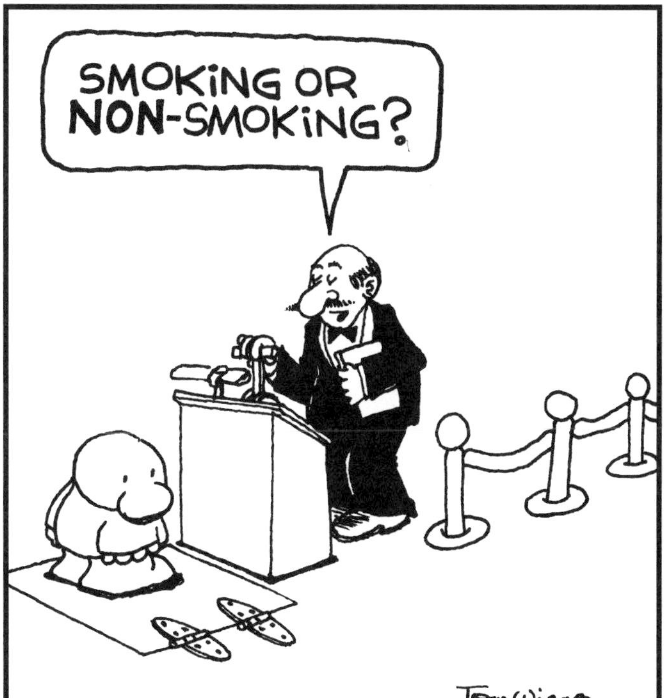
SMOKiNG OR NON-SMOKiNG?
Tom Wilson

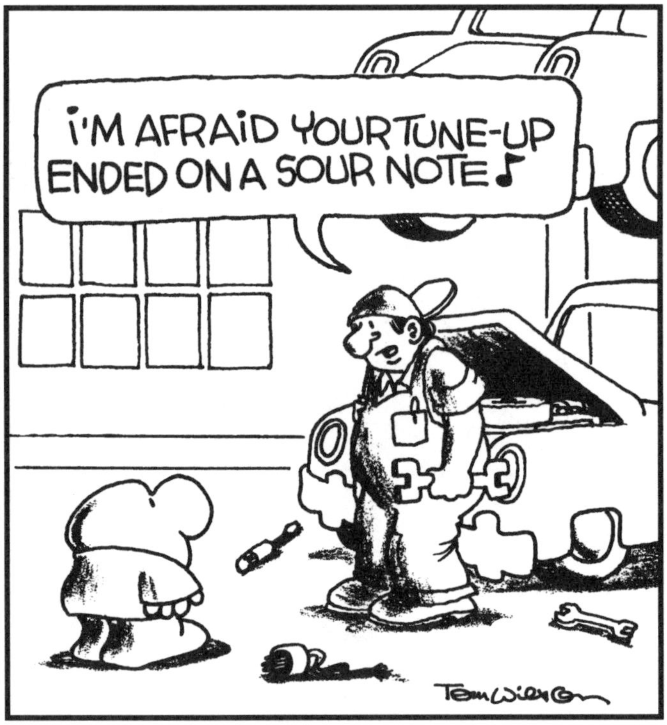
I'M AFRAID YOUR TUNE-UP ENDED ON A SOUR NOTE ♪
TOM WILSON

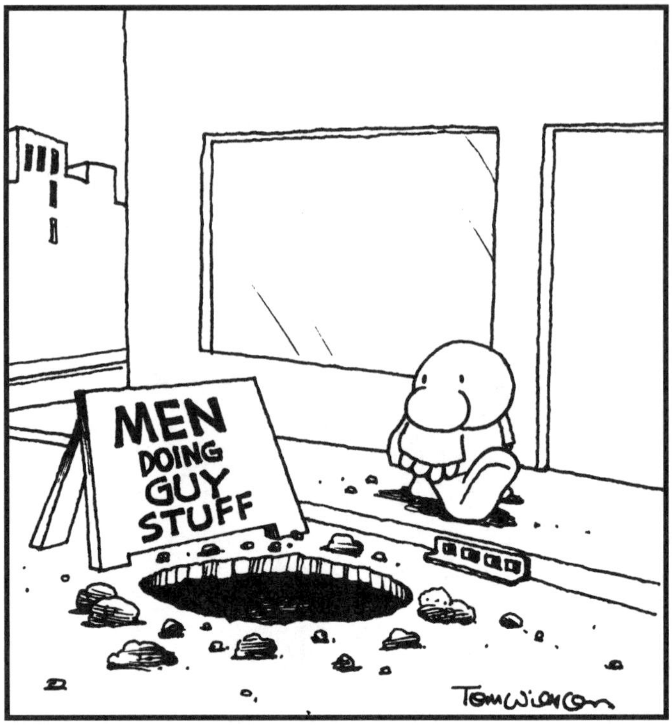
MEN DOING GUY STUFF
TOM WILSON

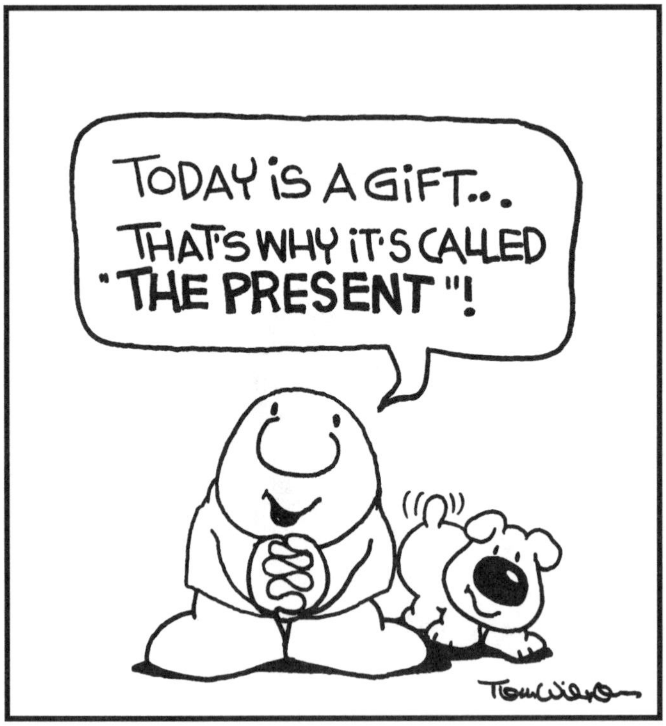
TODAY IS A GIFT... THAT'S WHY IT'S CALLED "THE PRESENT"!
TOM WILSON

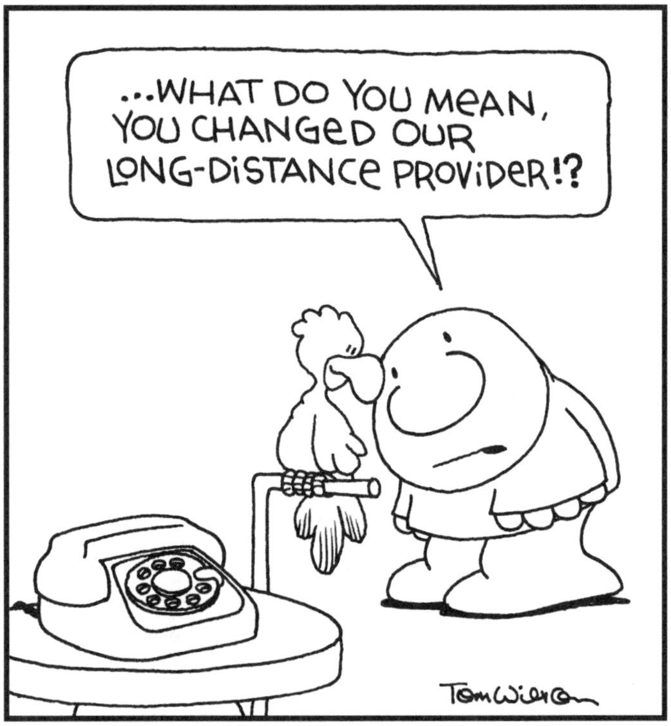
...WHAT DO YOU MEAN, YOU CHANGED OUR LONG-DISTANCE PROVIDER!?
TOM WILSON

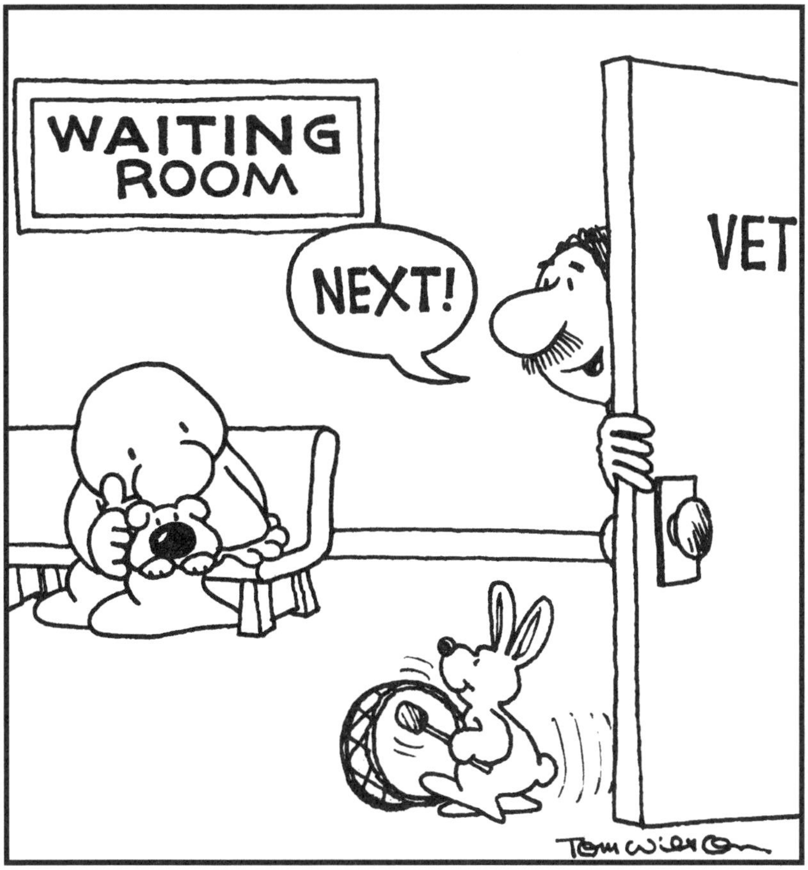
WAITING ROOM
NEXT!
VET
Tom Wilson

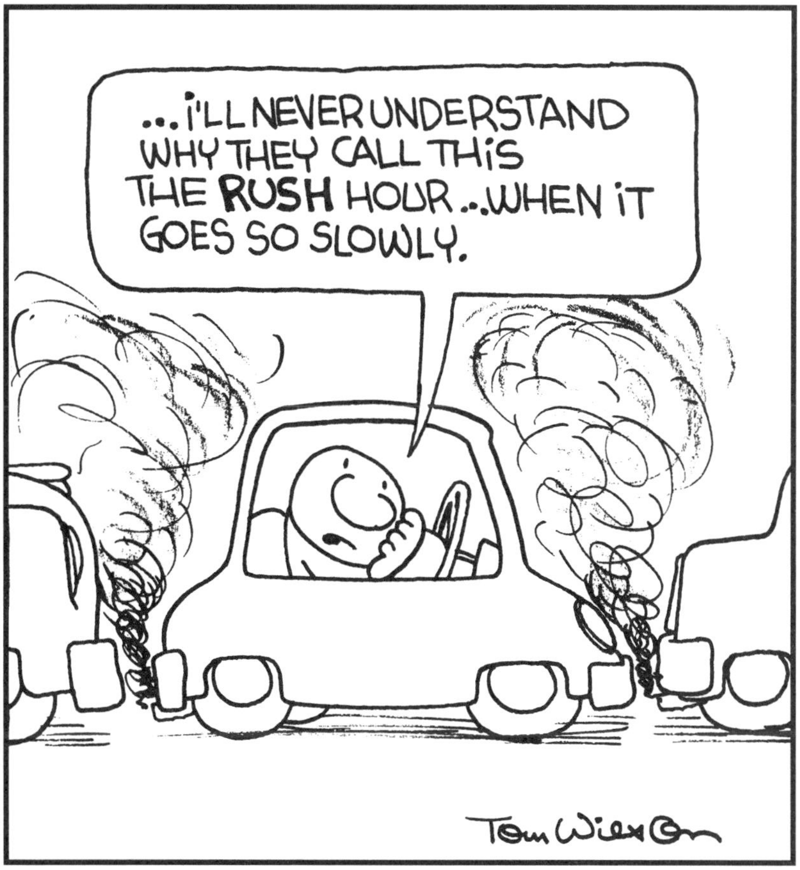
...I'LL NEVER UNDERSTAND WHY THEY CALL THIS THE RUSH HOUR...WHEN IT GOES SO SLOWLY.
Tom Wilson

Chapter VI
1996–2000

For thirty-five years *Ziggy* has touched the hearts and minds of millions. Rare is the person who at one time or another has not felt that *Ziggy* communicated exactly for them at a particular moment. Not only have I been able to enjoy Ziggy as a cartoon character, but I have had the honor of being personal friends with the "two Toms" that bring Ziggy to life every day. The creative energy they have and unselfishly share with those around them is rare and appreciated!

—Tom Thornton, former president and chief executive officer, Andrews McMeel Publishing

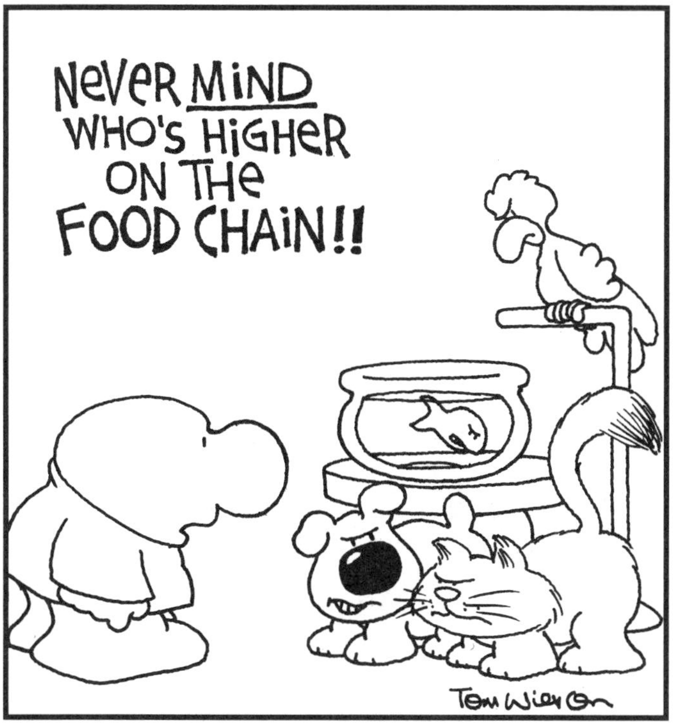
NEVER MIND WHO'S HIGHER ON THE FOOD CHAIN!!

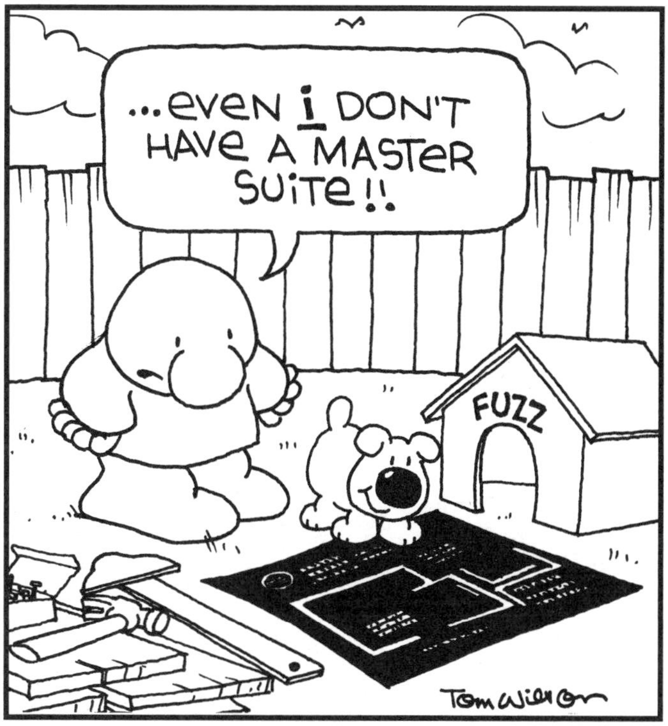
...EVEN I DON'T HAVE A MASTER SUITE!!
FUZZ

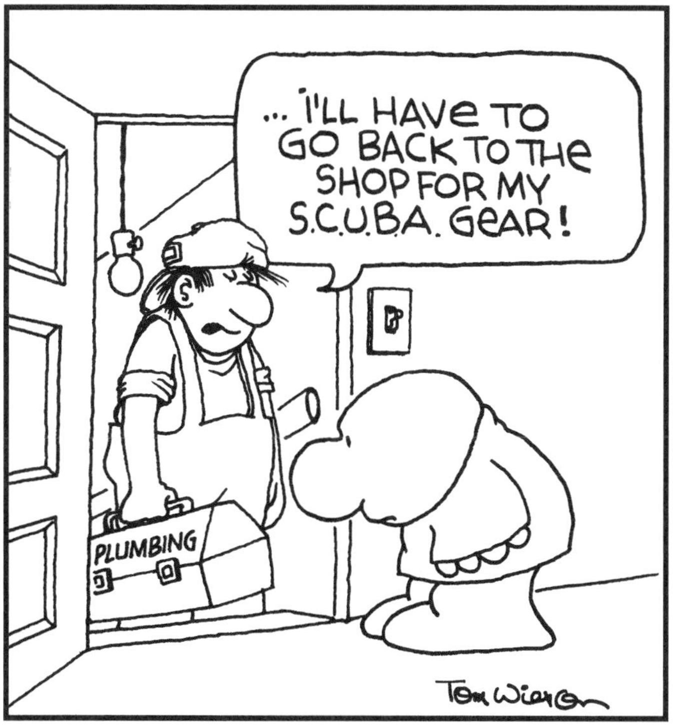
... I'LL HAVE TO GO BACK TO THE SHOP FOR MY S.C.U.B.A. GEAR!
PLUMBING

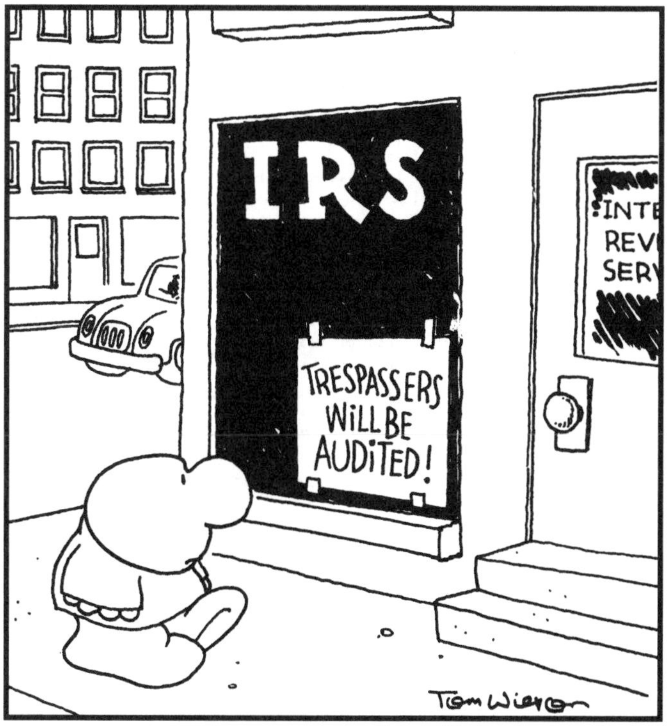
IRS
TRESPASSERS WILL BE AUDITED!

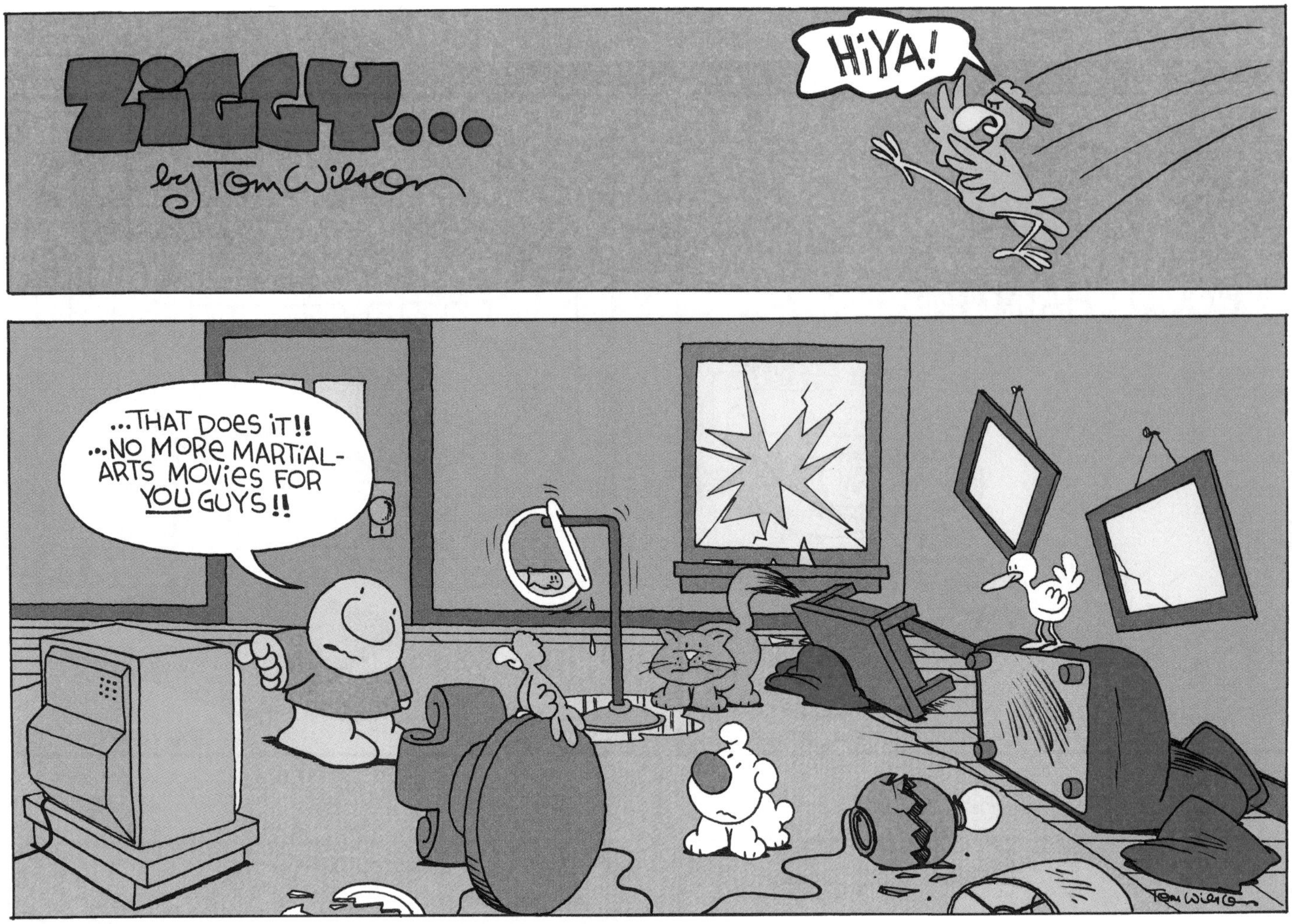
ZIGGY...
by Tom Wilson
HiYA!
...THAT DOes iT!! ...NO MORE MARTiAL-ARTS MOViES FOR YOU GUYS!!
Tom Wilson

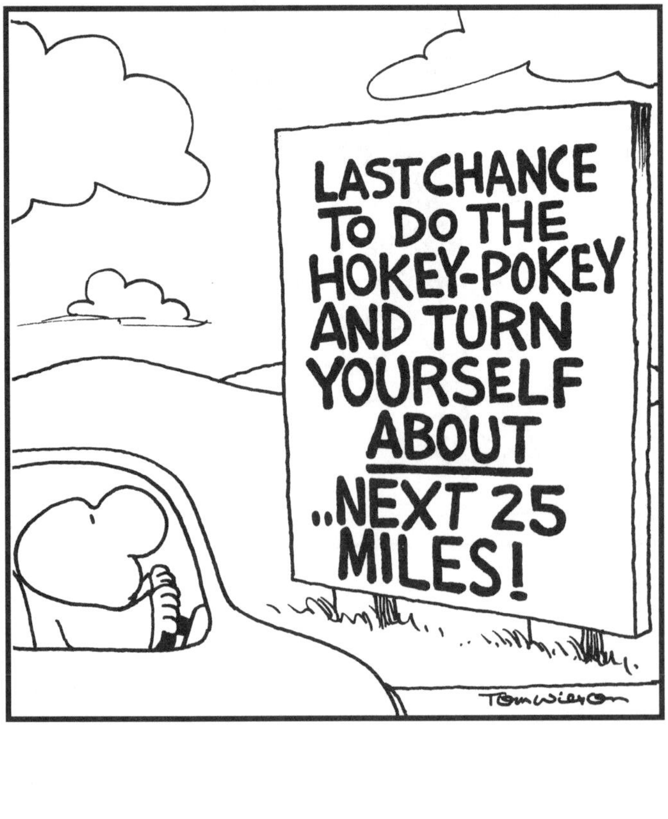
LAST CHANCE TO DO THE HOKEY-POKEY AND TURN YOURSELF ABOUT ..NEXT 25 MILES!
Tom Wilson

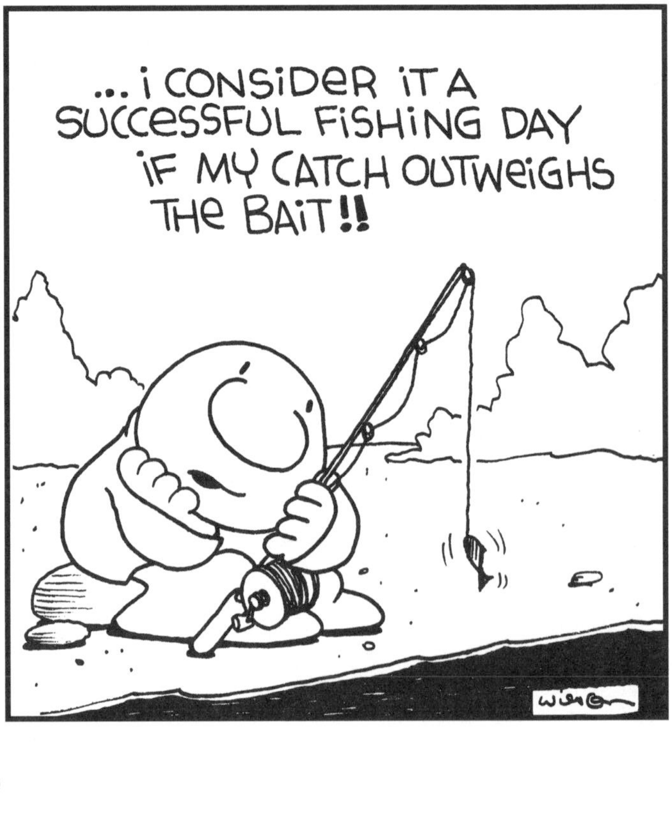
...i CONSiDeR iT A SUCCeSSFUL FiSHiNG DAY iF MY CATCH OUTWeiGHS THe BAiT!!
Wilson

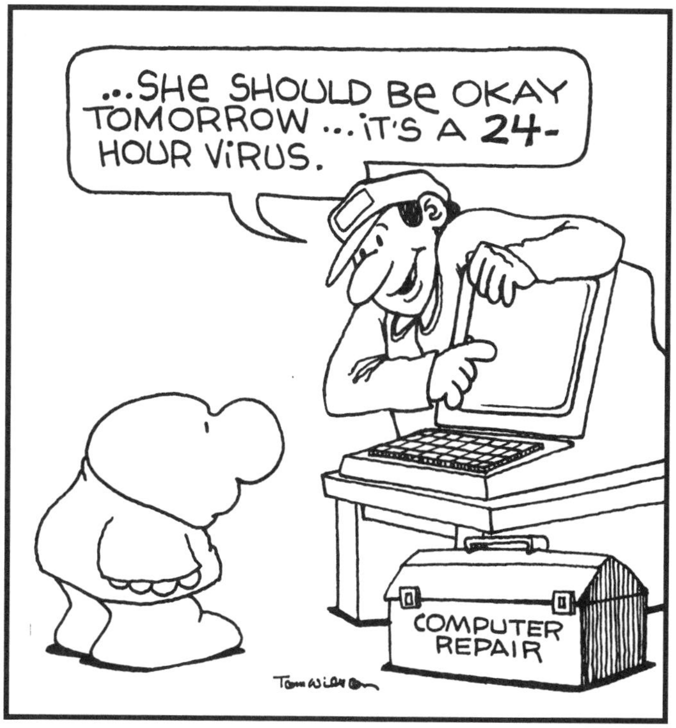
...SHE SHOULD BE OKAY TOMORROW ... IT'S A 24-HOUR VIRUS.
COMPUTER REPAIR
TOM WILSON

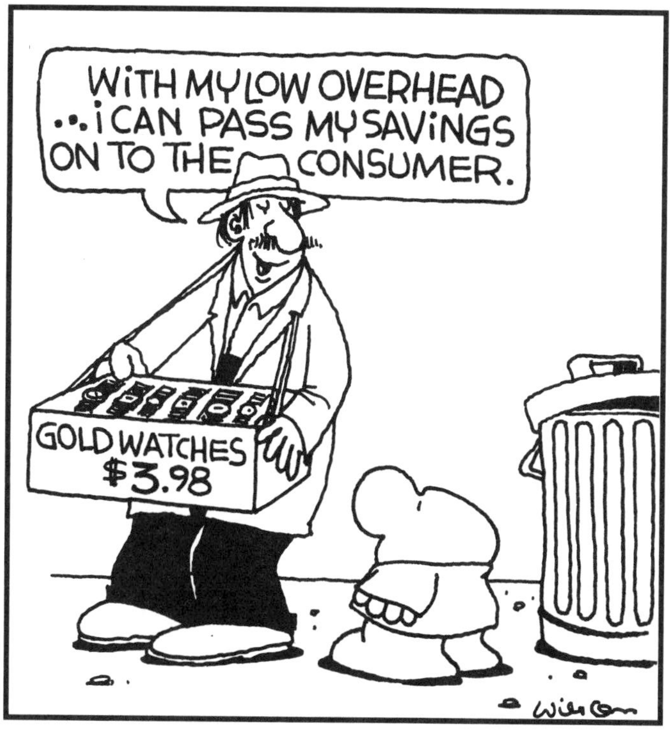
WITH MY LOW OVERHEAD ... I CAN PASS MY SAVINGS ON TO THE CONSUMER.
GOLD WATCHES $3.98
WILSON

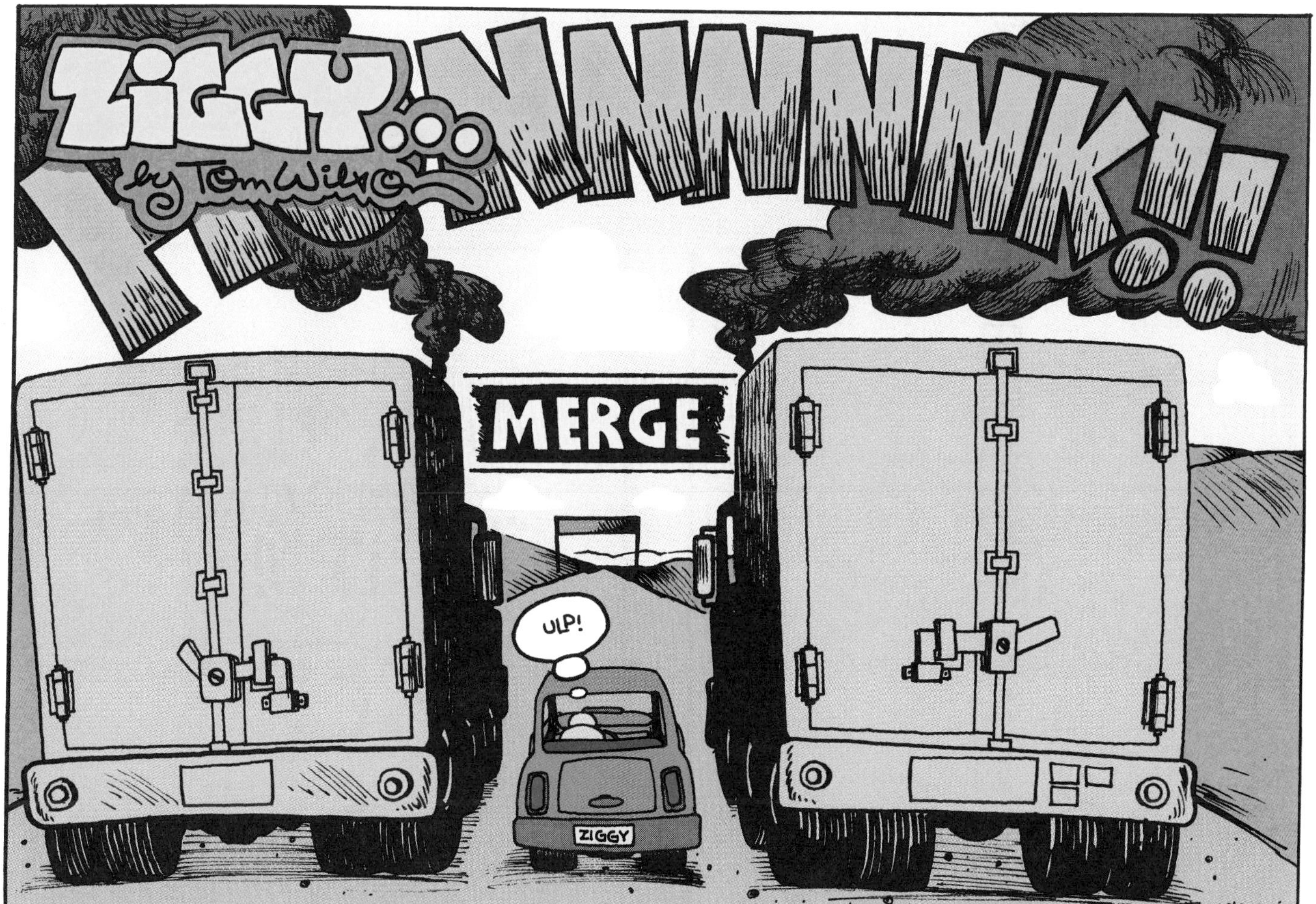
ZIGGY... by Tom Wilson
HNNNNNNK!!..
MERGE
ULP!
ZIGGY
TOM WILSON

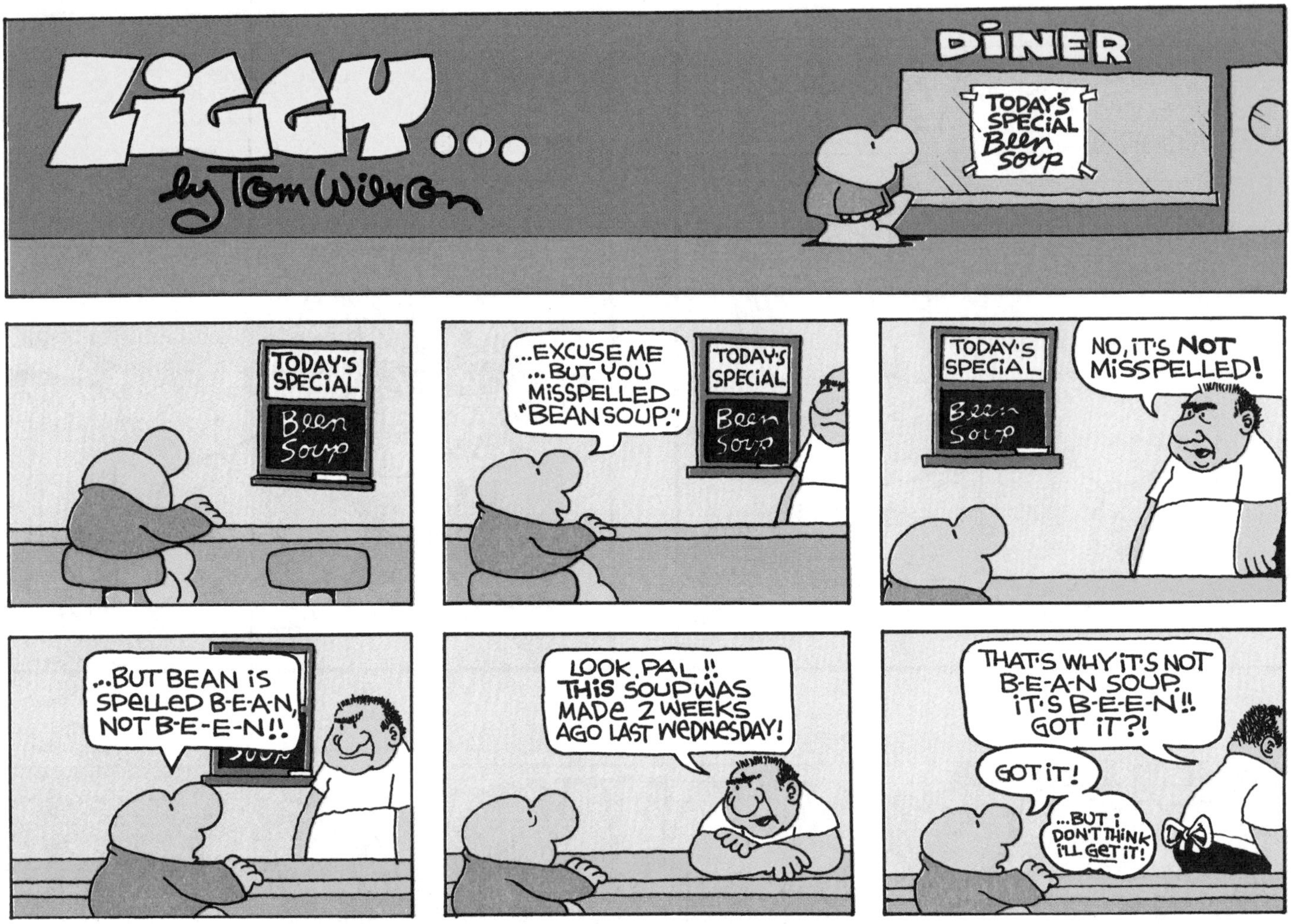
ZIGGY...
by Tom Wilson
DINER
TODAY'S SPECIAL Been Soup
TODAY'S SPECIAL
Been Soup
...EXCUSE ME ...BUT YOU MISSPELLED "BEAN SOUP."
NO, IT'S NOT MISSPELLED!
...BUT BEAN IS SPELLED B-E-A-N, NOT B-E-E-N!!
LOOK, PAL!! THIS SOUP WAS MADE 2 WEEKS AGO LAST WEDNESDAY!
THAT'S WHY IT'S NOT B-E-A-N SOUP. IT'S B-E-E-N!! GOT IT?!
GOT IT!
...BUT I DON'T THINK I'LL GET IT!

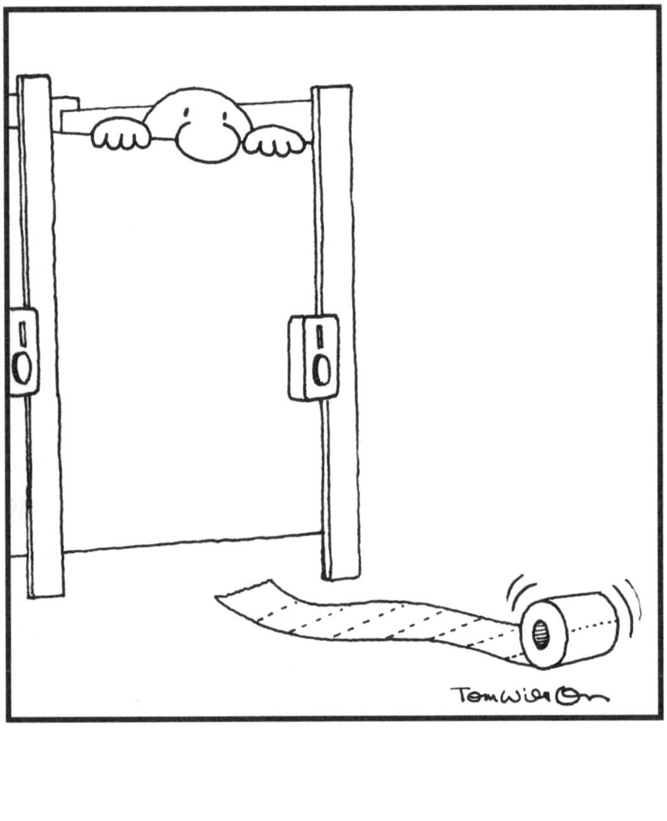
Tom Wilson

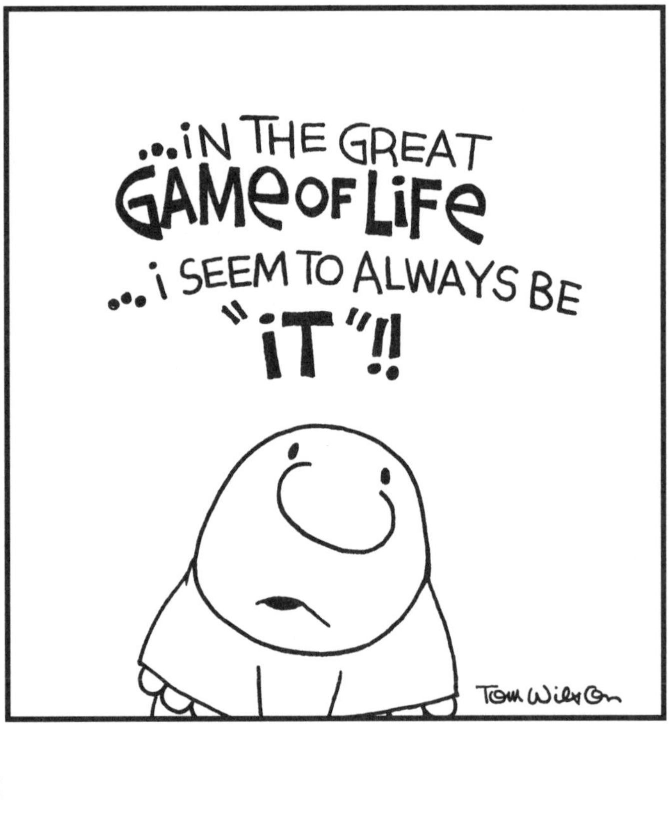
...IN THE GREAT GAME OF LIFE
...I SEEM TO ALWAYS BE "IT"!!
Tom Wilson

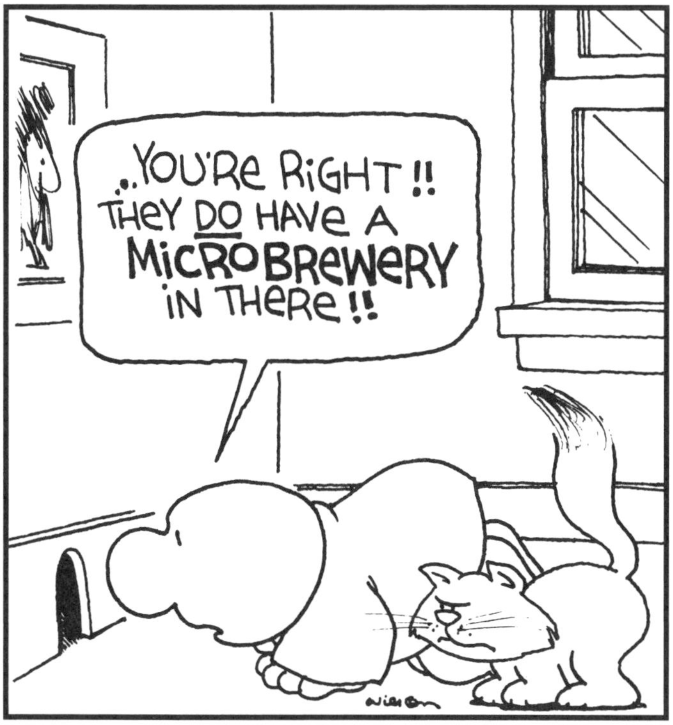
..YOU'RE RIGHT !!
THEY DO HAVE A
MICROBREWERY
IN THERE !!
WILSON

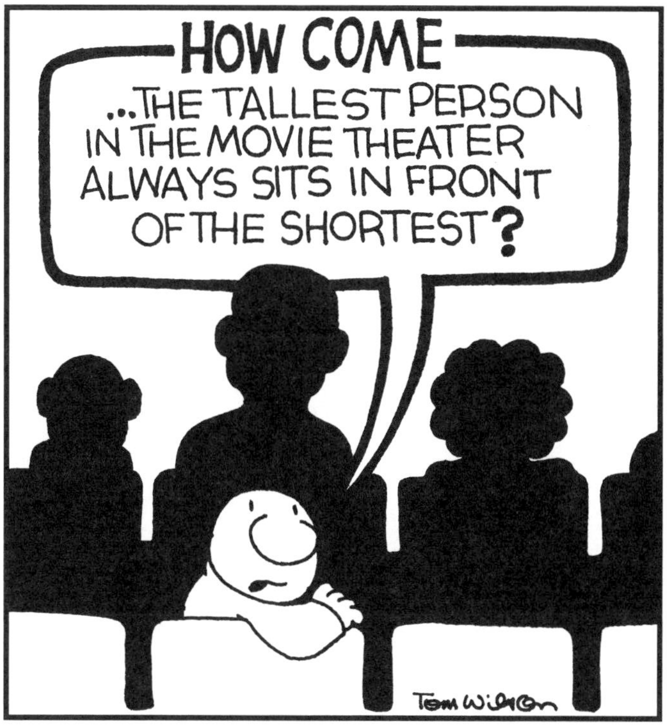
HOW COME
...THE TALLEST PERSON
IN THE MOVIE THEATER
ALWAYS SITS IN FRONT
OF THE SHORTEST?
TOM WILSON

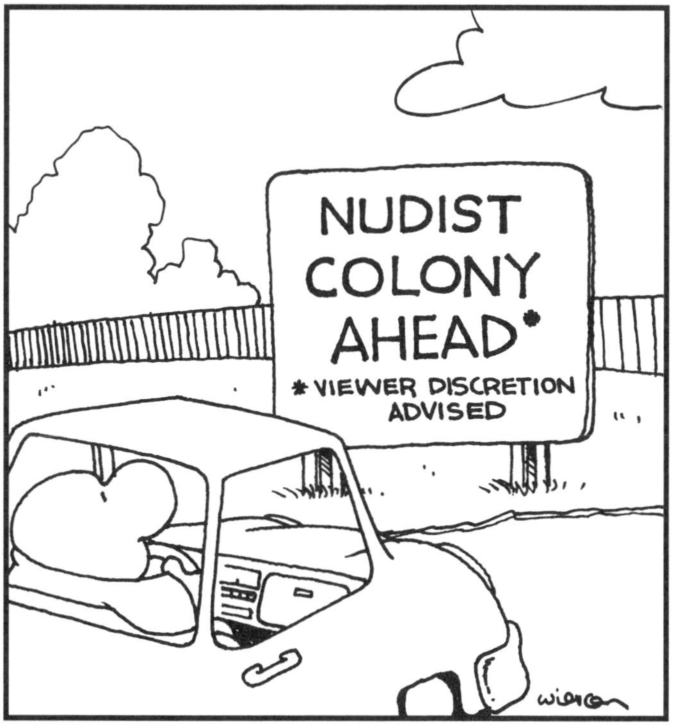
NUDIST
COLONY
AHEAD*
* VIEWER DISCRETION
ADVISED
WILSON

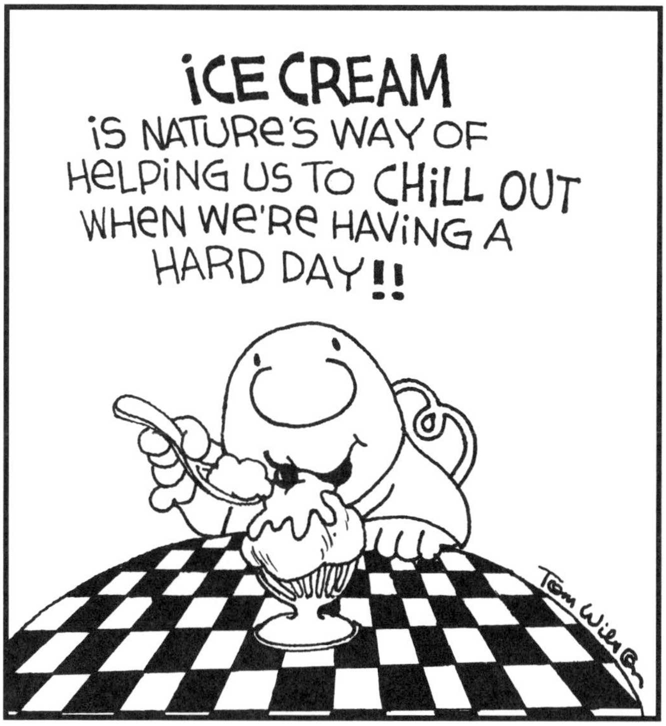
ICE CREAM
IS NATURE'S WAY OF
HELPING US TO CHILL OUT
WHEN WE'RE HAVING A
HARD DAY!!
TOM WILSON

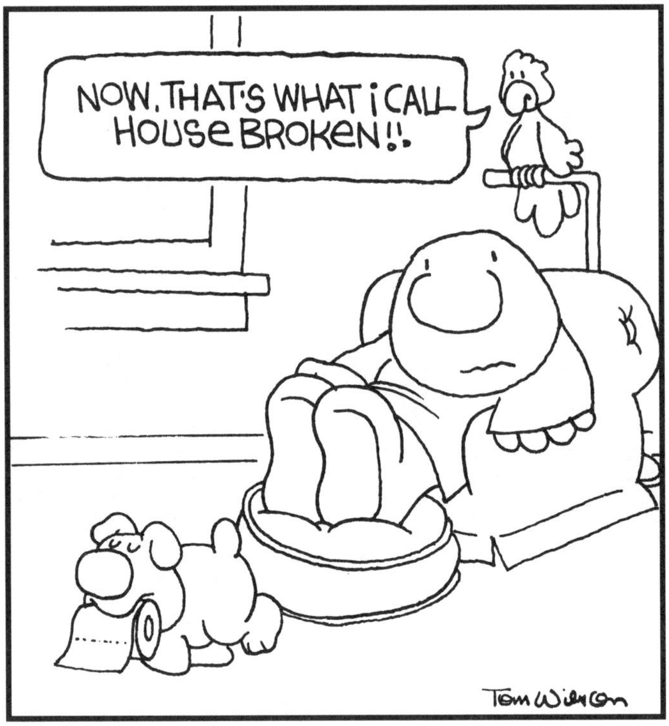
NOW, THAT'S WHAT I CALL HOUSE BROKEN!!
TOM WILSON

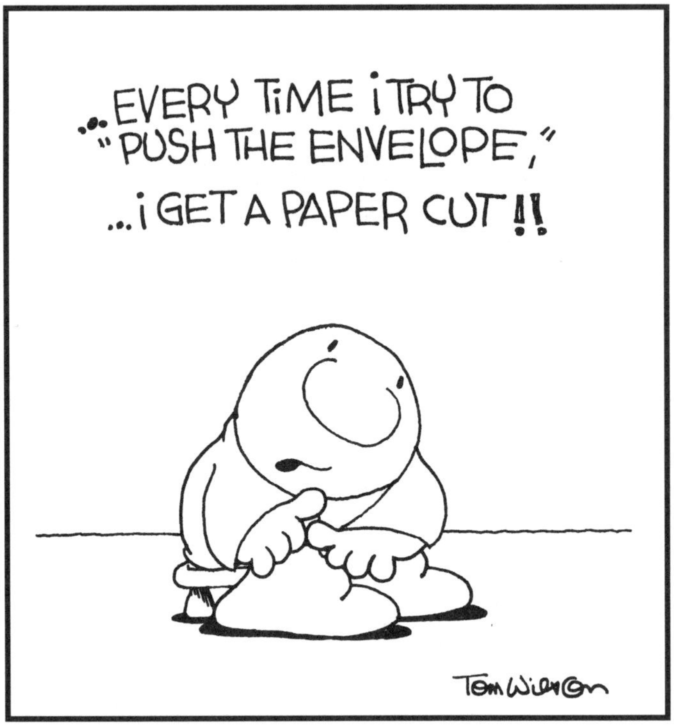
...EVERY TIME I TRY TO "PUSH THE ENVELOPE," ...I GET A PAPER CUT!!
TOM WILSON

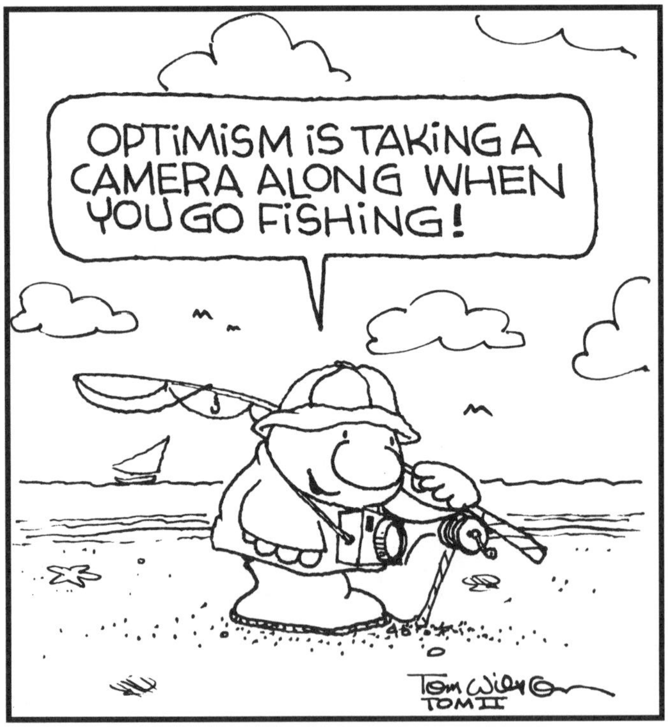
OPTIMISM IS TAKING A CAMERA ALONG WHEN YOU GO FISHING!
TOM WILSON
TOM II

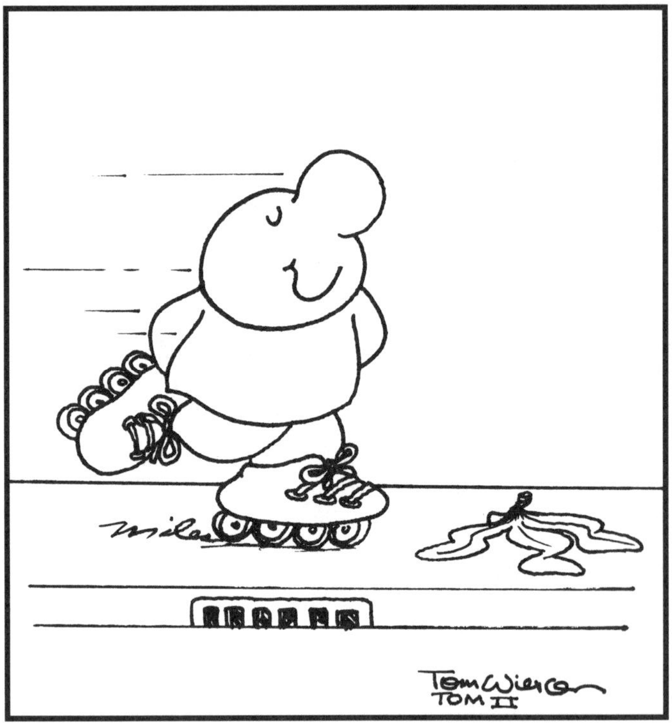
TOM WILSON
TOM II

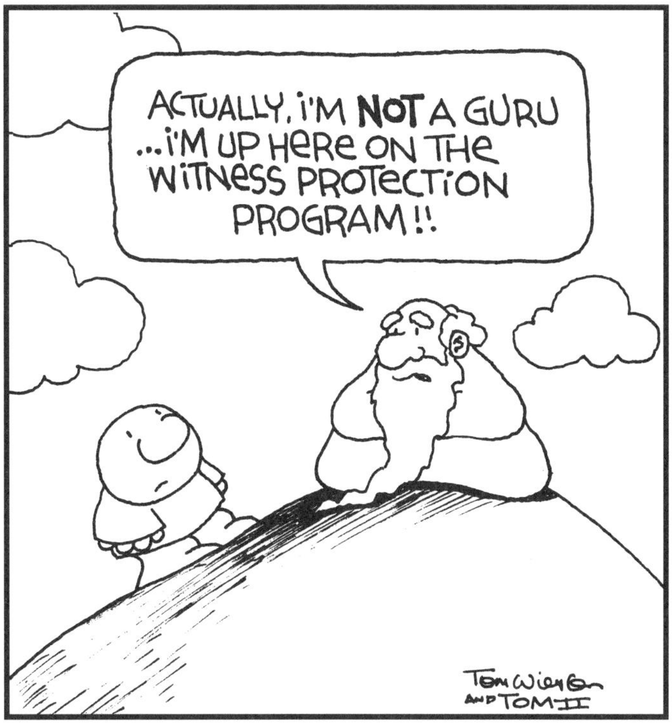
ACTUALLY, i'M **NOT** A GURU ...i'M UP HERE ON THE WITNESS PROTECTION PROGRAM!!
TOM WILSON AND TOM II

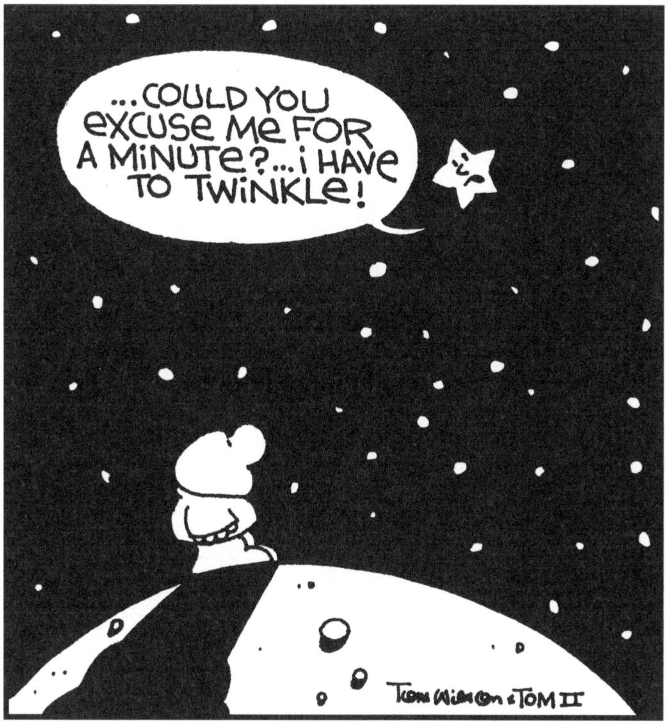
...COULD YOU EXCUSE ME FOR A MINUTE?...i HAVE TO TWINKLE!
TOM WILSON + TOM II

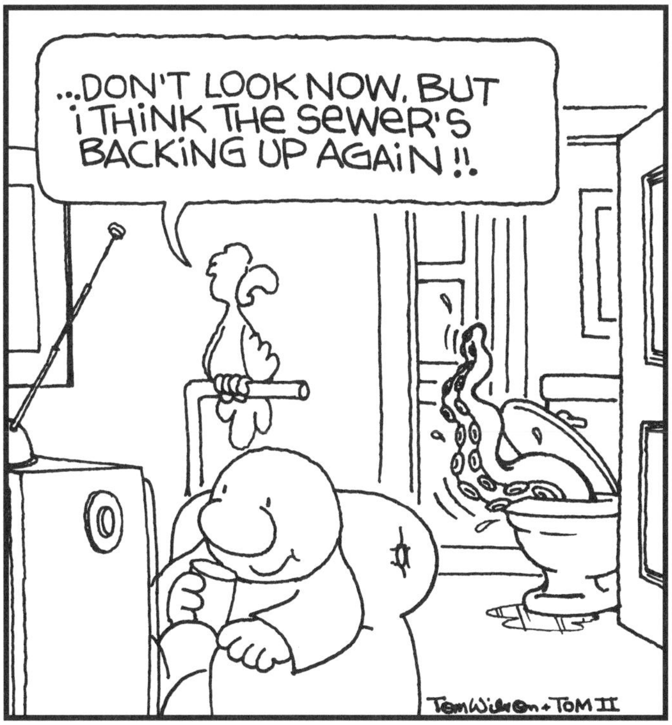
...DON'T LOOK NOW, BUT i THINK THE SEWER'S BACKING UP AGAIN!!
TOM WILSON + TOM II

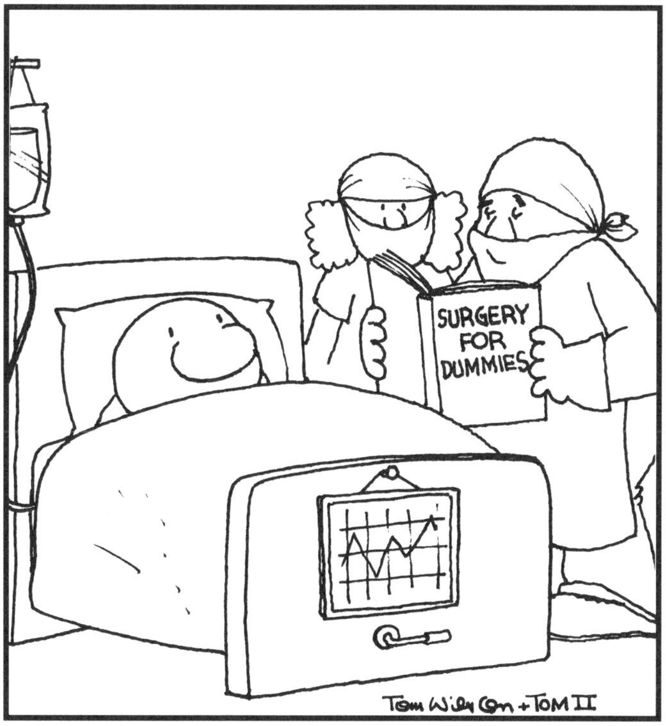
SURGERY FOR DUMMIES
TOM WILSON + TOM II

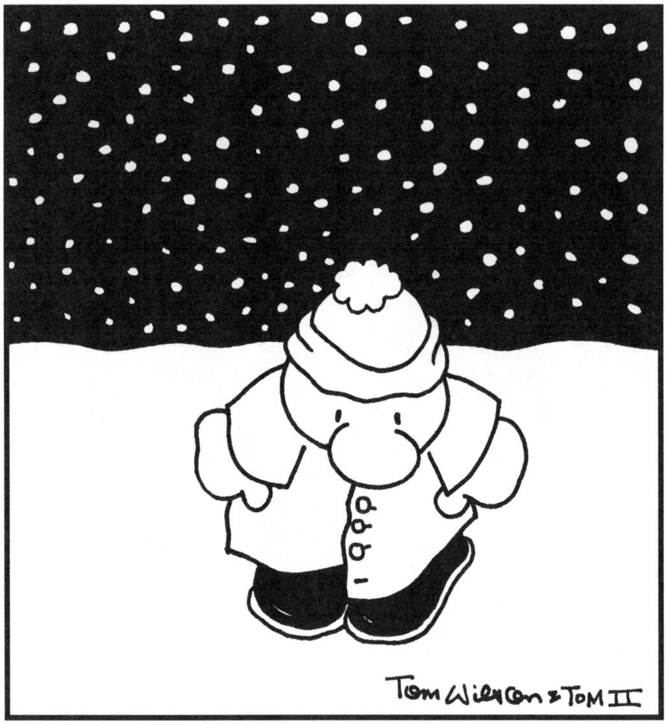
Tom Wilson & Tom II

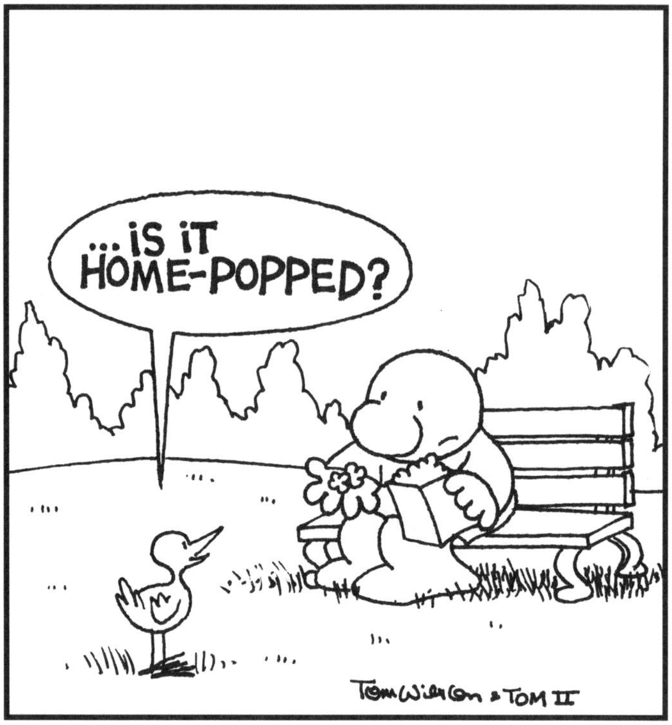
...iS iT HOME-POPPED?
Tom Wilson & Tom II

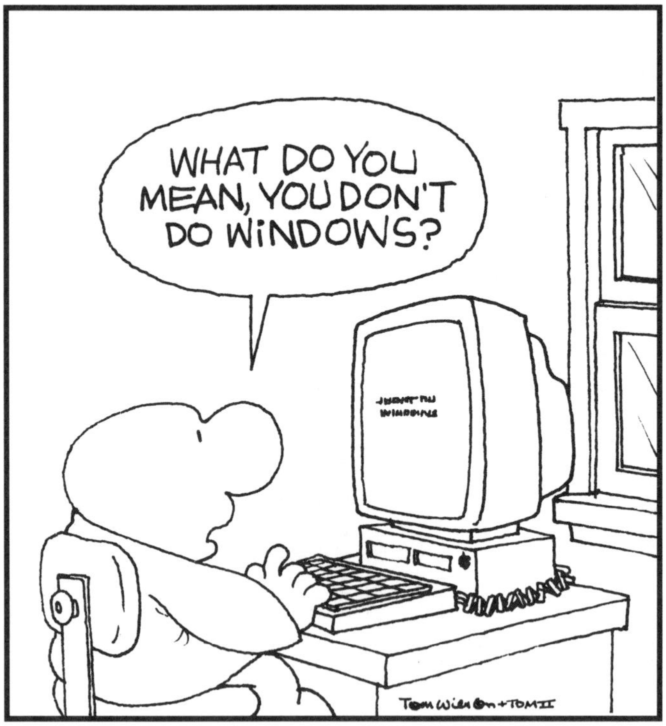
WHAT DO YOU MEAN, YOU DON'T DO WiNDOWS?
Tom Wilson + Tom II

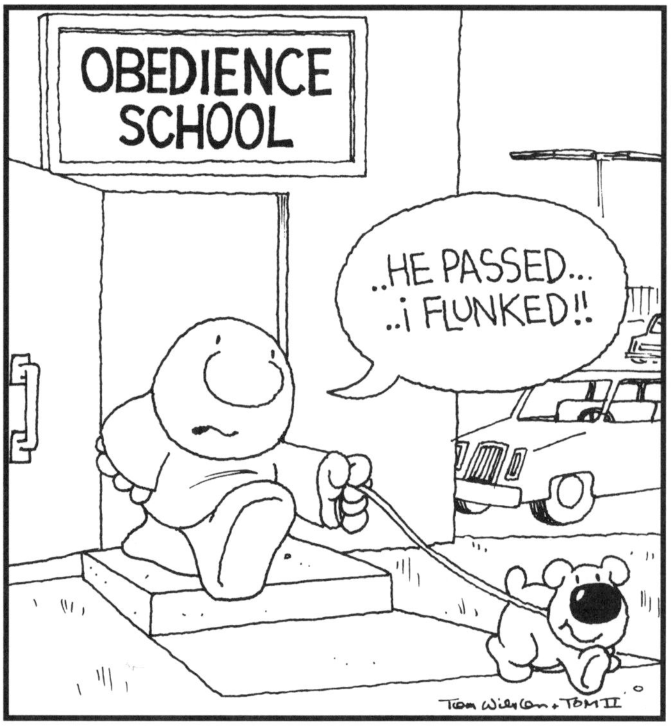
OBEDIENCE SCHOOL
..HE PASSED... ..i FLUNKED!!
Tom Wilson + Tom II

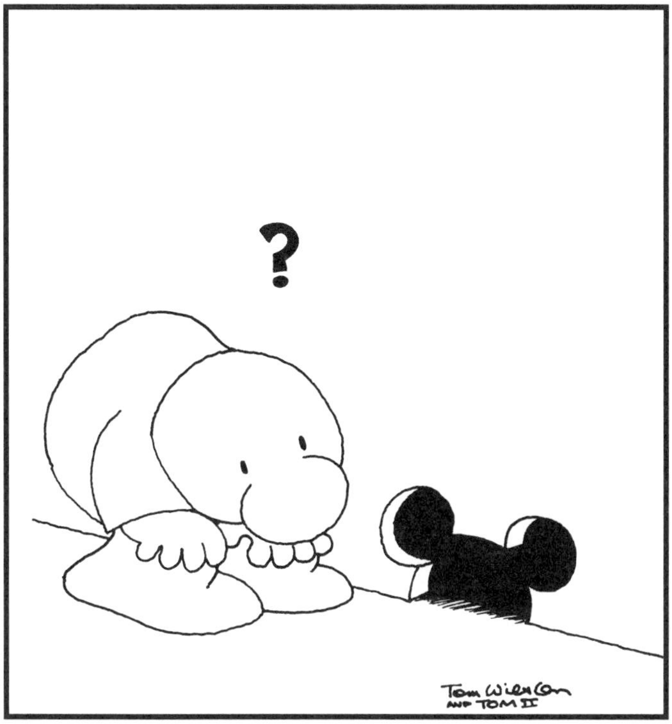
?
TOM WILSON AND TOM II

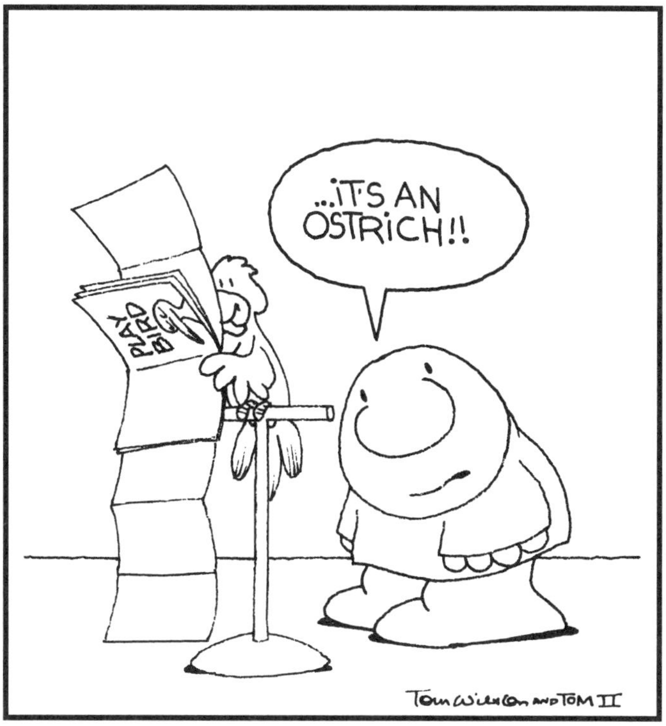
...IT'S AN OSTRICH!!
PLAY BIRD
TOM WILSON AND TOM II

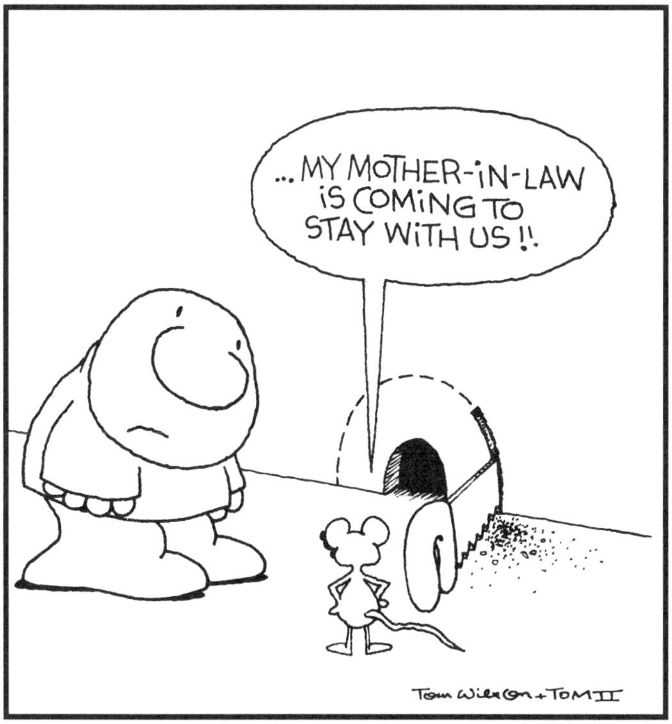
... MY MOTHER-IN-LAW IS COMING TO STAY WITH US!!
TOM WILSON + TOM II

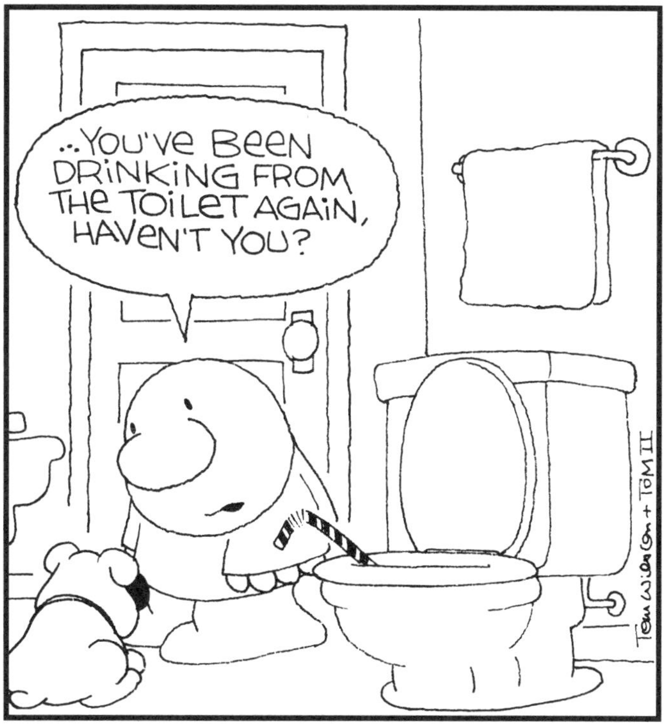
..YOU'VE BEEN DRINKING FROM THE TOILET AGAIN, HAVEN'T YOU?
TOM WILSON + TOM II

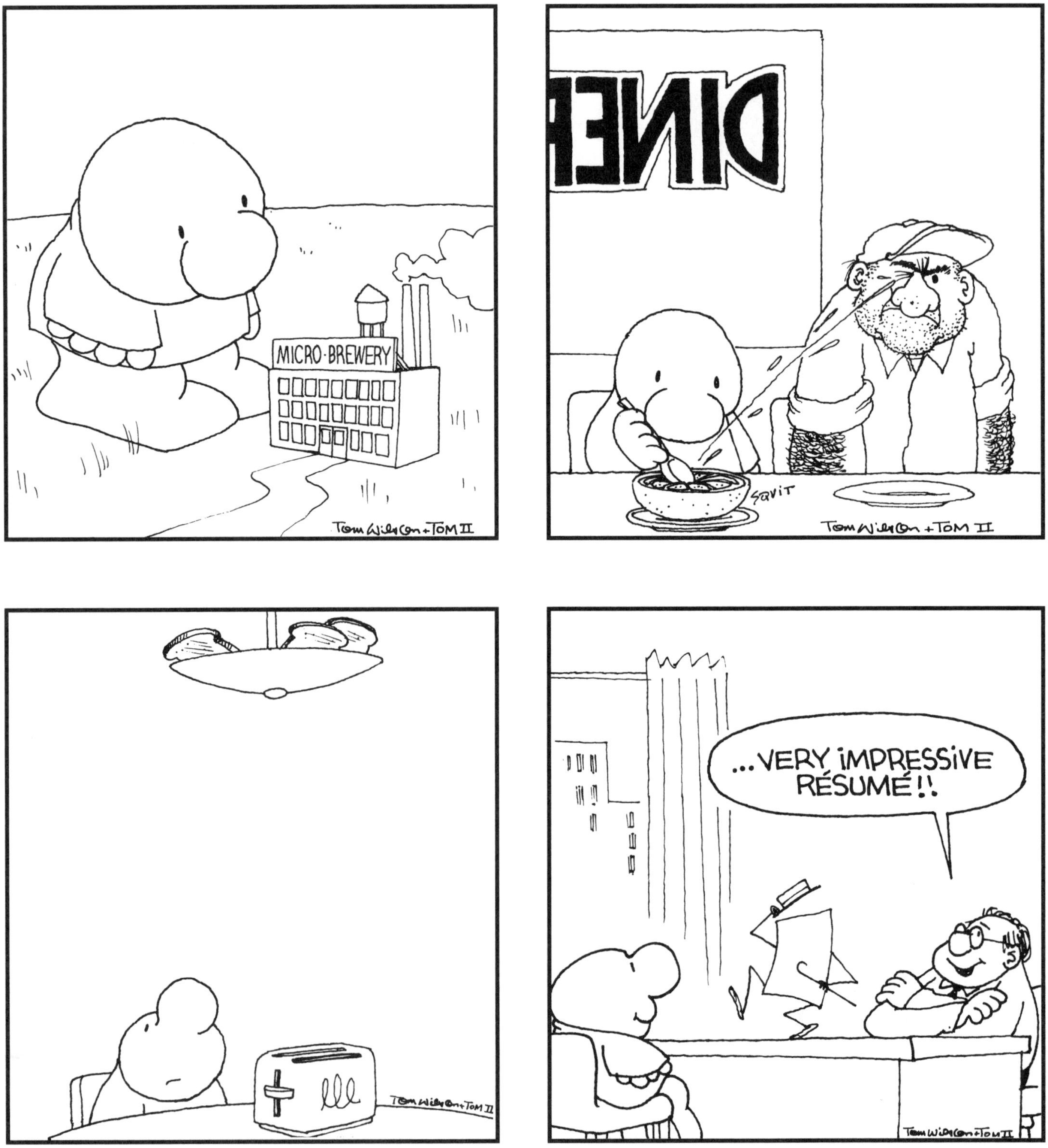
MICRO·BREWERY
Tom Wilson + TOM II
SQUIT
Tom Wilson + TOM II
Tom Wilson + TOM II
...VERY IMPRESSIVE RÉSUMÉ!!
Tom Wilson + TOM II

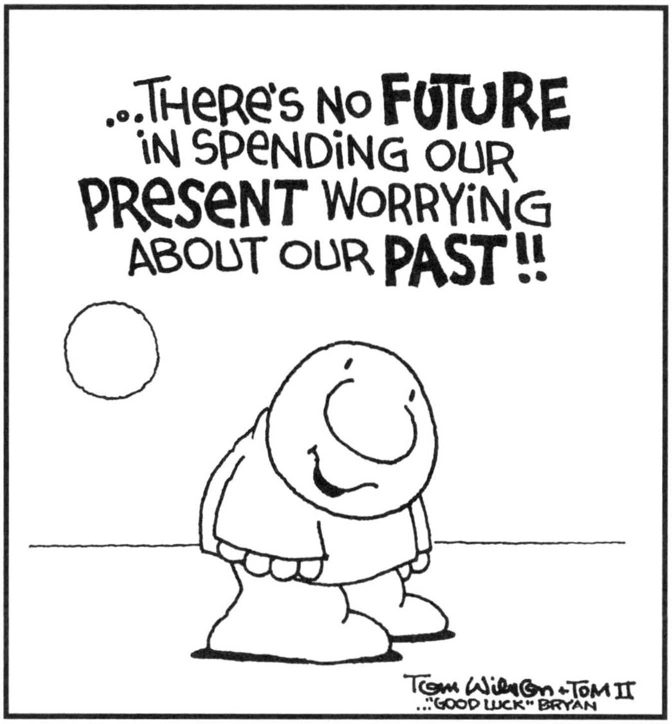
..There's no FUTURE in spending our PRESENT worrying about our PAST!!
Tom Wilson + Tom II
..."Good Luck" Bryan

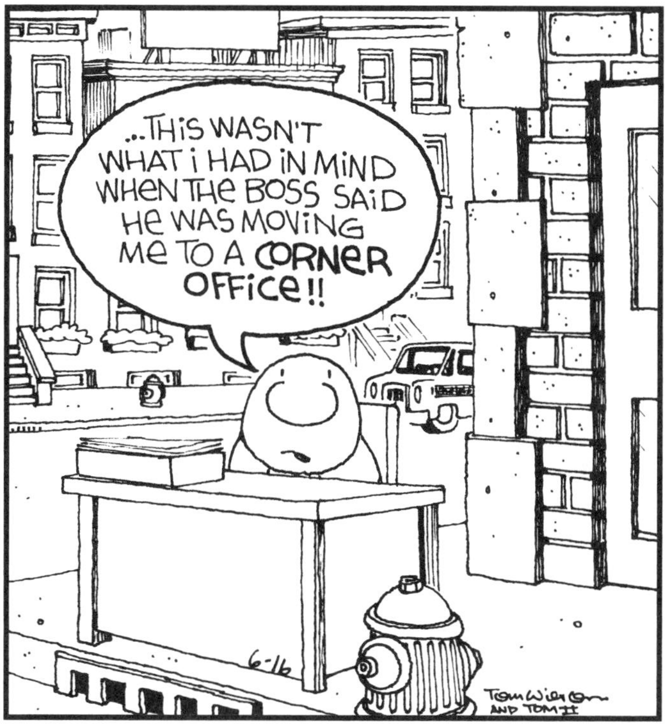
..This wasn't what i had in mind when the boss said he was moving me to a CORNER OFFICE!!
6-16
Tom Wilson and Tom II

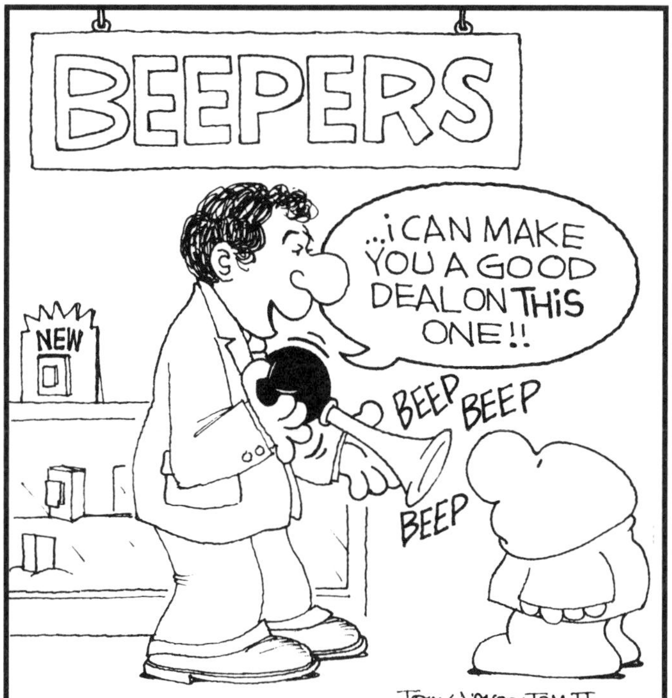
BEEPERS
NEW
..i can make you a good deal on this one!!
BEEP BEEP
BEEP
Tom Wilson + Tom II

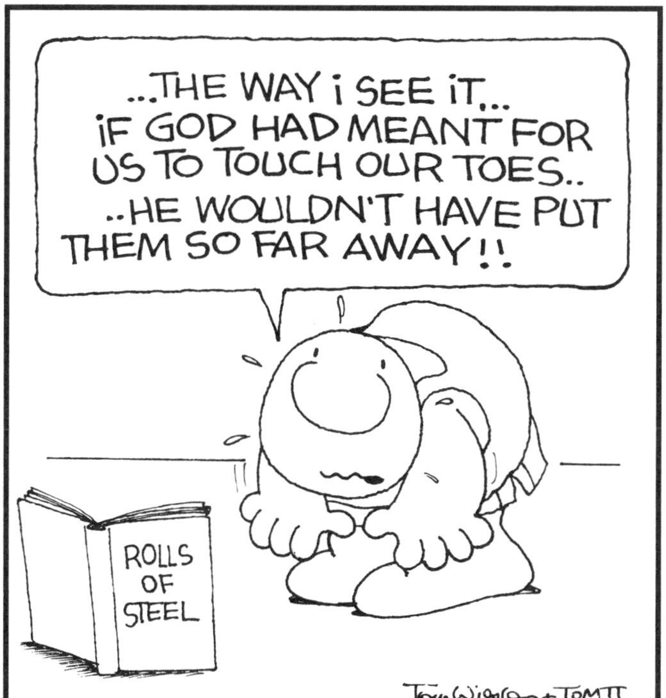
..The way i see it... if God had meant for us to touch our toes.. ..He wouldn't have put them so far away!!
ROLLS OF STEEL
Tom Wilson + Tom II

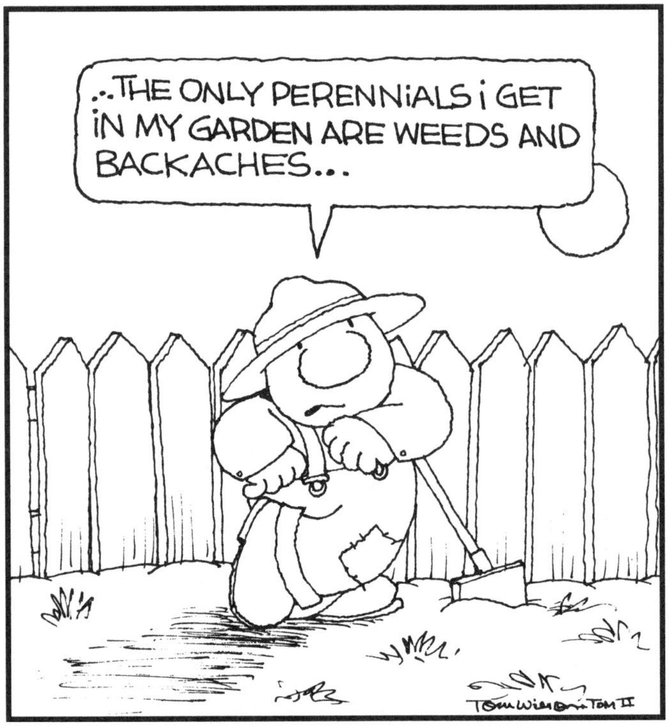
..THE ONLY PERENNIALS i GET iN MY GARDEN ARE WEEDS AND BACKACHES...
Tom Wilson + Tom II

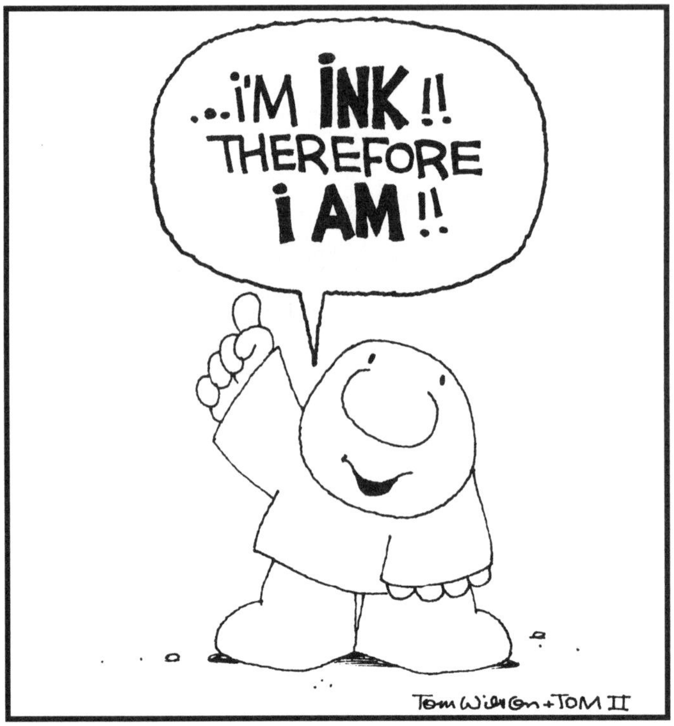
...i'M INK!! THEREFORE i AM!!
Tom Wilson + TOM II

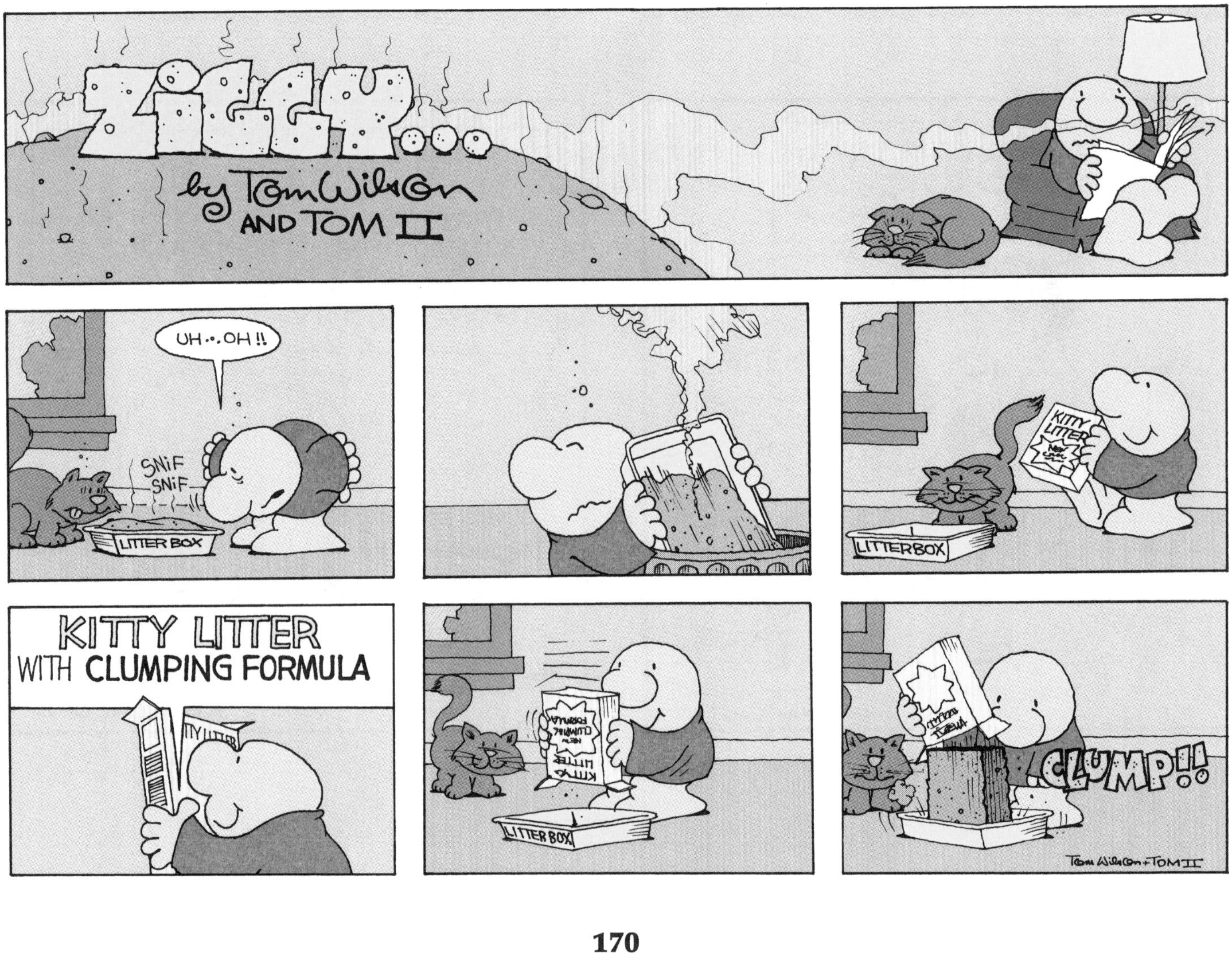
ZiGGY...
by Tom Wilson AND TOM II
UH..OH!!
SNiF
SNiF
LITTER BOX
KITTY LITTER
LITTERBOX
KITTY LITTER
WITH CLUMPING FORMULA
LITTER BOX
CLUMP!!
Tom Wilson + TOM II

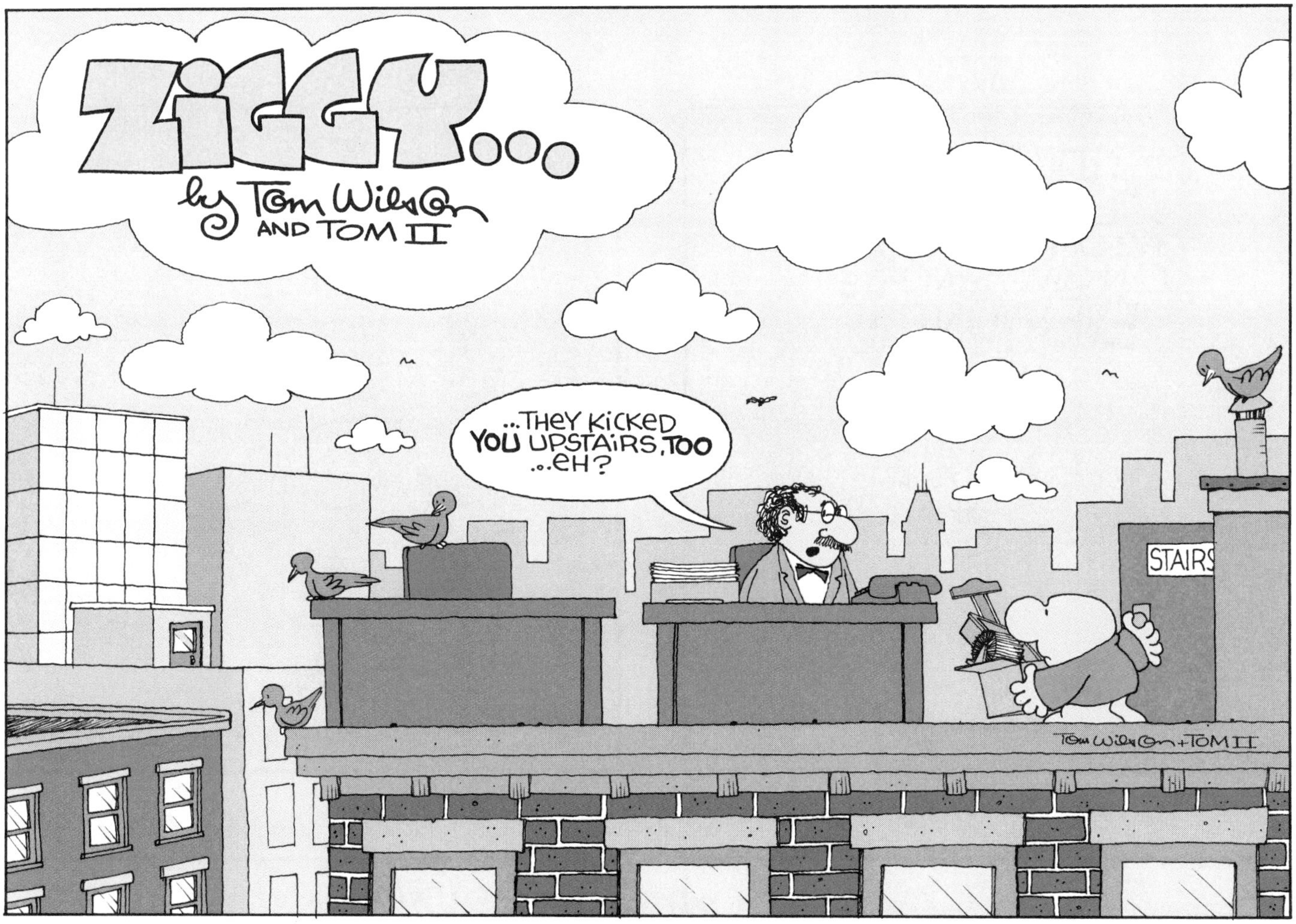
ZIGGY
by Tom Wilson
AND TOM II
...THEY KICKED YOU UPSTAIRS, TOO ...EH?
STAIRS
TOM WILSON + TOM II

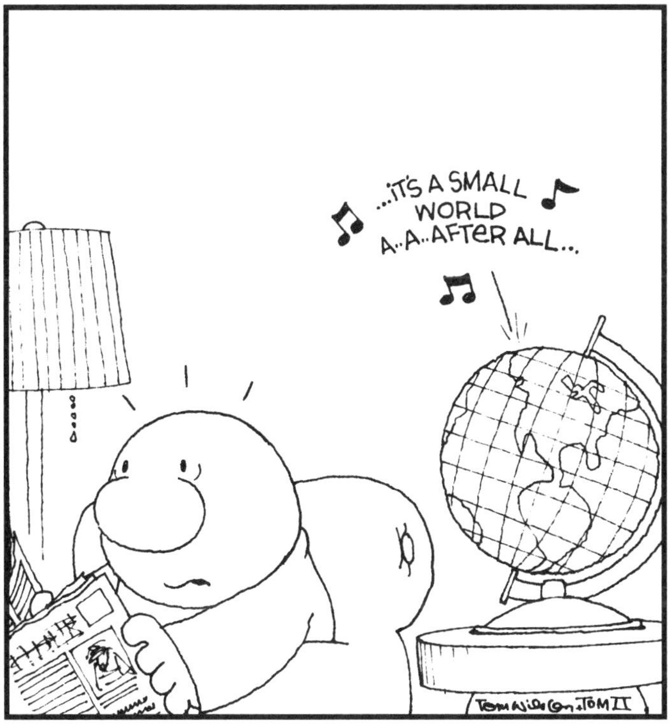
...IT'S A SMALL WORLD A..A..AFTER ALL...
TOM WILSON + TOM II

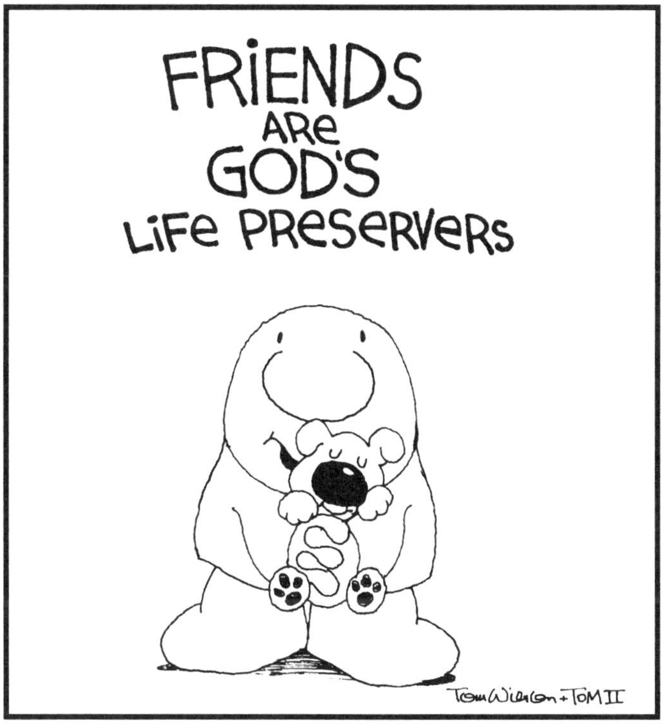
FRIENDS ARE GOD'S LIFE PRESERVERS
TOM WILSON + TOM II

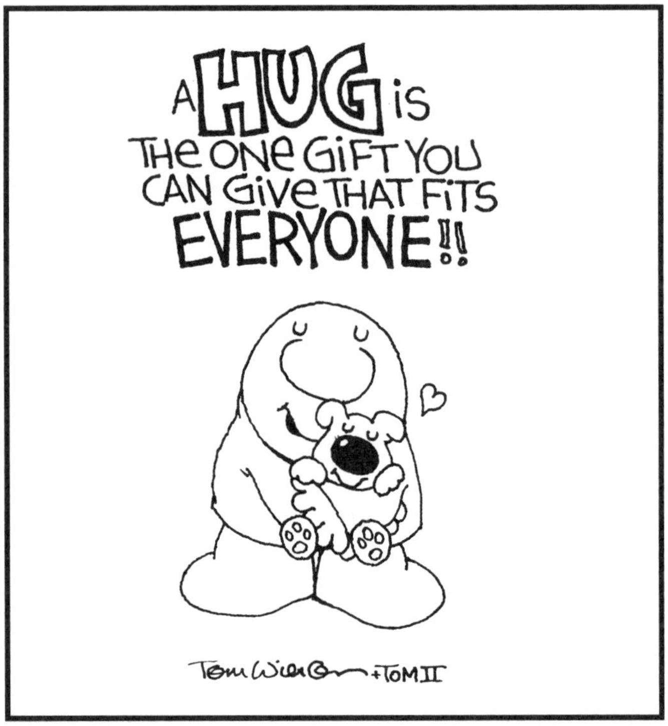
A HUG IS THE ONE GIFT YOU CAN GIVE THAT FITS EVERYONE!!
TOM WILSON + TOM II

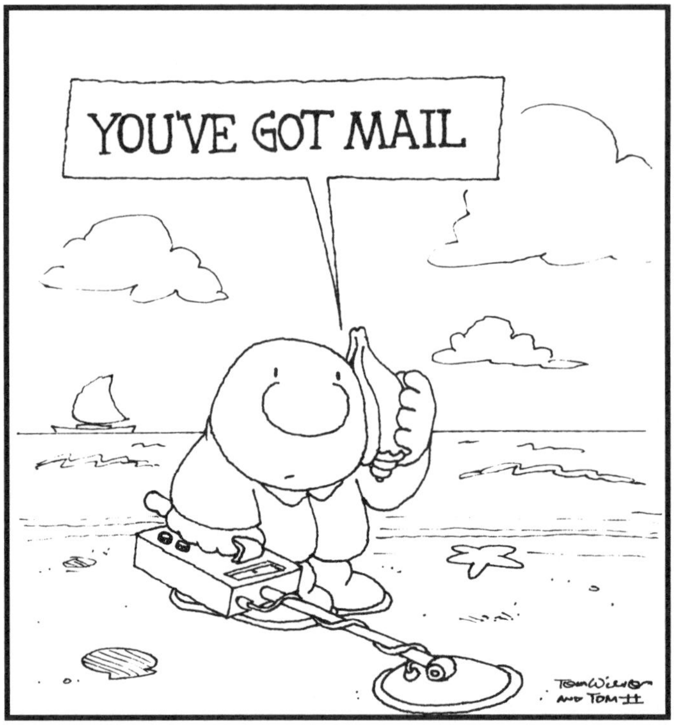
YOU'VE GOT MAIL

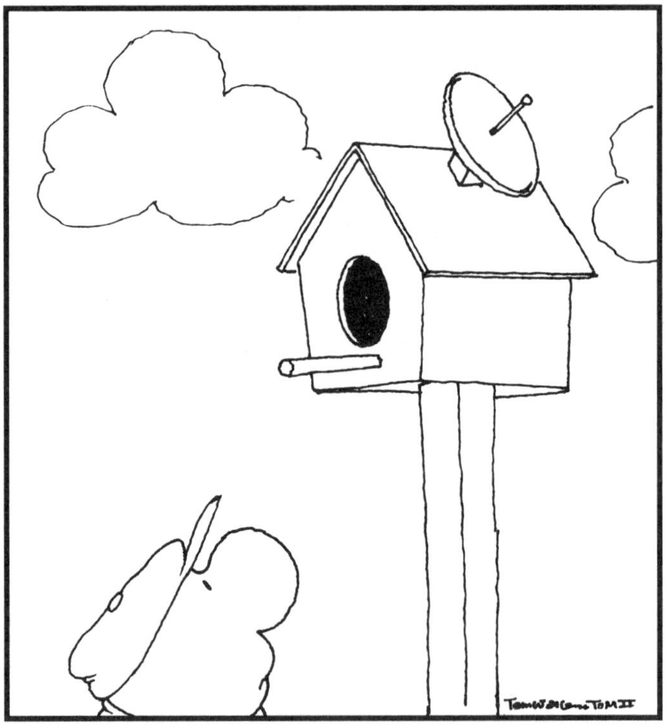

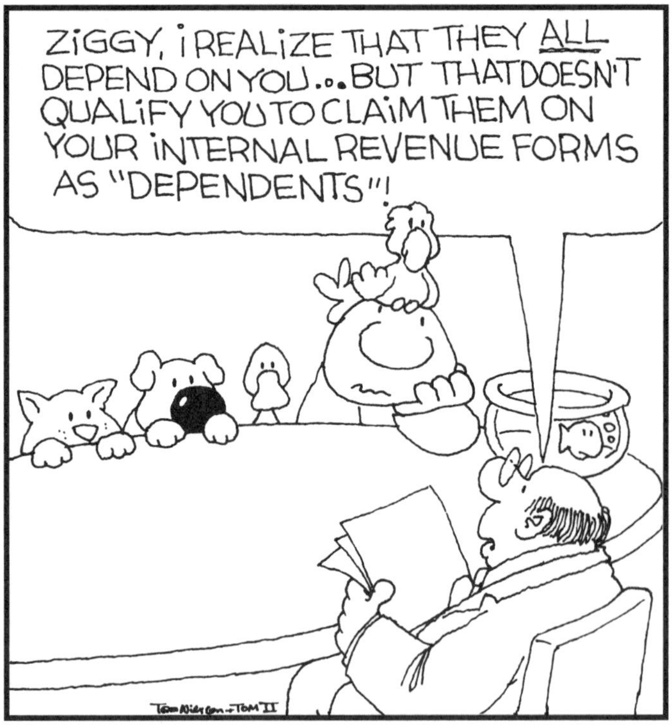
ZIGGY, I REALIZE THAT THEY ALL DEPEND ON YOU... BUT THAT DOESN'T QUALIFY YOU TO CLAIM THEM ON YOUR INTERNAL REVENUE FORMS AS "DEPENDENTS"!

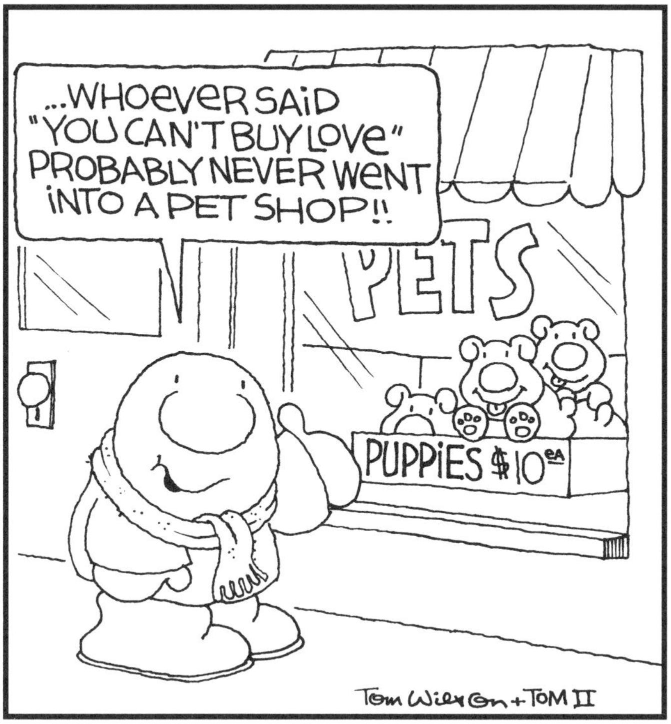
...WHOEVER SAID "YOU CAN'T BUY LOVE" PROBABLY NEVER WENT INTO A PET SHOP!!
PETS
PUPPIES $10 EA
Tom Wilson + TOM II

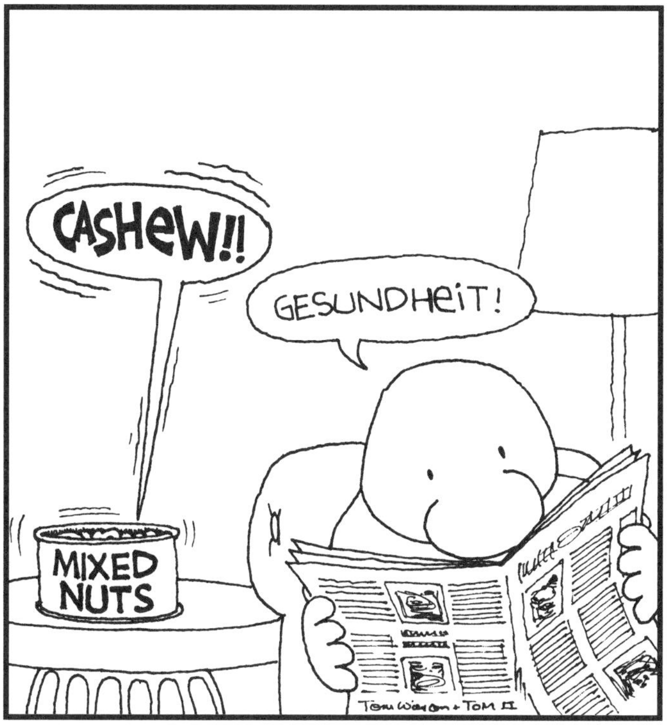
CASHEW!!
GESUNDHEIT!
MIXED NUTS
Tom Wilson + TOM II

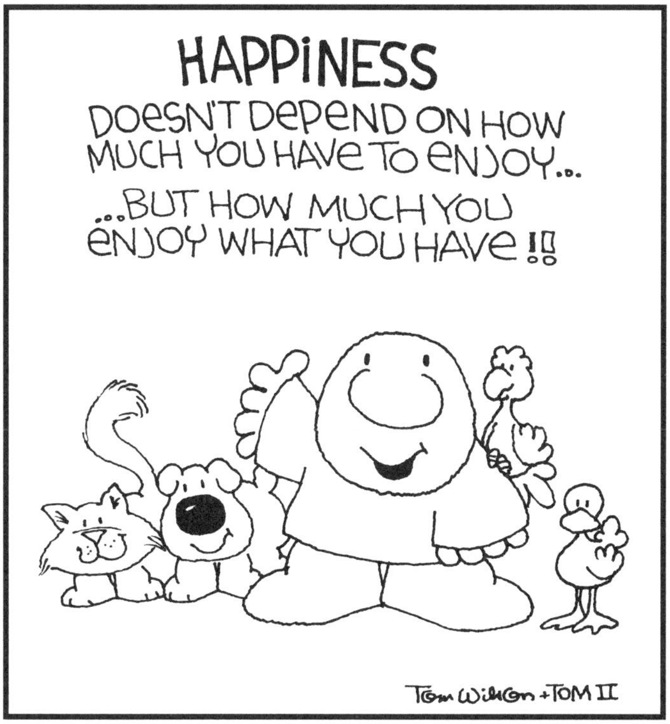
HAPPINESS DOESN'T DEPEND ON HOW MUCH YOU HAVE TO ENJOY...
...BUT HOW MUCH YOU ENJOY WHAT YOU HAVE!!
Tom Wilson + TOM II

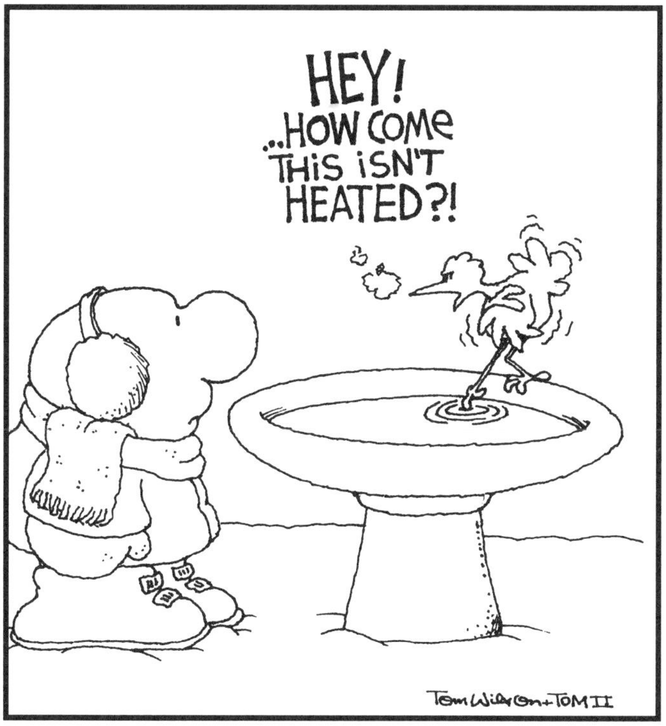
HEY! ..HOW COME THIS ISN'T HEATED?!
Tom Wilson + TOM II

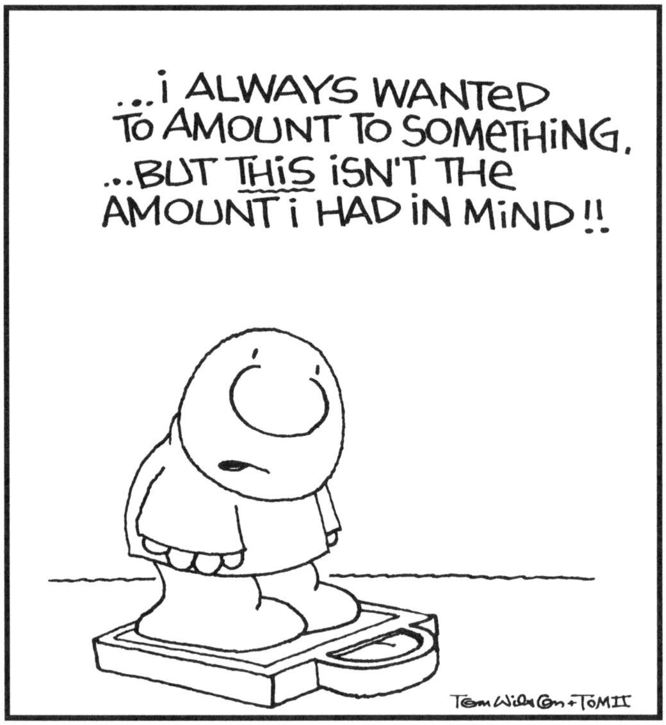
...i ALWAYS WANTED TO AMOUNT TO SOMETHING. ...BUT THIS isn'T THE AMOUNT i HAD iN MiND!!
Tom Wilson + Tom II

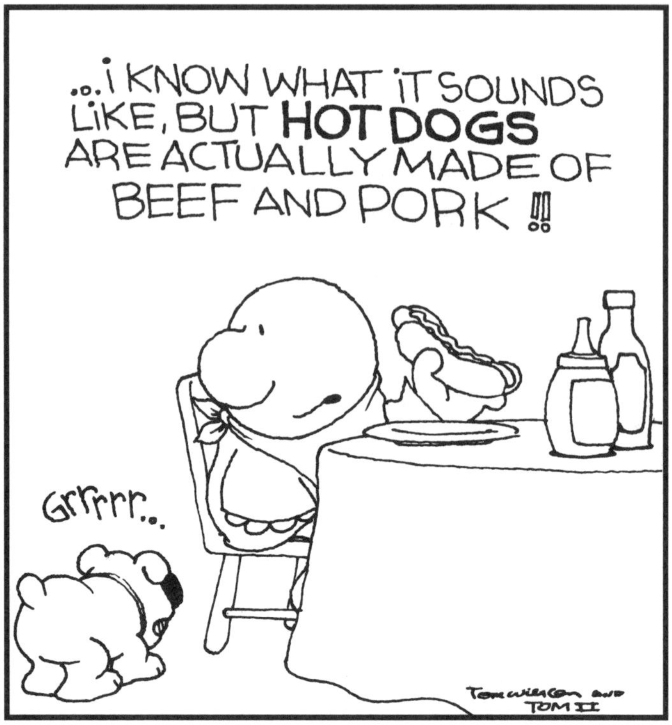
...i KNOW WHAT iT SOUNDS LiKE, BUT HOT DOGS ARE ACTUALLY MADE OF BEEF AND PORK!!
Grrrrr...
Tom Wilson and Tom II

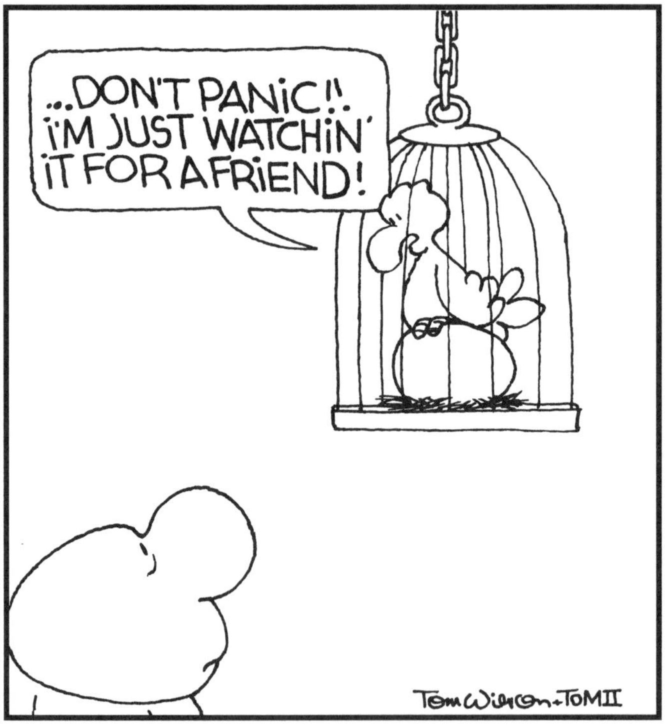
...DON'T PANIC!! i'M JUST WATCHiN' iT FOR A FRiEND!
Tom Wilson + Tom II

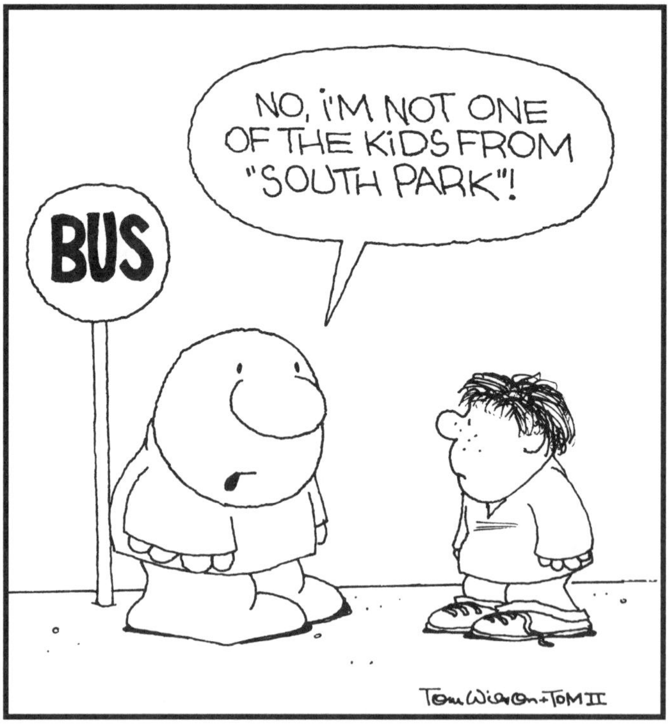
BUS
NO, i'M NOT ONE OF THE KiDS FROM "SOUTH PARK"!
Tom Wilson + Tom II

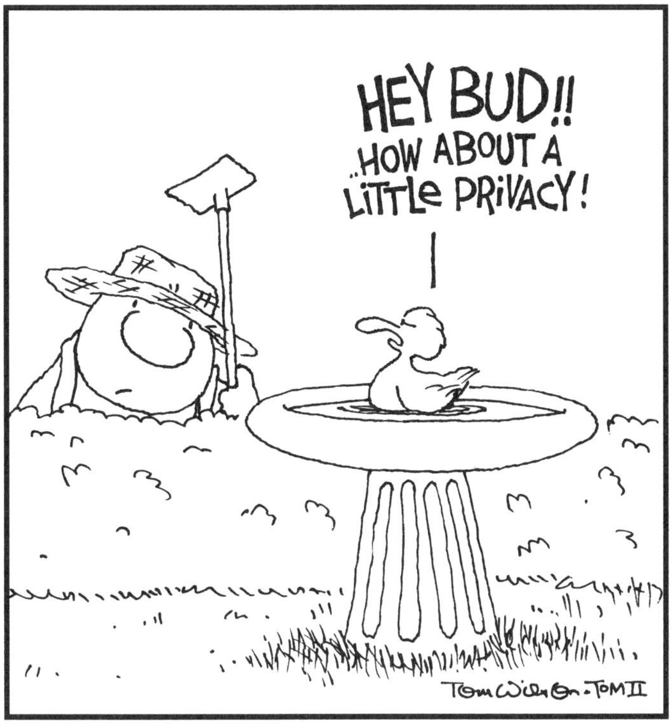
HEY BUD!! ..HOW ABOUT A LITTLE PRIVACY!
TOM WILSON + TOM II

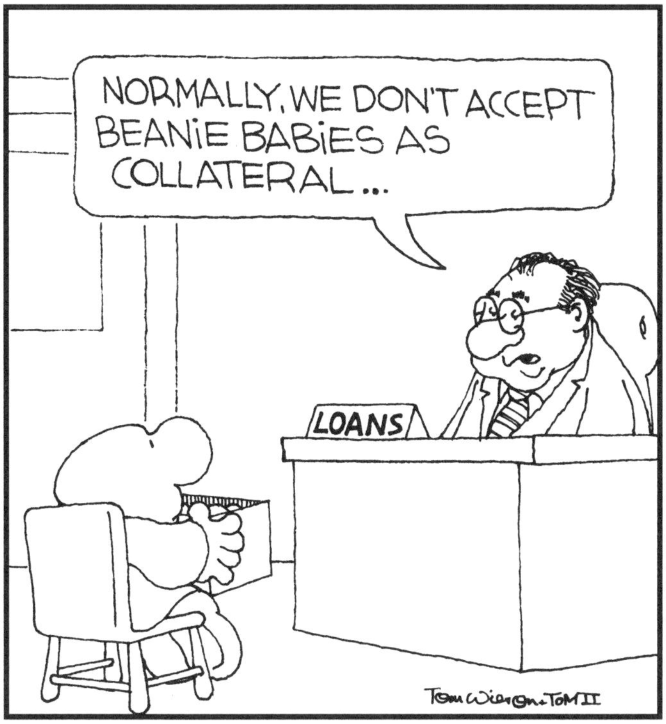
NORMALLY, WE DON'T ACCEPT BEANIE BABIES AS COLLATERAL...
LOANS
TOM WILSON + TOM II

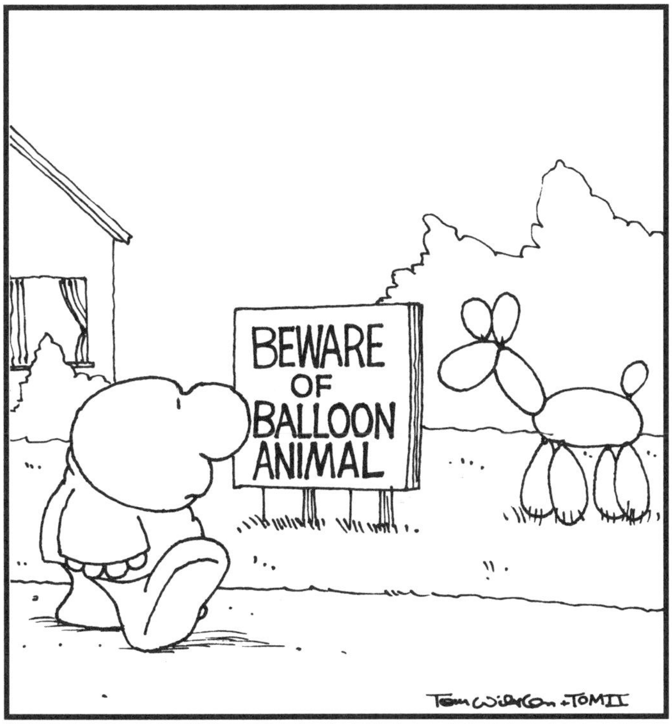
BEWARE OF BALLOON ANIMAL
TOM WILSON + TOM II

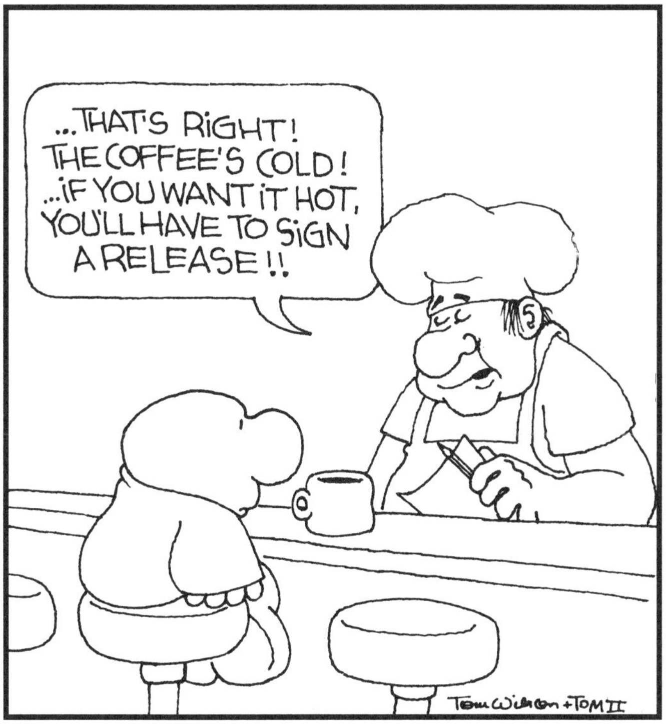
...THAT'S RIGHT! THE COFFEE'S COLD! ...IF YOU WANT IT HOT, YOU'LL HAVE TO SIGN A RELEASE!!
TOM WILSON + TOM II

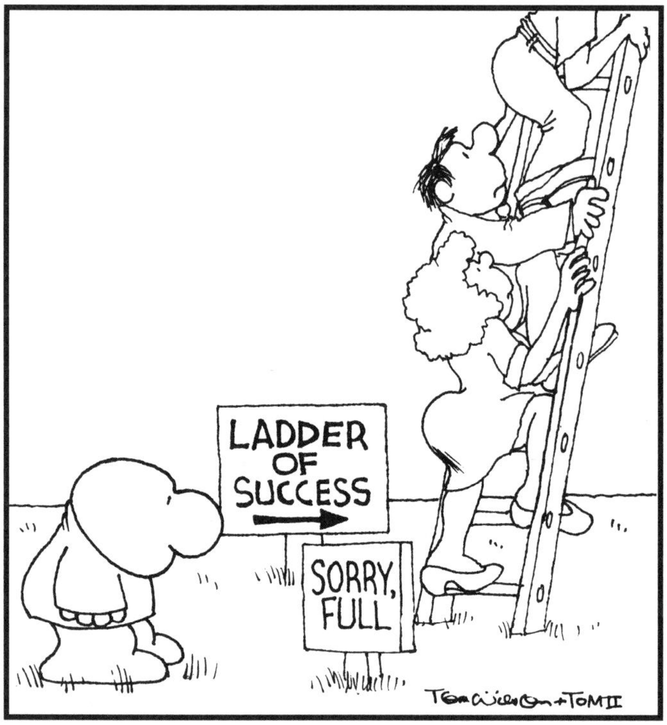
LADDER OF SUCCESS
SORRY, FULL
TOM WILSON + TOM II

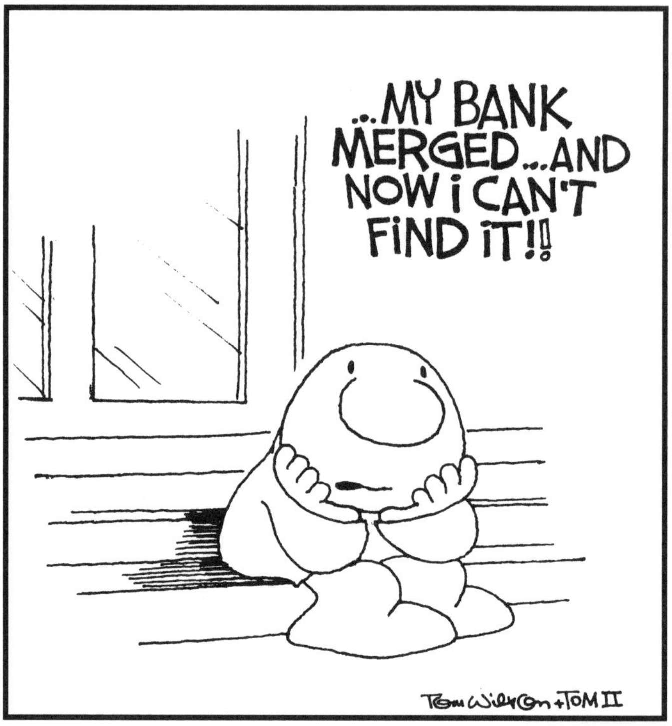
...MY BANK MERGED...AND NOW I CAN'T FIND IT!!
TOM WILSON + TOM II

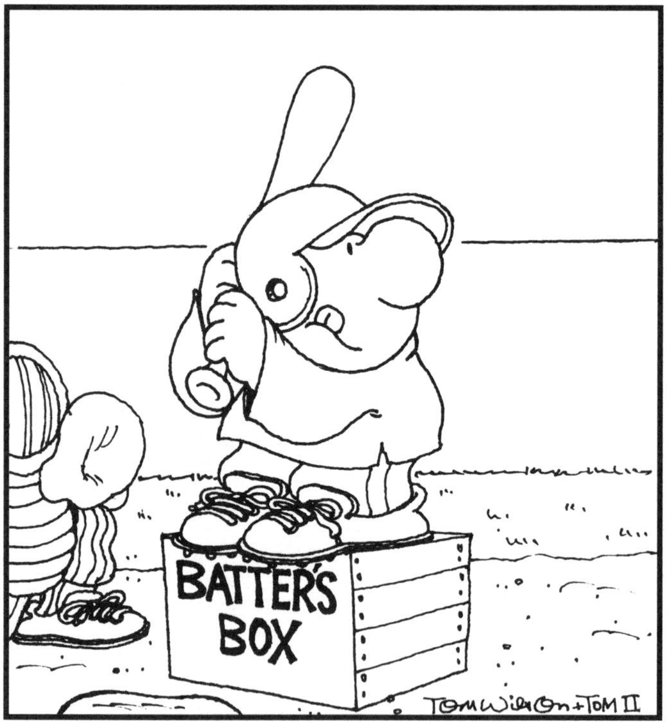
BATTER'S BOX
TOM WILSON + TOM II

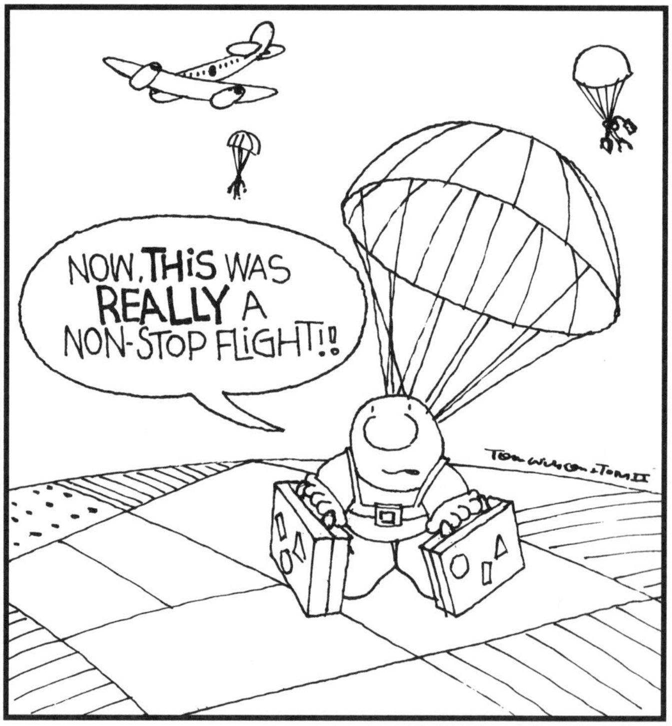
NOW, THIS WAS REALLY A NON-STOP FLIGHT!!
TOM WILSON + TOM II

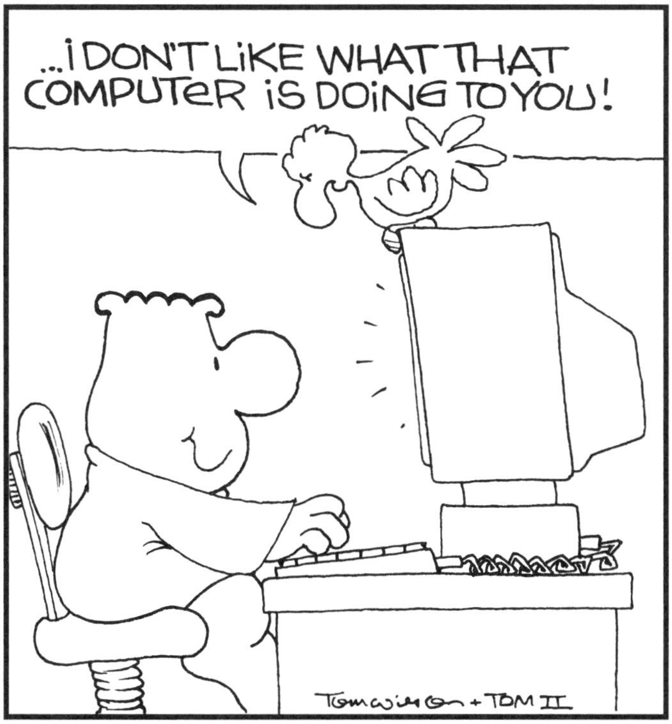
...I DON'T LIKE WHAT THAT COMPUTER IS DOING TO YOU!
TOM WILSON + TOM II

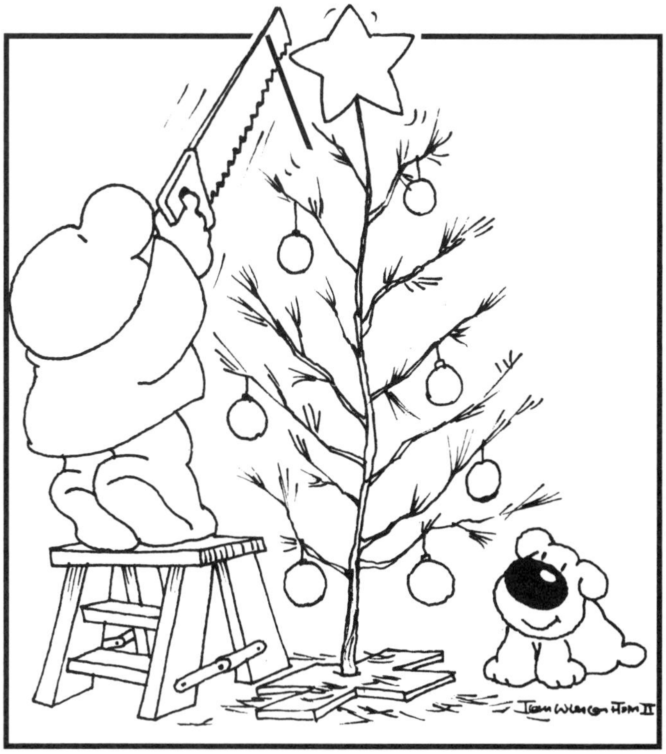
TOM WILSON + TOM II

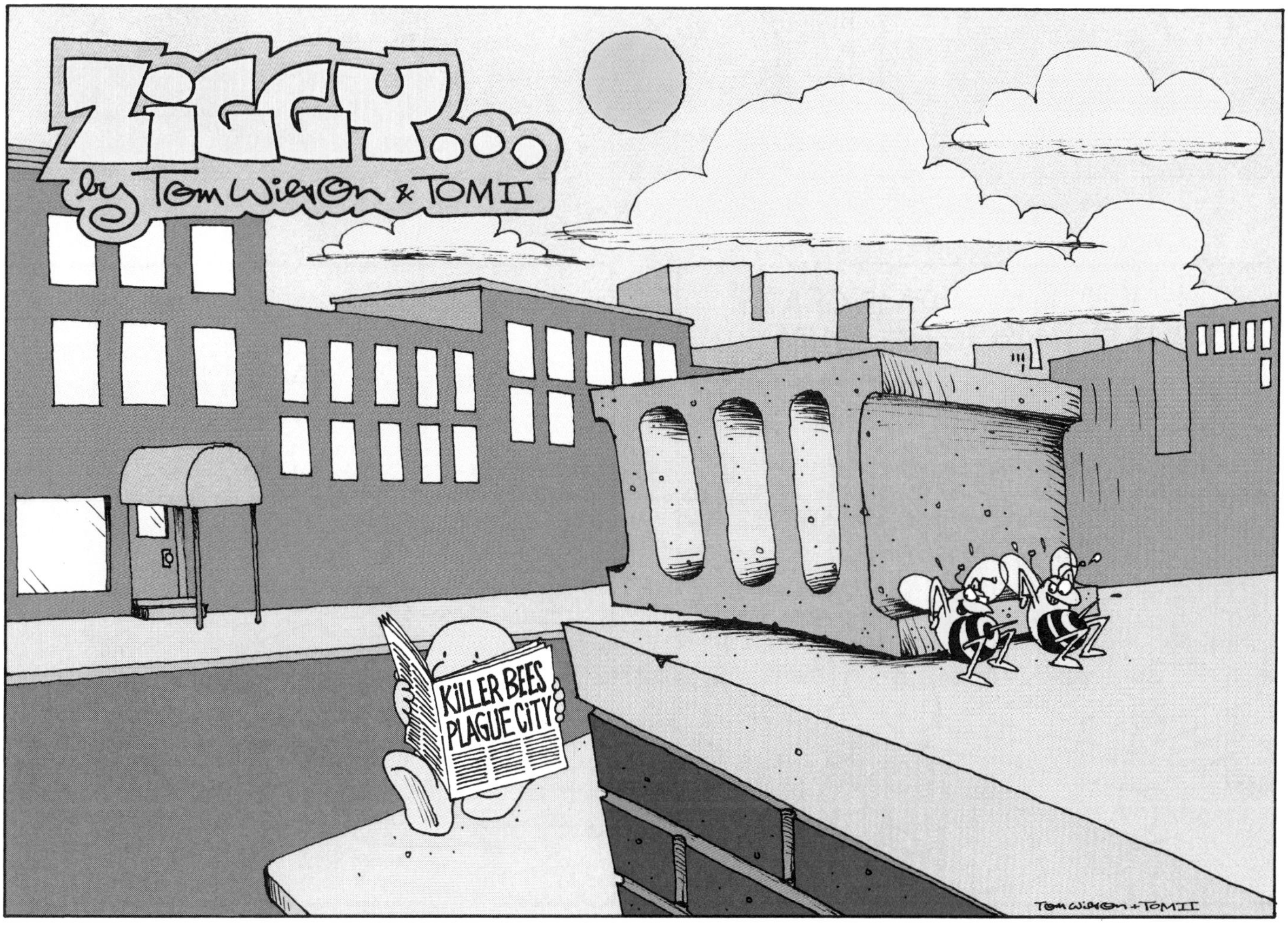
ZIGGY...
by TOM WILSON & TOM II
KILLER BEES PLAGUE CITY
TOM WILSON + TOM II

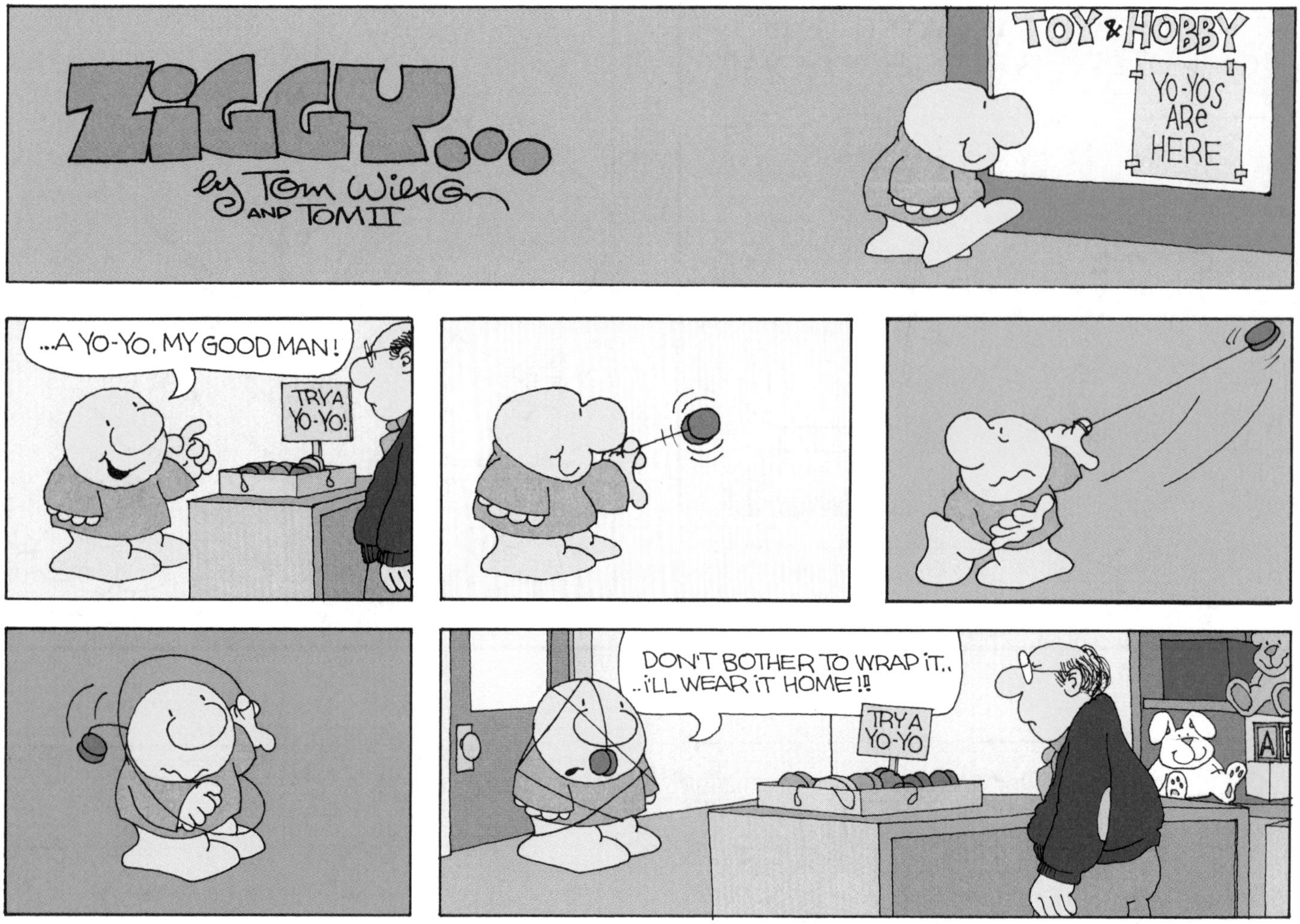
ZIGGY...
by Tom Wilson and Tom II
TOY & HOBBY
YO-YOS ARE HERE
...A YO-YO, MY GOOD MAN!
TRY A YO-YO!
DON'T BOTHER TO WRAP IT..
..I'LL WEAR IT HOME!!
TRY A YO-YO

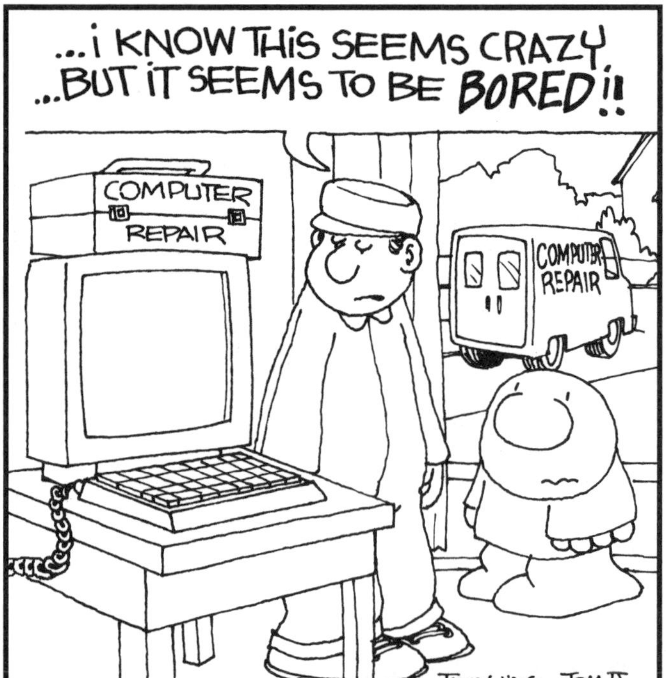
...I KNOW THIS SEEMS CRAZY
...BUT IT SEEMS TO BE BORED!!
COMPUTER REPAIR
COMPUTER REPAIR
Tom Wilson+Tom II

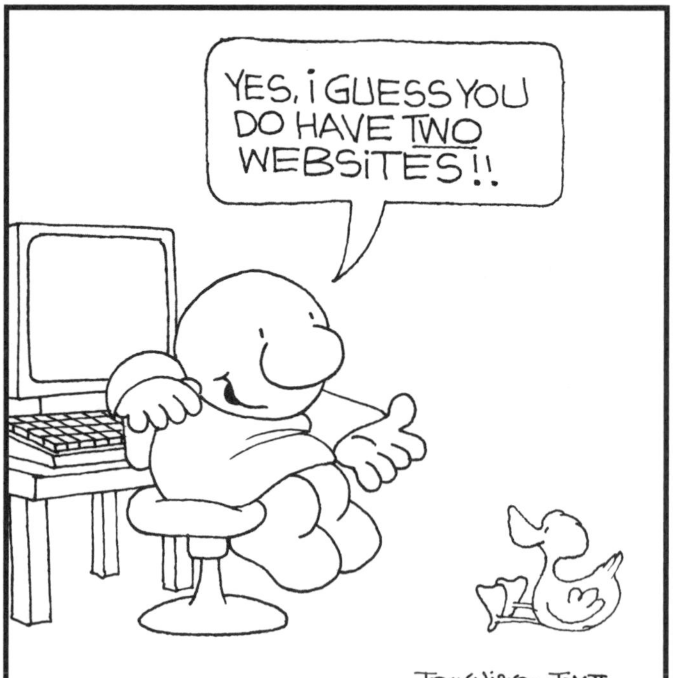
YES, I GUESS YOU DO HAVE TWO WEBSITES!!
Tom Wilson + Tom II

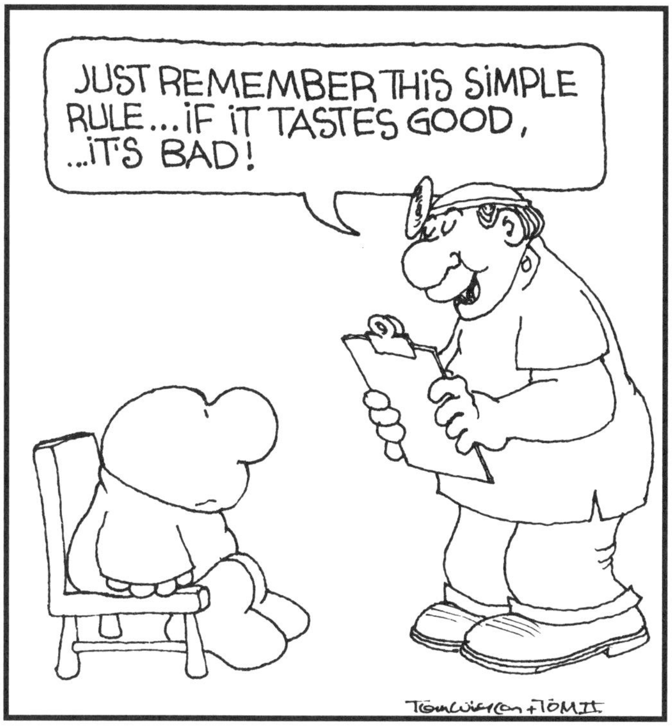
JUST REMEMBER THIS SIMPLE RULE...IF IT TASTES GOOD, ...IT'S BAD!

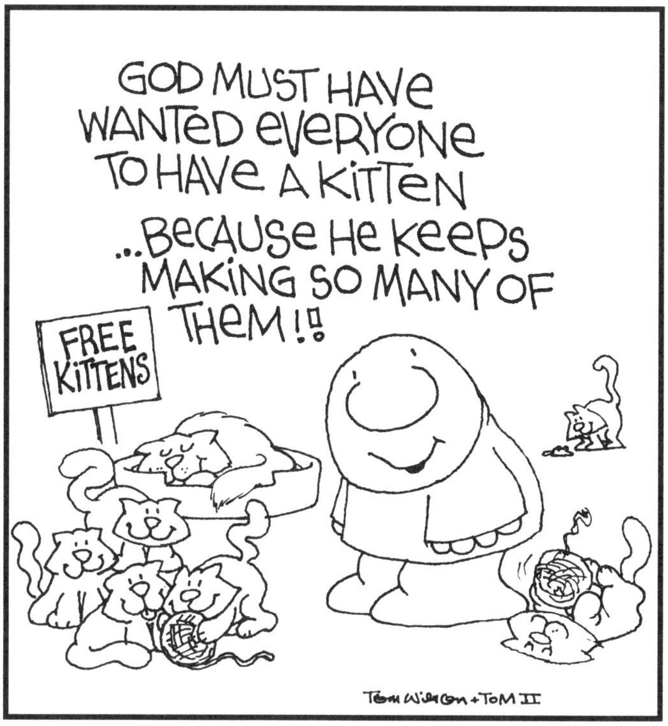
GOD MUST HAVE WANTED EVERYONE TO HAVE A KITTEN ...BECAUSE HE KEEPS MAKING SO MANY OF THEM!!
FREE KITTENS

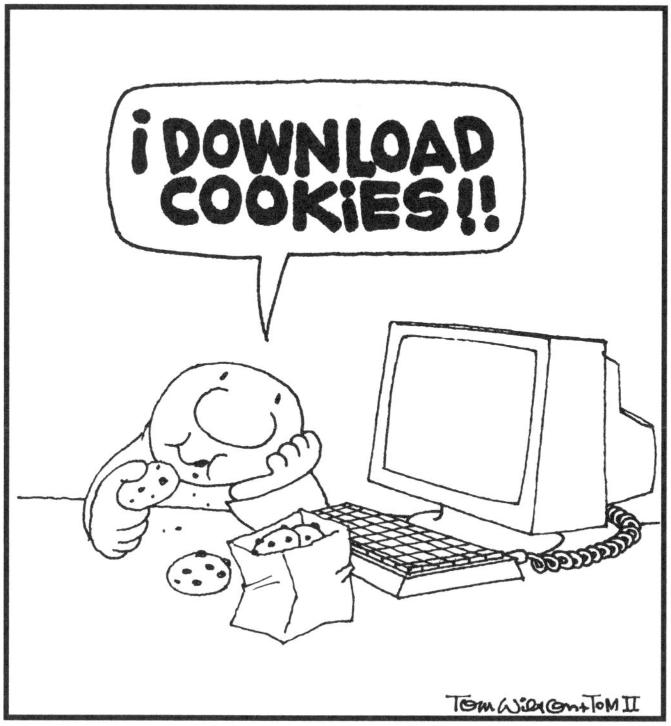
I DOWNLOAD COOKIES!!

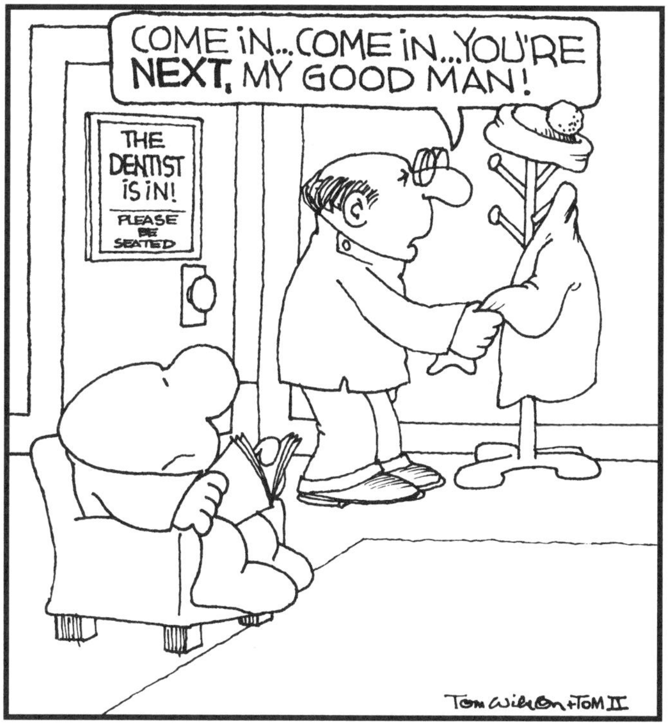
COME IN...COME IN...YOU'RE NEXT, MY GOOD MAN!
THE DENTIST IS IN!
PLEASE BE SEATED

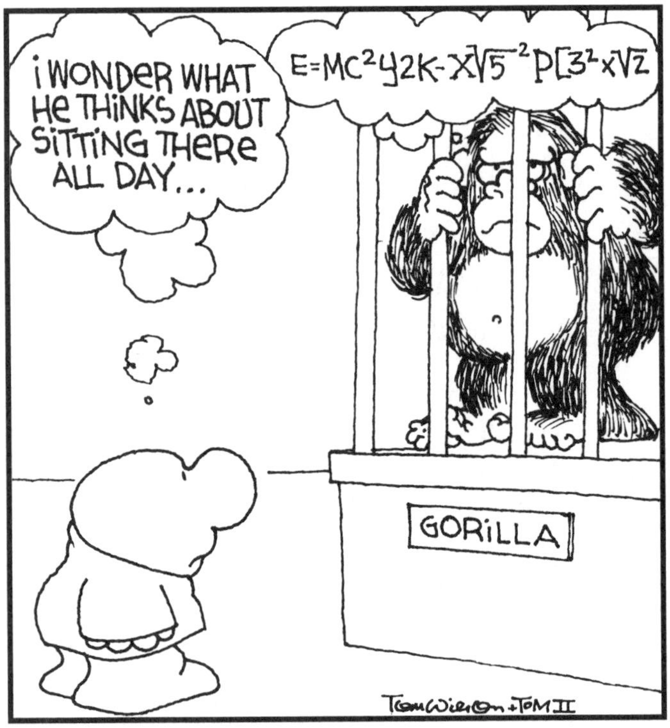
i WONDER WHAT HE THiNKS ABOUT SiTTiNG THeRe ALL DAY...
$E=MC^2 y2K-X\sqrt{5}^{-2}P[3^2 x\sqrt{2}$
GORiLLA

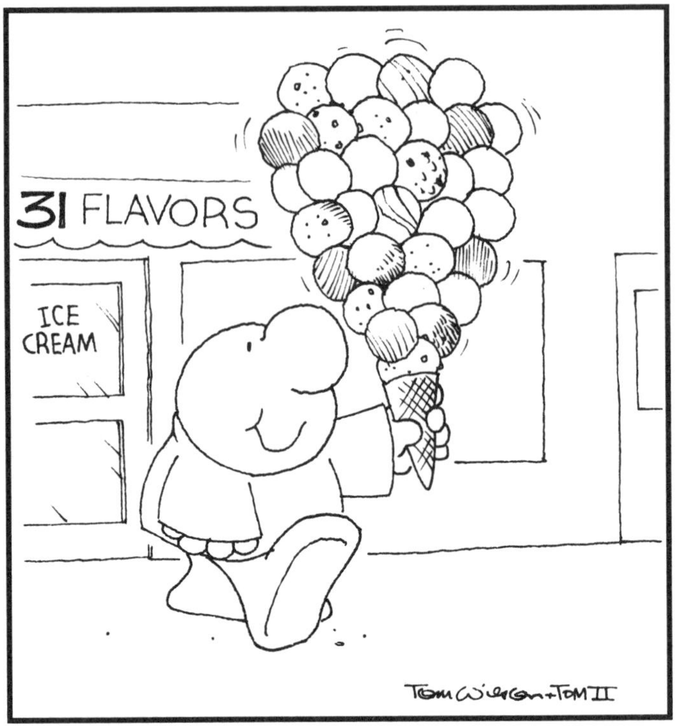
31 FLAVORS
ICE CREAM

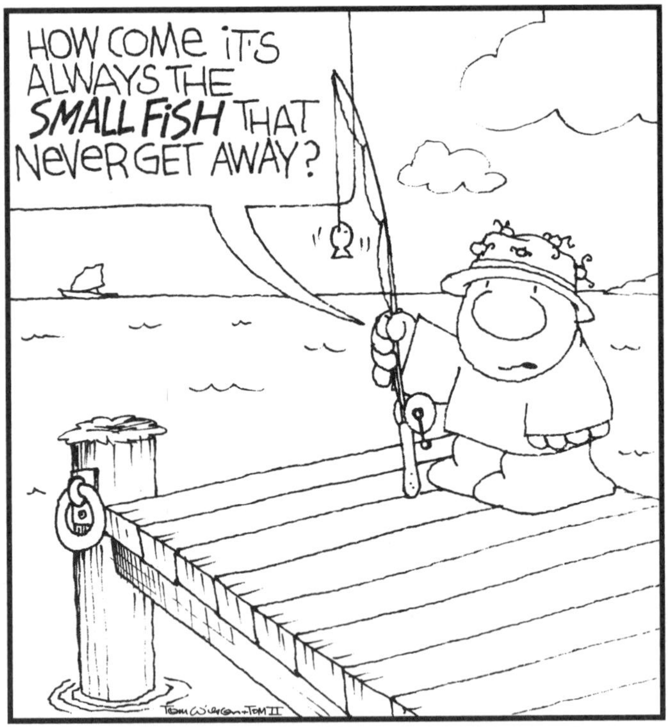
HOW COMe iT'S ALWAYS THE SMALL FiSH THAT NeVeR GET AWAY?

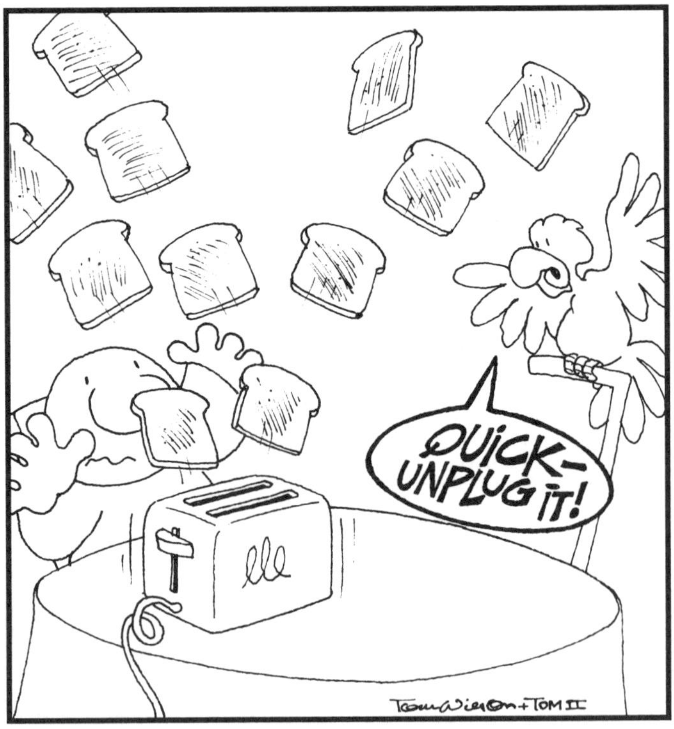
QUICK-UNPLUG iT!

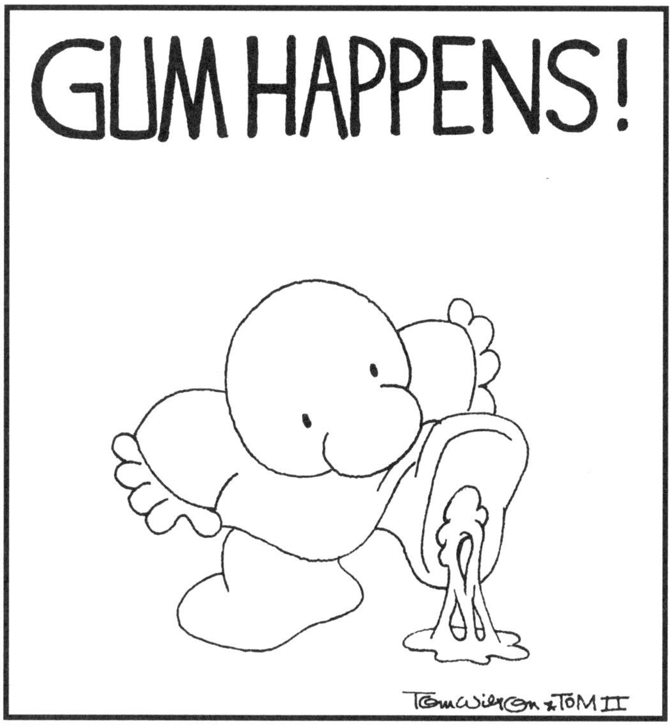
GUM HAPPENS!
Tom Wilson + TOM II

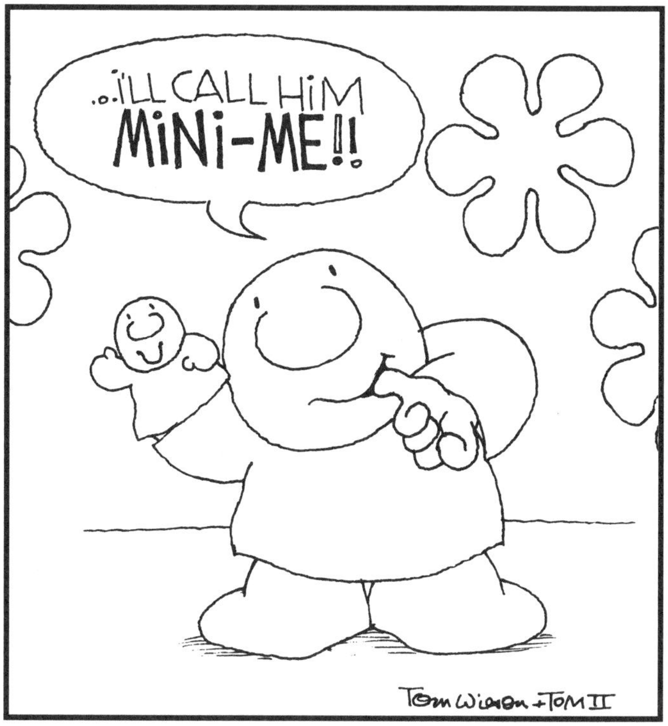
...I'LL CALL HIM MINI-ME!!
Tom Wilson + TOM II

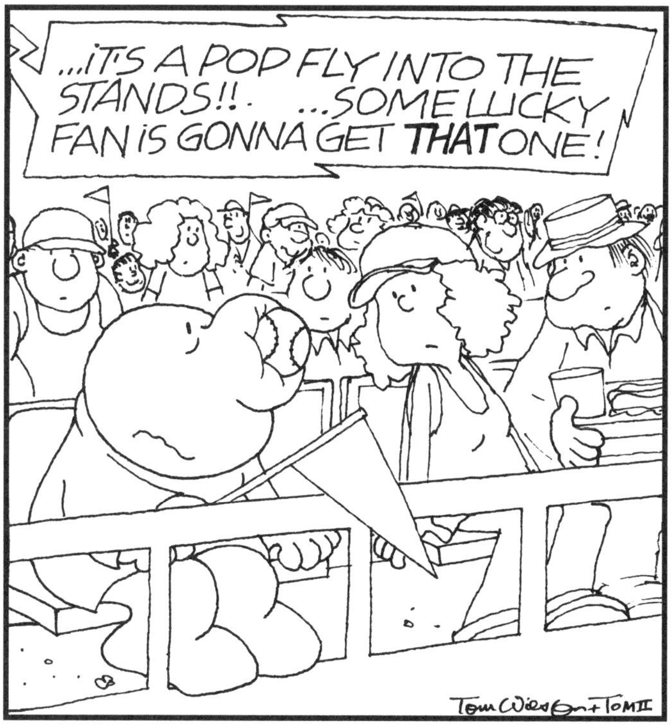
...IT'S A POP FLY INTO THE STANDS!! ...SOME LUCKY FAN IS GONNA GET THAT ONE!
Tom Wilson + TOM II

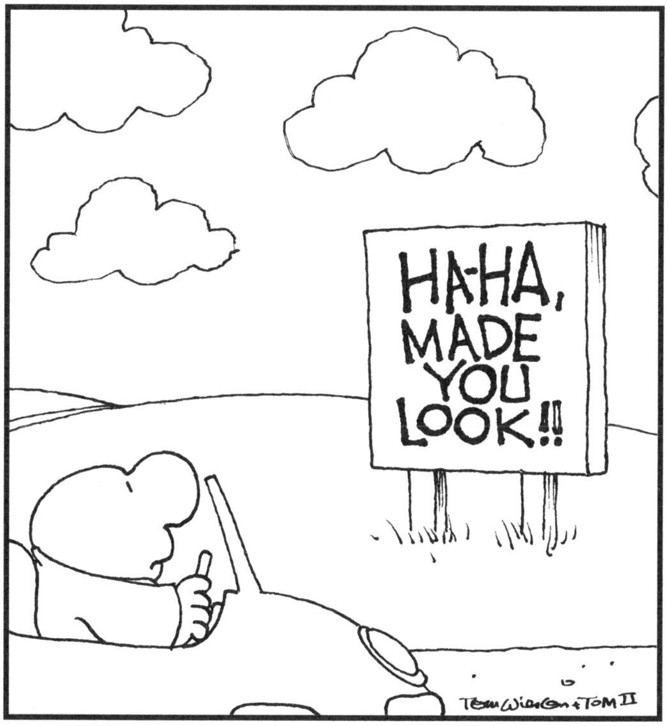
HA-HA, MADE YOU LOOK!!
Tom Wilson + TOM II

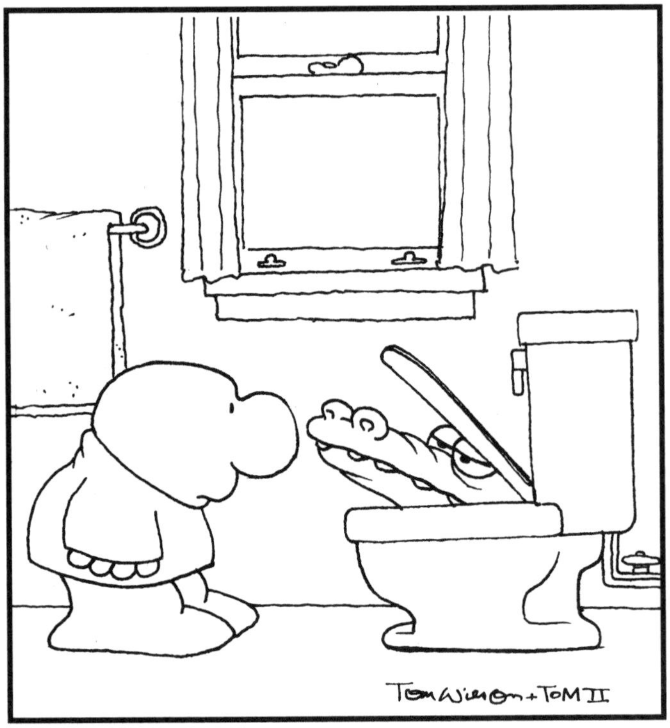
Tom Wilson + Tom II

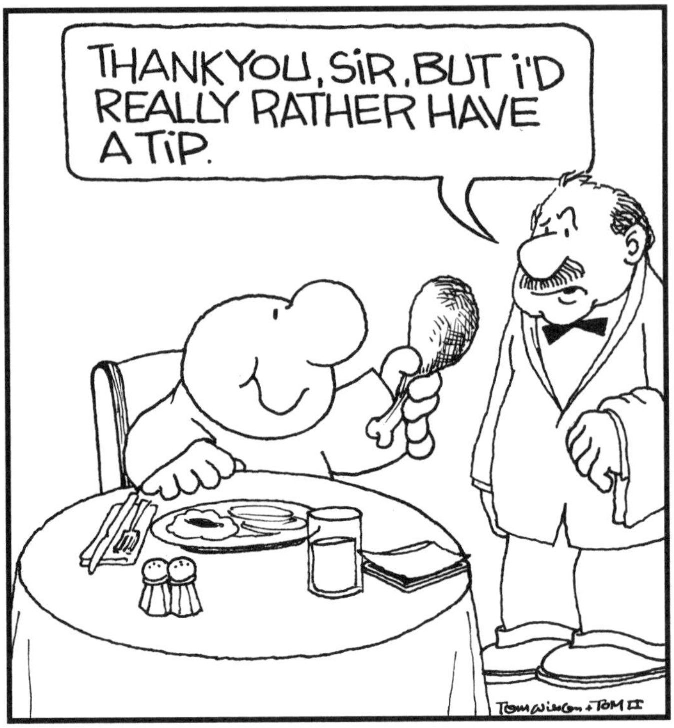
THANKYOU, SiR, BUT i'D REALLY RATHER HAVE A TiP.
Tom Wilson + Tom II

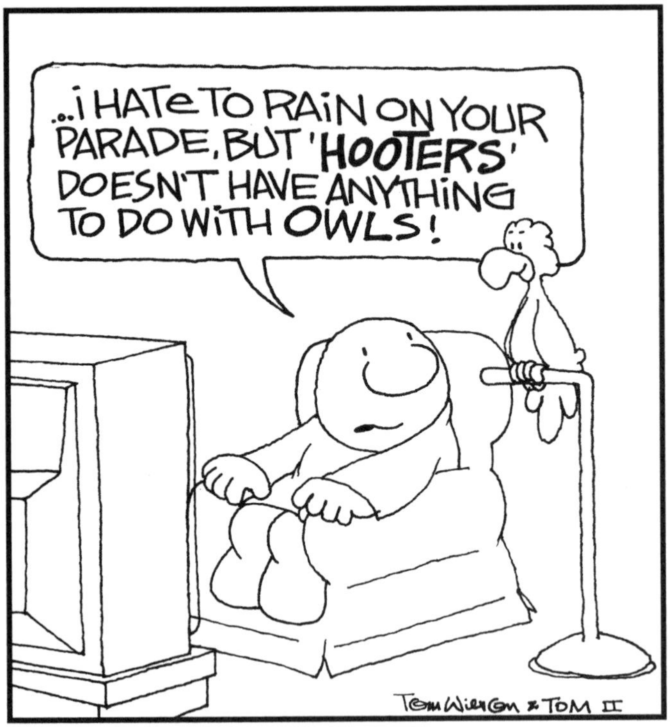
..i HATE TO RAIN ON YOUR PARADE, BUT 'HOOTERS' DOESN'T HAVE ANYTHING TO DO WITH OWLS!
Tom Wilson & Tom II

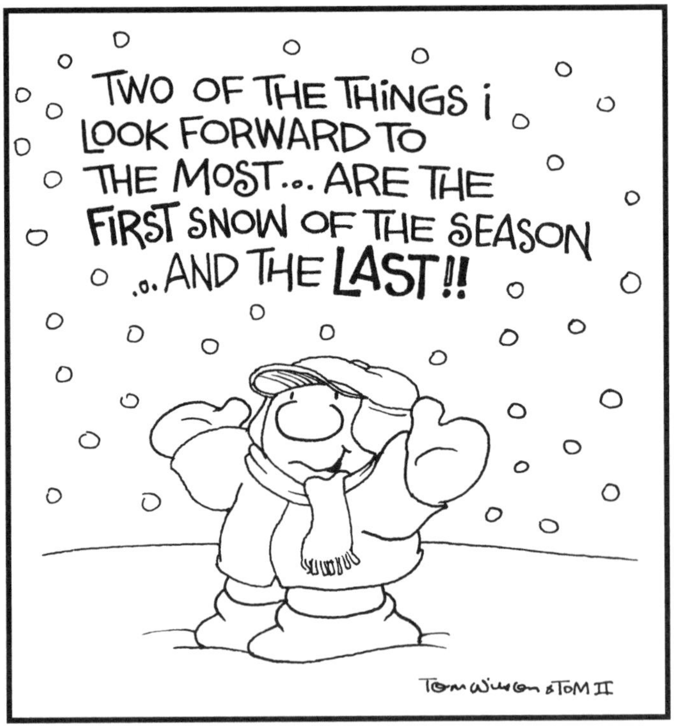
TWO OF THE THINGS i LOOK FORWARD TO THE MOST... ARE THE FIRST SNOW OF THE SEASON ...AND THE LAST!!
Tom Wilson & Tom II

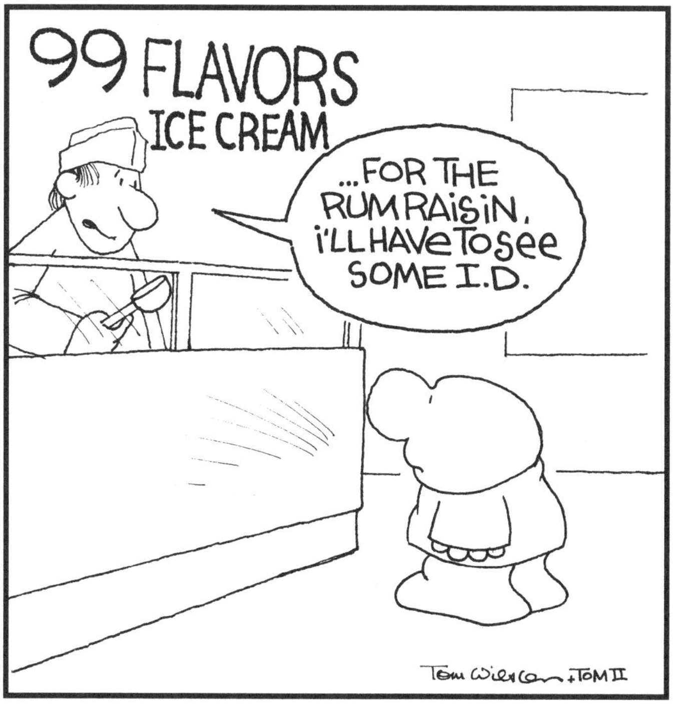
99 FLAVORS ICE CREAM
...FOR THE RUM RAISIN, i'LL HAVE TO SEE SOME I.D.
Tom Wilson + TOM II

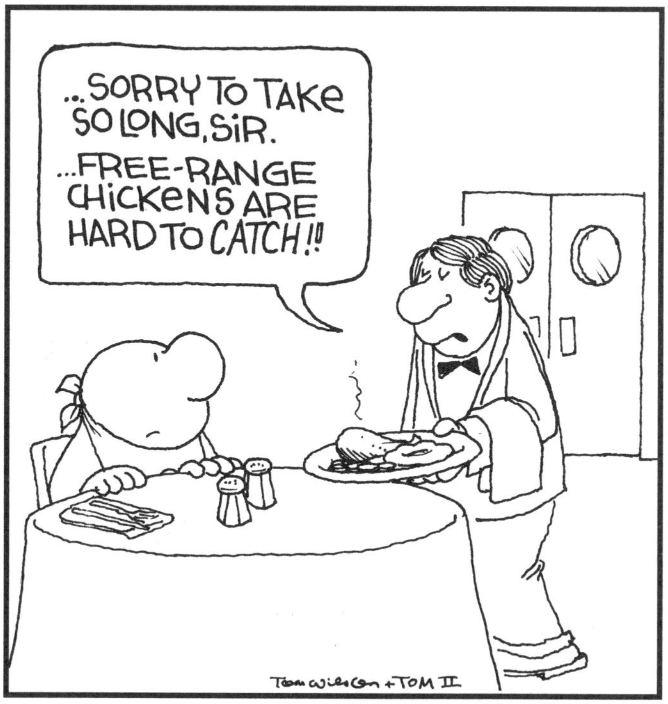
...SORRY TO TAKE SO LONG, SiR. ...FREE-RANGE CHiCKENS ARE HARD TO CATCH!!
Tom Wilson + TOM II

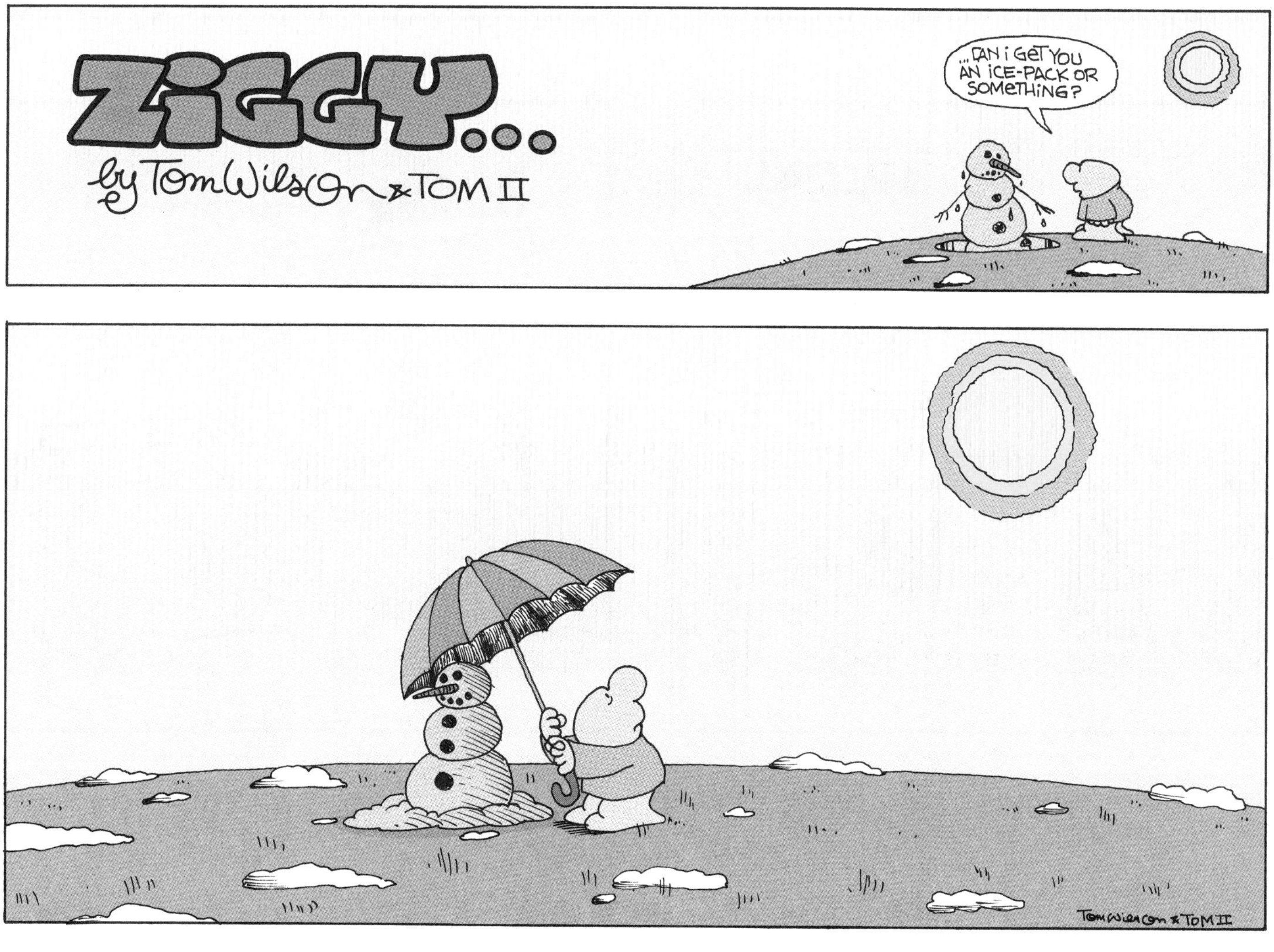
ZiGGY...
by Tom Wilson & TOM II
...CAN i GET YOU AN ICE-PACK OR SOMETHiNG?
Tom Wilson & TOM II

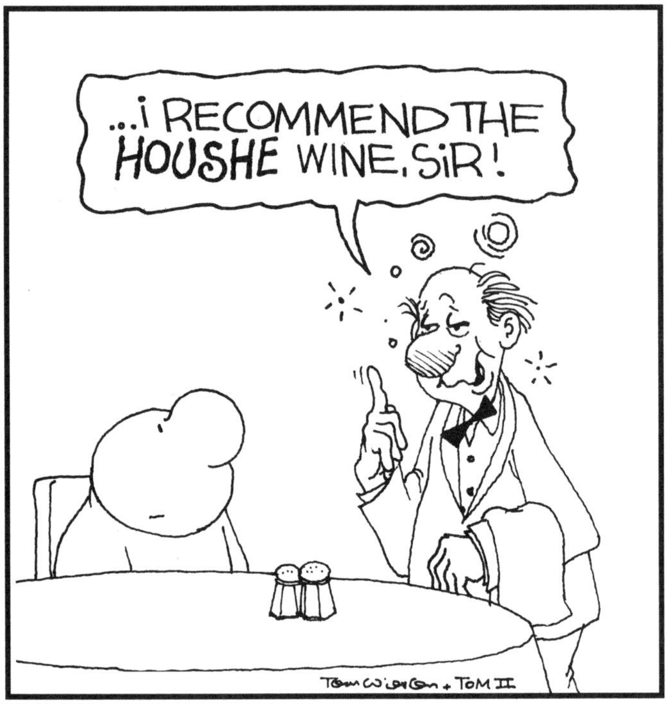
...I RECOMMEND THE HOUSHE WINE, SIR!

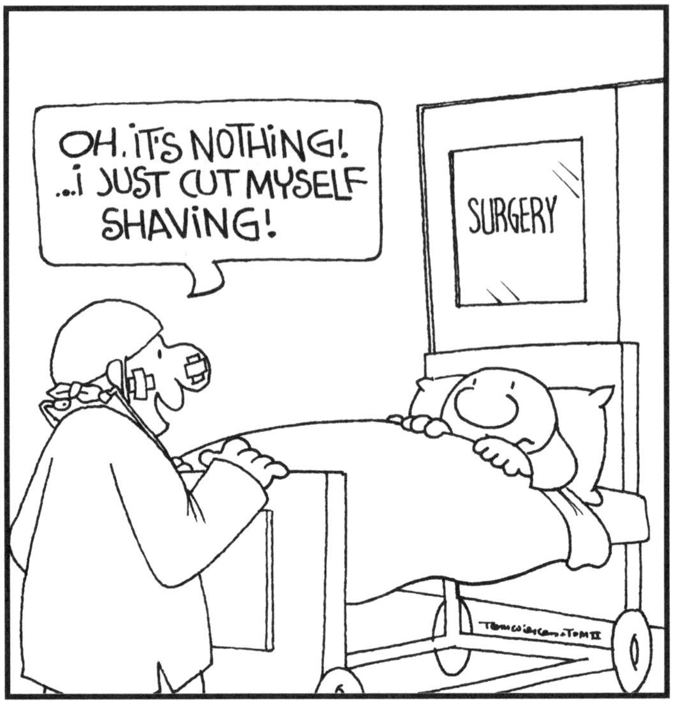
OH, IT'S NOTHING! ...I JUST CUT MYSELF SHAVING!
SURGERY

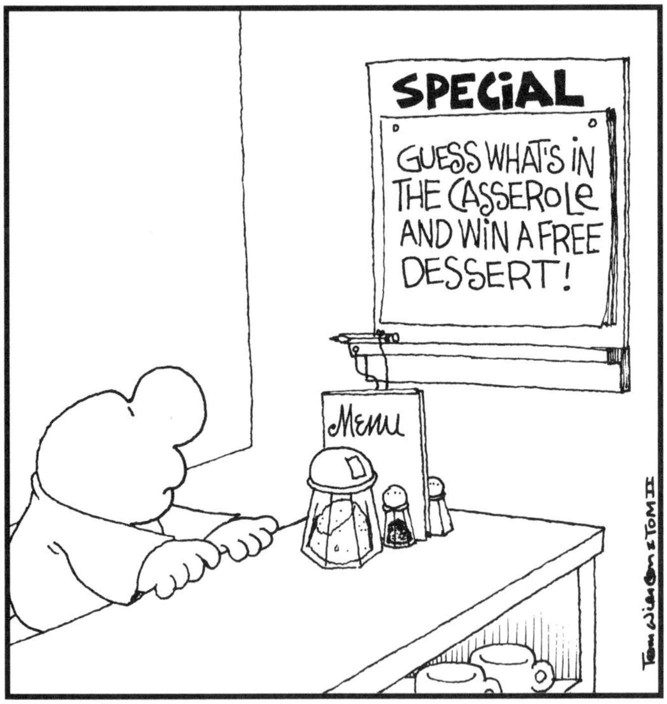
SPECIAL
GUESS WHAT'S IN THE CASSEROLE AND WIN A FREE DESSERT!
Menu

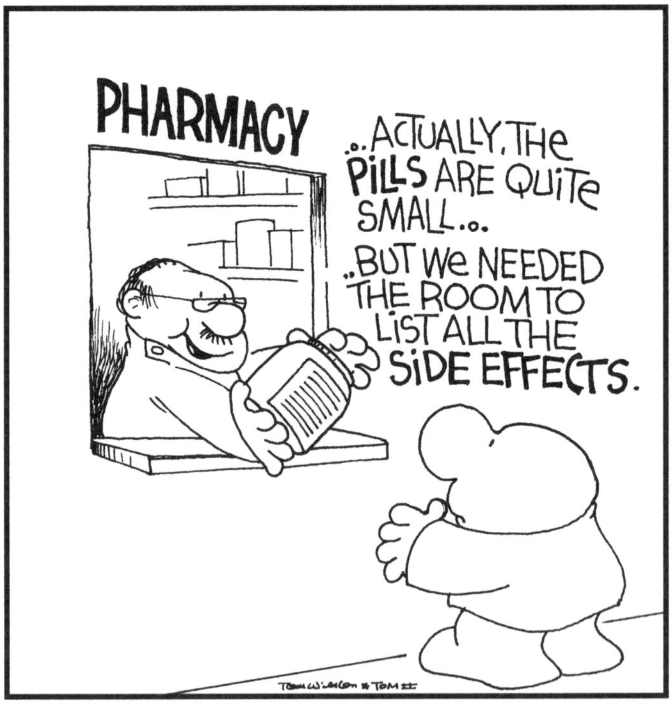
PHARMACY
...ACTUALLY, THE PILLS ARE QUITE SMALL...
..BUT WE NEEDED THE ROOM TO LIST ALL THE SIDE EFFECTS.

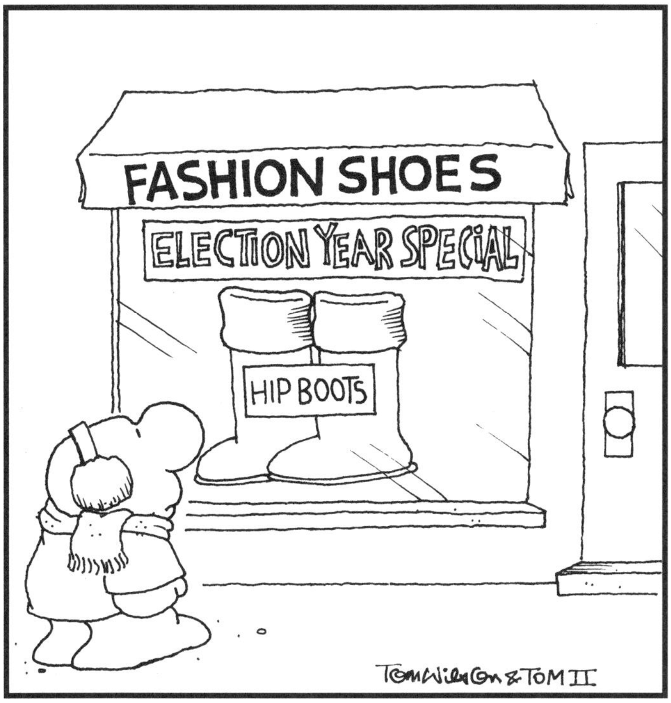
FASHION SHOES
ELECTION YEAR SPECIAL
HIP BOOTS
TomWilson & TOM II

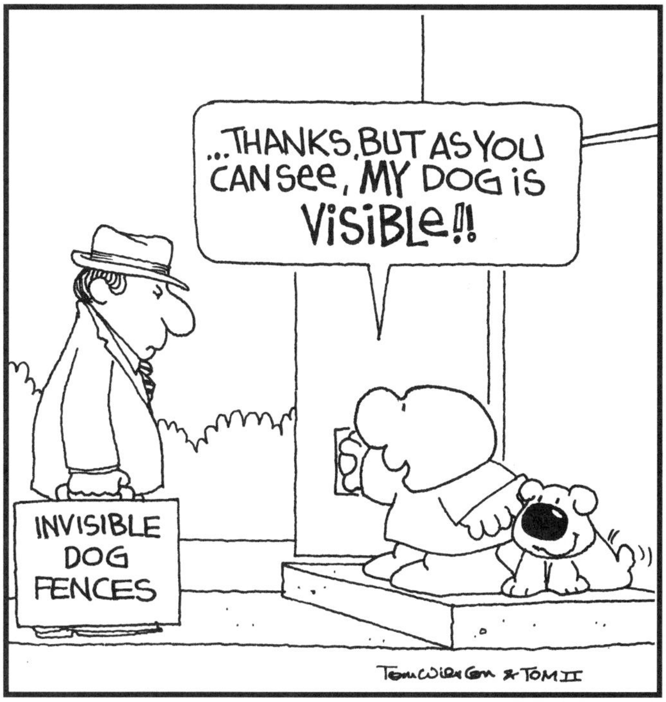
...THANKS, BUT AS YOU CAN SEE, MY DOG IS VISIBLE!!
INVISIBLE DOG FENCES
TomWilson & TOM II

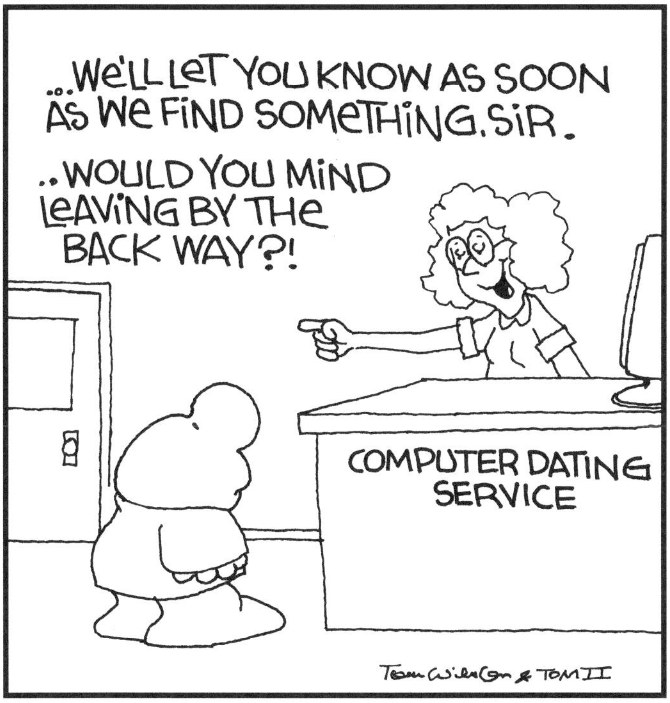
...WE'LL LET YOU KNOW AS SOON AS WE FIND SOMETHING, SIR.
..WOULD YOU MIND LEAVING BY THE BACK WAY?!
COMPUTER DATING SERVICE
TomWilson & TOM II

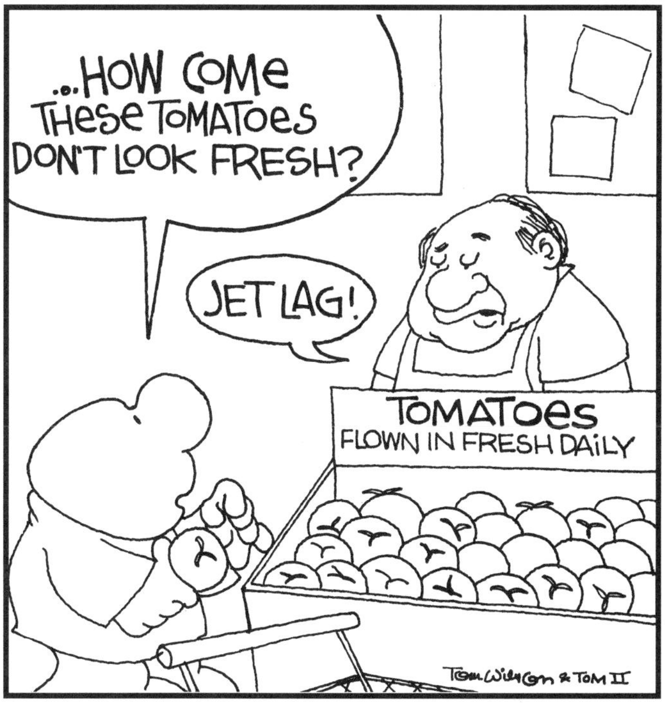
...HOW COME THESE TOMATOES DON'T LOOK FRESH?
JET LAG!
TOMATOES FLOWN IN FRESH DAILY
TomWilson & TOM II

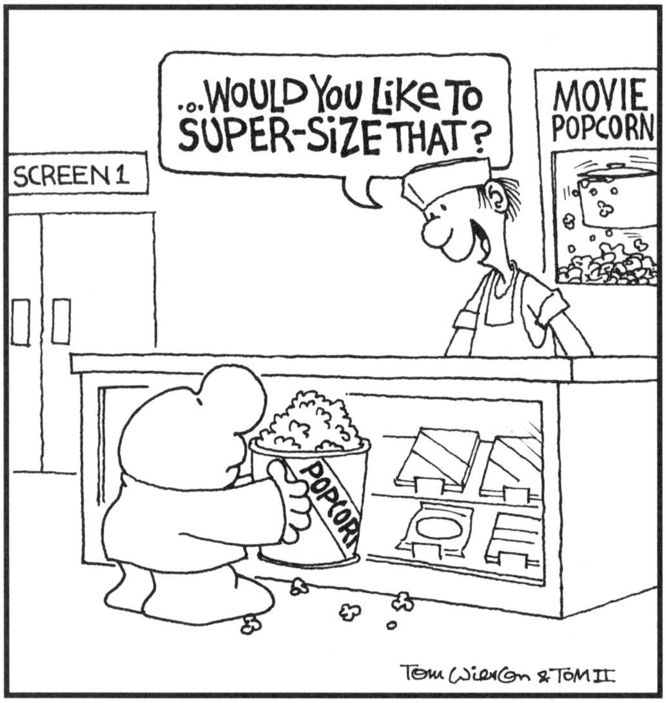
..WOULD YOU LIKE TO SUPER-SIZE THAT?
MOVIE POPCORN
SCREEN 1
Tom Wilson & TOM II

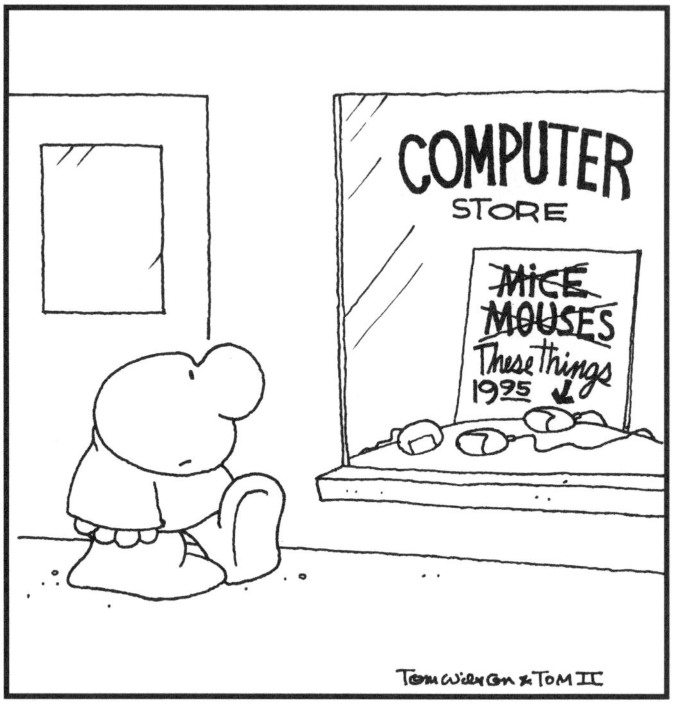
COMPUTER STORE
MICE
MOUSES
These things 1995
Tom Wilson & TOM II

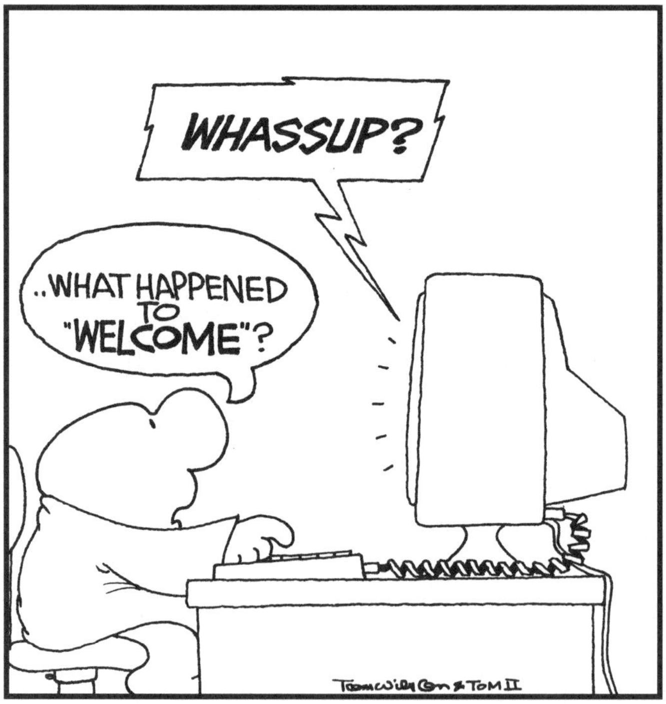
WHASSUP?
..WHAT HAPPENED TO "WELCOME"?
Tom Wilson & TOM II

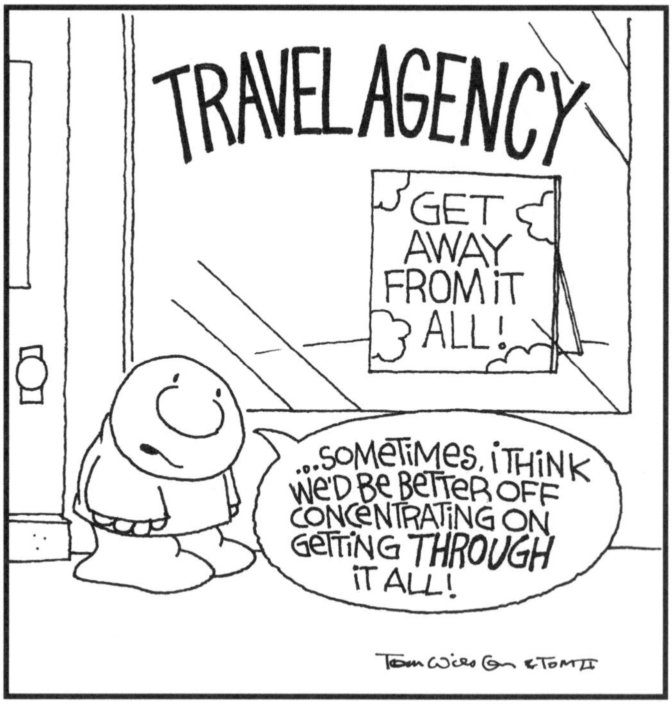
TRAVEL AGENCY
GET AWAY FROM IT ALL!
..SOMETIMES, I THINK WE'D BE BETTER OFF CONCENTRATING ON GETTING THROUGH IT ALL!
Tom Wilson & TOM II

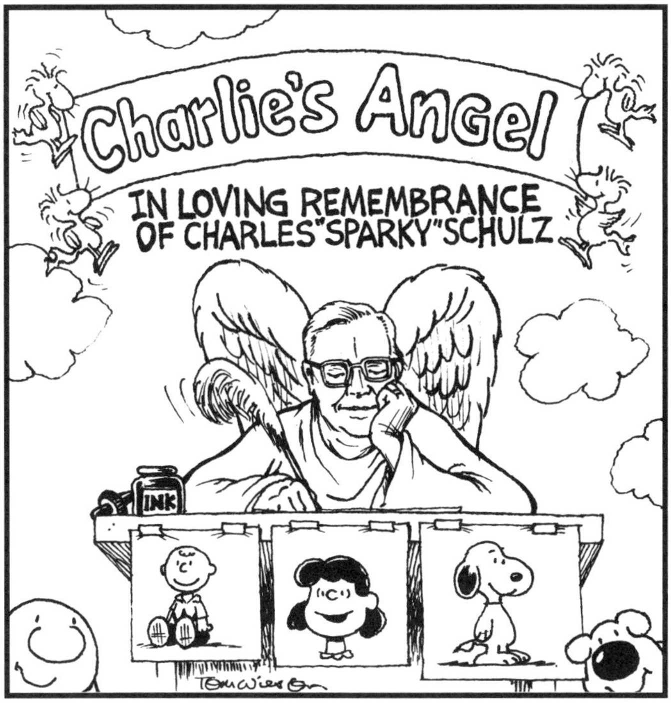
Charlie's Angel
IN LOVING REMEMBRANCE
OF CHARLES "SPARKY" SCHULZ
INK

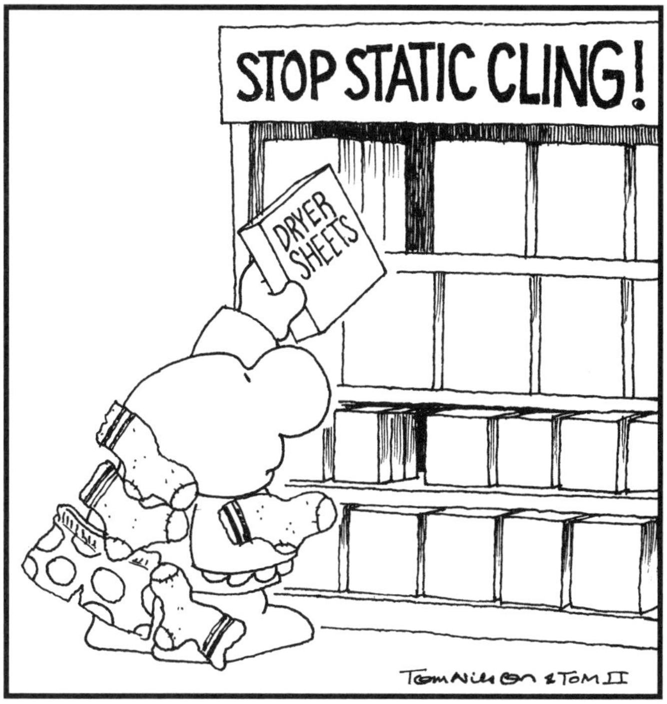
STOP STATIC CLING!
DRYER SHEETS

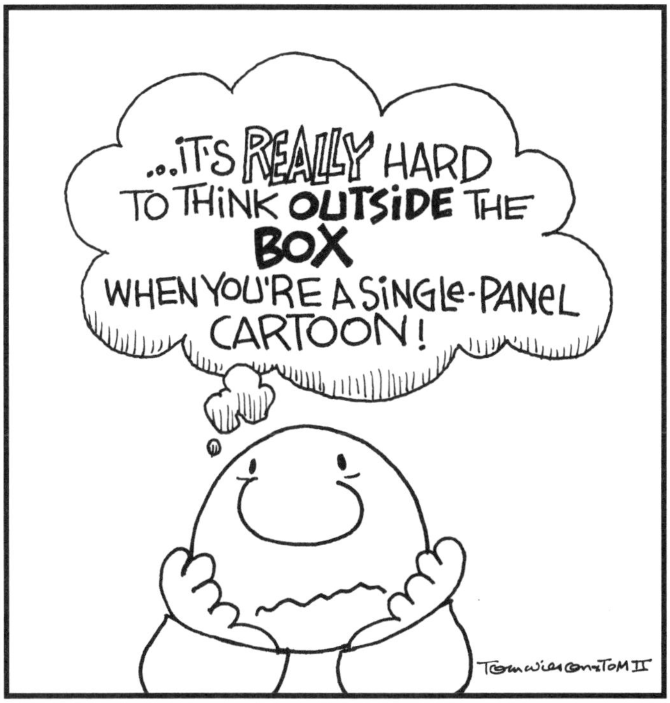
...IT'S REALLY HARD TO THINK OUTSIDE THE BOX WHEN YOU'RE A SINGLE-PANEL CARTOON!

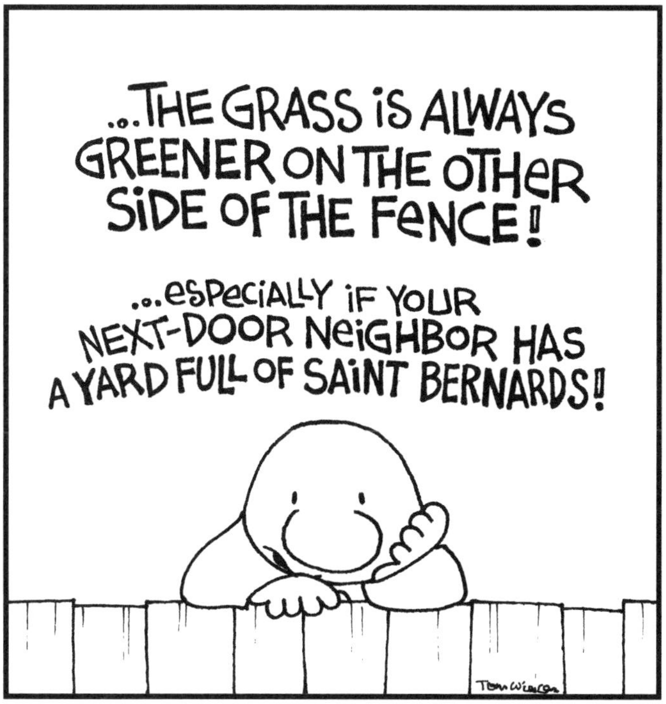
...THE GRASS IS ALWAYS GREENER ON THE OTHER SIDE OF THE FENCE!
...ESPECIALLY IF YOUR NEXT-DOOR NEIGHBOR HAS A YARD FULL OF SAINT BERNARDS!

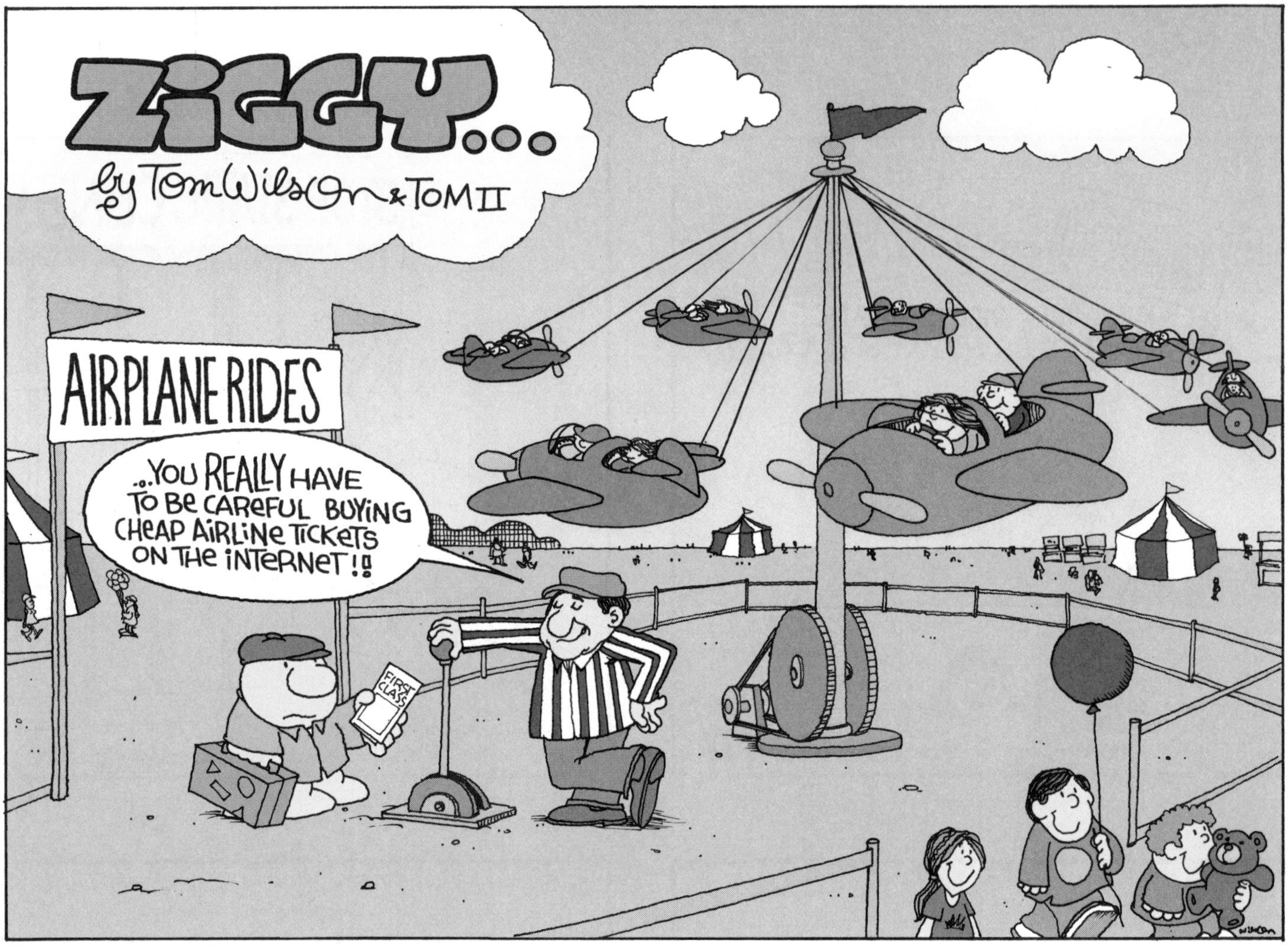
ZiGGY...
by Tom Wilson & Tom II
AIRPLANE RIDES
..YOU REALLY HAVE TO BE CAREFUL BUYING CHEAP AIRLINE TICKETS ON THE INTERNET!!
FIRST CLASS
Wilson

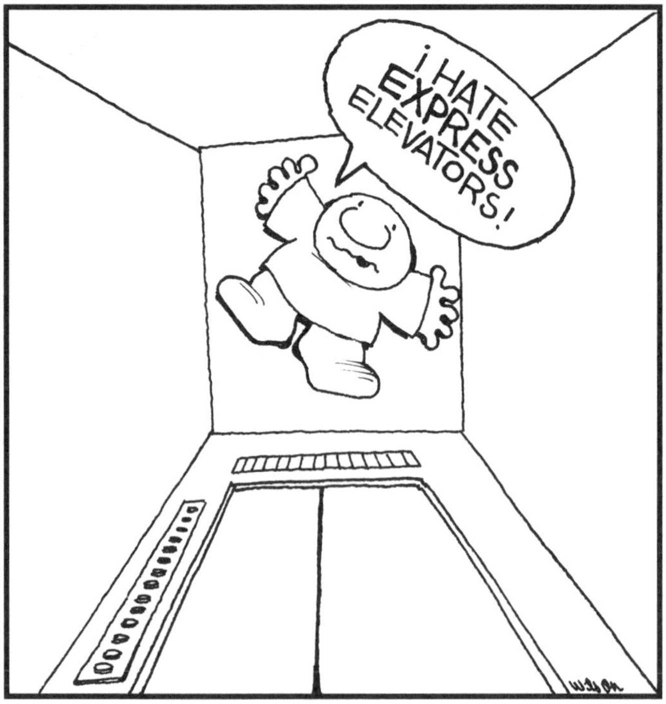
I HATE EXPRESS ELEVATORS!
Wilson

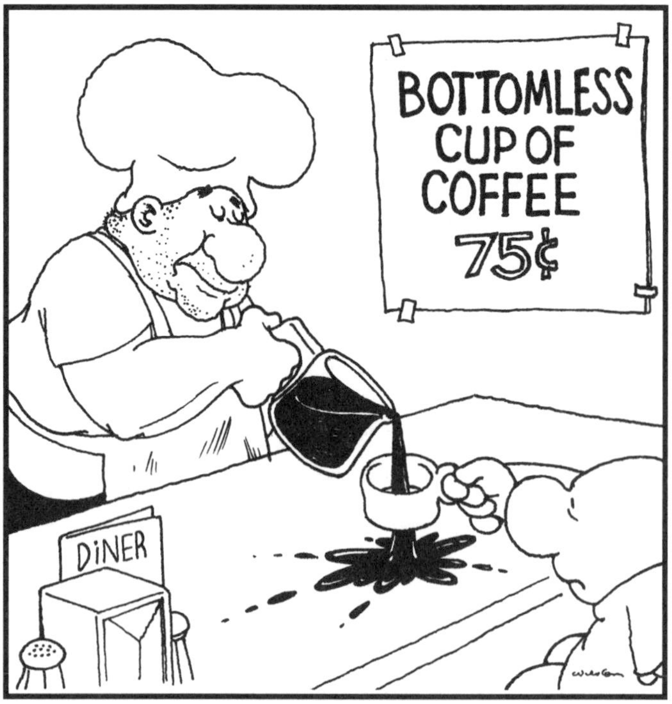
BOTTOMLESS CUP OF COFFEE 75¢
DINER
Wilson

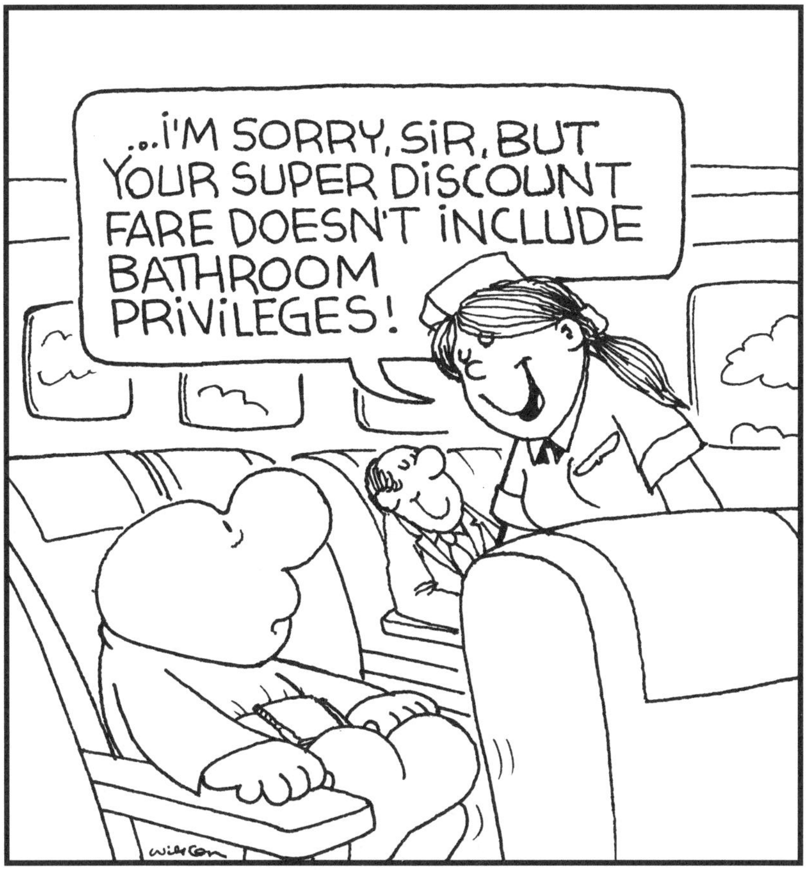
..I'M SORRY, SIR, BUT YOUR SUPER DISCOUNT FARE DOESN'T INCLUDE BATHROOM PRIVILEGES!

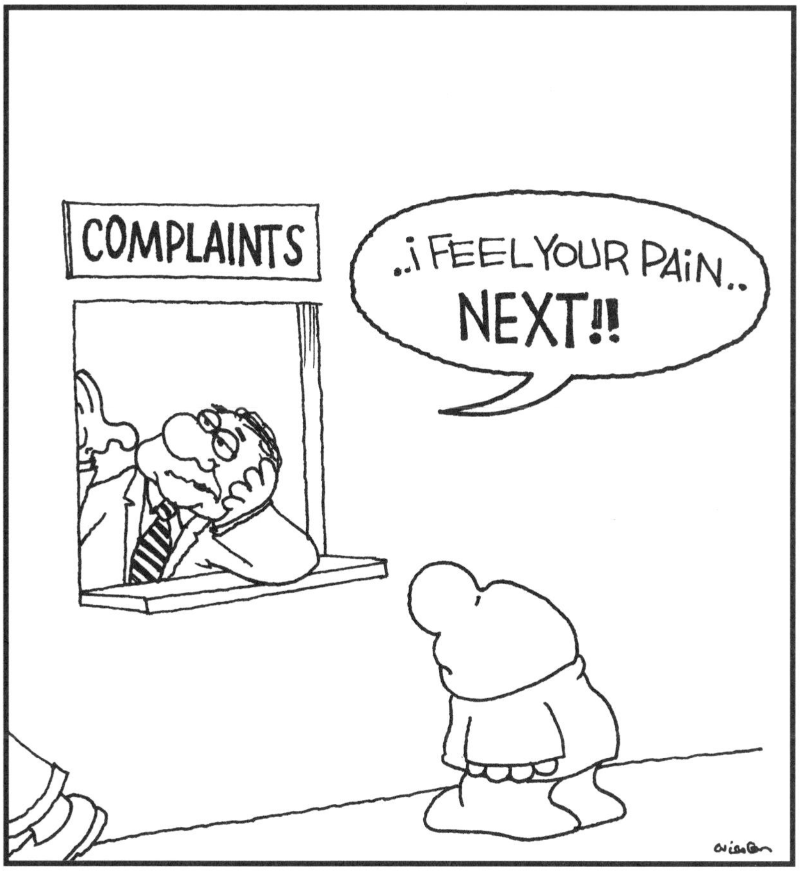
COMPLAINTS
..I FEEL YOUR PAIN.. NEXT!!

Chapter VII
2001–2006

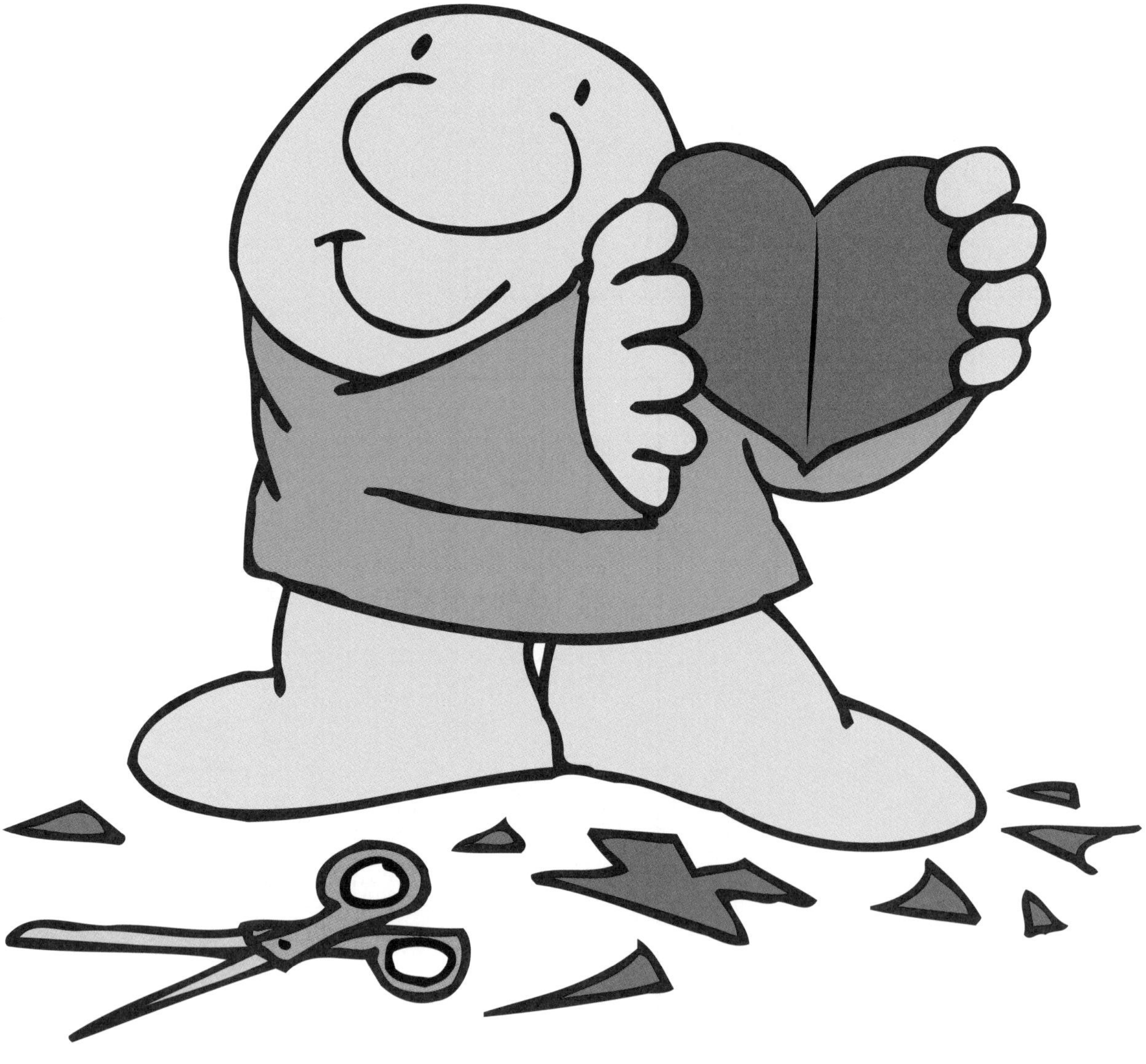

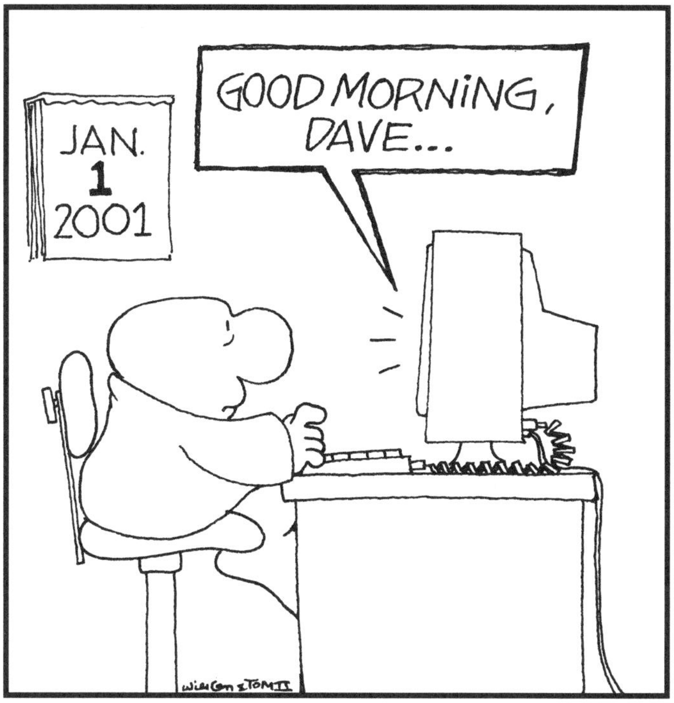
JAN.
1
2001
GOOD MORNING, DAVE...

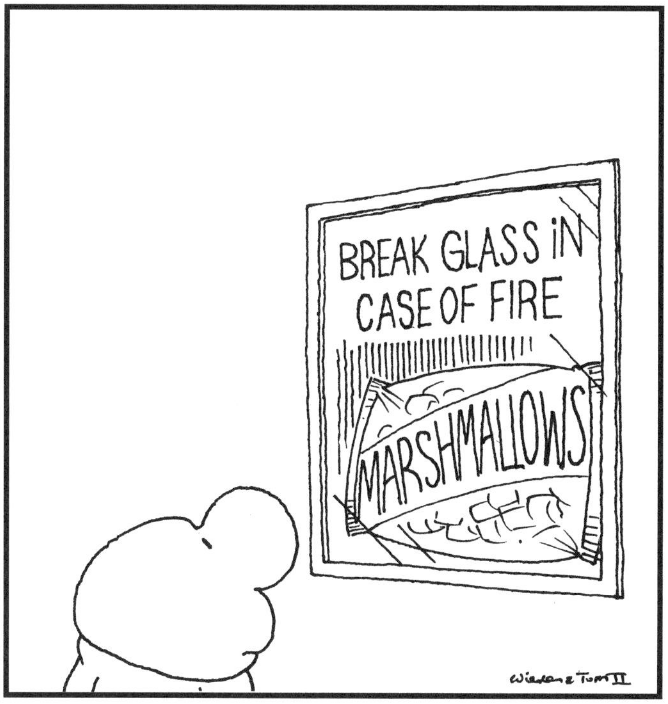
BREAK GLASS IN CASE OF FIRE
MARSHMALLOWS

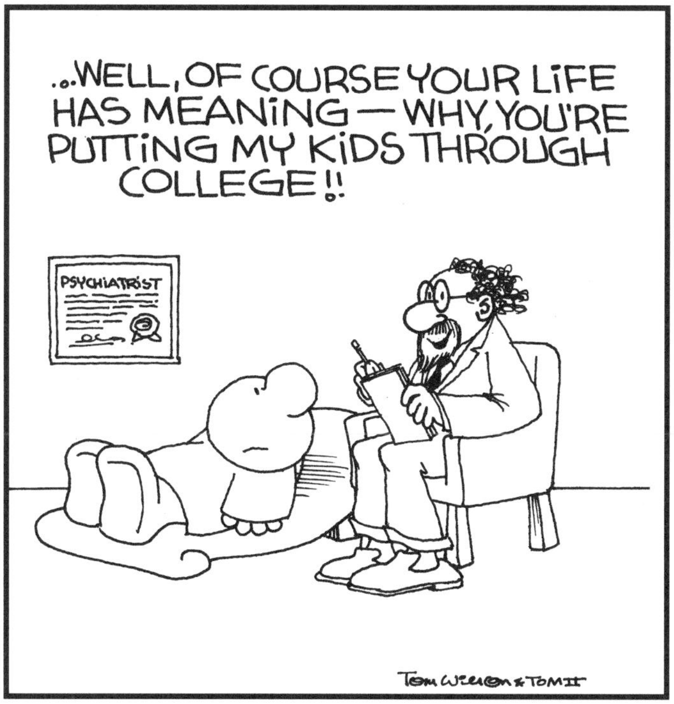
...WELL, OF COURSE YOUR LIFE HAS MEANING—WHY, YOU'RE PUTTING MY KIDS THROUGH COLLEGE!!
PSYCHIATRIST

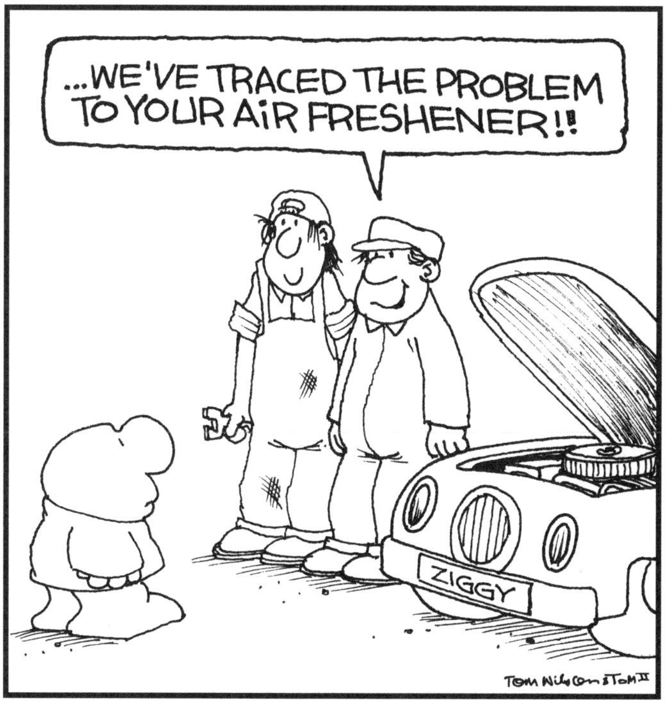
...WE'VE TRACED THE PROBLEM TO YOUR AIR FRESHENER!!
ZIGGY

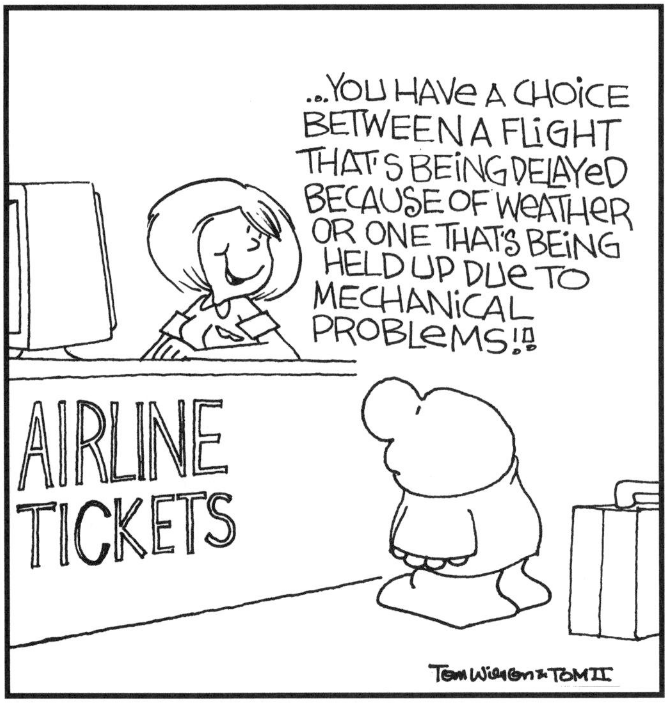
...YOU HAVE A CHOICE BETWEEN A FLIGHT THAT'S BEING DELAYED BECAUSE OF WEATHER OR ONE THAT'S BEING HELD UP DUE TO MECHANICAL PROBLEMS!!
AIRLINE TICKETS
Tom Wilson & Tom II

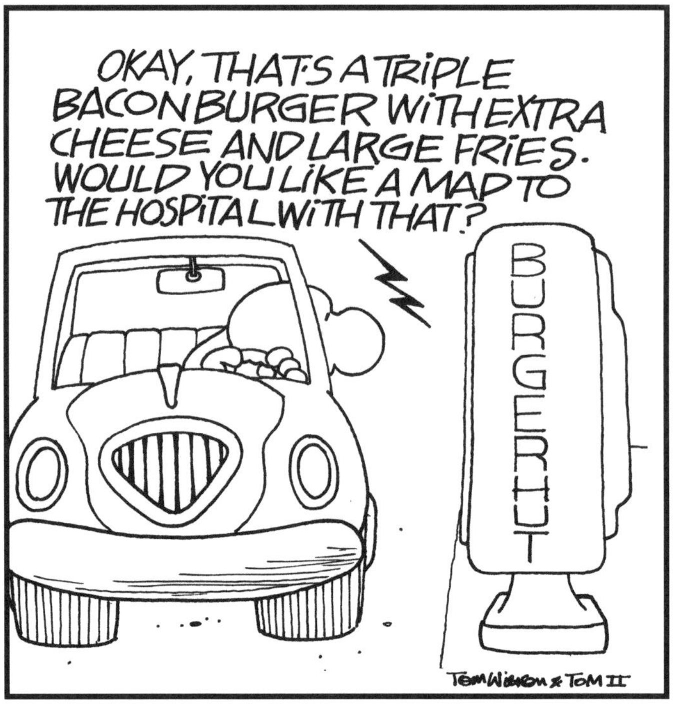
OKAY, THAT'S A TRIPLE BACON BURGER WITH EXTRA CHEESE AND LARGE FRIES. WOULD YOU LIKE A MAP TO THE HOSPITAL WITH THAT?
BURGERHUT
Tom Wilson & Tom II

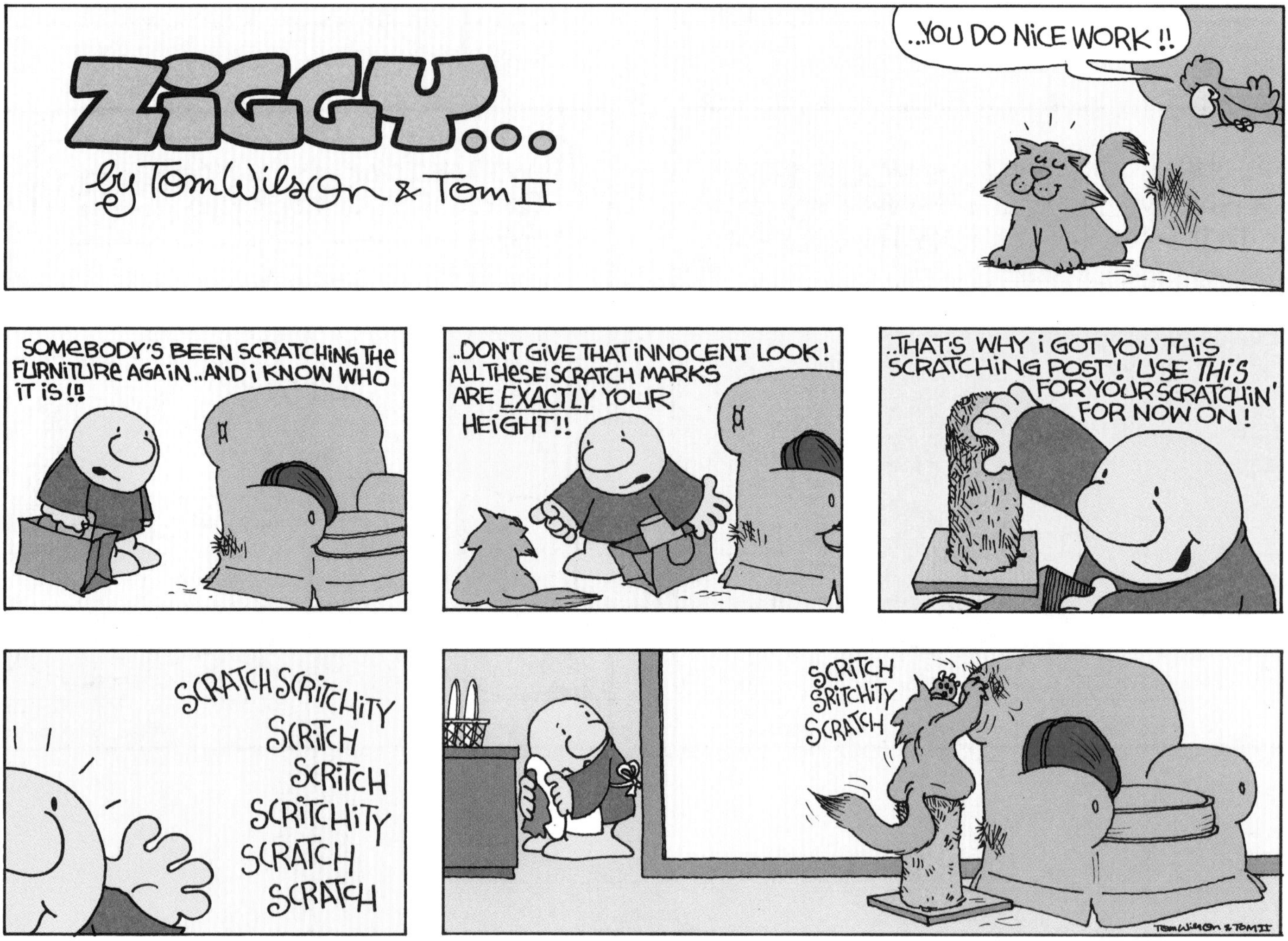
ZIGGY...
by Tom Wilson & Tom II
...YOU DO NICE WORK!!
SOMEBODY'S BEEN SCRATCHING THE FURNITURE AGAIN..AND I KNOW WHO IT IS!!
..DON'T GIVE THAT INNOCENT LOOK! ALL THESE SCRATCH MARKS ARE EXACTLY YOUR HEIGHT!!
..THAT'S WHY I GOT YOU THIS SCRATCHING POST! USE THIS FOR YOUR SCRATCHIN' FOR NOW ON!
SCRATCH SCRITCHITY SCRITCH SCRITCH SCRITCHITY SCRATCH SCRATCH
SCRITCH SRITCHITY SCRATCH
Tom Wilson & Tom II

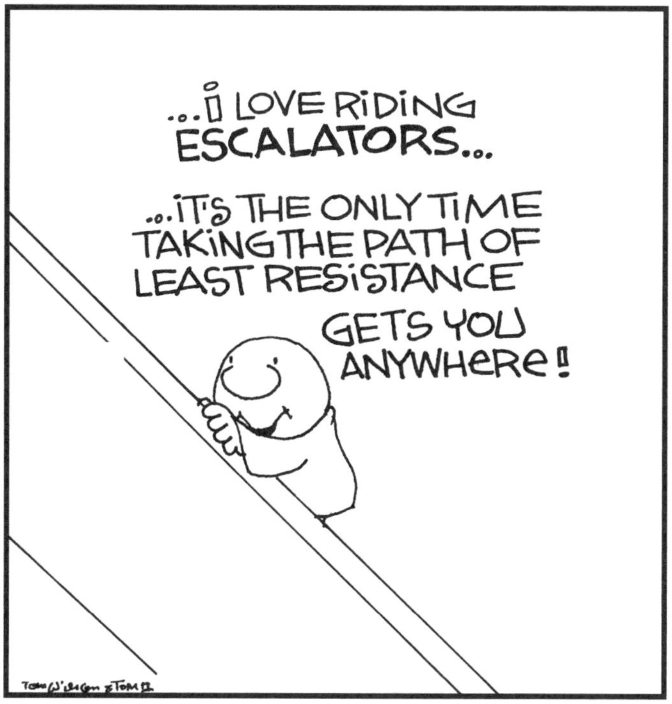
..I LOVE RIDING ESCALATORS...
..IT'S THE ONLY TIME TAKING THE PATH OF LEAST RESISTANCE
GETS YOU ANYWHERE!

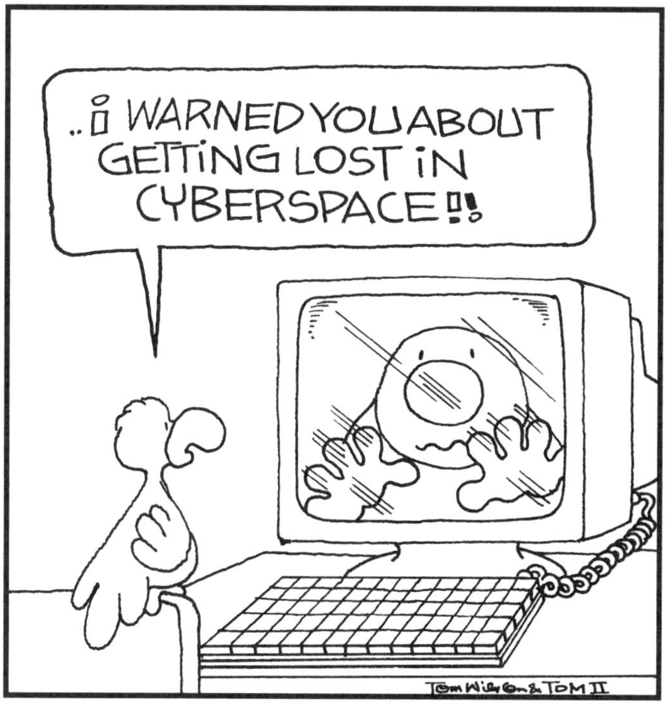
..I WARNED YOU ABOUT GETTING LOST IN CYBERSPACE!!
TOM WILSON & TOM II

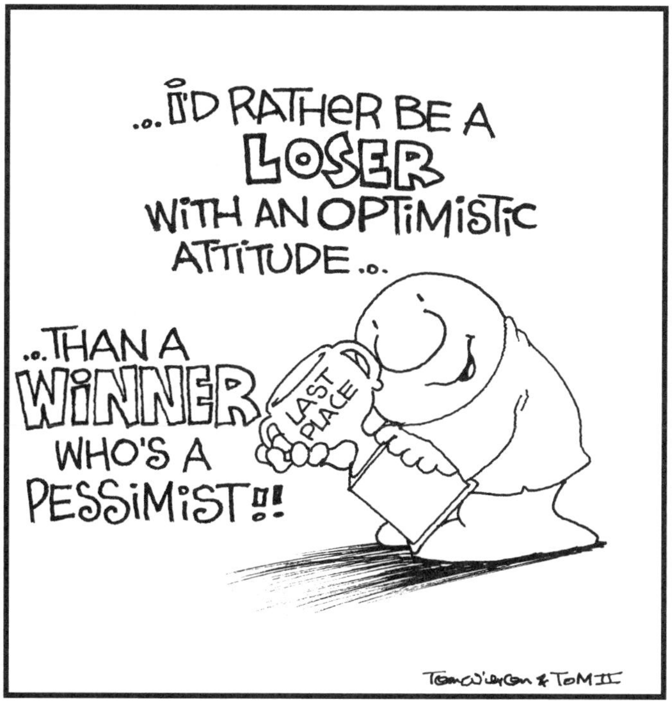
..I'D RATHER BE A LOSER WITH AN OPTIMISTIC ATTITUDE..
..THAN A WINNER WHO'S A PESSIMIST!!
LAST PLACE
TOM WILSON & TOM II

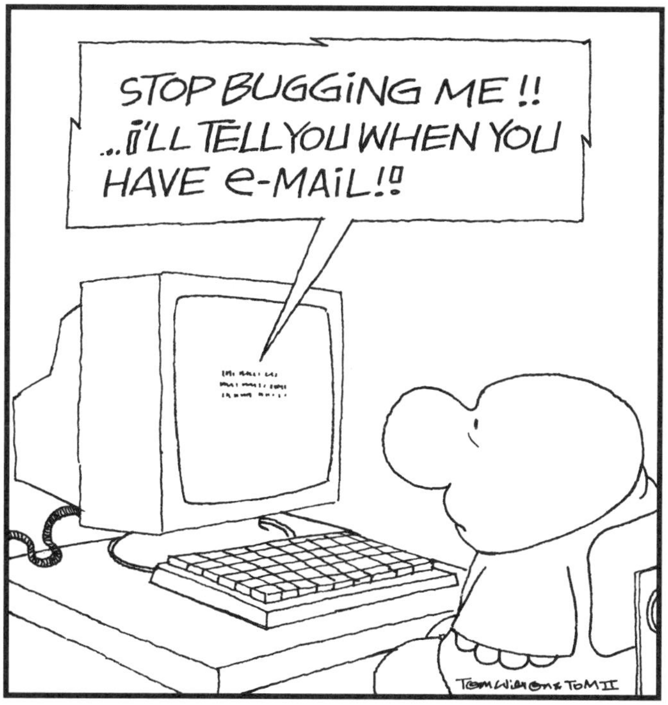
STOP BUGGING ME!! ..I'LL TELL YOU WHEN YOU HAVE E-MAIL!!
TOM WILSON & TOM II

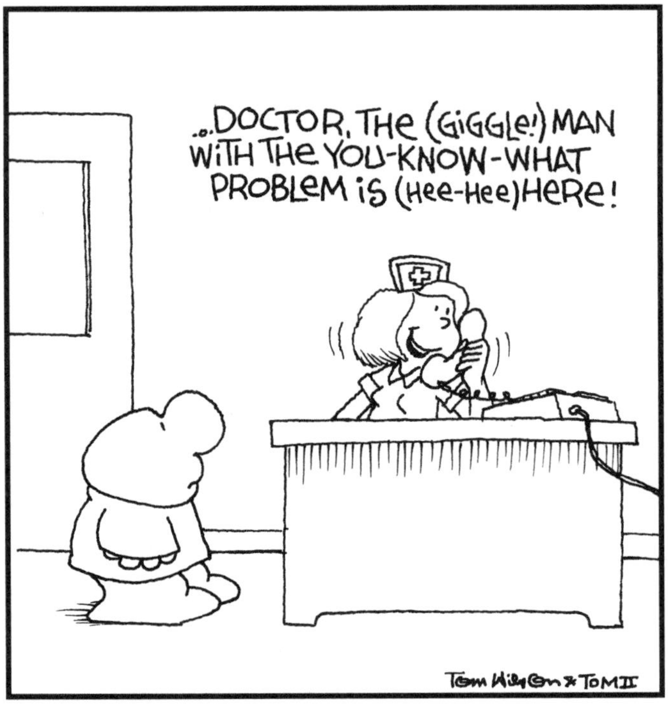
..DOCTOR, THE (GIGGLE!) MAN WITH THE YOU-KNOW-WHAT PROBLEM IS (HEE-HEE) HERE!
Tom Wilson & Tom II

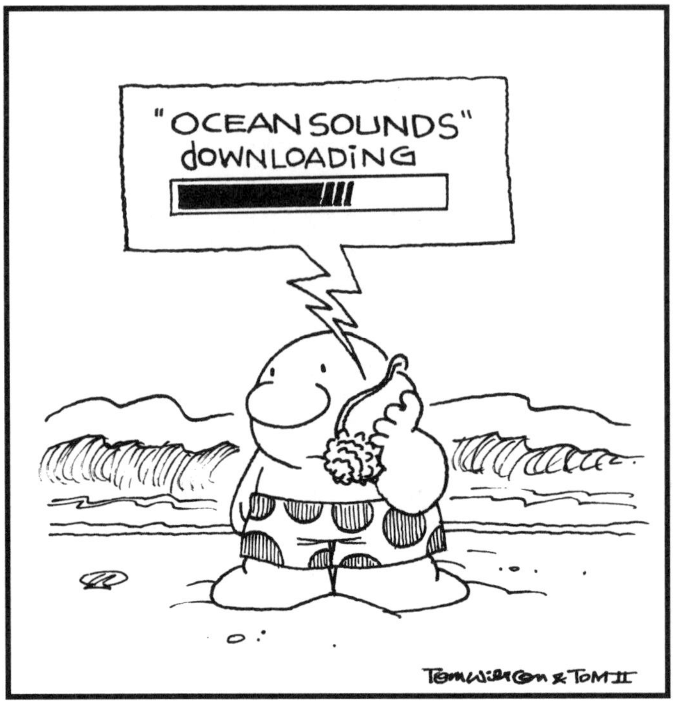
"OCEAN SOUNDS" DOWNLOADING
Tom Wilson & Tom II

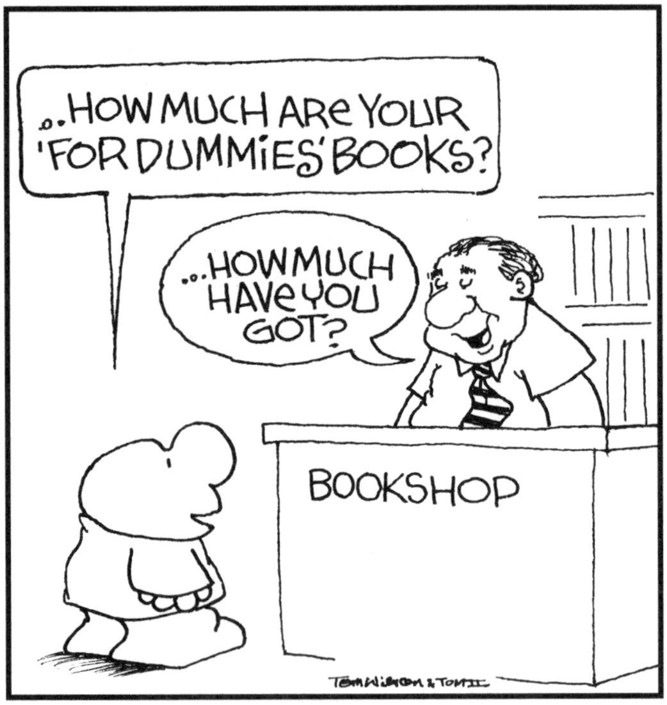
..HOW MUCH ARE YOUR 'FOR DUMMIES' BOOKS?
...HOW MUCH HAVE YOU GOT?
BOOKSHOP
Tom Wilson & Tom II

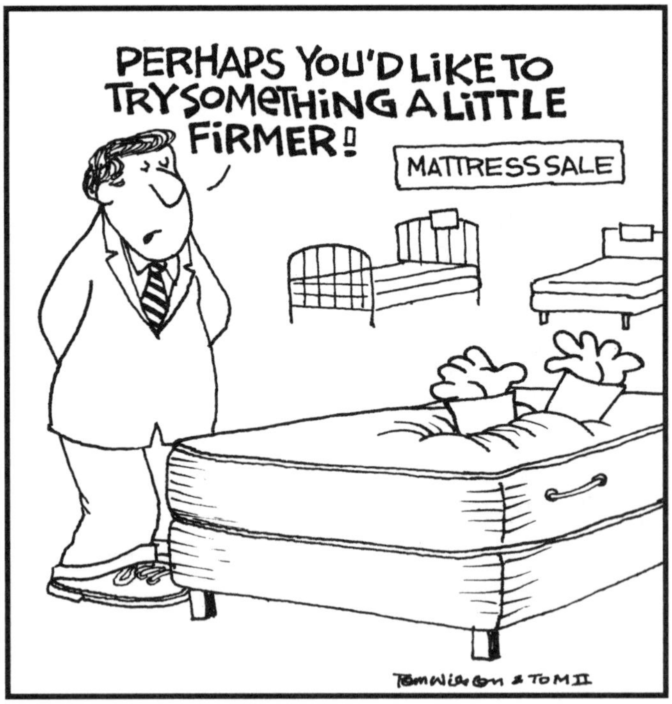
PERHAPS YOU'D LIKE TO TRY SOMETHING A LITTLE FIRMER!
MATTRESS SALE
Tom Wilson & Tom II

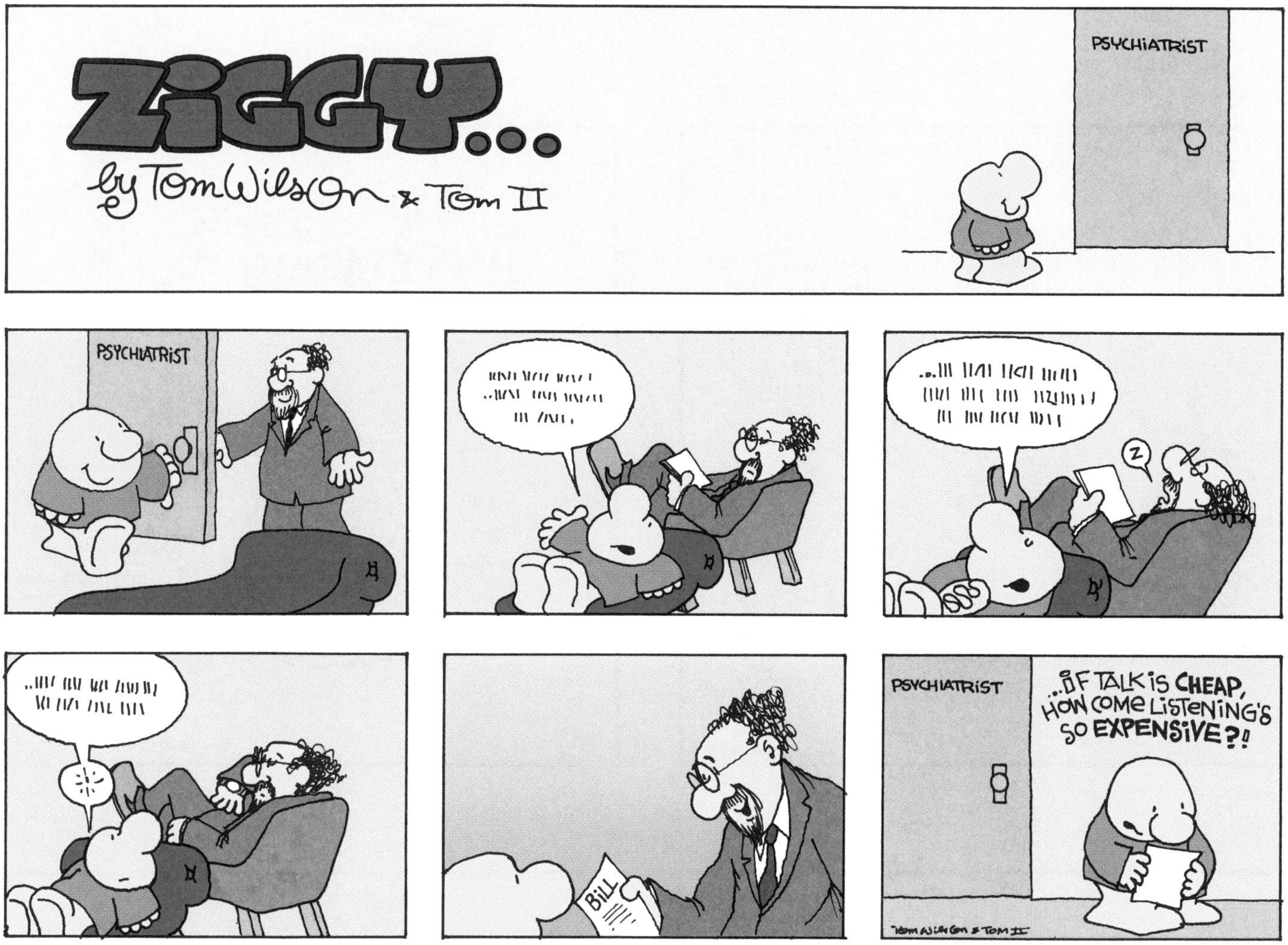
ZIGGY...
by Tom Wilson & Tom II
PSYCHIATRIST
PSYCHIATRIST
BILL
PSYCHIATRIST
...IF TALK IS CHEAP, HOW COME LISTENING'S SO EXPENSIVE?!
TOM WILSON & TOM II

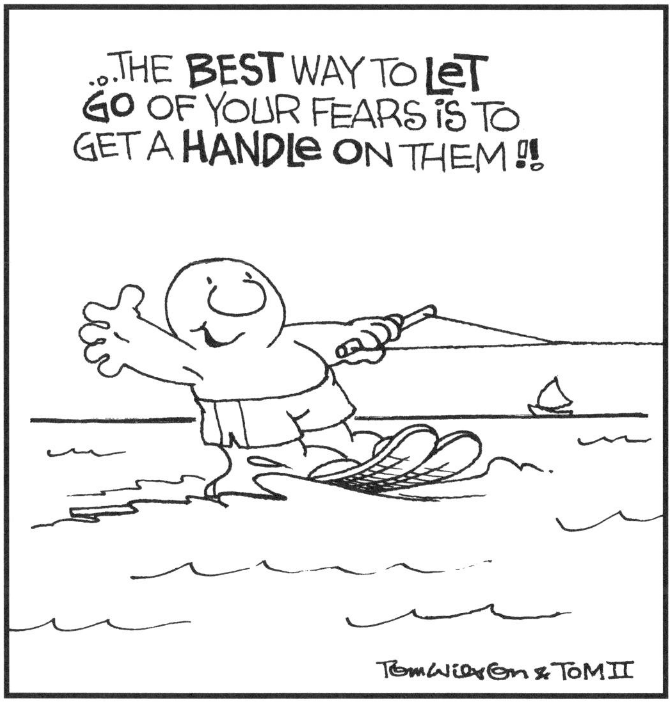
..THE BEST WAY TO LET GO OF YOUR FEARS IS TO GET A HANDLE ON THEM!!
TOM WILSON & TOM II

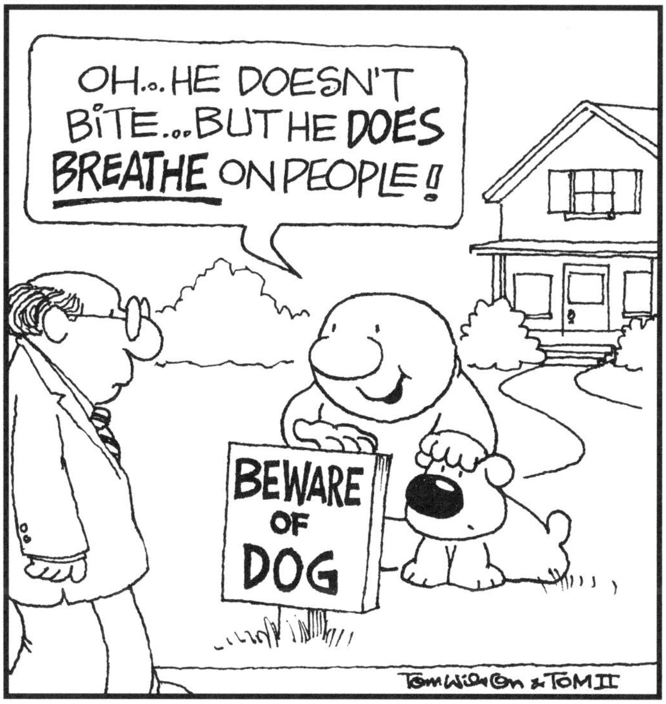
OH...HE DOESN'T BITE...BUT HE DOES BREATHE ON PEOPLE!
BEWARE OF DOG
TOM WILSON & TOM II

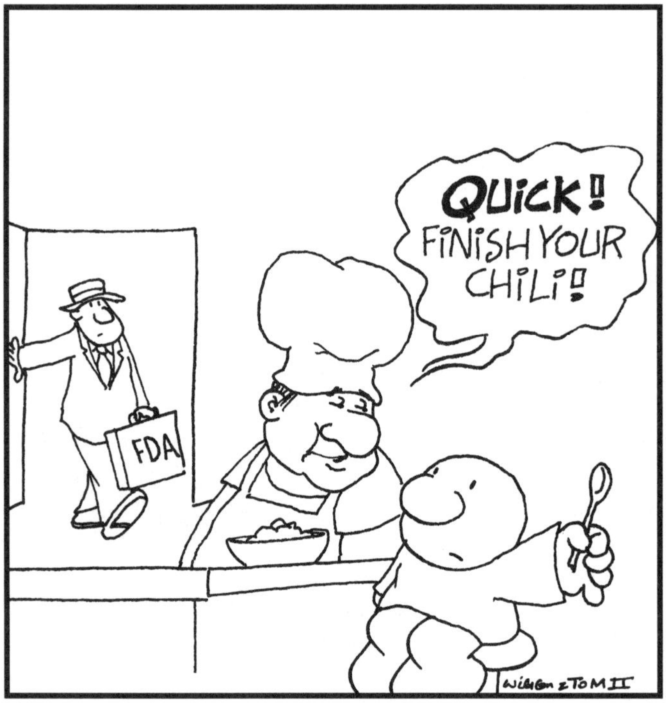
QUICK! FINISH YOUR CHILI!
FDA
WILSON & TOM II

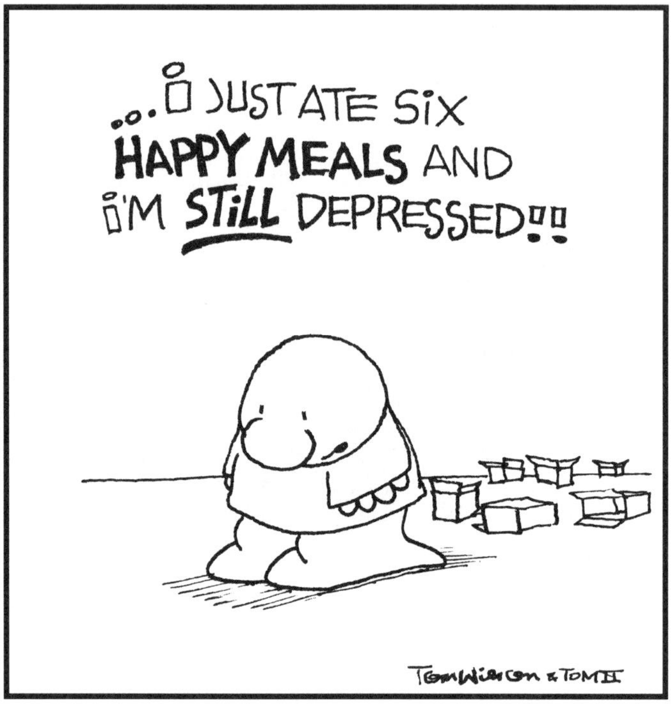
...I JUST ATE SIX HAPPY MEALS AND I'M STILL DEPRESSED!!
TOM WILSON & TOM II

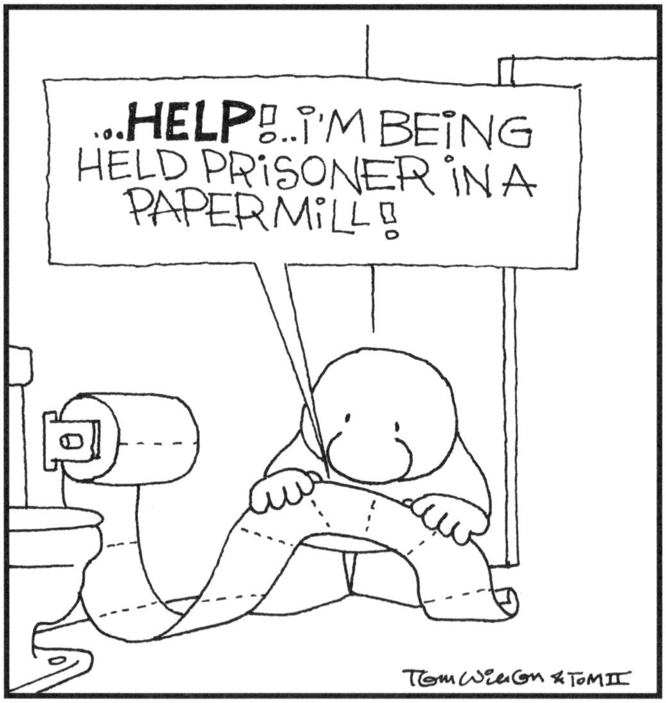
...HELP!..I'M BEING HELD PRISONER IN A PAPER MILL!
TOM WILSON & TOM II

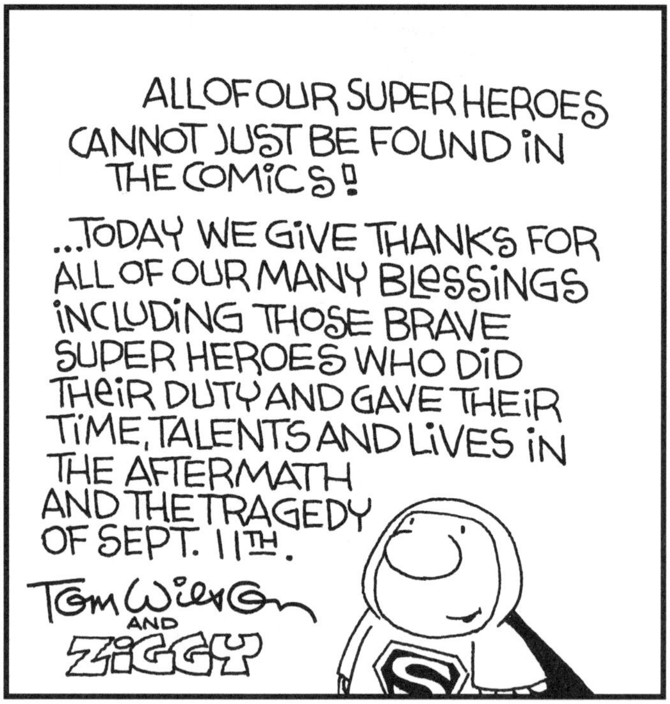
ALL OF OUR SUPER HEROES CANNOT JUST BE FOUND IN THE COMICS!
...TODAY WE GIVE THANKS FOR ALL OF OUR MANY BLESSINGS INCLUDING THOSE BRAVE SUPER HEROES WHO DID THEIR DUTY AND GAVE THEIR TIME, TALENTS AND LIVES IN THE AFTERMATH AND THE TRAGEDY OF SEPT. 11TH.
TOM WILSON AND ZIGGY

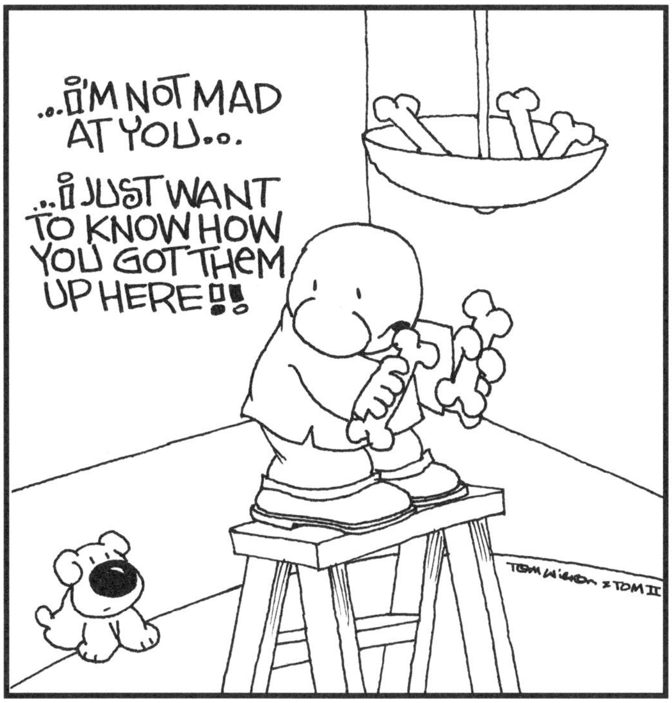
..I'M NOT MAD AT YOU..
..I JUST WANT TO KNOW HOW YOU GOT THEM UP HERE!!
TOM WILSON & TOM II

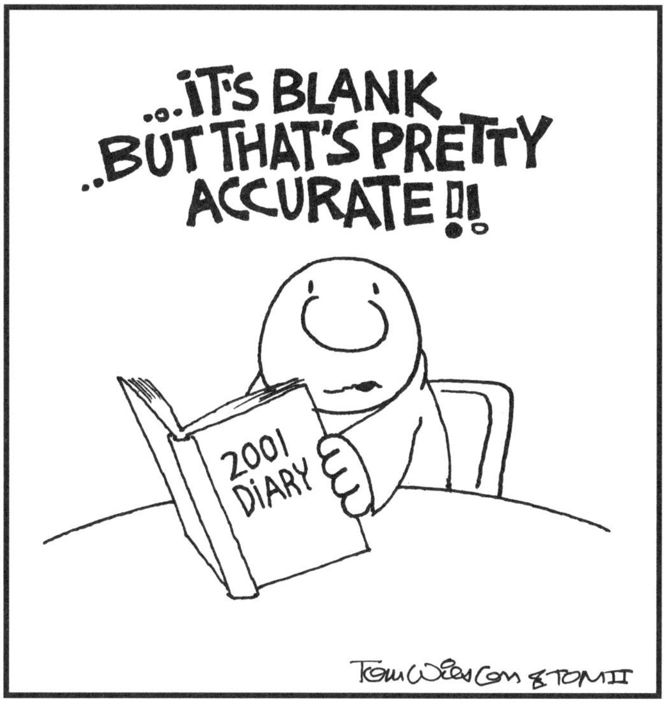
..IT'S BLANK ..BUT THAT'S PRETTY ACCURATE!!
2001 DIARY
TOM WILSON & TOM II

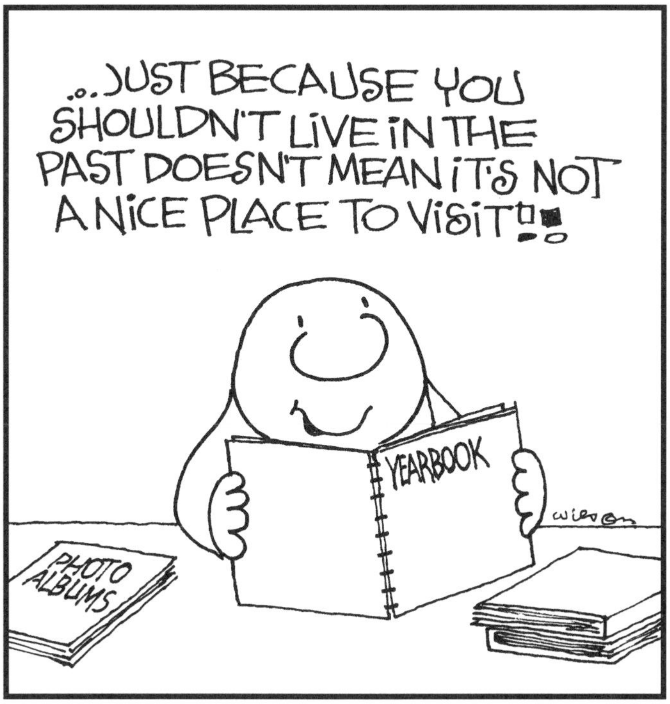
..JUST BECAUSE YOU SHOULDN'T LIVE IN THE PAST DOESN'T MEAN IT'S NOT A NICE PLACE TO VISIT!!
YEARBOOK
PHOTO ALBUMS
WILSON

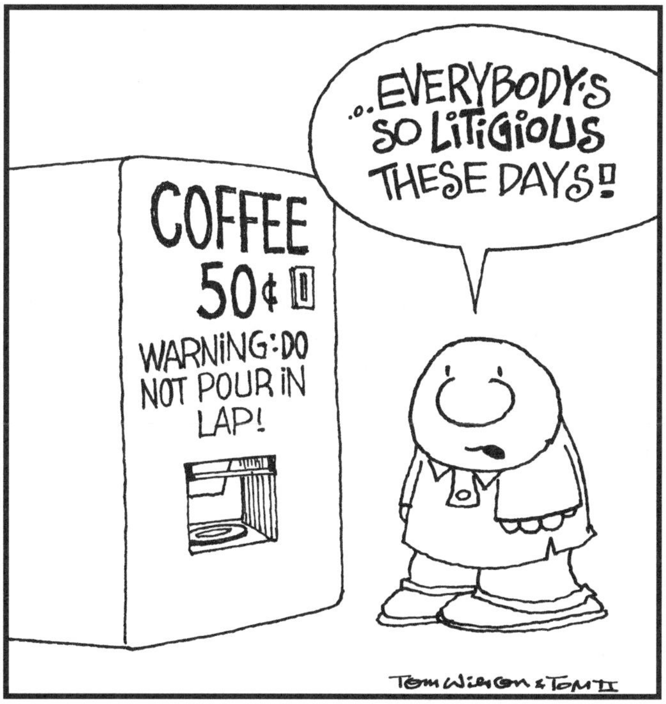
..EVERYBODY'S SO LITIGIOUS THESE DAYS!
COFFEE
50¢!
WARNING: DO NOT POUR IN LAP!
TOM WILSON & TOM II

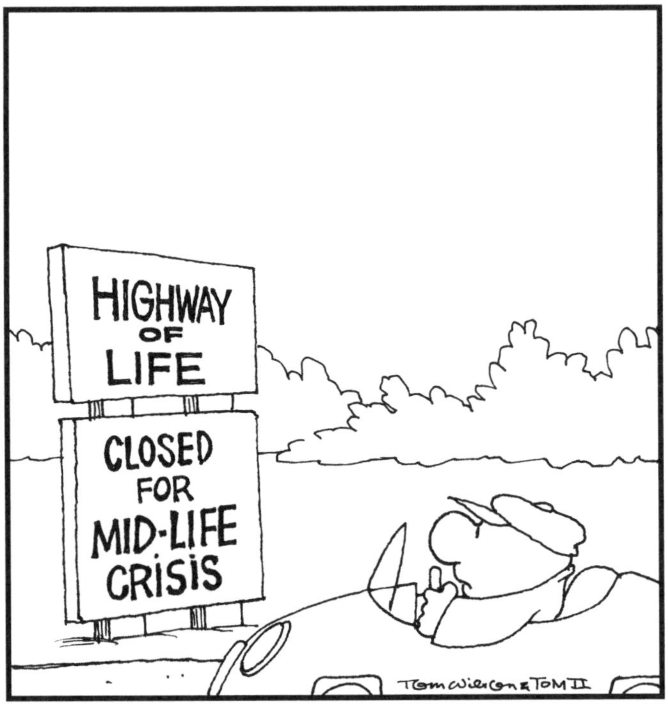
HIGHWAY OF LIFE
CLOSED FOR MID-LIFE CRISIS
TomWilson & TOM II

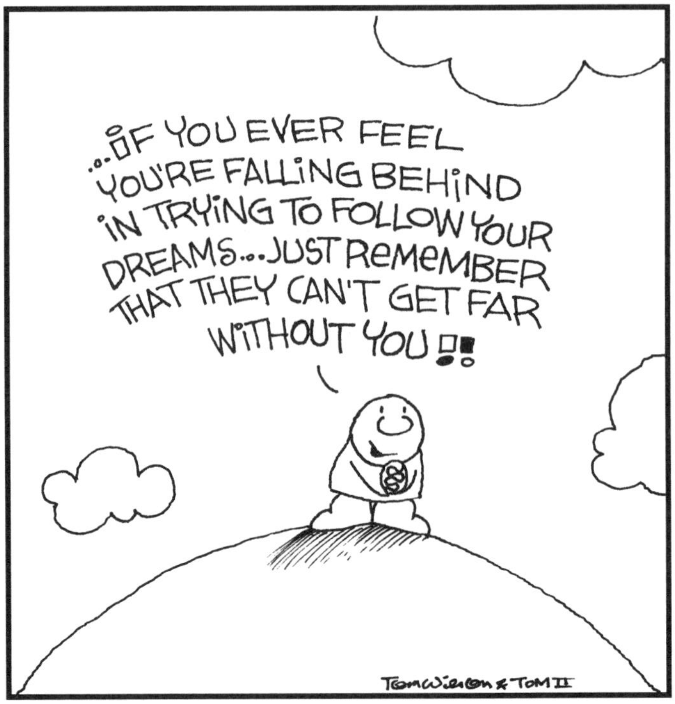
...IF YOU EVER FEEL YOU'RE FALLING BEHIND IN TRYING TO FOLLOW YOUR DREAMS...JUST REMEMBER THAT THEY CAN'T GET FAR WITHOUT YOU!!
TomWilson & TOM II

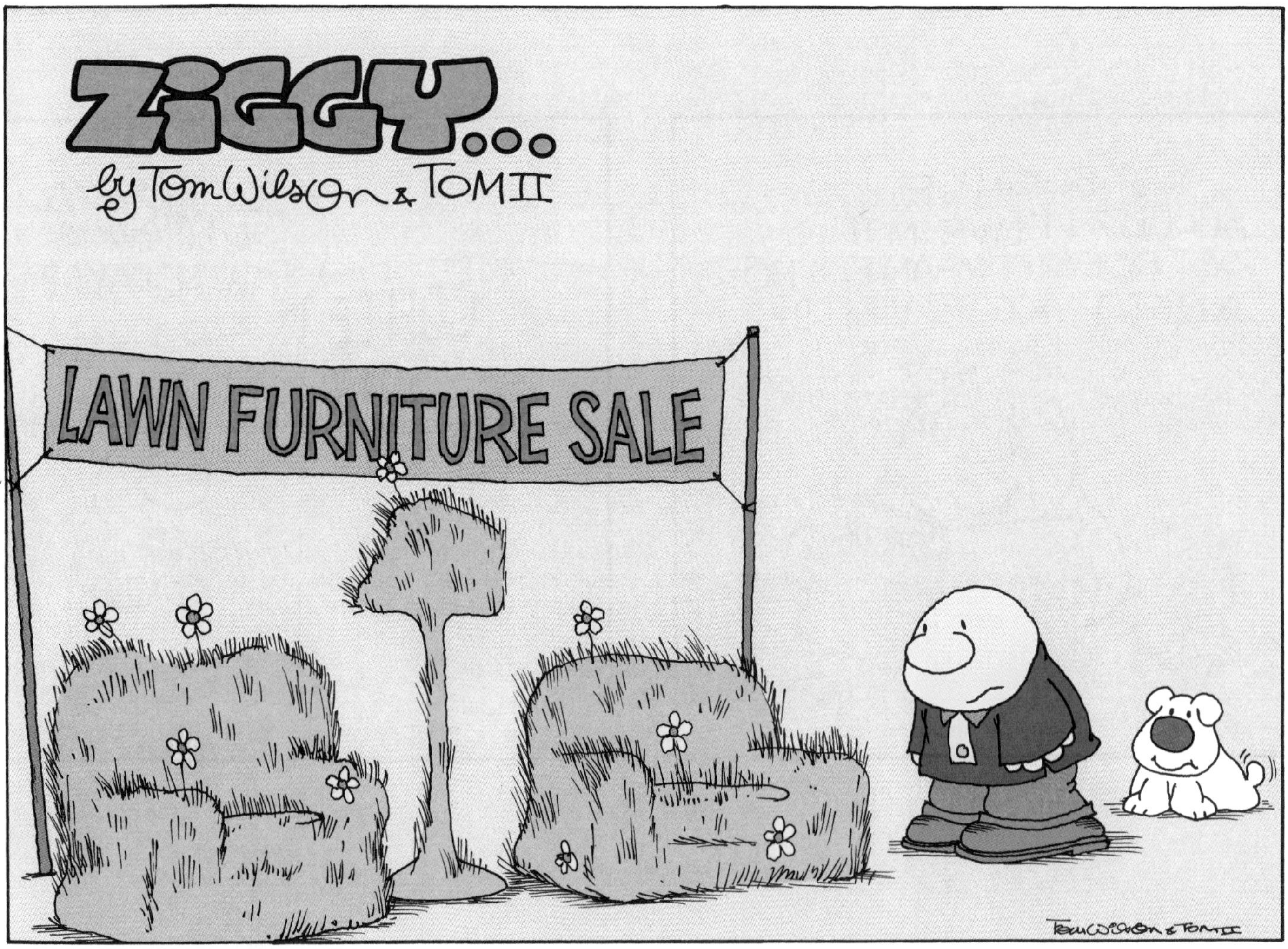
ZIGGY...
by TomWilson & TOM II
LAWN FURNITURE SALE
TomWilson & TOM II

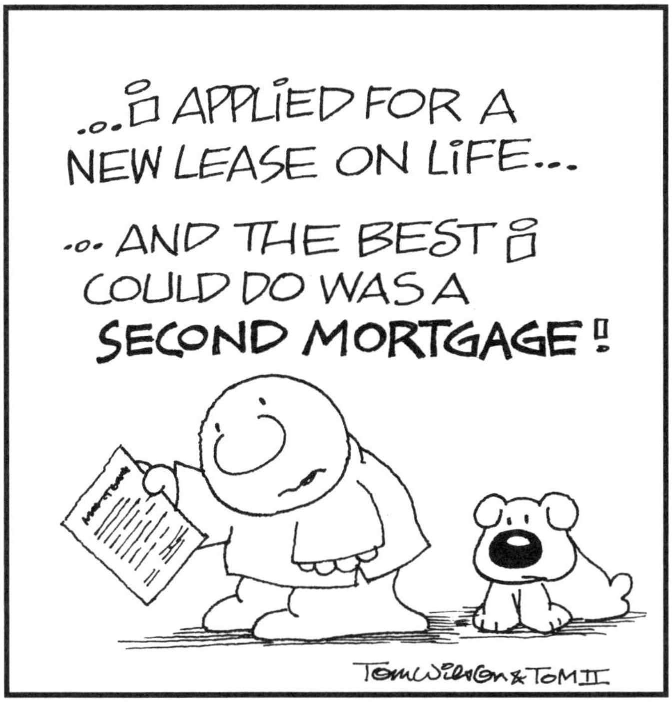
...I APPLIED FOR A NEW LEASE ON LIFE...
...AND THE BEST I COULD DO WAS A SECOND MORTGAGE!
Tom Wilson & Tom II

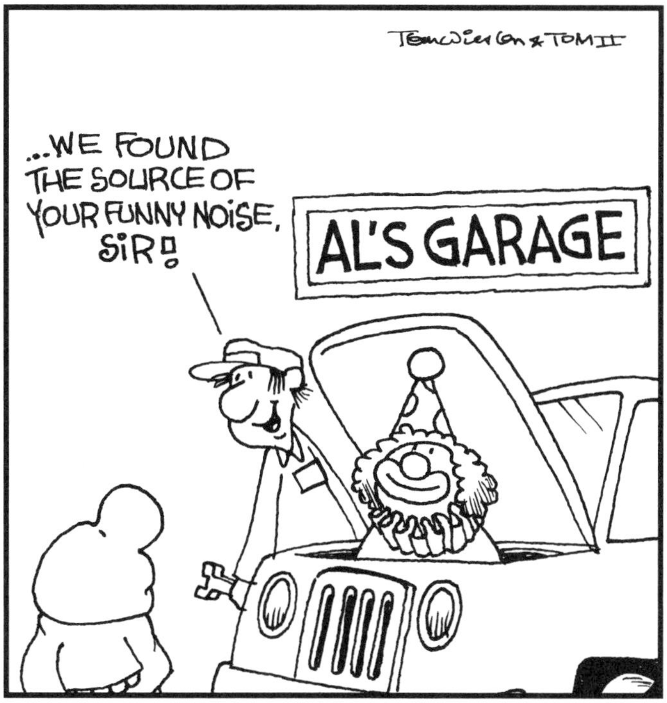
Tom Wilson & Tom II
...WE FOUND THE SOURCE OF YOUR FUNNY NOISE, SIR!
AL'S GARAGE

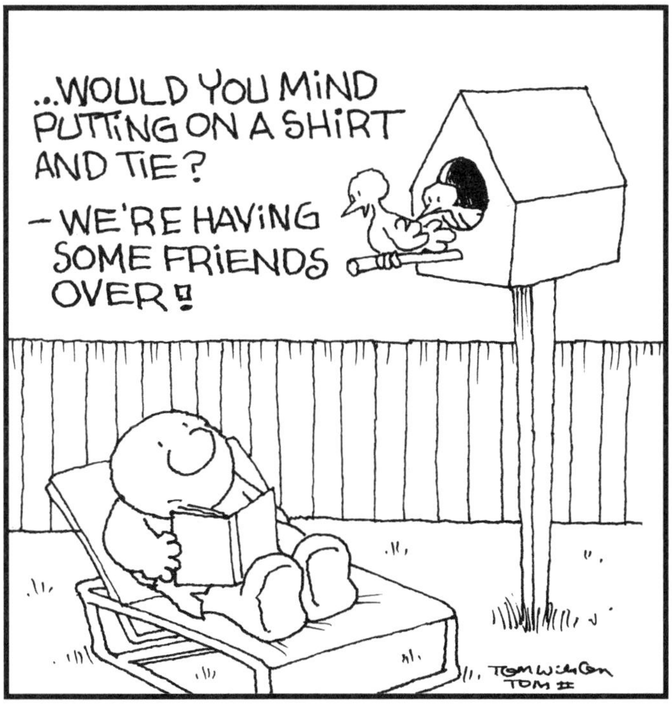
...WOULD YOU MIND PUTTING ON A SHIRT AND TIE?
– WE'RE HAVING SOME FRIENDS OVER!
Tom Wilson Tom II

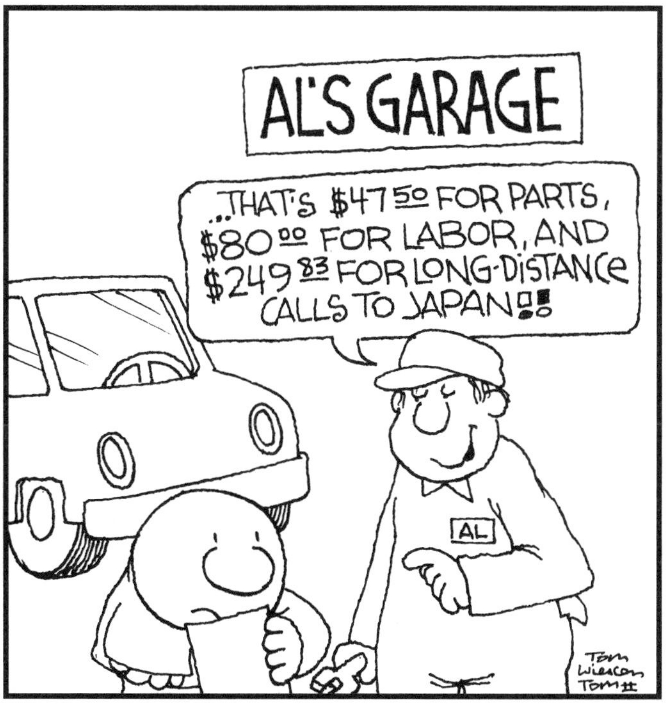
AL'S GARAGE
...THAT'S $47.50 FOR PARTS, $80.00 FOR LABOR, AND $249.83 FOR LONG-DISTANCE CALLS TO JAPAN!!
AL
Tom Wilson Tom II

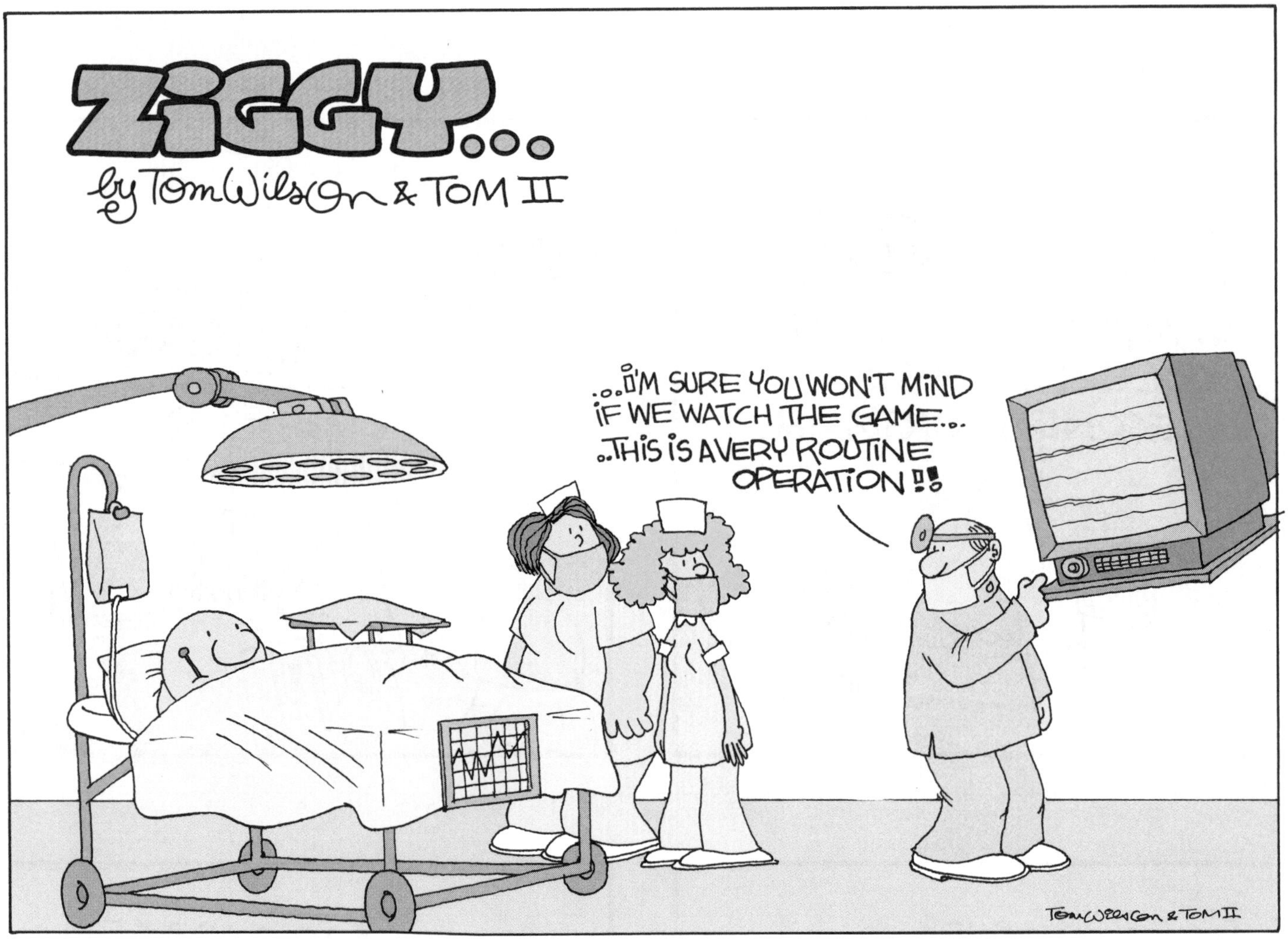
ZIGGY...
by Tom Wilson & Tom II
...I'M SURE YOU WON'T MIND IF WE WATCH THE GAME... ..THIS IS A VERY ROUTINE OPERATION!!
Tom Wilson & Tom II

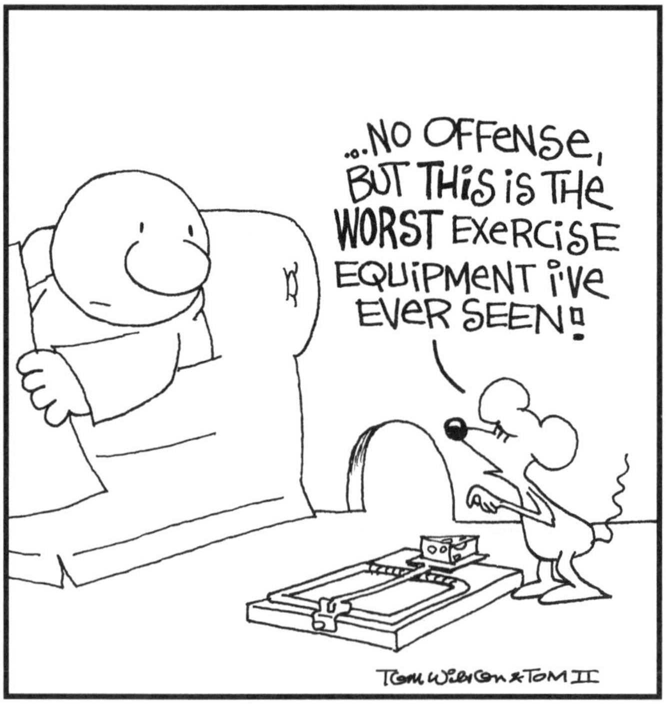
...NO OFFENSE, BUT THIS IS THE WORST EXERCISE EQUIPMENT I'VE EVER SEEN!
Tom Wilson & Tom II

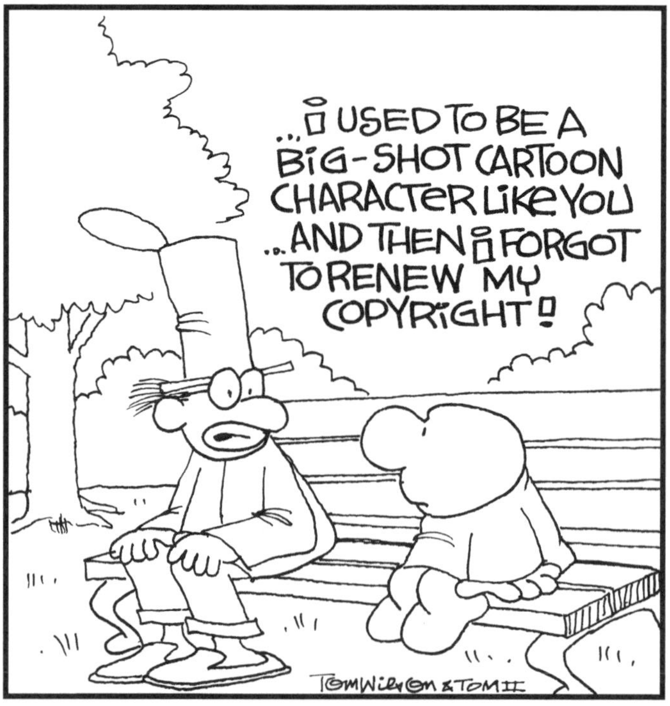
...I USED TO BE A BIG-SHOT CARTOON CHARACTER LIKE YOU ..AND THEN I FORGOT TO RENEW MY COPYRIGHT!
Tom Wilson & Tom II

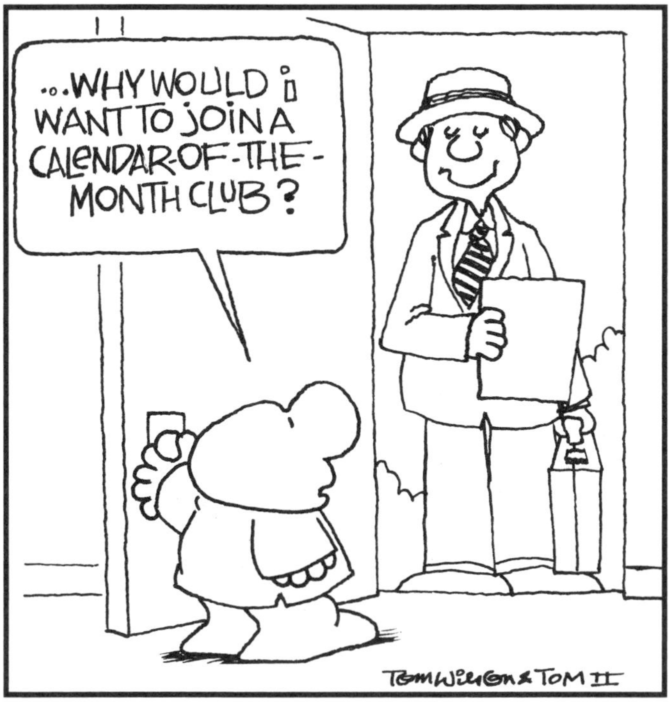
...WHY WOULD I WANT TO JOIN A CALENDAR-OF-THE-MONTH CLUB?
TOM WILSON & TOM II

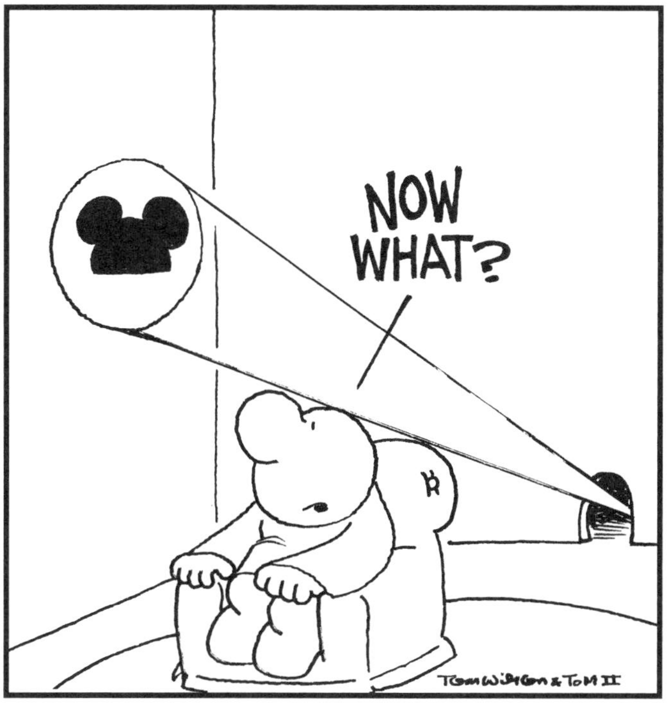
NOW WHAT?
TOM WILSON & TOM II

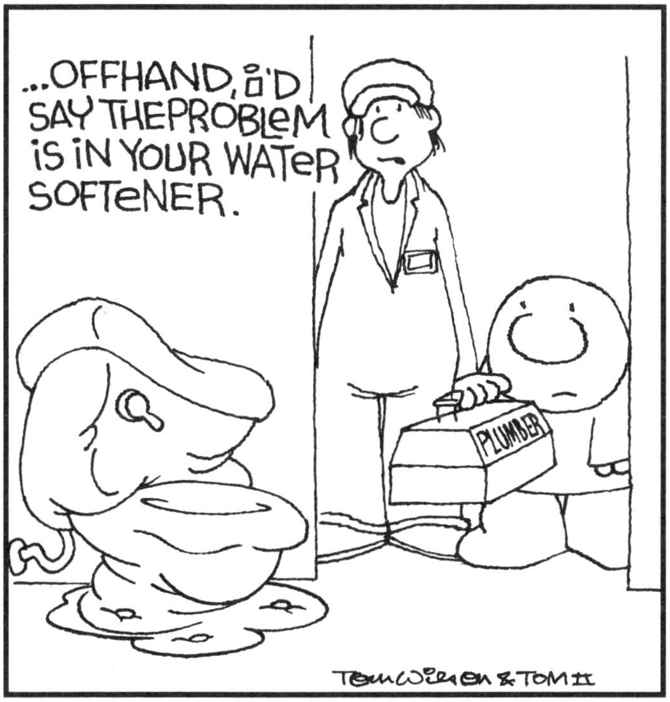
...OFFHAND, I'D SAY THE PROBLEM IS IN YOUR WATER SOFTENER.
PLUMBER
TOM WILSON & TOM II

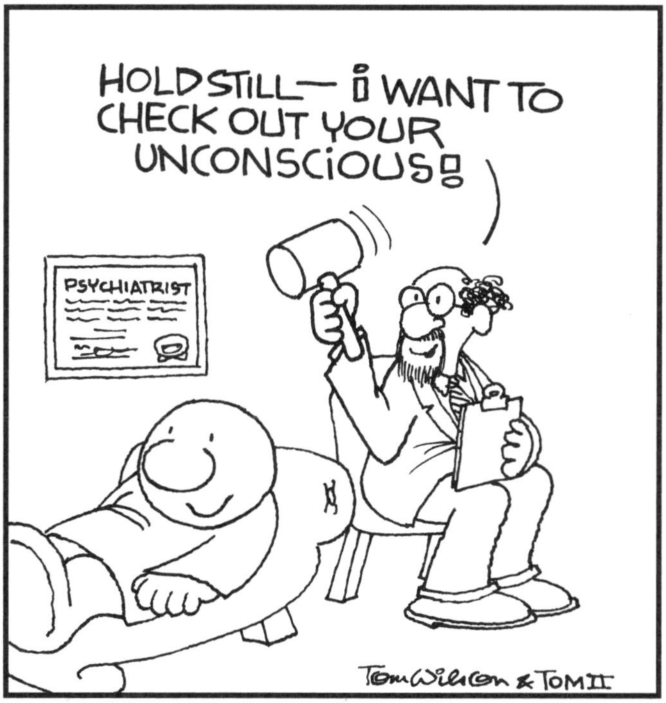
HOLD STILL— I WANT TO CHECK OUT YOUR UNCONSCIOUS!
PSYCHIATRIST
TOM WILSON & TOM II

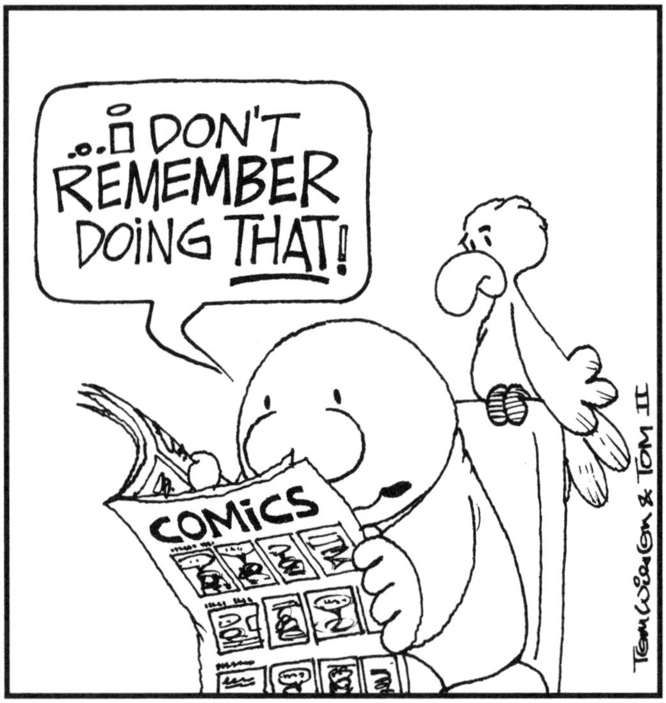
..I DON'T REMEMBER DOING THAT!
COMICS
Tom Wilson & Tom II

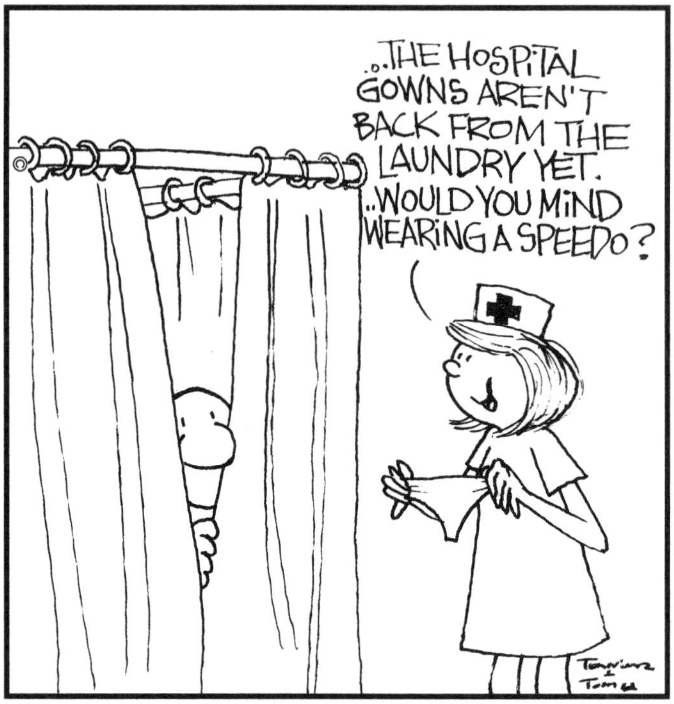
..THE HOSPITAL GOWNS AREN'T BACK FROM THE LAUNDRY YET. ..WOULD YOU MIND WEARING A SPEEDO?

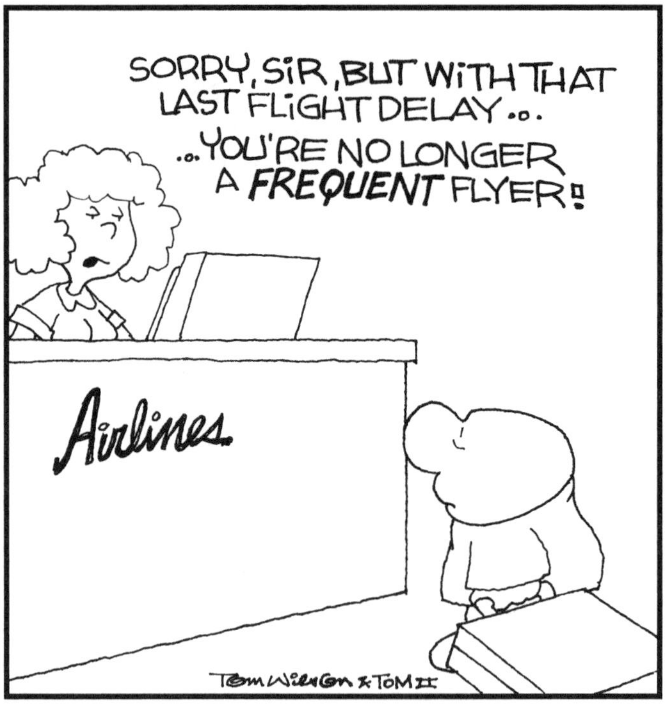
SORRY, SIR, BUT WITH THAT LAST FLIGHT DELAY...
...YOU'RE NO LONGER A FREQUENT FLYER!
Airlines
Tom Wilson & Tom II

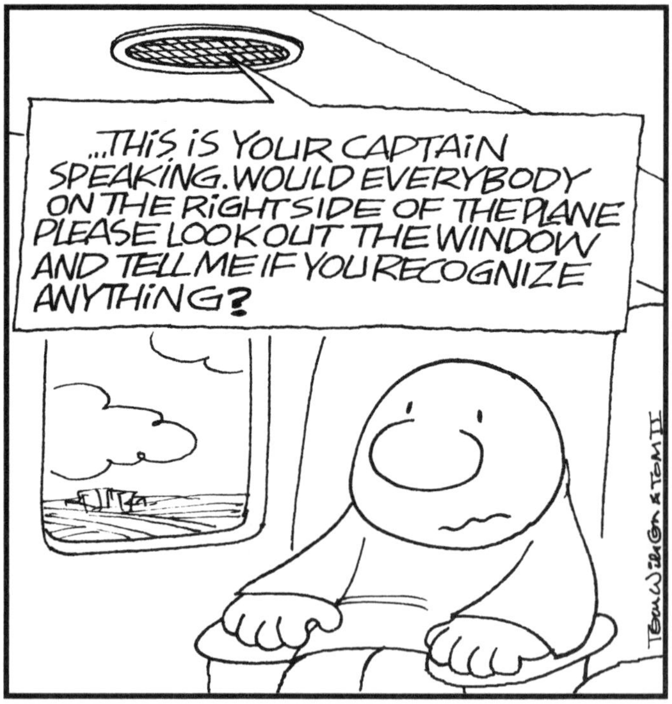
...THIS IS YOUR CAPTAIN SPEAKING. WOULD EVERYBODY ON THE RIGHT SIDE OF THE PLANE PLEASE LOOK OUT THE WINDOW AND TELL ME IF YOU RECOGNIZE ANYTHING?
Tom Wilson & Tom II

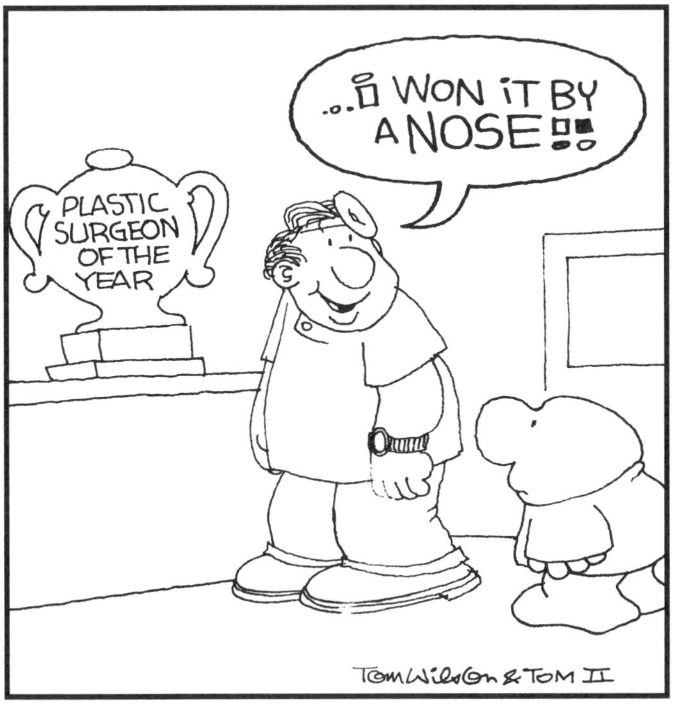
...I WON IT BY A NOSE!!
PLASTIC SURGEON OF THE YEAR
Tom Wilson & TOM II

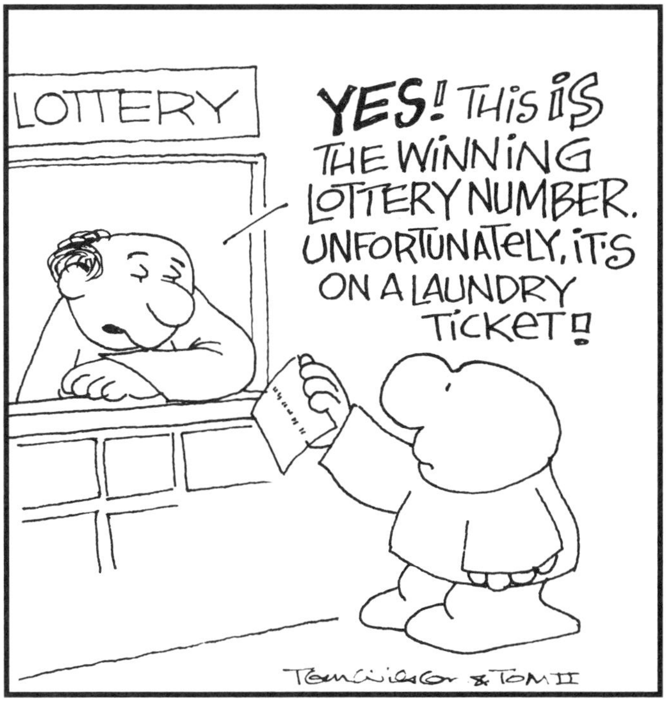
LOTTERY
YES! THIS IS THE WINNING LOTTERY NUMBER. UNFORTUNATELY, IT'S ON A LAUNDRY TICKET!
Tom Wilson & TOM II

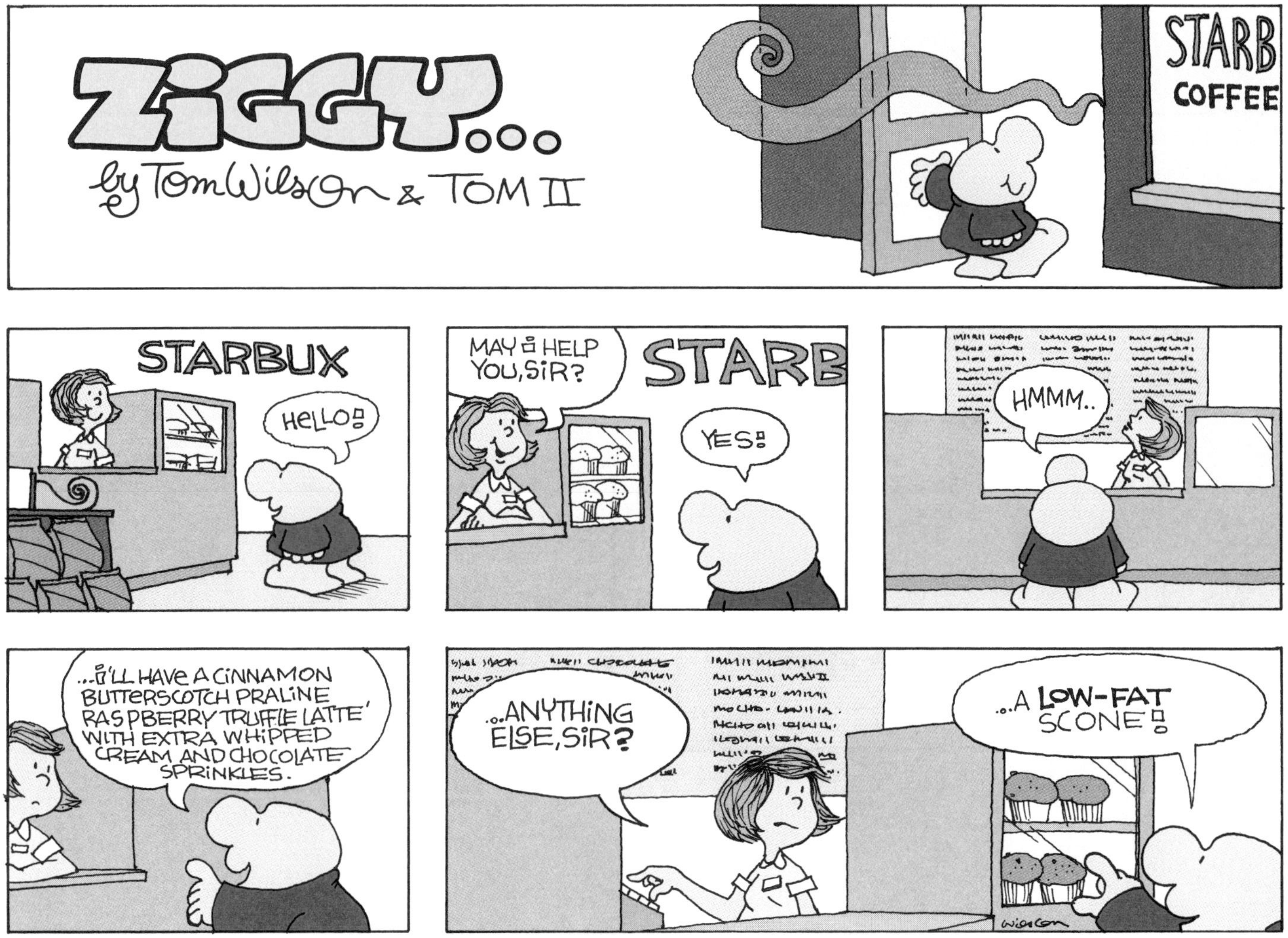
ZIGGY...
by Tom Wilson & TOM II
STARB
COFFEE
STARBUX
HELLO!
MAY I HELP YOU, SIR?
STARB
YES!
HMMM..
...I'LL HAVE A CINNAMON BUTTERSCOTCH PRALINE RASPBERRY TRUFFLE LATTE' WITH EXTRA WHIPPED CREAM AND CHOCOLATE SPRINKLES.
...ANYTHING ELSE, SIR?
...A LOW-FAT SCONE!
Wilson

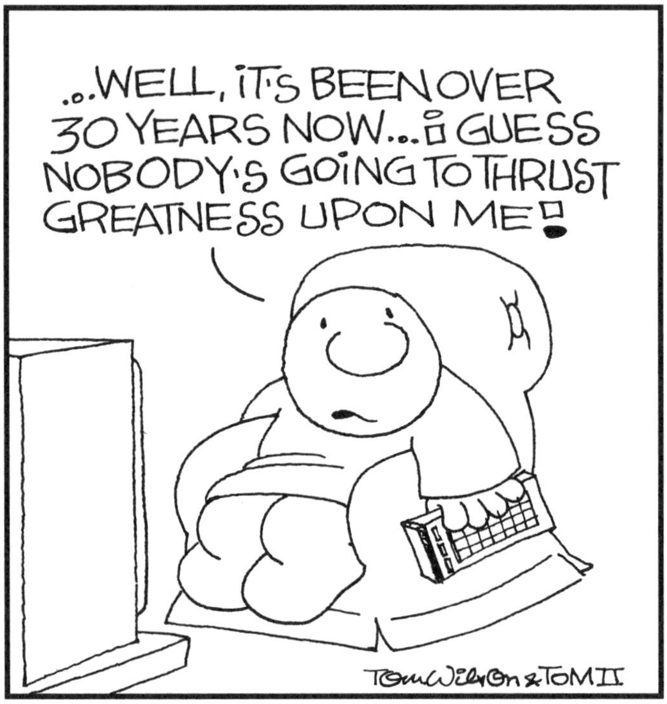
..WELL, iT'S BEEN OVER 30 YEARS NOW...i GUESS NOBODY'S GOING TO THRUST GREATNESS UPON ME!
TOM WILSON & TOM II

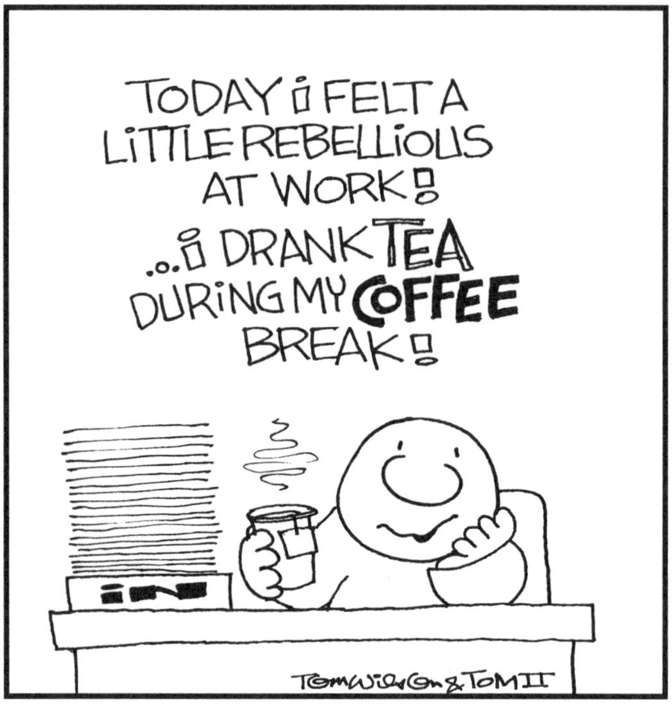
TODAY i FELT A LITTLE REBELLIOUS AT WORK!
..i DRANK TEA DURING MY COFFEE BREAK!
TOM WILSON & TOM II

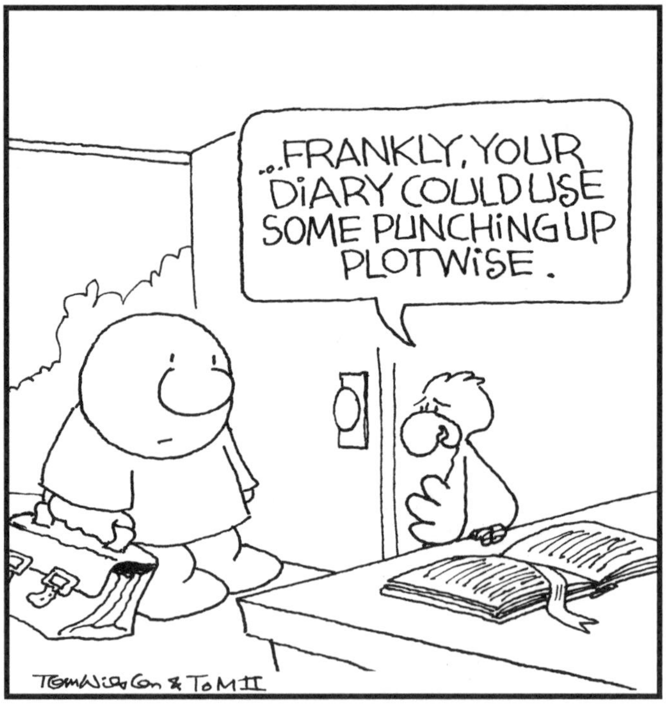
..FRANKLY, YOUR DIARY COULD USE SOME PUNCHING UP PLOTWISE.
TOM WILSON & TOM II

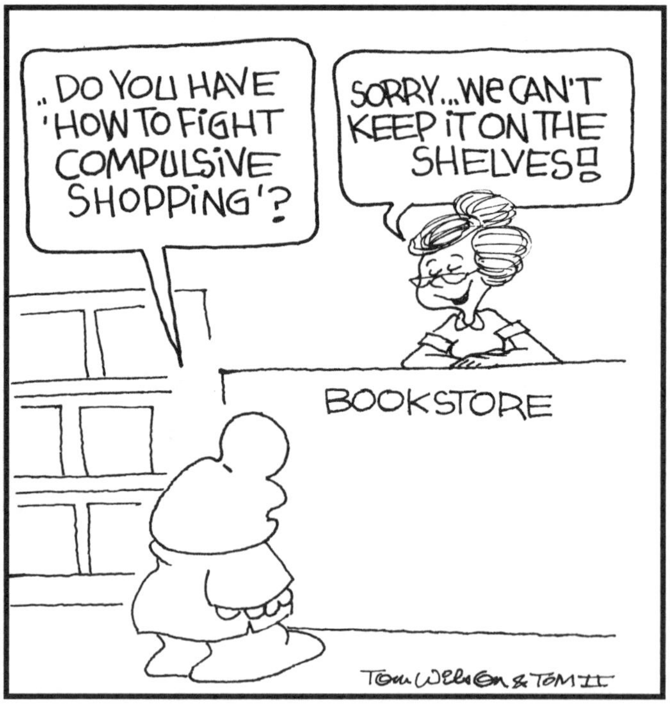
..DO YOU HAVE 'HOW TO FIGHT COMPULSIVE SHOPPING'?
SORRY...WE CAN'T KEEP IT ON THE SHELVES!
BOOKSTORE
TOM WILSON & TOM II

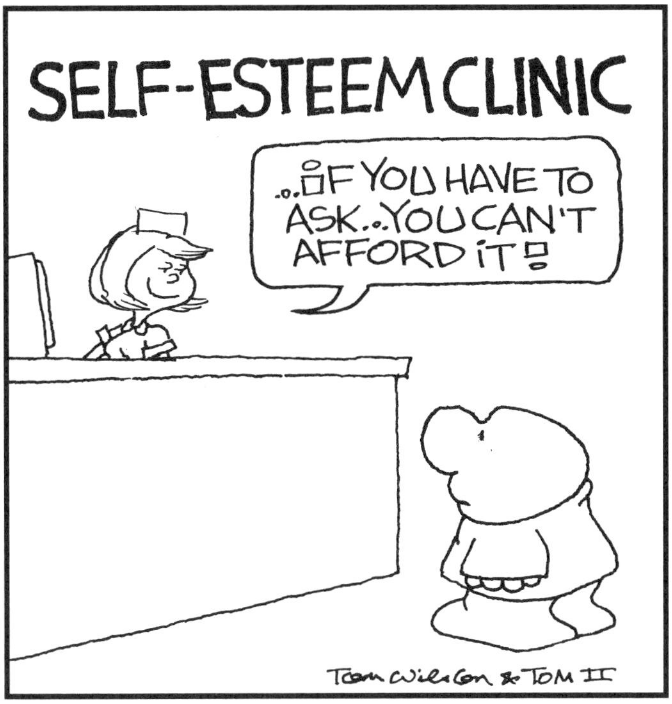
SELF-ESTEEM CLINIC
..o..IF YOU HAVE TO ASK..o..YOU CAN'T AFFORD IT!
TOM WILSON & TOM II

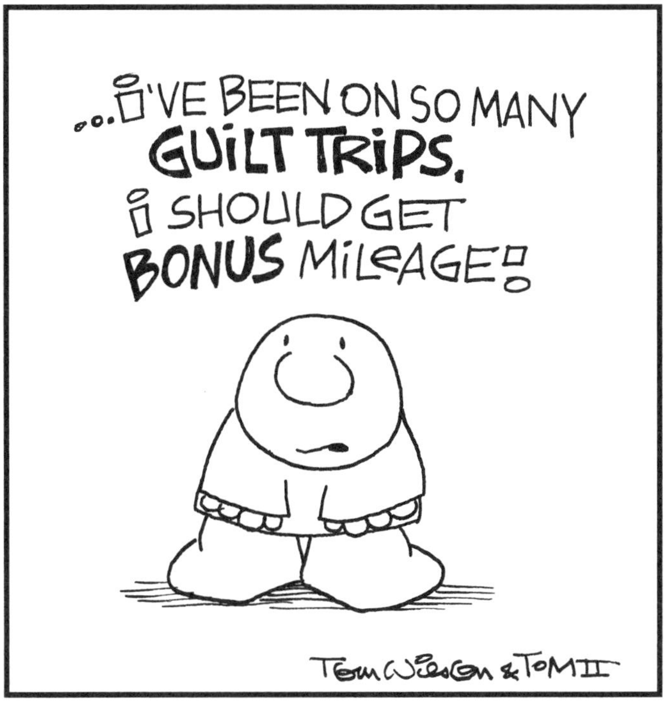
..o..I'VE BEEN ON SO MANY GUILT TRIPS, I SHOULD GET BONUS MILEAGE!
TOM WILSON & TOM II

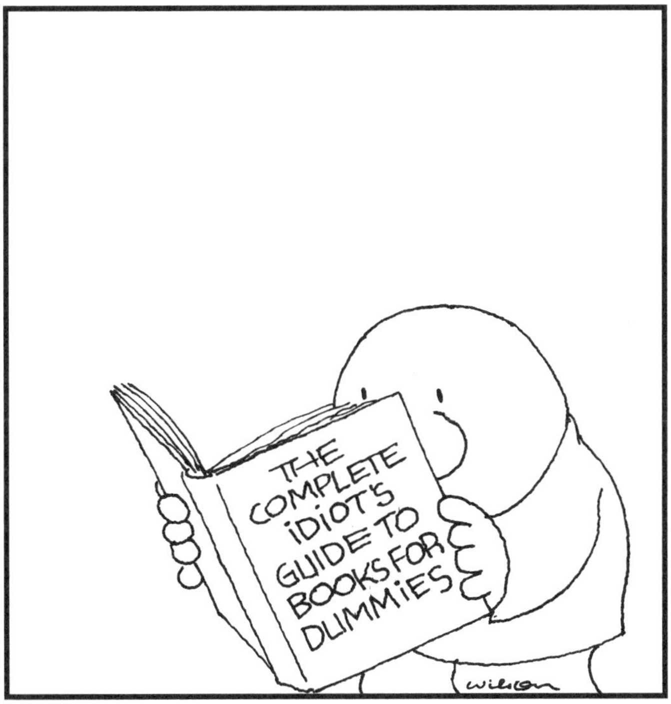
THE COMPLETE IDIOT'S GUIDE TO BOOKS FOR DUMMIES
WILSON

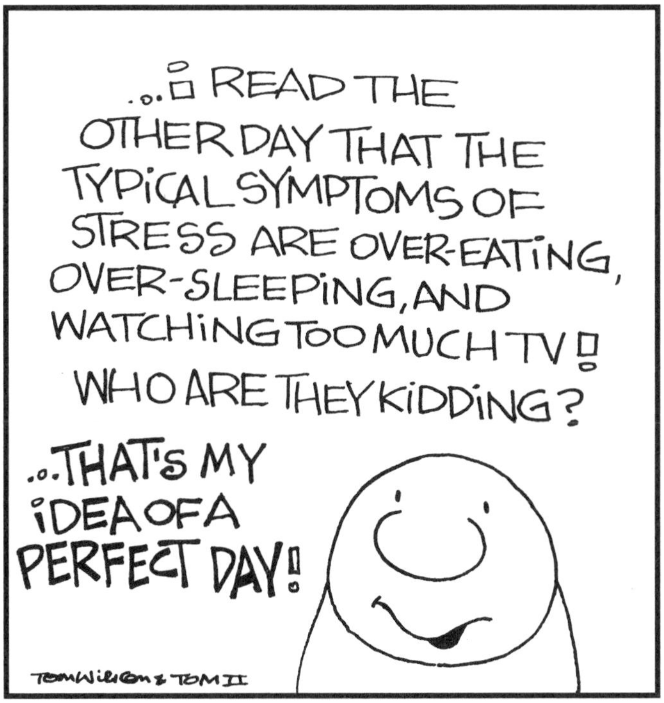
..o..I READ THE OTHER DAY THAT THE TYPICAL SYMPTOMS OF STRESS ARE OVER-EATING, OVER-SLEEPING, AND WATCHING TOO MUCH TV! WHO ARE THEY KIDDING?
..o..THAT'S MY IDEA OF A PERFECT DAY!
TOM WILSON & TOM II

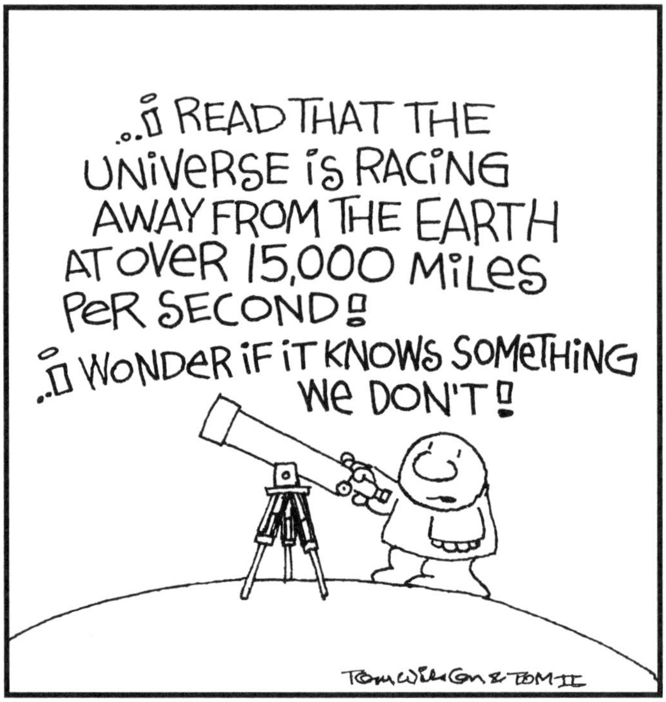
..I READ THAT THE UNIVERSE IS RACING AWAY FROM THE EARTH AT OVER 15,000 MILES PER SECOND!
..I WONDER IF IT KNOWS SOMETHING WE DON'T!

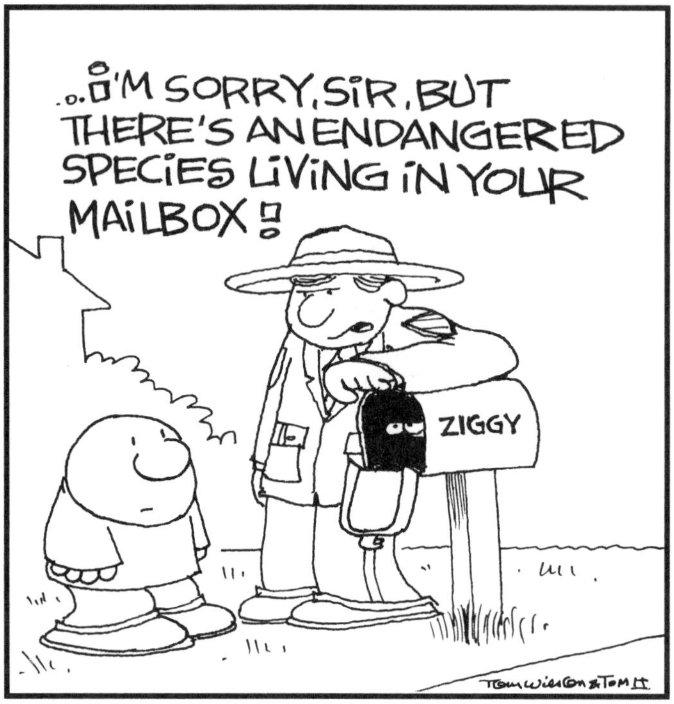
..I'M SORRY, SIR, BUT THERE'S AN ENDANGERED SPECIES LIVING IN YOUR MAILBOX!
ZIGGY

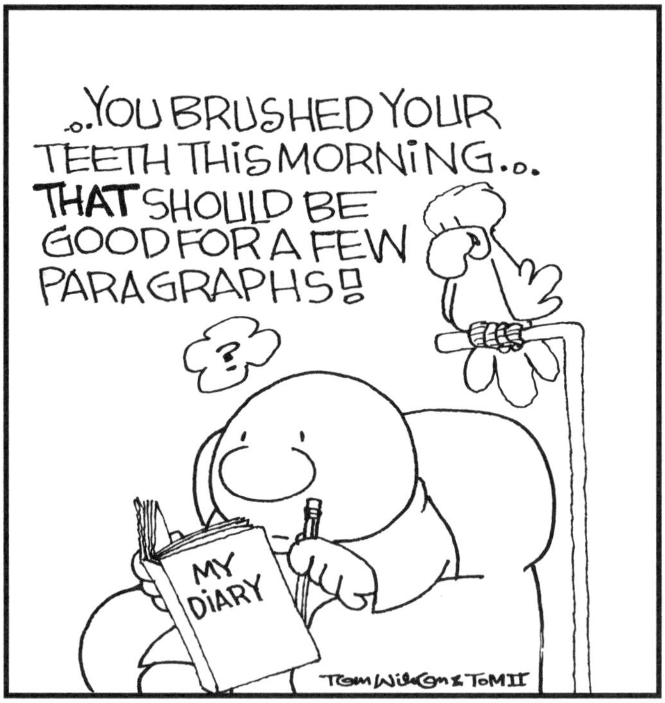
..YOU BRUSHED YOUR TEETH THIS MORNING.. THAT SHOULD BE GOOD FOR A FEW PARAGRAPHS!
?
MY DIARY

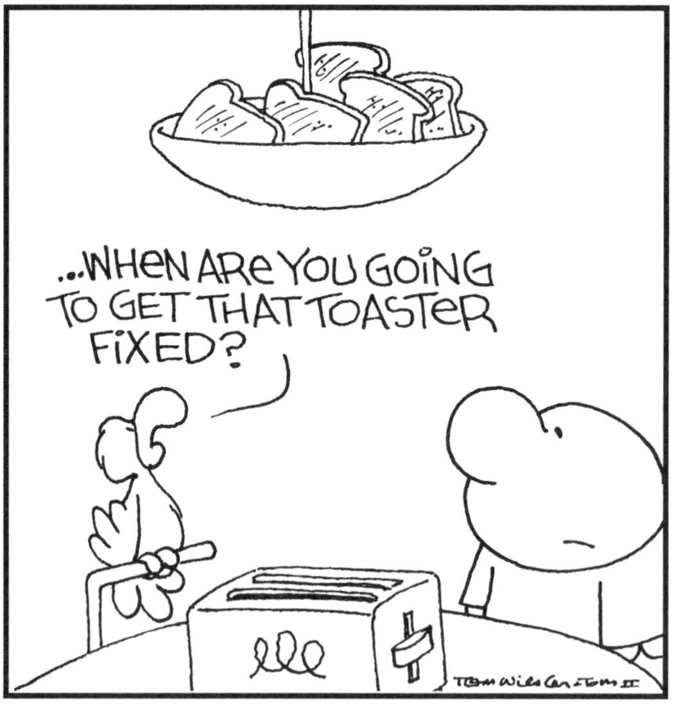
...WHEN ARE YOU GOING TO GET THAT TOASTER FIXED?

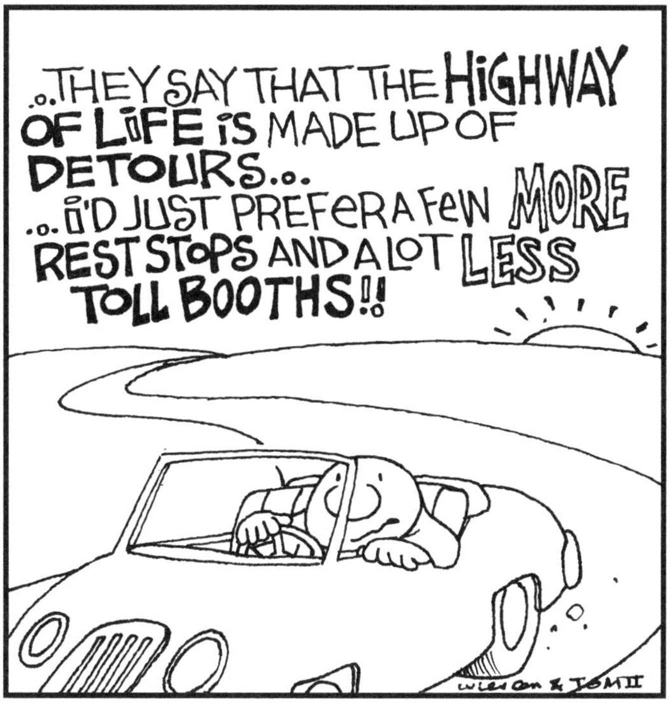
..THEY SAY THAT THE HIGHWAY OF LIFE IS MADE UP OF DETOURS...
..I'D JUST PREFER A FEW MORE REST STOPS AND A LOT LESS TOLL BOOTHS!!

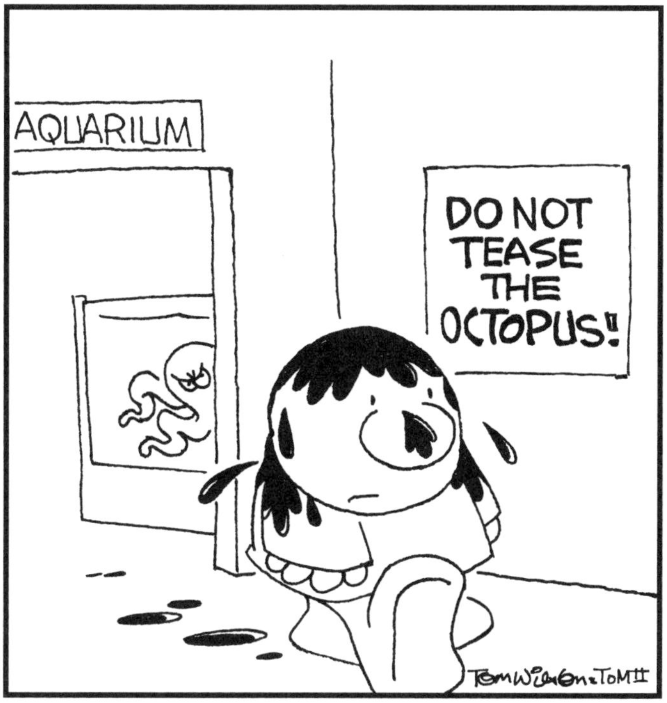
AQUARIUM
DO NOT TEASE THE OCTOPUS!

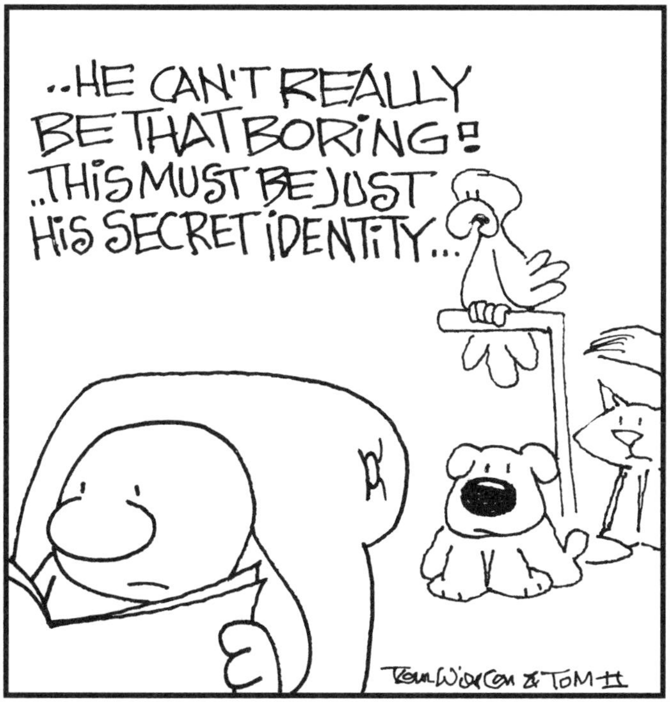
..HE CAN'T REALLY BE THAT BORING!
..THIS MUST BE JUST HIS SECRET IDENTITY...

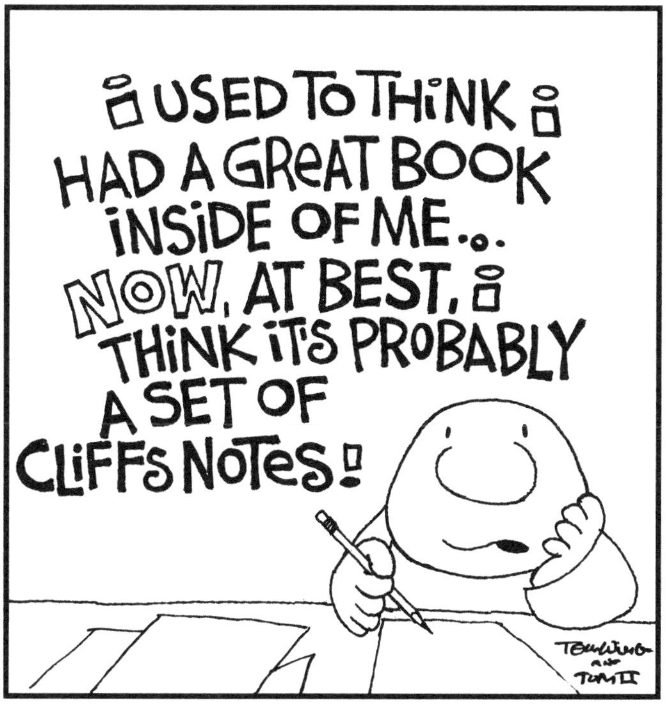
I USED TO THINK I HAD A GREAT BOOK INSIDE OF ME...
NOW, AT BEST, I THINK IT'S PROBABLY A SET OF CLIFFS NOTES!

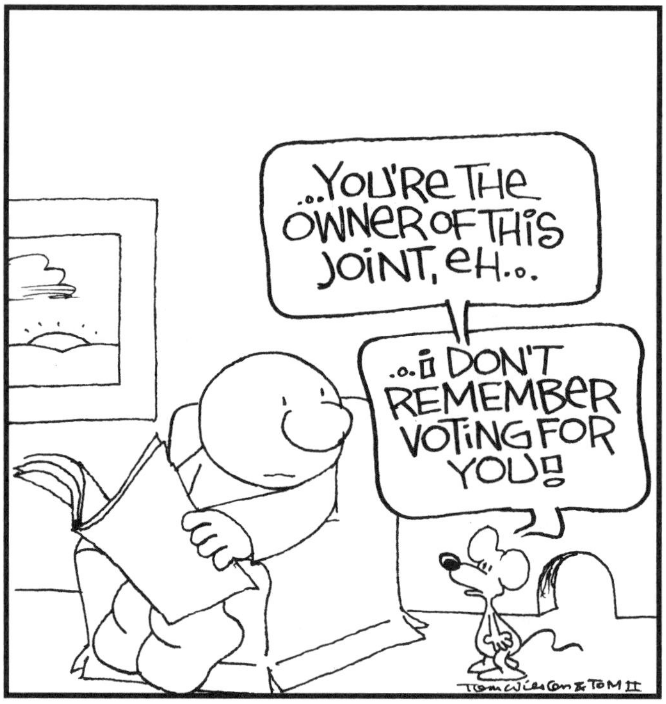
...YOU'RE THE OWNER OF THIS JOINT, EH...
...I DON'T REMEMBER VOTING FOR YOU!
TOM WILSON & TOM II

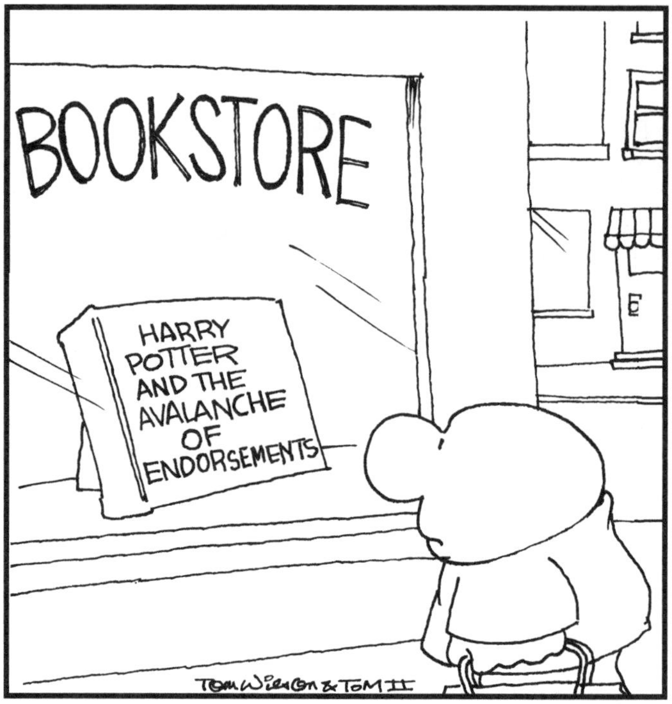
BOOKSTORE
HARRY POTTER AND THE AVALANCHE OF ENDORSEMENTS
TOM WILSON & TOM II

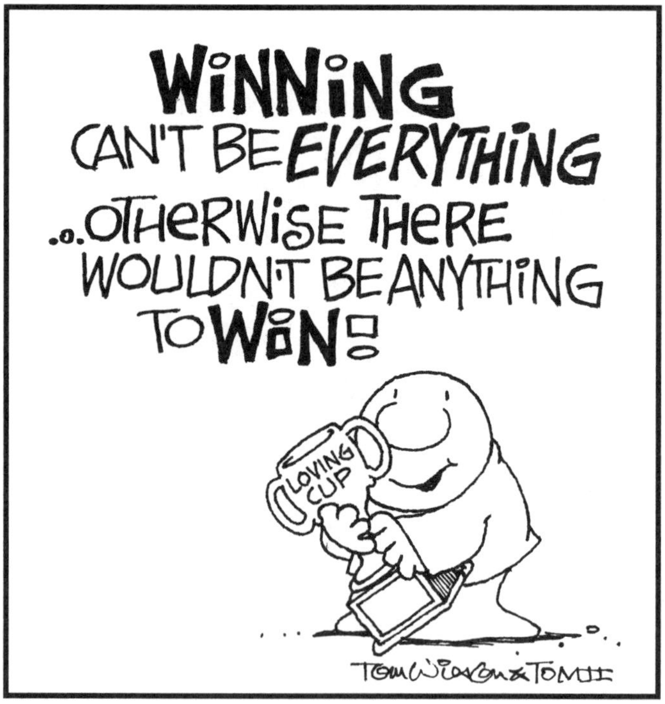
WINNING CAN'T BE EVERYTHING ...OTHERWISE THERE WOULDN'T BE ANYTHING TO WIN!
LOVING CUP
TOM WILSON & TOM II

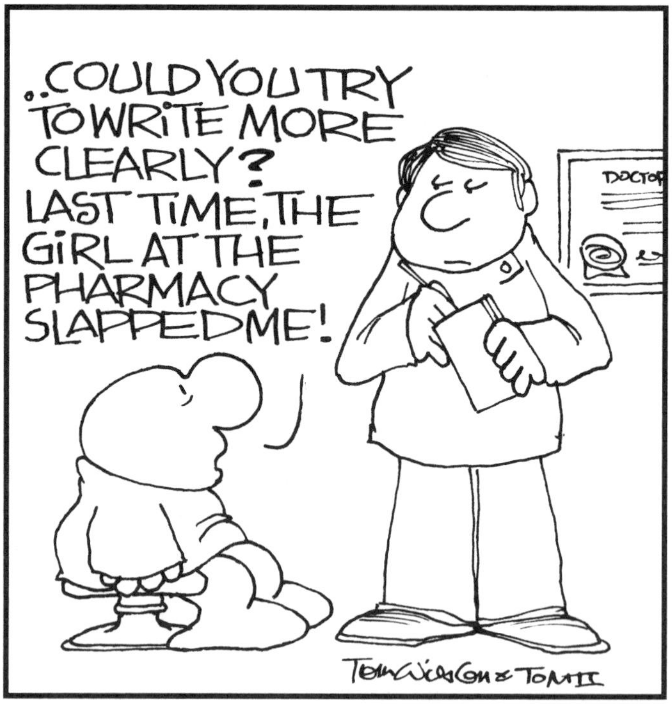
..COULD YOU TRY TO WRITE MORE CLEARLY? LAST TIME, THE GIRL AT THE PHARMACY SLAPPED ME!
DOCTOR
TOM WILSON & TOM II

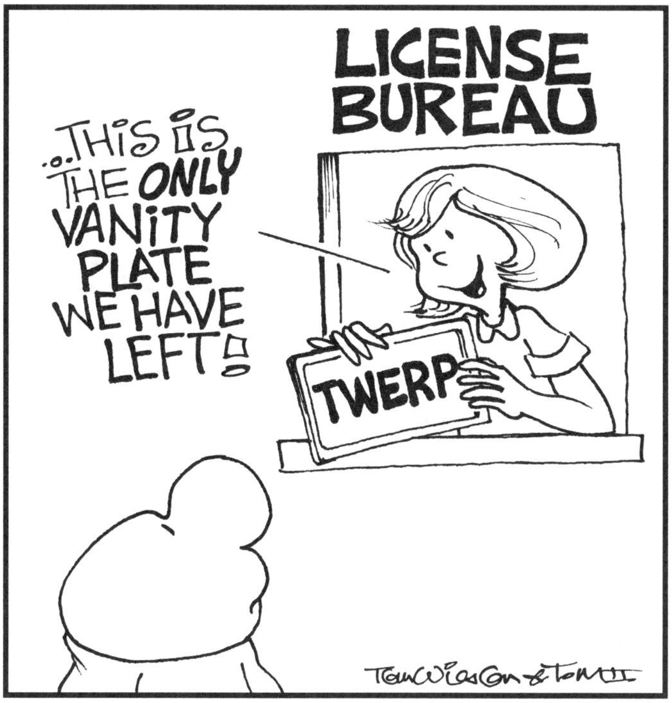
LICENSE BUREAU
..THIS IS THE ONLY VANITY PLATE WE HAVE LEFT!
TWERP

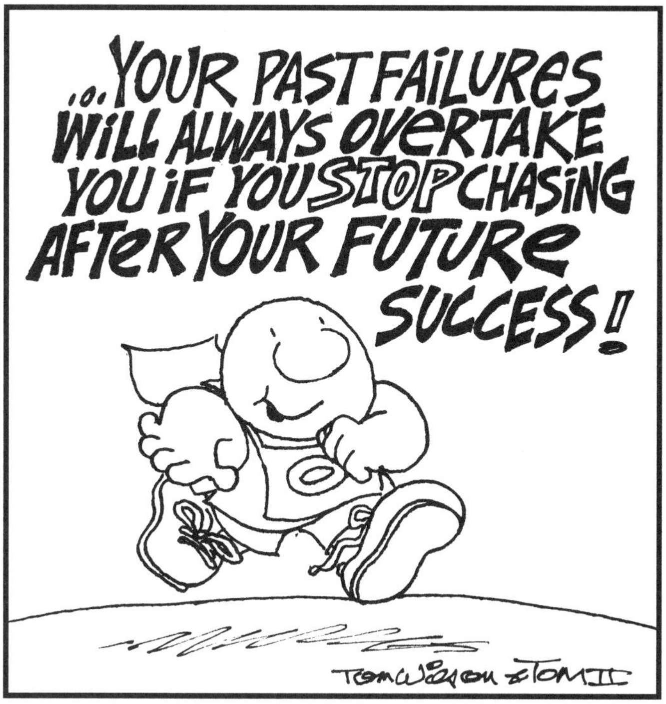
..YOUR PAST FAILURES WILL ALWAYS OVERTAKE YOU IF YOU STOP CHASING AFTER YOUR FUTURE SUCCESS!

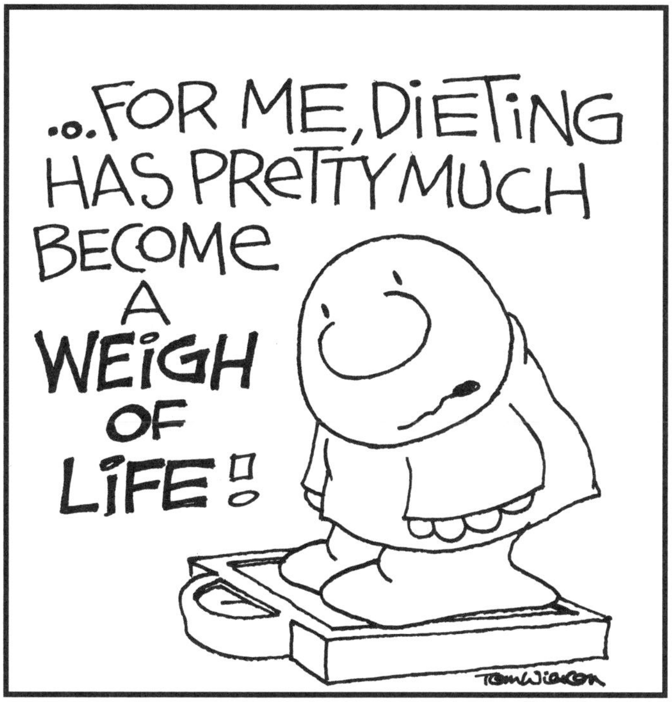
..FOR ME, DIETING HAS PRETTY MUCH BECOME A WEIGH OF LIFE!

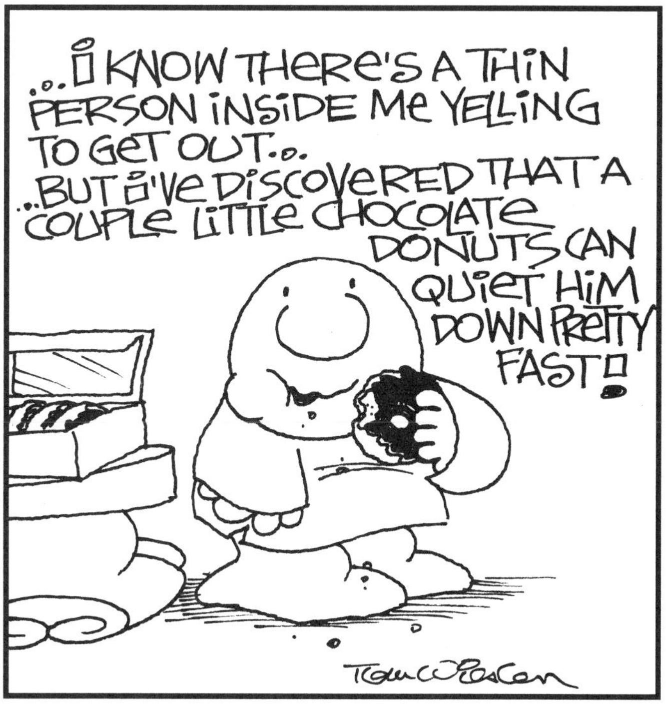
..I KNOW THERE'S A THIN PERSON INSIDE ME YELLING TO GET OUT..
..BUT I'VE DISCOVERED THAT A COUPLE LITTLE CHOCOLATE DONUTS CAN QUIET HIM DOWN PRETTY FAST!

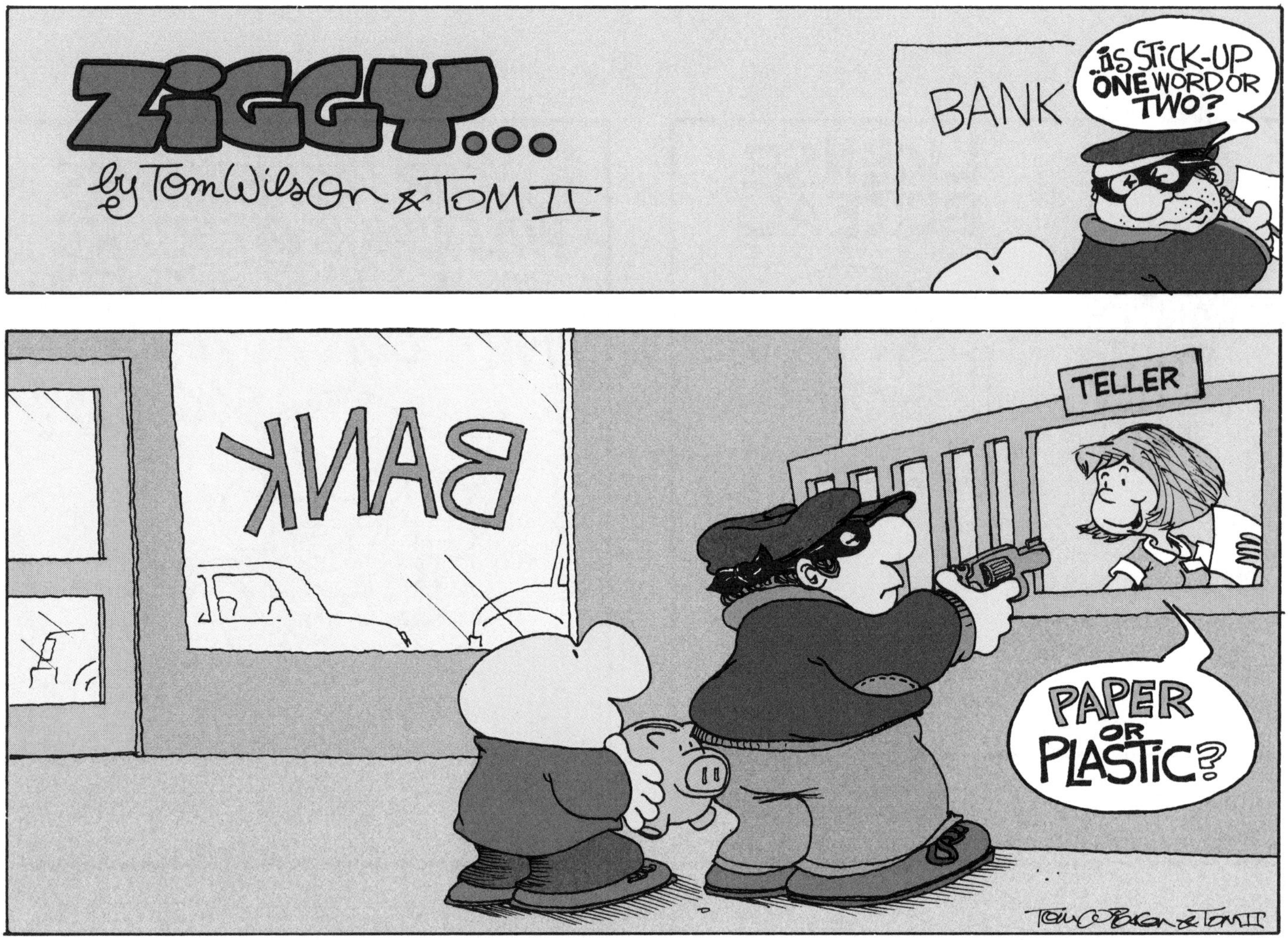
ZIGGY...
by Tom Wilson & Tom II
BANK
..IS STICK-UP ONE WORD OR TWO?
BANK
TELLER
PAPER OR PLASTIC?

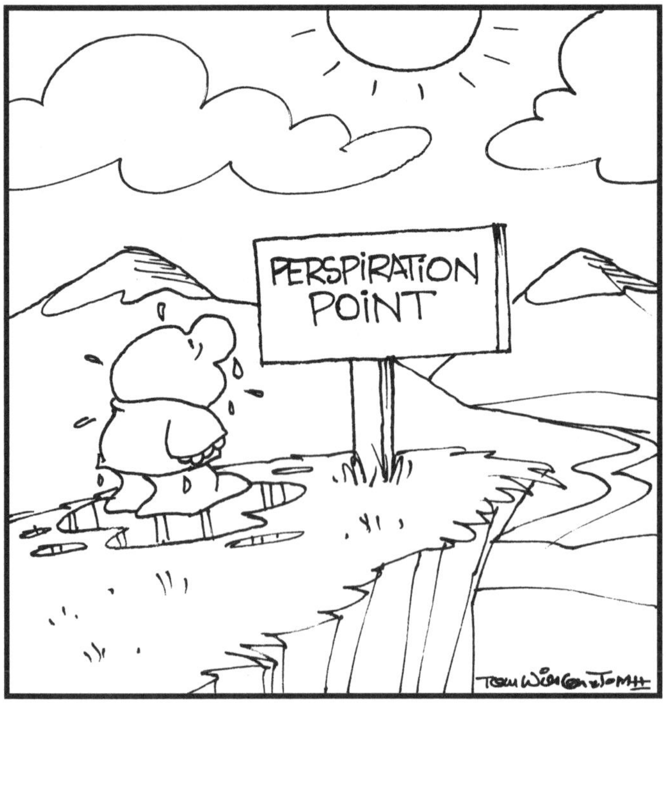
PERSPIRATION POINT

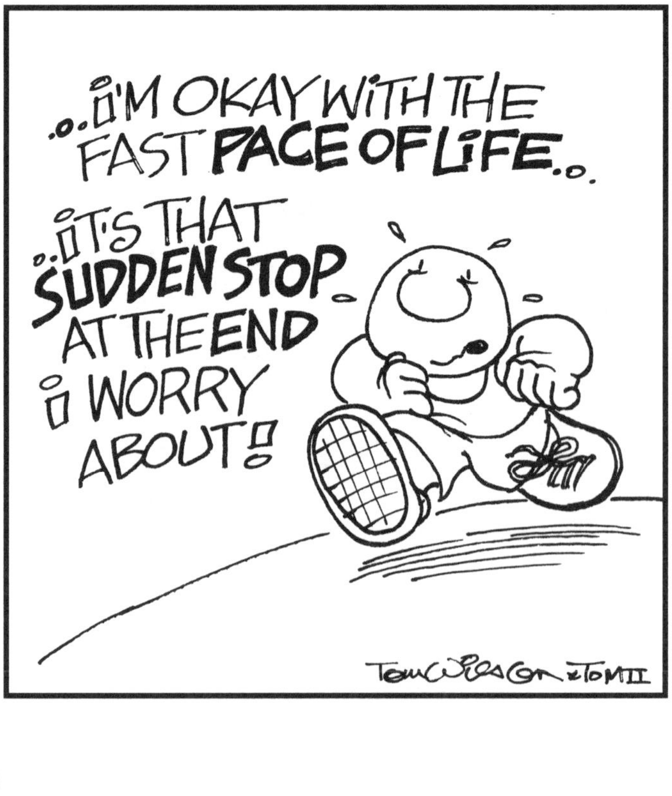
..o..I'M OKAY WITH THE FAST PACE OF LIFE..o.
..IT'S THAT SUDDEN STOP AT THE END I WORRY ABOUT!!

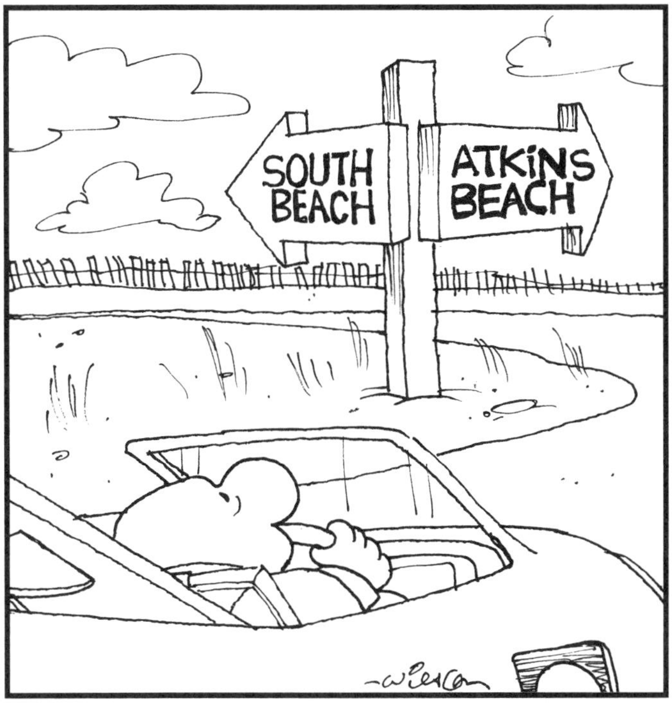
SOUTH BEACH
ATKINS BEACH

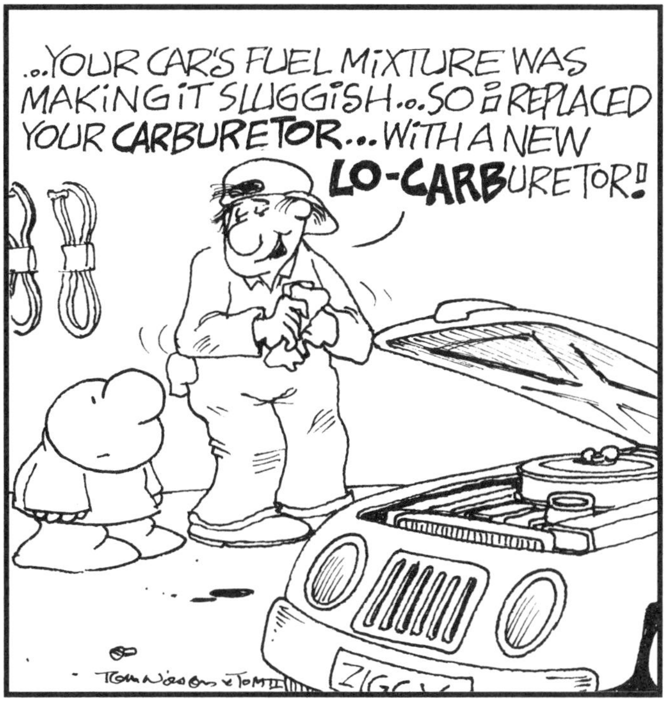
...YOUR CAR'S FUEL MIXTURE WAS MAKING IT SLUGGISH...SO I REPLACED YOUR CARBURETOR...WITH A NEW LO-CARBURETOR!

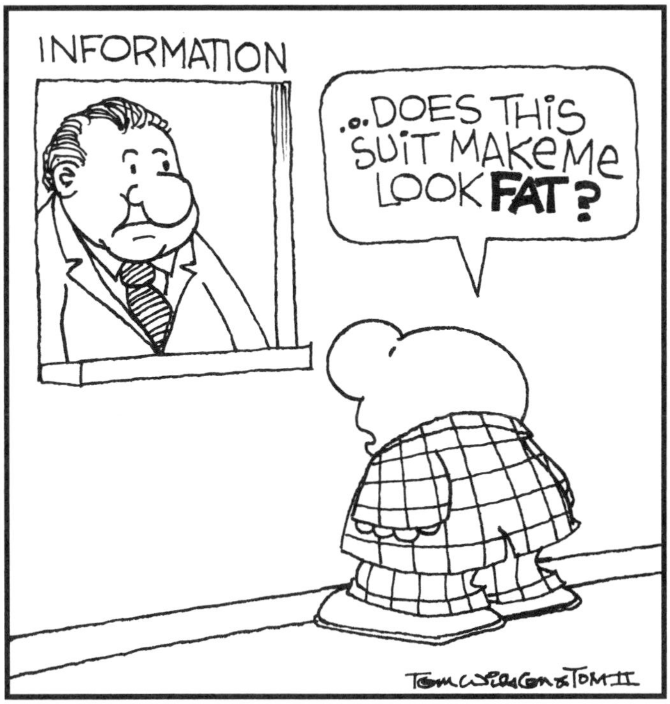
INFORMATION
...DOES THIS SUIT MAKE ME LOOK FAT?

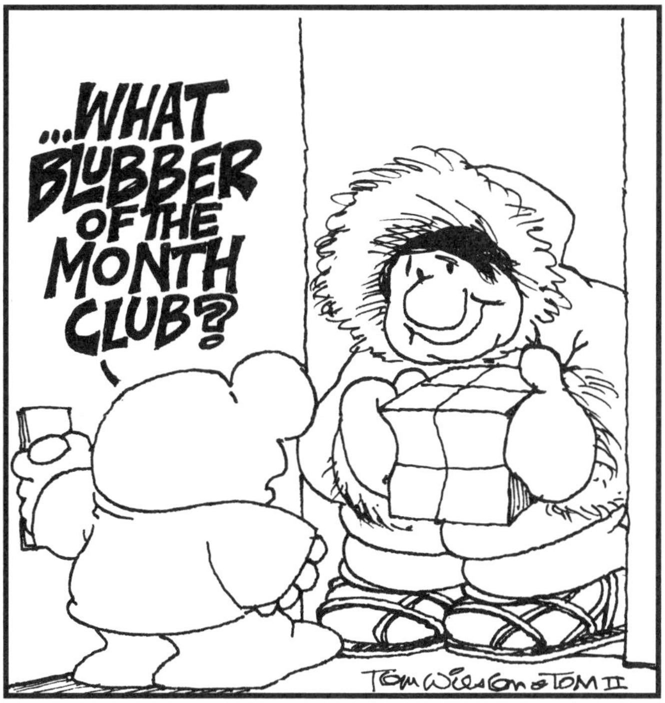
...WHAT BLUBBER OF THE MONTH CLUB?

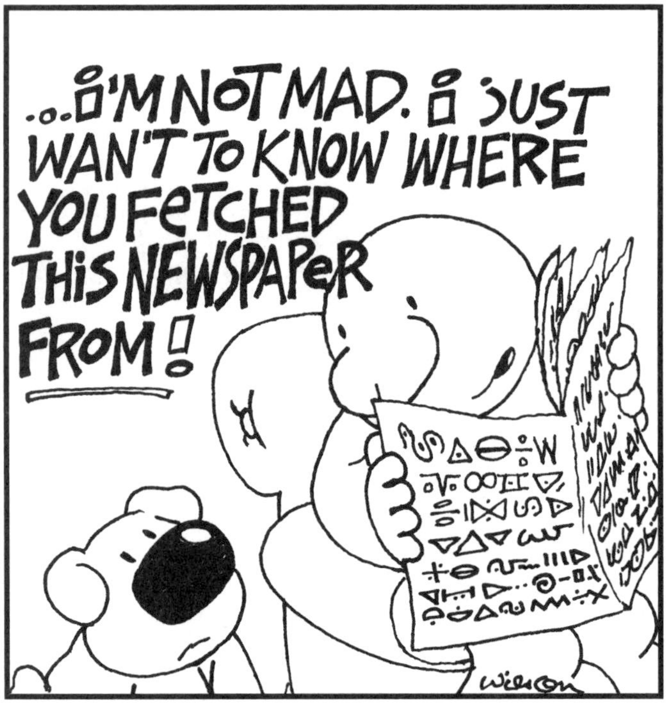
...I'M NOT MAD. I JUST WAN'T TO KNOW WHERE YOU FETCHED THIS NEWSPAPER FROM!
Wilson

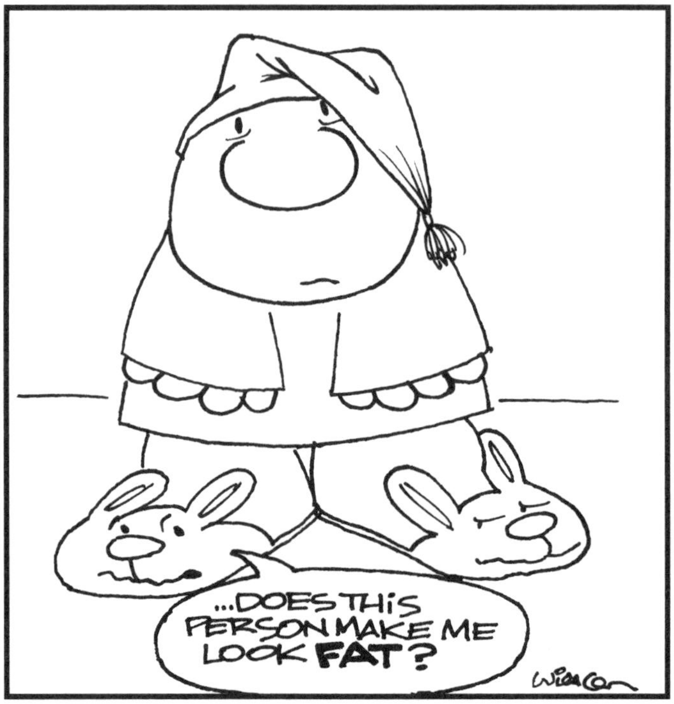
...DOES THIS PERSON MAKE ME LOOK FAT?
Wilson

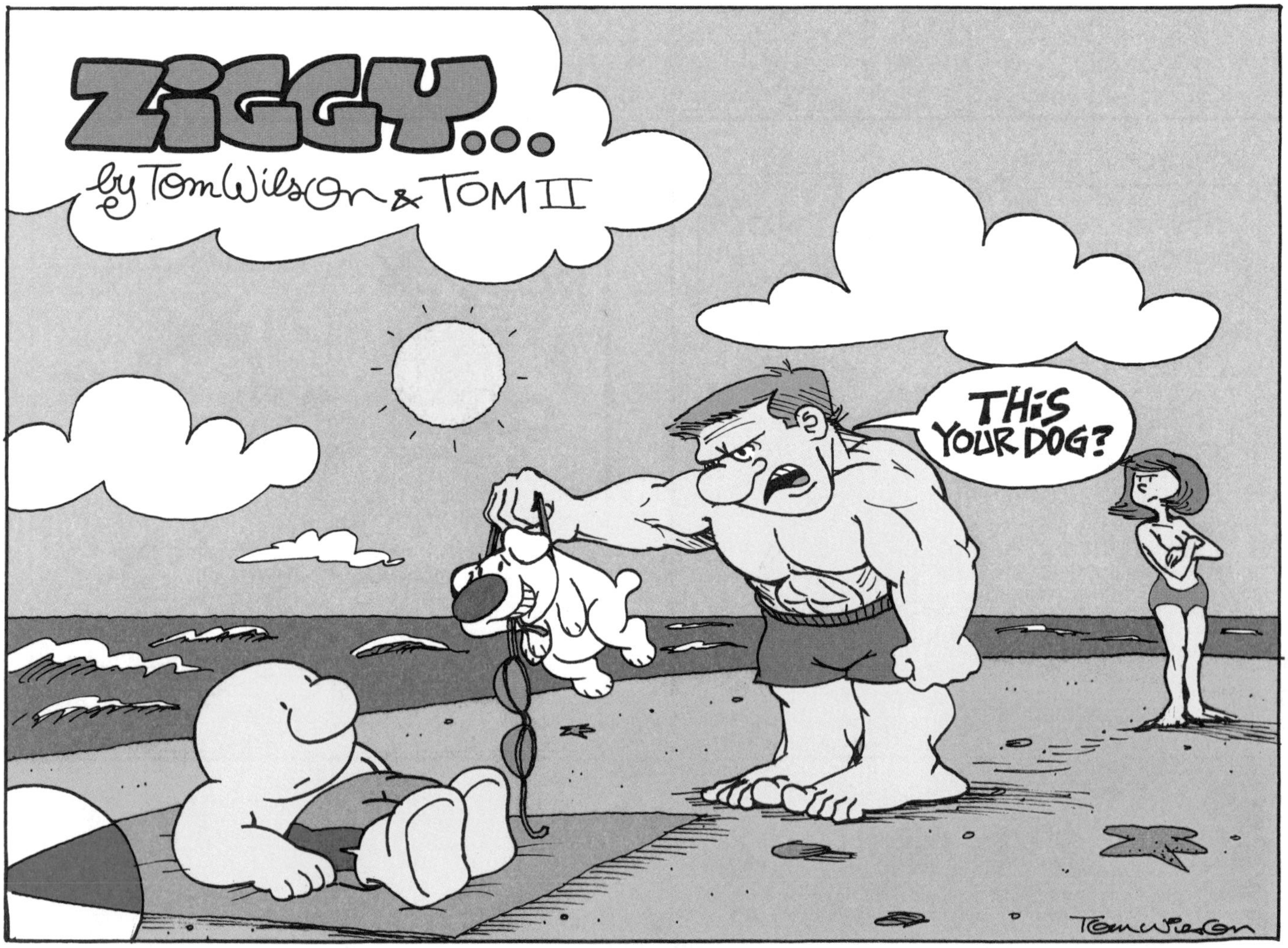
ZIGGY...
by Tom Wilson & TOM II
THIS YOUR DOG?
Tom Wilson

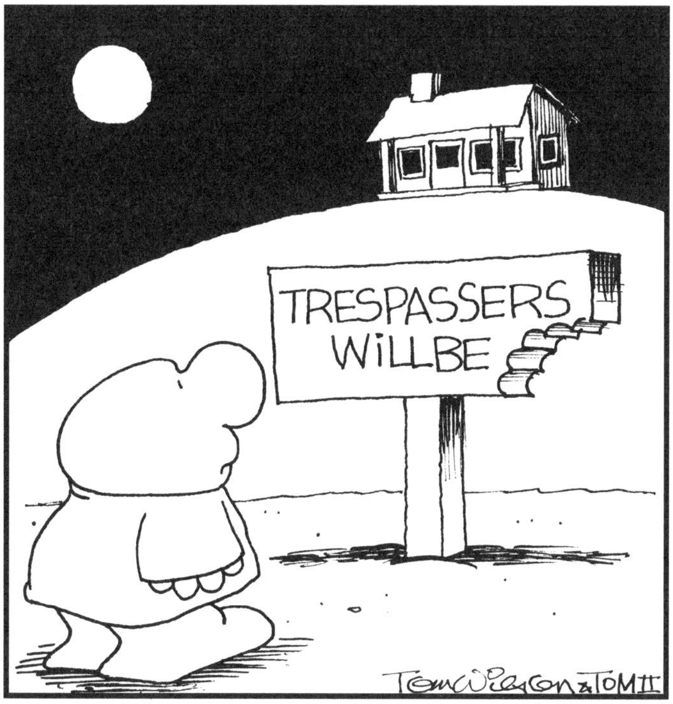
TRESPASSERS WILLBE
TOM WILSON & TOM II

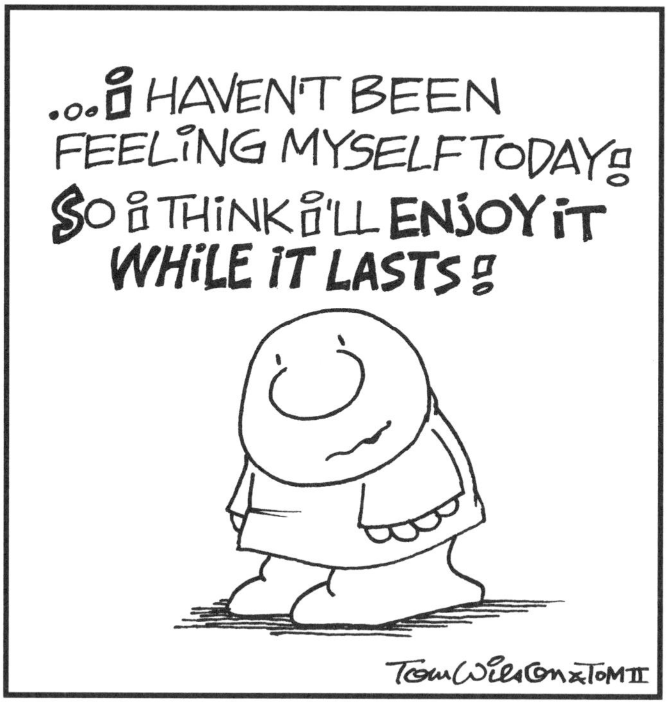
...I HAVEN'T BEEN FEELING MYSELF TODAY! SO I THINK I'LL ENJOY IT WHILE IT LASTS!
TOM WILSON & TOM II

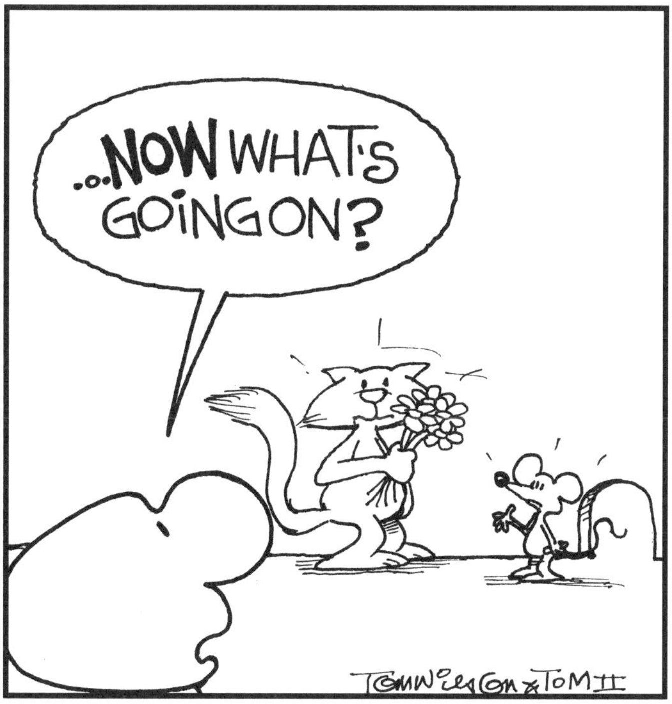
...NOW WHAT'S GOING ON?
TOM WILSON & TOM II

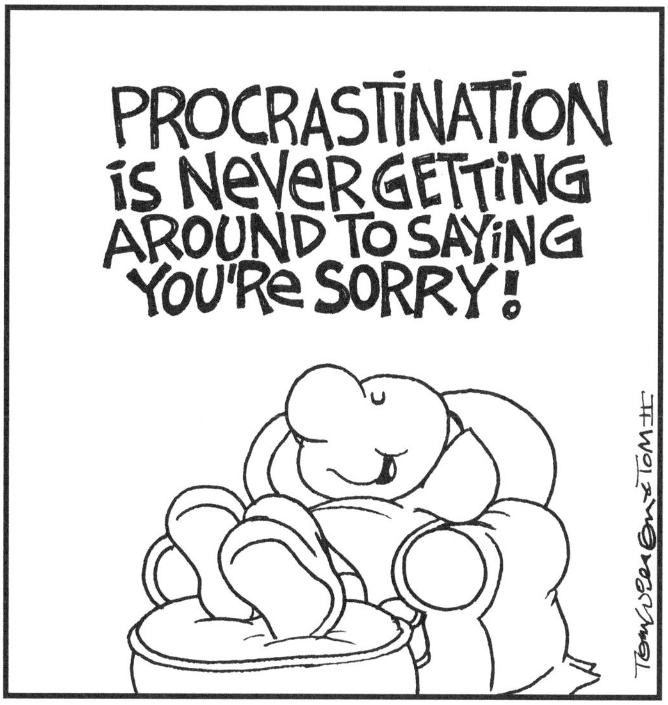
PROCRASTINATION IS NEVER GETTING AROUND TO SAYING YOU'RE SORRY!
TOM WILSON & TOM II

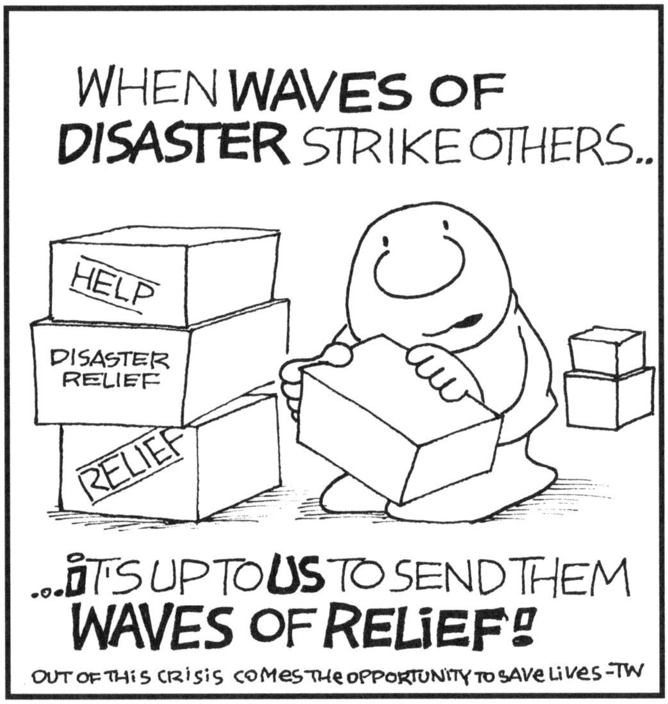
WHEN WAVES OF DISASTER STRIKE OTHERS..
HELP
DISASTER RELIEF
RELIEF
..o..IT'S UP TO US TO SEND THEM WAVES OF RELIEF!
OUT OF THIS CRISIS COMES THE OPPORTUNITY TO SAVE LIVES -TW

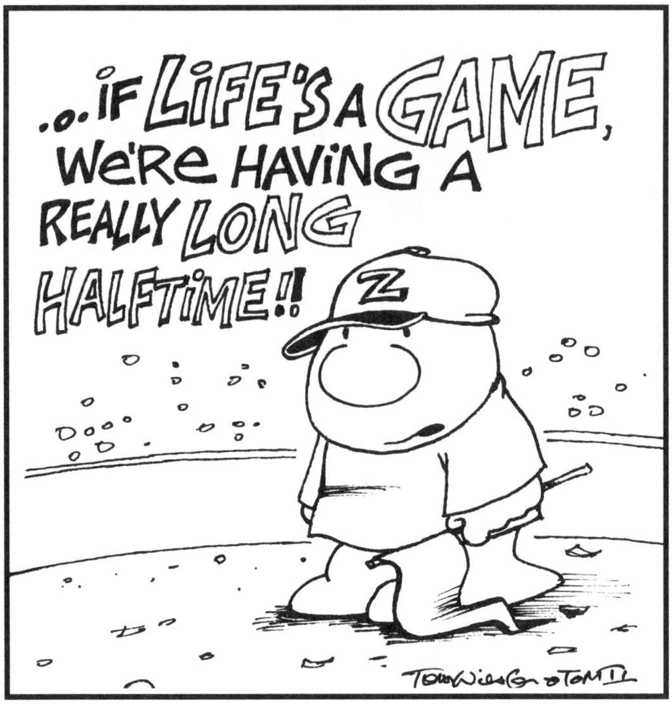
..o.. IF LIFE'S A GAME, WE'RE HAVING A REALLY LONG HALFTIME!!
Z

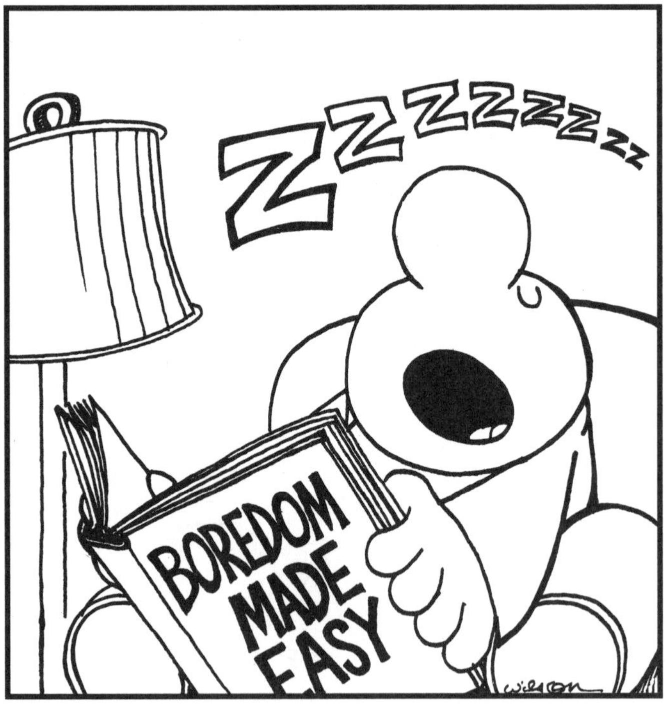
ZZZZZZZzz
BOREDOM MADE EASY

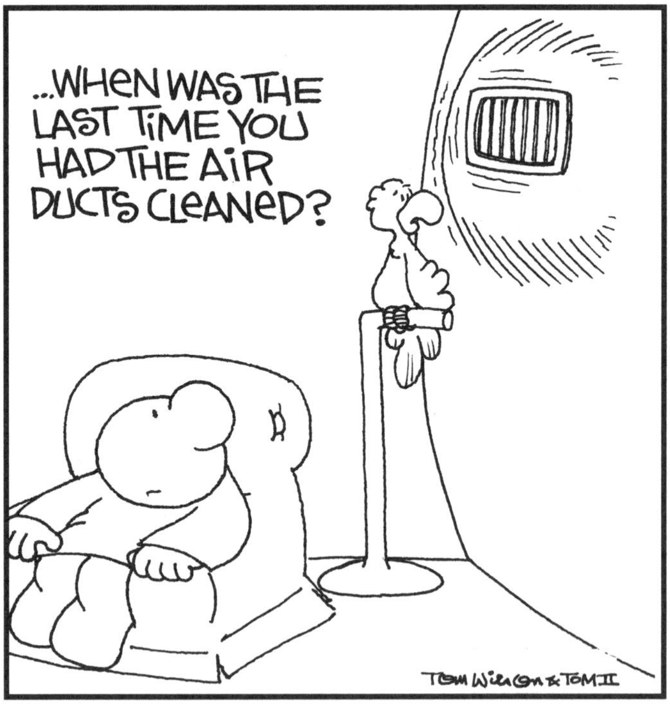
...WHEN WAS THE LAST TIME YOU HAD THE AIR DUCTS CLEANED?

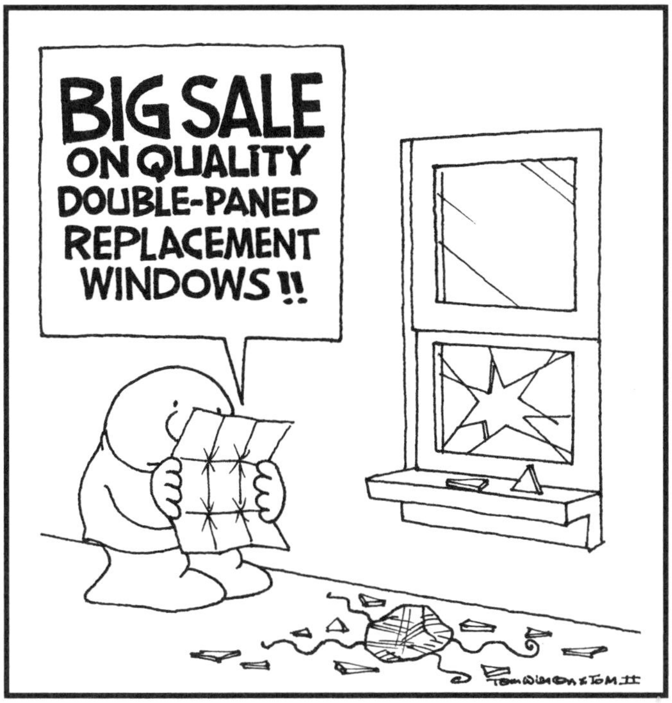
BIG SALE ON QUALITY DOUBLE-PANED REPLACEMENT WINDOWS!!

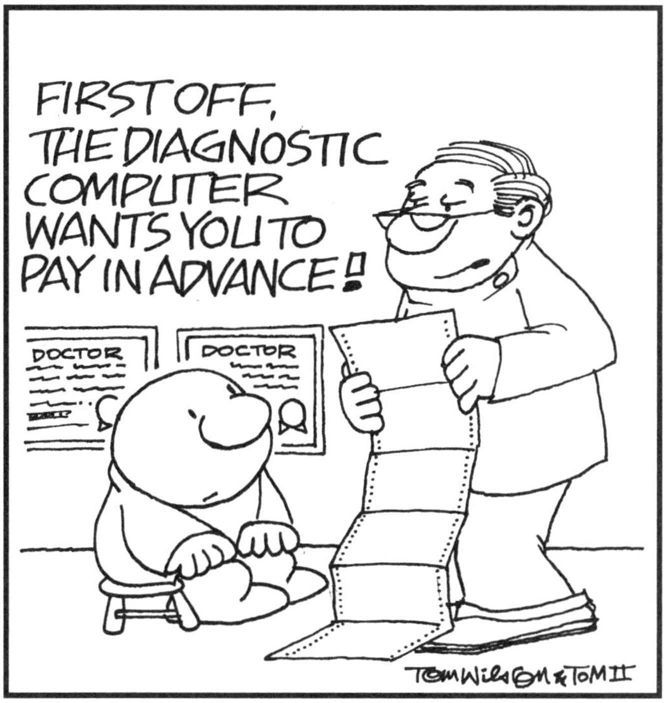
FIRST OFF, THE DIAGNOSTIC COMPUTER WANTS YOU TO PAY IN ADVANCE!!
DOCTOR
DOCTOR

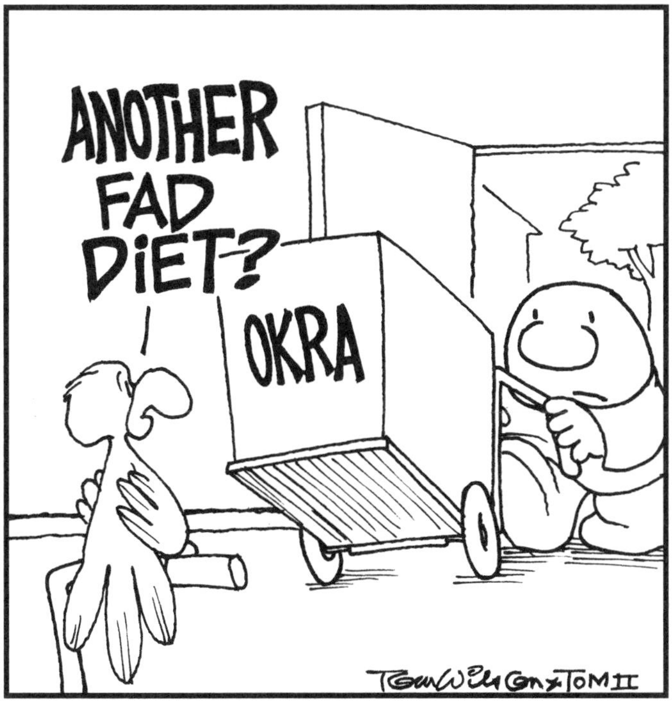
ANOTHER FAD DIET?
OKRA

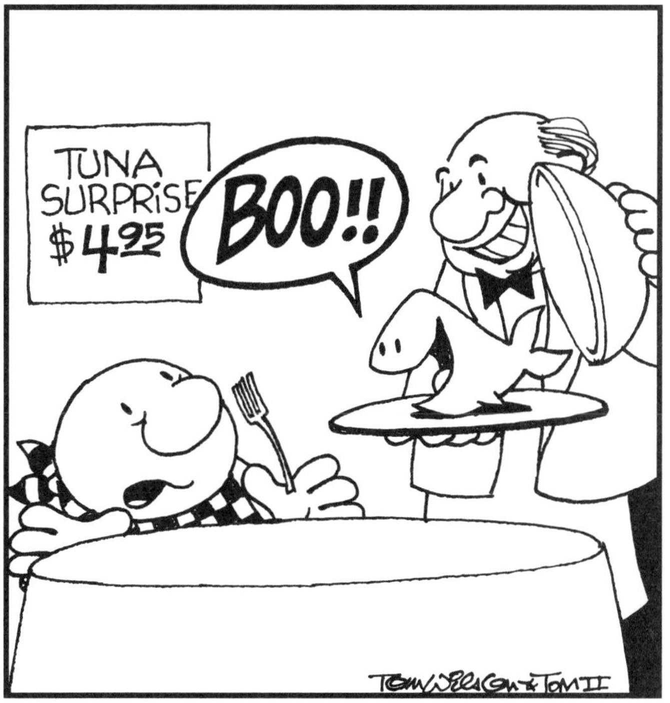
TUNA SURPRISE $4.95
BOO!!

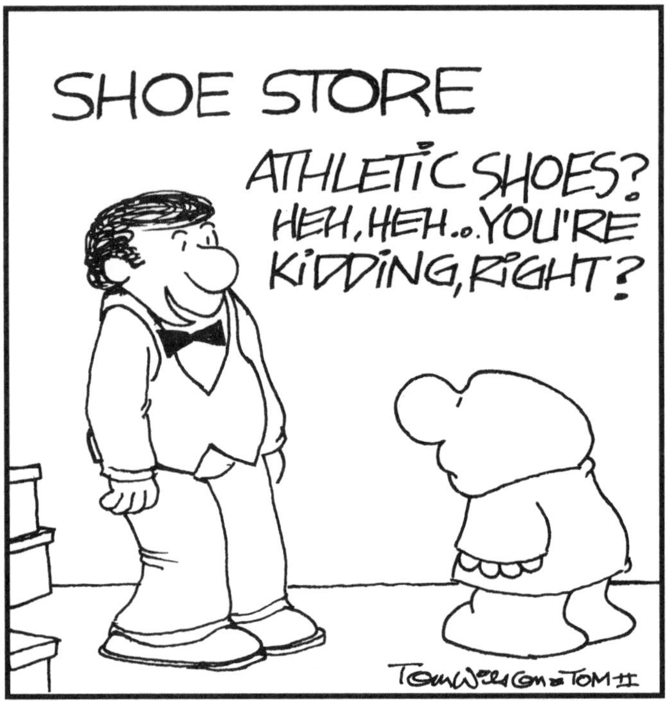
SHOE STORE
ATHLETIC SHOES? HEH, HEH... YOU'RE KIDDING, RIGHT?

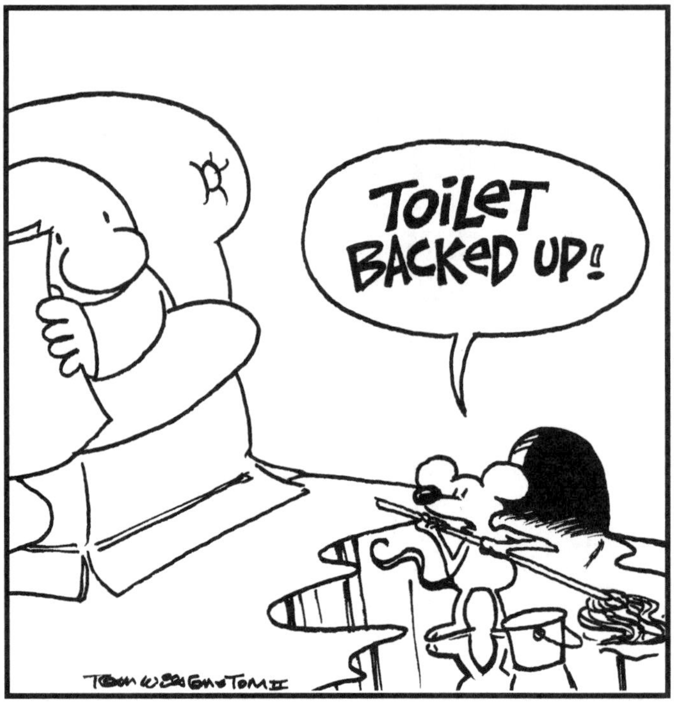
TOILET BACKED UP!

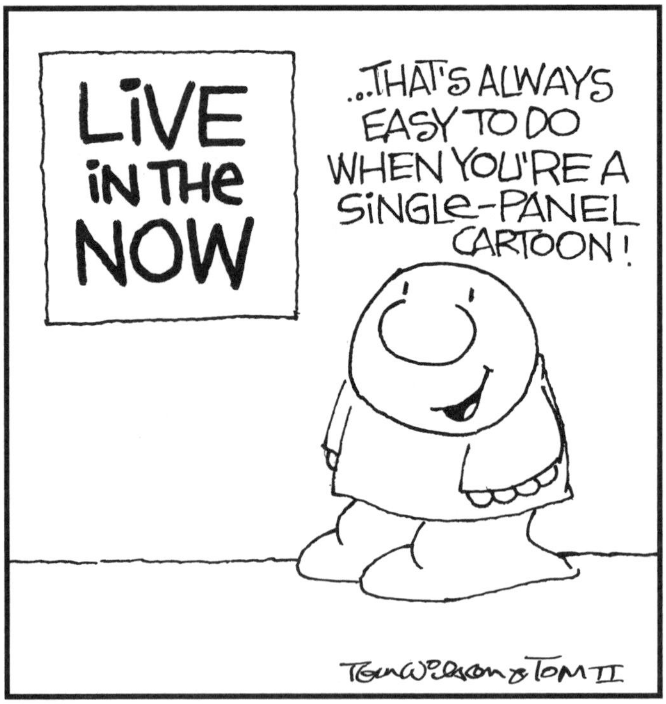
LIVE IN THE NOW
...THAT'S ALWAYS EASY TO DO WHEN YOU'RE A SINGLE-PANEL CARTOON!

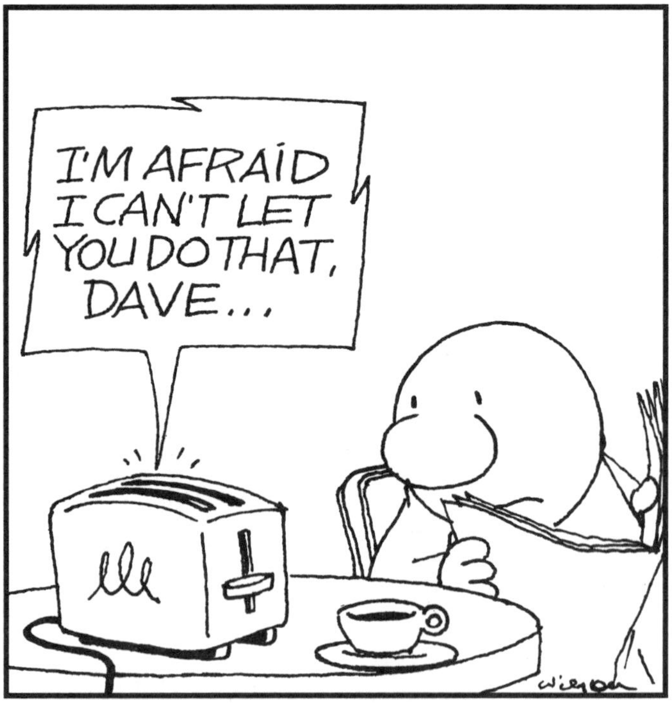
I'M AFRAID I CAN'T LET YOU DO THAT, DAVE...

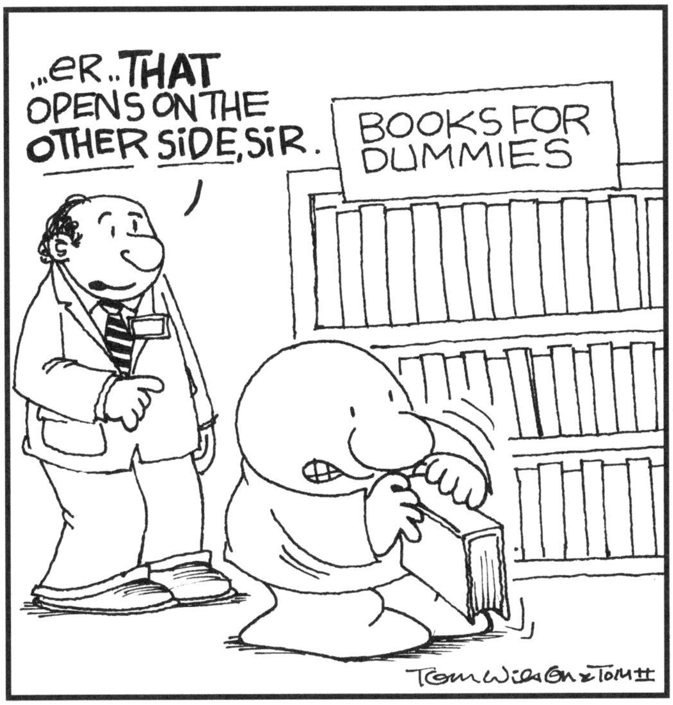
...er.. THAT OPENS ON THE OTHER SIDE, SIR.
BOOKS FOR DUMMIES
TomWilson & TOM II

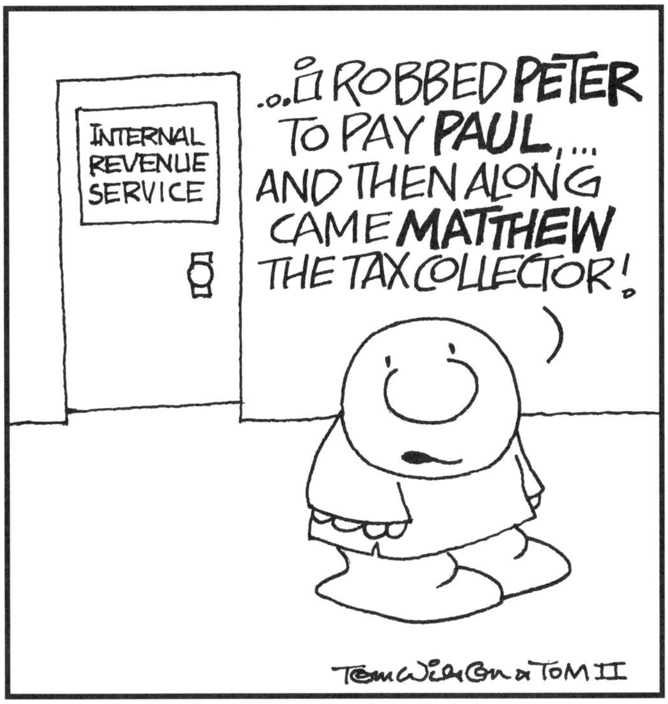
INTERNAL REVENUE SERVICE
..o..I ROBBED PETER TO PAY PAUL,... AND THEN ALONG CAME MATTHEW THE TAX COLLECTOR!
TomWilson & TOM II

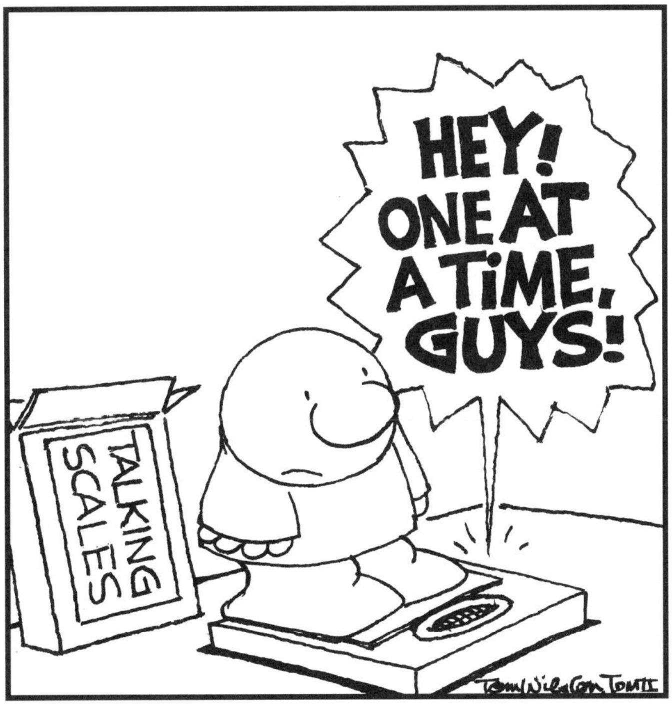
HEY! ONE AT A TIME, GUYS!
TALKING SCALES
TomWilson TOM II

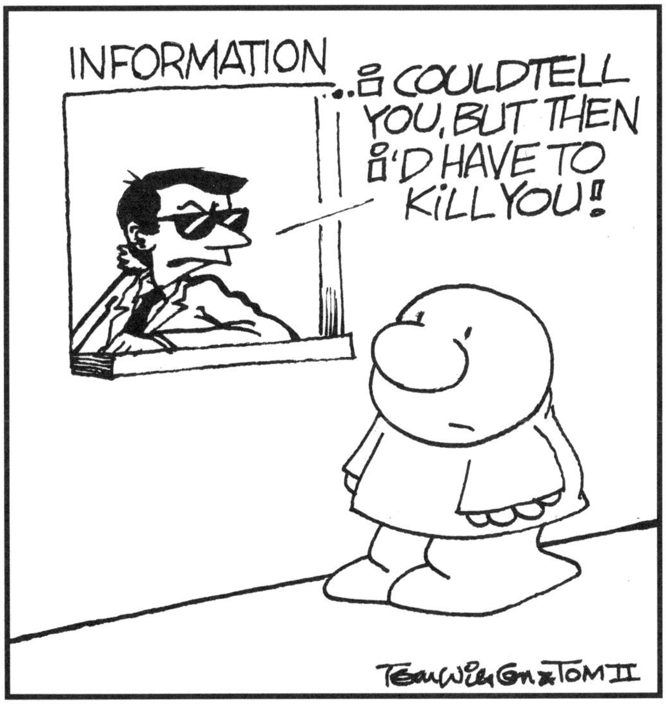
INFORMATION
..I COULD TELL YOU, BUT THEN I'D HAVE TO KILL YOU!!
TomWilson & TOM II

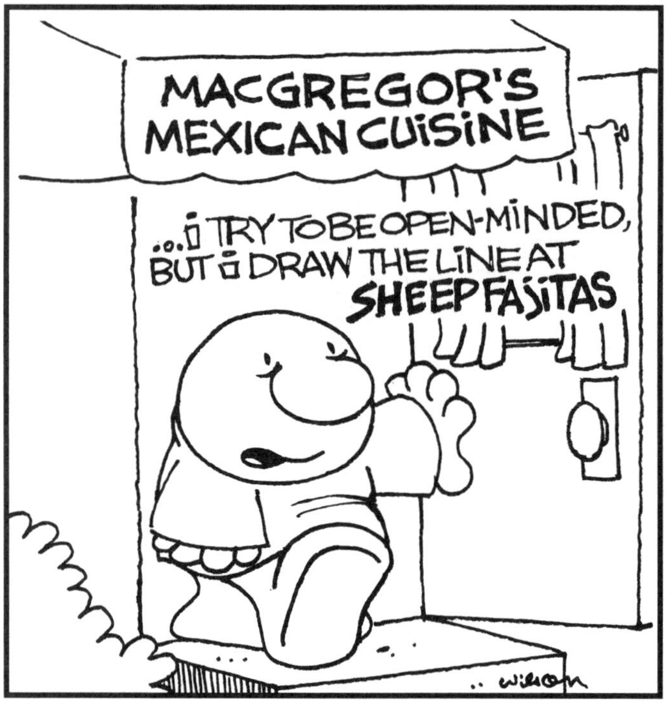
MACGREGOR'S
MEXICAN CUISINE
..I TRY TO BE OPEN-MINDED, BUT I DRAW THE LINE AT SHEEP FAJITAS

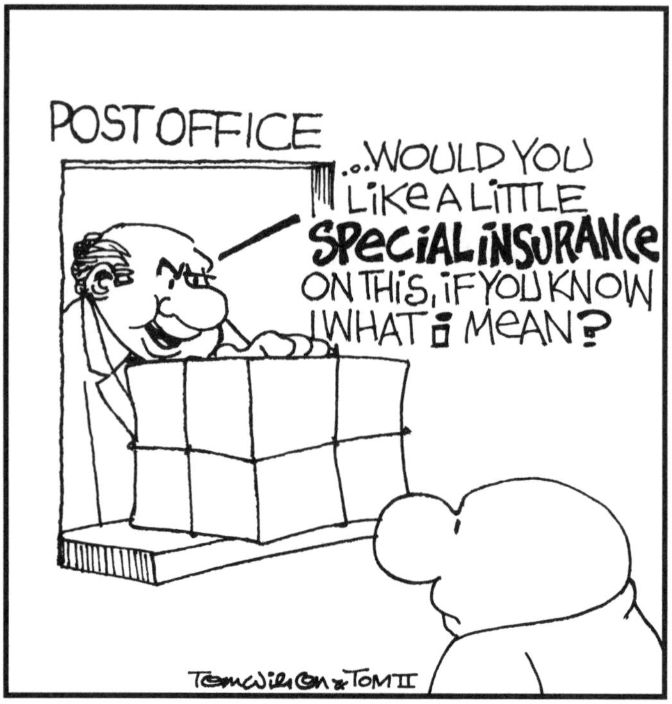
POST OFFICE
..WOULD YOU LIKE A LITTLE SPECIAL INSURANCE ON THIS, IF YOU KNOW WHAT I MEAN?
TOM WILSON & TOM II

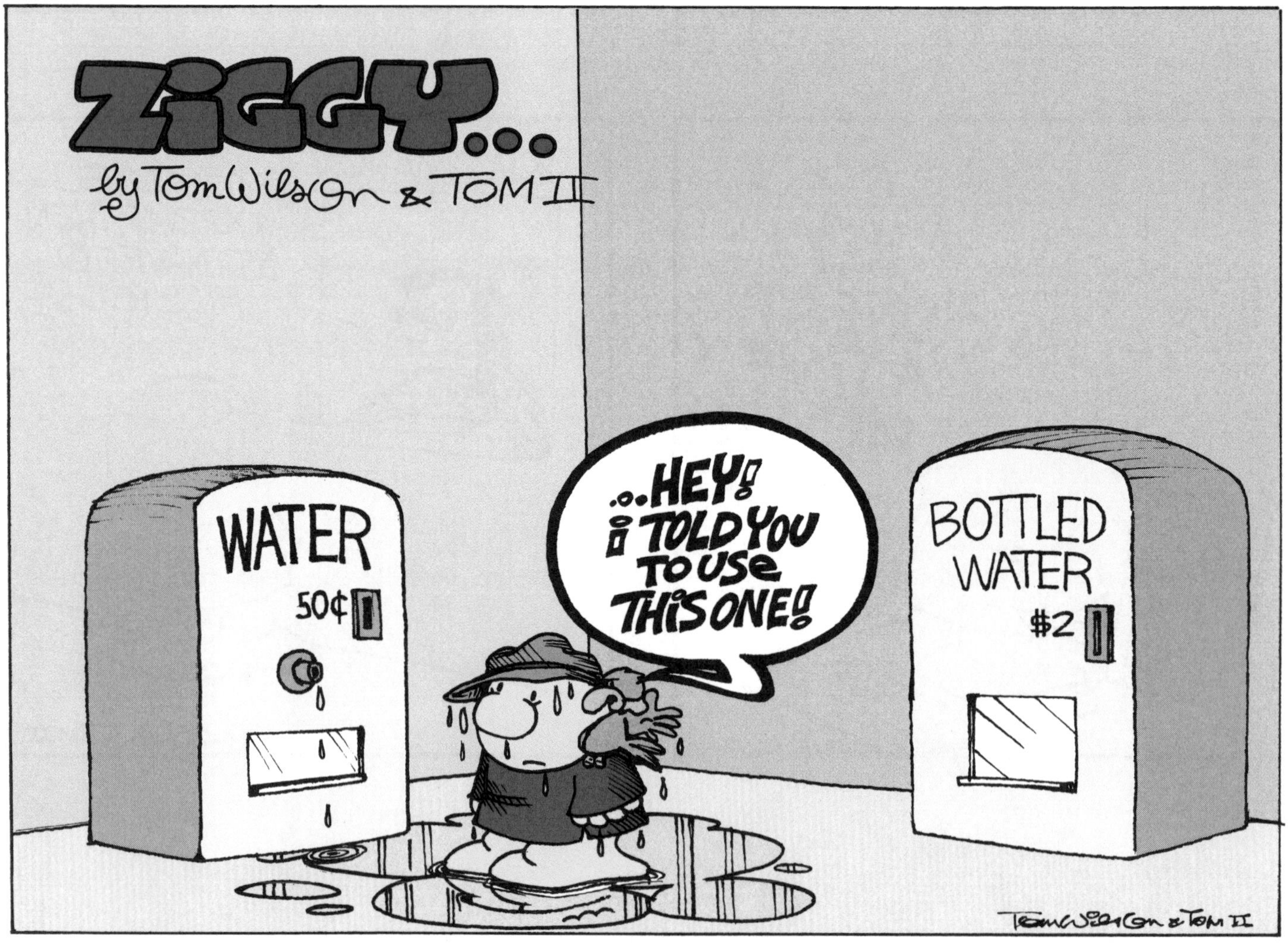
ZIGGY...
by Tom Wilson & TOM II
WATER
50¢
..HEY! I TOLD YOU TO USE THIS ONE!
BOTTLED WATER
$2
TOM WILSON & TOM II

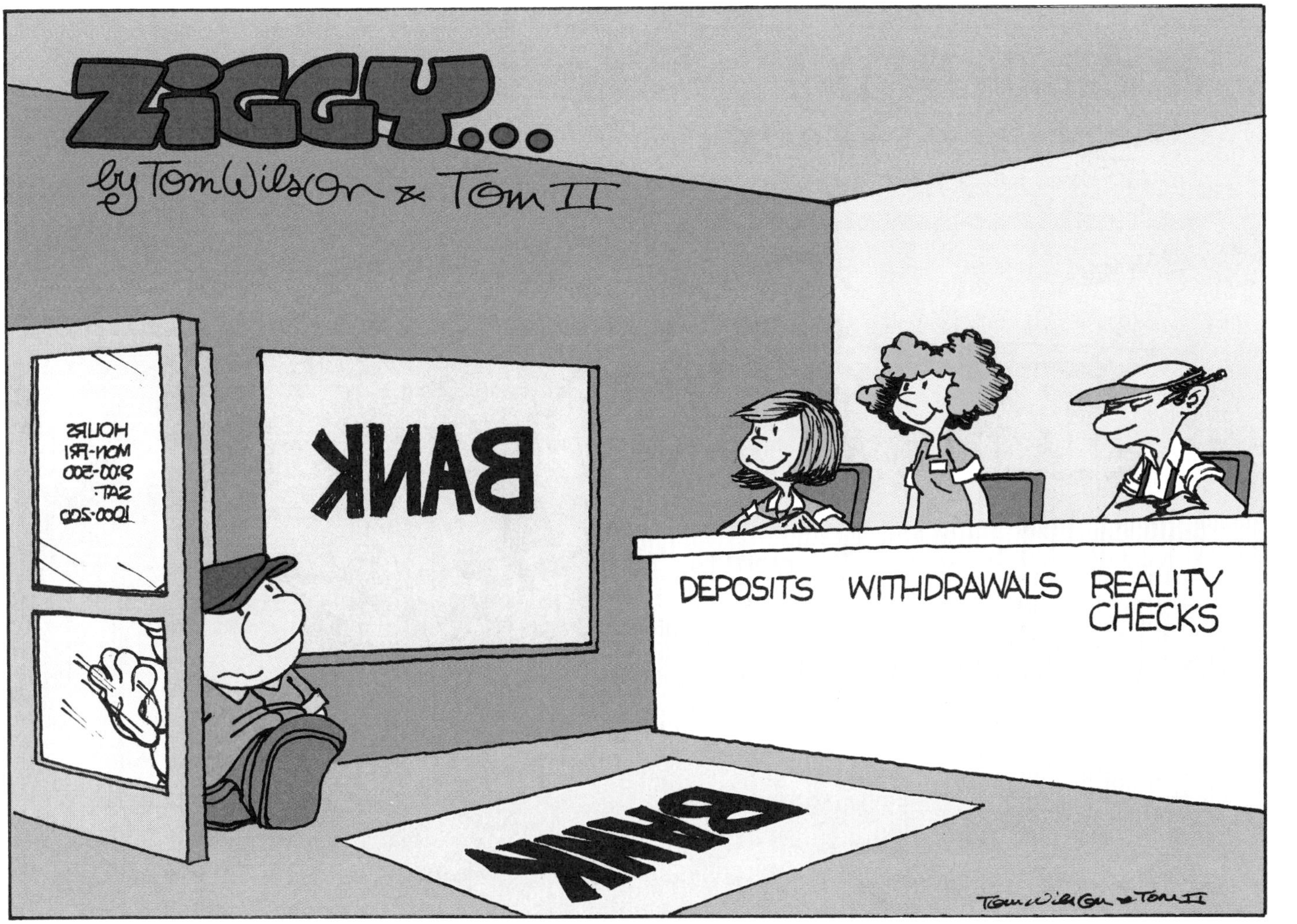
ZIGGY...
by Tom Wilson & Tom II
HOURS
MON-FRI
9:00-5:00
SAT
10:00-2:00
BANK
DEPOSITS
WITHDRAWALS
REALITY CHECKS
BANK
Tom Wilson & Tom II

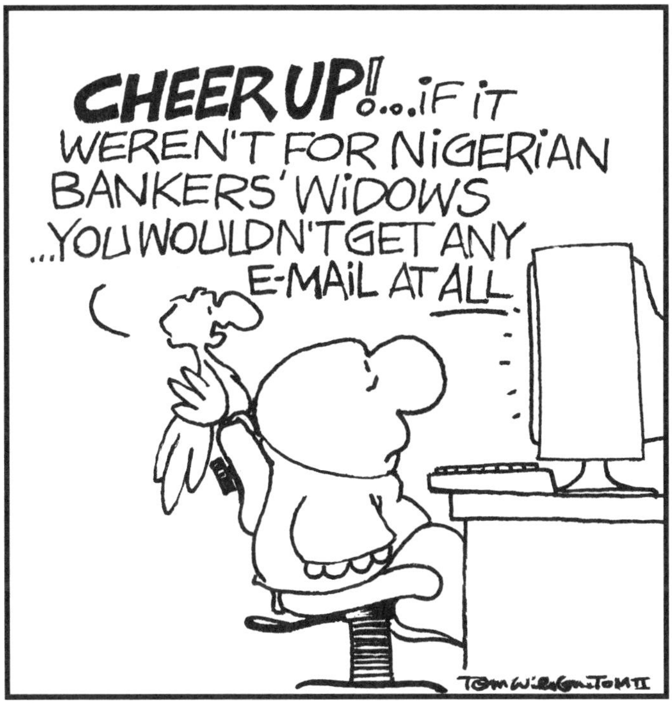
CHEER UP!...IF IT WEREN'T FOR NIGERIAN BANKERS' WIDOWS ...YOU WOULDN'T GET ANY E-MAIL AT ALL
Tom Wilson & Tom II

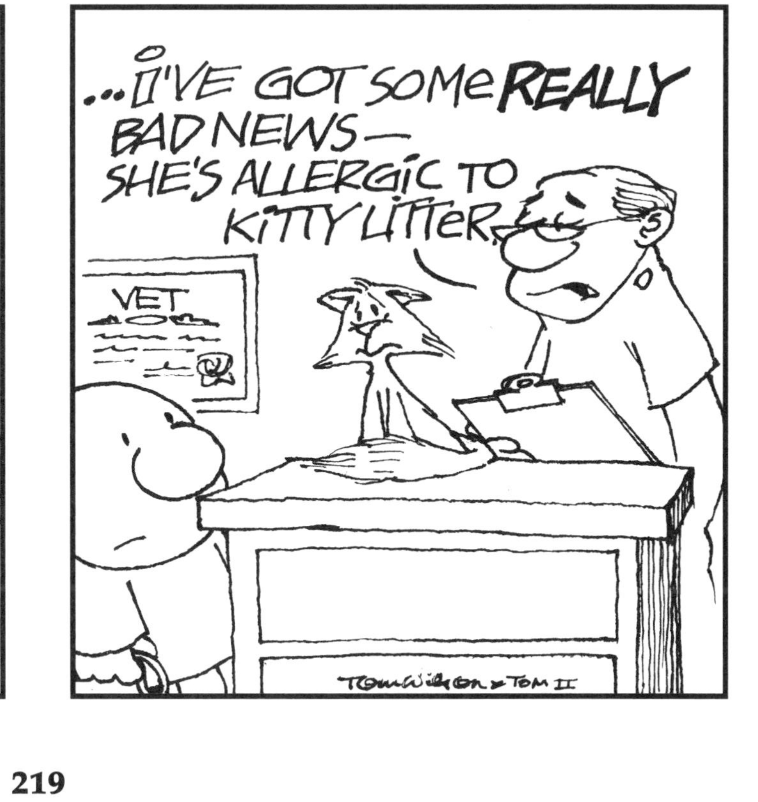
...I'VE GOT SOME REALLY BAD NEWS— SHE'S ALLERGIC TO KITTY LITTER
VET
Tom Wilson & Tom II

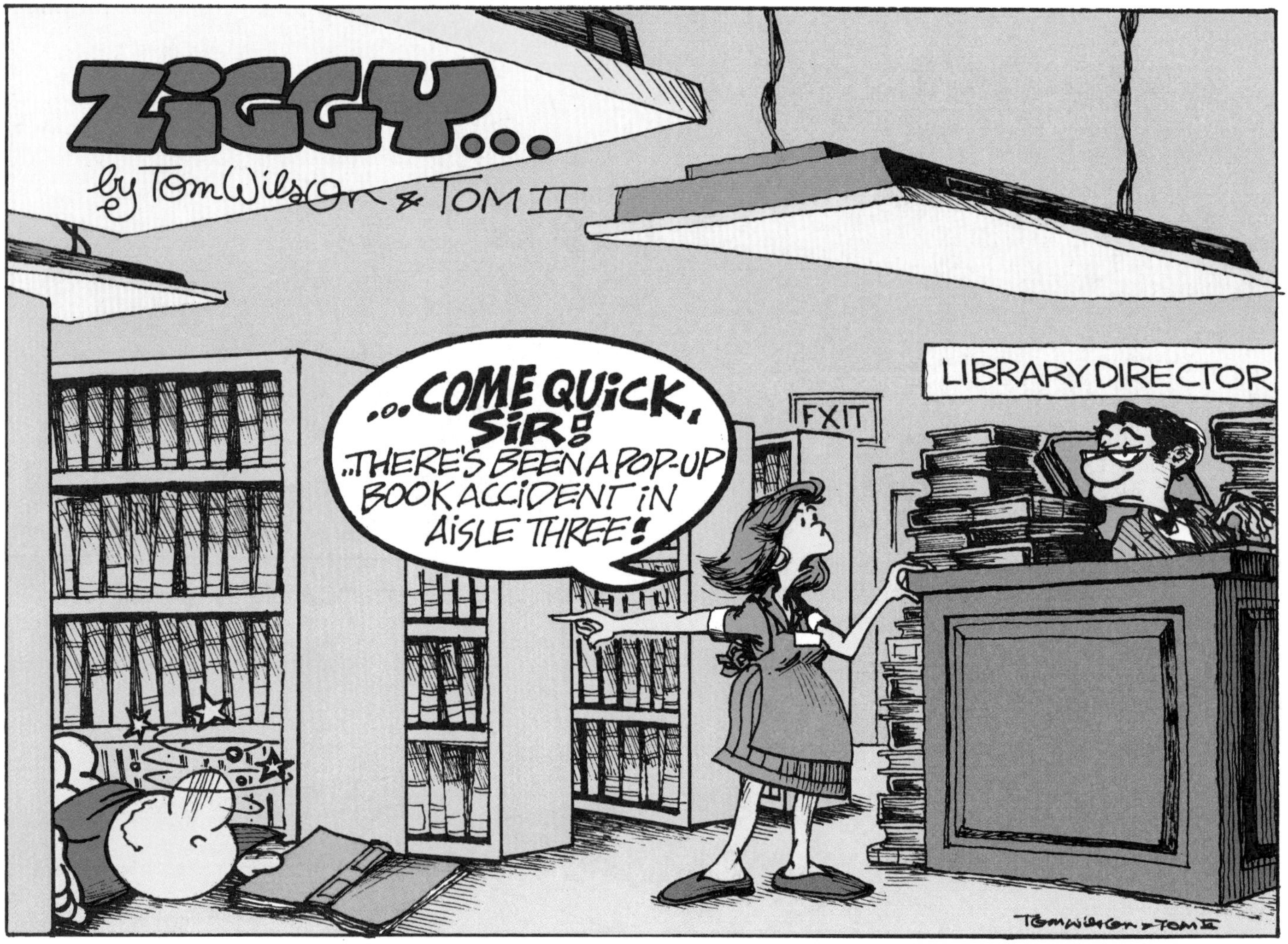
ZIGGY...
by Tom Wilson & TOM II
LIBRARY DIRECTOR
EXIT
...COME QUICK, SIR! ..THERE'S BEEN A POP-UP BOOK ACCIDENT IN AISLE THREE!

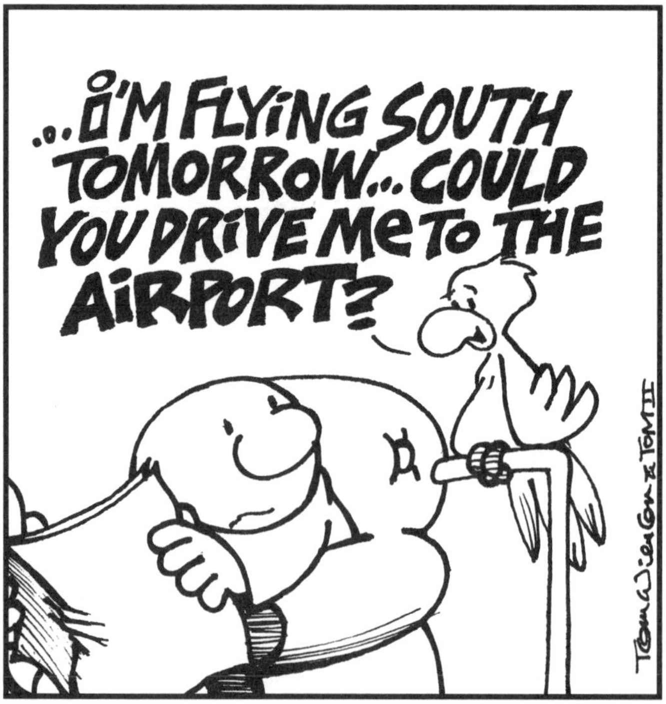
...I'M FLYING SOUTH TOMORROW... COULD YOU DRIVE ME TO THE AIRPORT?

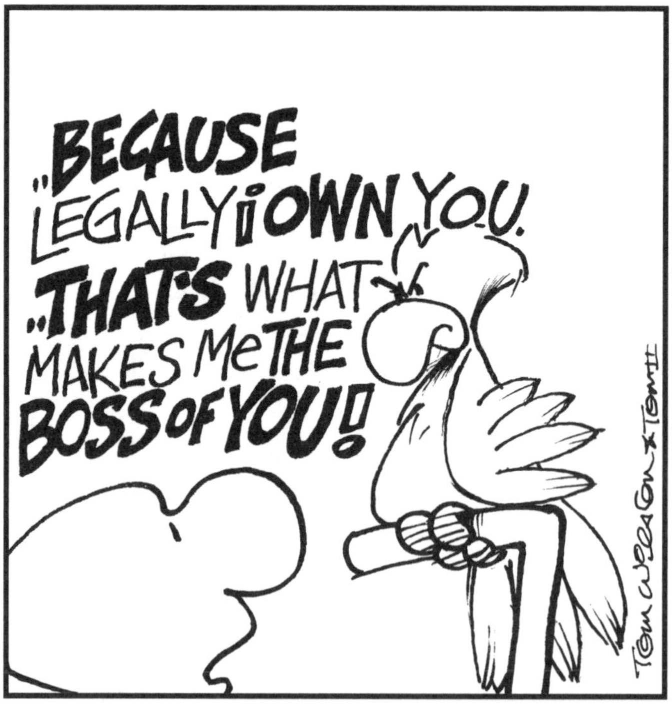
..BECAUSE LEGALLY I OWN YOU. ..THAT'S WHAT MAKES ME THE BOSS OF YOU!

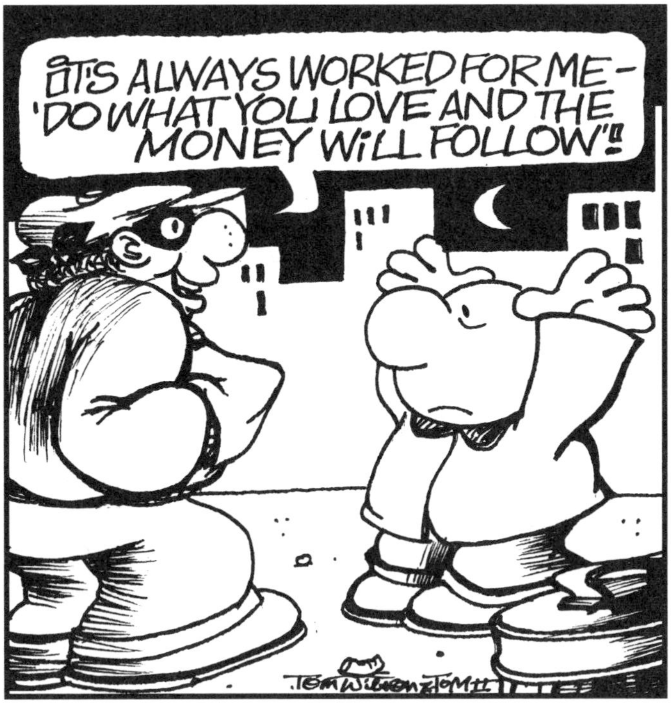
IT'S ALWAYS WORKED FOR ME- 'DO WHAT YOU LOVE AND THE MONEY WILL FOLLOW'!!

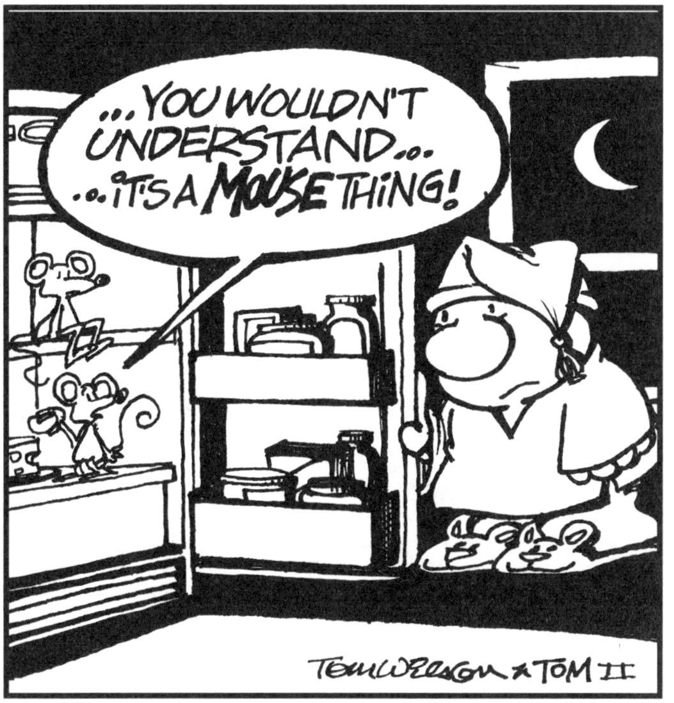
...YOU WOULDN'T UNDERSTAND... ...IT'S A MOUSE THING!

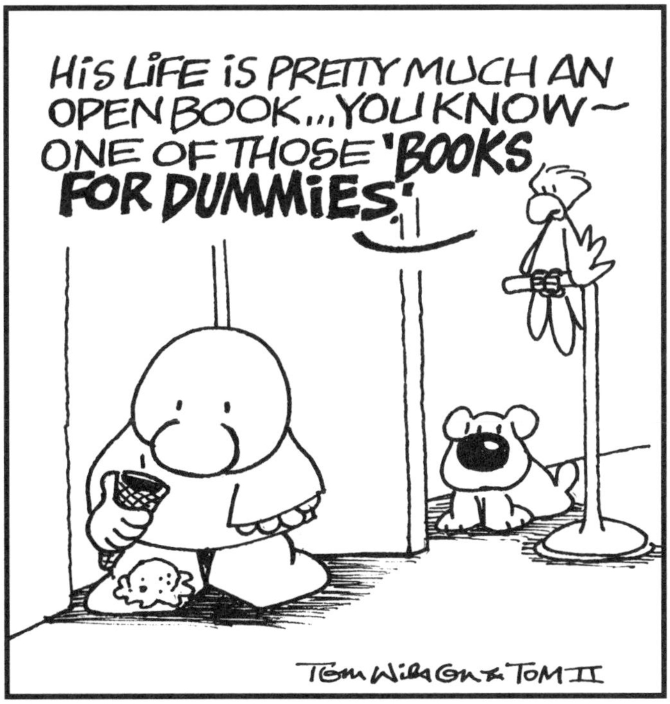
HIS LIFE IS PRETTY MUCH AN OPEN BOOK...YOU KNOW~ ONE OF THOSE 'BOOKS FOR DUMMIES'

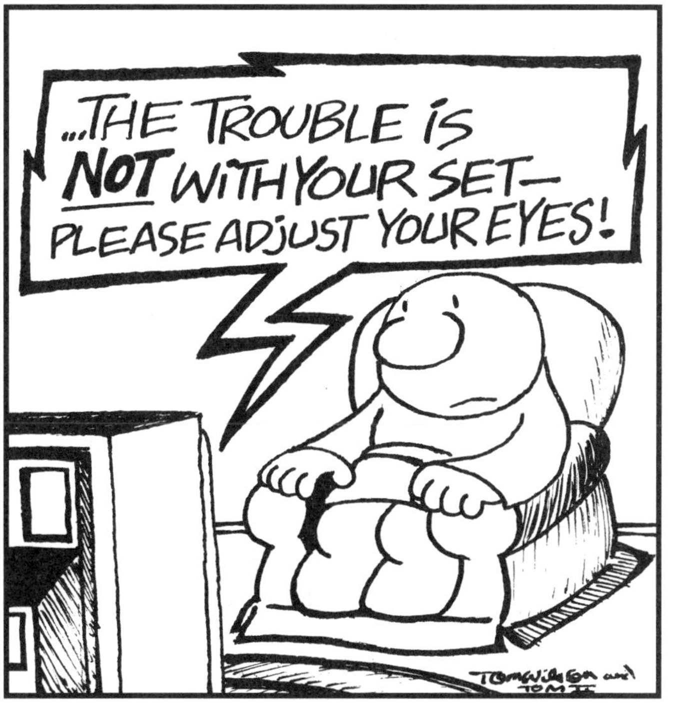
...THE TROUBLE IS NOT WITH YOUR SET- PLEASE ADJUST YOUR EYES!

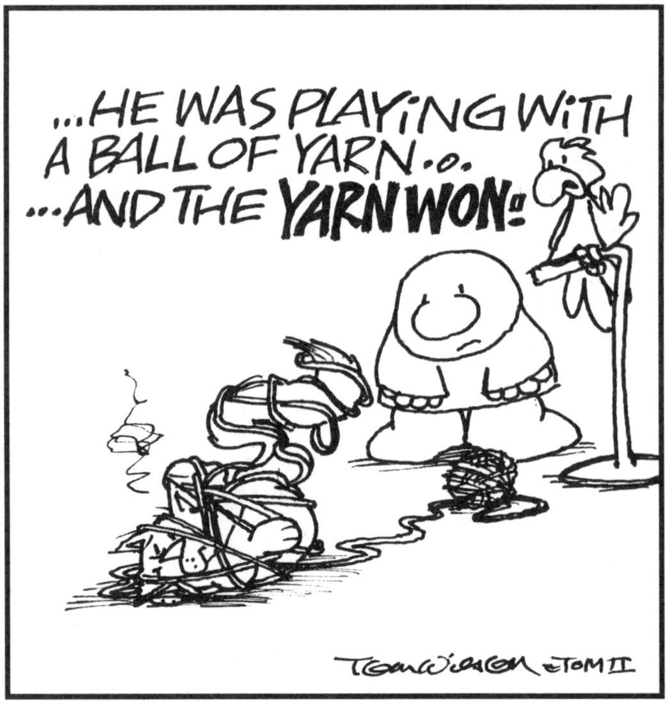
...HE WAS PLAYING WITH A BALL OF YARN...
...AND THE YARN WON!
TOM WILSON & TOM II

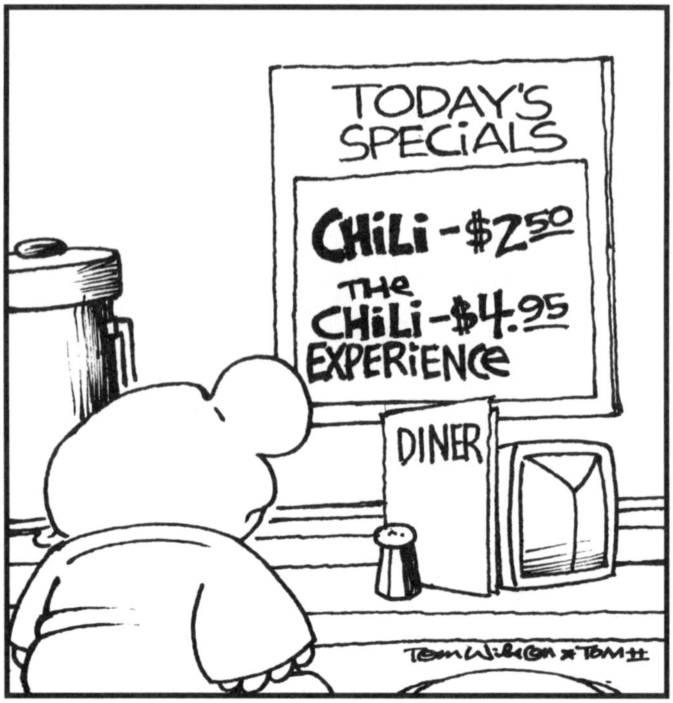
TODAY'S SPECIALS
CHILI - $2.50
THE CHILI EXPERIENCE - $4.95
DINER
TOM WILSON & TOM II

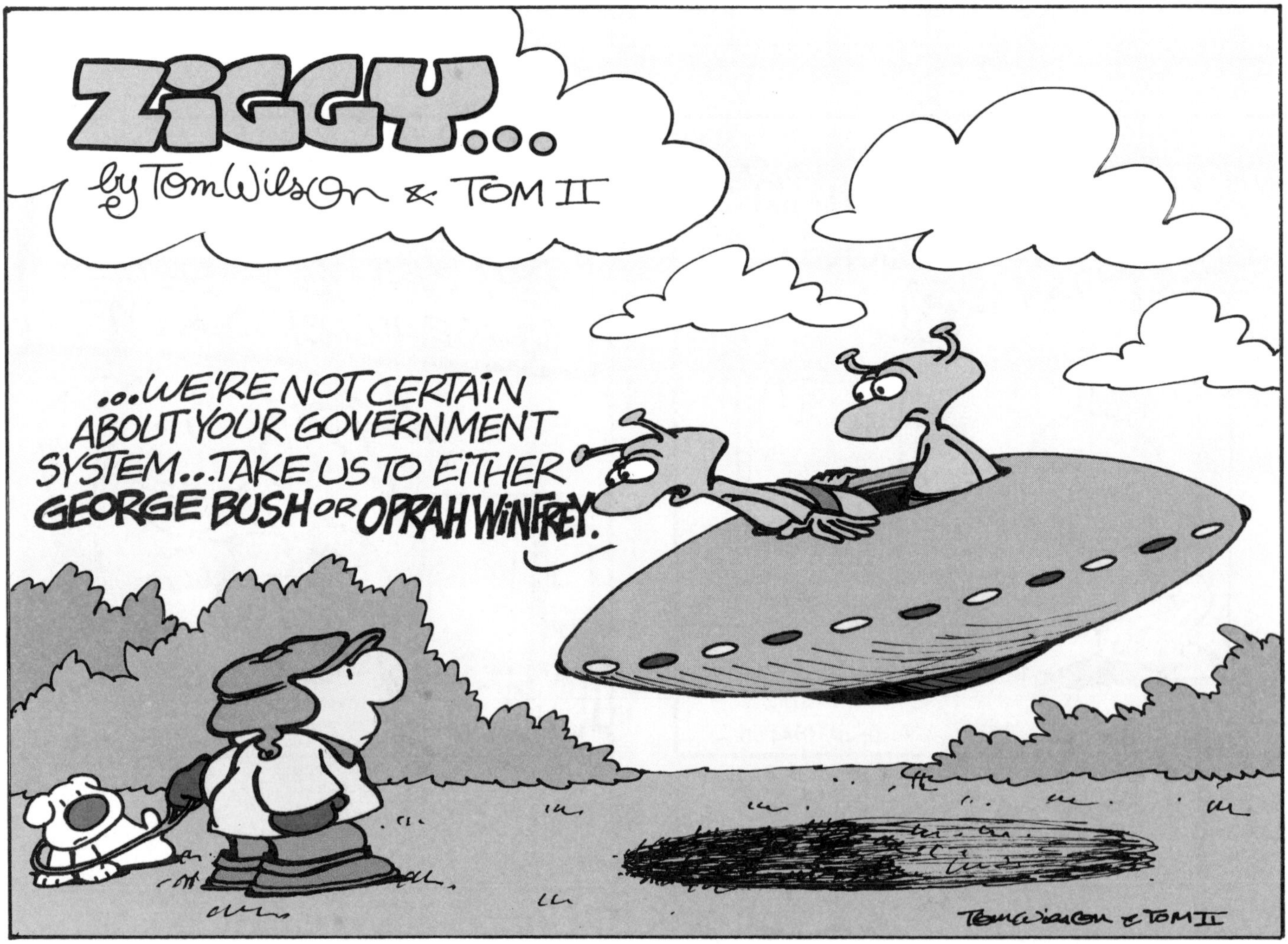
ZIGGY...
by Tom Wilson & TOM II
...WE'RE NOT CERTAIN ABOUT YOUR GOVERNMENT SYSTEM...TAKE US TO EITHER GEORGE BUSH OR OPRAH WINFREY.
TOM WILSON & TOM II

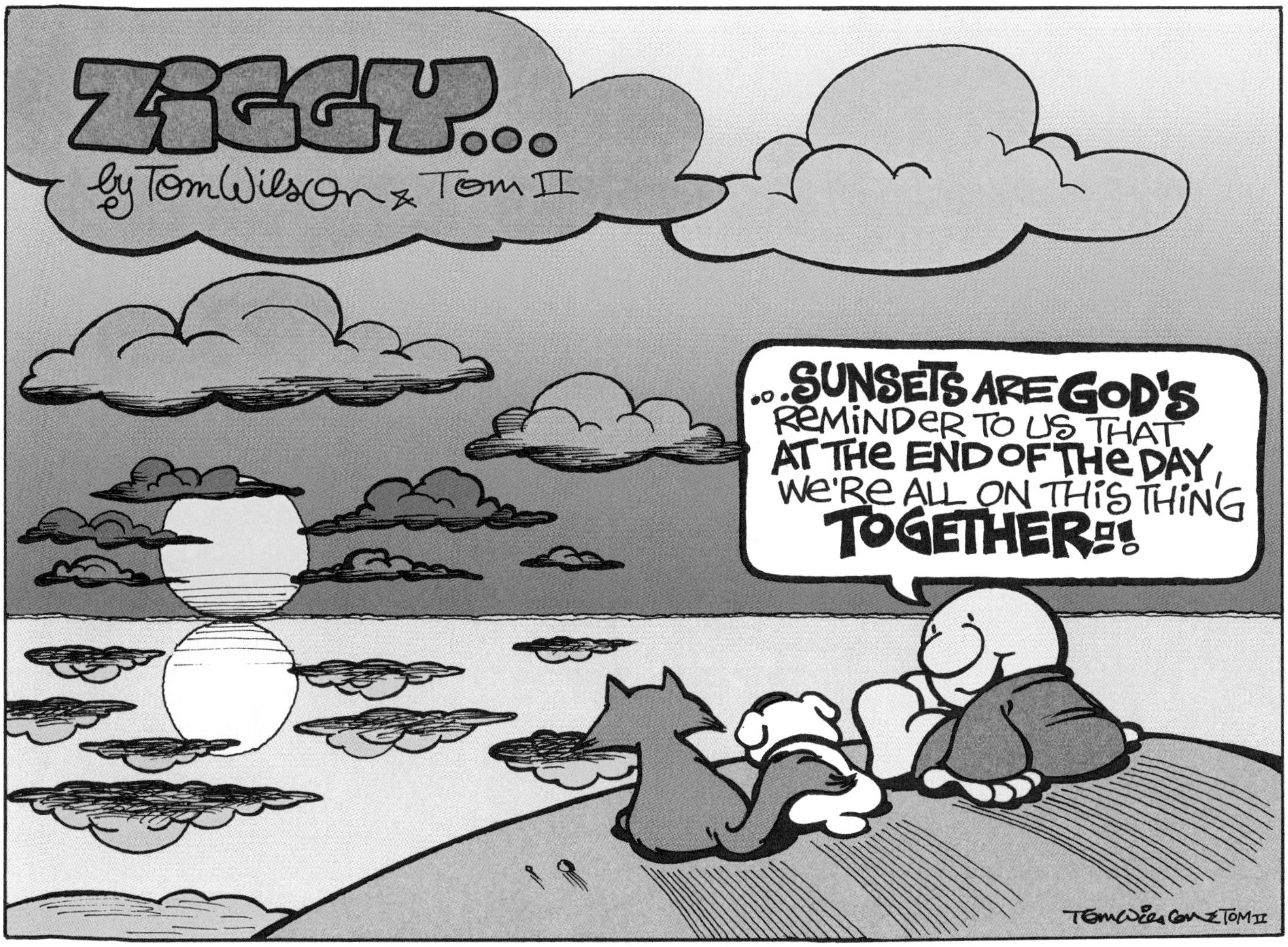
ZIGGY...
by Tom Wilson & Tom II
...SUNSETS ARE GOD'S REMINDER TO US THAT AT THE END OF THE DAY, WE'RE ALL ON THIS THING TOGETHER!!
TOM WILSON & TOM II

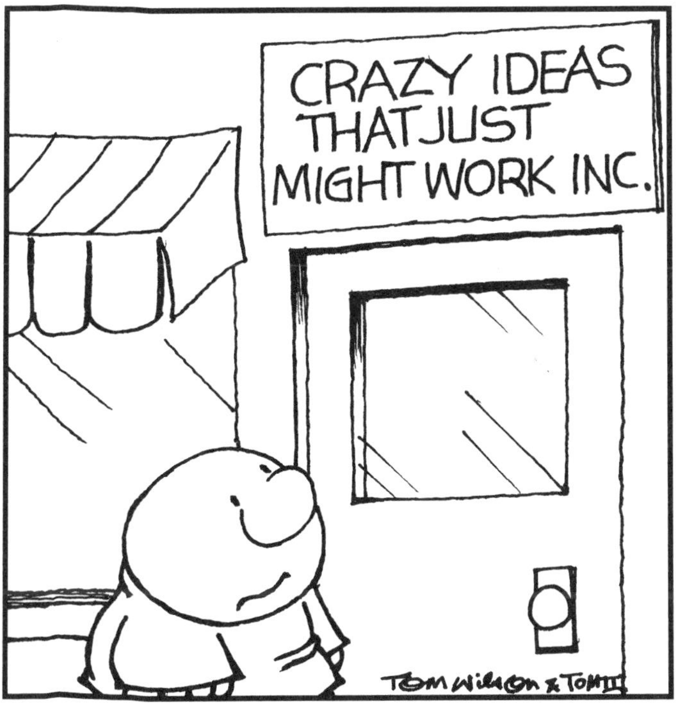
CRAZY IDEAS THAT JUST MIGHT WORK INC.
TOM WILSON & TOM II

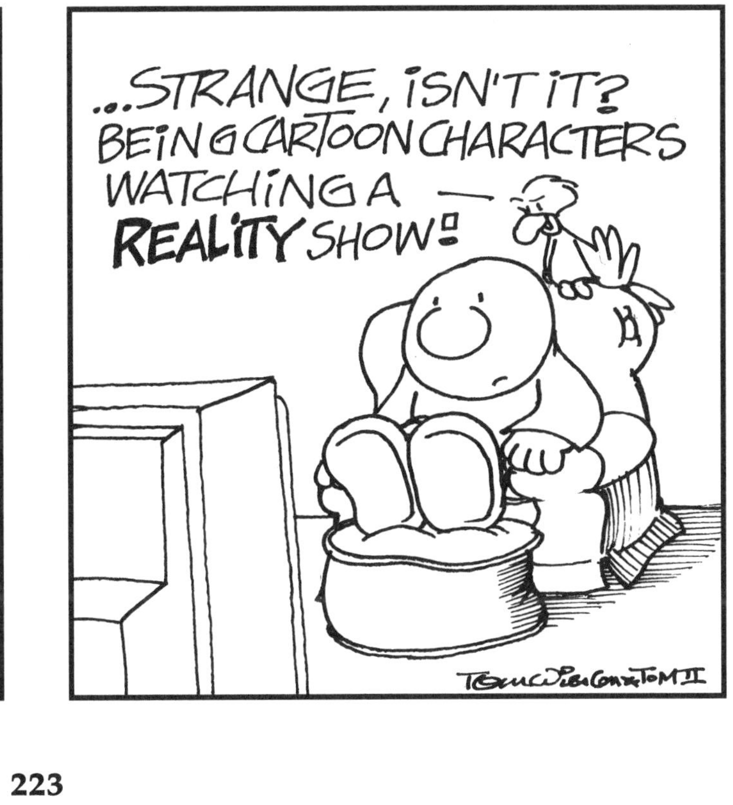
...STRANGE, ISN'T IT? BEING CARTOON CHARACTERS WATCHING A REALITY SHOW!
TOM WILSON & TOM II